ATLAS
OF THE
GREAT WESTERN RAILWAY
as at 1947

ATLAS
OF THE
GREAT WESTERN RAILWAY
as at 1947

REVISED EDITION

BY

R. A. COOKE

WILD SWAN PUBLICATIONS LTD.

ISBN 1 874103 38 0
First edition published 1988

Printed by Amadeus Press, Huddersfield

Published by
WILD SWAN PUBLICATIONS LIMITED
1-3 Hagbourne Road, Didcot, Oxon OX11 8DP

CONTENTS

INTRODUCTION AND ACKNOWLEDGEMENTS TO REVISED EDITION

At first glance, little difference will be detected between this and the first edition of nearly ten years ago. However, appearances can be deceptive, as the results of ongoing research have now been incorporated and numerous corrections made to the original. To bear testimony to the extent of the update, the index reflects 800 additional locations (indicated with an asterisk) and now contains over 9,200 entries. Long forgotten names such as Bulls Bridge, Clunt Bont Junction, Show Hill Junction and Dukes Lock Junction, amongst others now appear, together with many more collieries and other locations, all long extinct. The present has not been forgotten and the changes of the last ten years have also been included.

Appendix E 'Unknown Locations' has been radically updated but regretfully is now even longer than that in the first edition. Any help in this area would be particularly welcome.

One additional appendix has been added, 'Location names not adopted'. This was a very recent idea and is consequently far shorter than I suspect it should be. I would be very pleased to receive additional entries of this nature.

In a work of this kind a high level of integrity can only be achieved with the generous help of others and I am particularly grateful for extensive assistance from R.J. Caston, C. Chapman, J.H. Mann, G.H. Tilt and B.J. Wilson. Notwithstanding the above, I also owe a debt to M. Christensen, D.G. Coakham, Col. M.H. Cobb, M. Dawson, H. Edwards, E.A. Evans, R. Hellyer, R. Instone, G. Jacobs, A.M. Jervis, S.J. Kirby, Dr. G. Lambert, E. Langford Lewis, G.C. Lewthwaite, R. Maund, J.P. Morris, C.R. Potts, J.E. Tennent and C.E. Turner, and to any others that I may have inadvertently omitted, for their generous comments, corrections and suggestions on the first edition. I also wish to record my grateful thanks to the staff at the P.R.O. at Kew and to the B.R. Records Centre at Royal Oak.

R.A. Cooke
1997

INTRODUCTION

During the twenty-five years that I have been researching the lines of the Great Western Railway, I have often found it difficult to pinpoint a particular location and, in some cases, even understand the junction arrangements in a complex area. The absence of any fully comprehensive map led me to the idea of one day attempting to fill the gap.

As more information was pieced together, what had started out as a vague idea, gradually took shape. Inevitably my original thoughts of an atlas became modified and more ambitious, until the present format finally emerged. I make no apology for basing the design on the superb Midland Railway distance maps, which were probably not matched by any other company.

This atlas does not follow the usual practice of being constructed in strips of maps reading from left to right, then continuing with the next strip either above or below. There are two reasons for this departure. Firstly, at the scale used, some pages would be blank or have little or no content, and secondly, the use of a standard grid by which to divide the maps, would result in some larger railway centres being split over two, three, or even four pages. In order therefore to try and contain each 'centre' to one map, and also to make each map as complete as possible (e.g. the terminus of a branch, as far as possible, is not shown on a separate map from the branch itself – as would happen with a standard grid system), a line of route approach has been adopted (see list on page x). This in itself is not entirely satisfactory, especially in South Wales, but it is hoped that the 'reader' will not find it too difficult and, with the help of key maps, continuation numbers and the index, be able to find his way around.

The objective of any atlas is obviously to locate a specific place, and to that end, I have attempted to show every passenger station, halt or platform. In addition, every junction is named and all signal boxes are shown. Where an earlier (or later) box existed of a different name, then these, too, are included where known. The exception to this is if the earlier boxes were simply numbered 1, 2 and 3 or East and West, then in most cases only the latest box is shown. Finally,

all level crossings (including some that were closed), collieries (the majority closed), sidings (which bore their own name and were geographically distinct), engine sheds, water troughs, tunnels and viaducts have been included.

Although this is not an historical atlas with dates of openings and closures, all lines closed before 1947 and those opened since have been shown. The same applies to stations, halts, sidings and signal boxes, so there is much more to be found than just the GWR as it was at nationalisation. Only in the case of Margam and Briton Ferry have second maps been provided, as the changes that took place were so extensive as to be impossible to convey on a single map.

One of the most difficult and contentious issues will, I feel sure, be that of spelling. Some locations in Wales had two, three or even more versions, complicated by the use of English versus Welsh spellings. I have chosen to include every version that I came across in official railway documents, even though some will no doubt give rise to dispute. The main reason for adopting this approach is the extremely common feature of names with the same or similar spelling actually being geographically different locations.

Whilst I have endeavoured to ensure that this atlas is as accurate as possible, my researches are not yet complete. I would be very pleased therefore to receive comments on errors and omissions and in particular help regarding the locations in Appendix E, together with locations shown ø (which side of line not known) or * (precise position uncertain).

Finally, please study the two following pages of explanatory notes before attempting to use the atlas.

I do hope that the casual 'reader' will get as much interest out of browsing through this publication as I have had in preparing it. I also hope that the serious student of the Great Western Railway will find it of assistance in his researches.

R. A. Cooke,
Evergreen,
School Lane,
Harwell,
Oxfordshire

KEY AND EXPLANATORY NOTES

MAP GRID

The index refers to map references A to D and 1 to 6. Although the pages are not ruled across in a grid, the margins are annotated and thus the appropriate square can be identified.

singled track line

crossing place on single track line

double track line

four tracks, paired Up, Down, Up, Down

four tracks, paired Up, Up, Down, Down

loop on double track line

siding on double track line

LM & SR, Southern Rly, LNER or LPTB line

private line, siding or tramway, the full extent of which may not be shown

site of line closed before 1947 or opened post 1947

site of private line or tramway, the full extent of which may not be shown. In South Wales in particular, it is very often impossible to show all former tramways, many of which pre-dated the railways.

county boundary. These are shown (obviously based on the old counties) to give a broad indication, but cannot be taken as being absolutely accurate. For example, a boundary may be shown down the mid-course of a minor river, whereas in fact in may change from the centre to one or other of the banks.

canals. Many, although not all, are shown, even if partly derelict, but no attempt has been made to indicate locks. Canal basins have been shown only where these were served by the GWR except where the basins are of particular interest as at Stourport and Brimscombe Dock.

station, halt or platform (on single and on double line), open at 1947

station, halt or platform (on single and on double line), closed prior to 1947 or open post 1947

island platform on double line

signal box, open at 1947, closed prior to 1947 or opened post 1947. Note, S.B.'s shown as 'site of' may include boxes still standing but not in use or which have been converted to ground frames.

siding in existence at 1947, closed prior to 1947 or opened post 1947. Sidings at stations are not shown unless they were known by their own name.

level crossing

junction and single line junction

tunnel, mileages shown for each portal (see Appendix 'B' for full list)

viaduct (or major bridge). Mileage shown for mid point (see Appendix 'C' for full list)
the lengths shown for tunnels and viaducts are taken from contemporary records and some may vary from current details

underbridge and overbridge

flat crossing

water troughs

engine shed

☐	designation of line or branch as used by the Civil Engineer's Department (see also introduction to Appendix 'A')
JOINT	indicates that the line was joint with another company (see Appendix 'D')
– – – →	indicates the up direction of travel
(SITE OF) OR †	indicates a station, junction, siding or S.B. closed at 1947. When shown against a station it refers to passenger facilities. Goods facilities or private sidings may remain in use. On some maps where there is insufficient space, the symbol '†' has been used.
∅	platform, siding or S.B. shown, but which side of the line has not been confirmed
⑰	line continues on Map 17. Above, below or opposite indicates a continuation on the same page.
PENZANCE	– large print indicates the existence, at some time or other, of a passenger station, platform or halt. Changes of status between station, platform and halt are not shown.
(NA)	– station, platform or halt, not advertised to the public
[NORTH]	– station name suffix added post 1947
(NORTH)	– station name suffix added pre 1947
AKA	– also known or referred to (officially) as.
PREV–	– indicates that the location had previously been known under another name or with different spelling. Changes between station, halt and platform are not shown.
LATER –	– indicates that the location was renamed post 1947
123.42	– mileage (123 miles, 42 chains). All mileages are given in miles and chains, rounded to the nearest chain. Station mileages are measured at the mid-point of the platforms, except for terminal stations where stop-block mileage is used. Where the platforms are staggered, the mean distance is used and in some cases where the stagger is extreme, this results in a mileage midway between the platforms.

Mileages can and do differ as a result of site remeasurements, corrections, roundings or relaying work, and thus there will be some discrepancies with later figures.

It is also necessary to point out that even comparison with contemporary working timetables will show up many anomalies. More especially, the tables of distances between signal boxes were in many cases incorrect and occasionally significant errors occur. For example Box S.B. was shown as 1.18 from Corsham S.B. for several years, rather than the correct distance of 3.28.

Mileages for stations can also differ and, apart from errors, are often explained by the lengthening (or shortening) of platforms, thereby 'shifting' the mid point. Apparent discrepancies can also arise when a buffer stop mileage is adopted in place of the mid-point, a recent example being Milford Haven where the mid-point mileage of 284.65 was used up until 1982 when the line beyond the station to the dock was taken out of use and a buffer stop mileage of 284.71 was adopted.

It should be noted that all mileages
  West of Cogload Jcn are via Bristol T.M.
  West of Plymouth are via Bristol T.M. and Plymouth (Millbay) reverse
  Westbury to Weymouth are via Swindon
  North of Aynho Jcn are via Didcot and Oxford
  West of Severn Tunnel Jcn are via Swindon and Gloucester

123.42 = 17.31	– mileage at junction of two routes, or change of mileage
0.00	– zero point for line or branch
*	– approximate mileage or position

NOTE ON SCALES
Several different scales are used in this atlas, depending on the amount of detail to be shown. To assist in easy identification and comparison, each map or enlargement has the appropriate scale shown with a letter 'A' to 'D'. The letter 'E' is also used but covers a variety of larger scales according to requirements.

LIST OF MAPS

x

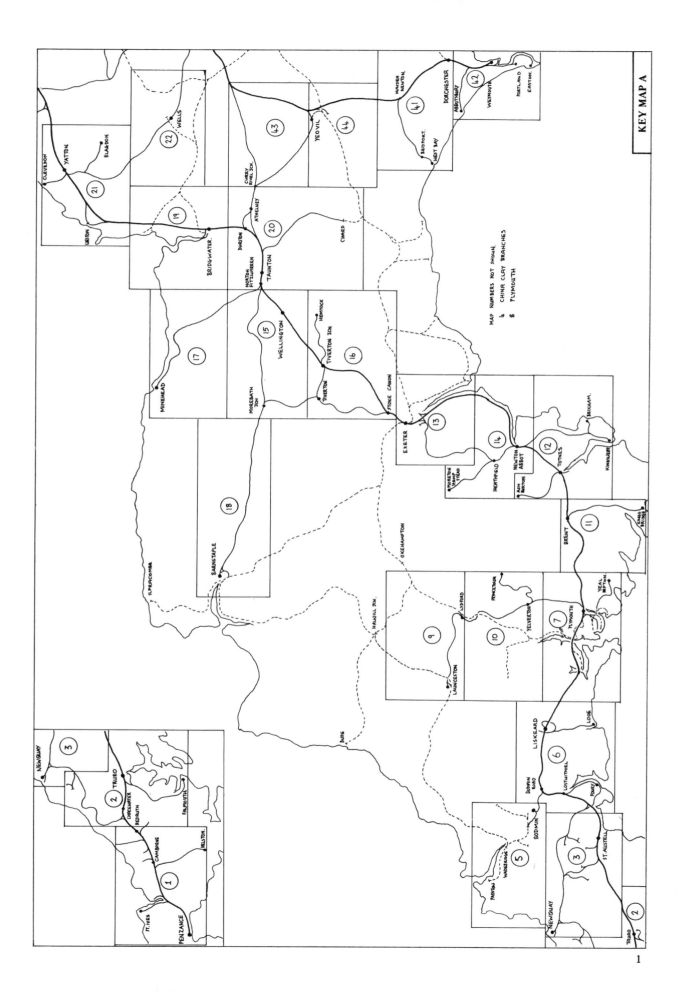

KEY MAP A

MAP NUMBERS NOT SHOWN:
4 CHINA CLAY BRANCHES
8 PLYMOUTH

1

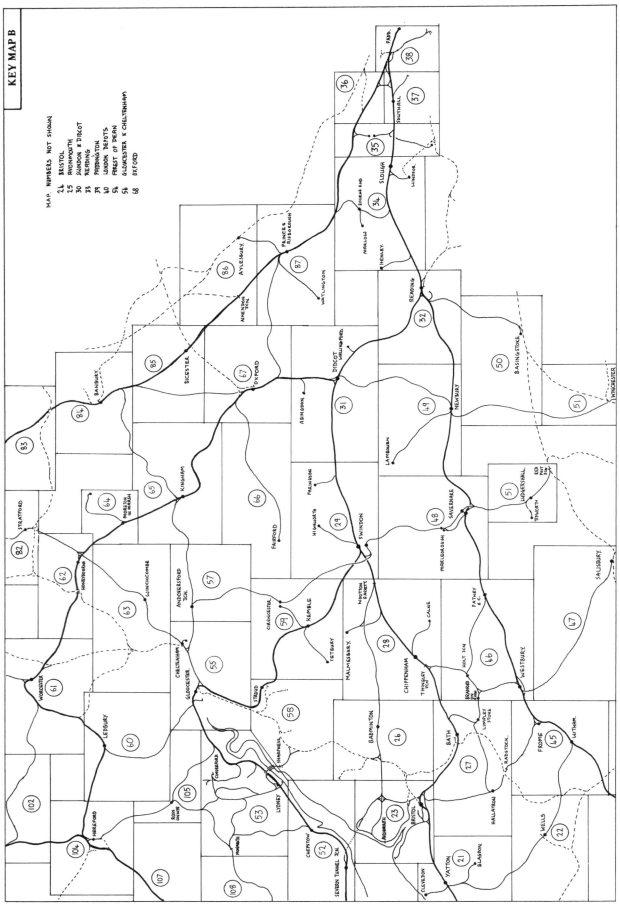

KEY MAP B

MAP NUMBERS NOT SHOWN
24   BRISTOL
25   AVONMOUTH
30   SWINDON & DIDCOT
33   READING
39   PADDINGTON
40   LONDON DEPOTS
54   FOREST OF DEAN
56   GLOUCESTER & CHELTENHAM
68   OXFORD

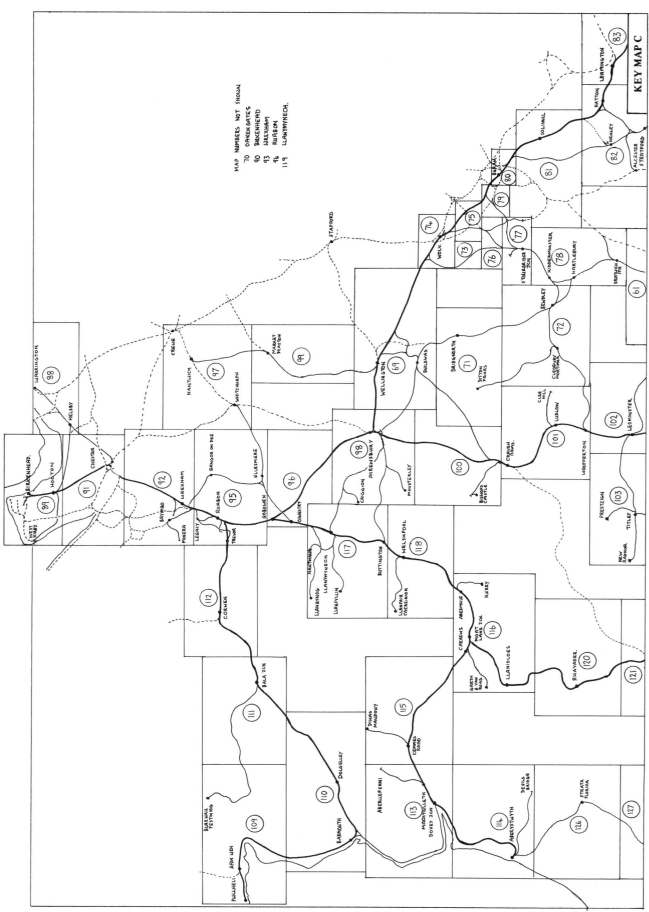

KEY MAP C

MAP NUMBERS NOT SHOWN
70 OAKEN GATES
90 BIRKENHEAD
93 WREXHAM
96 RUABON
119 LLANYMYNECH.

3

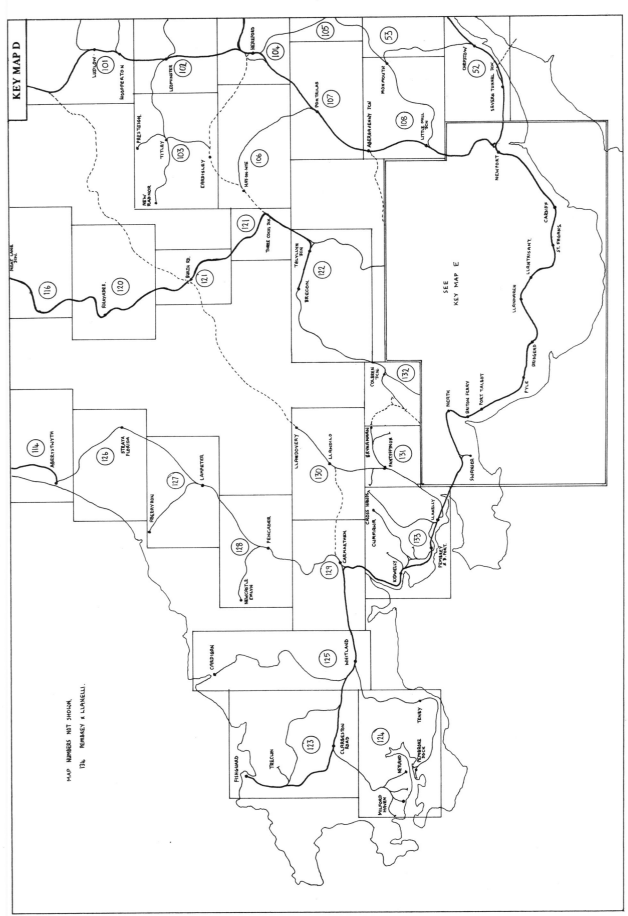

KEY MAP D

MAP NUMBERS NOT SHOWN.
134 PEMBREY & LLANELLI.

SEE KEY MAP E

101 LUDLOW — WOOFFERTON
102 LEOMINSTER
103 TITLEY — PRESTEIGN — NEW RADNOR — ERDISLEY
104 HEREFORD
105
106 HAY-ON-WYE
107 PON TRILAS
108 ABERGAVENNY JCN — LITTLE MILL JCN
52 CHEPSTOW — SEVERN TUNNEL JCN
53
MONMOUTH
NEWPORT
CARDIFF
ST. FAGANS
LLANTRISANT
LLANHARREN
BRIDGEND
PYLE
PORT TALBOT
BRITON FERRY
NEATH
SWANSEA
116 KNAP LANE JCN
120 RHAYADER — BUILTH RD.
121 THREE COCKS JCN — TALYLLYN JCN
122 BRECON
132 COLBREN JCN
131 PANTYFFYNON — BRYNAMMAN
130 LLANDOVERY — LLANDILO
114 ABERYSTWYTH
126 STRATA FLORIDA
127 LAMPETER — ABERAYRON
128 PENCADER — NEWCASTLE EMLYN
129 CARMARTHEN
133 CUMARFON — LLANELLY — KIDWELLY — PEMBREY & B. PORT — CROSS HANDS
125 WHITLAND
123 FISHGUARD — TRECWN
124 CLARBESTON ROAD — PEMBROKE DOCK — TENBY — MILFORD HAVEN — NEYLAND
CARDIGAN

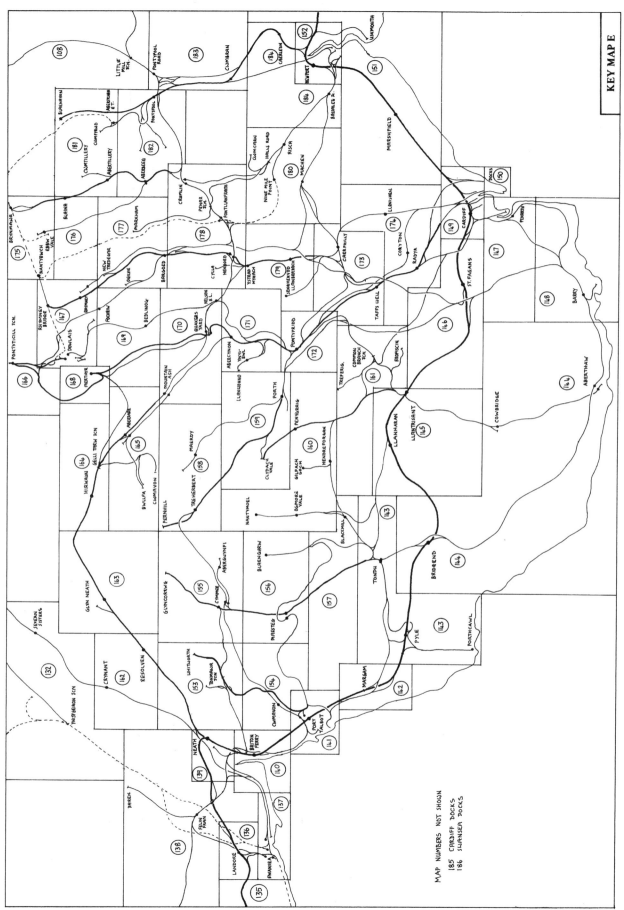

KEY MAP E

108

183

184

CLYDACH JN.
PONTYPOOL ROAD
CWMBRAN

CWMBRAN

LITTLE MILL JCN.

PONTYPOOL

181

182

ABERSYCHAN ET.

CWMFRWDD

BRYNMAWR

184

GWMCARN
HALLS ROAD

MARSHFIELD

NEWPORT

BASSALEG JN.

152

51

50

150

DOCKS

CRUMLIN

PENAR JCN.

RISCA

MACHEN

180

NINE MILE POINT

LLANISHEN

149

CARDIFF

177

176

ABERTILLERY

ABERBEEG

ABERTILLERY

BLAINA

BEAUFORT

EBBW VALE

NANTYBWCH

175

NEW TREDEGAR

OGILVIE

BRAGDED

CWM

HENGOED

178

YSTRAD MYNACH

179

SENGHENYDD
LLANBRADACH

CAERPHILLY

173

COBYTON

174

RADYR

167

RHYMNEY BRIDGE

DOWLAIS

PONTSTICILL JCN.

186

168

MERTHYR

ABERDARE

165

HIRWAUN

164

GELLI TARW JCN.

BWLLFA

CWMAVON

FERNHILL

TREHERBERT

158

MAERDY

RHYMNEY

PWLLYPANT

BEDLINOG

164

QUAKERS YARD

170

NELSON & L.

MOUNTAIN ASH

ABERCYNON

YNYS-BWL

171

LLANWONNO

PORTH

159

PENYGRAIG

160

GILFACH GOCH

HENDREFORGAN

PONTYPRIDD

172

TREFOREST

COMMON BRANCH JCN.

BROFISCIN

161

TAFFS WELL

146

ST. FAGANS

147

148

BARRY

144

ABERTHAW

COWBRIDGE

145

LLANHARAN

LLANTRISANT

143

BRIDGEND

144

163

GLYN NEATH

SEVERN SISTERS

132

CRYNANT

162

RESOLVEN

YNISDERWEN JCN.

ONLLWYN

155

ABERGWYNFI

CYMMER

156

BLAENGARW

NANTYMOEL

OGMORE VALE

BLACKMILL

TONDU

157

PARK SLIP

163

PYLE

143

PORTHCAWL

MARGAM

142

PORT TALBOT

141

NEATH

139

140

153

CWMAVON

154

BRITON FERRY

TONMAWR JCN.

WHITWORTH

DAREN

137

FELIN FRAN

136

138

LANDORE

SWANSEA

135

MAP NUMBERS NOT SHOWN
185 CARDIFF DOCKS
186 SWANSEA DOCKS

5

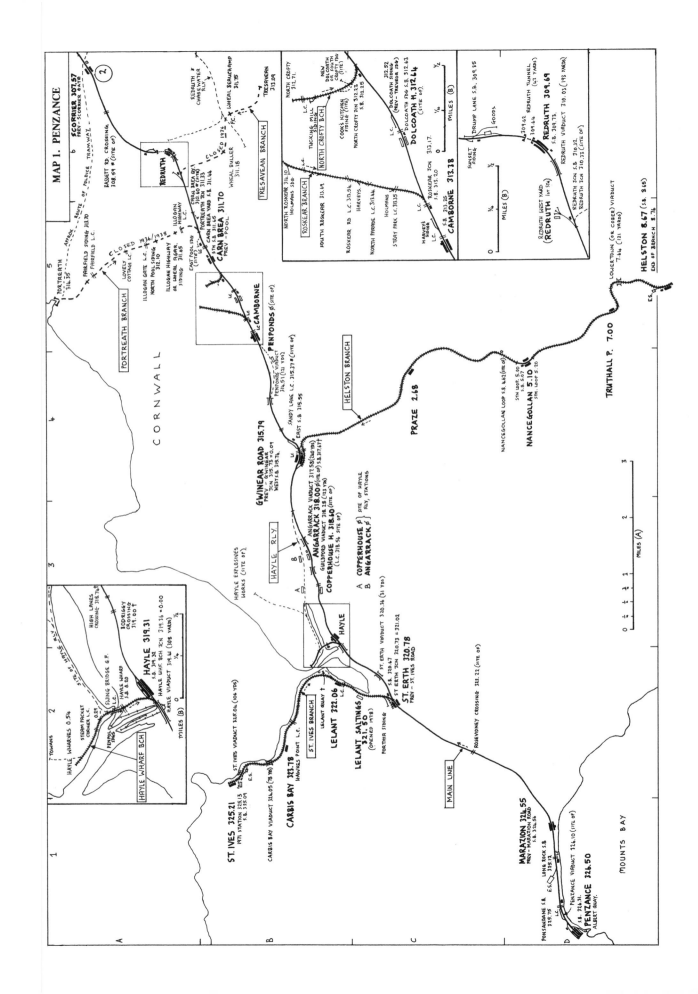

MAP 1. PENZANCE

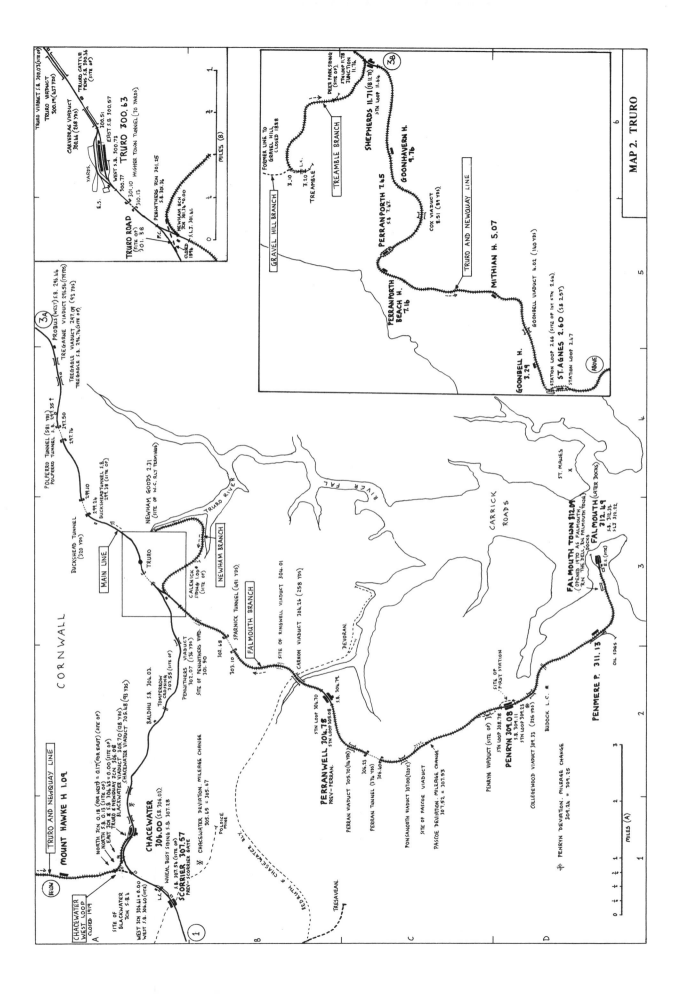

MAP 2. TRURO

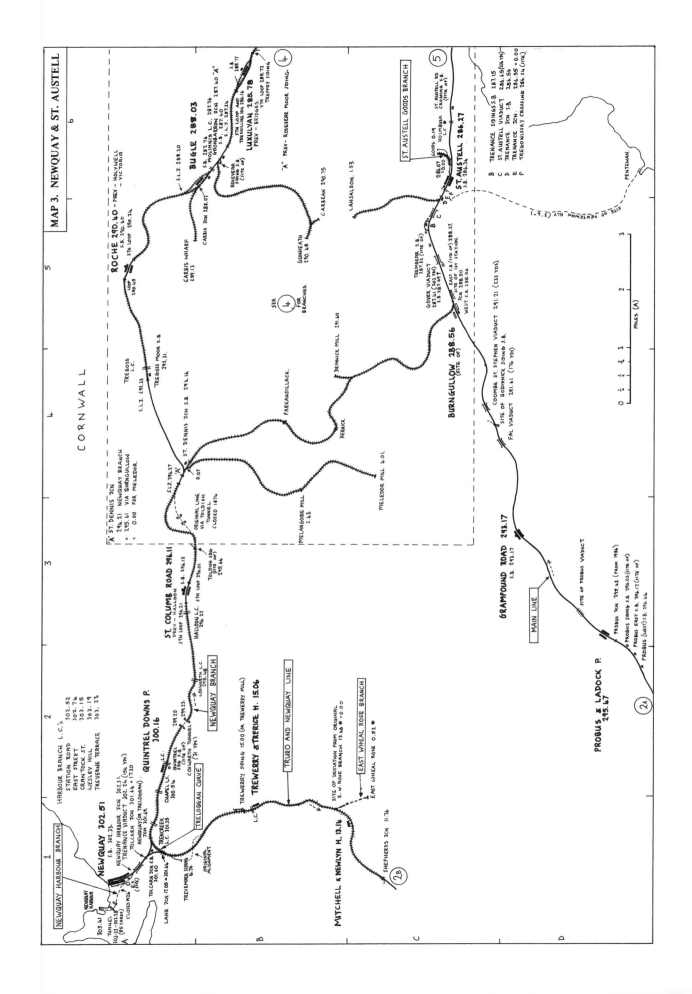

MAP 3. NEWQUAY & ST. AUSTELL

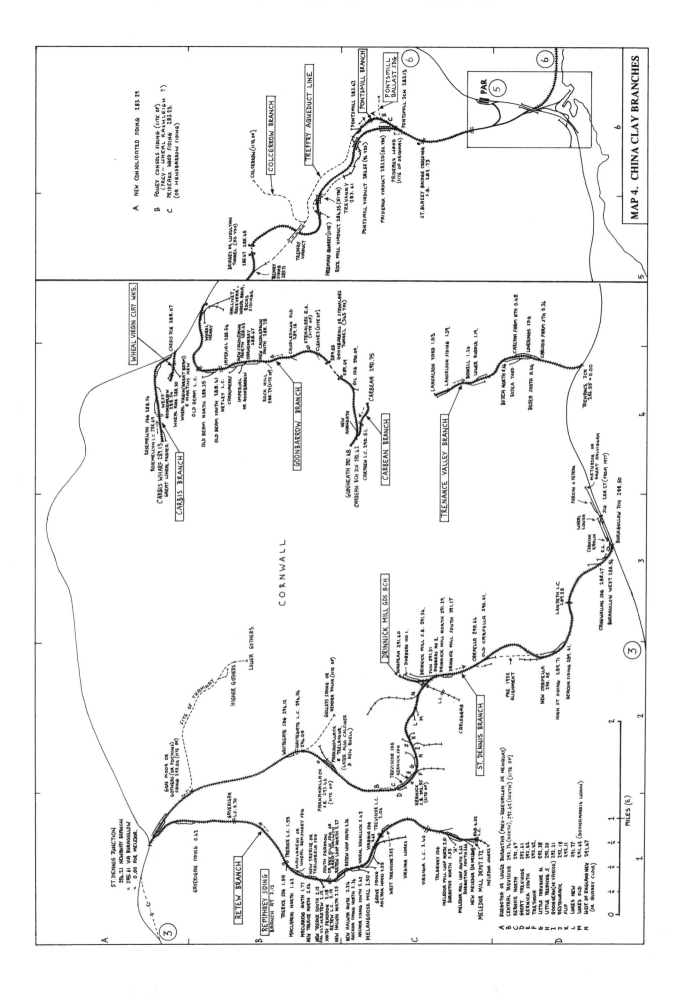

MAP 4. CHINA CLAY BRANCHES

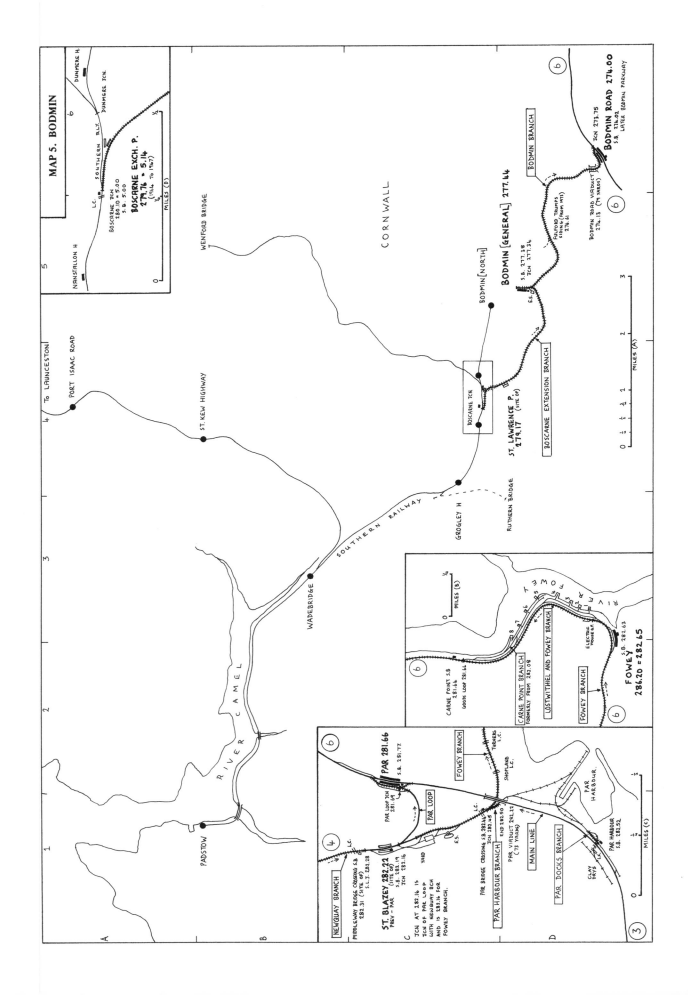

MAP 5. BODMIN

CORNWALL

BOSCARNE EXCH. P.
279.76 = 5.114
(1964 TO 1967)

BOSCARNE JCN 280.10 = 5.00
S.B. 5.00

DUNMERE H.
DUNMERE JCN.
SOUTHERN RLY.
NANSTALLON H.
WENFORD BRIDGE

BODMIN ROAD 274.00
S.B. 274.02
LATER BODMIN PARKWAY
JCN 273.75
BODMIN ROAD VIADUCT 274.13 (74 YARDS)
BODMIN BRANCH
GILFORD TRUMPS SIDING (FROM 1971) 274.61

BODMIN (GENERAL) 277.44
S.B. 277.38
JCN 277.34
E.S. 277.34

BODMIN (NORTH)

ST. LAWRENCE P. 279.17 (SITE OF)
BOSCARNE JCN
BOSCARNE EXTENSION BRANCH

MILES (A)
0 1 2 3

To LAUNCESTON
PORT ISAAC ROAD
ST. KEW HIGHWAY
RIVER CAMEL
SOUTHERN RAILWAY
GROGLEY H.
RUTHERN BRIDGE
WADEBRIDGE
PADSTOW

FOWEY 286.20 = 282.65
S.B. 282.63
RIVER FOWEY
8 7 6 5 4 3 2 1
CARNE POINT S.B. 281.64
(GOODS LOOP FROM 281.44)
CARNE POINT BRANCH FORMERLY FROM 282.08
LOSTWITHIEL AND FOWEY BRANCH
FOWEY BRANCH
ELECTRIC HOUSE B.R.
MILES (B)
0 1/4

PAR 281.66
S.B. 281.77
PAR LOOP JCN 281.64
PAR LOOP
FOWEY BRANCH
TURNERS L.C.
SHOPLAND L.C.
PAR HARBOUR
PAR VIADUCT 282.21 END 282.50 (73 YARDS)
PAR BRIDGE CROSSING S.B. 282.41 JCN 282.45
E.S.
MAIN LINE
PAR HARBOUR BRANCH
PAR DOCKS BRANCH
CLAY DRYS
PAR HARBOUR S.B. 281.52
L.C.

NEWQUAY BRANCH
MIDDLEWAY BRIDGE CROSSING S.B. 282.31 (SITE OF)
S.L.J. 282.28
ST. BLAZEY 282.22 (SITE OF) PREV - PAR
S.B. 282.19
JCN 282.16
JCN AT 282.16 IS JCN OF PAR LOOP WITH NEWQUAY BCH AND IS 282.16 FOR FOWEY BRANCH.
YARD
L.C.
MILES (C)
0 1/4 1/2 3/4

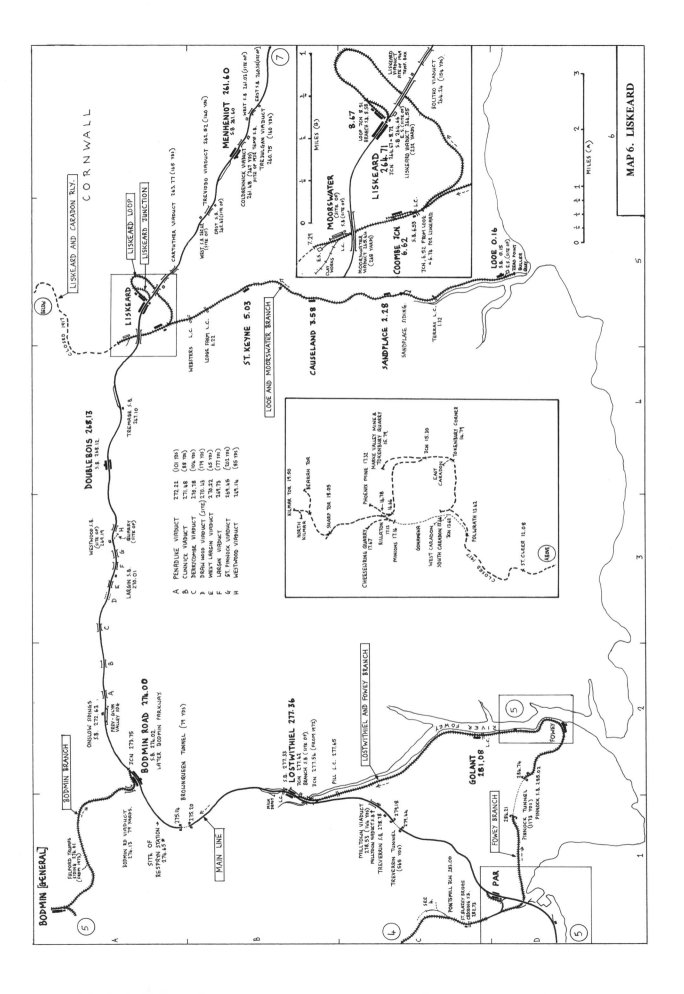

MAP 6. LISKEARD

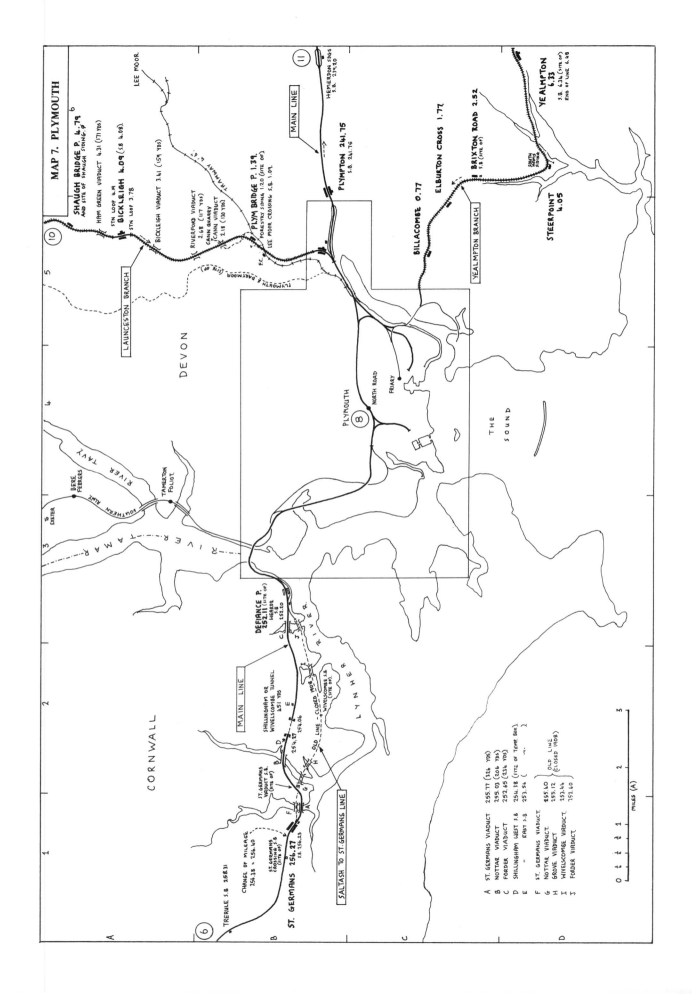

MAP 7. PLYMOUTH

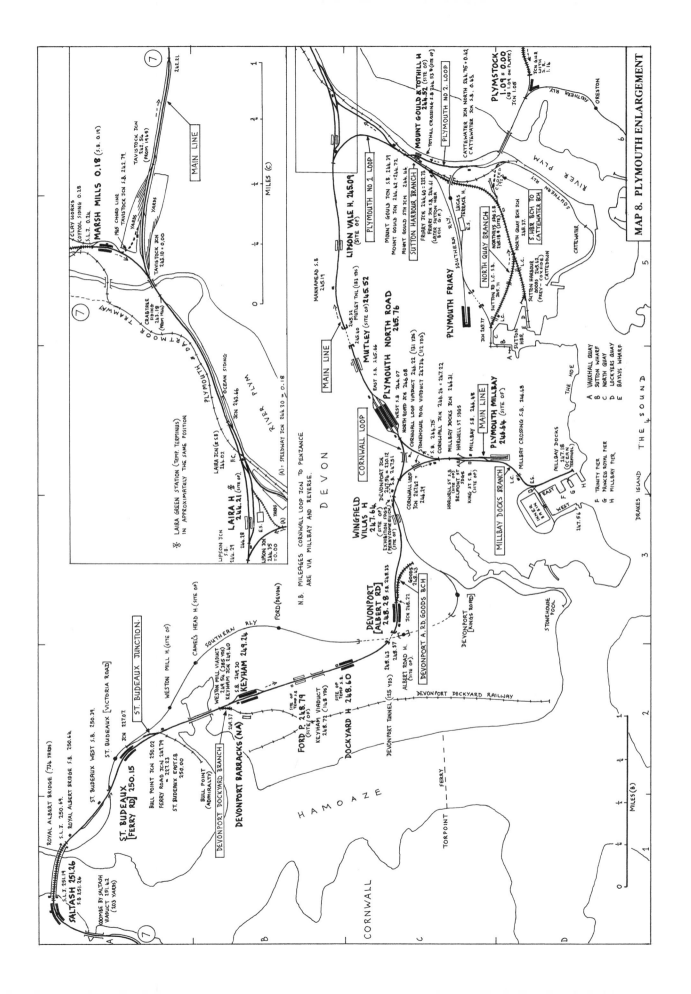

MAP 8. PLYMOUTH ENLARGEMENT

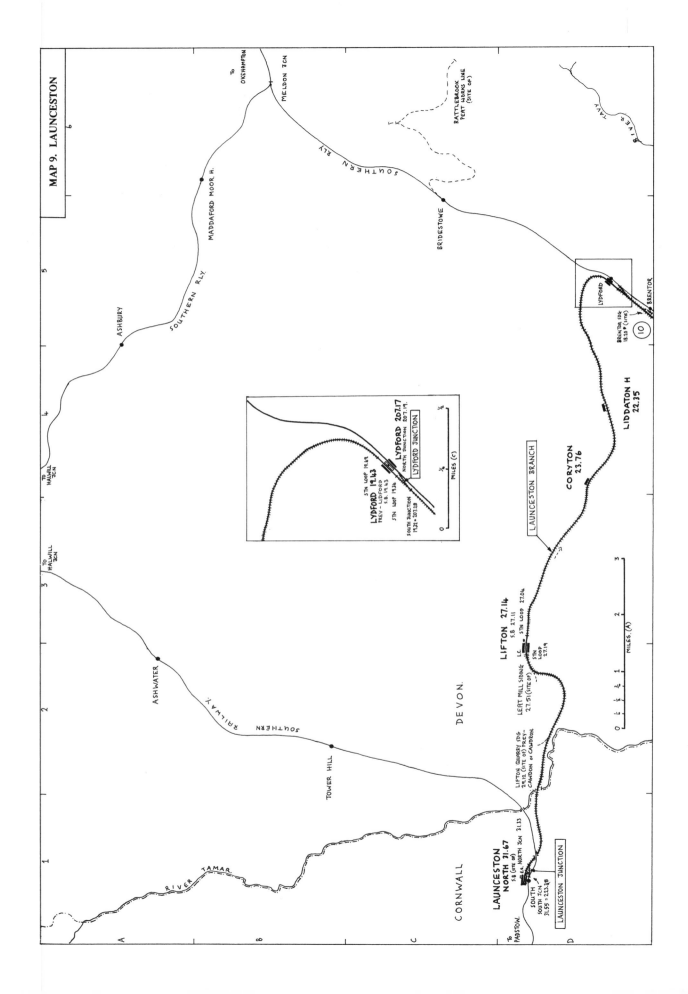

MAP 9. LAUNCESTON

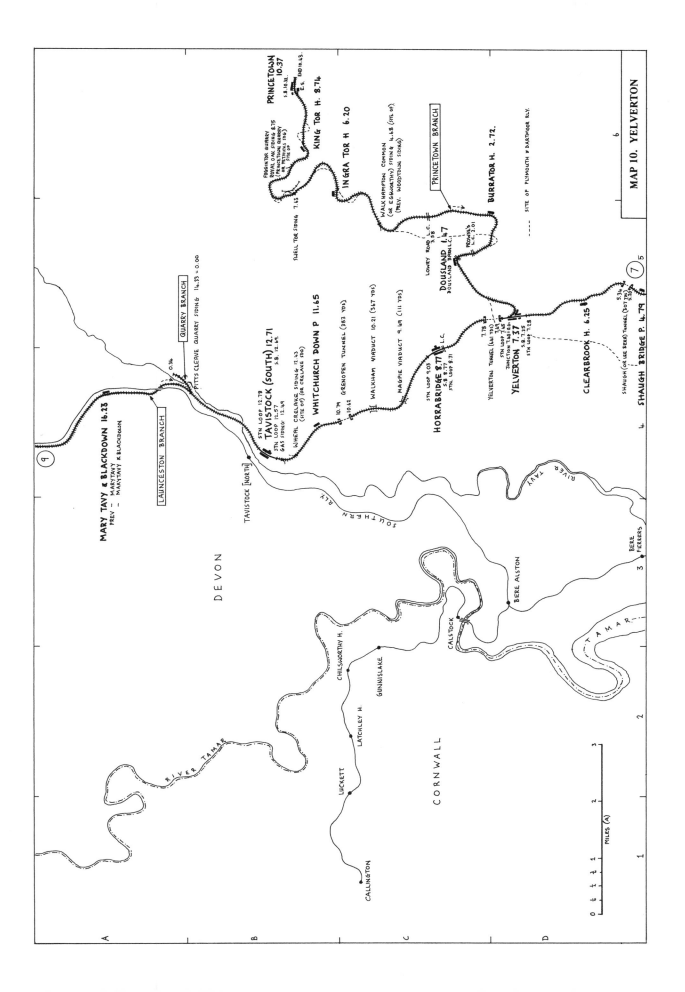

MAP 10. YELVERTON

PRINCETOWN 10.37
S.B. 10.32.
END 10.43.
E.S.
KING TOR H. 8.74
FOGGINTOR QUARRY
ROYAL OAK SIDING 8.75
(PRINCETOWN QUARRY
OR PETHICKS SDG)
SITE OF.
INGRA TOR H. 6.20
WALKHAMPTON COMMON
(OR EGGWORTHY) SIDING & 4.68 (SITE OF).
(PREV. WOODYTOWN SIDING)
SWELL TOR SIDING 7.63

PRINCETOWN BRANCH

BURRATOR H. 2.72.

LOWERY ROAD L.C.
3.58
PROWSE'S
L.C. 2.01
SITE OF PLYMOUTH & DARTMOOR RLY.

DOUSLAND 1.47
DOUSLAND BARN L.C.

(7)

CLEARBROOK H. 6.25
5.34
S.B. 5.30
SHAUGH (OR LEE MOOR) TUNNEL (307 YDS)
SHAUGH BRIDGE P. 4.79

YELVERTON TUNNEL (641 YDS)
YELVERTON 7.37
JUNCTION 7 & 0.00
STN LOOP 7.45
7.44
STN LOOP 7.28
S.B. 7.25

HORRABRIDGE 8.77
L.C.
S.B. 8.77
STN LOOP 8.71
7.78

MAGPIE VIADUCT 9.49 (111 YDS)

WALKHAM VIADUCT 10.21 (367 YDS)

GRENOFEN TUNNEL (363 YDS)
10.74
10.62

WHITCHURCH DOWN P 11.65

WHEAL CRELAKE SIDING 12.43
(SITE OF) (OR CRELAKE SDG)

TAVISTOCK (SOUTH) 12.71
S.B. 12.69.
STN LOOP 12.57
GAS SIDING 12.49
STN LOOP 12.78

PITTS CLEAVE QUARRY SIDING 14.33 = 0.00

QUARRY BRANCH

0.34

0.36

LAUNCESTON BRANCH

MARY TAVY & BLACKDOWN 16.23
PREV. – MARYTAVY
– MARYTAVY & BLACKDOWN

(9)

TAVISTOCK [NORTH]

DEVON

RIVER TAMAR

SOUTHERN RLY.

RIVER TAVY

RIVER TAVY

CALLINGTON

LUCKETT

LATCHLEY H.

CHILSWORTHY H.

GUNNISLAKE

CALSTOCK

BERE ALSTON

BERE
FERRERS

CORNWALL

TAMAR

A

B

C

D

MILES (A)

0   ¼ ½ ¾ 1   2   3

1   2   3   4   5   6

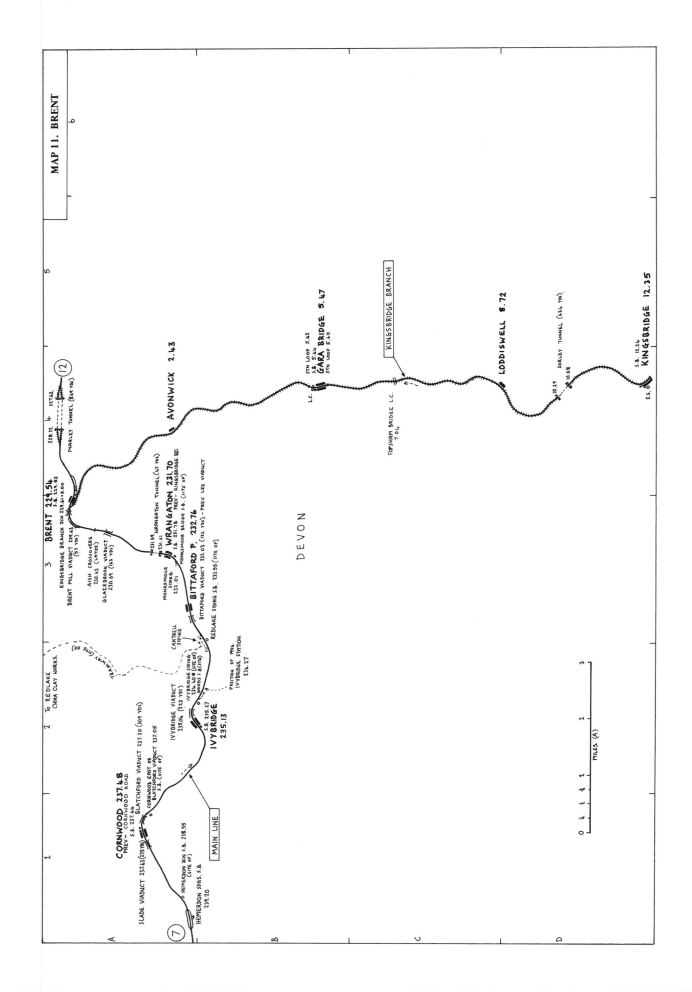

MAP 11. BRENT

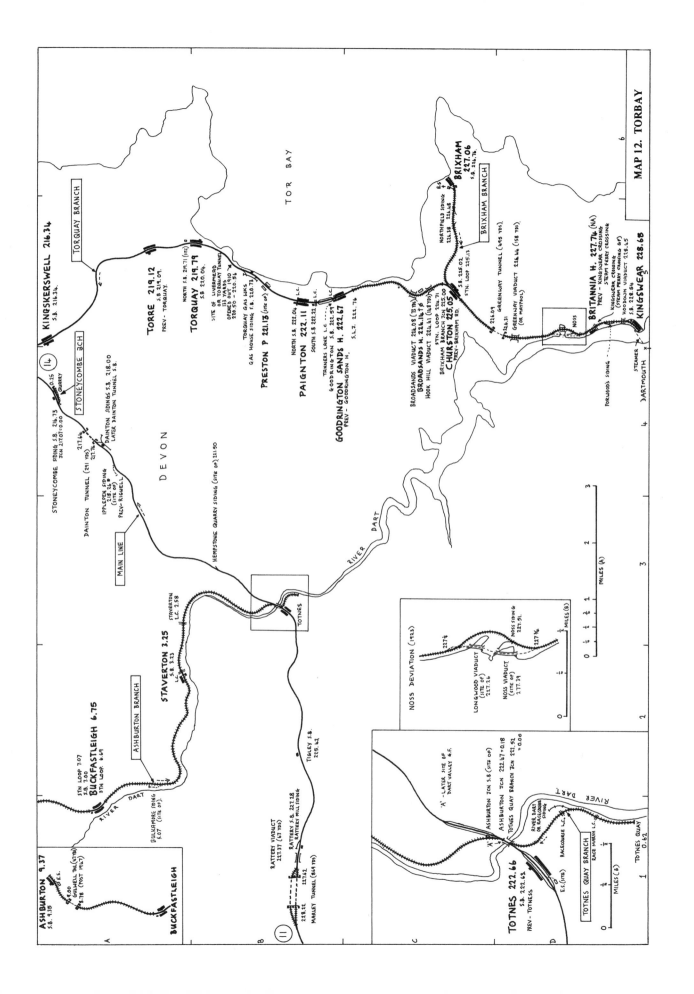

MAP 12. TORBAY

KINGSKERSWELL 216.34
S.B. 216.36.

TORQUAY BRANCH

TORRE 219.12
PREV - TORQUAY.

TORQUAY 219.79
S.B. 220.06.
NORTH S.B. 219.71 (SITE)

SITE OF LIVERMEAD
OR TORQUAY TUNNEL
133 YARDS
OPENED OUT 1910
210.50 - 220.56

STONEYCOMBE SIDING S.B. 216.73
STONEYCOMBE BCH
JCN 217.07 - 0.00
STONEYCOMBE
QUARRY
0.25
14

STONEYCOMBE 217.44
217.74

DAINTON SIDING S.B. 218.00
LATER DAINTON TUNNEL S.B.
DAINTON TUNNEL (291 YDS)
IPPLEPEN SIDING
218.26 (SITE OF)
PREV - RIGWELL.

MAIN LINE

TORQUAY GAS WKS
GAS HOUSE SIDING S.B. 220.73

PRESTON P 221.13 (SITE OF)

PAIGNTON 222.11
NORTH S.B. 222.04
SOUTH S.B. 222.22

TANNERS LANE L.C.
GOODRINGTON S.B. 222.59
GOODRINGTON SANDS H. 222.67
PREV - GOODRINGTON H.
S.L.T. 222.76

HEMPSTONE QUARRY SIDING (SITE OF) 221.50

BROADSANDS VIADUCT 223.08 (13 YDS)
BROADSANDS H. 224.16. T.P
HOOK HILL VIADUCT 224.41 (167 YDS)

STN. LOOP 224.71
BRIXHAM JCN 225.00
CHURSTON 225.05
PREV - BRIXHAM RD.

NORTHFIELD SIDING
226.18 226.48

BRIXHAM 227.06
S.B. 226.76.

BRIXHAM BRANCH

S.B. 225.02
STN. LOOP 225.13

224.09

224.31
GREENWAY TUNNEL (495 YDS.)
GREENWAY VIADUCT 226.44 (158 YDS.)
(OR MAYPOOL)

NOSS

BRITANNIA H. 227.74 (NA)
PREV - KINGSWEAR CROSSING
(STEAM FERRY CROSSING OF)
HOODOWN VIADUCT 219.45
KINGSWEAR 228.65
S.B. 228.54

FORWOODS SIDING

STEAMER

DARTMOUTH

TOR BAY

DEVON

RIVER DART

NOSS DEVIATION (1923)
LONGWOOD VIADUCT
(SITE OF)
227.26
NOSS SIDING 227.51.
NOSS VIADUCT
(SITE OF)
227.39
227½
227¾

MILES (B)
0 ¼ ½ ¾ MILE

ASHBURTON 9.37
S.B. 9.18

GULWELL TNL (47 YD)
9.00   E.S.
9.78 (POST MILT)

BUCKFASTLEIGH

STN LOOP 7.07
S.B. 7.00
BUCKFASTLEIGH 6.75
STN LOOP 6.69

ASHBURTON BRANCH

BULKAMORE SIDING
(SITE OF).
9.07

STAVERTON 3.25
L.C. 3.23
STAVERTON
L.C. 2.58

RIVER DART

TOTNES

RATTERY VIADUCT
223.37 (47 YDS)
RATTERY S.B. 223.28
RATTERY MILL SIDING

MARLEY TUNNEL (864 YDS)
223.21   223.42

TIGLEY S.B.
223.42

11

ASHBURTON JCN S.B. 222.47 - 0.018 (SITE OF)
TOTNES QUAY BRANCH JCN 221.52
0.00
'A'
RIVER DART OR RACECOURSE
SIDING
TOTNES QUAY BRANCH
RACE MARSH L.C.
'A' = LATER SITE OF DART VALLEY G.F.
RACECOURSE L.C.
TOTNES QUAY 0.62

TOTNES 222.66
S.B. 222.65.
PREV - TOTNES.
E.S. (SITE)

RIVER DART

MILES (A)
3 3 2 1 1
MILES (B)
0 1 2
MILES (B)
0 1

A

B

C

D

5 4 3
6

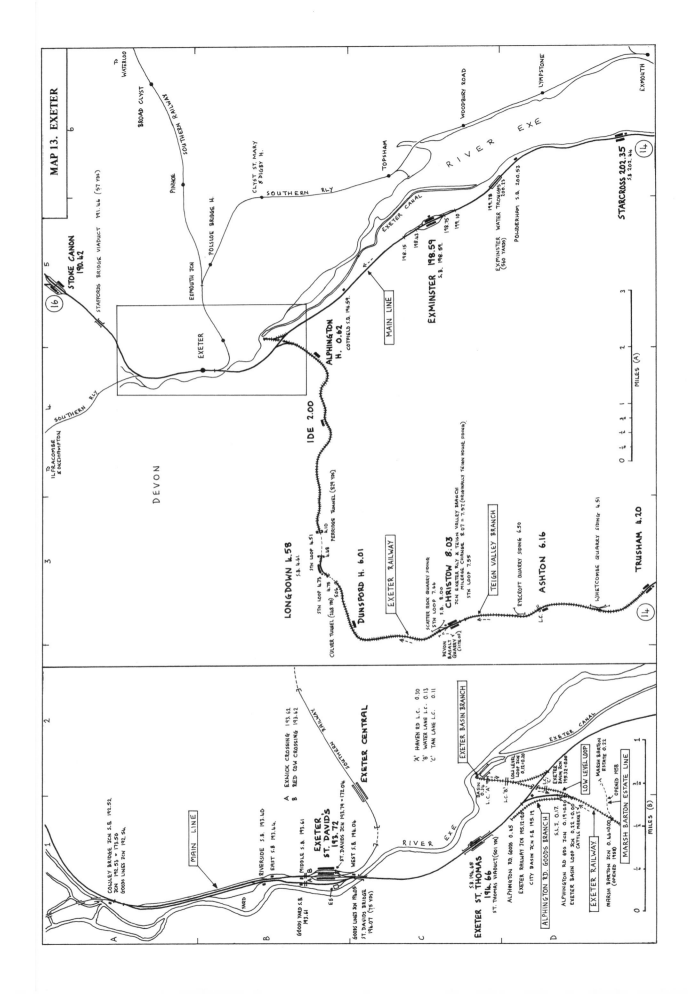

MAP 13. EXETER

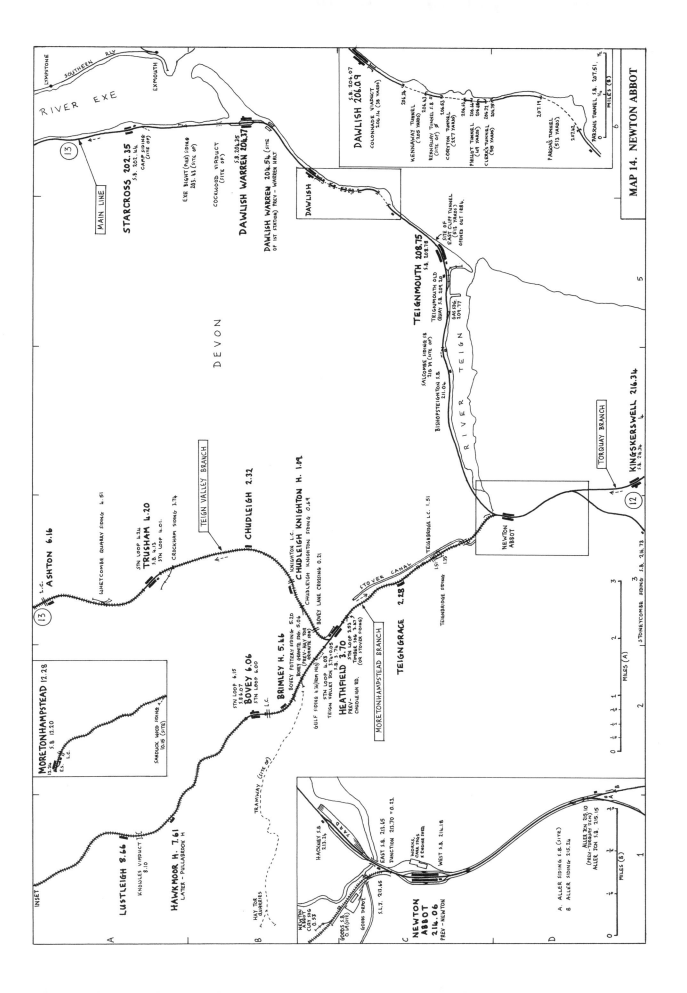

MAP 14. NEWTON ABBOT

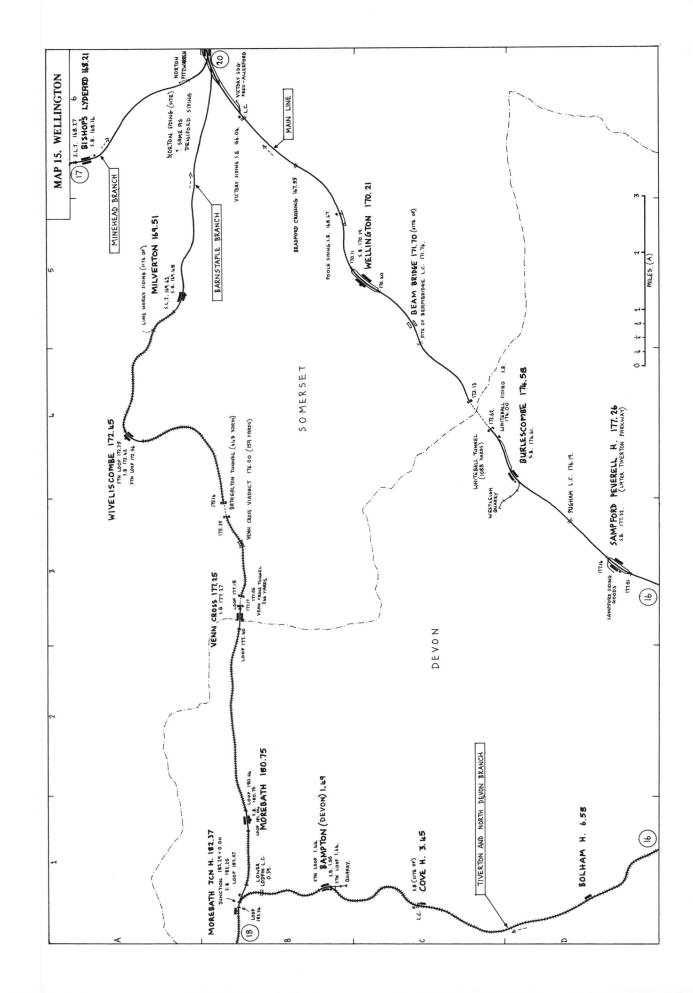

MAP 15. WELLINGTON

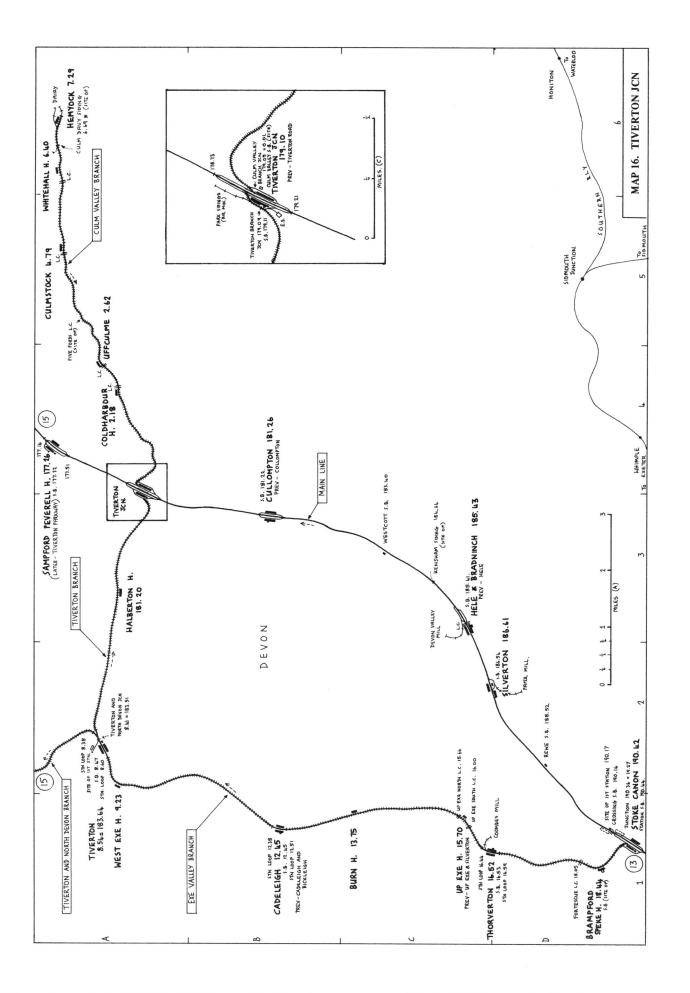

MAP 16. TIVERTON JCN

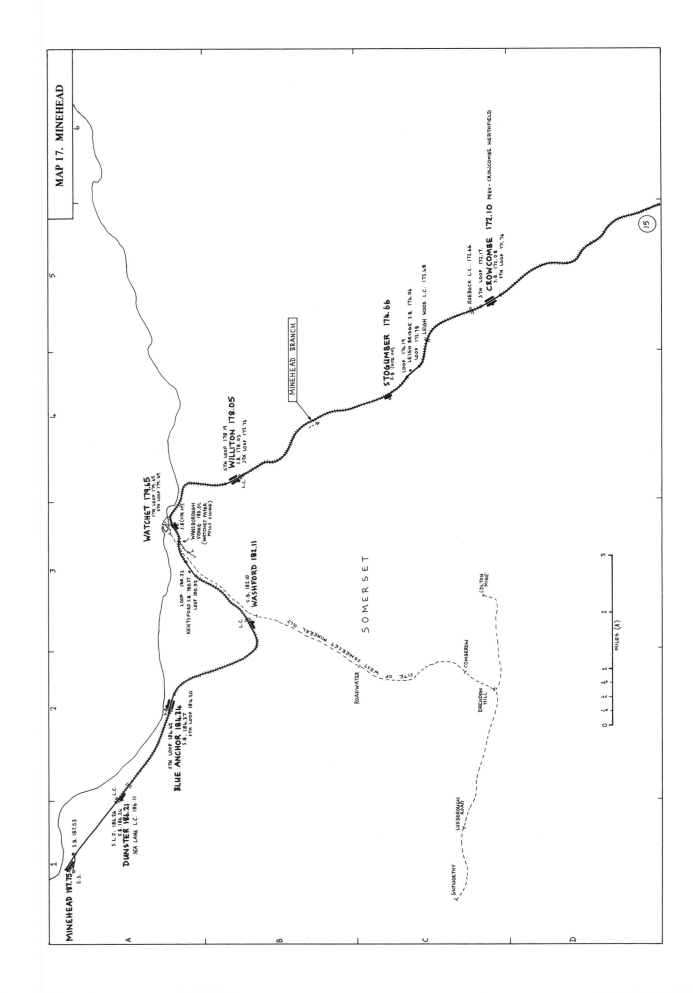

MAP 17. MINEHEAD

MINEHEAD BRANCH

SOMERSET

MINEHEAD 187.75
E.S.
S.B. 187.53

S.L.3. 186.24 L.C.
S.B. 186.24
DUNSTER 186.21
SEA LANE L.C. 186.11

BLUE ANCHOR 184.34
STN LOOP 184.42
S.B. 184.37
STN LOOP 184.20

WASHFORD 182.11
S.B. 182.10
L.C.

WATCHET 179.65
STN LOOP 179.65
STN LOOP 179.44

S.B. (NTH OP.)
WANSBOROUGH
SIDING 180.01
(WATCHET PAPER
MILLS SIDING)
KENTSFORD S.B. 180.37
LOOP 180.37
LOOP 180.57

WILLITON 178.05
STN LOOP 178.14
S.B. 178.03
STN LOOP 177.76
L.C.

STOGUMBER 174.66
S.B. (NTH OP.)
LOOP 174.14
LEIGH BRIDGE S.B. 174.06
LEIGH WOOD L.C. 173.48
LOOP 173.78

CROWCOMBE 172.10 PREV - CROWCOMBE HEATHFIELD
S.B. 172.08
STN LOOP 171.76
STN LOOP 172.17
ROEBUCK L.C. 172.66

SITE OF WEST SOMERSET MINERAL RLY

ROADWATER

COMBEROW

BRENDON HILL

LUXBOROUGH ROAD

GUPWORTHY

COLTON MINE

MILES (A)
0   ½   1   1½   2   3

15

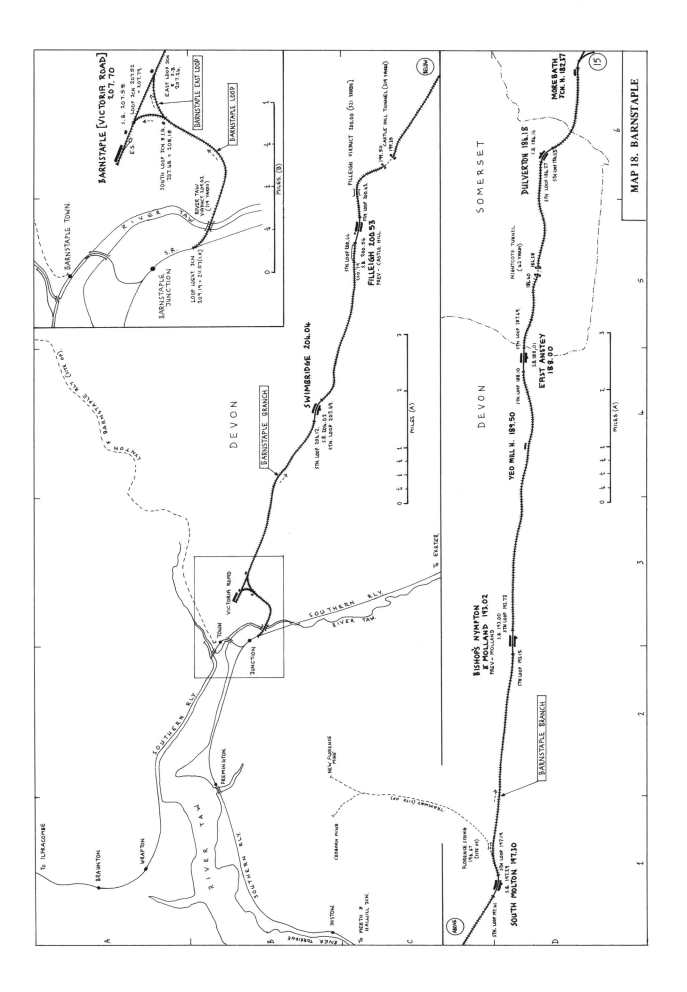

MAP 18. BARNSTAPLE

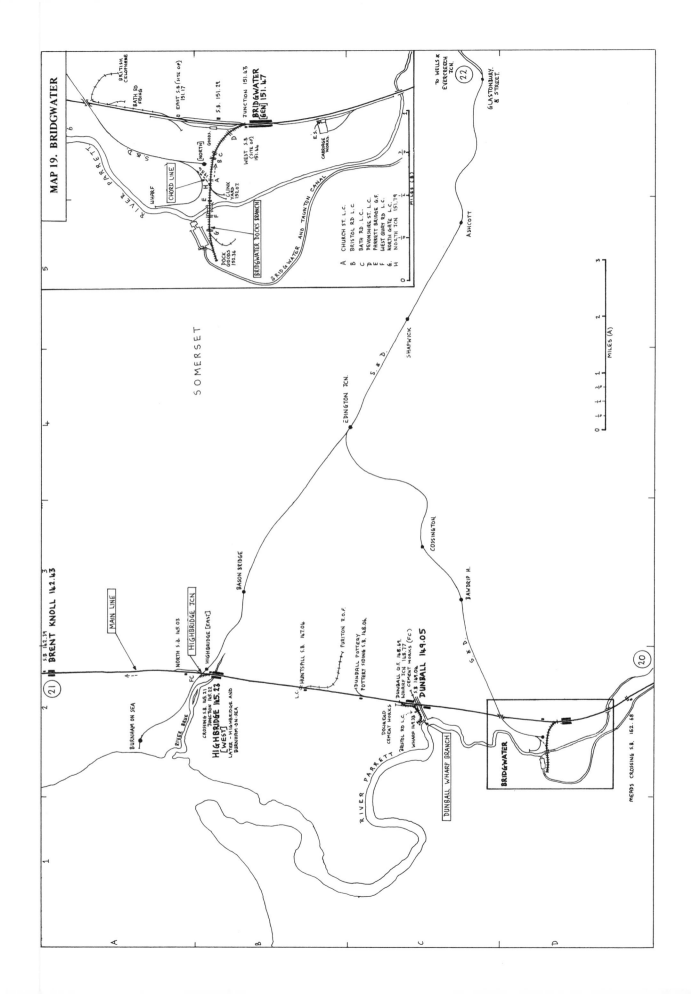

MAP 19. BRIDGWATER

SOMERSET

A CHURCH ST. L.C.
B BRISTOL RD L.C.
C BATH RD L.C.
D PEVONHIRE ST. L.C.
E WEST QUAY RD L.C.
F PARRETT BRIDGE G.F.
G NORTH GATE L.C.
H NORTH JCN 151.79

RIVER PARRETT

BRITISH CELOPHANE
EAST S.B (SITE OF) 151.17
BATH RD SIDING
[NORTH]
GOODS.
S.B. 151.24
JUNCTION 151.43
BRIDGWATER [GEN] 151.47
WEST S.B (SITE OF) 151.44
E.S.
CABBAGE WORKS.
CHORD LINE
WHARF
LINK YARD 151.07
BRIDGWATER DOCKS BRANCH
DOCK GOODS 151.36
BRIDGWATER AND TAUNTON CANAL

TO WELLS & EVERCREECH JCN.
GLASTONBURY & STREET.
ASHCOTT
SHAPWICK
S & D
EDINGTON JCN.
COSSINGTON
BAWDRIP H.
S & D

MILES (B)

MILES (A)

BRENT KNOLL 142.43
S.B. 142.39
MAIN LINE
BASON BRIDGE
HIGHBRIDGE [EAST]
NORTH S.B. 145.03
HIGHBRIDGE JCN
FC
CROSSING S.B. 145.21
JUNCTION 145.22
HIGHBRIDGE [WEST]
LATER - HIGHBRIDGE AND BURNHAM-ON-SEA
BURNHAM ON SEA
RIVER BRUE
HUNTSPILL S.B. 147.04
L.C.
PURITON R.O.F.
DUNBALL POTTERY
POTTERY SIDING S.B. 148.04.
DUNBALL G.F. 148.64
DUNBALL JCN 148.77
S.B 148.06
DUNBALL 149.05
CEMENT WORKS (FC)
DUNBALL WHARF JCN
COGNARD CEMENT WORKS
BRISTOL RD L.C.
WHARF 149.23
WHARF
DUNBALL WHARF BRANCH
RIVER PARRETT
BRIDGWATER
MERDS CROSSING S.B. 162.68

21
20
22

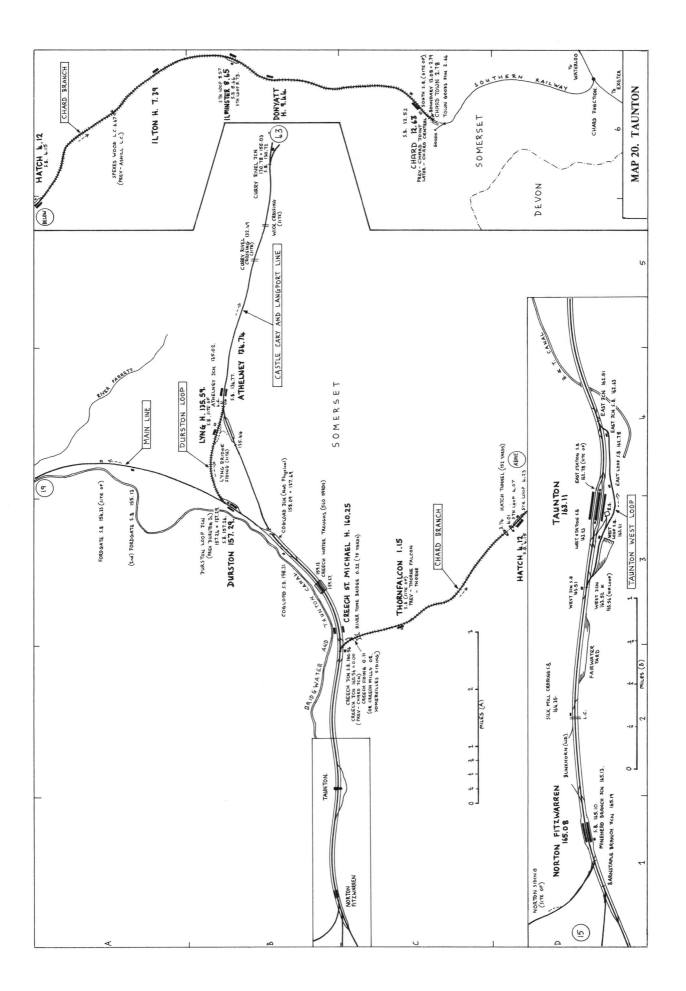

MAP 20. TAUNTON

HATCH 4.12
S.B. 4.15

ILTON H. 7.39

CHARD BRANCH

SPEKES WOOD L.C. 6.47
(PREV - ASHILL L.C.)

ILMINSTER 8.65
STN. LOOP 8.57
STN. LOOP 8.73

DONYATT H. 9.44

CURRY RIVEL JCN
130.73 = 156.03
S.B. 130.72

CURRY RIVEL 132.49
(SITE OF)

WICK CROSSING
(SITE)

CASTLE CARY AND LANGPORT LINE

CHARD 12.63
PREV - CHARD JOINT
LATER - CHARD CENTRAL

S.B. 12.52

SOUTH S.B. (SITE OF)
BOUNDARY 13.08 = 2.79
CHARD TOWN 2.78
TOWN GOODS JCN 2.46
GOODS

SOMERSET

SOUTHERN RAILWAY

To WATERLOO

CHARD JUNCTION

To EXETER

DEVON

SOMERSET

RIVER PARRETT

BRIDGWATER AND TAUNTON CANAL

MAIN LINE

DURSTON LOOP

LYNG H. 135.59.
S.B. SITE OF
ATHELNEY JCN 135.02.

ATHELNEY 136.74

S.B. 136.77

LYNG BRIDGE
SIDING (SITE OF)
135.44

FORDGATE S.B. 154.11 (SITE OF)
(2nd) FORDGATE S.B. 155.13

DURSTON LOOP JCN
(PREV DURSTON JC.)
157.24 = 157.26
S.B. 157.26.

DURSTON 157.29.

COGLOAD S.B. 158.31

COGLOAD JCN (NOT PHYSICAL)
158.04 = 157.68.

CREECH WATER TROUGHS (560 YARDS)

154.11
CREECH WATER 154.17

CREECH ST. MICHAEL H. 160.25

CREECH JCN S.B. 160.56
(PREV - CHARD JCN)
CREECH SIDING 0.11
(OR CREECH MILLS OR
SOMERVILLES SIDING)
R. RIVER TONE BRIDGE 0.21 (78 YARDS)

THORNFALCON 1.15
S.B. (SITE OF)
(PREV - THORNE FALCON
OR - THORNE)

CHARD BRANCH

HATCH 4.12
S.B. 4.15

3.74 HATCH TUNNEL (91 YARDS)
4.01
STN. LOOP 4.07
STN. LOOP 4.23

ABOVE

T. CANAL

EAST JCN 162.61
EAST JCN
EAST LOOP S.B. 162.63
EAST S.B. 162.78

TAUNTON 163.11

EAST STATION S.B. 161.78 (SITE OF)

WEST STATION S.B. 163.13
E.S.

WEST S.B. 163.51
WEST JCN
163.52 E
163.56 (WEST LOOP)
WEST S.B.
163.31

WEST LOOP S.B.

TAUNTON WEST LOOP

FAIRWATER YARD

SILK MILL CROSSING S.B. 164.15
L.C.

BUNKHORN (sub).

NORTON FITZWARREN 165.08

NORTON SIDING (SITE OF)

S.B. 165.10
MINEHEAD BRANCH JCN 165.13.
BARNSTAPLE BRANCH JCN 165.19

TAUNTON.

NORTON FITZWARREN

TAUNTON.

19

BELOW

43

5

6

4

3

2

1

15

A

B

C

D

0 ¼ ½ ¾ 1   2   3
MILES (A)

0 ¼ ½ ¾ 1
MILES (B)

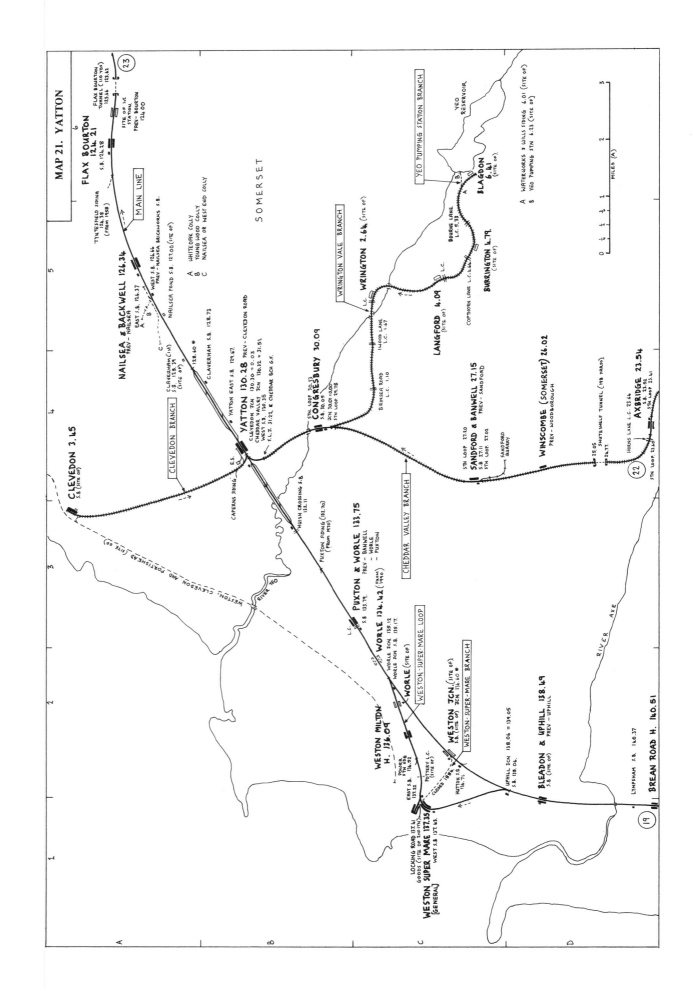

MAP 21. YATTON

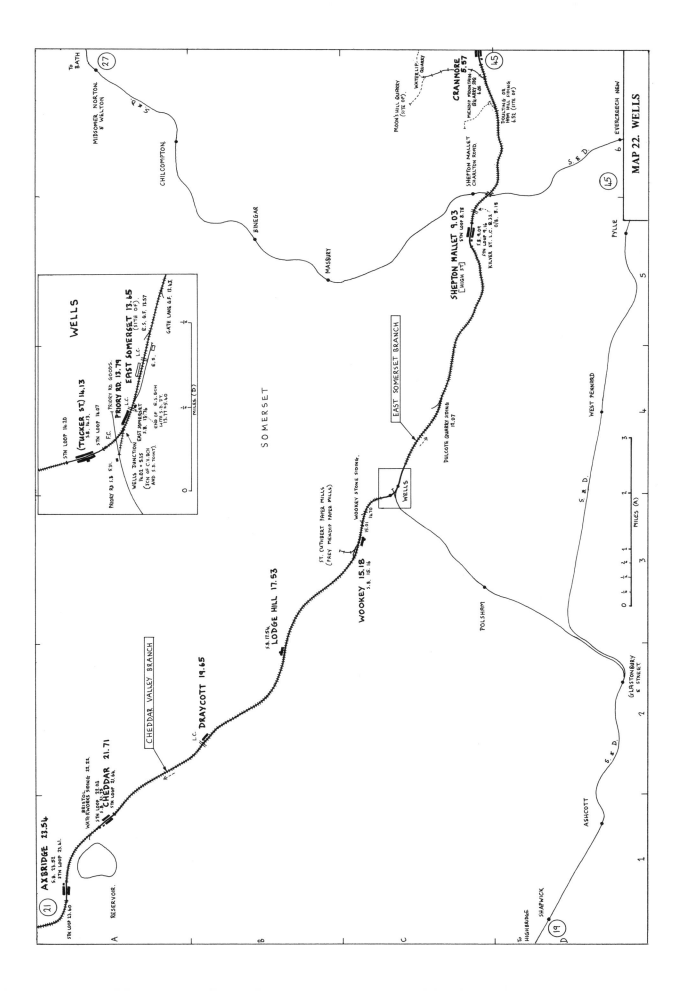

MAP 22. WELLS

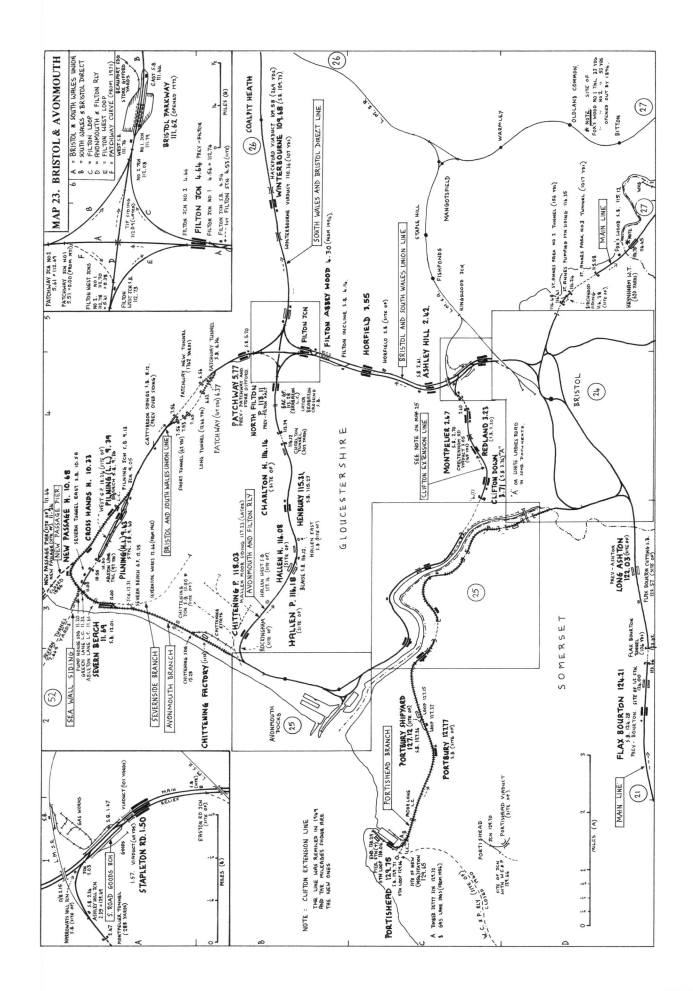

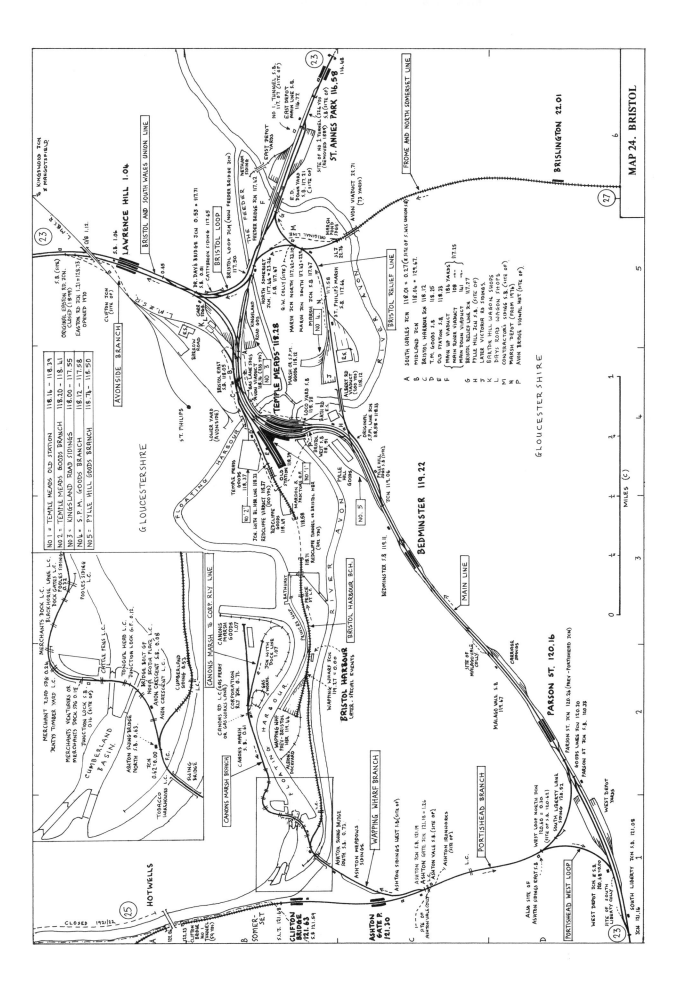

MAP 24. BRISTOL

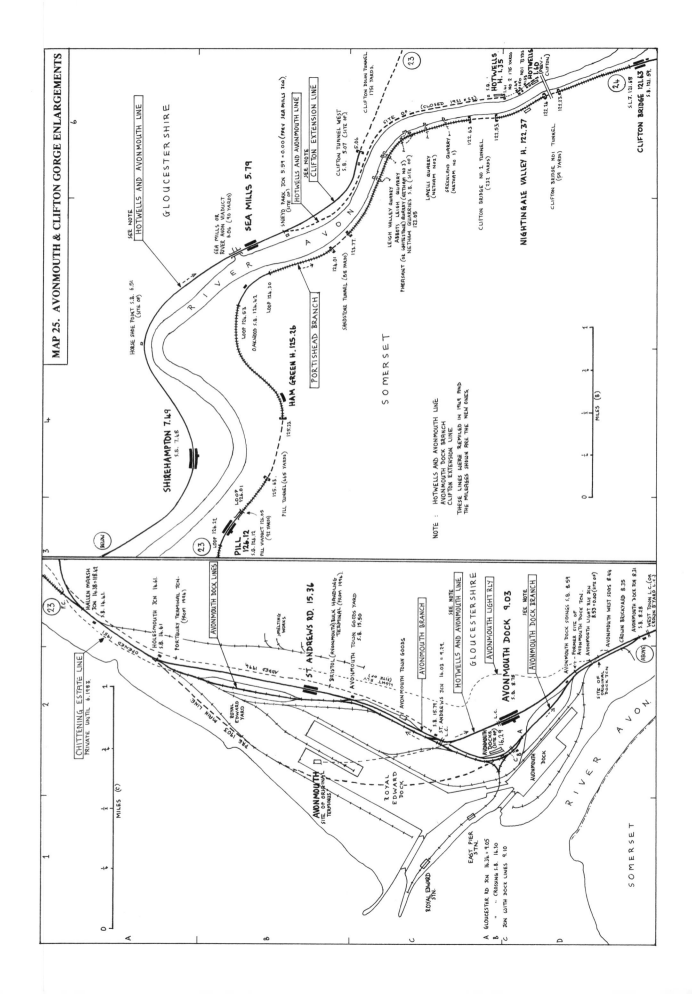

MAP 25. AVONMOUTH & CLIFTON GORGE ENLARGEMENTS

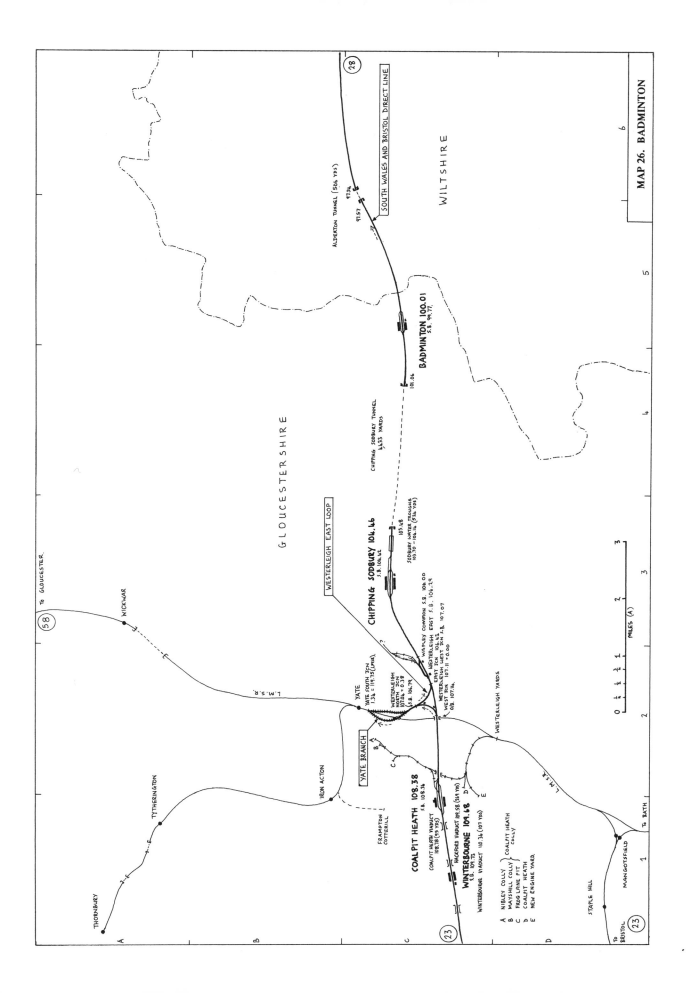

THORNBURY

TYTHERINGTON

WICKWAR

⑤⑧ TO GLOUCESTER.

TO GLOUCESTER.

L.M.S.R.

YATE

YATE SOUTH JCN 1.34 = 119.75 (L.M.S.)

WESTERLEIGH NORTH JCN 107.04 = 0.38

WESTERLEIGH NORTH JCN S.B. 104.74

⑤⑧

IRON ACTION

FRAMPTON COTTERILL

YATE BRANCH

WESTERLEIGH EAST LOOP

CHIPPING SODBURY 104.46
S.B. 106.42

WAPLEY COMMON S.B. 106.00

EAST JCN 106.41

WESTERLEIGH EAST S.B. 104.29

WEST JCN 107.11 = 0.00

0/B. 107.14

WESTERLEIGH WEST JCN S.B. 107.07

WESTERLEIGH YARDS

105.48

SODBURY WATER TROUGHS (524 YDS)
103.70 - 104.14

CHIPPING SODBURY TUNNEL 4433 YARDS

101.04

BADMINTON 100.01
S.B. 99.77

ALDERTON TUNNEL (506 YDS)

97.14

97.57

SOUTH WALES AND BRISTOL DIRECT LINE

②⑧

GLOUCESTERSHIRE

WILTSHIRE

COALPIT HEATH 108.38
S.B. 108.34

COALPIT HEATH VIADUCT 108.78 (95 YDS)

HACKFORD VIADUCT 108.58 (369 YDS)

WINTERBOURNE 109.68
S.B. 109.73

WINTERBOURNE VIADUCT 110.36 (107 YDS)

NIBLEY COLLY.
MAYSHILL COLLY. } COALPIT HEATH COLLY.

A NIBLEY COLLY.
B MAYSHILL COLLY.
C FROG LANE PIT
D COALPIT HEATH
E NEW ENGINE YARD.

L.M.S.R.

STAPLE HILL

MANGOTSFIELD

②③

TO BRISTOL

TO BATH

MILES (A)

0 ¼ ½ ¾ 1 1½ 2 2½ 3

MAP 26. BADMINTON

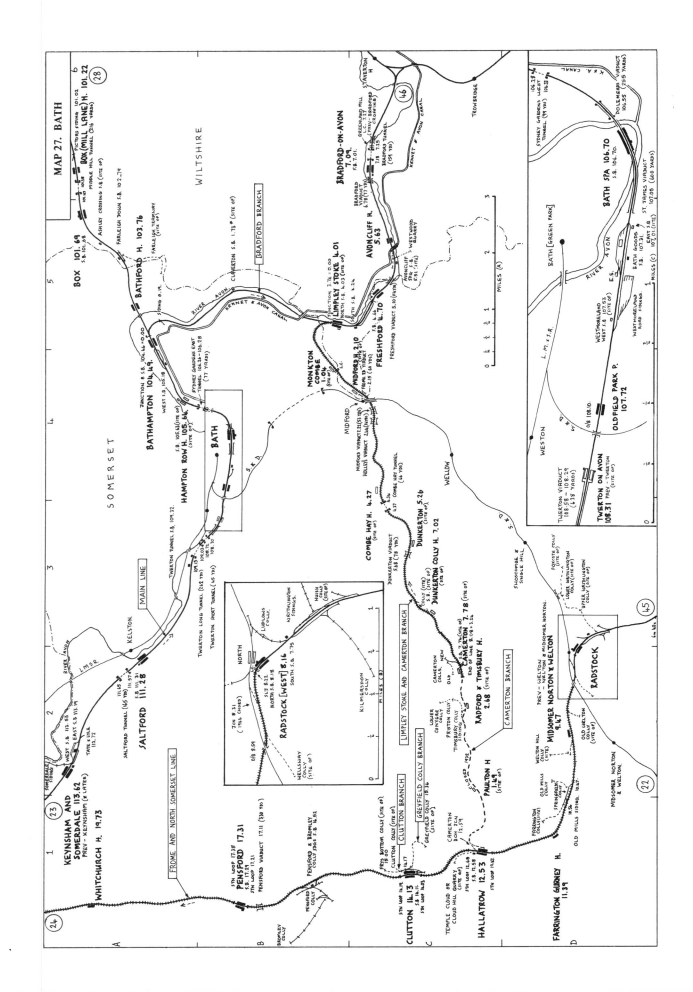

MAP 27. BATH

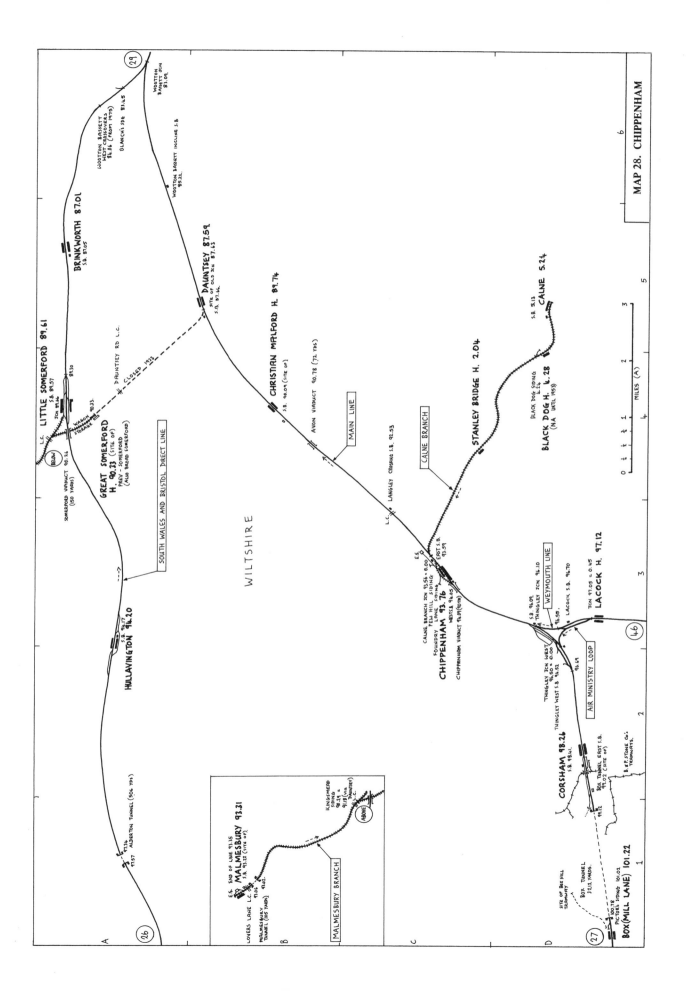

MAP 28. CHIPPENHAM

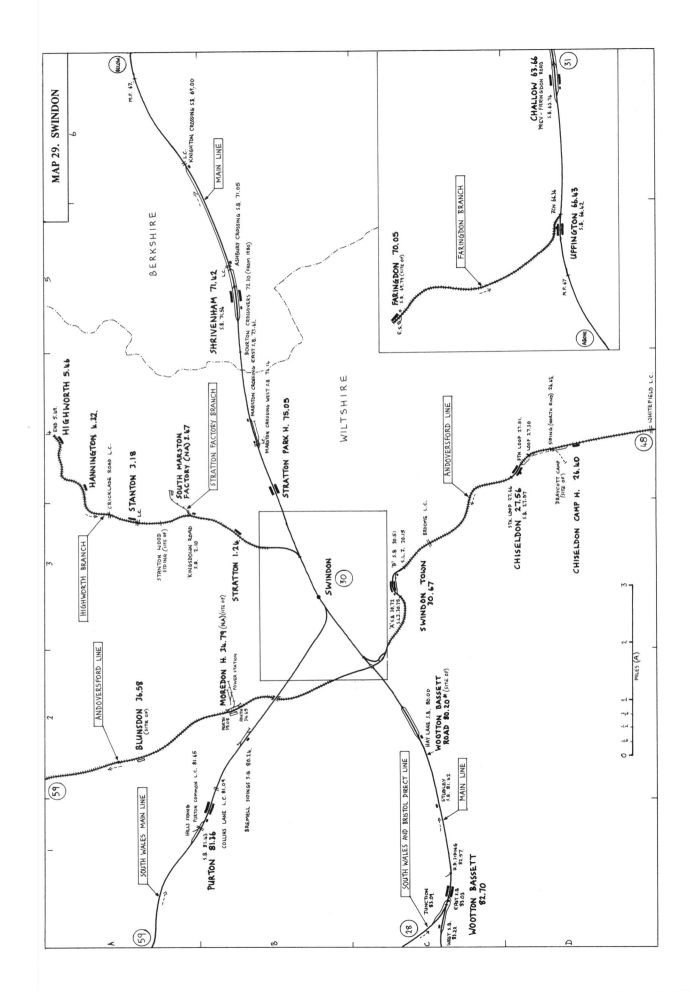

MAP 29. SWINDON

BERKSHIRE

WILTSHIRE

HIGHWORTH 5.46

HANNINGTON 4.32

STANTON 3.18

SOUTH MARSTON FACTORY (NA) 2.67

STRATTON FACTORY BRANCH

HIGHWORTH BRANCH

END 5.49

CRICKLADE ROAD L.C.

STANTON WOOD SIDING (SITE OF)

KINGSDOWN ROAD S.B. 2.10

STRATTON 1.24

STRATTON PARK H. 75.05

SHRIVENHAM 71.42
S.B. 71.54

MARSTON CROSSING WEST S.B. 74.14

BOURTON CROSSOVERS 72.10 (FROM 1986)

MARSTON CROSSING EAST S.B. 71.61

ASHBURY CROSSING S.B. 71.05

L.C. KNIGHTON CROSSING S.B. 69.00

MAIN LINE

M.P. 47

BELOW

6

5

SWINDON

30

ANDOVERSFORD LINE

BLUNSDON 36.58 (SITE OF)

MOREDON H. 34.79 (NA)(SITE OF)

POWER STATION

NORTH 34.08

SOUTH 34.45

BROOME L.C.

'A'S.B. 34.72
S.L.3.30.75

'B' S.B. 30.51
S.L.T. 30.15

SWINDON TOWN 30.67

STN. LOOP 27.51.

CHISELDON 27.56
S.B. 27.57

LOOP 27.30

STN. LOOP 27.66

CHISELDON CAMP H. 26.40

DRAYCOTT CAMP SIDING (NORTH END) 26.63.
SIDING (SITE OF)

WHITEFIELD L.C.

48

ANDOVERSFORD LINE

SOUTH WALES MAIN LINE

BLUNSDON 36.58 (SITE OF)

HILLS SIDING
PURTON COMMON L.C. 81.65

COLLINS LANE L.C. 81.04

BREMELL SIDINGS S.B. 80.24.

PURTON 81.36
S.B. 81.43

HAY LANE S.B. 80.00

WOOTTON BASSETT ROAD 80.20 *(SITE OF)

STURLEY S.B. 81.42

SOUTH WALES AND BRISTOL DIRECT LINE

MAIN LINE

U.D. SIDING 82.57

WOOTTON BASSETT 82.70

JUNCTION 83.09

EAST S.B. 83.03

WEST S.B. 83.21

28

59

59

FARINGDON 70.05

FARINGDON BRANCH

CHALLOW 63.66
PREV.-FARINGDON ROAD
S.B. 63.76

UFFINGTON 66.43
S.B. 66.42

TCH 64.34

M.P. 67

E.S.Q.5.57.71 (SITE OF)

ABOVE

31

MILES (A)

0   ¼   ½   ¾   1   2   3

1

2

3

A

B

C

D

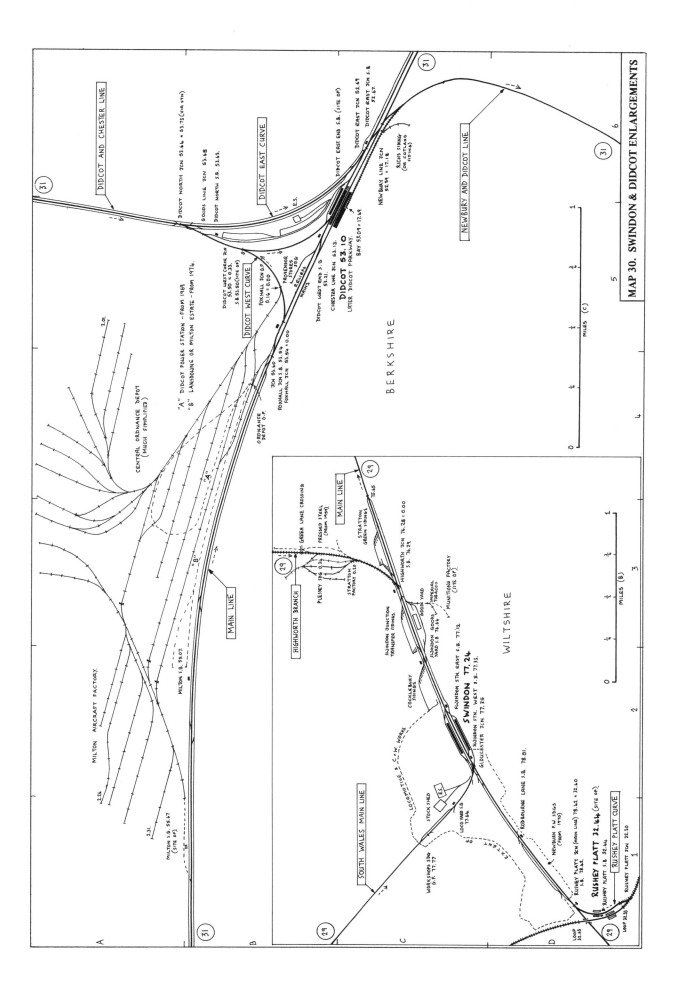

MAP 30. SWINDON & DIDCOT ENLARGEMENTS

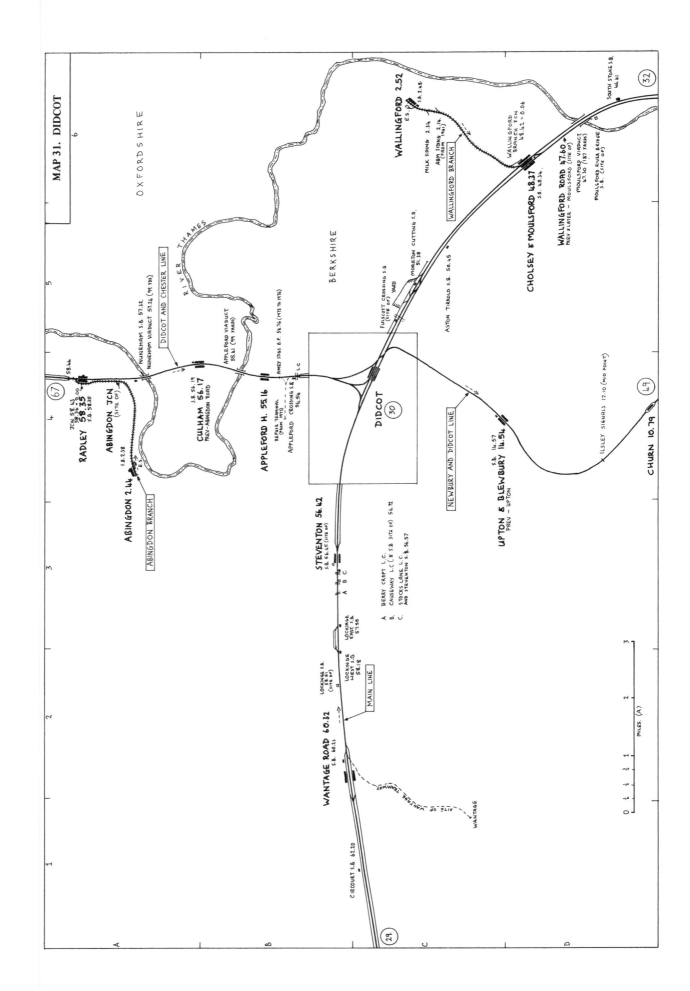

MAP 31. DIDCOT

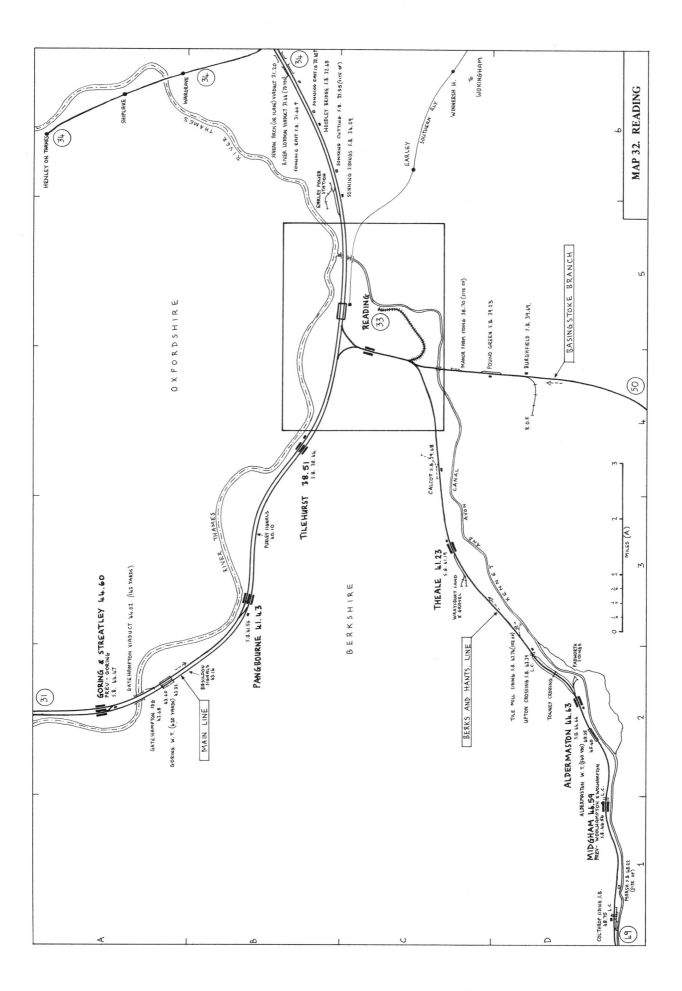

MAP 32. READING

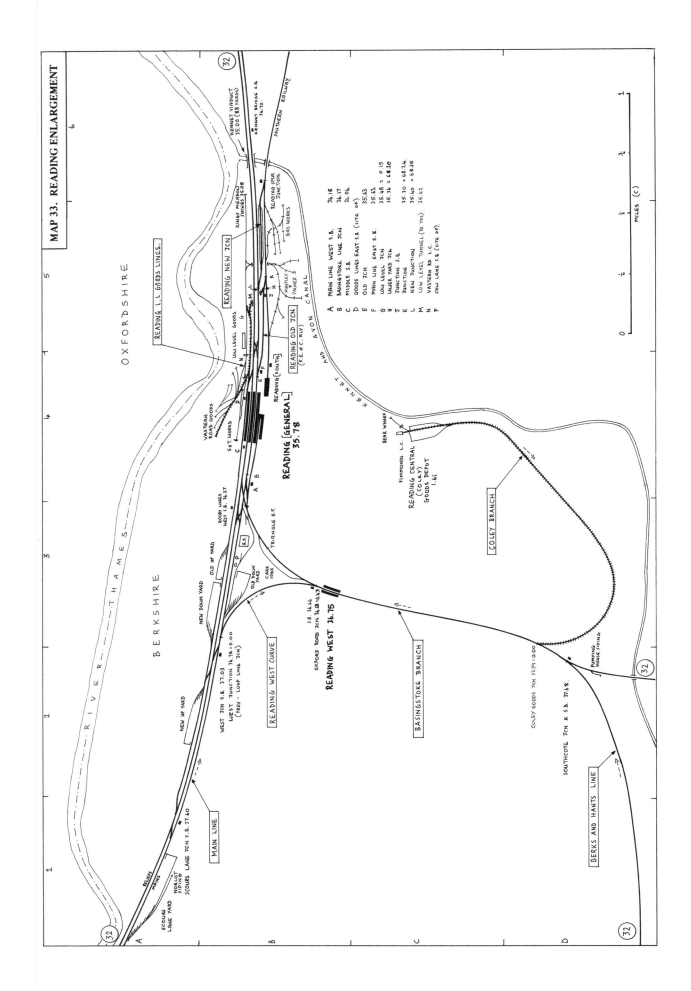

MAP 33. READING ENLARGEMENT

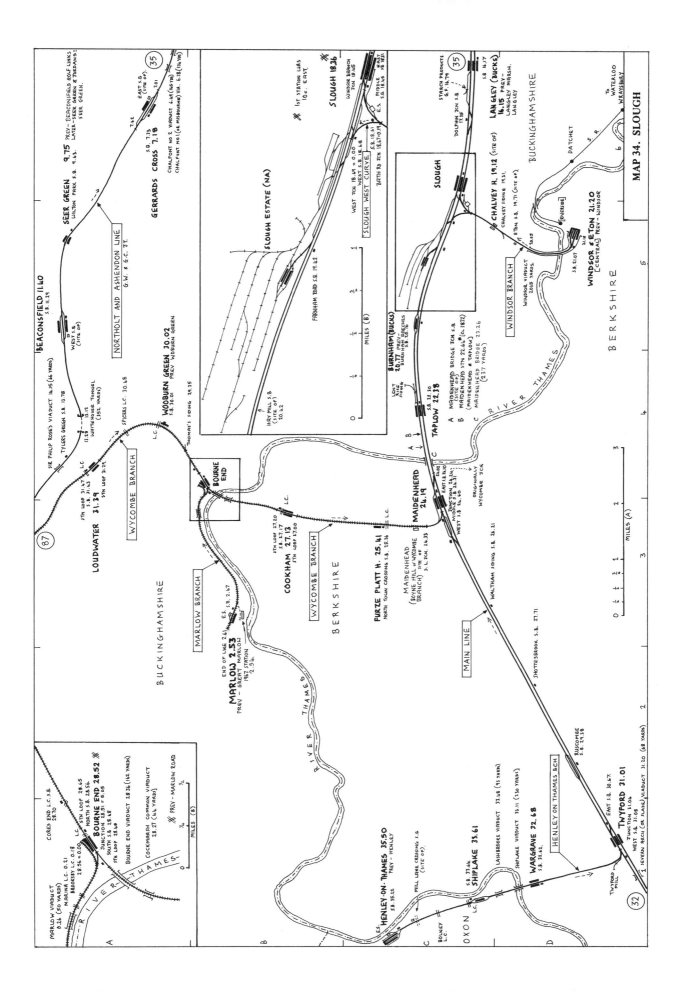

MAP 34. SLOUGH

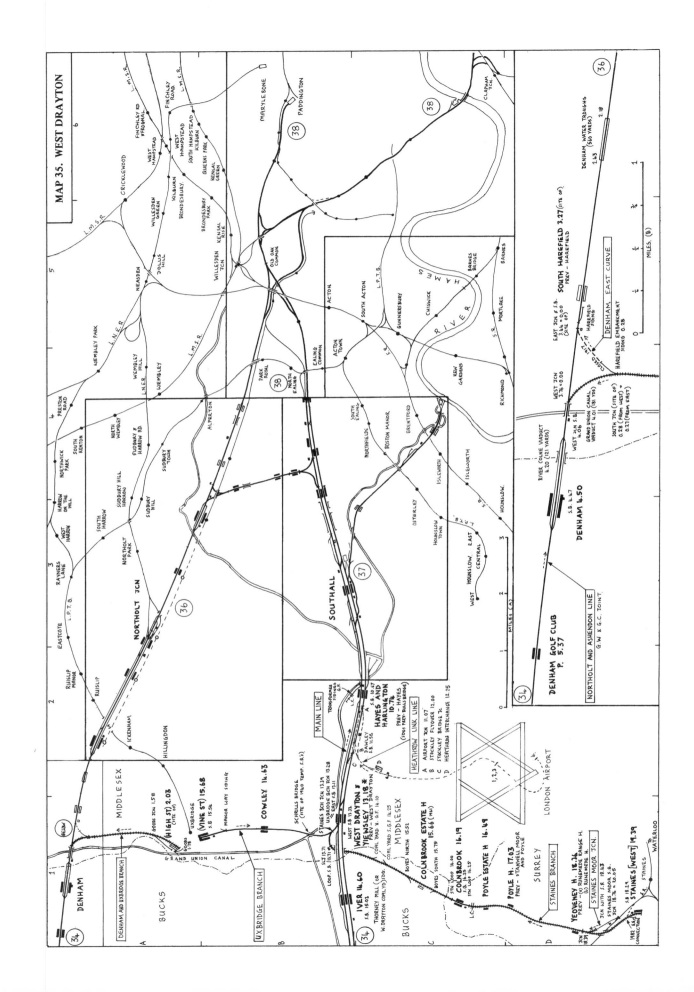

MAP 35. WEST DRAYTON

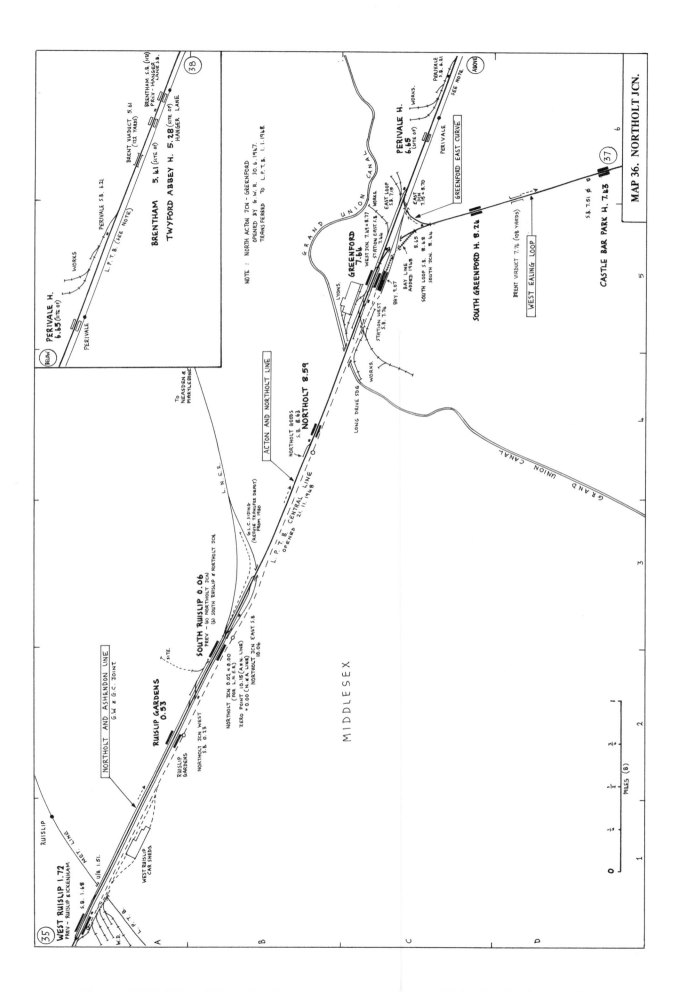

MAP 36. NORTHOLT JCN.

MIDDLESEX

NOTE : NORTH ACTON JCN - GREENFORD
OPENED BY G.W.R. 30.6.1947.
TRANSFERRED TO L.P.T.B. 1.1.1948.

PERIVALE H.
6.65 (SITE OF)

BRENTHAM 5.61 (SITE OF)
TWYFORD ABBEY H. 5.28 (SITE OF)
HANGER LANE

BRENT VIADUCT 5.61 (712 YARDS)
BRENTHAM S.B. 5.61 PREV. HANGER LANE S.B.

PERIVALE S.B. 6.21

PERIVALE H. 6.65 (SITE OF)
PERIVALE

GRAND UNION CANAL

GREENFORD 7.64
WEST JCN 7.63 = 8.77
STATION EAST S.B. 7.44
EAST LOOP S.B. 7.19
EAST JCN 7.15 = 8.70
STATION WEST S.B. 7.74
BAY. 9.07
BAY LINE ADDED 1948
SOUTH LOOP S.B. 8.58
SOUTH JCN. 8.44

GREENFORD EAST CURVE

SOUTH GREENFORD H. 8.24

WEST EALING LOOP
BRENT VIADUCT 7.76 (108 YARDS)

CASTLE BAR PARK H. 7.43
S.B. 7.51 Ø 0

ACTION AND NORTHOLT LINE

NORTHOLT 8.59
NORTHOLT ROADS S.B. 8.63

LYONS.

LONG DRIVE SDG.

WORKS.

GRAND UNION CANAL

To NEASDEN & MARYLEBONE

L.N.E.R.

W.L.C. SIDING (REFUSE TRANSFER DEPOT) FROM 1950

L.P.T.B & CENTRAL LINE
OPENED 21.11.1948

SOUTH RUISLIP 0.06
PREV - (a) NORTHOLT JCN (b) SOUTH RUISLIP & NORTHOLT JCN
NORTHOLT JCN 0.02 = 8.00 (PAR L.N.E.R.)
ZERO POINT (0.15 (A.&N. LINE) * 0.00 (N.&A LINE)
NORTHOLT JCN EAST S.B. 10.06

NORTHOLT JCN WEST S.B. 0.23

RUISLIP GARDENS 0.53
RUISLIP GARDENS

NORTHOLT AND ASHENDON LINE
G.W. & G.C. JOINT

WEST RUISLIP 1.72
PREV.- RUISLIP & ICKENHAM

RUISLIP

MET. LINE
MET. 1.51
U/B 1.68
S.B. 1.68

WEST RUISLIP CAR SHEDS
B.L.
W.D.

MILES (B)
0   1/4   1/2   3/4   1   1   2

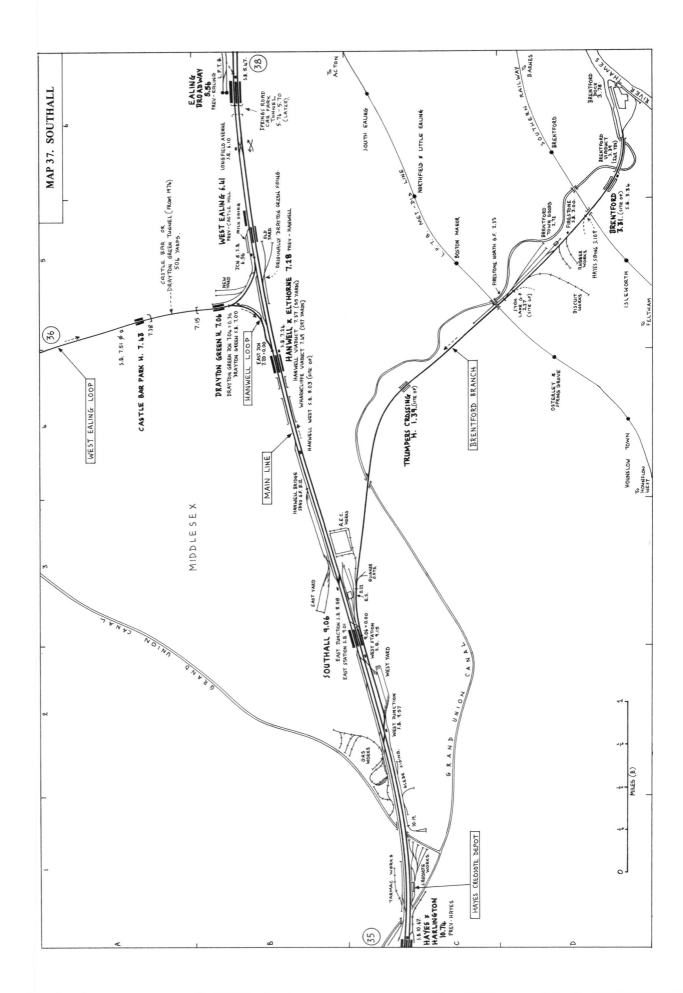

MAP 37. SOUTHALL

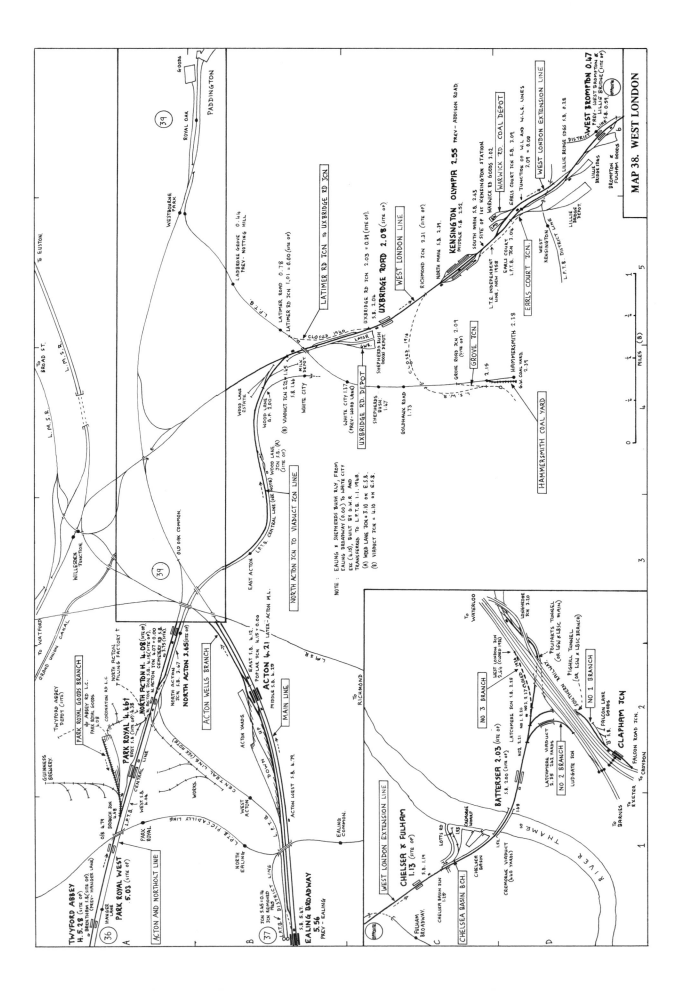

MAP 38. WEST LONDON

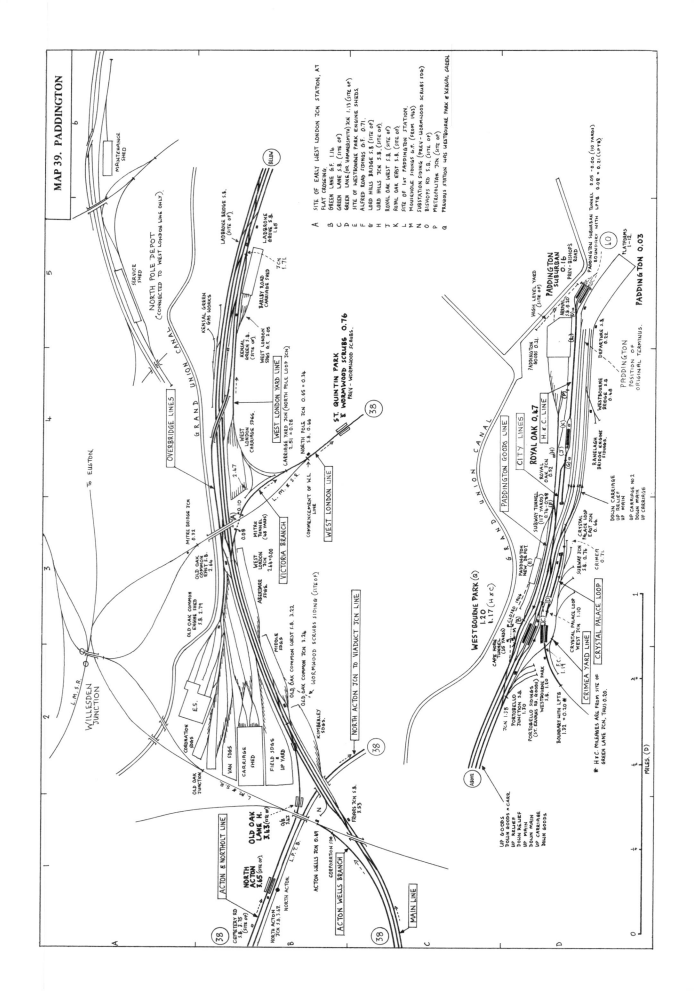

MAP 39. PADDINGTON

A. SITE OF EARLY WEST LONDON JCN STATION, AT FLAT CROSSING.
B. GREEN LANE G.F. 1.14.
C. GREEN LANE S.B. (SITE OF)
D. GREEN LANE (OR WORMWOOD) JCN 1.13 (SITE OF)
E. SITE OF WESTBOURNE PARK ENGINE SHEDS.
F. ALFRED ROAD SIDINGS G.F. 0.71.
G. LORD HILLS BRIDGE S.B. (SITE OF)
H. LORD HILLS JCN S.B. (SITE OF)
J. ROYAL OAK WEST S.B. (SITE OF)
K. ROYAL OAK EAST S.B. (SITE OF)
L. SITE OF 1ST PADDINGTON STATION.
M. MOUSEHOLE SIDINGS (PREV - WORMWOOD SCRUBS 10G) (FROM 1963)
N. SUBSTATION SIDING (PREV - WORMWOOD SCRUBS 10G)
O. BISHOPS RD S.B. (SITE OF)
P. METROPOLITAN JCN (SITE OF)
Q. PREVIOUS STATION WAS WESTBOURNE PARK & KENSAL GREEN.

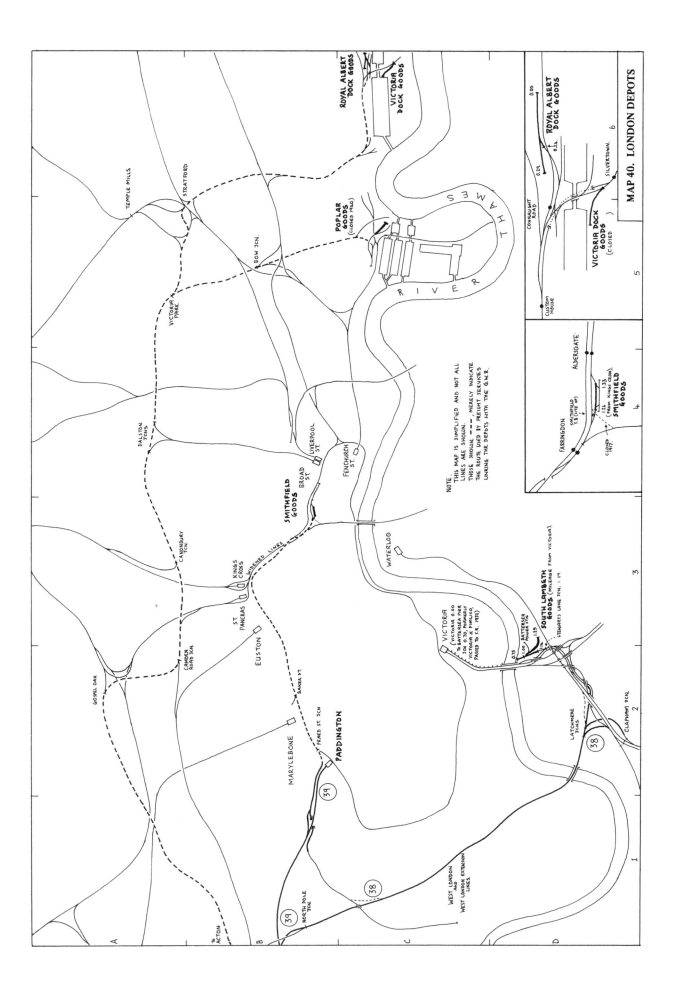

MAP 40. LONDON DEPOTS

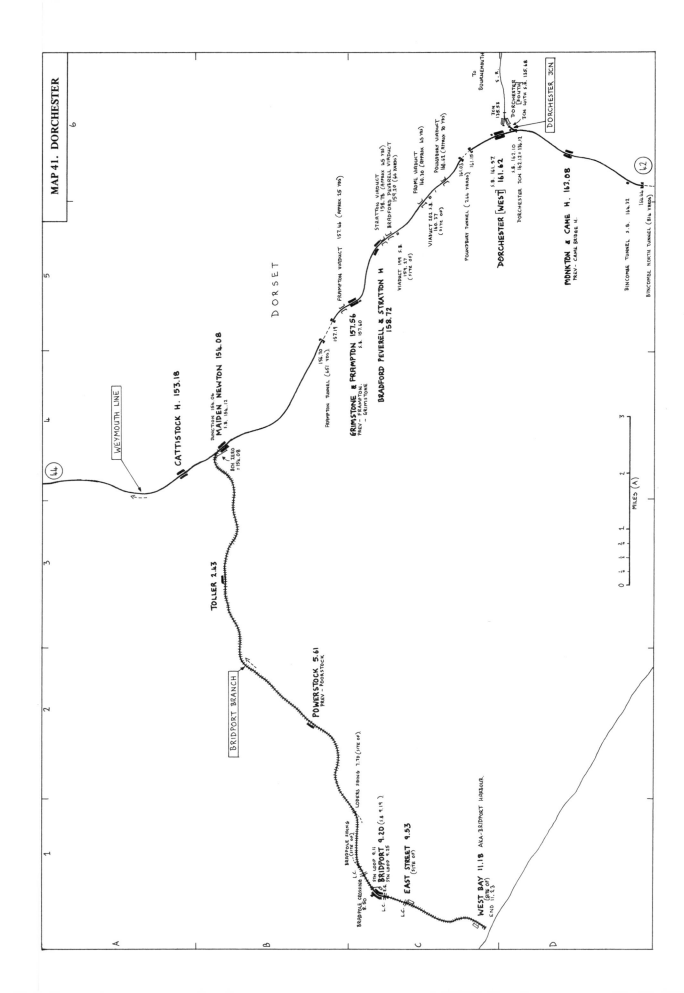

MAP 41. DORCHESTER

DORSET

WEYMOUTH LINE

CATTISTOCK H. 153.18

JUNCTION 154.08
MAIDEN NEWTON 154.08   S.B. 154.12

BCH ZERO 154.08

TOLLER 2.43

BRIDPORT BRANCH

POWERSTOCK 5.61
PREV - POORSTOCK

LODERS SIDING 7.70 (SITE OF)

BRADPOLE SIDING (SITE OF)

BRADPOLE CROSSING 9.50
L.C.

STN LOOP 9.11
BRIDPORT 9.20 (S.B. 9.19)
L.C.   STN LOOP 9.25

EAST STREET 9.53
(SITE OF)

L.C.

WEST BAY 11.18 AKA-BRIDPORT HARBOUR.
(SITE OF)

END 11.23

FRAMPTON TUNNEL (651 YDS)

FRAMPTON VIADUCT 157.46 (APPROX 15 YDS)

GRIMSTONE & FRAMPTON 157.56
PREV - FRAMPTON.   S.B. 157.60
- GRIMSTONE

BRADFORD PEVERELL & STRATTON H.
158.72

VIADUCT 199 S.B.
159.27
(SITE OF)

STRATTON VIADUCT
159.78 (APPROX 45 YDS)
BRADFORD PEVERELL VIADUCT
159.20 (44 YARDS)

FROME VIADUCT
160.30 (APPROX 45 YDS)

VIADUCT 202 S.B.
160.37
(SITE OF)

POUNDBURY VIADUCT
160.61 (APPROX 30 YDS)

POUNDBURY TUNNEL (244 YARDS)

161.03 ?   161.15 ?

To
BOURNEMOUTH

JCN
135.52

DORCHESTER
[SOUTH]
JCN WITH S.R. 115.48

DORCHESTER JCN

DORCHESTER [WEST] 161.62   S.B. 161.57

DORCHESTER JCN 162.12 = 136.12

MONKTON & CAME H. 163.08
PREV - CAME BRIDGE H.

BINCOMBE TUNNEL S.B. 164.32

BINCOMBE NORTH TUNNEL (814 YARDS)
164.44

44

42

0   ½   1   2   3
MILES (A)

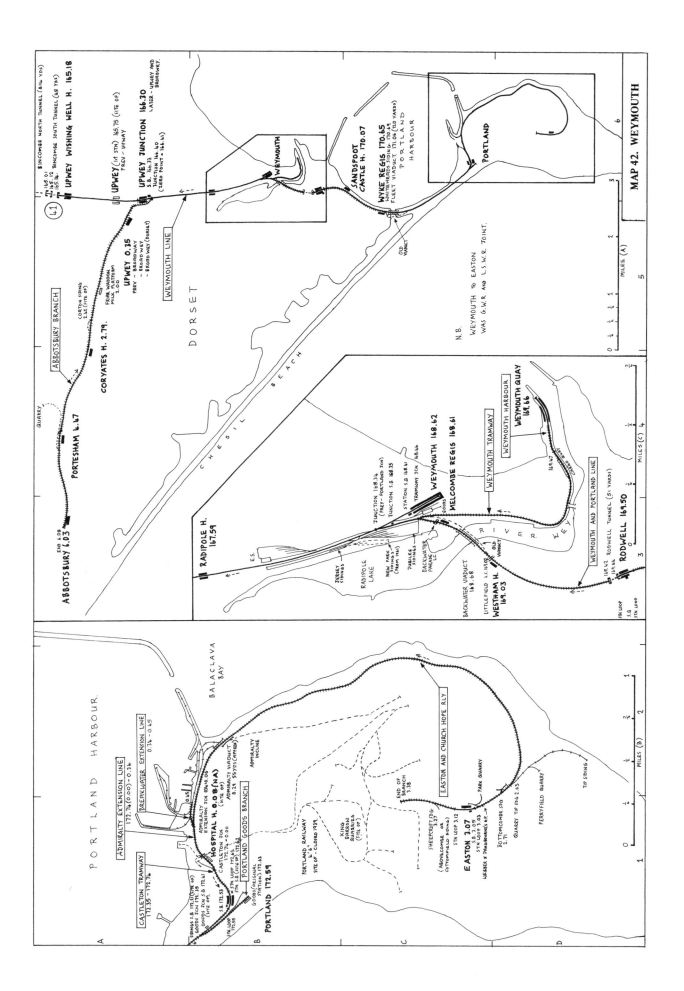

MAP 42. WEYMOUTH

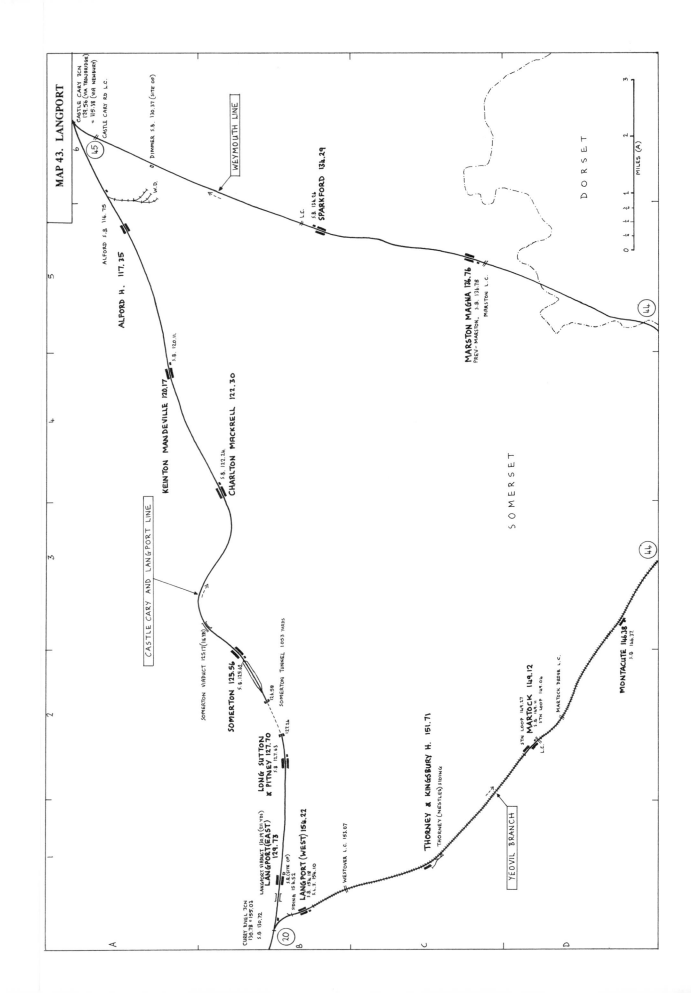

MAP 43. LANGPORT

CASTLE CARY JCN
129.56 (VIA TROWBRIDGE)
= 115.38 (VIA NEWBURY)
CASTLE CARY RD L.C.

DIMMER S.B. 130.37 (SITE OF)

WEYMOUTH LINE

W.D.

ALFORD S.B. 116.75

ALFORD H. 117.35

S.B. 134.56

SPARKFORD 136.29

S.B. 120.11.

KEINTON MANDEVILLE 120.17

MARSTON MAGNA 136.76
PREV-MARSTON. S.B. 136.78
MARSTON L.C.

S.B. 122.24

CHARLTON MACKRELL 122.30

CASTLE CARY AND LANGPORT LINE

SOMERSET

DORSET

MILES (A)

SOMERTON VIADUCT 125.17 (116YD)

S.B. 125.60

SOMERTON 125.56

124.59

SOMERTON TUNNEL 1053 YARDS

127.24

LONG SUTTON
& PITNEY 127.70
S.B 127.65

MONTACUTE 146.38
S.B 146.37

STN LOOP 144.37

MARTOCK 144.12
S.B. 144.11
STN LOOP 144.06
L.C. MARTOCK DROVE L.C.

YEOVIL BRANCH

THORNEY & KINGSBURY H. 151.71
THORNEY (NESTLES) SIDING

CURRY RIVEL JCN
130.78 = 155.03
S.B 130.72.

LANGPORT VIADUCT 130.19 (211 YDS)

LANGPORT (EAST)
129.73
S.B. (SITE OF)

SIDING 154.52

LANGPORT (WEST) 154.22
S.B. 154.18
S.L.T. 154.10

WESTOVER L.C. 151.07

20

44

44

45

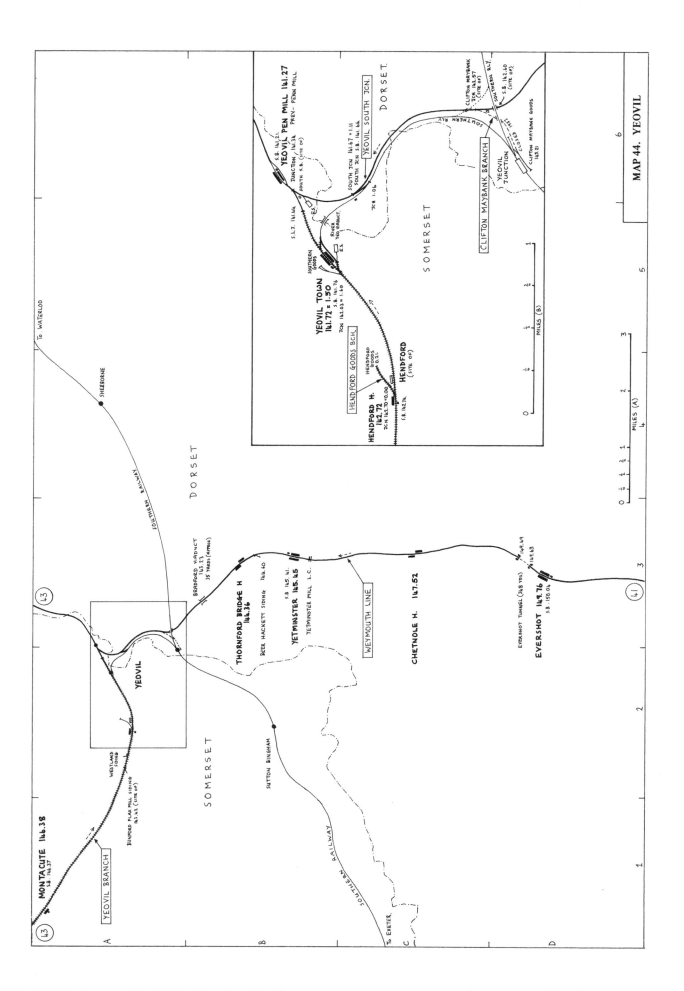

MAP 44. YEOVIL

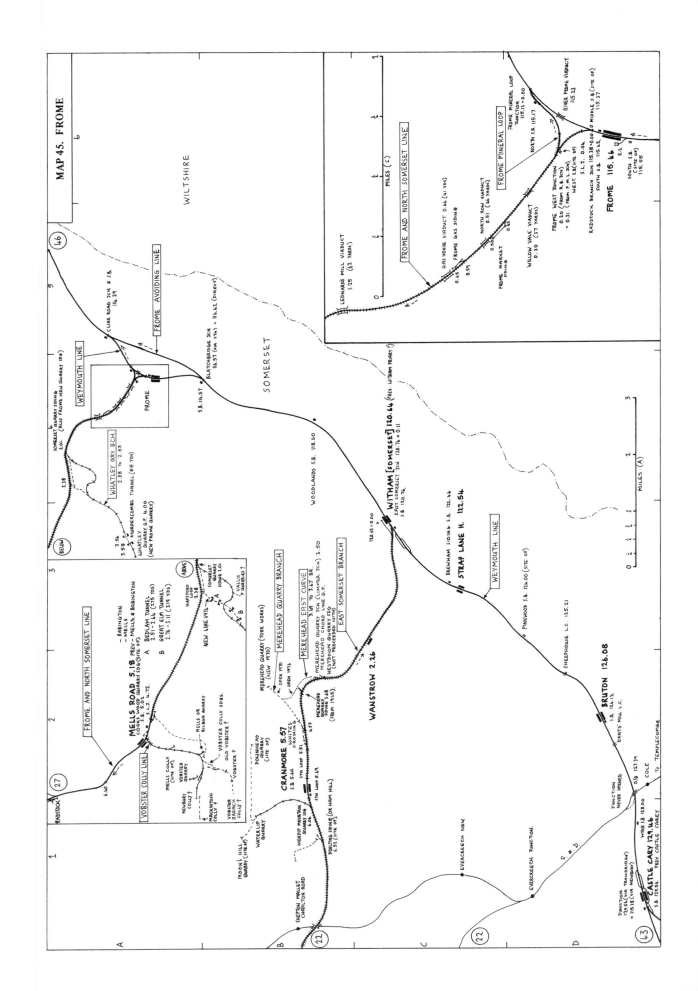

MAP 45. FROME

WILTSHIRE

SOMERSET

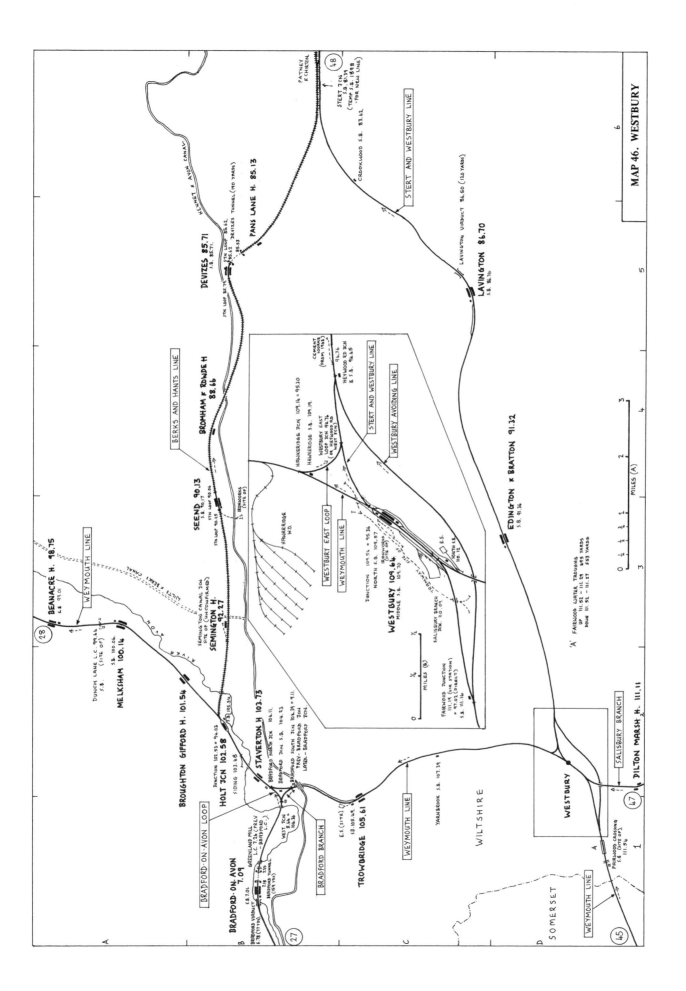

MAP 46. WESTBURY

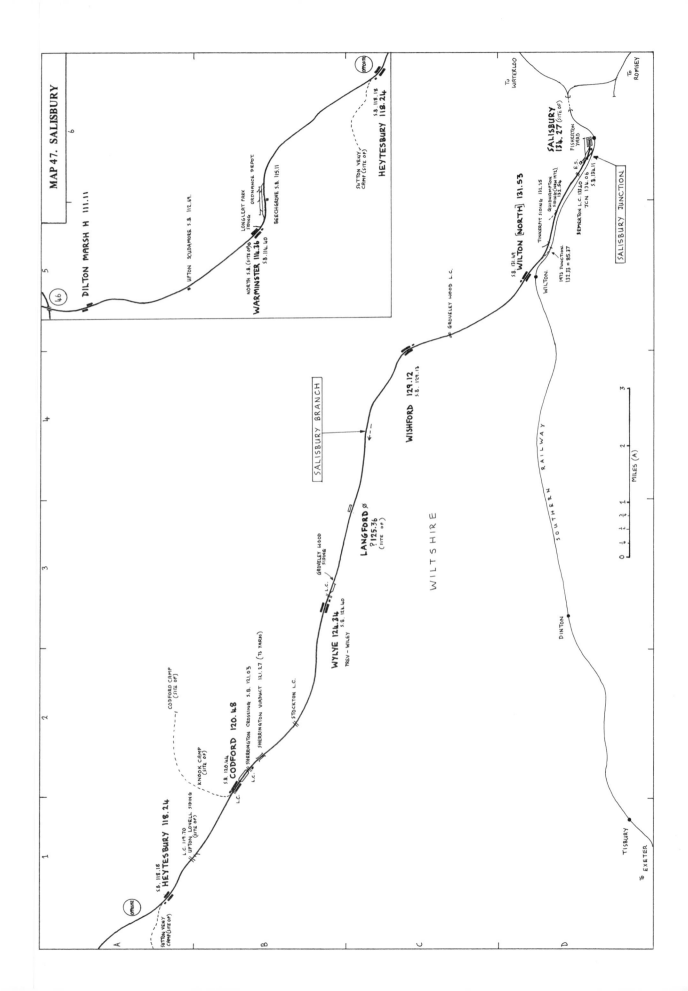

MAP 47. SALISBURY

DILTON MARSH H 111.11

UPTON SCUDAMORE S.B. 112.69

LONGLEAT PARK
SIDING   ORDNANCE DEPOT
NORTH S.B. (SITE OF) 114.96
WARMINSTER 114.36
S.B. 114.40

BEECHGROVE S.B. 115.11

SUTTON VENY
CAMP (SITE OF)

HEYTESBURY 118.24
S.B. 118.18

OFFSPRING

WILTSHIRE

SALISBURY BRANCH

GROVELEY WOOD L.C.

WISHFORD 129.12
S.B. 129.13

LANGFORD Ø
125.36
(SITE OF)

GROVELEY WOOD
SIDING

L.C.

WYLYE 124.34
PREV - WILEY
S.B. 124.40

SHERRINGTON CROSSING S.B. 121.03
L.C. SHERRINGTON VIADUCT 121.27 (15 YARDS)

STOCKTON L.C.

CODFORD 120.48
S.B. 120.44
L.C.

KNOOK CAMP
(SITE OF)

CODFORD CAMP
(SITE OF)

L.C. 119.70
UPTON LOVELL SIDING
(SITE OF)

HEYTESBURY 118.24
S.B. 118.18

SUTTON VENY
CAMP (SITE OF)

OFFSPRING

TO EXETER

TISBURY

DINTON

SOUTHERN RAILWAY

WILTON (NORTH) 131.53
S.B. 131.49

TUNKERAFT SIDING 131.15
QUIDHAMPTON
SIDING (NR. MFTS) 131.54

WILTON.

WILTON.
WTG JUNCTION
132.33 = 85.37

GROVELEY WOOD L.C.

SALISBURY
134.27 (SITE OF)

FISHERTON
YARD

E.S.
BEMERTON L.C. 133.60
JCN 134.06
S.B. 134.11

SALISBURY JUNCTION

TO WATERLOO

TO ROMSEY

0   ¼ ½ 1   2   3
MILES (A)

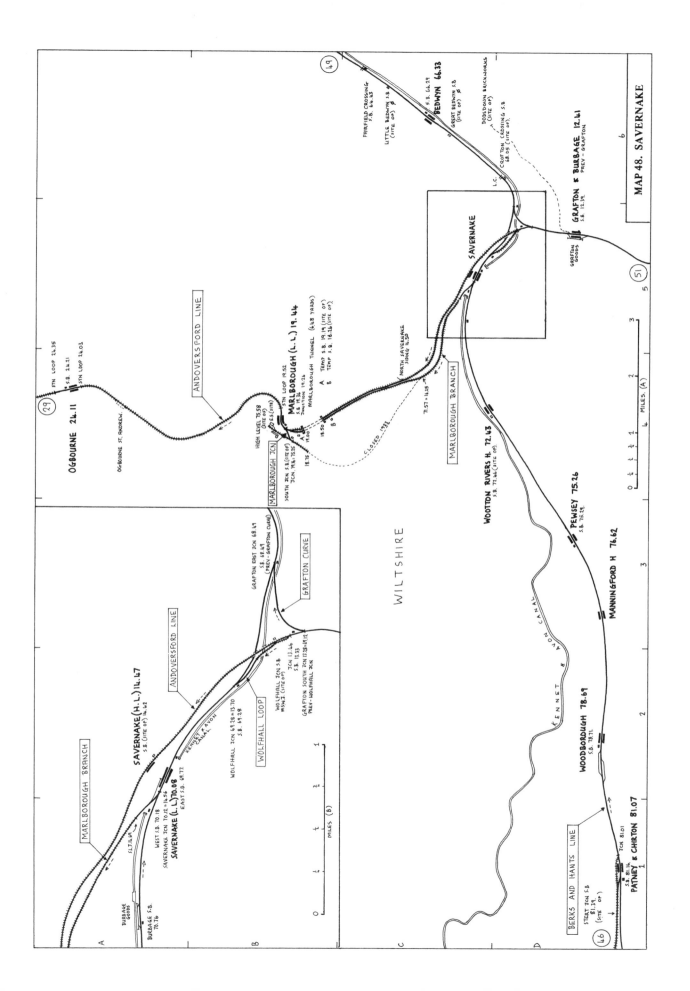

MAP 48. SAVERNAKE

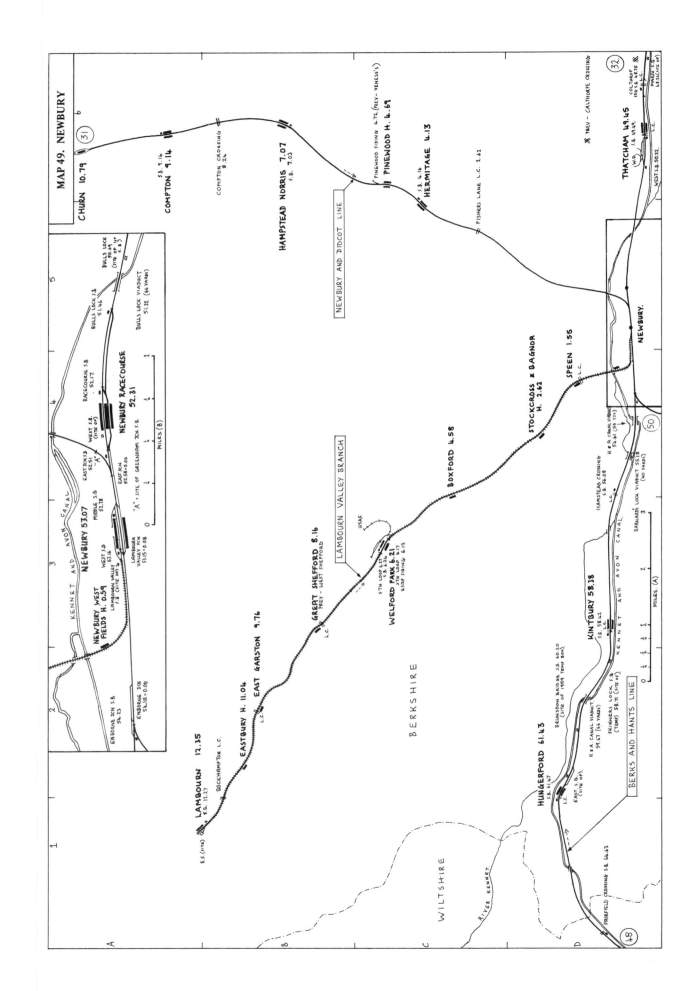

MAP 49. NEWBURY

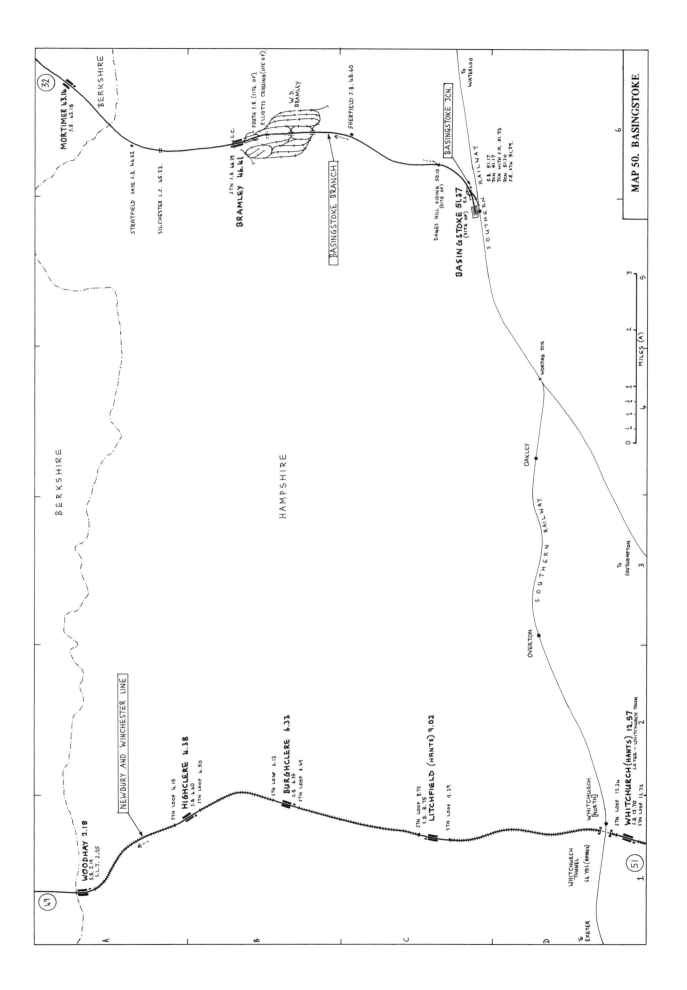

MAP 50. BASINGSTOKE

MORTIMER 43.14
S.B. 43.18

BERKSHIRE

BERKSHIRE

HAMPSHIRE

STRATFIELD SAYE S.B. 44.62
SILCHESTER L.C. 45.23

STN S.B. 46.39
BRAMLEY 46.41

SOUTH S.B. (SITE OF)
ELLIOTTS CROSSING (SITE OF)
W.D. BRAMLEY

SHERFIELD S.B. 48.60

SHERFIELD S.B. 48.60

BASINGSTOKE BRANCH

BASINGSTOKE JCN.

To WATERLOO

DANES HILL SIDING 50.10
(SITE OF)

BASINGSTOKE 51.37
(SITE OF)

SOUTHERN RAILWAY

S.B. 51.17
JCN 51.17
JCN WITH S.R. 51.23
JCN 51.30
S.R. STN 51.39

NEWBURY AND WINCHESTER LINE

WOODHAY 2.18
S.B. 2.19
S.L.T. 2.25

STN LOOP 4.15
HIGHCLERE 4.38
S.B. 4.40
JTN LOOP 4.50

STN LOOP 6.13
BURGHCLERE 6.33
S.B. 6.35
STN LOOP 6.44

STN LOOP 8.71
S.B. 8.75
LITCHFIELD (HANTS) 9.02
STN LOOP 9.29

WHITCHURCH TUNNEL
66 YDS (APPROX)

WHITCHURCH (NORTH)

STN LOOP 12.34
WHITCHURCH (HANTS) 12.57
LATER - WHITCHURCH TOWN
S.B. 12.70
STN LOOP 12.72

To EXETER

OVERTON

OAKLEY

WORTING TCN.

To SOUTHAMPTON

SOUTHERN RAILWAY

MILES (A)

0   ¼ ½ ¾ 1   2   3
                  5

49

51

32

To WATERLOO

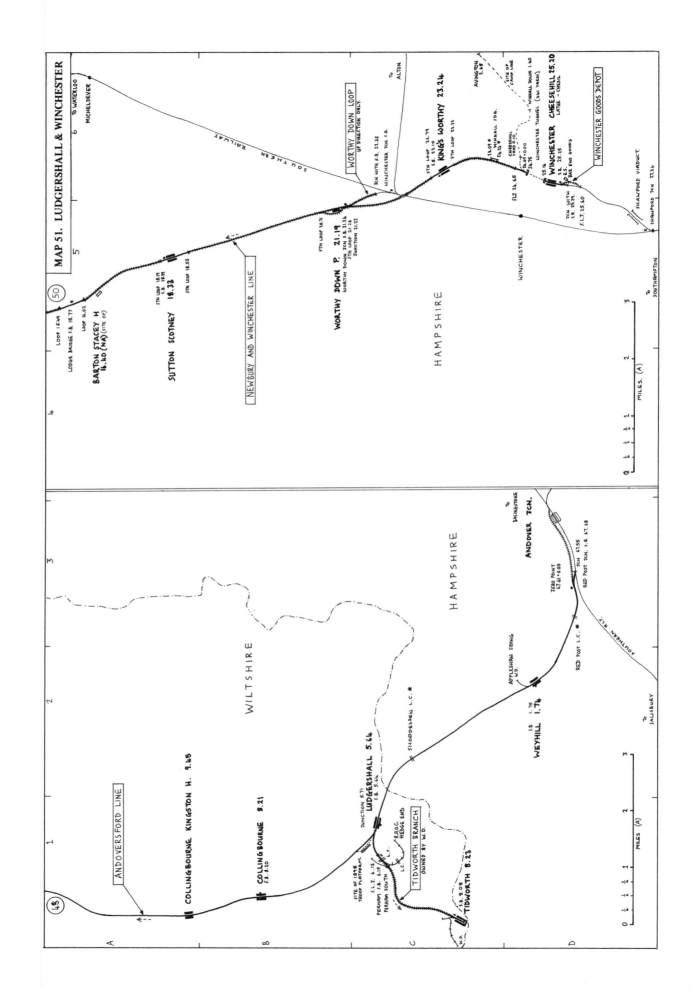

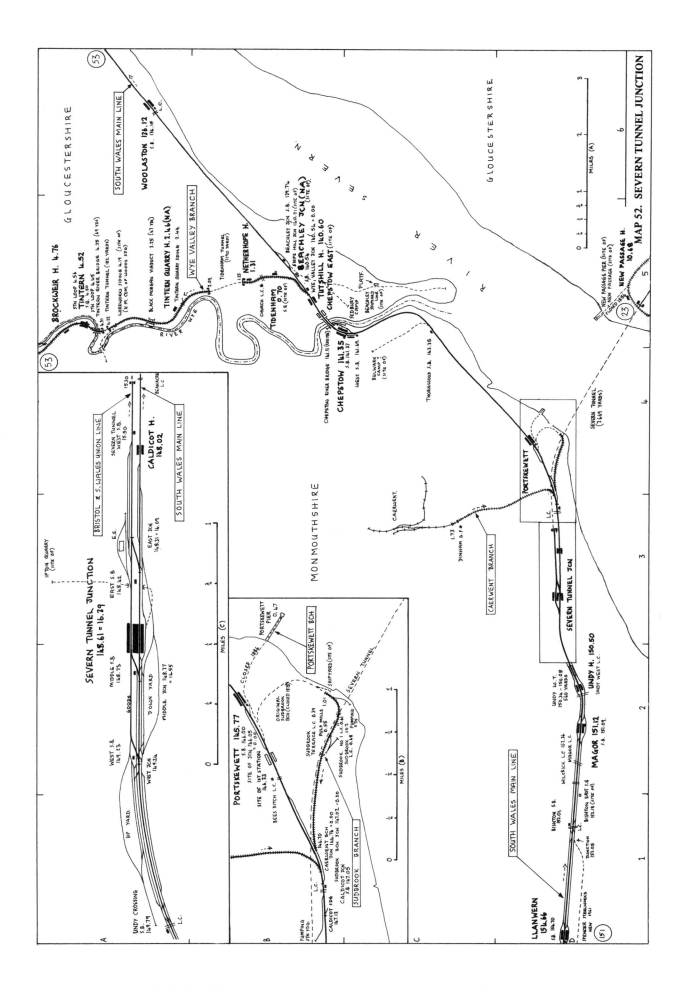

MAP 52. SEVERN TUNNEL JUNCTION

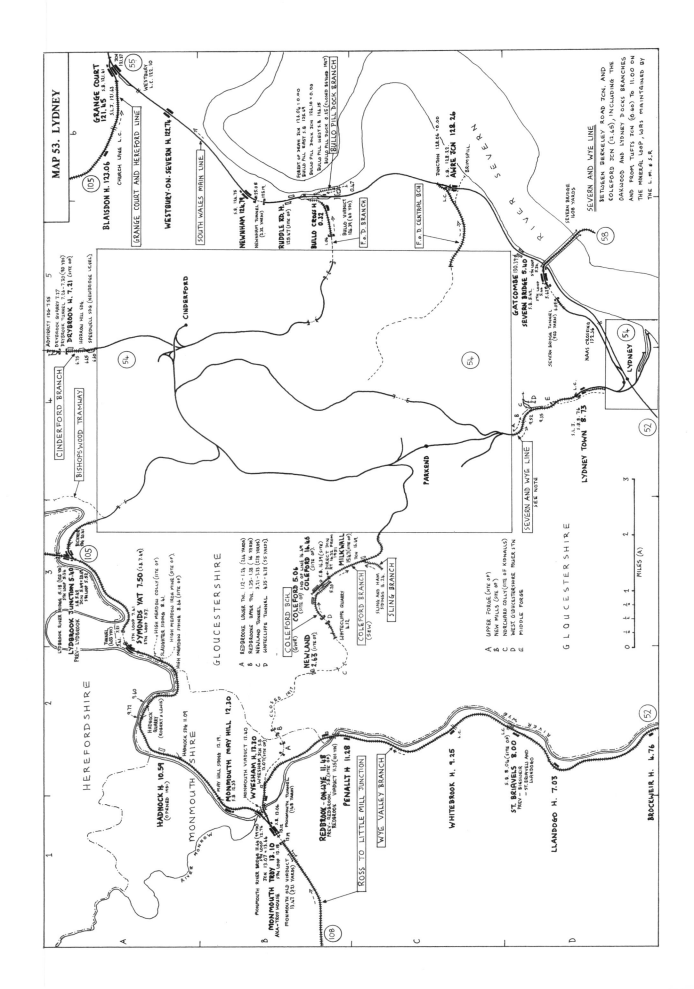

MAP 53. LYDNEY

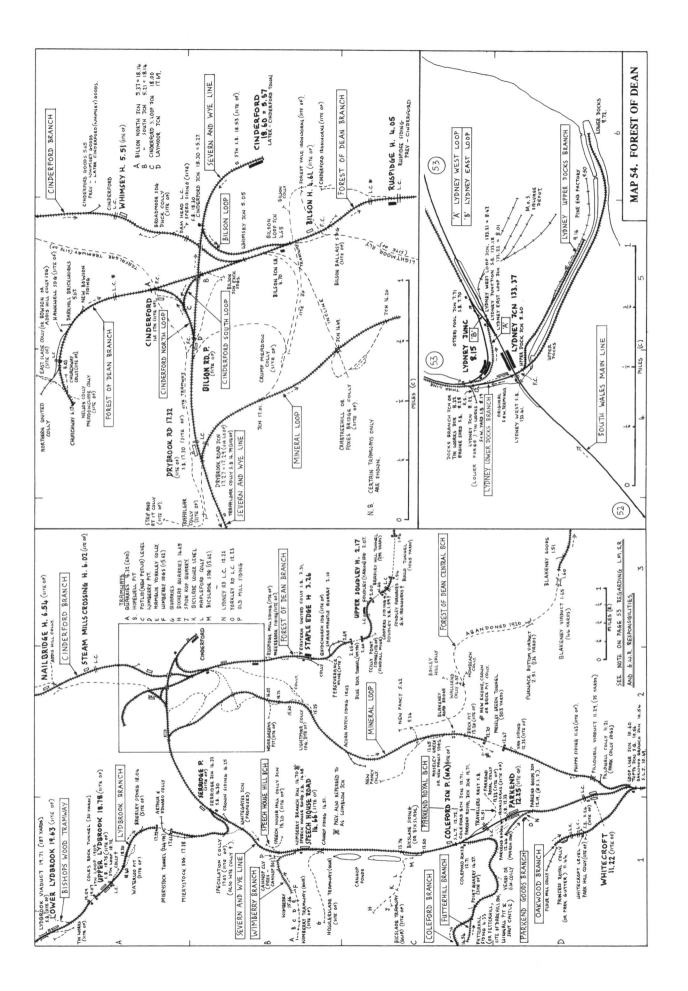

MAP 54. FOREST OF DEAN

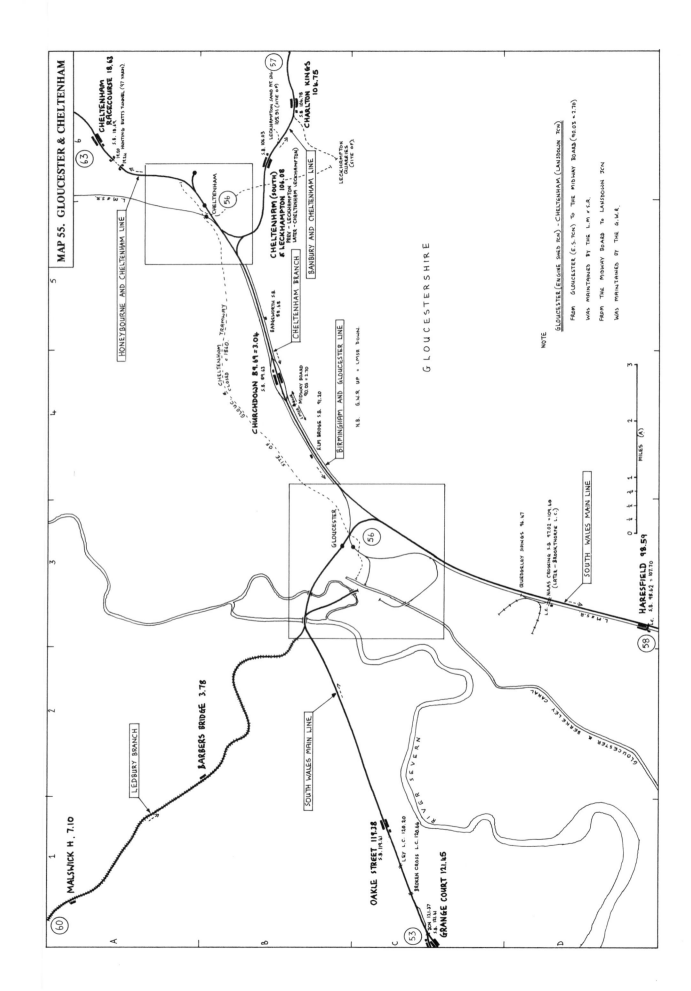

MAP 55. GLOUCESTER & CHELTENHAM

CHELTENHAM RACECOURSE 18.63
S.B. 18.24
1630 HUNTING BUTTS TUNNEL (97 YARDS).

HONEYBOURNE AND CHELTENHAM LINE

Cheltenham

J.B. 106.03
LECKHAMPTON SAND PIT SDG
105.51 (SITE OF)

CHARLTON KINGS 104.75
104.78
S.B. 104.78

LECKHAMPTON QUARRIES (SITE OF)

CHELTENHAM (SOUTH)
& LECKHAMPTON 104.08
PREV - LECKHAMPTON
LATER - CHELTENHAM-LECKHAMPTON

BANBURY AND CHELTENHAM LINE

CHELTENHAM TRAMWAY
CLOSED c/1860.

CHELTENHAM BRANCH

BARNWOOD S.B.
98.55

CHURCHDOWN 89.69 = 3.04
S.B. 99.63

LMSR MIDWAY BOARD
90.03 = 2.70

ELM BRIDGE S.B. 91.20

BIRMINGHAM AND GLOUCESTER LINE

N.B. G.W.R UP = LMSR DOWN.

GLOUCESTERSHIRE

GLOUCESTER

QUEDGELEY SIDINGS S.B. 97.02 = 109.60

NAAS CROSSING 98.02 = 109.60
(LATER - BROOKTHORPE L.C.)
L.C.

SOUTH WALES MAIN LINE

HARESFIELD 98.59
L.C. S.B. 98.62 = 107.70

LEDBURY BRANCH

BARBERS BRIDGE 3.78

SOUTH WALES MAIN LINE

MALSWICK H. 7.10

RIVER SEVERN

GLOUCESTER & BERKELEY CANAL

OAKLE STREET 119.28
S.B. 119.41

LEY L.C. 120.20
BROKEN CROSS L.C. 120.86

SIGN 121.37
S.B. 121.41

GRANGE COURT 121.45

NOTE

GLOUCESTER (ENGINE SHED JCN) - CHELTENHAM (LANSDOWN JCN)

FROM GLOUCESTER (E.S. JCN) TO THE MIDWAY BOARD (90.03 = 2.70)
WAS MAINTAINED BY THE L.M & S.R.
FROM THE MIDWAY BOARD TO LANSDOWN JCN
WAS MAINTAINED BY THE G.W.R.

0   ¼ ½ ¾ 1   2   3
MILES (A)

A

B

C

D

60

63

56

57

58

53

5

1   2   3   4   5

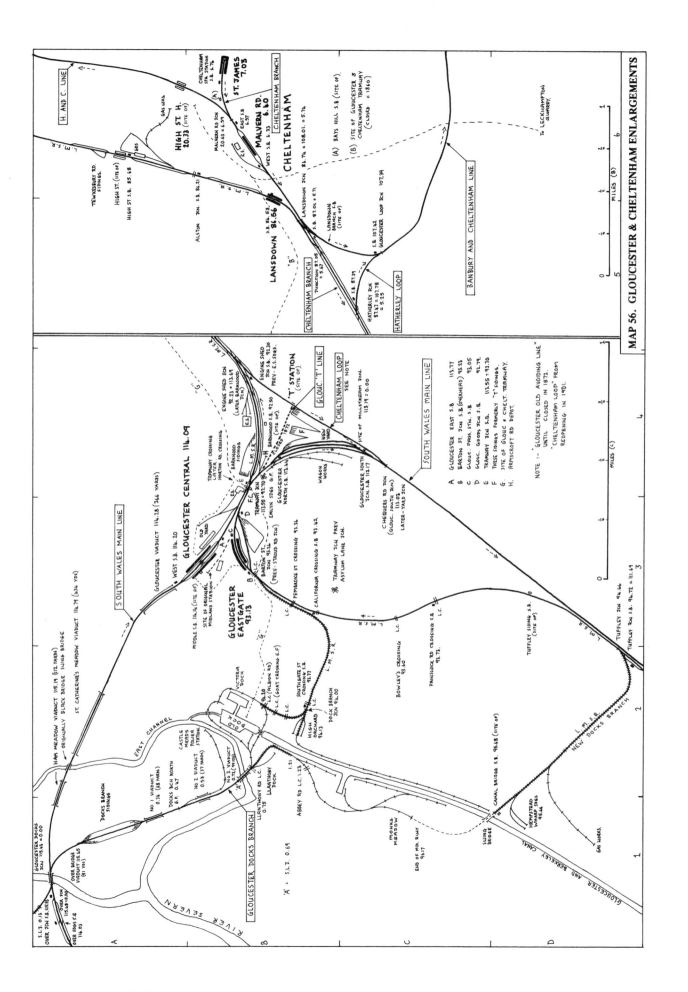

MAP 56. GLOUCESTER & CHELTENHAM ENLARGEMENTS

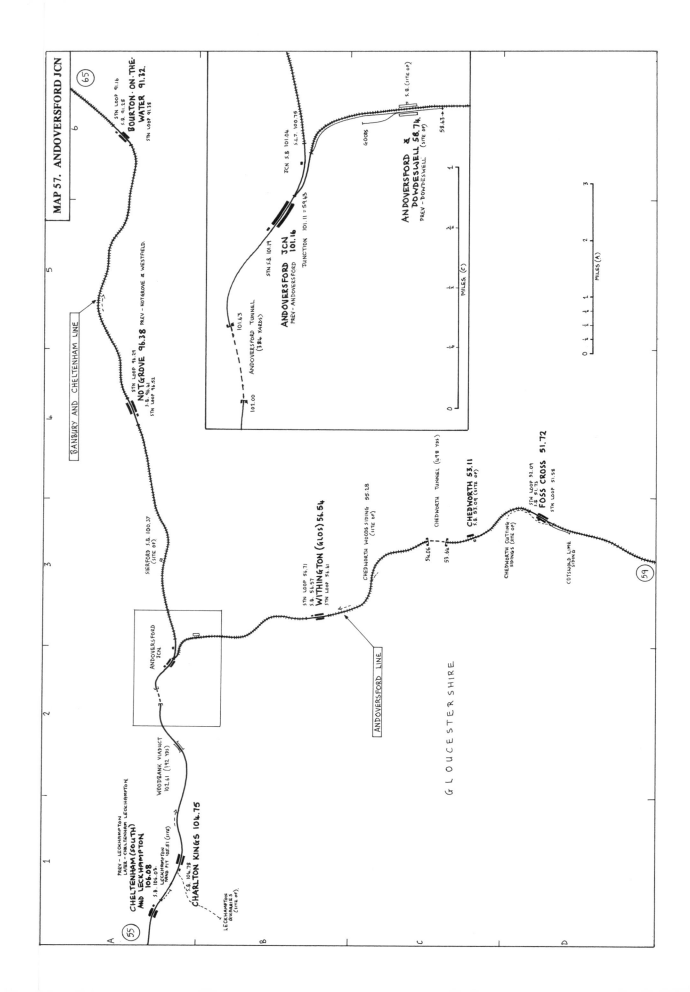

MAP 57. ANDOVERSFORD JCN

(65)

STN LOOP 91.16
S.B. 91.28
BOURTON·ON·THE·
WATER 91.32.
STN LOOP 91.38

BANBURY AND CHELTENHAM LINE

5

STN LOOP 96.24
NOTGROVE 96.38 PREV·NOTGROVE & WESTFIELD.
S.B. 96.44
STN LOOP 96.52

4

SIGNFORD S.B. 100.37 (SITE OF)

JCN S.B. 101.04
S.L.7. 100.75
ANDOVERSFORD JCN 101.16
PREV·ANDOVERSFORD
JUNCTION 101.11 = 59.43

ANDOVERSFORD TUNNEL (384 YARDS)

STN S.B. 101.19

GOODS

ANDOVERSFORD & DOWDESWELL, 58.74.
PREV·DOWDESWELL (SITE OF)

S.B. (SITE OF)

101.63

101.00

102.00

58.63

0   ¼   ½   ¾   1   1¼
MILES (C)

0   ¼   ½   1   2   3
MILES (A)

3

ANDOVERSFORD JCN

STN LOOP 56.71
S.B. 56.57
WITHINGTON (GLOS) 56.54
STN LOOP 56.41

ANDOVERSFORD LINE

CHEDWORTH WOODS SIDING 55.18 (SITE OF)

54.06

53.64

CHEDWORTH TUNNEL (484 YDS)

CHEDWORTH 53.11
S.B. 53.09 (SITE OF)

CHEDWORTH CUTTING SIDINGS (SITE OF)

STN LOOP 51.09
S.B. 51.73
FOSS CROSS 51.72
STN LOOP 51.58

COTSWOLD LIME SIDING

(59)

GLOUCESTERSHIRE

2

WOODBANK VIADUCT 102.61 (192 YDS)

1

PREV·LECKHAMPTON
LATER·CHELTENHAM LECKHAMPTON
CHELTENHAM (SOUTH) AND LECKHAMPTON 106.08
S.B. 106.03.

LECKHAMPTON SAND PIT 105.51 (SITE)

S.B. 104.79
CHARLTON KINGS 104.75

LECKHAMPTON QUARRIES (SITE OF)

(55)

A

B

C

D

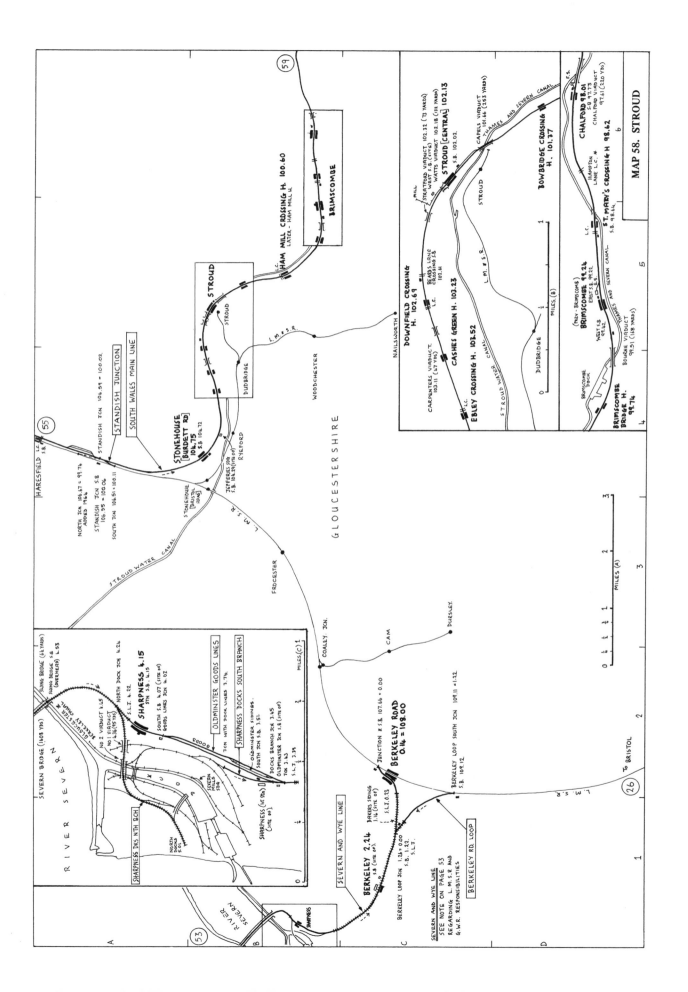

MAP 58. STROUD

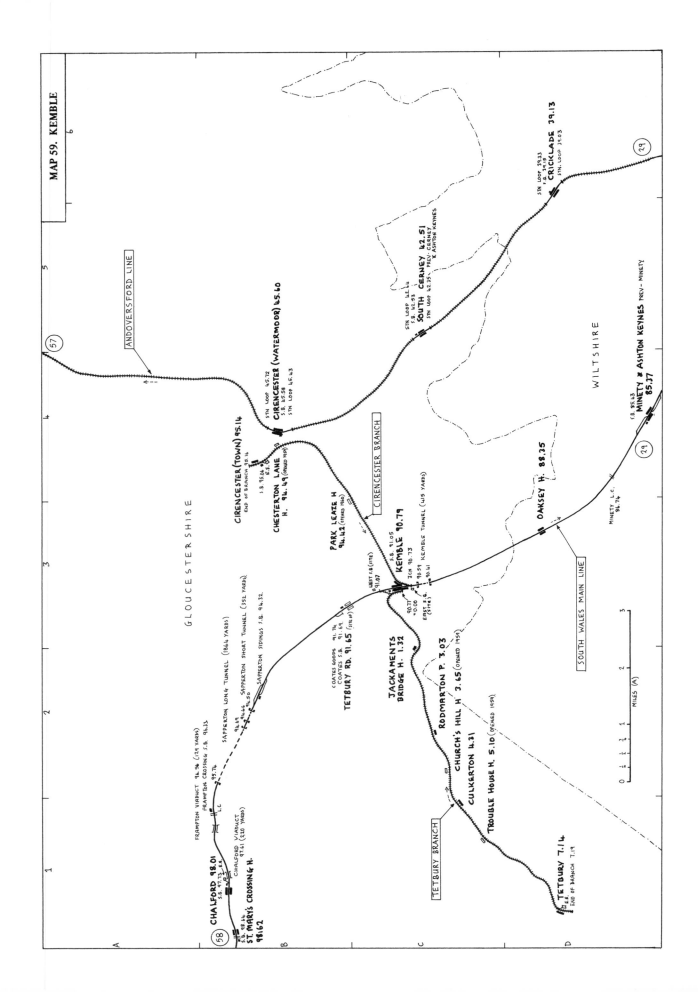

MAP 59. KEMBLE

ANDOVERSFORD LINE

GLOUCESTERSHIRE

WILTSHIRE

FRAMPTON VIADUCT 96.56 (124 YARDS)
FRAMPTON CROSSING S.B. 96.33
95.74
L.C.
CHALFORD VIADUCT
97.61 (210 YARDS)
CHALFORD 98.01
S.B. 97.73 . 6.S.
98.46
S.B.
ST. MARYS CROSSING H.
98.62

SAPPERTON LONG TUNNEL (1864 YARDS)
94.49 SAPPERTON SHORT TUNNEL (352 YARDS)
94.46
94.50
SAPPERTON SIDINGS S.B. 94.32.

CIRENCESTER (TOWN) 95.14
END OF BRANCH 95.16
S.B. 95.04 . 6.S.
6.S.0.
CHESTERTON LANE
H. 94.49 (OPENED 1959)

PARK LEAZE H.
94.42 (OPENED 1960)

CIRENCESTER (WATERMOOR) 45.60
STN LOOP 45.72
S.B. 45.58
STN LOOP 46.43

STN LOOP 42.64
S.B. 42.53
SOUTH CERNEY 42.51
STN LOOP 42.35. PREV. CERNEY
X ASHTON KEYNES

STN LOOP 39.33
S.B. 39.19
CRICKLADE 39.13
STN LOOP 39.03

CIRENCESTER BRANCH

COATES GOODS 91.74
COATES S.B. 91.69
TETBURY RD. 91.65 (SITE #F)
WEST S.B. (SITE)
91.07
S.B. 91.05
KEMBLE 90.79
7CM 90.73
90.59 KEMBLE TUNNEL (415 YARDS)
90.41
90.17
0.00
EAST S.B.
(SITE)

JACKAMENTS
BRIDGE H. 1.32

RODMARTON P. 3.03
CHURCH'S HILL H. 3.65 (OPENED 1959)
CULKERTON 4.31
TROUBLE HOUSE H. 5.10 (OPENED 1959)

TETBURY 7.14
END OF BRANCH 7.19

TETBURY BRANCH

OAKSEY H. 88.35

MINETY L.C. 86.74

S.B. 85.43
MINETY X ASHTON KEYNES PREV. MINETY
85.37

SOUTH WALES MAIN LINE

57

58

29

29

MILES (A)
0   1/4 1/2 3/4 1   2   3

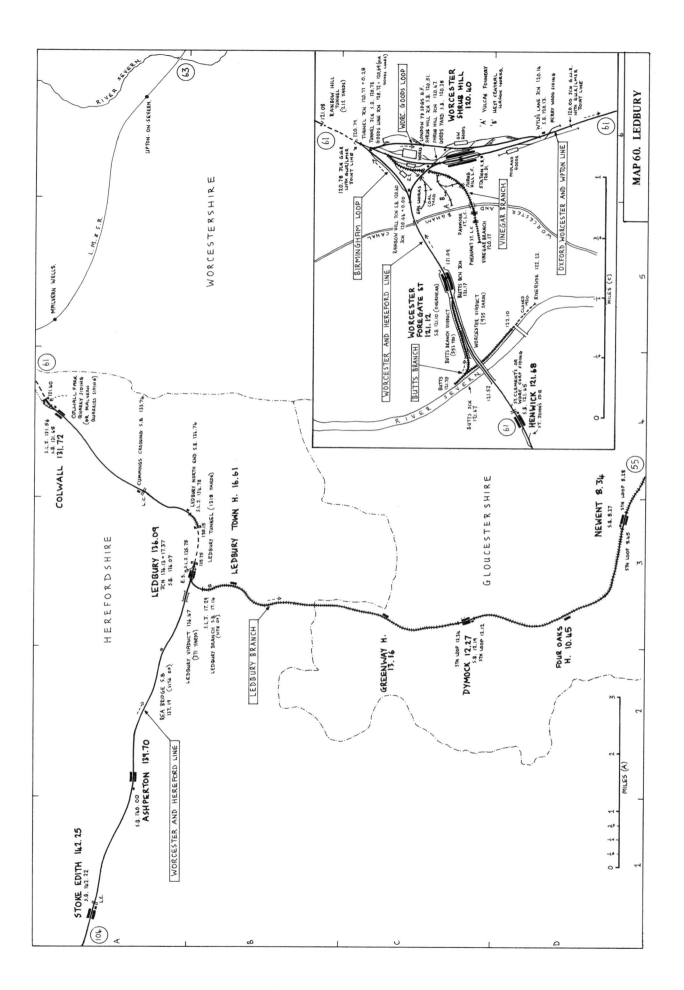

MAP 60. LEDBURY

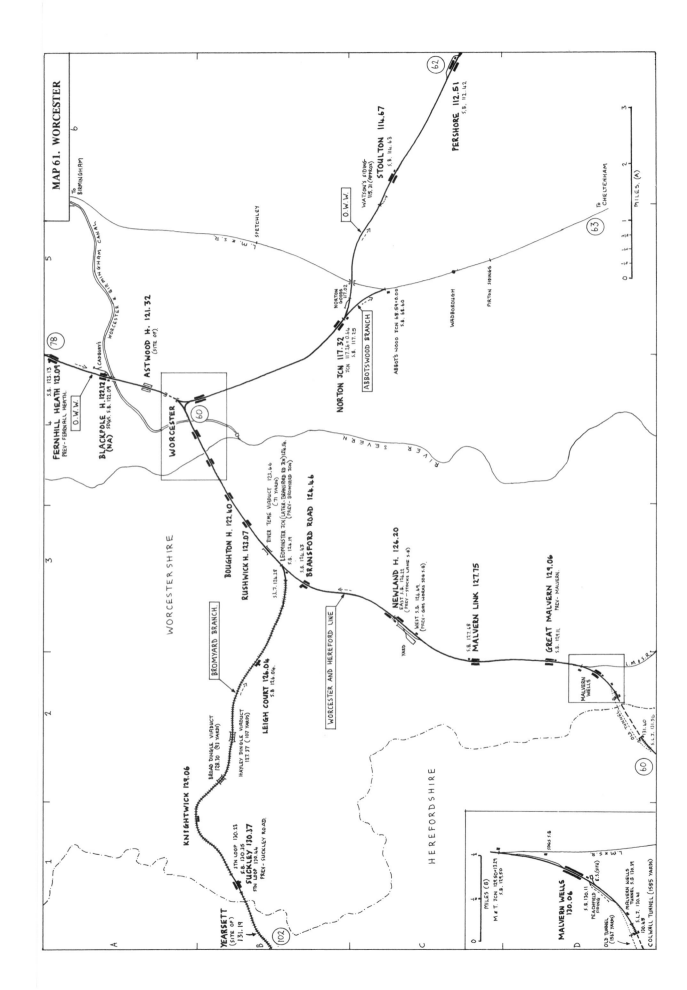

MAP 61. WORCESTER

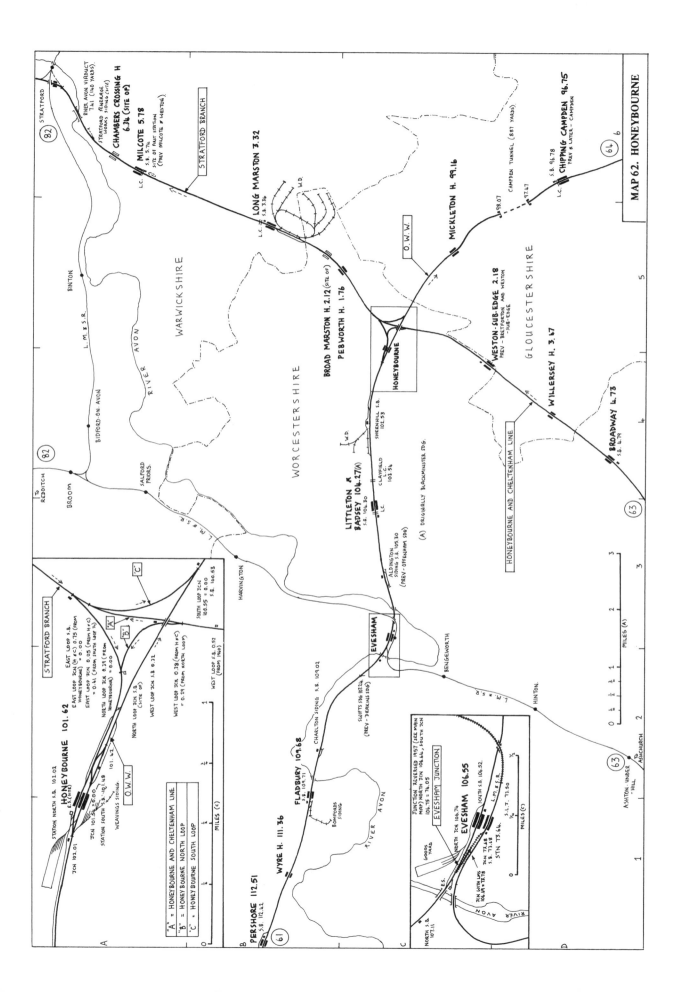

MAP 62. HONEYBOURNE

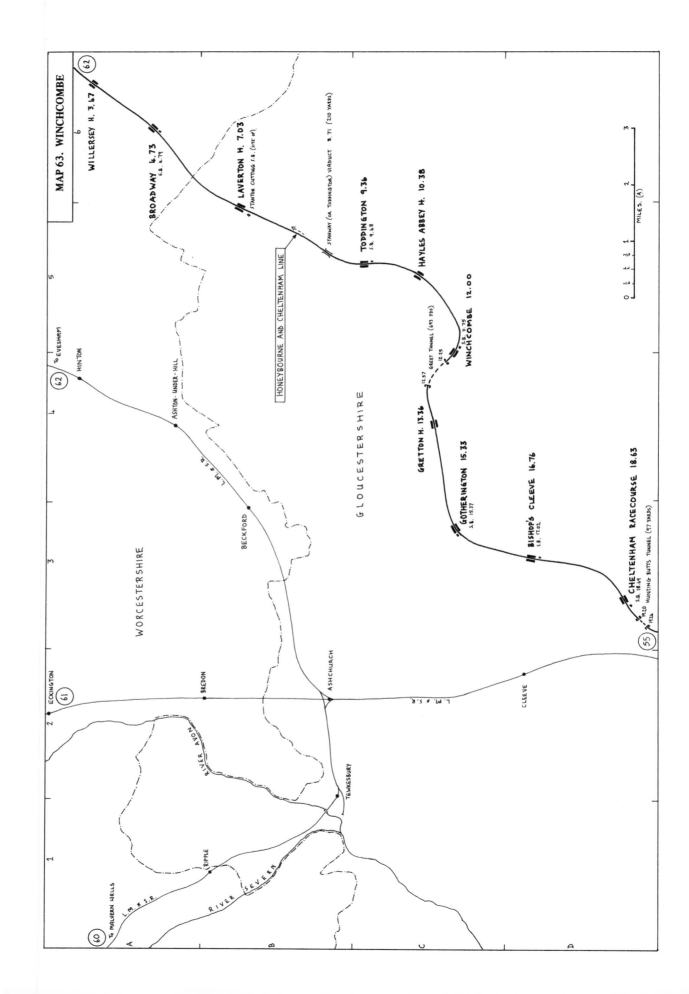

MAP 63. WINCHCOMBE

WILLERSEY H. 3.47

BROADWAY 4.73
S.B. 4.79

LAVERTON H. 7.03
STANTON CUTTING S.B. (SITE OF)

STANWAY (OR TODDINGTON) VIADUCT B. 71 (210 YARDS)

HONEYBOURNE AND CHELTENHAM LINE

TODDINGTON 9.36
S.B. 9.68

HAYLES ABBEY H. 10.38

WINCHCOMBE 12.00
S.B. 11.75
12.25

GREET TUNNEL (693 YDS)

GRETTON H. 13.36
12.57

GOTHERINGTON 15.23
S.B. 15.37

BISHOP'S CLEEVE 16.76
S.B. 17.02

CHELTENHAM RACECOURSE 18.63
S.B. 18.69
18.20
HUNTING BUTTS TUNNEL (57 YARDS)
18.26

GLOUCESTERSHIRE

WORCESTERSHIRE

To EVESHAM
HINTON
ASHTON-UNDER-HILL

L.M. & S.R.
BECKFORD

RIVER AVON

ECKINGTON
BREDON

RIPPLE

To MALVERN WELLS
L.M. & S.R.

RIVER SEVERN

TEWKESBURY

ASHCHURCH

L.M. & S.R.
CLEEVE

MILES. (A)
0   ¼ ½ ¾ 1   2   3

60
61
62
62
55

A
B
C
D

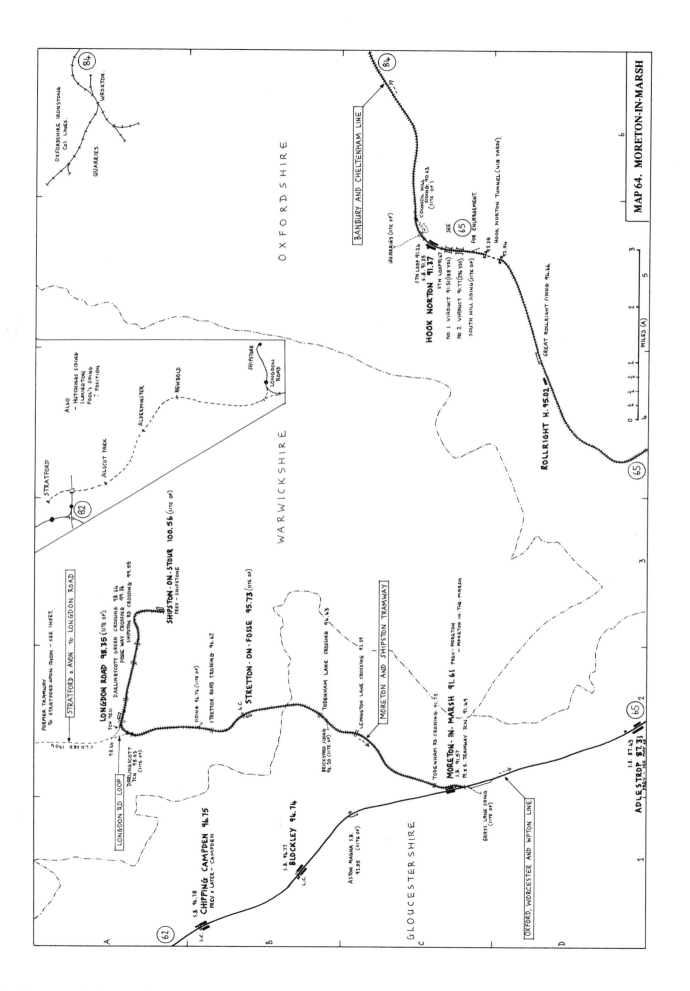

MAP 64. MORETON-IN-MARSH

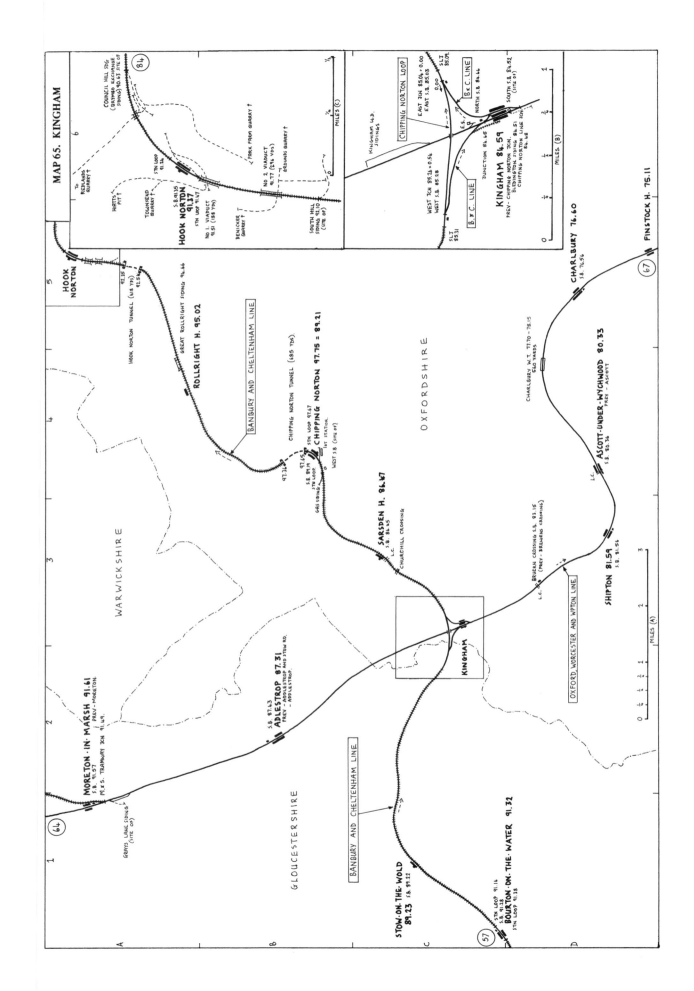

MAP 65. KINGHAM

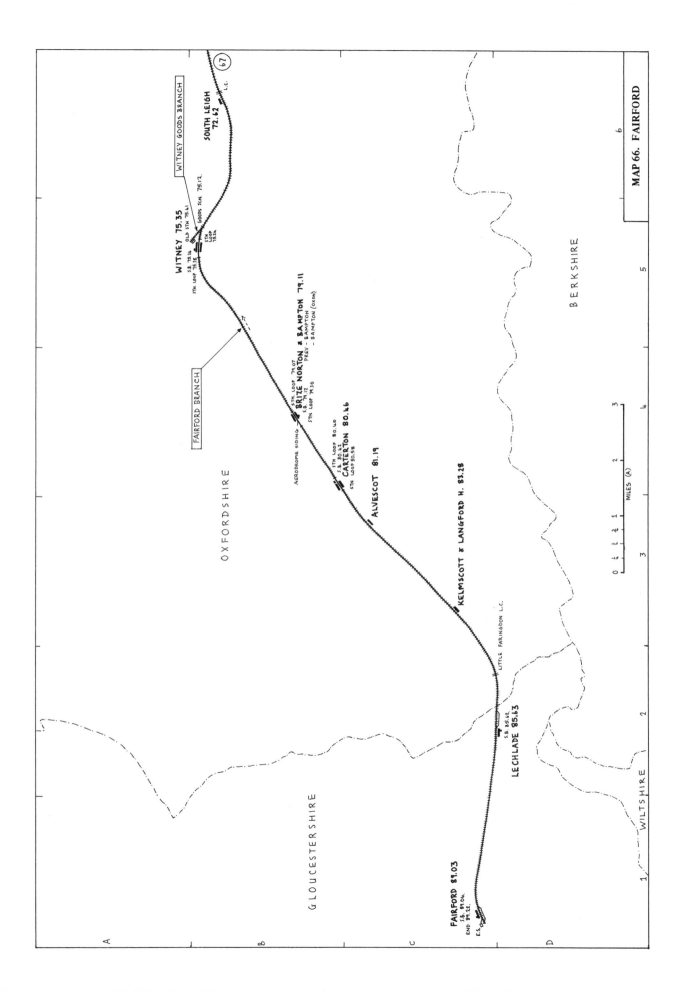

SOUTH LEIGH
72.62

WITNEY GOODS BRANCH

WITNEY 75.35
OLD STN 75.41
S.B. 75.36
GOODS JCN 75.12.
STN LOOP 75.24.
STN LOOP 75.41

FAIRFORD BRANCH

STN LOOP 79.07
BRIZE NORTON & BAMPTON 79.11
S.B. 79.12
STN LOOP 79.30
PREV - BAMPTON
- BAMPTON (OXON)

AERODROME SIDING

STN LOOP 80.40
S.B. 80.42
CARTERTON 80.46
STN LOOP 80.58

ALVESCOT 81.19

KELMSCOTT & LANGFORD H. 83.28

LITTLE FARINGDON L.C.

S.B. 85.62
LECHLADE 85.63

FAIRFORD 89.03
S.B. 89.04.
END 89.22.
E.S.

OXFORDSHIRE

GLOUCESTERSHIRE

BERKSHIRE

WILTSHIRE

67
L.C.

MAP 66. FAIRFORD

MILES (A)

0   ¼ ½ ¾ 1
0 ¼ ½ ¾ 1   2   3
1   2   3   4   5   6

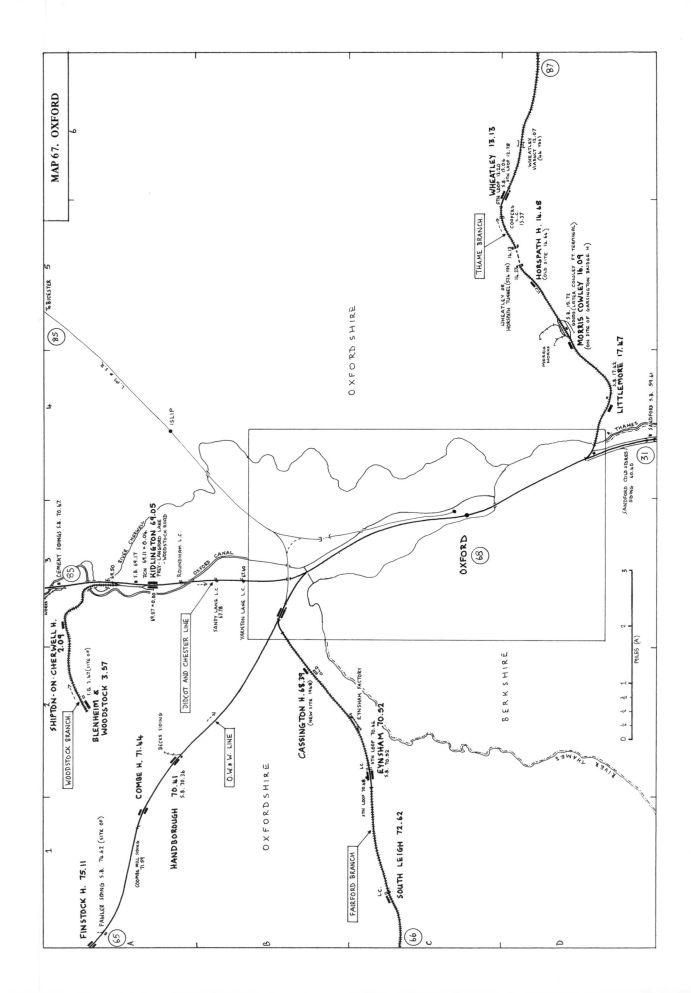

MAP 67. OXFORD

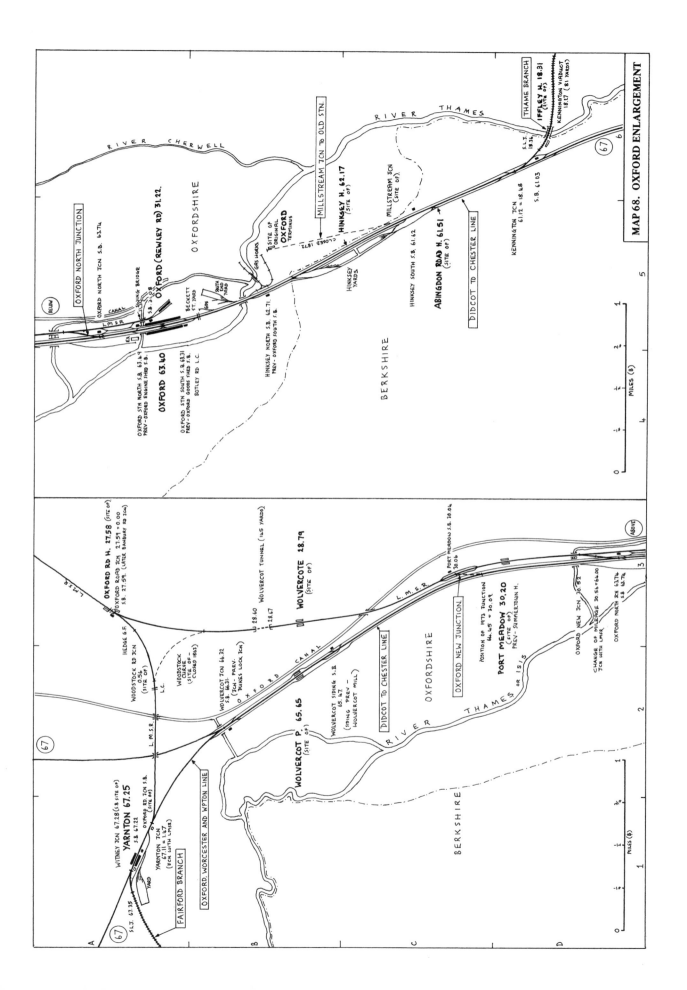

MAP 68. OXFORD ENLARGEMENT

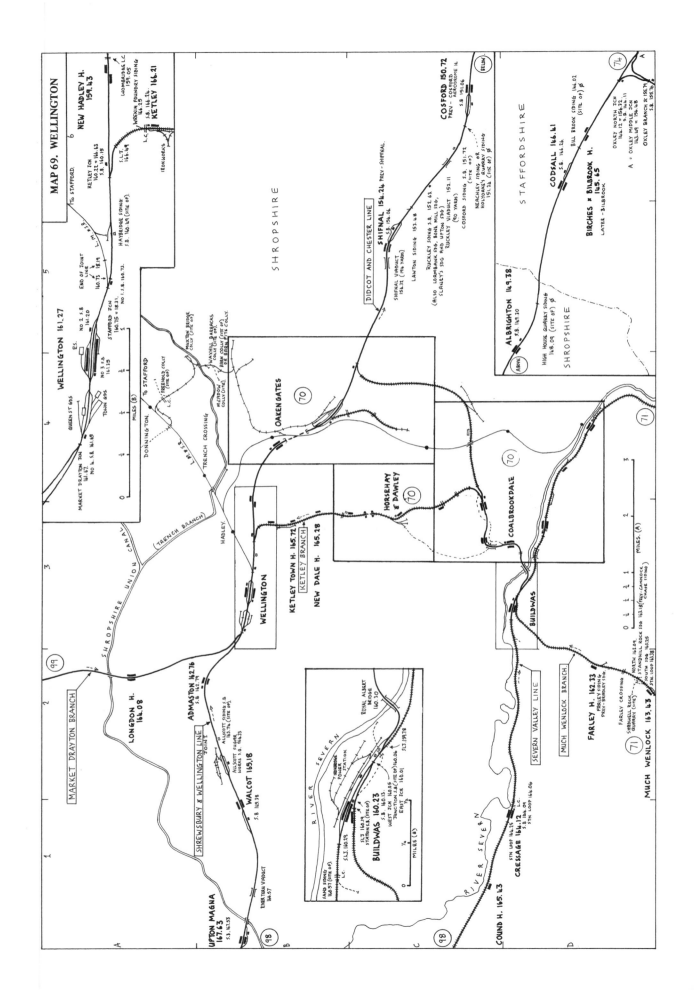

MAP 69. WELLINGTON

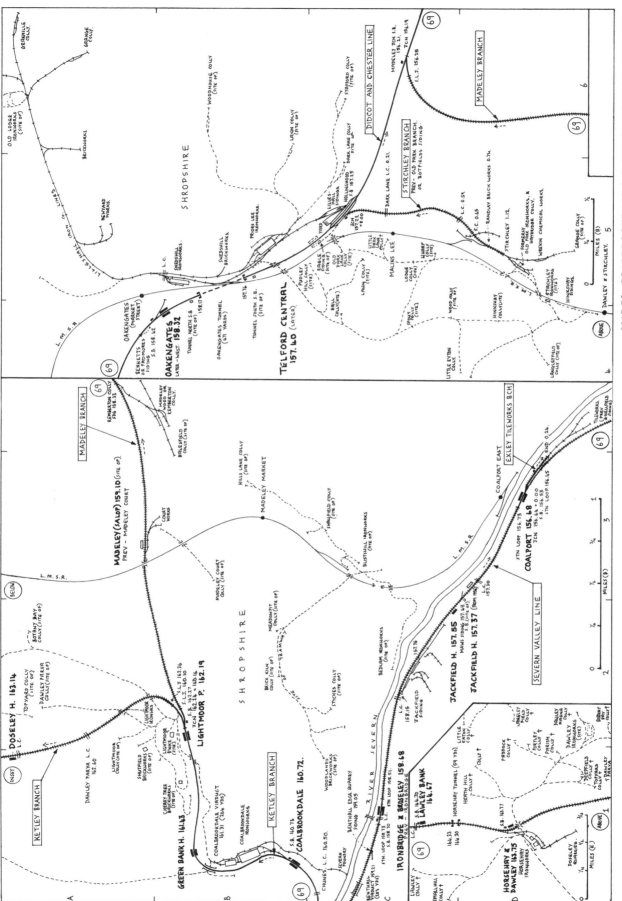

MAP 70. COALBROOKDALE & OAKENGATES ENLARGEMENTS

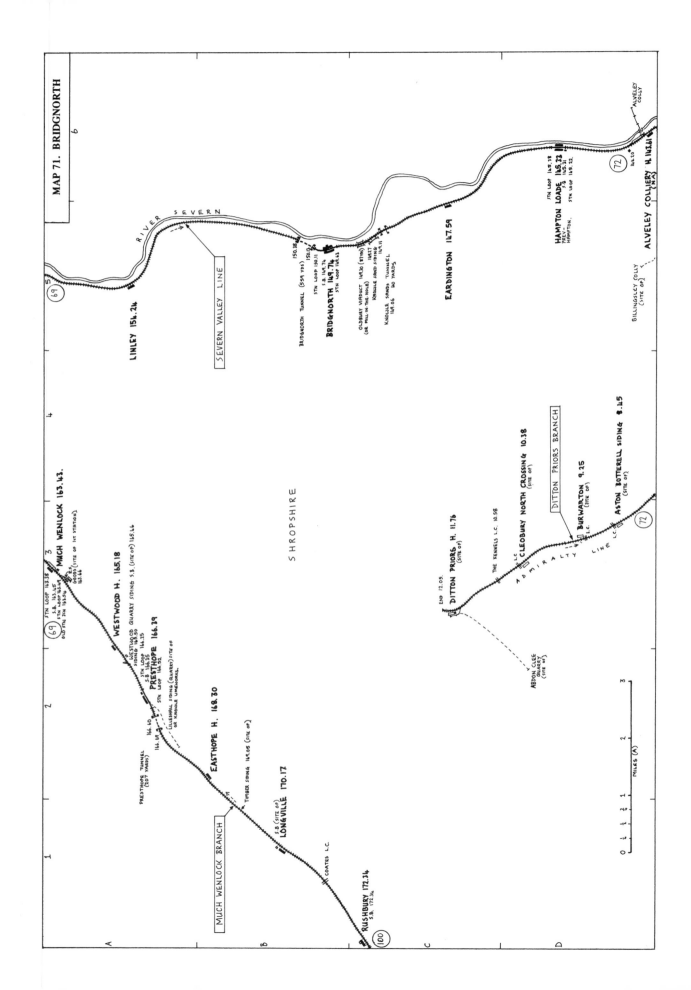

MAP 71. BRIDGNORTH

RIVER SEVERN

SEVERN VALLEY LINE

LINLEY 156.24

BRIDGNORTH TUNNEL (550 YDS)
150.18
150.13
STN LOOP 150.11
S.B. 149.74
STN LOOP 149.63
BRIDGNORTH 149.74
OLDBURY VIADUCT 149.30 (9THS)
(OR PULL IN THE HOLE)
149.17
KNOWLE SAND SIDING 149.11
KNOWLE SANDS TUNNEL 149.06
140 YARDS

EARDINGTON 146.59

HAMPTON LOADE 145.38
PREV.-
HAMPTON.
STN LOOP 145.31
S.B. 145.23
STN LOOP 145.22

BILLINGSLEY COLLY.
(SITE OF)

ALVELEY COLLIERY H. 143.66
(M2)
143.10
ALVELEY
COLLY.

SHROPSHIRE

MUCH WENLOCK 163.43.
STN LOOP 163.58
S.B. 163.45
STN LOOP 163.46
OLD STN 163.54
GOODS (SITE OF 1ST STATION)
163.44

WESTWOOD H. 165.18
WESTWOOD SIDING 164.75
WESTWOOD QUARRY SIDING S.B. (SITE OF) 165.66

PRESTHOPE 166.39
STN LOOP 166.52
S.B. 166.35
STN LOOP 166.52

LILLESHALL SIDING (QUARRY)(SITE OF)
OR KNOWLE LIMEWORKS.

EASTHOPE H. 168.80

PRESTHOPE TUNNEL (207 YARDS)
166.40
166.55

TIMBER SIDING 169.05 (SITE OF)

LONGVILLE 170.17
S.B. (SITE OF)

COATES L.C.

RUSHBURY 172.34
S.B. 172.34

MUCH WENLOCK BRANCH

DITTON PRIORS BRANCH

DITTON PRIORS H. 11.76
(SITE OF)

END 12.05

THE KENNELS L.C. 10.58

CLEOBURY NORTH CROSSING H. 10.38
(SITE OF)

BURWARTON 9.25
(SITE OF)
L.C.

ASTON BOTTERELL SIDING 8.45
(SITE OF)
L.C.

ADMIRALTY LINE

ABDON CLEE QUARRY
(SITE OF)

MILES (A)
0 ¼ ½ ¾ 1   2   3

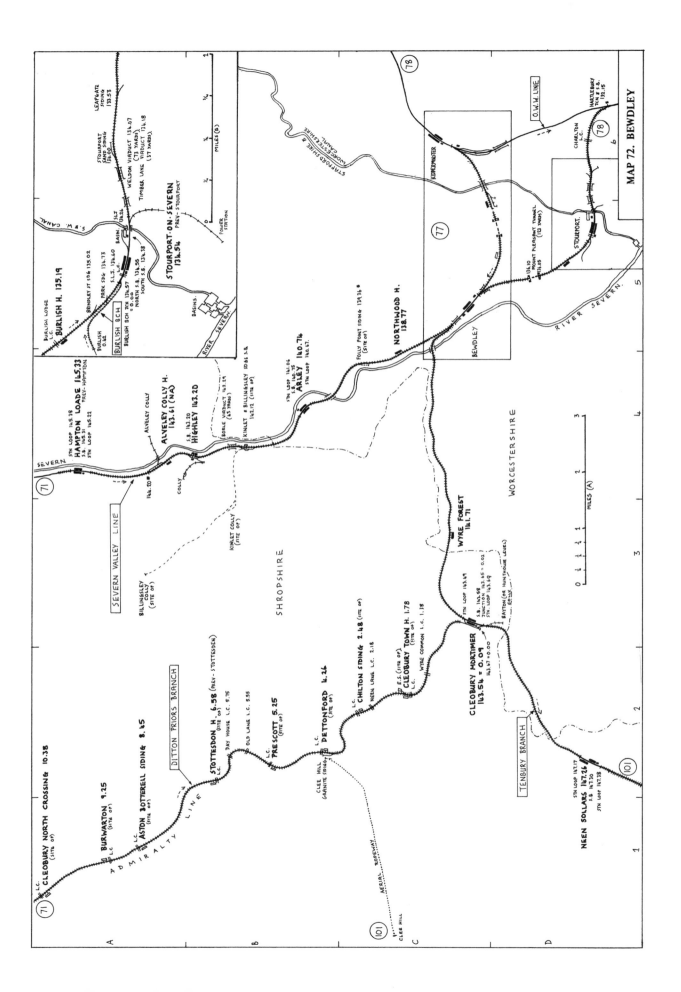

MAP 72. BEWDLEY

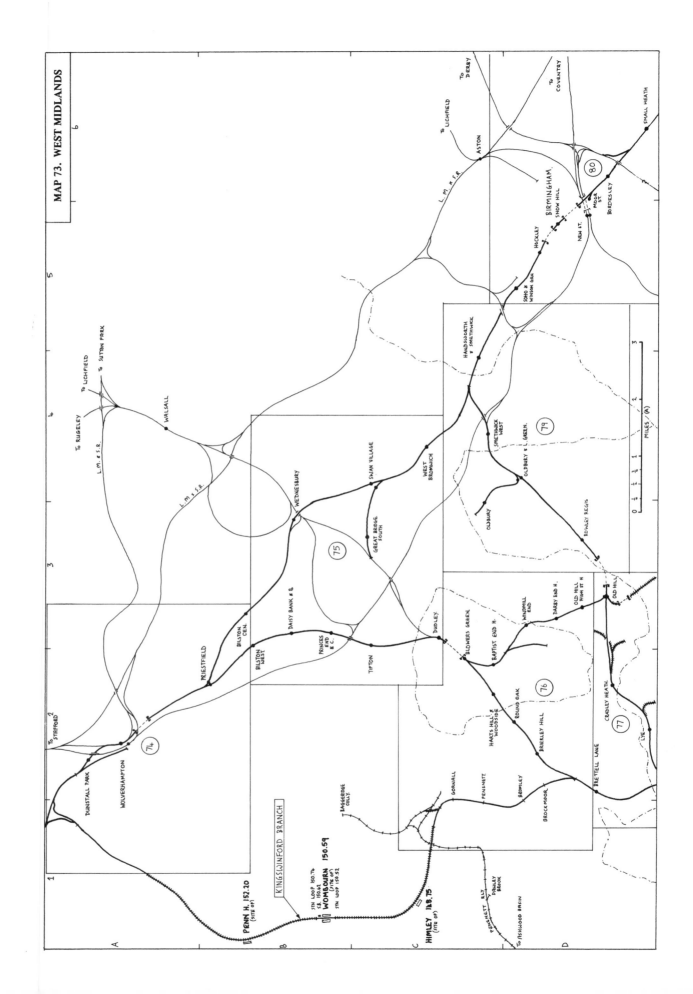

MAP 73. WEST MIDLANDS

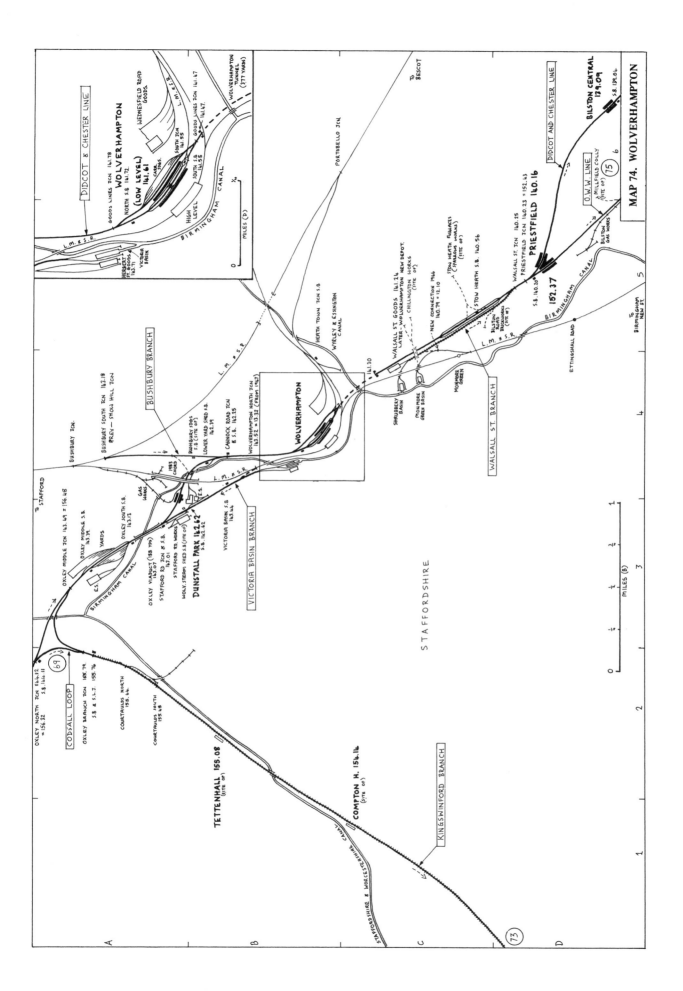

MAP 74. WOLVERHAMPTON

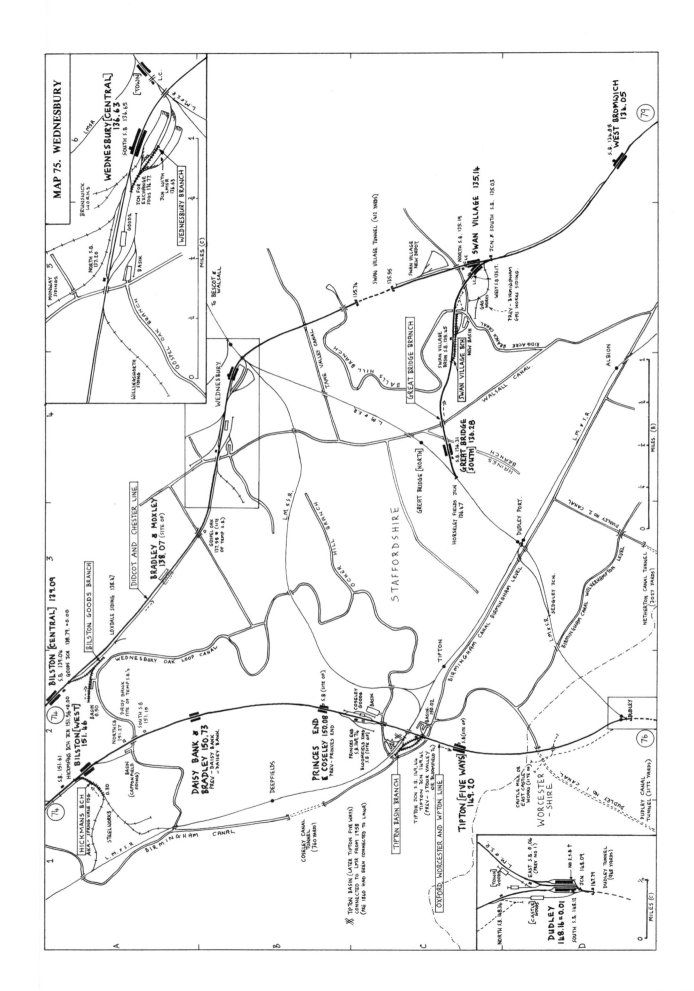

MAP 75. WEDNESBURY

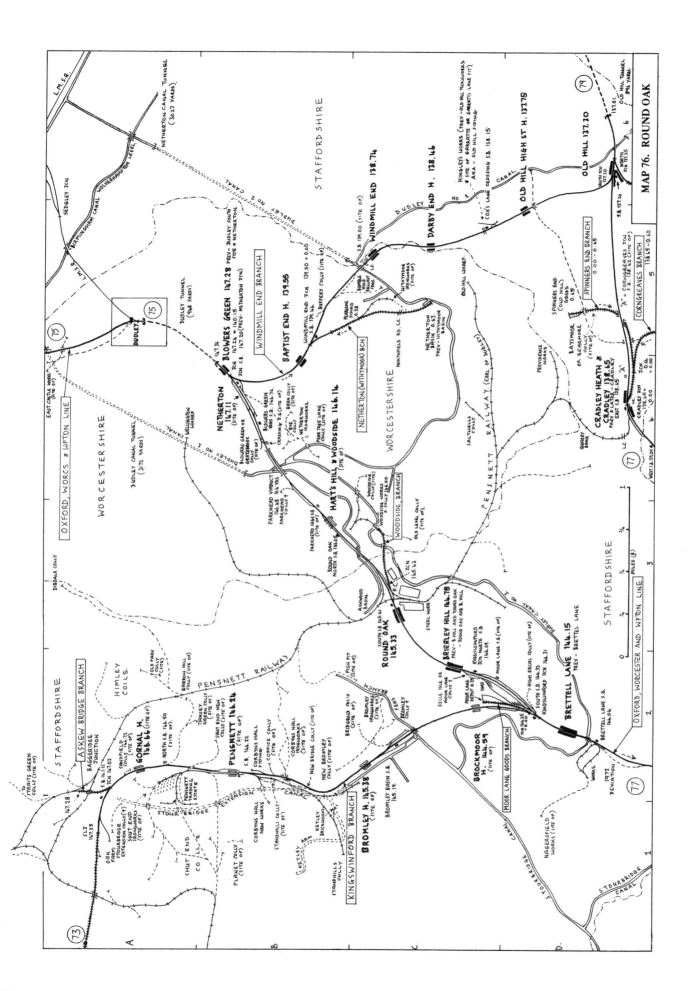

MAP 76. ROUND OAK

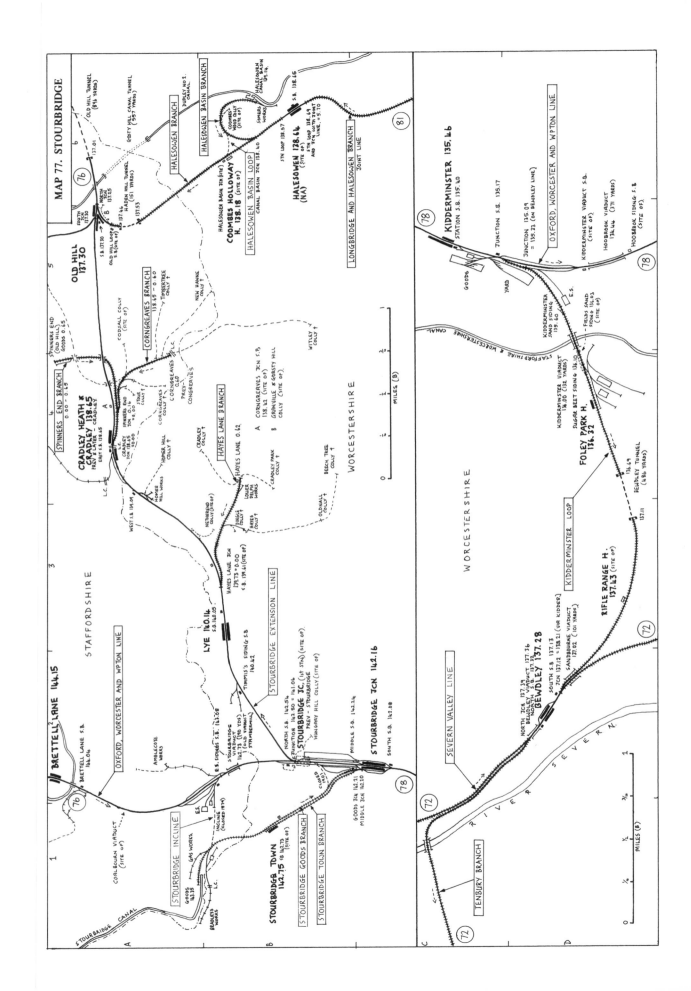

MAP 77. STOURBRIDGE

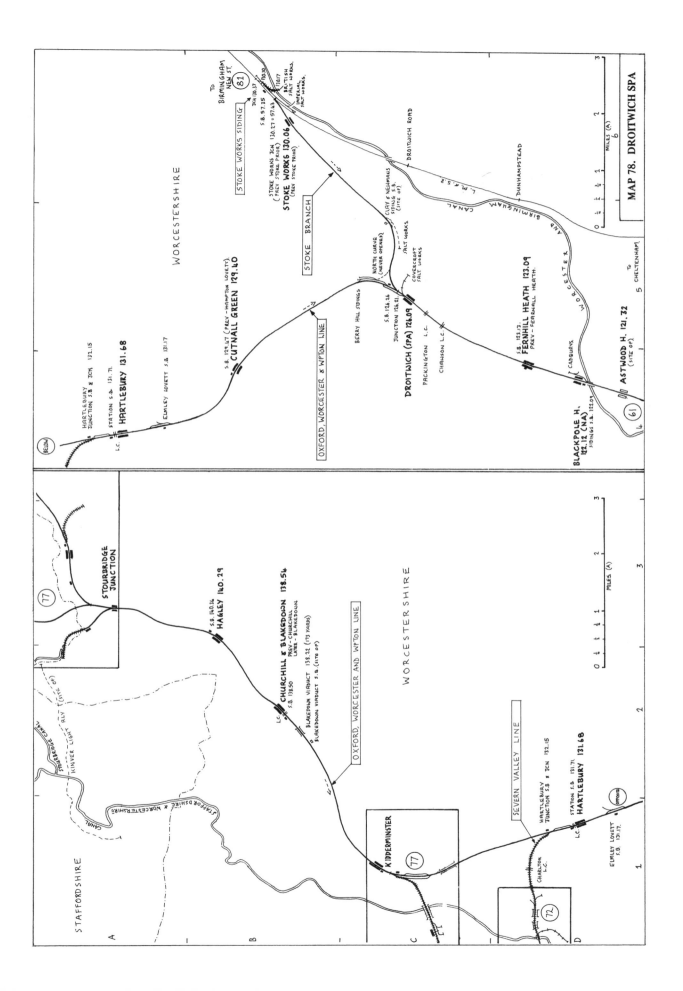

MAP 78. DROITWICH SPA

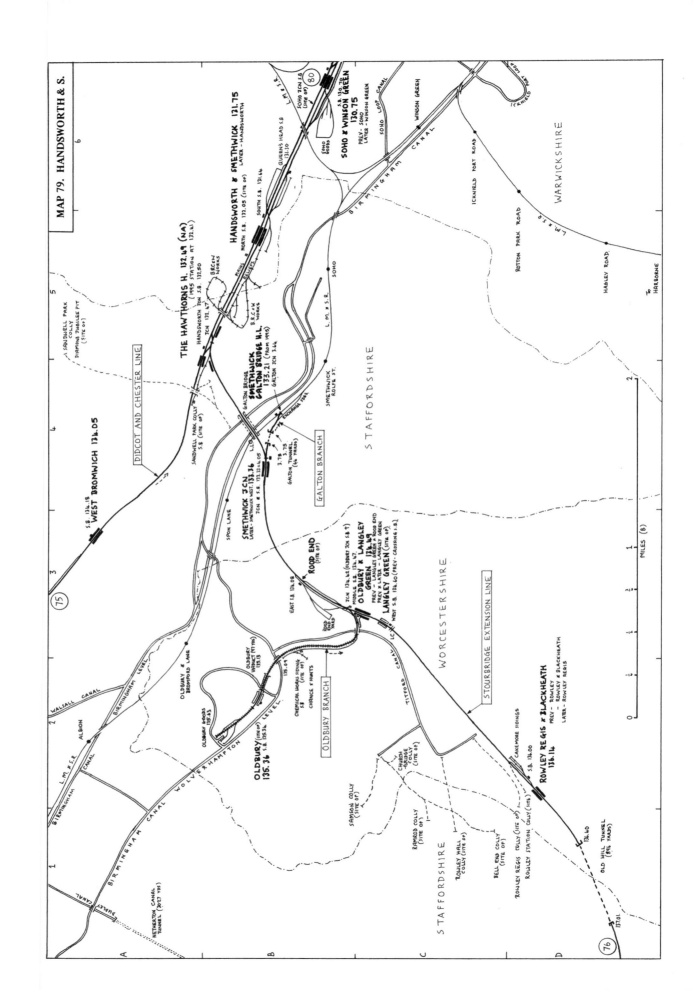

MAP 79. HANDSWORTH & S.

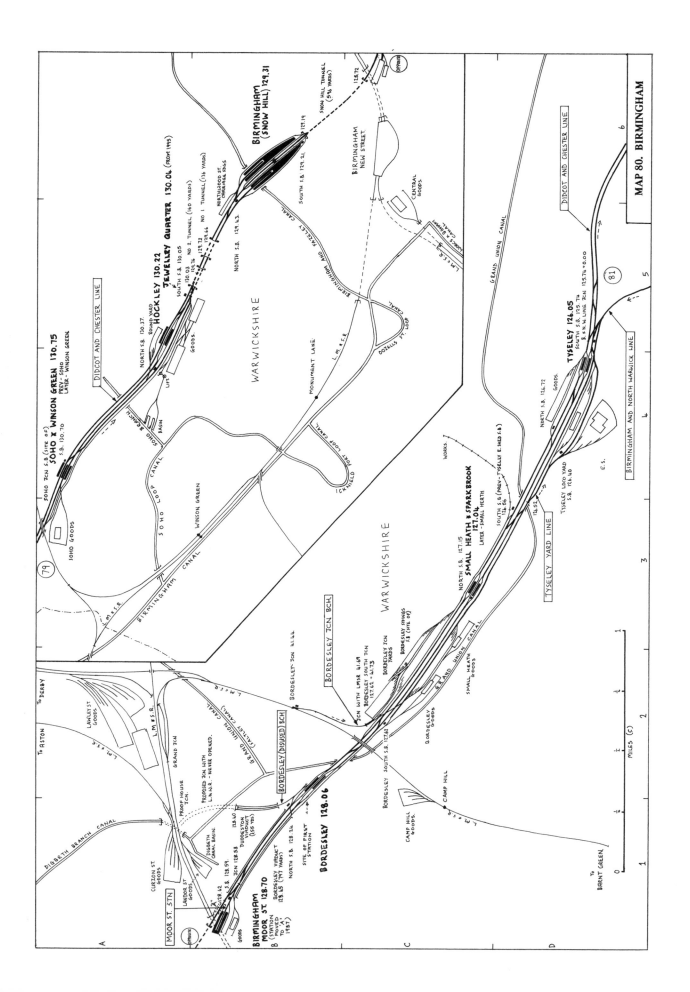

MAP 80. BIRMINGHAM

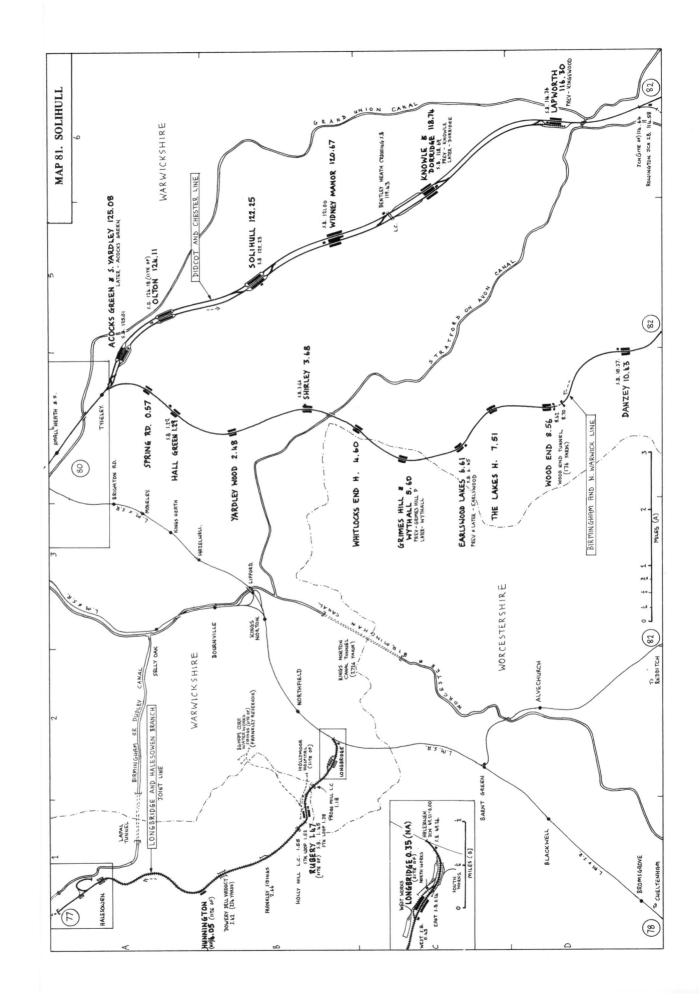

MAP 81. SOLIHULL

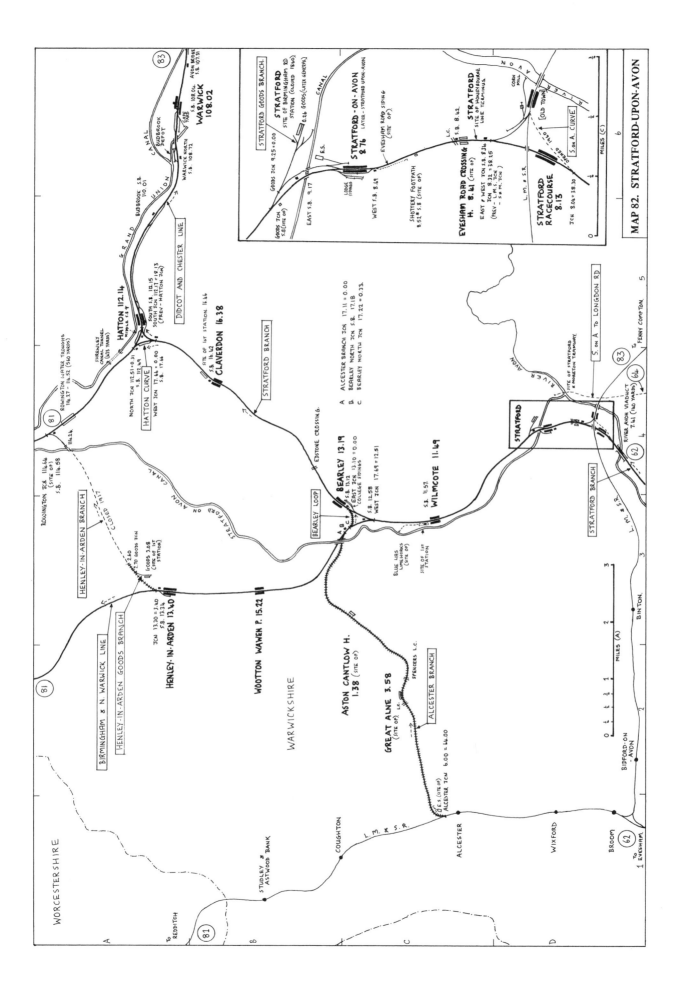

MAP 82. STRATFORD-UPON-AVON

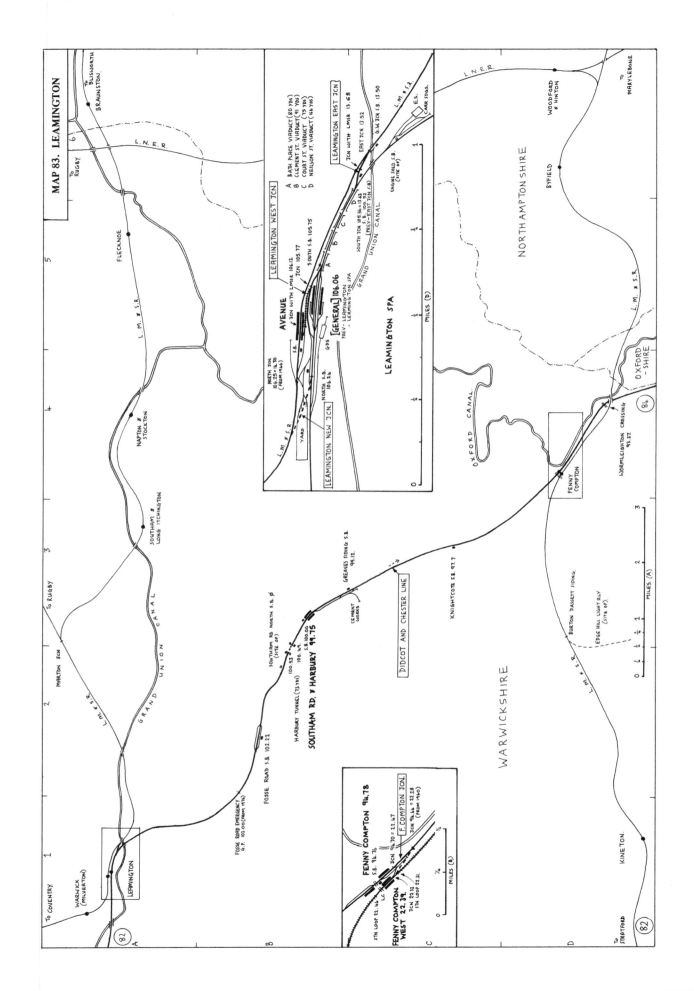

MAP 83. LEAMINGTON

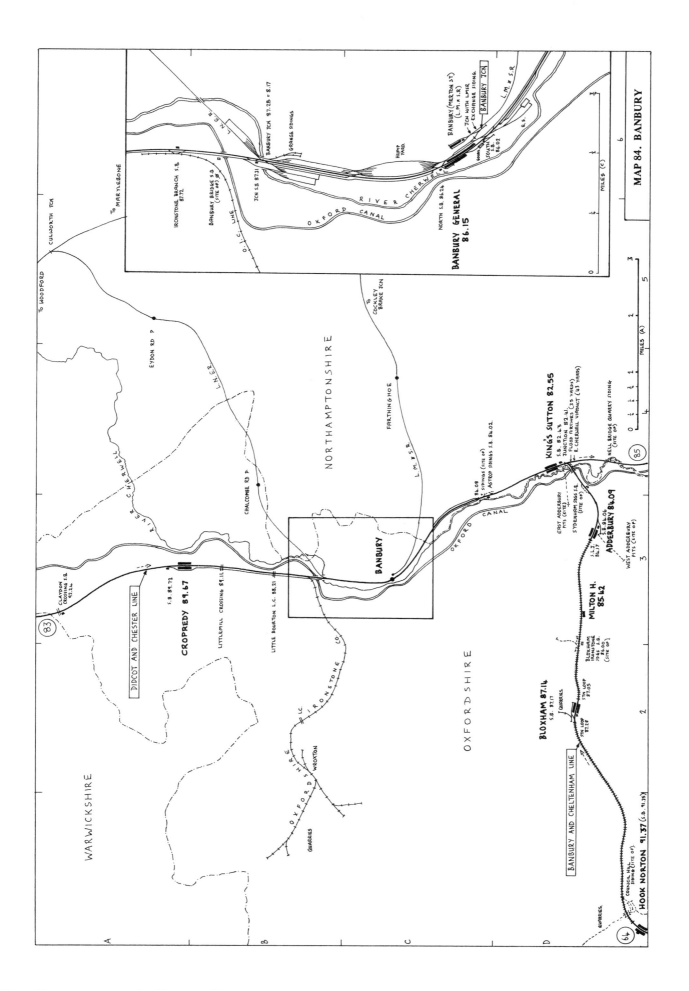

MAP 84. BANBURY

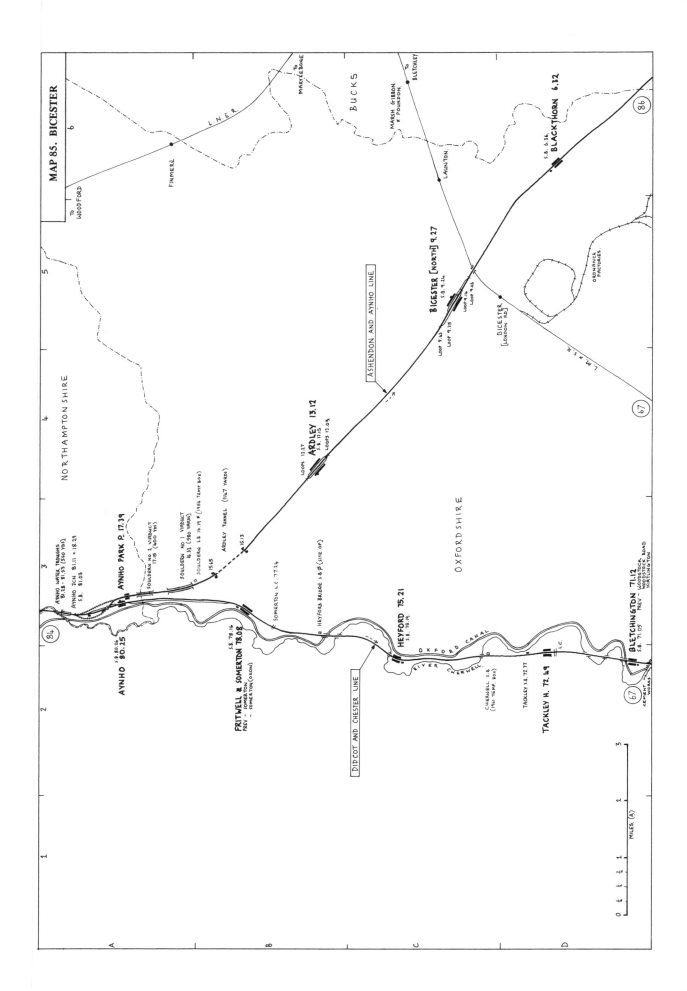

MAP 85. BICESTER

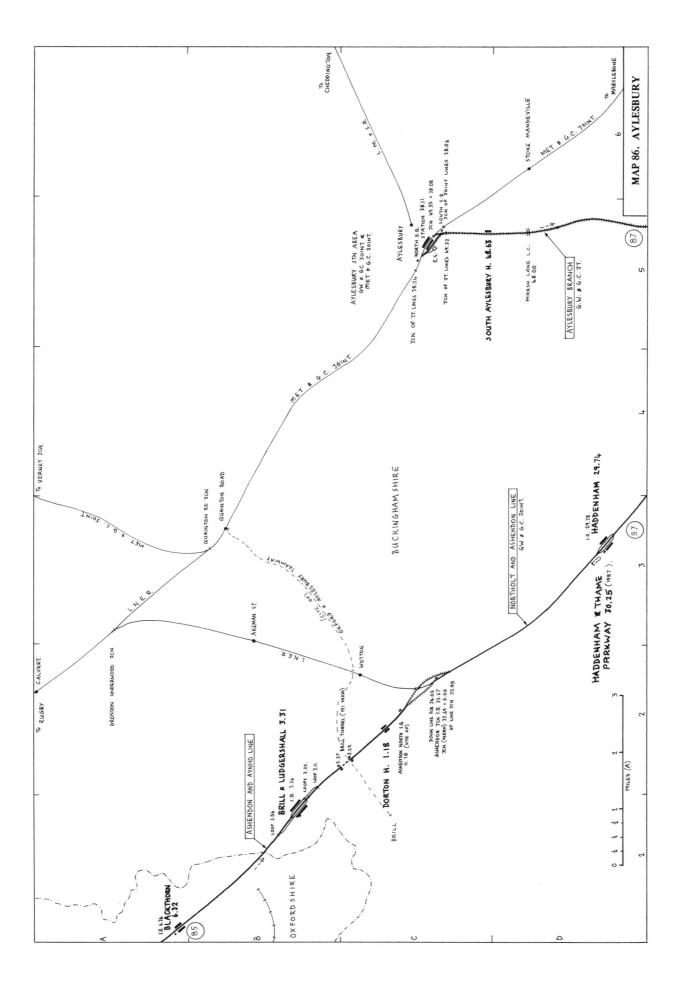

MAP 86. AYLESBURY

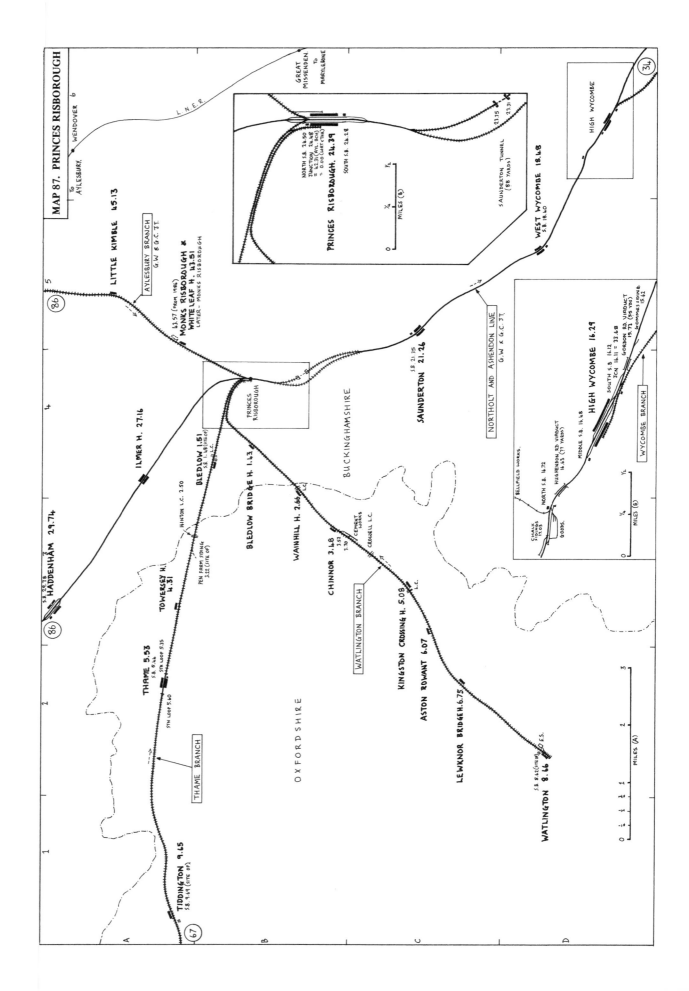

MAP 87. PRINCES RISBOROUGH

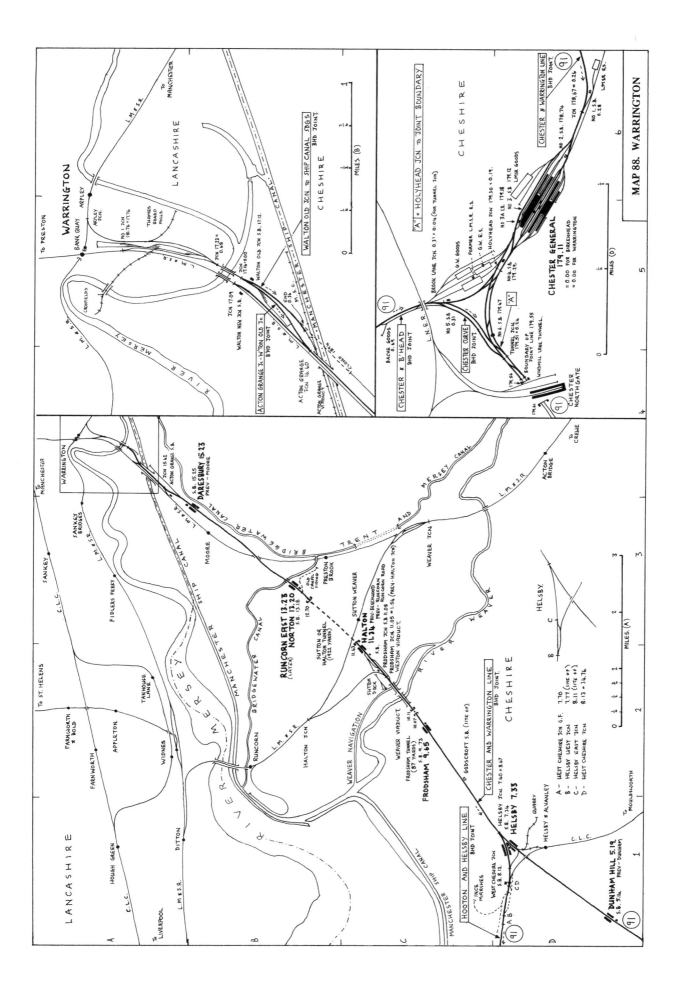

MAP 88. WARRINGTON

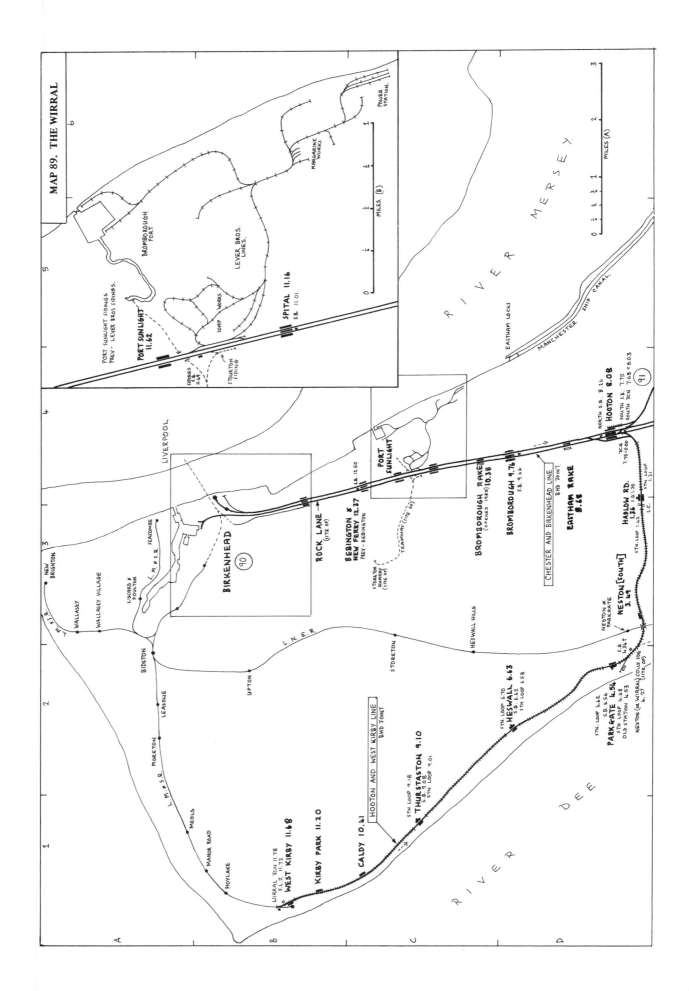

MAP 89. THE WIRRAL

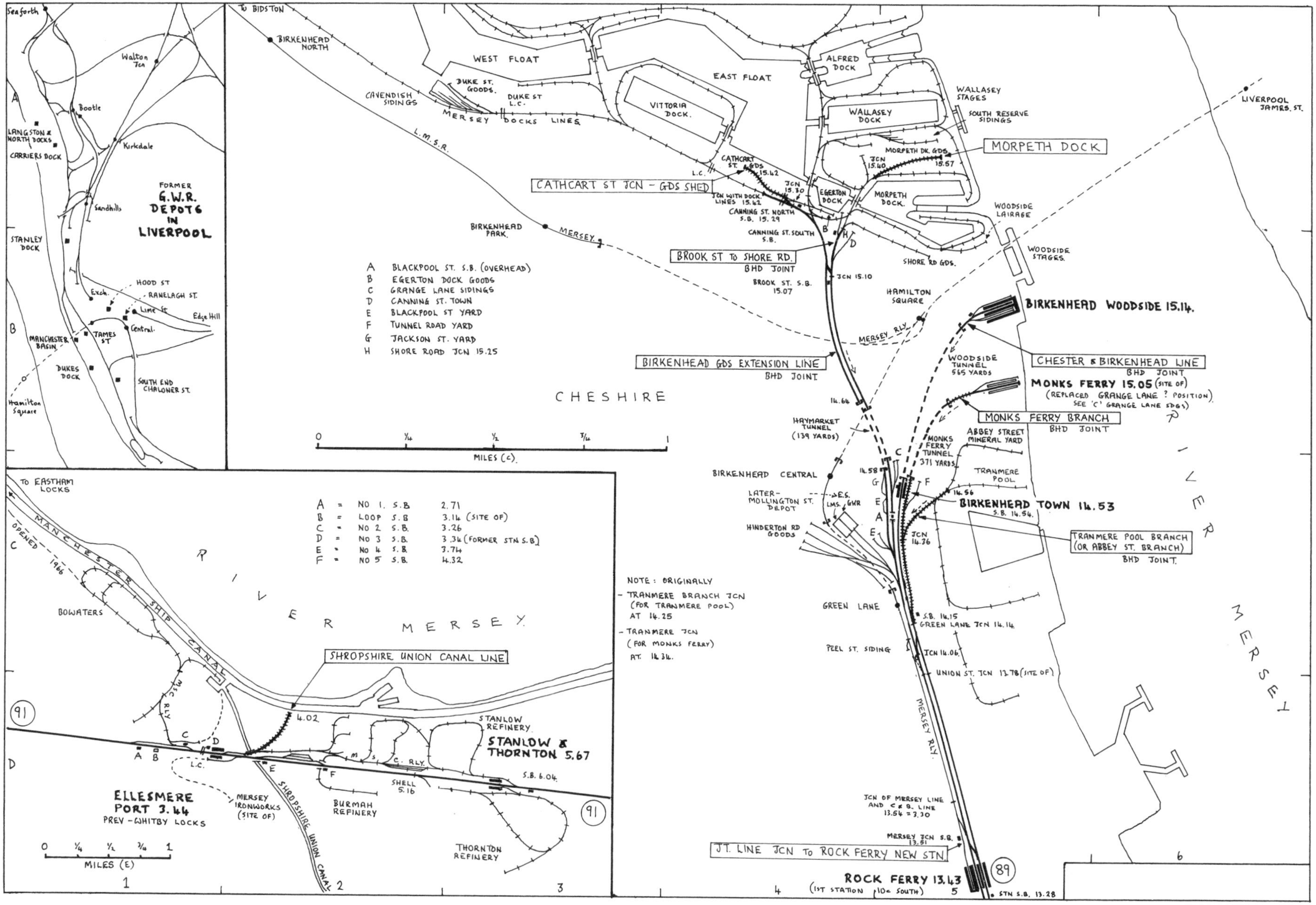

MAP 90. BIRKENHEAD ENLARGEMENT

Key labels (Birkenhead enlargement):

LIVERPOOL JAMES. ST.

RIVER MERSEY

MORPETH DOCK

WOODSIDE STAGES
WOODSIDE LAIRAGE
SOUTH RESERVE SIDINGS
WALLASEY STAGES

BIRKENHEAD WOODSIDE 15.14.

CHESTER & BIRKENHEAD LINE
MONKS FERRY 15.05 (SITE OF)
(RENAMED GRANGE LANE ? POSITION
SEE 'C' GRANGE LANE SDGS)
BHD JOINT

MONKS FERRY BRANCH
BHD JOINT

BIRKENHEAD TOWN 14.53

TRANMERE POOL BRANCH
(OR ABBEY ST. BRANCH)
BHD JOINT.

WALLASEY DOCK
ALFRED DOCK
EAST FLOAT
VICTORIA DOCK

MORPETH DK. GDS. 15.67
MORPETH DOCK
JCN 15.40
JCN 15.42
EGERTON DOCK
CATHCART ST. GDS. 15.42
JCN WITH DOCK LINES 15.40
CANNING ST. NORTH S.B.
CANNING ST. SOUTH S.B.

SHORE TO GDS.

HAMILTON SQUARE
MERSEY RLY

JCN 15.10

BROOK ST. S.B.
BHD JOINT
BROOK ST. 15.07

WOODSIDE TUNNEL
545 YARDS

MONKS FERRY
TUNNEL
371 YARDS

ABBEY STREET
MINERAL YARD
TRANMERE POOL
14.54
JCN 14.26

BIRKENHEAD TOWN
S.B. 14.54.

14.58

HAYMARKET
TUNNEL
(159 YARDS)

BIRKENHEAD CENTRAL

LAIRD-
MOLLINGTON ST.
DEPOT
LMS LNWR

HINDERTON RD.
GOODS

GREEN LANE

PEEL ST. SIDINGS

S.B. 14.15
GREEN LANE JCN 14.14.
JCN 14.06
UNION ST. JCN 13.78 (SITE OF)

MERSEY RLY

JCN OF MERSEY LINE
AND C & B. LINE
13.54 = 3.30

ROCK FERRY 13.43
(1ST STATION 10. SOUTH)

MERSEY JCN S.B.
ROCK FERRY NEW STN
STN S.B. 13.28

JT. LINE JCN TO ROCK FERRY NEW STN.

(Cathcart St Jcn – Gds Shed box):

CATHCART ST JCN – GDS SHED

WEST FLOAT
DUKE ST L.C.
CAVENDISH SIDINGS
MERSEY DOCKS LINES
L.M.S.R.
DUKE ST. GOODS.

BIRKENHEAD PARK
MERSEY

CHESHIRE

TO BIDSTON
BIRKENHEAD NORTH

(Brook St to Shore Rd box):

BROOK ST. TO SHORE RD.
BHD JOINT
BIRKENHEAD GDS EXTENSION LINE
BHD JOINT

A   BLACKPOOL ST. S.B. (OVERHEAD)
B   EGERTON DOCK GOODS
C   GRANGE LANE SIDINGS
D   CANNING ST. TOWN
E   BLACKPOOL ST YARD
F   TUNNEL ROAD YARD
G   JACKSON ST. YARD
H   SHORE ROAD JCN 15.25

MILES (C)
0   ¼   ½   ¾

NOTE: ORIGINALLY –
TRANMERE BRANCH JCN
(FOR TRANMERE POOL)
AT 14.25
– TRANMERE JCN
(FOR MONKS FERRY)
AT 14.34.

(Former G.W.R. Depots in Liverpool box):

FORMER G.W.R. DEPOTS IN LIVERPOOL

SEAFORTH
LANGTON & NORTH DOCKS
CANADA DOCK
STANLEY DOCK
MANCHESTER BASIN
HAMILTON SQUARE
WALTON JCN
BOOTLE
KIRKDALE
SANDHILLS
EXCH.
TRANMERE ST.
DUKES DOCK
SEACOMBE
RANELAGH ST.
HOOD ST.
LIME ST.
CENTRAL
SOUTH END CHALONER ST.
EGG HILL

A
B

(Ellesmere Port / Stanlow box):

RIVER MERSEY

SHROPSHIRE UNION CANAL LINE

STANLOW & THORNTON 5.67

STANLOW
REFINERY
S.B. 6.04.
THORNTON
REFINERY

SHELL
5.16
C. RLY.
BURMAH REFINERY
M.S.C. RLY.

ELLESMERE PORT 3.44
PREV. – WHITBY LOCKS

SHROPSHIRE UNION CANAL
MERSEY IRONWORKS
(SITE OF)
M.S.C. RLY
L.C.
14.02

MANCHESTER SHIP CANAL
OPENED 1896
BOWATERS
TO EASTHAM LOCKS

A = NO 1. S.B.   2.71
B = LOOP S.B.   3.14 (SITE OF)
C = NO 2. S.B.   3.26
D = NO 3. S.B.   3.34 (FORMER STA S.B.)
E = NO 4. S.B.   3.74.
F = NO 5. S.B.   4.32

MILES (E)
0   ¼   ½   ¾   1

89   91

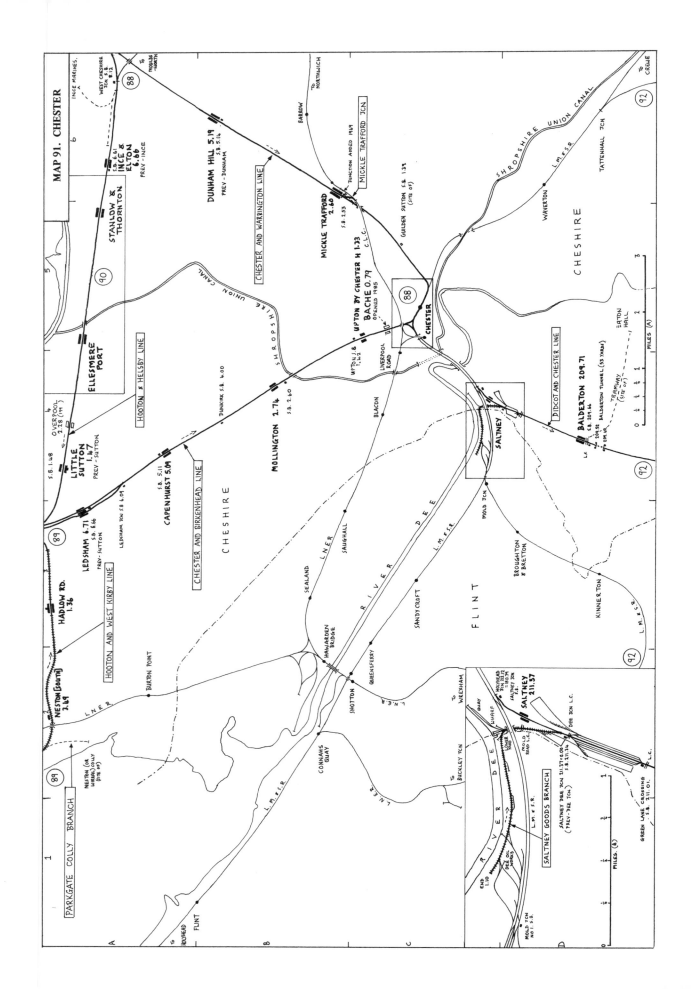

MAP 91. CHESTER

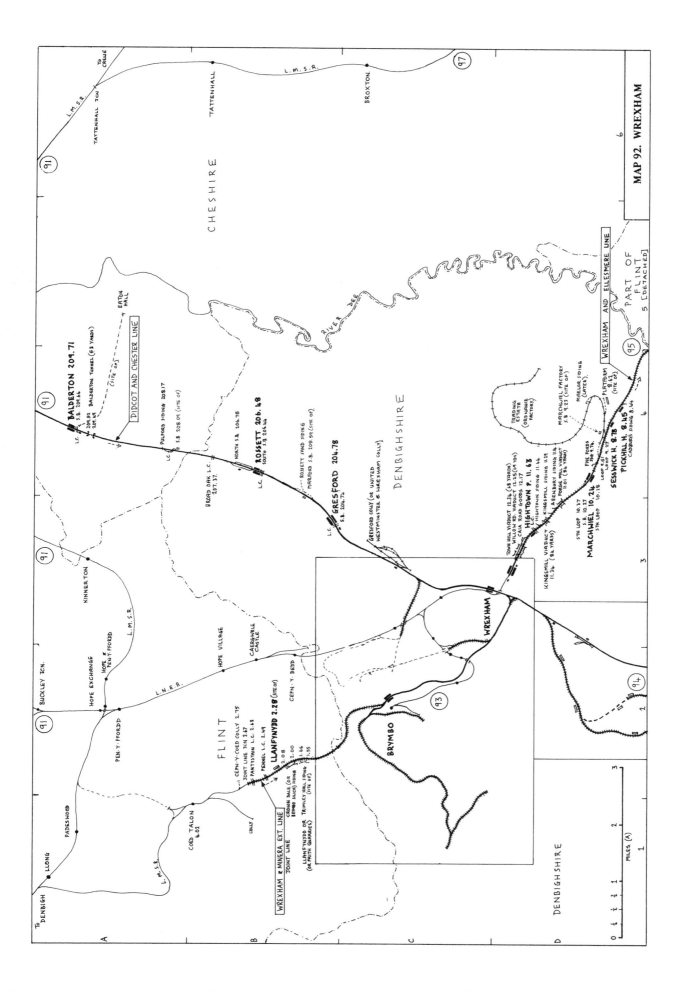

MAP 92. WREXHAM

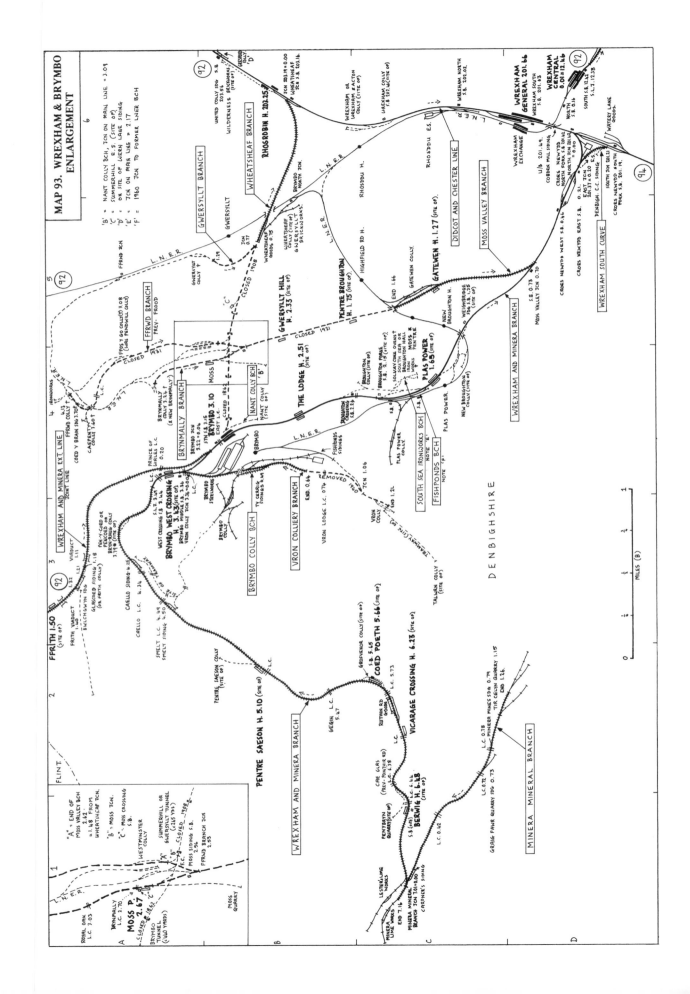

MAP 93. WREXHAM & BRYMBO ENLARGEMENT

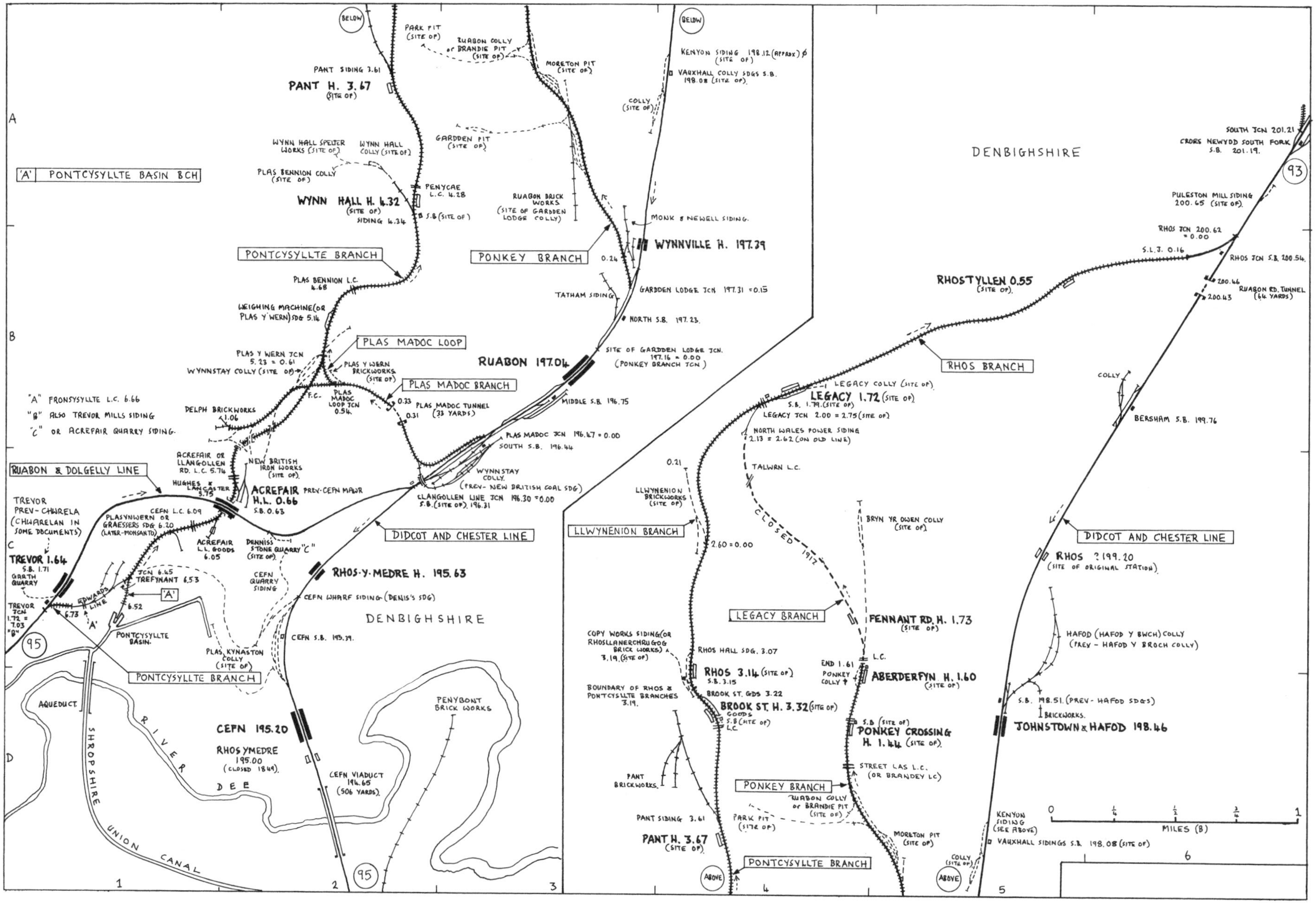

MAP 94. RUABON BRANCHES ENLARGEMENT

DENBIGHSHIRE

SOUTH TCN 201.21
CROES NEWYDD SOUTH FORK
S.B. 201.19.
PULESTON MILL SIDING 200.65 *0.00
RHOS TCN 200.62
RHOS TCN S.B. 200.54
200.46
200.43
RUABON RD. TUNNEL (64 YARDS)
S.I.T. 0.16
BERSHAM S.B. 199.76
COLLY (SITE OF)

RHOSTYLLEN 0.55 (SITE OF)

RHOS BRANCH

RHOS 2 199.20 (SITE OF ORIGINAL STATION)
DIDCOT AND CHESTER LINE

HAFOD (HAFOD Y BWCH COLLY) (PREV - HAFOD Y BRWCH COLLY)
S.B. 198.51 (PREV - HAFOD SDGS)
TOWNSTOWN x HAFOD 198.46
BRICKWORKS
KENYON SIDING (SEE ABOVE)
VAUXHALL SIDINGS S.B. 198.08 (SITE OF)

LEGACY 1.72 (SITE OF)
LEGACY TCN (SITE OF)
S.B. 1.71 (SITE OF)
NORTH WALES POWER SIDING 2.00 = 1.75 (SITE OF)
2.13 = 2.62 (ON OLD LINE)
TALWRN L.C.

CLOSED 1917

LEGACY BRANCH
2.60 = 0.00
0.21
LLWYNENION BRICKWORKS
0.24 (SITE OF)

LLWYNENION BRANCH

BRYN YR OWEN COLLY (SITE OF)

PENNANT RD. H. 1.73 (SITE OF)
ABERDERFYN H. 1.60 (SITE OF)
END 1.61
PONKEY COLLY
S.B. (SITE OF)
PONKEY CROSSING & H. 1.44 (SITE OF)
STREET LAS L.C. (OR BRANDEY LC)
MORETON PIT (SITE OF)
PONKEY BRANCH
RUABON COLLY OR BRANDIE PIT (SITE OF)
PARK PIT (SITE OF)
PONTCYSYLLTE BRANCH
COLLY (SITE OF)
ABOVE

RHOS 3.14 (SITE OF)
RHOS HALL SDG. 3.07
S.B. 3.15
BROOK ST. GDS 3.22
GOODS
BROOK ST. H. 3.32 (SITE OF)
S.B. (SITE OF) L.C.
COPY WORKS SIDING (OR RHOSLLANERCHRUGOG BRICK WORKS) 3.14 (SITE OF)
BOUNDARY OF RHOS & PONTCYSYLLTE BRANCHES 3.14.
PANT BRICKWORKS
PANT SIDING 2.61
PANT H. 3.67 (SITE OF)

PANT H. 3.67 (SITE OF)
PANT SIDING 2.61 (BELOW)

KENYON SIDING 198.12 (RPPROX)
(SITE OF)
VAUXHALL COLLY SDGS S.B. 198.08 (SITE OF)
COLLY (SITE OF)

WYNNVILLE H. 197.39

MONK & NEWELL SIDING
GARDDEN LODGE TCN 197.31 = 0.15
GARDDEN LODGE TCN 197.13
NORTH S.B. 197.13
0.24
SITE OF GARDDEN LODGE TCN. (PONKEY BRANCH TCN)
TATHAM SIDING
S.B. 196.75
MIDDLE TCN
PLAS MADOC TCN 196.67 = 0.00
SOUTH S.B.
WYNNSTAY COLLY.
PLAS MADOC TCN 196.64
PLAS Y SABN BRICKWORKS (SITE OF)
(PREV - NEW BRITISH GAL SDG)
LLANGOLLEN LINE TCN 196.20 *0.00
F.B. 196.31

RUABON 197.04

PLAS MADOC BRANCH

PLAS MADOC LOOP

0.33 PLAS MADOC TUNNEL (31 YARDS)
0.31 LLANGOLLEN LINE TCN 196.20

DIDCOT AND CHESTER LINE

RHOS-Y-MEDRE H. 195.63 (DENNIS'S SDG)
CEFN S.B. 195.19.
CEFN WHARF SIDING (SITE OF)

DENBIGHSHIRE

PENYBONT BRICK WORKS

CEFN 195.20
RHOSYMEDRE H. (CLOSED 18 M.)
CEFN VIADUCT H.L.145 (500 YARDS)

95

RIVER DEE

UNION CANAL
SHROPSHIRE
AQUEDUCT

PONTCYSYLLTE BASIN BRANCH

PANT H. 3.67 (SITE OF)

PARK PIT (SITE OF)
RUABON COLLY OR BRANDIE PIT (SITE OF)
GARDDEN PIT (SITE OF)
MORETON PIT (SITE OF)
PENYCAE L.C. 4.28 (SITE OF)
S.B. 4.56 (SITE OF)
PLAS FENNION COLLY (SITE OF)
WYNN HALL SPELTER WORKS (SITE OF)
WYNN HALL COLLY (SITE OF)
WYNN HALL H. 4.32
SIDING 4.34
PONTCYSYLLTE BRANCH

PLAS BENNION L.C.
WEIGHING MACHINE (OR PLAS Y WERN) SDG 5.14
PLAS Y WERN TCN 5.13 = 0.01
WYNNSTAY COLLY (SITE OF)
DELPH BRICKWORKS
ACREFAIR OR LLANGOLLEN RD L.C. 5.76
HUGHES L. (SITE OF)
ACREFAIR H.L. 0.66
S.B. 0.63
ACREFAIR L.L. GOODS 6.05
NEW BRITISH IRON WORKS (SITE OF)
PREV - CEFN MAWR
DENNIS'S STONE QUARRY "C" (SITE OF)
CEFN QUARRY SIDING
PLAS KYNASTON (SITE OF)
PONTCYSYLLTE BRANCH
PONTCYSYLLTE BASIN

PLAS Y WERN L.C. 6.66
ALSO TREVOR MILLS SIDING
OR ACREFAIR QUARRY SIDING

RUABON & DOLGELLY LINE

"A" FRONSYSYLLTE L.C.
"B" ALSO CHWAREL AN (CHWARELAN IN SOME DOCUMENTS)
"C" OR ACREFAIR QUARRY SIDING

PLASYNWAERN OR GRAESSERS SDG 6.10 (LATER-MORGAN LTD)
TCN 6.45 TREFYNANT 6.53
6.52
BRANCH TCN
TREVOR TCN
L.T.3.73
"A"
"B"

TREVOR 1.64
S.B. 1.71
TREVOR PREV - CHWAREL AN
GARTH QUARRY

95
93

DENBIGHSHIRE

A

B

C

D

1   2   3   4   5   6

MILES (B)
0   ¼   ½   ¾   1

MAP 94. RUABON BRANCHES ENLARGEMENT

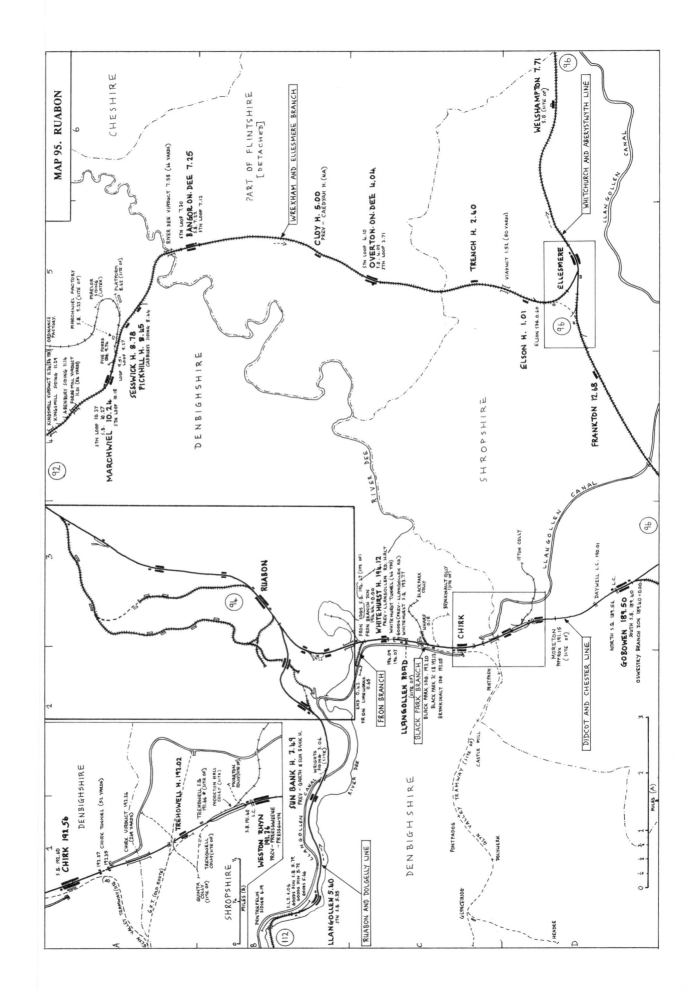

MAP 95. RUABON

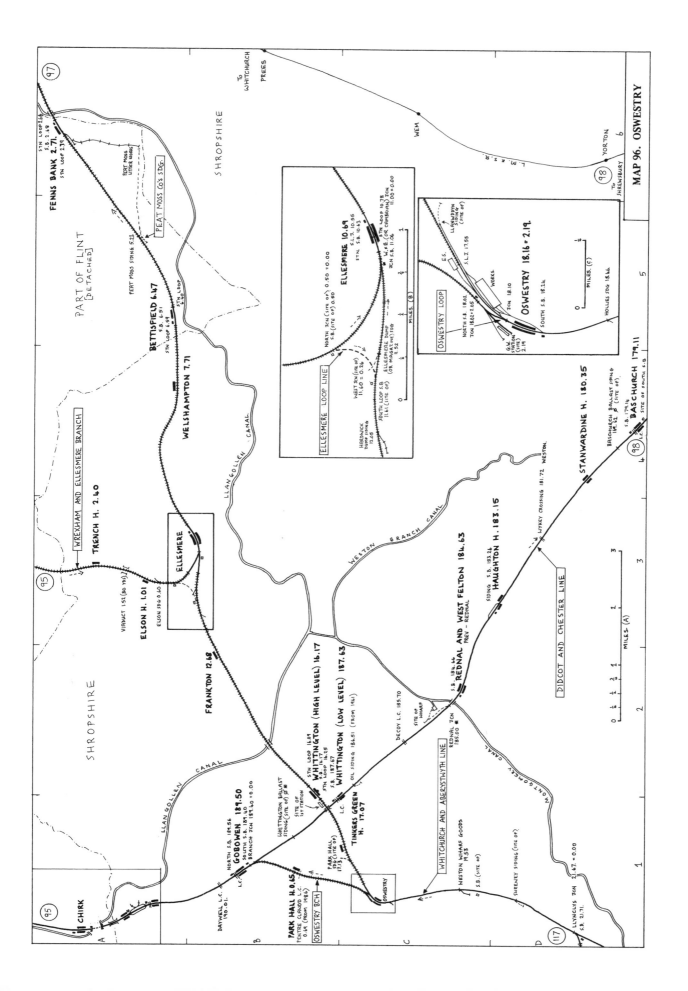

MAP 96. OSWESTRY

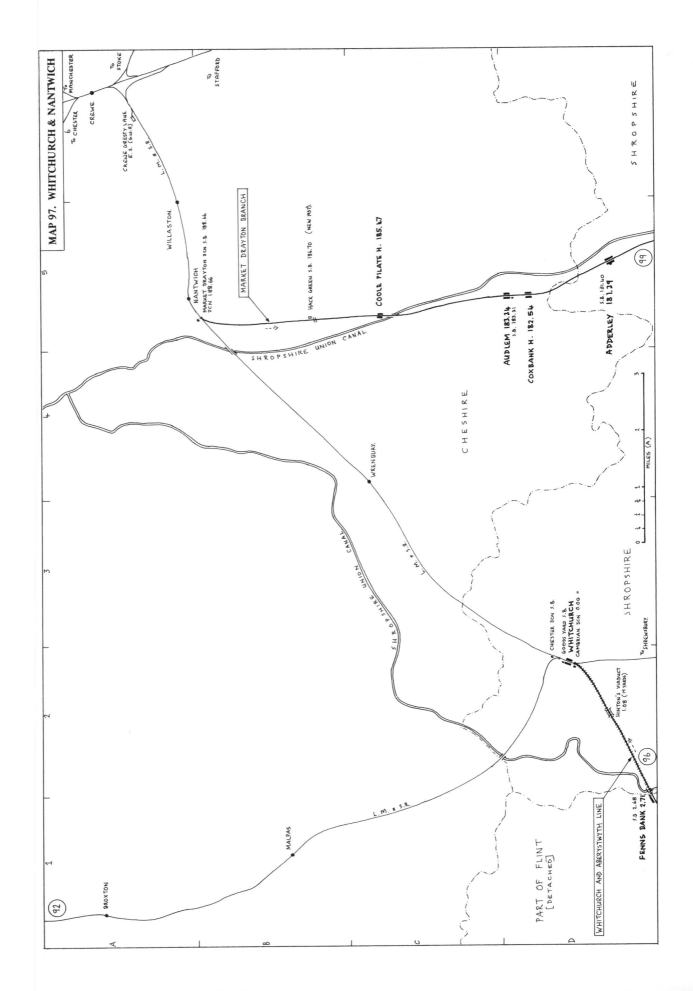

MAP 97. WHITCHURCH & NANTWICH

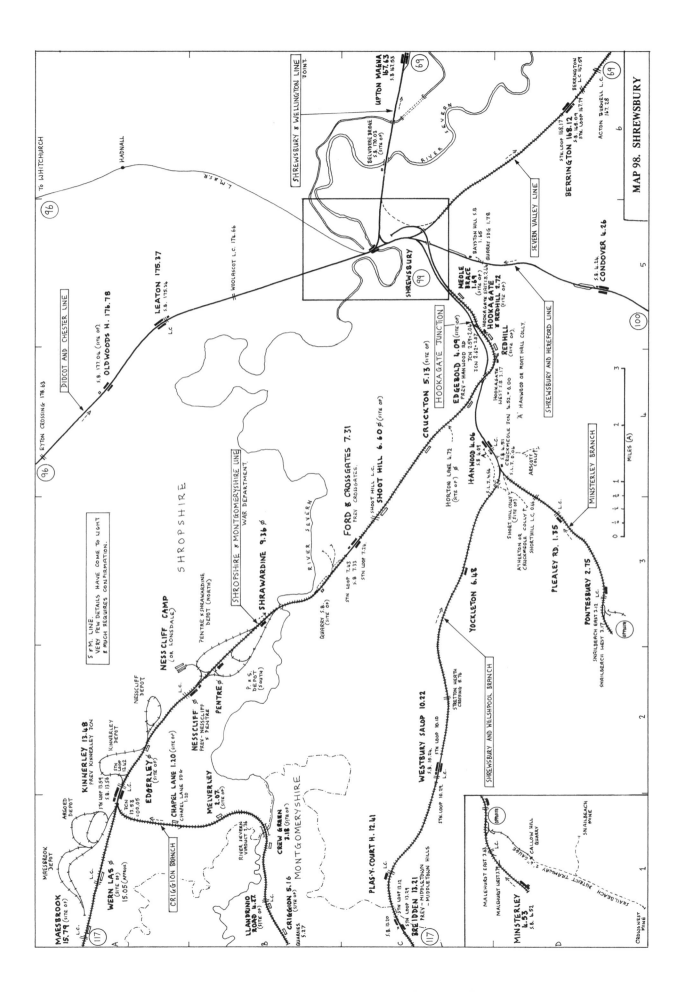

MAP 98. SHREWSBURY

MAP 99. SHREWSBURY & MKT DRAYTON

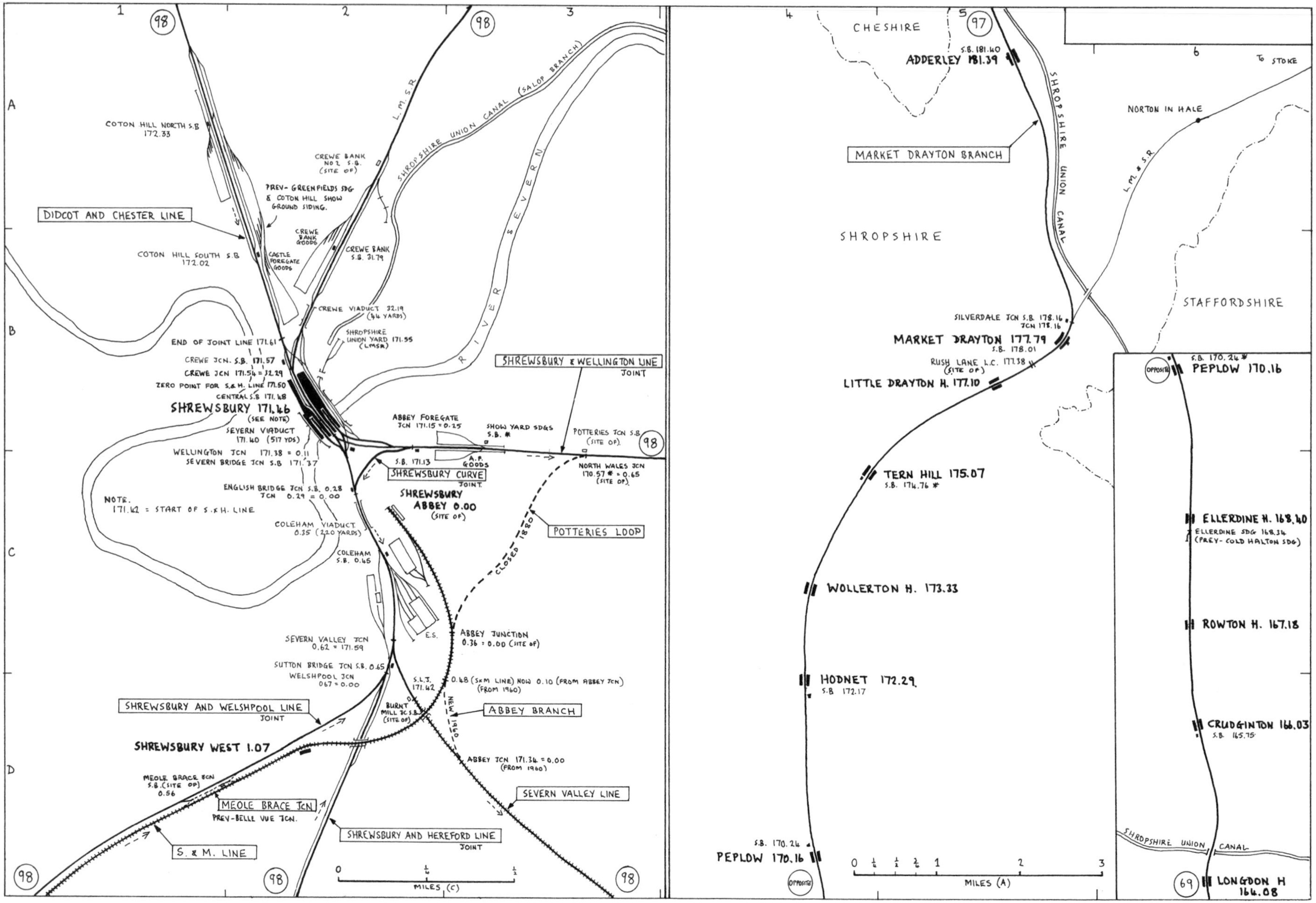

to STOKE

STAFFORDSHIRE

NORTON IN HALE

L.M.S.R.

SHROPSHIRE UNION CANAL

CHESHIRE

ADDERLEY 181.39
S.B. 181.40

MARKET DRAYTON BRANCH

SHROPSHIRE

SILVERDALE JCN S.B. 178.14
JCN 178.16

MARKET DRAYTON 177.79
RUSH LANE L.C. 177.38 S.B. 178.01
(SITE OF)

LITTLE DRAYTON H. 177.10

TERN HILL 175.07
S.B. 174.74 #

WOLLERTON H. 173.33

HODNET 172.29
S.B. 172.17

PEPLOW 170.16
S.B. 170.24

PEPLOW 170.16
S.B. 170.24 #
(OFFICE)

ELLERDINE H. 168.40
ELLERDINE SIDG 168.31
(PREV-COLD HATTON SDG)

ROWTON H. 167.18

CRUDGINTON 166.03
S.B. 165.75

LONGDON H. 164.08

SHROPSHIRE UNION CANAL

SUROPSHIRE UNION CANAL

MILES (A)
0 ¼ ½ ¾ 1 2 3

97   95   5   4   3

69

Left panel

COTON HILL NORTH S.B. 172.55

CREWE BANK NO 1 S.B. (SITE OF)

PREV- GREENFIELDS SDG & COTON HILL SHUNT GROUND SIDING

COTON HILL SOUTH S.B. 172.02

CREWE BANK S.B. 31.79

CREWE BANK GOODS

CASTLE FOREGATE GOODS

CREWE JCN. S.B. 171.57
CREWE JCN 171.54 = 31.79
CENTRAL S.B. 171.68
ZERO POINT FOR S&M LINE 171.50

END OF JOINT LINE 171.61

SEVERN VIADUCT 171.40 (517 YDS)
WELLINGTON JCN 171.38 = 0.11
ENGLISH BRIDGE JCN S.B. 0.18 0.35 = 171.37
COLEHAM VIADUCT 0.35 (220 YARDS)
SEVERN BRIDGE JCN S.B. 171.37
TCN 171.42 = 0.00

NOTE:
171.42 = START OF S.&H. LINE

SHREWSBURY 171.46 (SEE NOTE)

SHROPSHIRE UNION CANAL (CANAL BRANCH)

L.M.S.R.

RIVER SEVERN

DIDCOT AND CHESTER LINE

SHREWSBURY VIADUCT 32.19 (94 YARDS)

SHROPSHIRE UNION YARD 171.55 (L.M.S.R.)

SHREWSBURY-WELLINGTON LINE JOINT

POTTERIES JCN S.B. (SITE OF)

NORTH WALES JCN 170.57 # = 0.45 (SITE OF)

SHOD YARD SDGS
S.B. #

ABBEY FOREGATE JCN 171.15 = 0.15

GOODS
S.B. 171.13

SHREWSBURY CURVE JOINT

SHREWSBURY ABBEY 0.00 (SITE OF)

POTTERIES LOOP

CLOSED 1960

COLEHAM S.B. 0.45

E.S.

ABBEY JUNCTION 0.36 = 0.00 (SITE OF)

0.48 (S&M LINE) NO.2 0.10 (FROM ABBEY JCN)
NEW 1960

SEVERN VALLEY JCN 0.62 = 171.59

SUTTON BRIDGE JCN S.B. 0.45
WELSHPOOL JCN 0.67 = 0.00

S.I.T. 171.42
BURNT MILL JCS.B. (SITE OF)

ABBEY BRANCH

ABBEY JCN 171.34 = 0.00 (FROM 1960)

SEVERN VALLEY LINE

SHREWSBURY AND HEREFORD LINE JOINT

SHREWSBURY AND WELSHPOOL LINE JOINT

SHREWSBURY WEST 1.07

MEOLE BRACE JCN
S.B. (SITE OF)
0.56

MEOLE BRACE JCN
PREV-BELLE VUE JCN

S. & M. LINE

MILES (C)
0 ¼ ½ ¾ 1

98

1 2 3

A

B

C

D

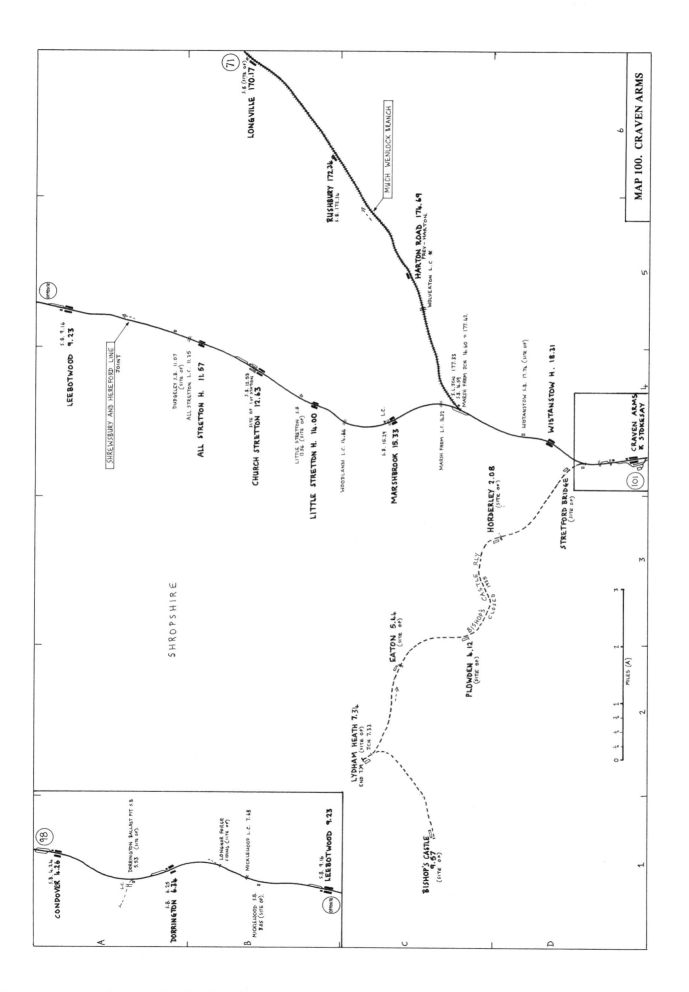

MAP 100. CRAVEN ARMS

SHROPSHIRE

MUCH WENLOCK BRANCH

LONGVILLE 170.17   S.B. (SITE OF)

RUSHBURY 172.34   S.B. 172.34

HARTON ROAD 174.69   PREV - HARTON.   WOLVERTON L.C. *

71

LEEBOTWOOD 9.23   S.B. 9.16

SHREWSBURY AND HEREFORD LINE
JOINT

DUDGELEY S.B. 11.07   (SITE OF)

ALL STRETTON H. 11.57   ALL STRETTON L.C. 11.15

CHURCH STRETTON 12.63   S.B. 12.55   SITE OF 1ST STATION

LITTLE STRETTON H. 14.00   LITTLE STRETTON S.B 13.56 (SITE OF)

WOODLANDS L.C. 14.66

MARSHBROOK 15.33   S.B. 15.29   L.C.

MARSH FARM L.C. 16.42

S.L. 3CA1 177.33   S.B. 16.59   MARSH FARM JCN 16.60 = 177.42

WISTANSTOW S.B. 17.74 (SITE OF)

WISTANSTOW H. 18.31

HORDERLEY 2.08   (SITE OF)

STRETFORD BRIDGE   (SITE OF)

CRAVEN ARMS
& STOKESAY

101

EATON 5.44   (SITE OF)

PLOWDEN 4.12   (SITE OF)

BISHOPS CASTLE RLY.
CLOSED 1935

LYDHAM HEATH 7.34   (SITE OF)
END 7.79   JCN 7.33

BISHOP'S CASTLE 9.57   (SITE OF)

MILES (A)
3   2   1   0   ½   1   2   3

CONDOVER 4.26   S.B. 4.24

DORRINGTON BALLAST PIT S.B. 5.53   (SITE OF)

LONGNOR FORGE SIDING (SITE OF)   7.48

DORRINGTON 6.34   S.B. 6.25

MICKLEWOOD L.C. 7.48

MICKLEWOOD S.B. 8.05 (SITE OF)

LEEBOTWOOD 9.23   S.B. 9.16

98

A

B

C

D

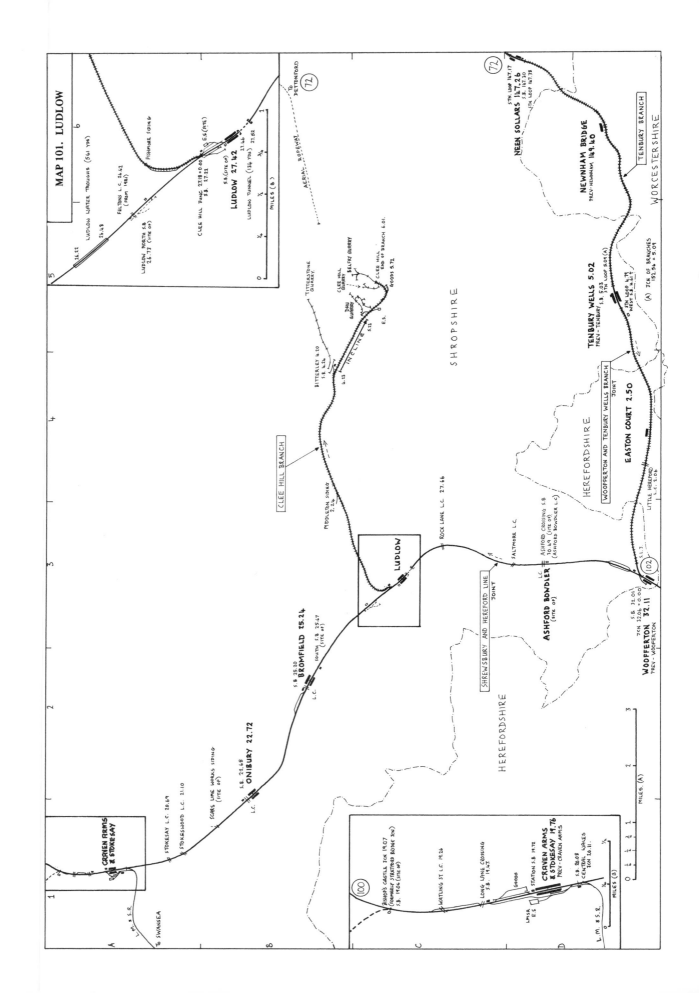

MAP 101. LUDLOW

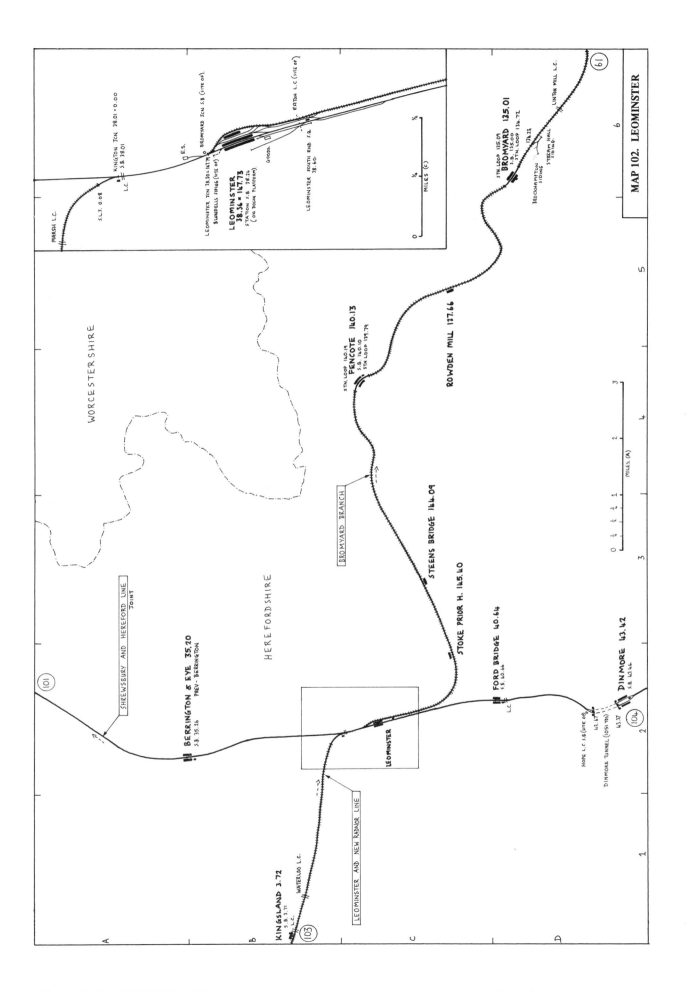

MAP 102. LEOMINSTER

MARSH L.C.

KINGTON JCN 38.01 = 0.00
S.B. 38.01
L.C.
S.L.T. 0.08

E.S.
BROMYARD JCN S.B. (SITE OF)
LEOMINSTER JCN 78.30 = 147.79
BLUNDELLS SIDING (SITE OF)
EATON L.C (SITE OF)

LEOMINSTER
38.34 = 147.73
STATION S.B. 78.74
(ON DOWN PLATFORM)

GOODS.

LEOMINSTER SOUTH END S.B.
38.60

MILES (C)
0   ¼   ½   ¾

WORCESTERSHIRE

STN.LOOP 135.09
BROMYARD 135.01
S.B. 135.00
STN. LOOP 134.72
134.33
BROCKHAMPTON SIDING
STREAM HALL SIDING
LINTON MILL L.C.

19

6

STN.LOOP 140.19
PENCOTE 140.13
S.B. 140.10
STN.LOOP 139.79

ROWDEN MILL 137.66

5

BROMYARD BRANCH

STEENS BRIDGE 164.09

STOKE PRIOR H. 165.40

HEREFORDSHIRE

MILES (A)
0 ¼ ½ ¾ 1   2   3
3   4

SHREWSBURY AND HEREFORD LINE
JOINT

101

BERRINGTON & EYE 35.20
S.B. 35.16
PREV-BERRINGTON

FORD BRIDGE 40.64
S.B. 40.64
L.C.

LEOMINSTER

DINMORE 43.42
S.B. 43.44

HOPE L.C S.B (SITE OF)
42.67
42.67¾
DINMORE TUNNEL (1051 YDS)
43.37
104

KINGSLAND 3.72
S.B. 3.71
L.C.
WATERLOO L.C.

LEOMINSTER AND NEW RADNOR LINE

103

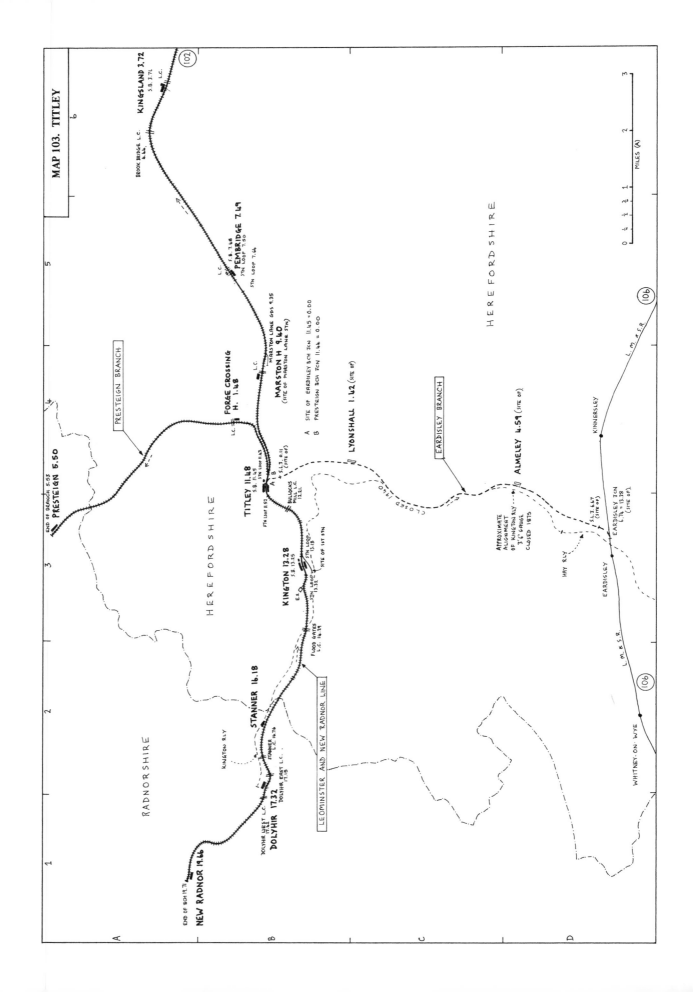

MAP 103. TITTLEY

KINGSLAND 3.72
S.B. 3.7L
BROOK BRIDGE L.C.
4.44

PEMBRIDGE 7.49
F.B. 7.48
STN LOOP 7.50
STN LOOP 7.44
L.C.

PRESTEIGN BRANCH

MARSTON LANE GDS 7.35
MARSTON H 9.40
(SITE OF MARSTON LANE STN)
L.C.

FORGE CROSSING
H. 1.48
L.C.

END OF BRANCH 5.53
PRESTEIGN 6.50

A SITE OF EARDISLEY BCH JCN 11.45 = 0.00
B PRESTEIGN BCH JCN 11.46 = 0.00

LYONSHALL 1.42 (SITE OF)

TITTLEY 11.48
S.B. 11.49
STN LOOP 11.43
A B + S.L.T. 0.11
(SITE OF)

STN LOOP 11.52
BULLOCKS
MILL L.C.
12.21

EARDISLEY BRANCH

ALMELEY 4.59 (SITE OF)

CLOSED 1940

APPROXIMATE
ALIGNMENT
OF KINGTON RLY
3' 6" GAUGE
CLOSED 1875

HAY RLY

KINNERSLEY

S.L.T. 6.47
(SITE OF)
EARDISLEY JCN
6.7L = 13.28
(SITE OF)

EARDISLEY

L.M. & S.R.

WHITNEY-ON-WYE

HEREFORDSHIRE

HEREFORDSHIRE

STANNER 16.18

KINGTON RLY

STANNER L.C. 16.76

DOLYHIR WEST L.C.
DOLYHIR 17.32
DOLYHIR EAST L.C.
(SITE OF) 17.15

KINGTON 13.28
S.B. 13.25
STN LOOP 13.18
SITE OF 1ST STN
E. & STN LOOP 13.32

FLOOD GATES
L.C. 14.29

LEOMINSTER AND NEW RADNOR LINE

END OF BCH 17.71
NEW RADNOR 19.66

RADNORSHIRE

MILES (A)
0 ¼ ½ ¾ 1 1½ 2 3

(102)

(106)

(106)

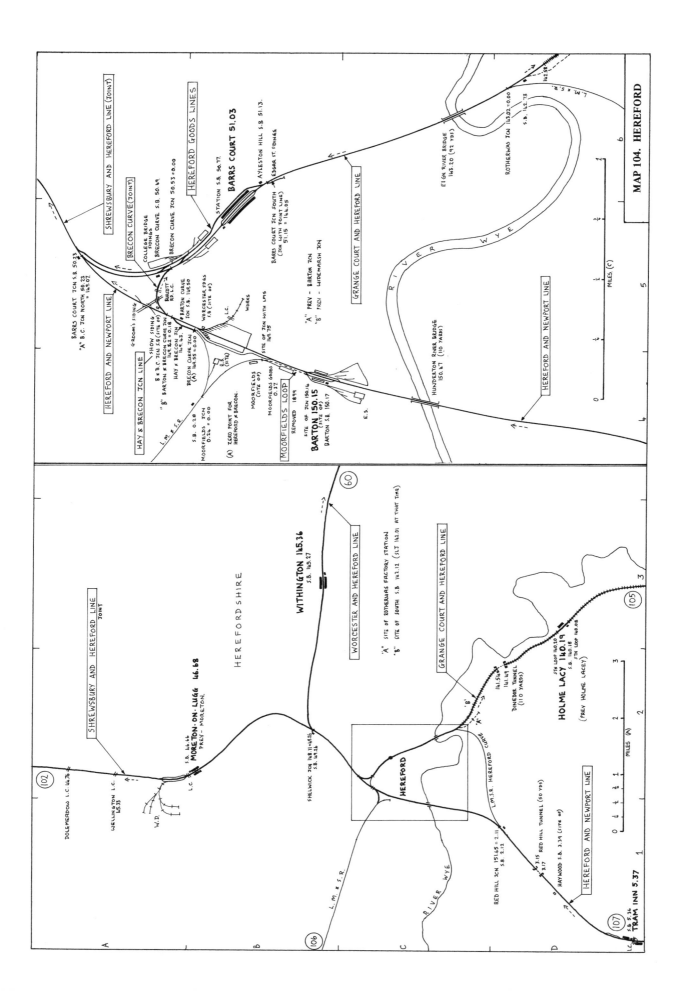

MAP 104. HEREFORD

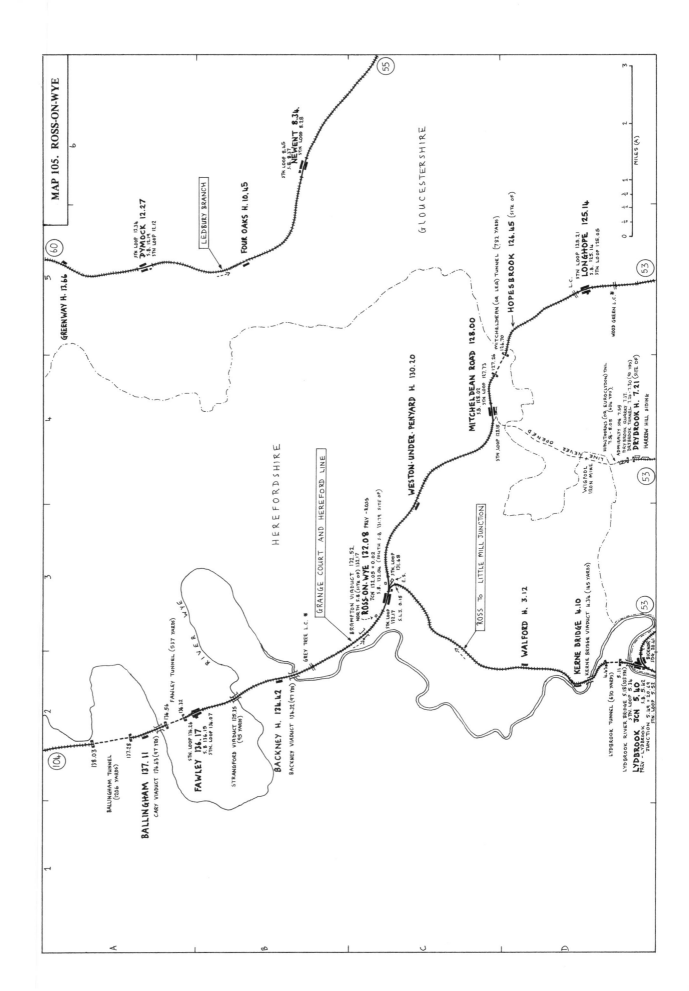

MAP 105. ROSS-ON-WYE

GREENWAY H. 13.66

STN LOOP 13.34
DYMOCK 12.27
S.B. 12.14
STN LOOP 11.12

LEDBURY BRANCH

FOUR OAKS H. 10.45

STN LOOP 8.45
S.B. 8.17
NEWENT 8.34
STN LOOP 8.28

GLOUCESTERSHIRE

BALLINGHAM TUNNEL
(206 YARDS)

CARY VIADUCT 136.63 (47 YDS)

BALLINGHAM 137.11

138.03

137.28

FAWLEY TUNNEL (537 YARDS)

136.56

136.32

STN LOOP 136.26
FAWLEY 136.17
S.B. 136.15
STN LOOP 136.07

RIVER WYE

STRANGFORD VIADUCT 135.25 (55 YARDS)

BACKNEY H. 134.42
BACKNEY VIADUCT 134.32 (47 YDS)

GREY TREE L.C. ✳

HEREFORDSHIRE

BRAMPTON VIADUCT 132.52,
NORTH S.B. (SITE OF) 132.17

ROSS-ON-WYE 132.08 PREV. ROSS
STN 132.05 = 0.02
S.B. 132.04 (SOUTH) J.B. 131.79 SITE OF)

STN LOOP 132.17

GRANGE COURT AND HEREFORD LINE

E.S. 131.68

STN LOOP 131.17

S.L.J. 0.16

WESTON-UNDER-PENYARD H. 130.20

WALFORD H. 3.12

ROSS TO LITTLE MILL JUNCTION

STN LOOP 128.15

MITCHELDEAN ROAD 128.00
S.B. 128.02
STN LOOP 127.73

127.26 MITCHELDEAN (OR LEA) TUNNEL (792 YARDS)
126.70

HOPESBROOK 126.45 (SITE OF)

LINE NEVER OPENED

WIGPOOL
IRON MINE

KERNE BRIDGE 4.10
KERNE BRIDGE VIADUCT 4.34 (145 YARDS)

LYDBROOK RIVER BRIDGE 5.18 (107YD)
LYDBROOK TUNNEL (630 YARDS)

LYDBROOK JCN 5.40
PREV. LYDBROOK
JUNCTION 5.44 = 20.49
STN LOOP 5.52

BACKNOR
5.11
STN LOOP 20.41

HORRIDGE ✳

STN LOOP 125.21
LONGHOPE 125.14
S.B. 125.14
STN LOOP 125.05

WOOD GREEN L.C. ✳

HOPSTHORNS (OR EUROCLYDON) TNL.
7.96 - 8.05 (434 YARDS)

ADMIRALTY SDG 7.56
DRYBROOK QUARRY 7.21
DRYBROOK TUNNEL 7.14 - 7.30 (90 YDS)
DRYBROOK H. 7.21 (SITE OF)
HARROW HILL SIDING

MILES (A)
0   ¼ ½ ¾ 1   2   3

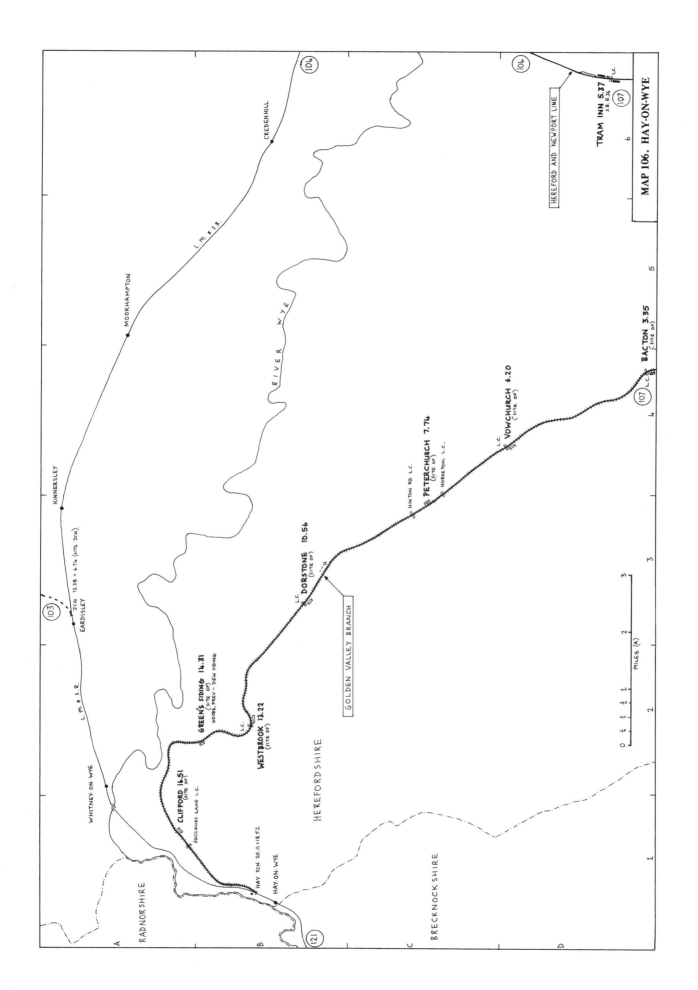

MAP 106. HAY-ON-WYE

HEREFORD AND NEWPORT LINE

TRAM INN 5.37
S.B. 6.76

L.C.

BACTON 3.35
(SITE OF)

L.C.

VOWCHURCH 6.20
(SITE OF)

L.C.

PETERCHURCH 7.74
(SITE OF)

HORSEPOOL L.C.

HINTON RD L.C.

DORSTONE 10.56
(SITE OF)

L.C.

GOLDEN VALLEY BRANCH

GREEN'S SIDING 14.31
(SITE OF)
GOODS, PREV - DEW SIDING

WESTBROOK 13.22
(SITE OF)

L.C.

CLIFFORD 16.51
(SITE OF)

SUCCOURS LANE L.C.

HAY TCN 20.11 = 19.52

HAY-ON-WYE

CREDENHILL

L. M & S.R.

MOORHAMPTON

R I V E R   W Y E

KINNERSLEY

JCN 13.38 = 6.74 (SITE JCN)

EARDISLEY

L. M & S.R.

WHITNEY-ON-WYE

HEREFORDSHIRE

RADNORSHIRE

BRECKNOCKSHIRE

MILES (A)

0   ¼   ½   ¾   1   2   3

A

B

C

D

104

103

121

107

107

104

104

6

5

4

3

2

1

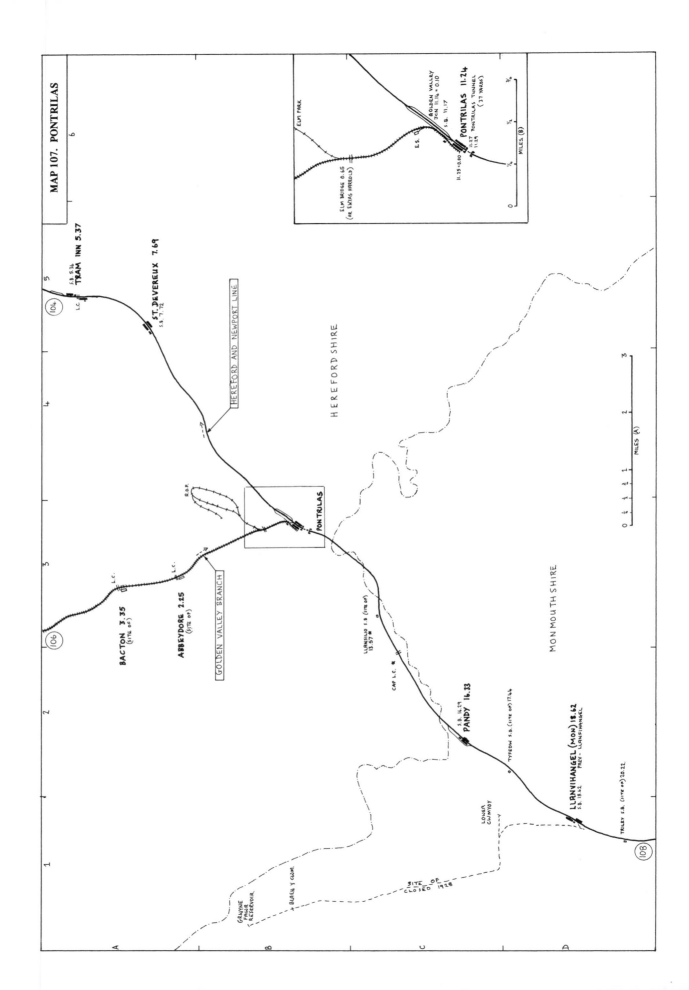

MAP 107. PONTRILAS

TRAM INN 5.37
S.B. 5.36

ST. DEVEREUX 7.69
S.B. 7.72

HEREFORD AND NEWPORT LINE

HEREFORDSHIRE

BACTON 3.35
(SITE OF)

ABBEYDORE 2.25
(SITE OF)

GOLDEN VALLEY BRANCH

R.O.P.

PONTRILAS

LLANSILLO S.B. 13.57 *
(SITE OF)

CWM L.C.

PANDY 16.33
S.B. 16.29

TYFEDW S.B. (SITE OF) 17.44

LLANVIHANGEL (MON) 18.62
S.B. 18.62   PREV- LLANFIHANGEL

TRILEY S.B. (SITE OF) 20.22.

MONMOUTHSHIRE

GRWYNE FAWR
RESERVOIR

BLAEN Y CWM

LOWER CWMYOY

SITE OF
CLOSED 1928

0   ¼   ½   1   2   3
MILES (A)

Inset:

ELM PARK

ELM BRIDGE 0.65
(AR EWYAS HAROLD)

E.S.

GOLDEN VALLEY
JCN 11.14 • 0.10

PONTRILAS 11.24
S.B. 11.17

11.15 • 0.00

11.27   PONTRILAS TUNNEL
11.29   (37 YARDS)

0   ¼   ½   ¾
MILES (B)

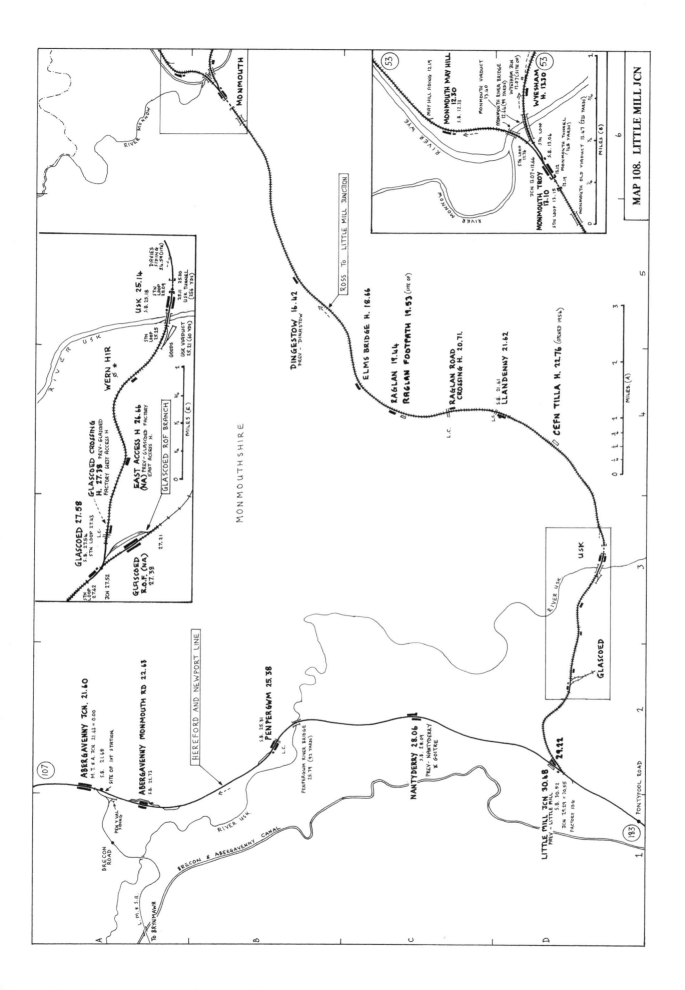

MAP 108. LITTLE MILL JCN

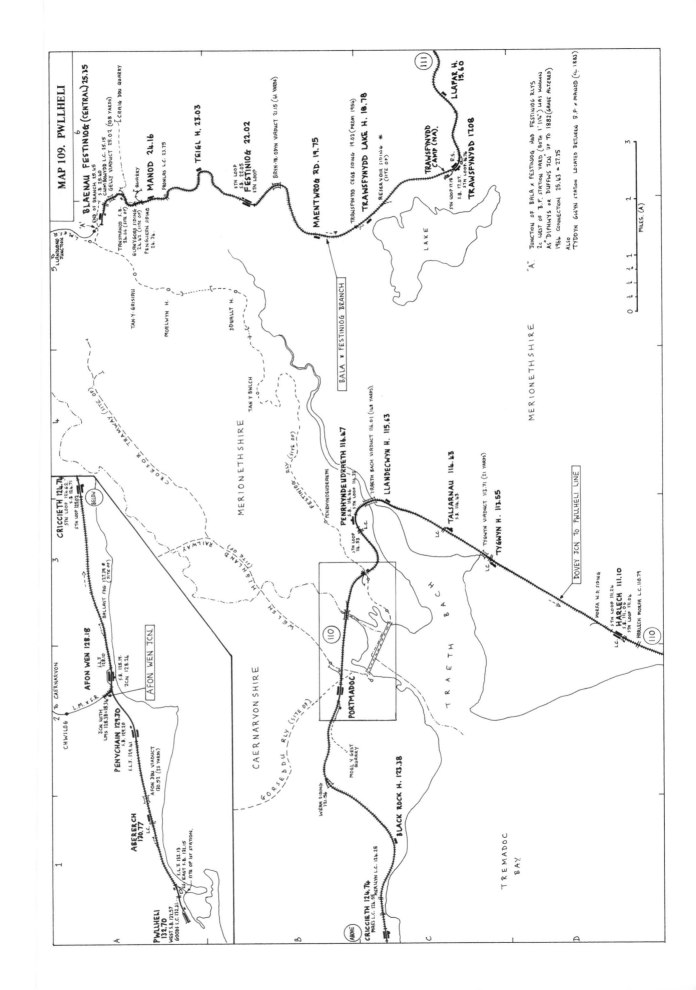

MAP 109. PWLLHELI

BLAENAU FESTINIOG (CENTRAL) 25.35

LLAFAR H. 15.60

TEIGL H. 23.03

FESTINIOG 22.02

MANOD 24.16

MAENTWROG RD. 19.75

TRAWSFYNYDD LAKE H. 18.78

TRAWSFYNYDD CAMP (NA).

TRAWSFYNYDD 17.08

BALA & FESTINIOG BRANCH

MERIONETHSHIRE

PENRHYNDEUDRAETH 116.67

LLANDECWYN H. 115.63

TALSARNAU 116.43

TYGWYN H. 113.55

HARLECH 111.10

DOVEY JCN TO PWLLHELI LINE

TRAETH BACH

MERIONETHSHIRE

CRICCIETH 124.74

AFON WEN JCN.

PENYCHAIN 129.70

ABERERCH 130.77

PWLLHELI 131.70

CAERNARVONSHIRE

PORTMADOC

BLACK ROCK H. 123.38

CRICCIETH 124.74

TREMADOC BAY

MILES. (A)

"A" JUNCTION OF BALA & FESTINIOG RLYS
2c WEST OF B.F. STATION YARD (BOTH 1'11½") WAS MANAGED
AS "DIPHWYS OR DUFFWS JCN" UP TO 1882 (GAUGE ALTERED
1966 CONNECTION 25.43 = 27.35)
ALSO
TYDDYN GWYN STATION LOCATED BETWEEN B.F. & MANOD (-C. 1883)

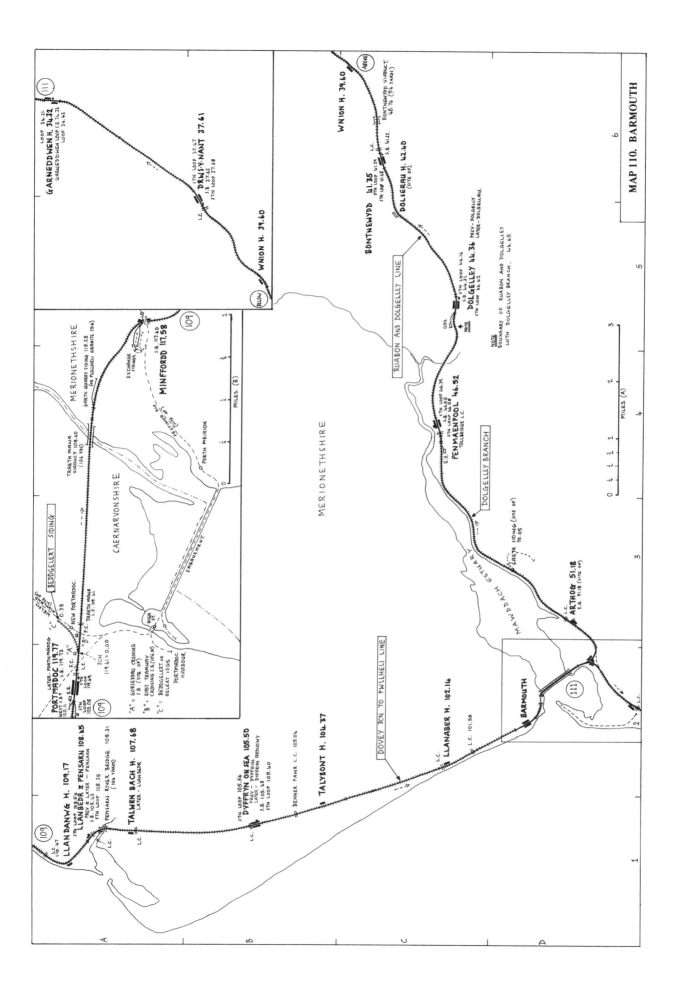

MAP 110. BARMOUTH

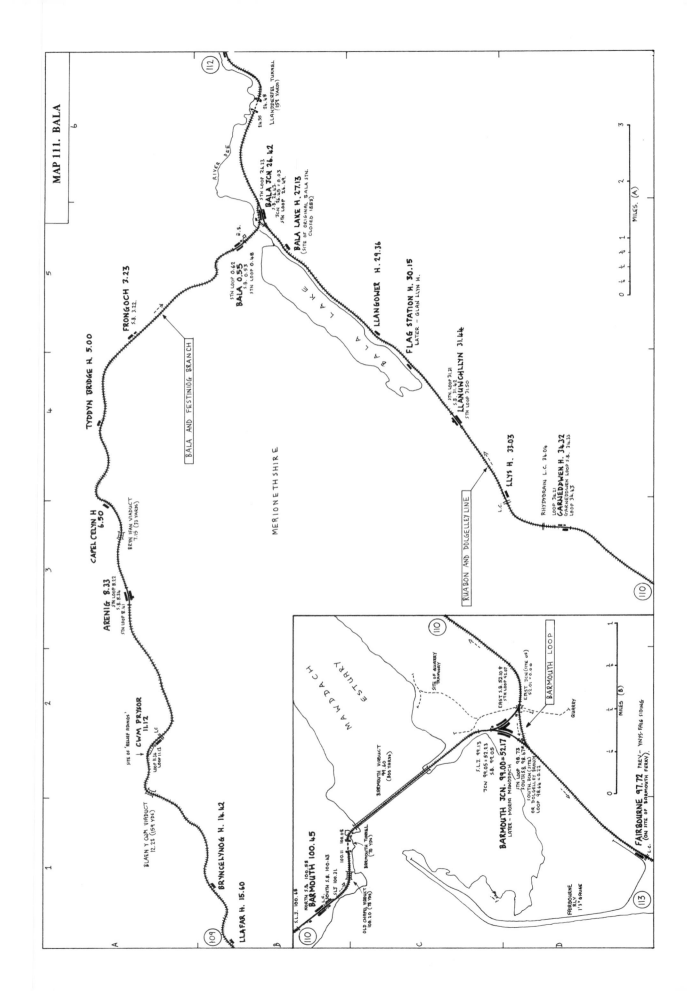

MAP 111. BALA

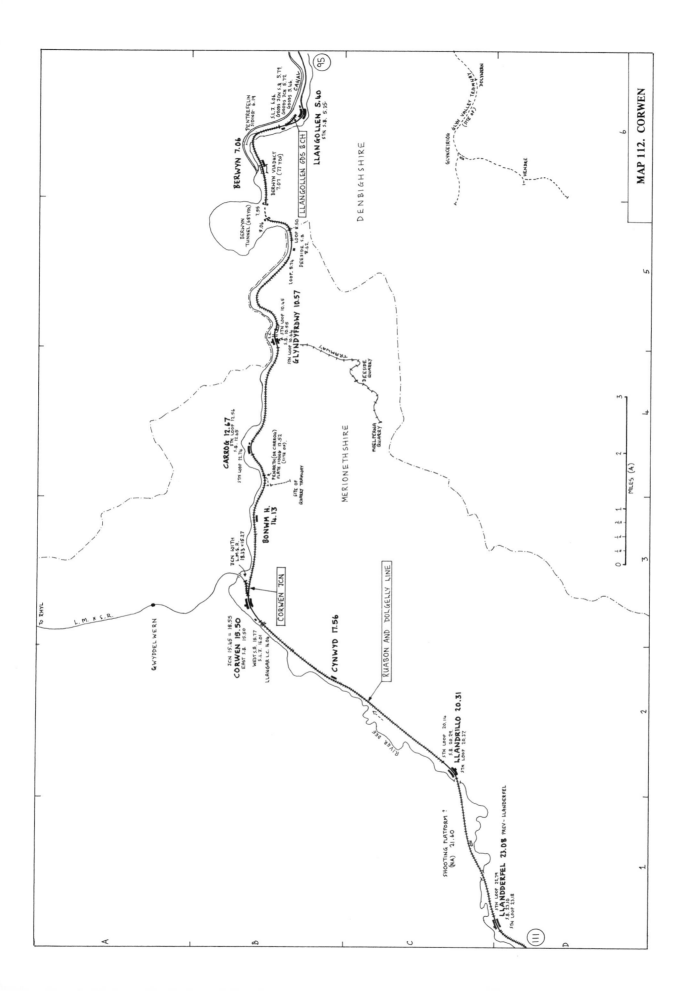

MAP 112. CORWEN

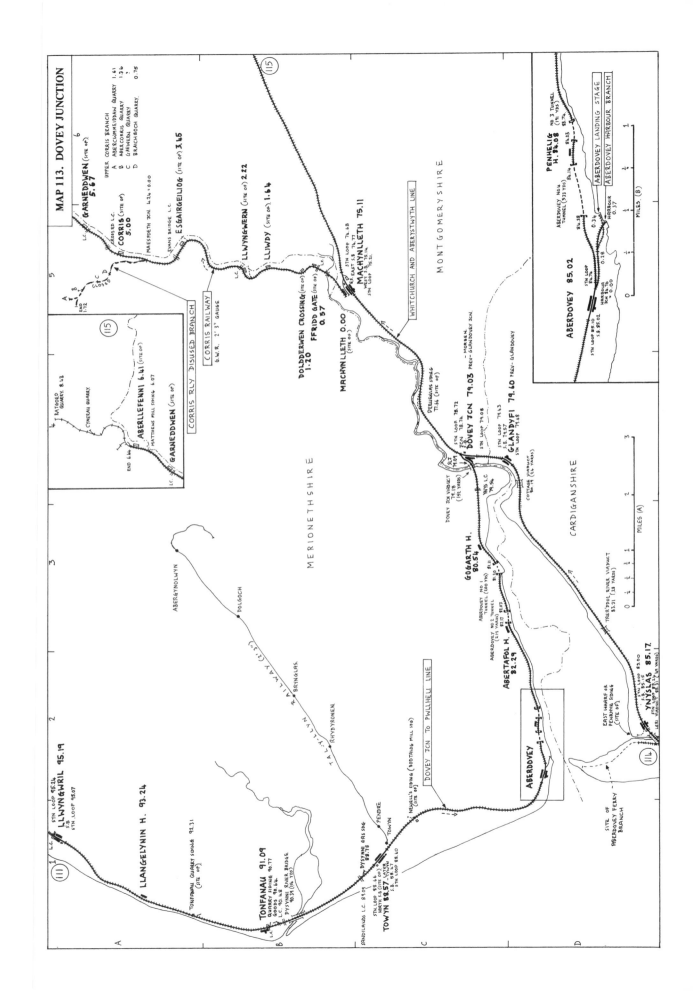

MAP 113. DOVEY JUNCTION

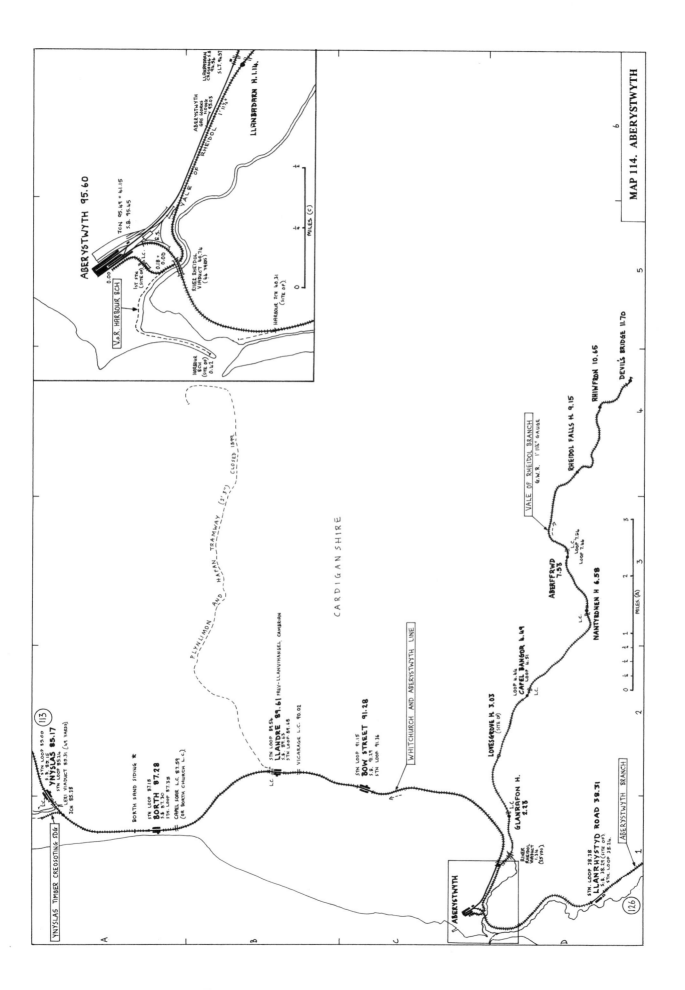

YNYSLAS TIMBER CREOSOTING SDG

113

YNYSLAS 85.17
STN LOOP 85.00
S.B. 85.15
(LERI VIADUCT 85.31 (49 YARDS)
STN LOOP 85.31
ICN 85.38

BORTH SAND SIDING ✳

BORTH 87.28
STN LOOP 87.18
S.B. 87.30
STN LOOP 87.38
CAPEL SOAR L.C. 87.59
(OR BORTH CHURCH L.C.)

LLANDRE 89.61 PREV-LLANVIHANGEL CAMBRIAN
STN LOOP 89.54
S.B. 89.65
STN LOOP 89.68
VICARAGE L.C. 90.01

PLYNLIMON AND HAFAN TRAMWAY (2'3") CLOSED 1899

CARDIGANSHIRE

BOW STREET 91.28
STN LOOP 91.15
S.B. 91.29
STN LOOP 91.36

WHITCHURCH AND ABERYSTWYTH LINE

GLANRAFON H. 2.28
L.C.

LOVESGROVE H. 3.03
(SITE OF)

LOOP 4.44
CAPEL BANGOR 4.49
LOOP 4.51
L.C.

ABERFFRWD 7.53
L.C.
LOOP 7.34

NANTYRONEN H 6.58

L.C.
LOOP 7.44

VALE OF RHEIDOL BRANCH
G.W.R. 1'11½" GAUGE

RHEIDOL FALLS H. 9.15

RHIWFRON 10.65

DEVIL'S BRIDGE 11.7D

ABERYSTWYTH BRANCH

LLANRHYSTYD ROAD 38.31
STN LOOP 38.38
S.B. 38.23 (SITE OF)
STN LOOP 38.24

RIVER RHEIDOL VIADUCT 1.36 (55 YDS)

ABERYSTWYTH

126

ABERYSTWYTH 95.60

V.O.R. HARBOUR BCH

1ST STN
(SITE OF)
0.00

0.18 =
0.00
L.C.

RIVER RHEIDOL VIADUCT 40.74 (64 YARDS)

HARBOUR BCH
(SITE OF)
0.42

HARBOUR TCN 40.31
(SITE OF)

7CN 95.49 = 41.15
S.B. 95.45

ABERYSTWYTH GWR GOODS 95.05

VALE OF RHEIDOL

LLANBADARN CROSSING 41.16
95.56
S.L.T 95.57

LLANBADARN H. 1.14.

ABERYSTWYTH GWR 95.56

MILES (C)

MAP 114. ABERYSTWYTH

MILES (A)

WHITCHURCH AND ABERYSTWYTH LINE

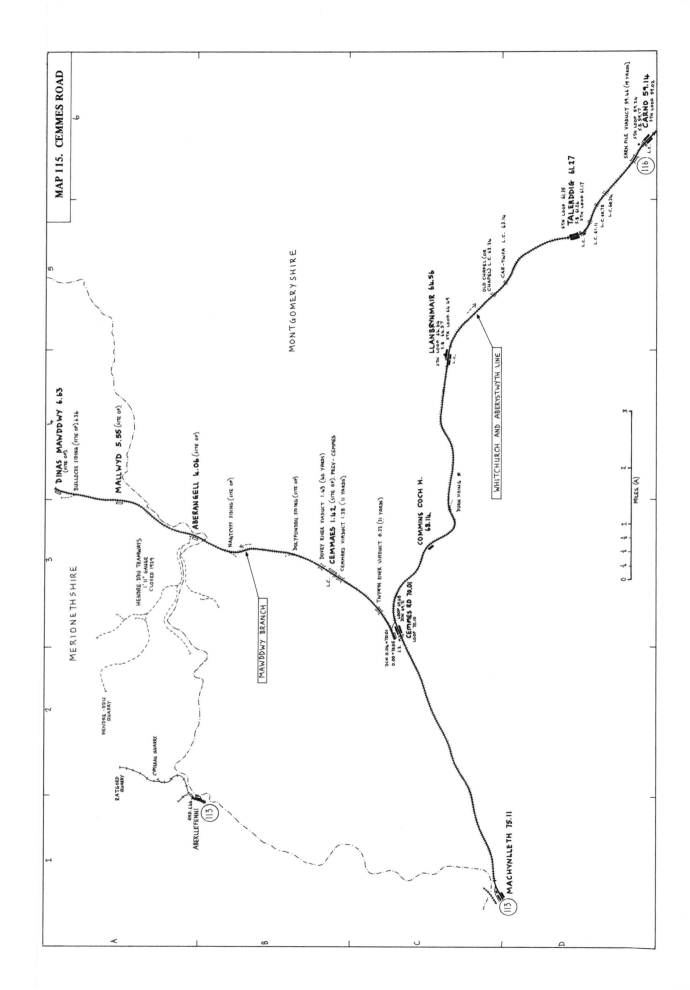

MAP 115. CEMMES ROAD

MERIONETHSHIRE

MONTGOMERYSHIRE

DINAS MAWDDWY 6.63 (SITE OF)
BULLOCKS SIDING (SITE OF) 6.16

MALLWYD 5.55 (SITE OF)

ABERANGELL 6.06 (SITE OF)

HENDRE DDU TRAMWAYS
1'11" GAUGE
CLOSED 1939

HENDRE-DDU QUARRY

CYMERAU QUARRY

RATGOED QUARRY

ABERLLEFENNI
END 6.44
113

NANTCYFF SIDING (SITE OF)

MAWDDWY BRANCH

DOLYFONDDU SIDING (SITE OF)

CEMMAES 6.42 (SITE OF). PREV - CEMMES
L.C.
DOVEY RIVER VIADUCT 6.43 (40 YARDS)
CEMMAES VIADUCT 6.38 (11 YARDS)
TWYMYN RIVER VIADUCT 6.33 (31 YARDS)

CEMMES RD 70.01
LOOP 70.10
3CH 0.04 70.01
0.00 70.05
L.B.
LOOP 69.70
3CN 69.70

COMMINS COCH H.
68.14

DURN SIDING

MACHYNLLETH 75.11
113

LLANBRYNMAIR 66.56
STN LOOP 66.64
S.B. 66.57
STN LOOP 66.49
L.C.

OLD CHAPEL (OR CHAPEL) L.C. 63.34

CAE-TWPA L.C. 63.14

WHITCHURCH AND ABERYSTWYTH LINE

STN LOOP 61.35
TALERDDIG 61.27
S.B. 61.24
STN LOOP 61.17
L.C. 61.11
L.C. 60.78
L.C. 60.34

SARN PILE VIADUCT 59.44 (14 YARDS)
STN LOOP 59.26
S.B. 59.17
CARND 59.14
STN LOOP 59.02
L.C.
116

MILES (A)

0   ¼   ½   ¾   1   2   3

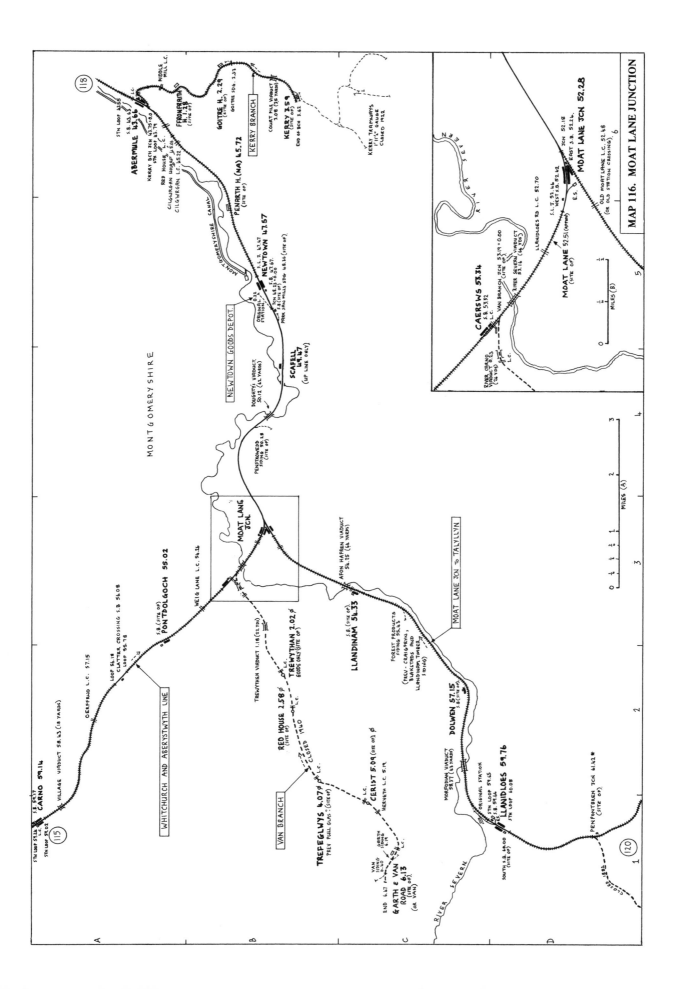

MAP 116. MOAT LANE JUNCTION

MONTGOMERYSHIRE

KERRY BRANCH

NEWTOWN GOODS DEPOT.

WHITCHURCH AND ABERYSTWYTH LINE

MOAT LANE JCN TO TALYLLYN

VAN BRANCH

ABERMULE 43.66
FFRONFRAITH H. 1.18 (SITE OF)
GOITRE H. 2.24 (SITE OF)
PENARTH H. (NA) 45.72
KERRY 3.54 (SITE OF)
NEWTOWN 47.57
SCAFELL 49.47 (UP LINE ONLY)
PONTDOLGOCH 55.02
CARNO 59.14
TREFEGLWYS 4.07∮ PREV PALL GLAS.? (SITE OF)
CERIST 5.04 (SITE OF) ∮
GARTH & VAN ROAD 6.13 (SITE OF) (OR VAN)
TREWYTHAN 2.02∮ GOODS ONLY (SITE OF)
RED HOUSE 2.58∮ (SITE OF) CLOSED 1940
LLANDINAM 51.33
DOLWEN 57.15 S.B (SITE OF)
LLANIDLOES 59.76

CAERSWS 53.34
S.B. 53.52
MOAT LANE JCN 52.28
MOAT LANE 52.51 (SITE OF)
EAST S.B. 52.24
OLD MOAT LANE L.C. 52.48 (OR OLD STATION CROSSING)
JCN 52.18
W.S.T. 52.66 WEST S.B. 52.42
LLANIDLOES RD L.C. 52.70
RIVER SEVERN VIADUCT 53.16 (44 YDS)
VAN BRANCH JCN 53.00 (SITE OF)
RIVER GRAND VIADUCT 53.73 (24 YDS)
RIVER SEVERN

MILES (B)
0   ¼   ½   ¾   1   2   3

MILES (A)
0   ¼   ½   ¾   1   2   3   4

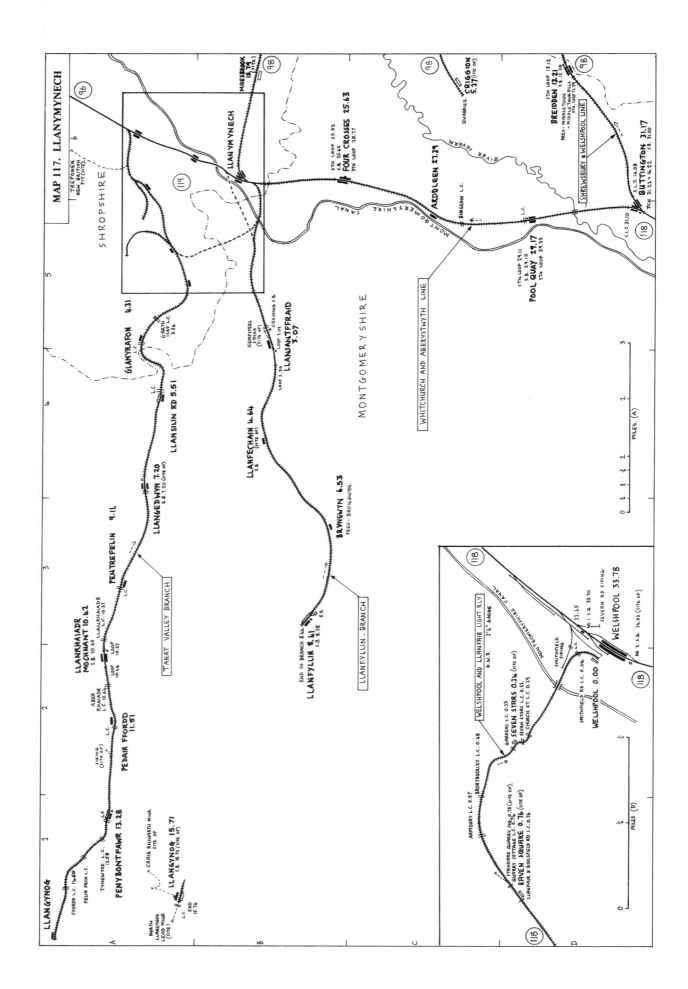

MAP 117. LLANYMYNECH

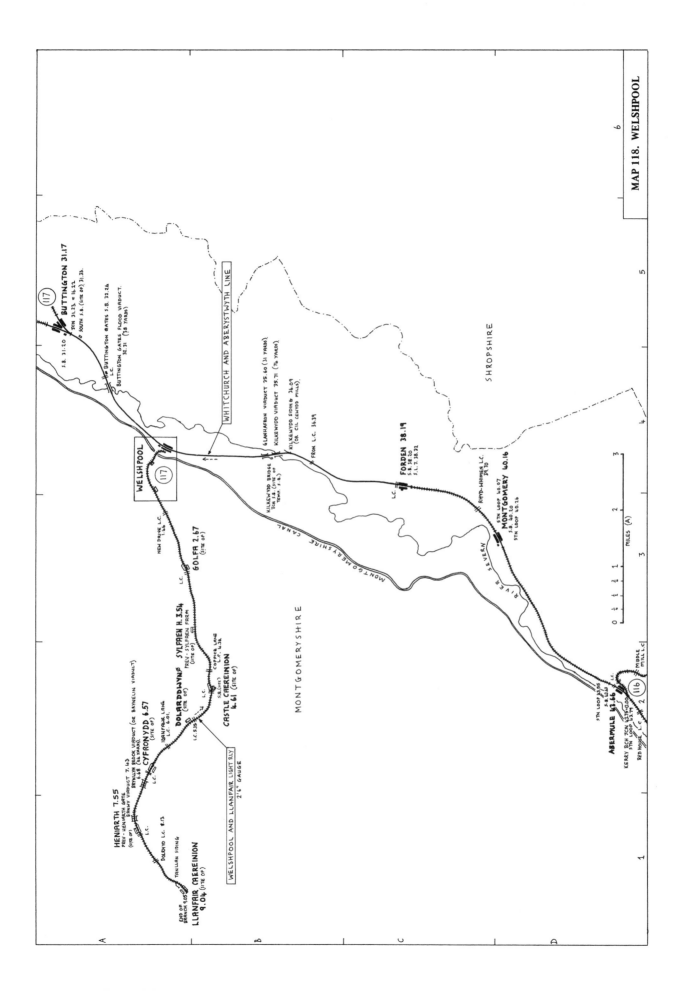

MAP 118. WELSHPOOL

SHROPSHIRE

MONTGOMERYSHIRE

WHITCHURCH AND ABERYSTWYTH LINE

WELSHPOOL AND LLANFAIR LIGHT RLY
2' 6" GAUGE

BUTTINGTON 31.17
TCN 31.23 = 16.22.
S.B. 31.20
L.C. BUTTINGTON GATES S.B. 32.26
BUTTINGTON GATES FLOOD VIADUCT
32.31 (38 YARDS)
SOUTH S.B. (SITE OF) 31.33

WELSHPOOL

LLANHAFREN VIADUCT 35.60 (31 YARDS)
KILKEWYDD VIADUCT 35.71 (74 YARDS)
KILKEWYDD SIDING 36.09
(OR CIL CEWYDD MILLS)
KILKEWYDD BRIDGE
TCN S.B. (SITE OF
TEMPY. S.B.)
FRON L.C. 36.39

FORDEN 38.19
S.B. 38.20
S.L. 7. 38.22

L.C.

NEW DRIVE L.C.
1.66

GOLFA 2.67
(SITE OF)

STN LOOP 40.07
RHYD-WHIMEN L.C.
39.70
MONTGOMERY 40.16
S.B. 40.10
STN LOOP 40.26

RIVER SEVERN

MONTGOMERYSHIRE CANAL

SYLFAEN H.3.54
PREV-SYLFAEN FARM
(SITE OF)

DOLARDDDYND
(SITE OF)
LLANFAIR LANE
L.C. 6.01
L.C.
L.C. S.35

S.B. (SITE)
COPPICE LANE
L.F. 4.34

CASTLE CAEREINION 4.61 (SITE OF)

CYFRONYDD 6.57
(SITE OF)

BRYNLLWYN
6.48
BRYNELLOCK VIADUCT (OR BRYNELLIN VIADUCT)
6.68 (44 YARDS)

HENIARTH 7.55
PREV-HENIARTH GATE
(SITE OF)
S'BNWY VIADUCT 7.43
L.C.
DOLRHYD L.C. 8.13
TRANLLAN SIDING

END OF
BRANCH 9.05
LLANFAIR CAEREINION
9.04 (SITE OF)

STN LOOP 43.55
L.C.
ABERMULE 43.66
KERRY BCH 7CN 43.75 43.00
STN LOOP 43.77
RED HOUSE L.C.
S.B. 43.65

MIDDLE
MILL L.C.

MILES (A)

117

117

116

0 ½ 1 2 3

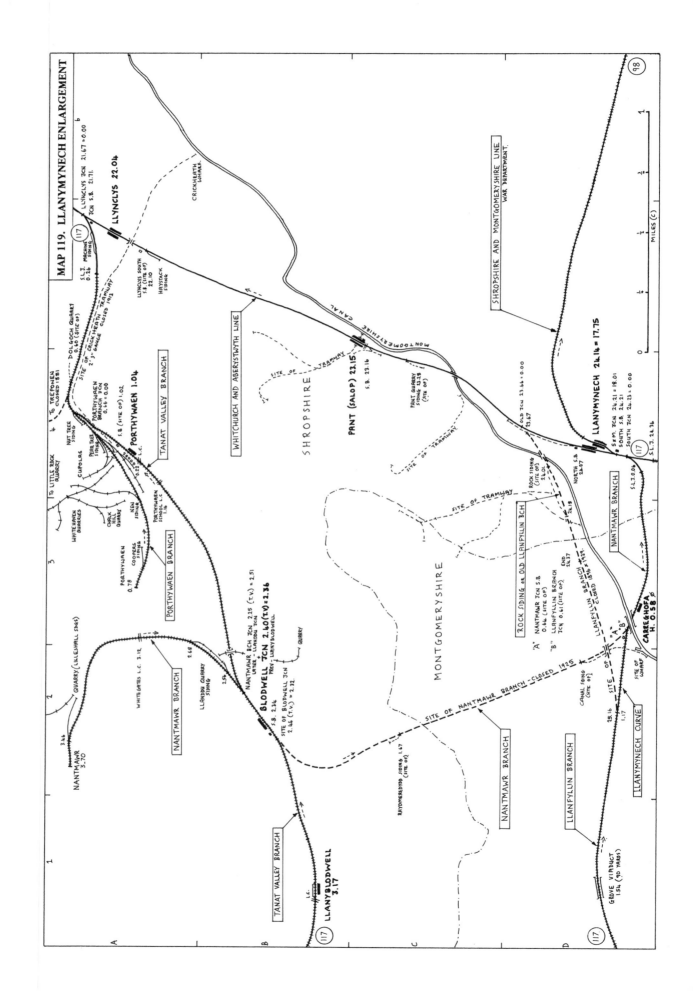

MAP 119, LLANYMYNECH ENLARGEMENT

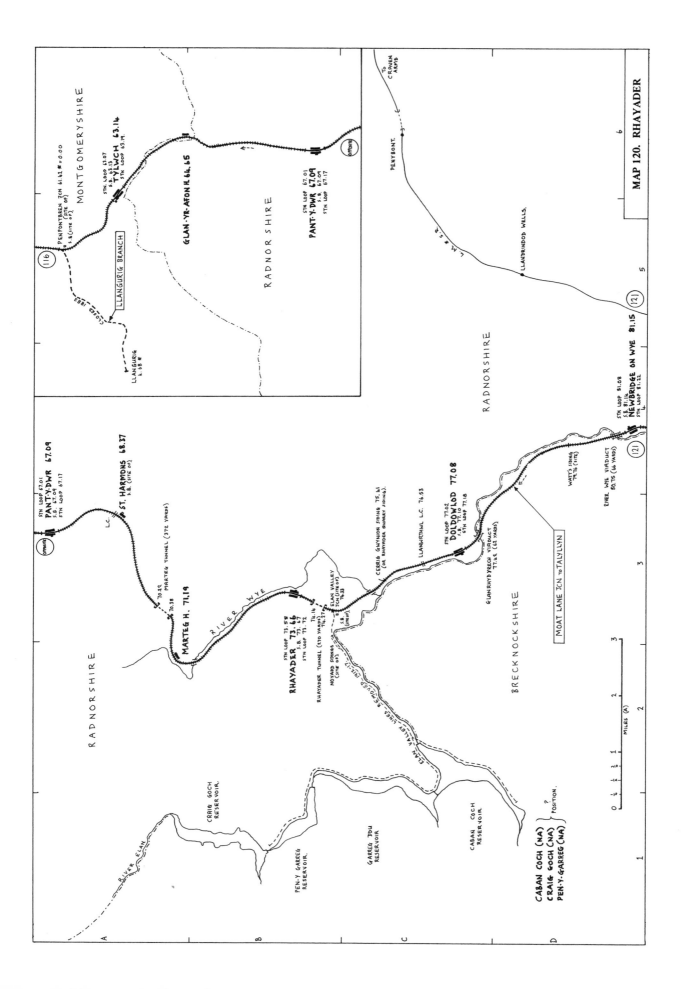

MAP 120. RHAYADER

MONTGOMERYSHIRE

RADNORSHIRE

PENPONTBREN JCN 61.61 *=0.00
(SITE OF)
S.B.(SITE OF)

STN LOOP 63.07
ST. HILWCH 63.14
STN LOOP 63.19

LLANGURIG BRANCH

CLOSED 1883

LLANGURIG
k.88 *

GLAN-Yr-AFON H. 66.65

STN LOOP 67.01
PANT-Y-DWR 67.09
S.B.
STN LOOP 67.17

116

121

TO CRAVEN ARMS

PENYBONT.

LLANDRINDOD WELLS.

L.M.S.R.

RADNORSHIRE

RADNORSHIRE

STN LOOP 67.01
PANT-Y-DWR 67.09
S.B. (SITE OF)
STN LOOP 67.17

OFFGURIG

L.C.

ST. HARMONS 68.37
S.B. (SITE OF)

70.84
MARTEG TUNNEL (372 YARDS)
70.38

MARTEG H. 71.14

RIVER WYE

STN LOOP 73.58
RHAYADER 73.66
S.B. 73.67
STN LOOP 73.72

RHAYADER TUNNEL (170 YARDS)
74.16
74.27½

NOYARD SIDINGS
(SITE OF)

ELAN VALLEY
JCN (SITE OF)
76.23

S.B. (SITE OF)

CEFRIG GWYNION SIDING 75.61
(OR RHAYADER QUARRY SIDING).

LLANURTHWL L.C. 76.53

STN LOOP 77.02
DOLDOWLOD 77.08
F.B. 77.10
STN LOOP 77.18

GLANRHYDYBEECH VIADUCT
77.41 (42 YARDS)

MOAT LANE JCN TO TALYLLYN

WATT'S SIDING
74.76 (SITE)

RIVER WYE VIADUCT
80.75 (66 YARDS)

STN LOOP 81.08
NEWBRIDGE ON WYE 81.15
S.B. 81.16
STN LOOP 81.22

BRECKNOCKSHIRE

121

121

CRAIG GOCH RESERVOIR.

PEN-Y-GARREG RESERVOIR.

GARREG DDU RESERVOIR

CABAN COCH RESERVOIR.

RIVER ELAN

ELAN VALLEY WATER-WORKS LINES
REMOVED 1916-17.

CABAN COCH (NA)
CRAIG GOCH (NA) ? POSITION.
PEN-Y-GARREG (NA)

MILES (A)

0   ½   1   2   3

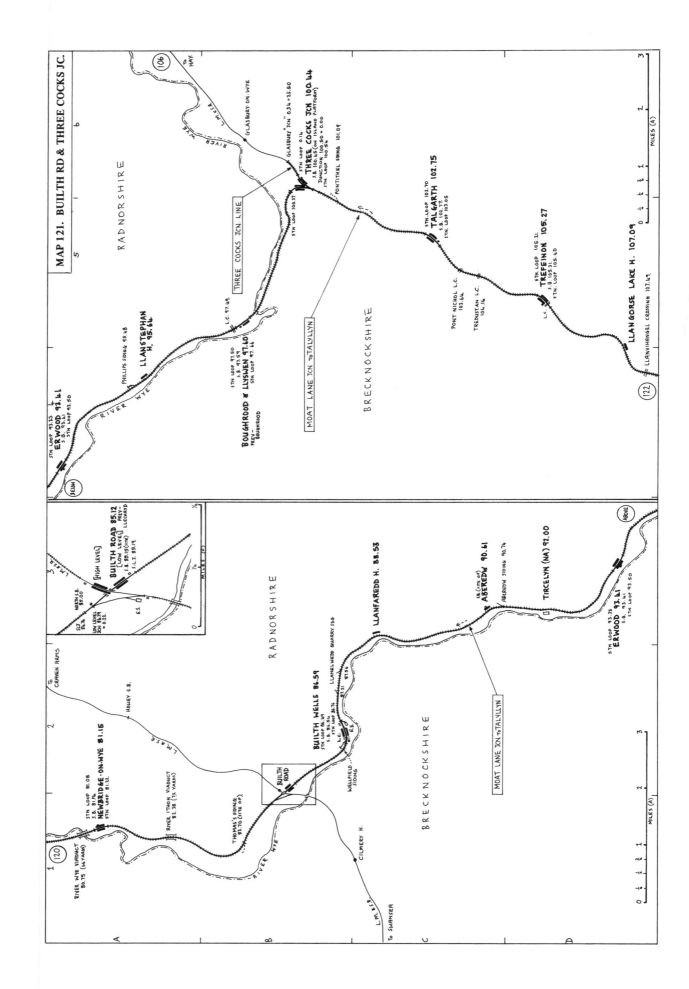

MAP 121. BUILTH RD & THREE COCKS JC.

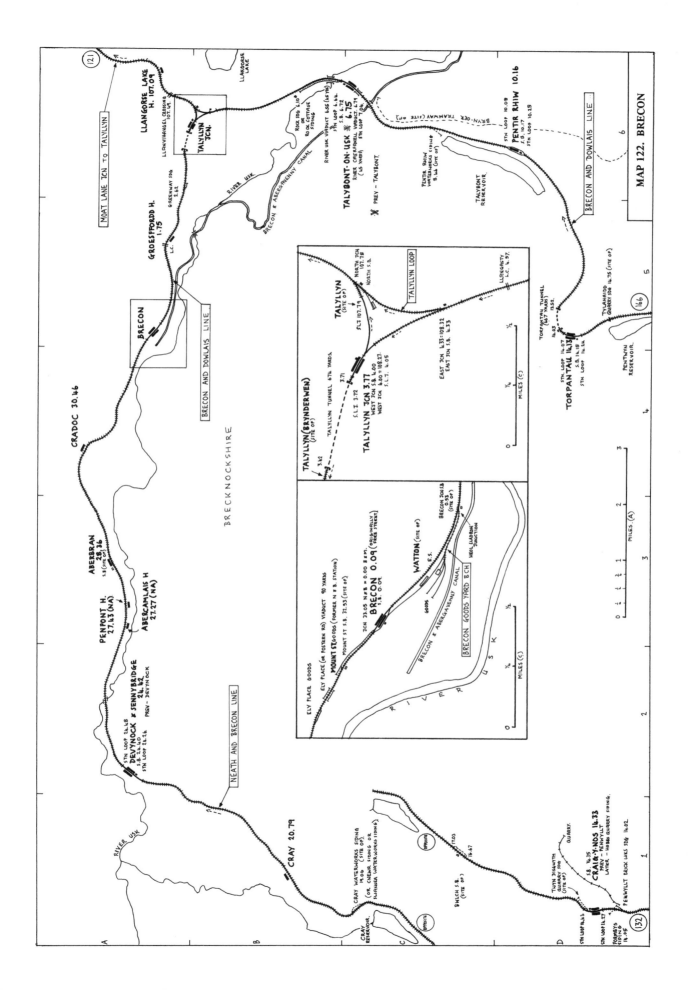

MAP 122. BRECON

BRECKNOCKSHIRE

MOAT LANE JCN TO TALYLLYN

LLANGORSE LAKE H. 107.09
LLANGOOSE LAKE

LLANVIHANGEL CROSSING 107.44

TALYLLYN JCN.

GREENWAY SDG 2.62

GROESFFORDD H. 1.75

L.C.

RIVER USK

BRECON & ABERGAVENNY CANAL

BRECON

BRECON AND DOWLAIS LINE

ROCK SDG 4.10 OR
ROD OL COTTAGE SIDING

RIVER USK VIADUCT 6.55 (46 YDS)
STN LOOP 6.64

TALYBONT-ON-USK ✱ 6.75
RIVER CRICKARRELL VIADUCT 6.71
(45 YARDS)
S.B. 6.72
STN LOOP 7.06

✱ PREV - TALYBONT

PENTR RHIW WATERBANKEG SIDING
B. 6.6 (SITE OF)

PENTR RHIW 10.16
STN LOOP 10.08
S.B. 10.17
STN LOOP 10.19

BRYN-DER TRAMWAY (SITE OF)

TALYBONT RESERVOIR.

BRECON AND DOWLAIS LINE

TALYLLYN (BRYNDERWEN) (SITE OF)
3.42

TALYLLYN TUNNEL 674 YARDS
3.71

TALYLLYN (SITE OF)
S.L.J 107.79
S.L.I 3.72

TALYLLYN JCN 3.77
WEST JCN S.B. 4.00
WEST JCN 4.00=108.27
S.L.T. 4.05

NORTH JCN 107.79
NORTH S.B.

TALYLLYN LOOP

LLANGORSE
L.C. 4.97

EAST JCN 4.33=108.12
EAST JCN S.B. 4.33

MILES (c.)
0   ¼   ½   ¾   1

ELY PLACE GOODS

ELY PLACE (OR POSTERN RD) VIADUCT 40 YARDS

MOUNT ST (GOODS (FORMER N & B. STATION)
MOUNT ST S.B. 32.53 (SITE OF)

JCN 33.05 N&B = 0.00 B&M.
BRECON 0.09 (ORIGINALLY FREE STREET)
S.B. 0.09

WATTON (SITE OF)
E.S.
GOODS

BRECON 30JS.B. 0.53 (SITE OF)

HEOL LLADRON JUNCTION

BRECON & ABERGAVENNY CANAL

BRECON GOODS YARD B'CH

RIVER USK

MILES (c.)
0   ¼   ½   ¾   1

CRADOC 30.46

ABERBRAN 28.26
S.B (SITE OF)

PENPONT H. 27.43 (NA)

ABERCAMLAIS H 27.27 (NA)

DEVYNOCK & SENNYBRIDGE 24.42
PREV - DEVYNOCK

STN LOOP 24.48
S.B 24.40
STN LOOP 24.26

NEATH AND BRECON LINE

RIVER USK

CRAY 20.79

CRAY WATERWORKS SIDING H.06 (SITE OF)
(OR CNEWR SIDING OR SWANSEA WATERWORKS SIDING)

CRAY RESERVOIR.

OFFING

OFFING

BWLCH S.B. (SITE OF)

17.03

17.67

TWYN DISGWYLFA QUARRY SDG (SITE OF)

QUARRY.

S.B. 14.35
CRAIG-Y-NOS 14.33
PREV - PENWYLLT
LATER - HOMBS QUARRY SIDING.

PENWYLLT BRICK OKKS SDG 14.02

STN LOOP 14.43
PENWYLLT 14.37

PENWYLLT
STN LOOP 14.14

PENWYLLT 14.05

MILES (A)
0 ¼ ½ ¾ 3

TORPANTAU TUNNEL (667 YARDS)
14.03   13.52

STN LOOP 14.07
TORPANTAU 14.13
S.B. 14.15
STN LOOP 14.14

PENTWYN RESERVOIR.

TORPANTAU TUNNEL
TYLAHAIDD
TYLANAIDD QUARRY SDG 14.75 (SITE OF)

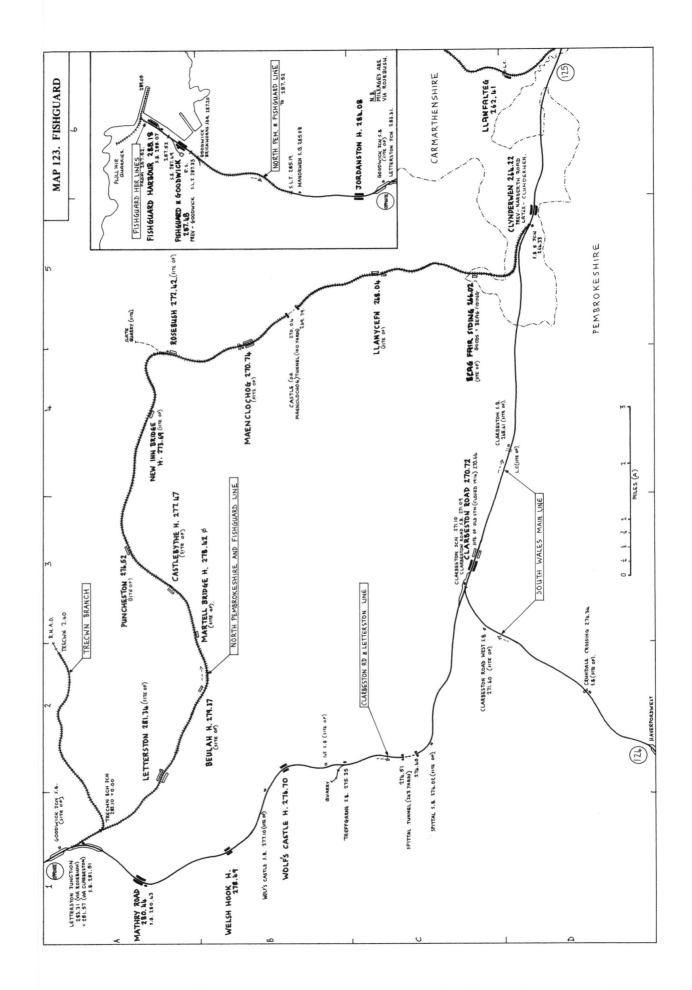

MAP 123. FISHGUARD

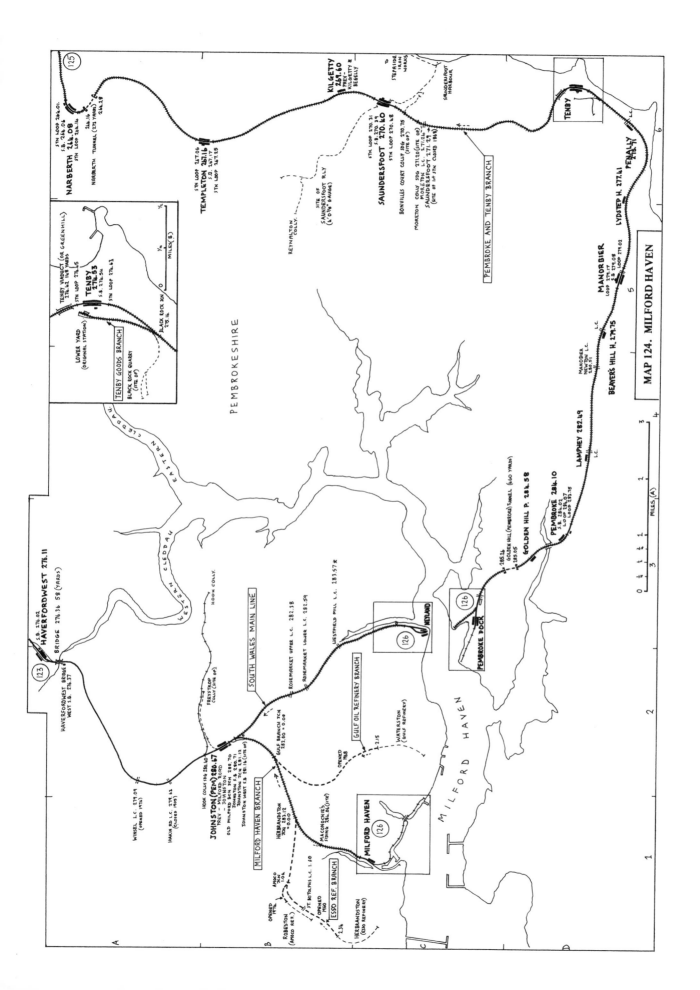

MAP 124. MILFORD HAVEN

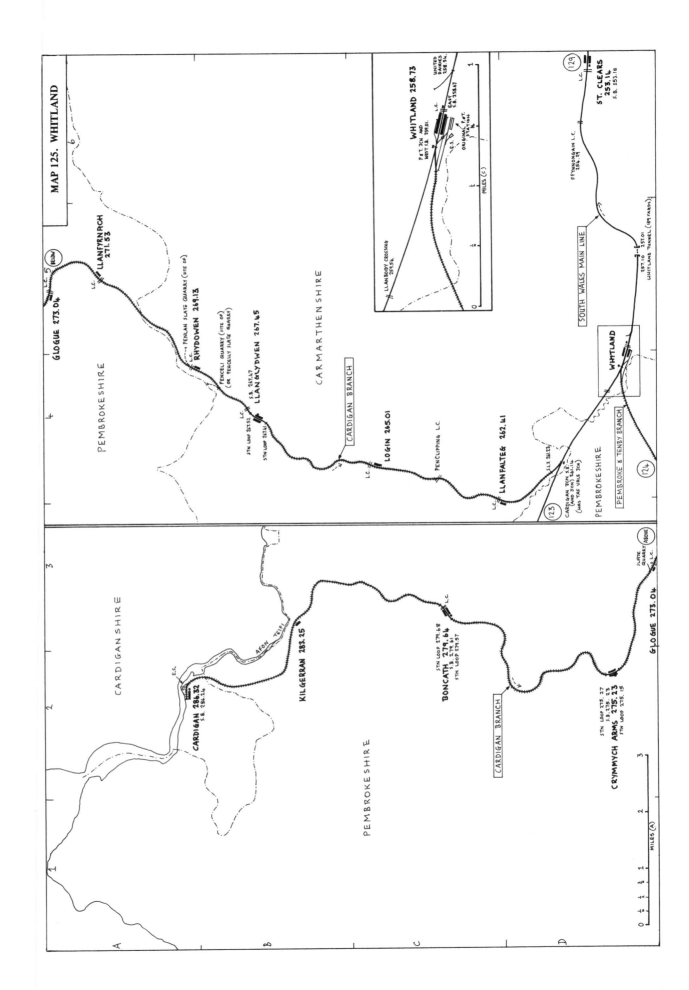

MAP 125. WHITLAND

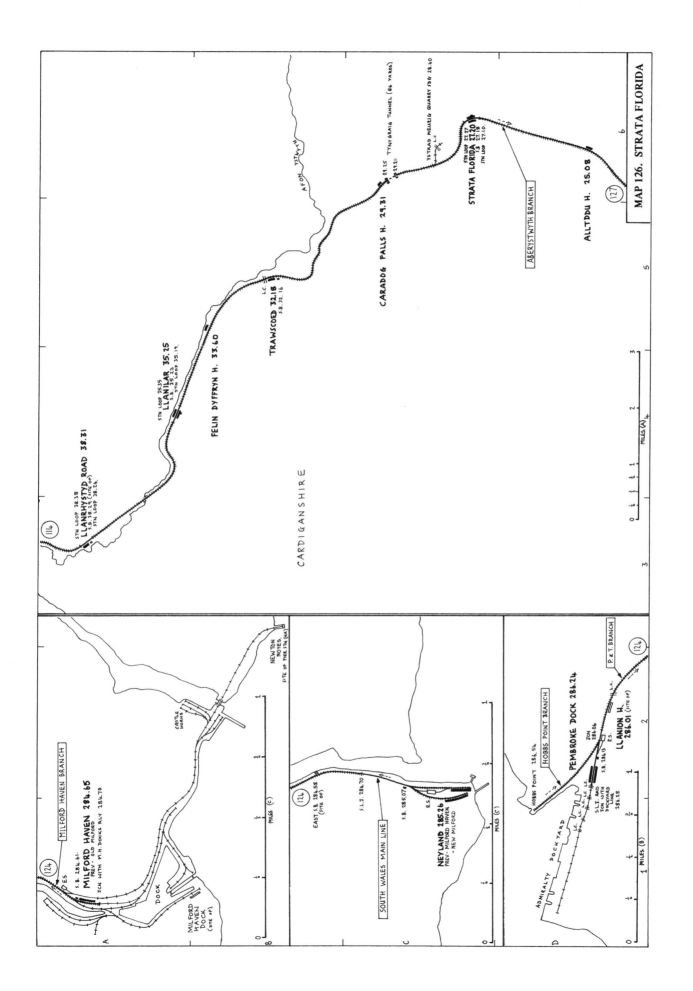

MAP 126. STRATA FLORIDA

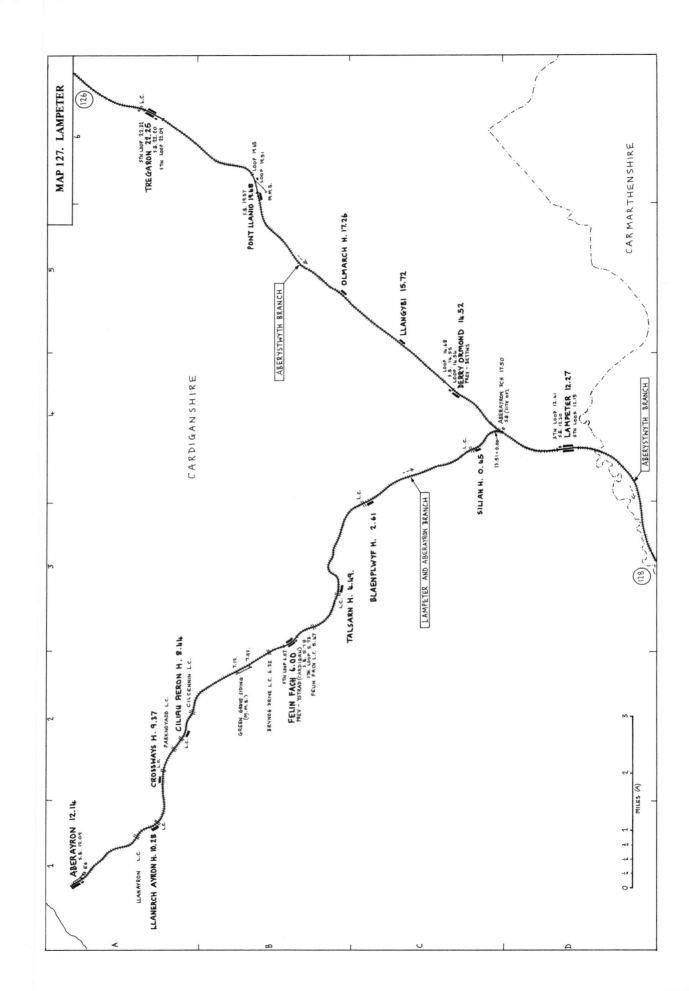

MAP 127. LAMPETER

CARDIGANSHIRE

CARMARTHENSHIRE

ABERAYRON 12.14
S.B. 12.09

LLANERCH AYRON H. 10.28

CROSSWAYS H. 9.37

CILIAU AERON H. 8.44

GREEN GROVE SIDING 7.13

FELIN FACH 6.00
PREV - YSTRAD (CARDIGAN)
STN. LOOP 5.79
FELIN FACH L.C. 5.47

TALSARN H. 4.49.

BLAENPLWYF H. 2.61

LAMPETER AND ABERAYRON BRANCH

SILIAN H. 0.45

ABERAYRON BRANCH

OLMARCH H. 17.26

PONT LLANIO H.48
S.B. 19.57

TREGARON 22.26
S.B. 22.20
STN LOOP 22.31
STN LOOP 22.09

LLANGYBI 15.72

DERRY ORMOND 14.52
PREV - BETTWS
LOOP 14.55
S.B. 14.54
LOOP 14.68

13.51 + 0.00
ABERAYRON TCH 17.50
S.B. (SITE OF)

LAMPETER 12.27
STN LOOP 12.10
S.B. 12.20
STN LOOP 12.41
STN LOOP 12.15

ABERYSTWYTH BRANCH

LOOP 19.51
M.M.B.

MILES (A)

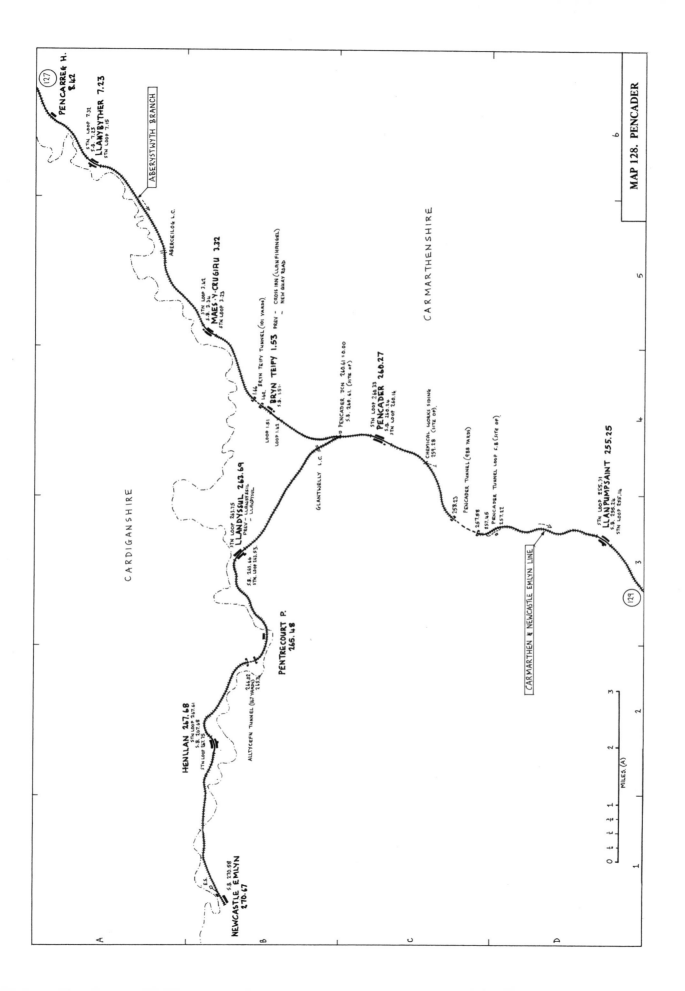

MAP 128. PENCADER

(127)

PENCARREG H. 8.42
STN LOOP 7.31
S.B. 7.23
LLANYBYTHER 7.23
STN LOOP 7.15

ABERYSTWYTH BRANCH

ABERCEILLOG L.C.

STN LOOP 3.41
S.B. 3.34
MAES-Y-CRUGIRU 3.32
STN LOOP 3.23

BRYN TEIFY TUNNEL (101 YARDS)
BRYN TEIFY 1.53 PREV - CROSS INN (LLANFIHANGEL)
- NEW QUAY ROAD

CARDIGANSHIRE

CARMARTHENSHIRE

LOOP 1.51
LOOP 1.41
1.44
S.B. 1.51

PENCADER JCN 260.61=0.00 (SITE OF)

STN LOOP 260.33
PENCADER 260.27
S.B. 260.24
STN LOOP 260.14

CHEMICAL WORKS SIDING
259.28 (SITE OF)

GLANTWELLY L.C.

STN LOOP 263.75
LLANDYSSUL 263.69 PREV - LLANDYSSIL
- LLANDYSUL

S.B. 263.46
STN LOOP 263.53

PENCADER TUNNEL (488 YARDS)
258.23
PENCADER TUNNEL LOOP S.B (SITE OF)
257.58
257.45
257.41

HENLLAN 267.68
STN LOOP 267.61
S.B. 267.68
STN LOOP 267.75

PENTRECOURT P. 265.48

ALLTYCEFN TUNNEL (167 YARDS)
264.02
263.74

STN LOOP 255.31
S.B. 255.24
LLANPUMPSAINT 255.25
STN LOOP 255.14

CARMARTHEN & NEWCASTLE EMLYN LINE

(129)

NEWCASTLE EMLYN 270.67
E.S.
S.B. 270.68

MILES. (A)
0 ¼ ½ ¾ 1   2   3

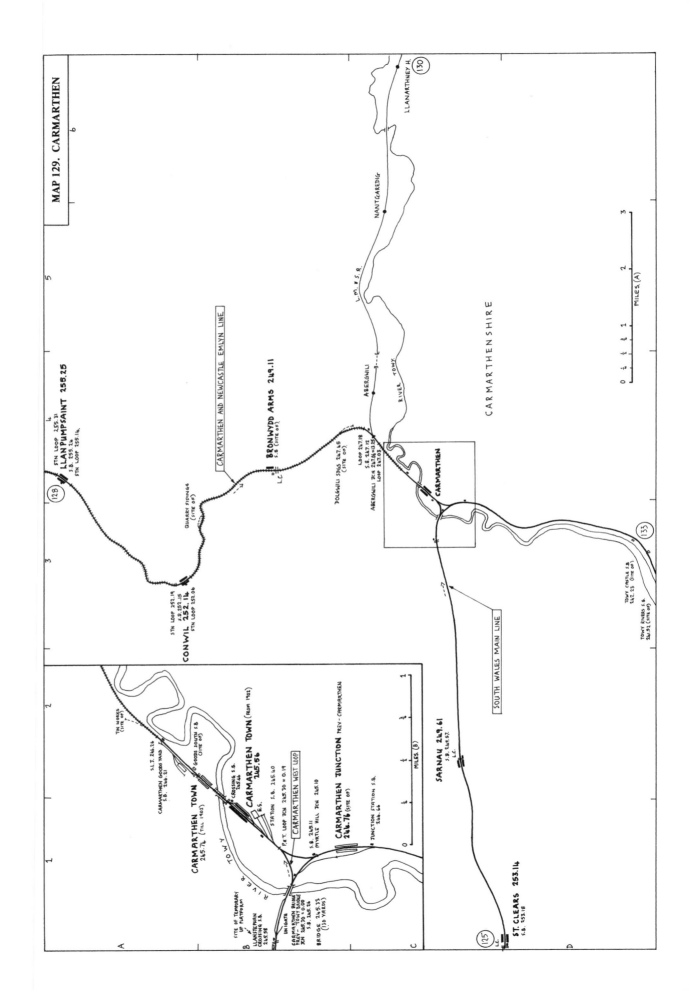

MAP 129. CARMARTHEN

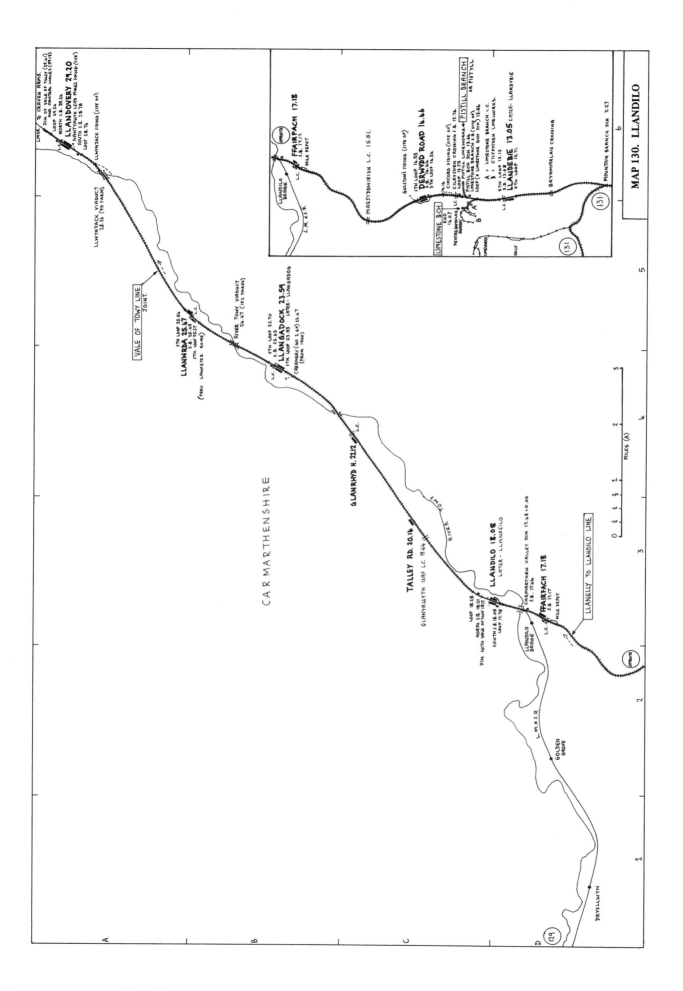

MAP 130. LLANDILO

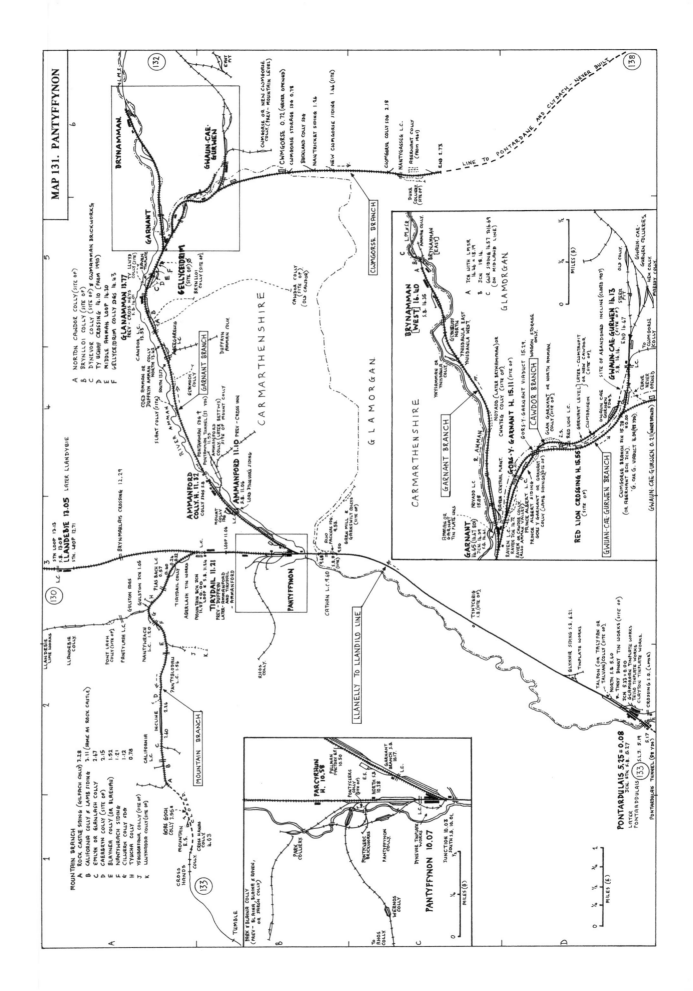

MAP 131. PANTYFFYNON

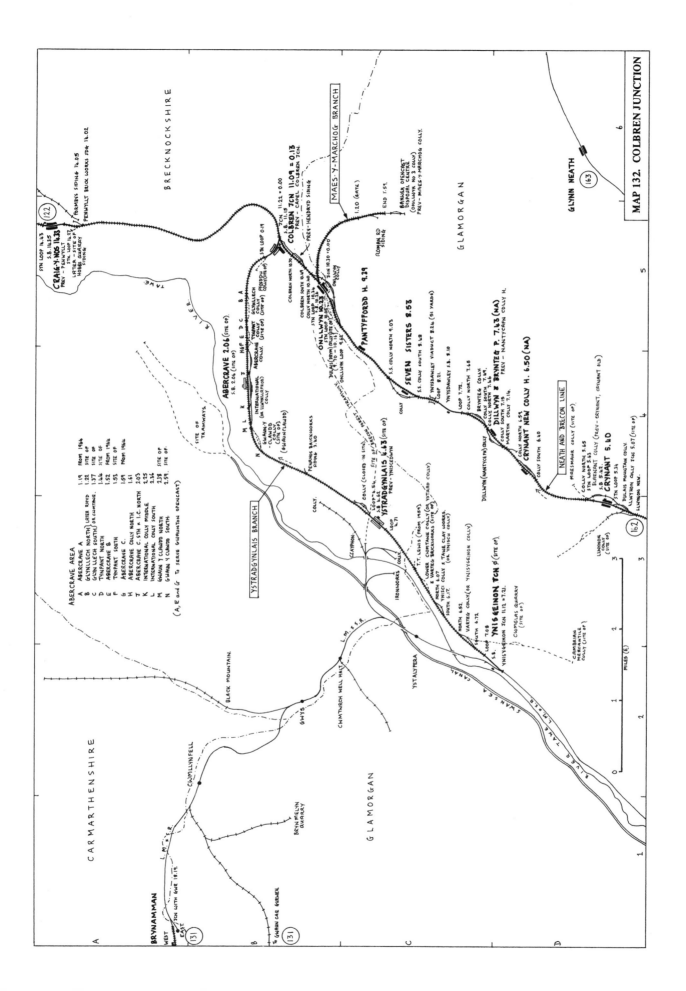

MAP 132. COLBREN JUNCTION

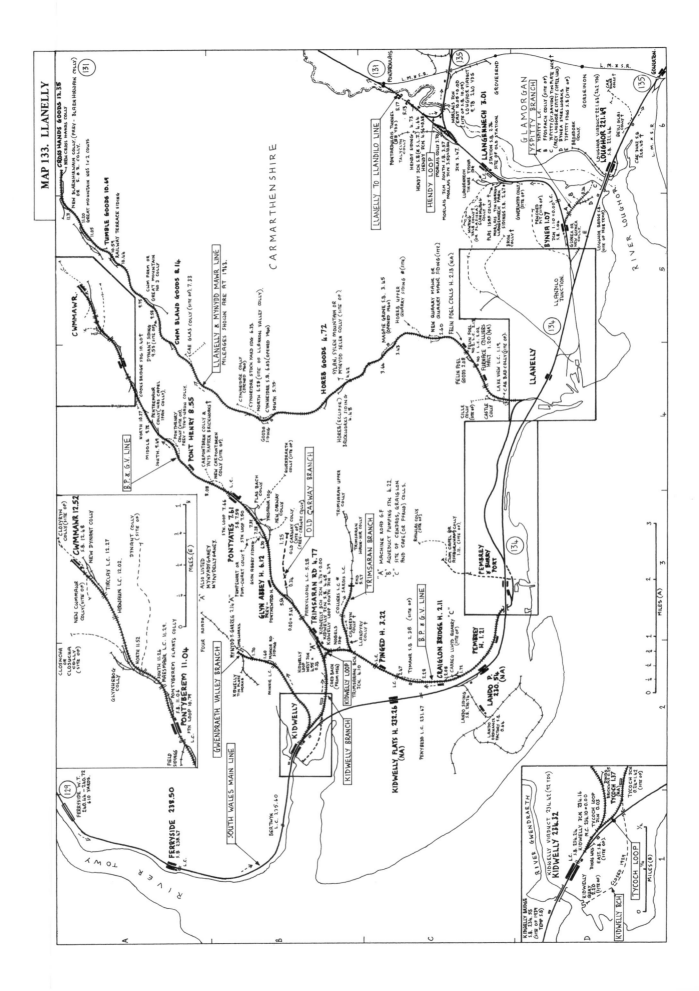

MAP 133. LLANELLY

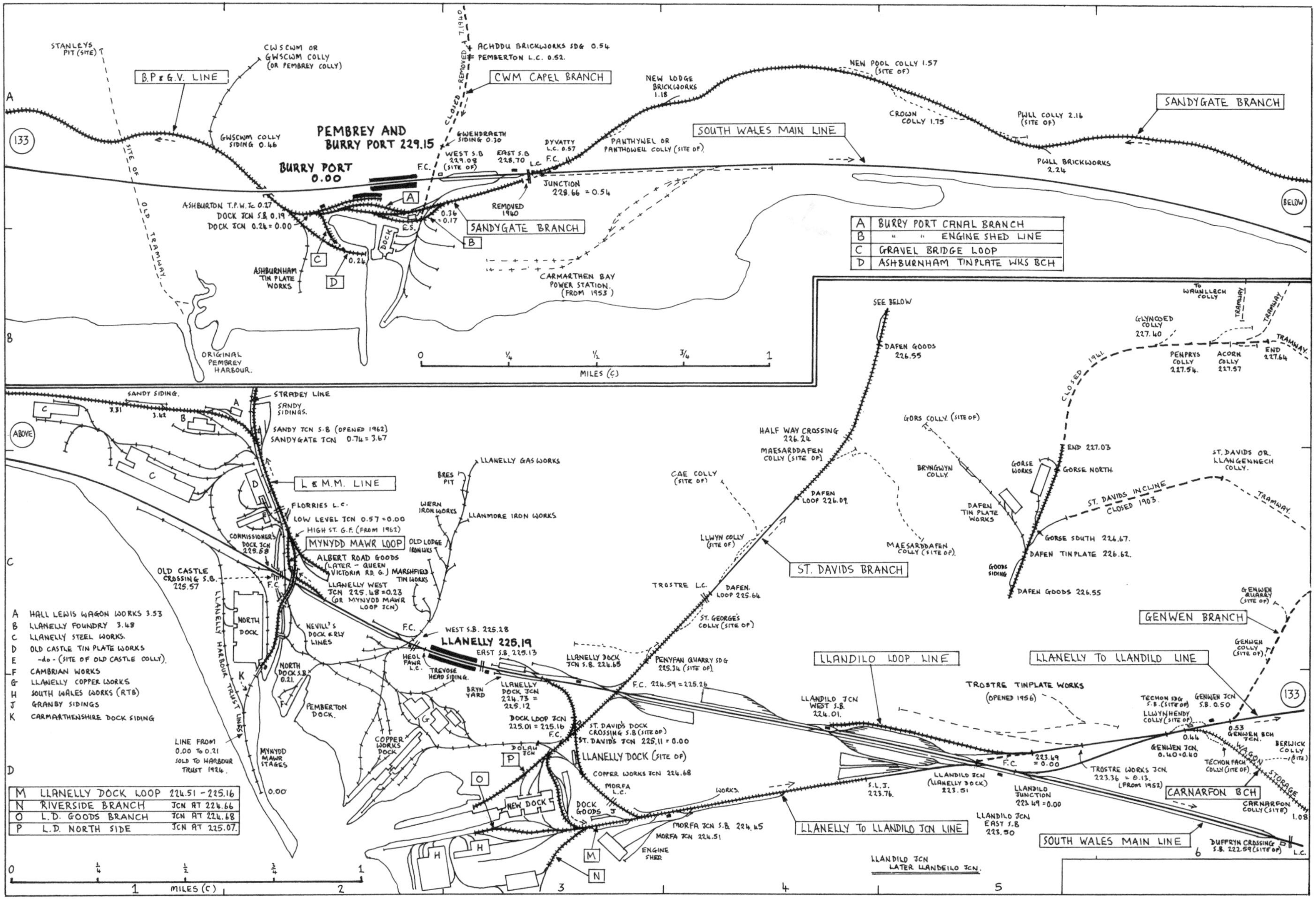

MAP 134. PEMBREY AND LLANELLY ENLARGEMENT

SANDYGATE BRANCH

PAALL COLLY 2.16 (SITE OF)
PAALL BRICKWORKS 2.24

NEW POOL COLLY 1.57 (SITE OF)
CROAN COLLY 1.75

NEW LODGE BRICKWORKS 1.18
PANTHWEL OR PANTHOWELL COLLY (SITE OF)

SOUTH WALES MAIN LINE

ACHDDU BRICKWORKS SDG 0.54
PEMBERTON L.C. 0.52.   CLOSED
CLOSED   7.1940
CWM CAPEL BRANCH
REMOVED

GWSCWM COLLY SIDING 0.46
CWSCWM OR GWSCWM COLLY (OR PEMBREY COLLY)

STANLEYS PIT (SITE OF)
B.P. & G.V. LINE

B.P. & G.V. LINE

ASHBURNHAM T.P.W. L.C. 0.27
DOCK JCN E.S.B. 0.19
DOCK JCN 0.24 = 0.00
ASHBURNHAM TIN PLATE WORKS

PEMBREY AND BURRY PORT 229.15
BURRY PORT 0.00

ORIGINAL PEMBREY HARBOUR

SITE OF OLD TRAMWAY

	A	BURRY PORT CANAL BRANCH
	C	ENGINE SHED LINE
	C	GRAVEL BRIDGE LOOP
	D	ASHBURNHAM TINPLATE WKS BCH

SHREWSBROTH SIDING 0.10
WEST S.B. 221.98 (SITE OF)
EAST S.B. 228.70
JUNCTION 229.66 = 0.54
SYVATY L.C. 0.57
PWLLTHYNEL L.C.

SANDYGATE BRANCH

RENAMED 1940

CARMARTHEN BAY POWER STATION (FROM 1953)

MILES (C.)

SEE BELOW

DAFEN GOODS 226.55

HALF WAY CROSSING 226.24
MAESARDDAFEN COLLY (SITE OF)

CAE COLLY (SITE OF)

GORS COLLY (SITE OF)

LLWYN COLLY (SITE OF)

TROSTRE L.C.
ST. GEORGES COLLY (SITE OF)
DAFEN LOOP 225.64
PENYFAN QUARRY SDG 225.31a (SITE OF)

GORSE WORKS
GORSE SOUTH
DAFEN TINPLATE 226.61
GORSE NORTH   END 227.03
DAFEN GOODS 226.55
GOODS SIDING
BRYNGWYN COLLY

ST DAVIDS OR LLANGENNECH COLLY
ST DAVIDS INCLINE CLOSED 1903
TRAMWAY

GENWEN BRANCH

LLANELLY TO LLANDILO LINE

TROSTRE TINPLATE WORKS (OPENED 1956)

WARMULLECH COLLY
TRAMWAY

GWYNGOED 227.40
ACORN COLLY 227.56
TRAMWAY END 227.44

PENYRES COLLY 227.57a

LLANDILO LOOP LINE

LLANDILO JCN WEST S.B. 224.01
F.L.T. 213.76
LLANDILO JCN EAST S.B. 224.51 = 225.16

TECHRON FACH 0.15 (SITE OF)
BERWICK COLLY (SITE OF)
GENWEN JCN S.B. 0.50
GENWEN JCN 0.40 = 0.00
TECHRON END S.B. (SITE OF)
LLWYNHENDY COLLY (SITE OF)
TECHRON FACH S.B. 0.63 (SITE OF)
TROSTRE WORKS (FROM 1952)

LLANDILO JCN 213.51 (LLANELLY DOCK)
LLANDILO JCN 223.49 = 0.00

CARNARFON BCH
CARNARFON COLLY (SITE OF)

WAGON STORAGE

DUFFRYN CROSSING S.B. 222.54 (SITE OF)
L.C.

SOUTH WALES MAIN LINE

LLANDILO JCN LATER LLANDILO JCN.

STRADEY LINE

LLANELLY GAS WORKS
BRES PIT
WERN IRON WORKS
LLANMORE IRON WORKS

SANDY JCN S.B. (OPENED 1962)
SANDY JCN 224.75 = 3.67
SANDYGATE JCN 0.74 = 3.67
FLORRIES L.C.
LOW LEVEL JCN 0.57 = 0.00
HIGH ST. G.F. (FROM 1963)
OLD LODGE FERMILY

L. & M.M. LINE

MYNYDD MAWR LOOP
ALBERT ROAD GOODS
VICTORIA RD. G.J
LLANELLY WEST JCN 225.28 = 0.23
MARGARET (LATER - QUEEN VICTORIA RD. G.) OR MYNYDD MAWR LOOP JCN

LLANELLY 225.19
LLANELLY WEST S.B. 225.28
LLANELLY EAST S.B. 225.13
HEOL FAWR
TREVOISE HEAD SIDING
BREW YARD

NEVILL'S DOCK & RLY. LINES
NORTH DOCK G.F.
F.C.

ST DAVIDS DOCK CROSSING S.B. (SITE OF)
ST. DAVIDS JCN 225.11 = 0.00
F.C. 224.51a = 225.16
DOCK LOOP JCN 225.16
LLANELLY DOCK JCN 5.B. 224.75

LLANELLY DOCK
LLANELLY DOCK 7CN S.B. 224.68
F.C. 224.51a = 225.16

MORFA JCN S.B. 224.45
MORFA JCN 224.51

COPPER WORKS JCN 224.68

ENGINE SHED

PEMBERTON DOCK
MYNYDD MAWR (L. & M.M.)
N
O
P
H
H
J
K

COMMISSIONERS DOCK JCN S.B.

NORTH DOCK

LLANELLY HARBOUR TRUST LINES

OLD CASTLE CROSSING S.B. 225.57

SANDY SIDING

GRANBY SIDINGS
CARMARTHENSHIRE DOCK SIDING

| | MILES (C.) |

A	HALL LEWIS WAGON WORKS 3.53
B	LLANELLY FOUNDRY 3.49
C	LLANELLY STEEL WORKS
D	OLD CASTLE TIN PLATE WORKS
E	-do- (SITE OF OLD CASTLE COLLY.)
F	CAMBRIAN WORKS
G	LLANELLY COPPER WORKS
H	SOUTH WALES WORKS (R.T.B.)
J	GRANBY SIDINGS
K	CARMARTHENSHIRE DOCK SIDING
M	LLANELLY DOCK LOOP 224.51 - 225.16
N	RIVERSIDE BRANCH JCN RT 224.66
O	L.D. GOODS BRANCH JCN RT 224.18
P	L.D. NORTH SIDE JCN RT 225.07

LINE FROM 0.00 to 0.31 SOLD TO HARBOUR TRUST 1926

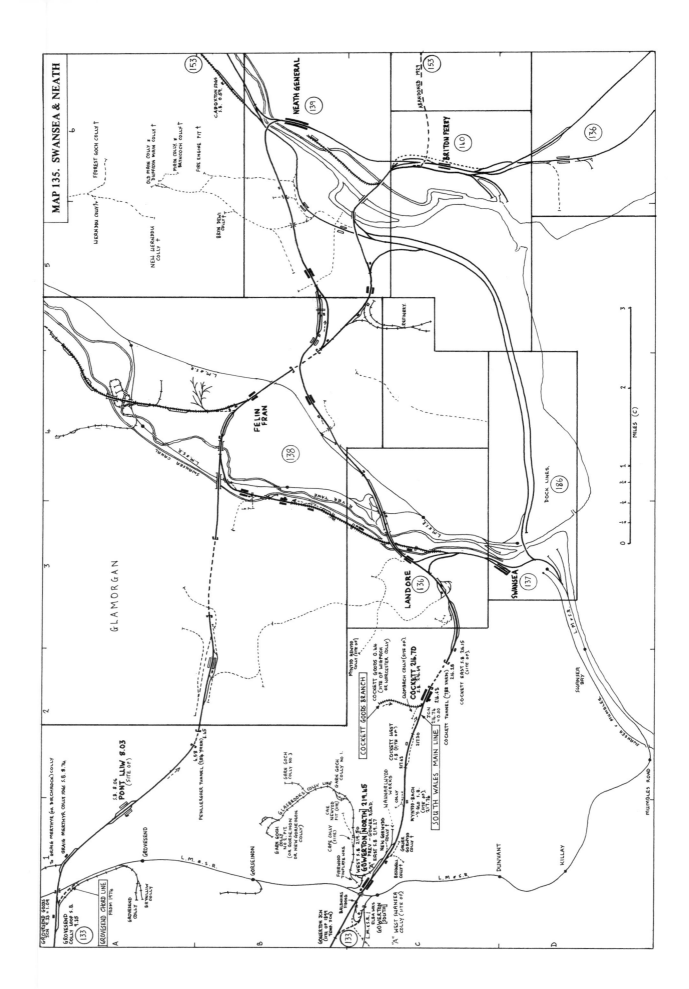

MAP 135. SWANSEA & NEATH

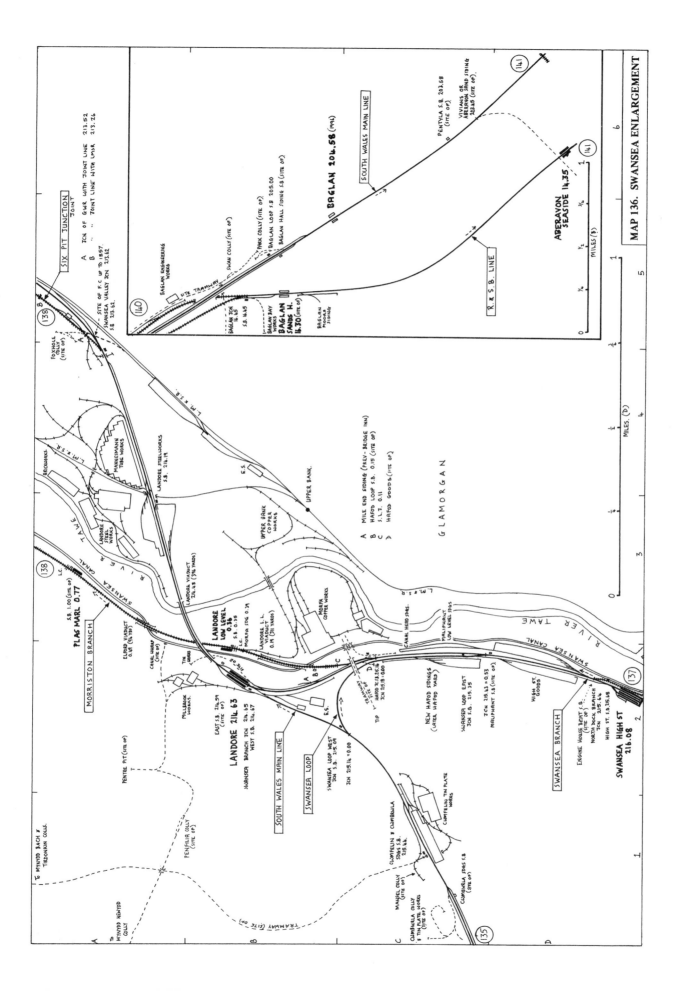

MAP 136. SWANSEA ENLARGEMENT

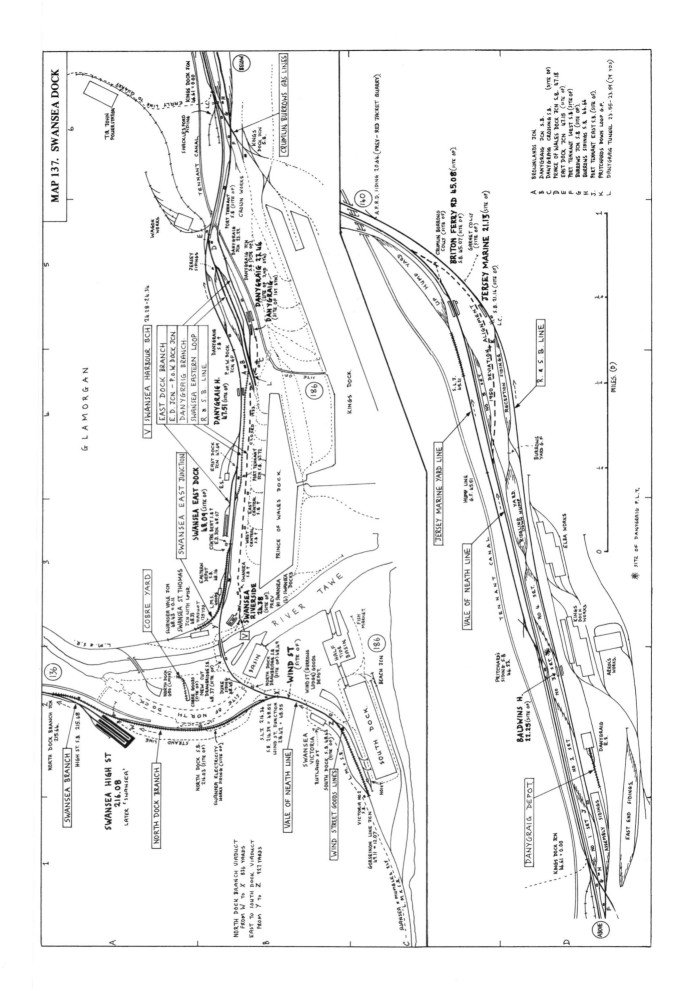

MAP 137. SWANSEA DOCK

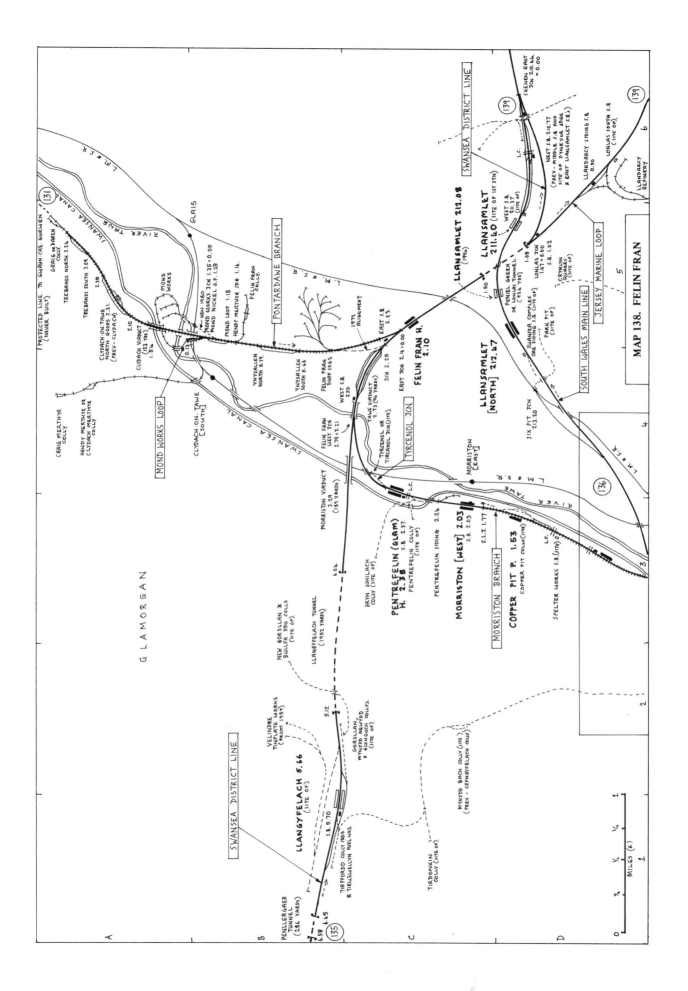

MAP 138. FELIN FRAN

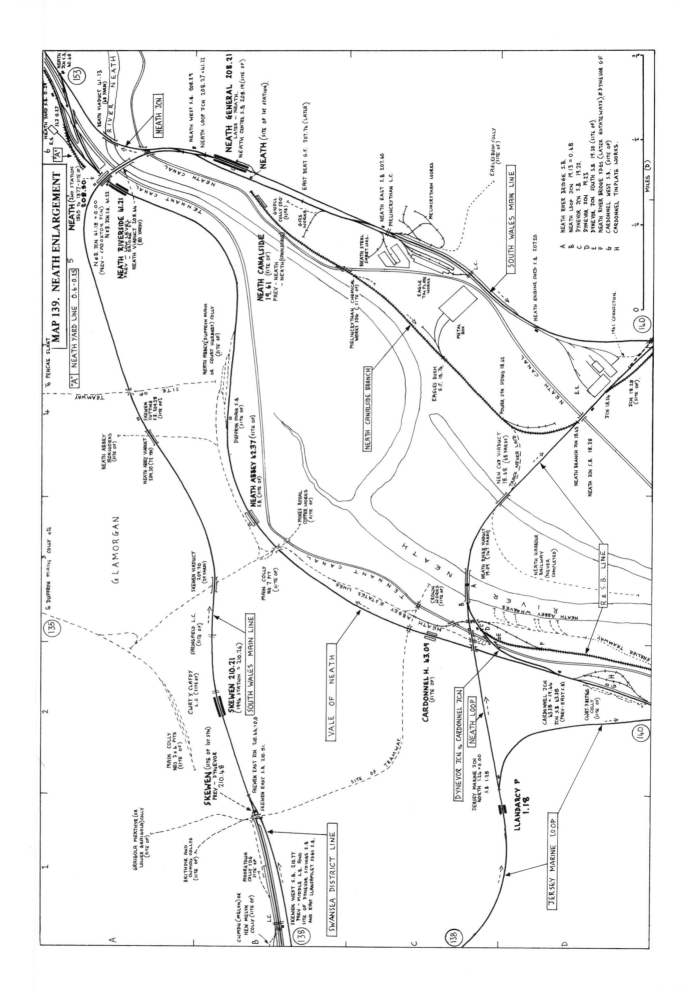

MAP 139. NEATH ENLARGEMENT

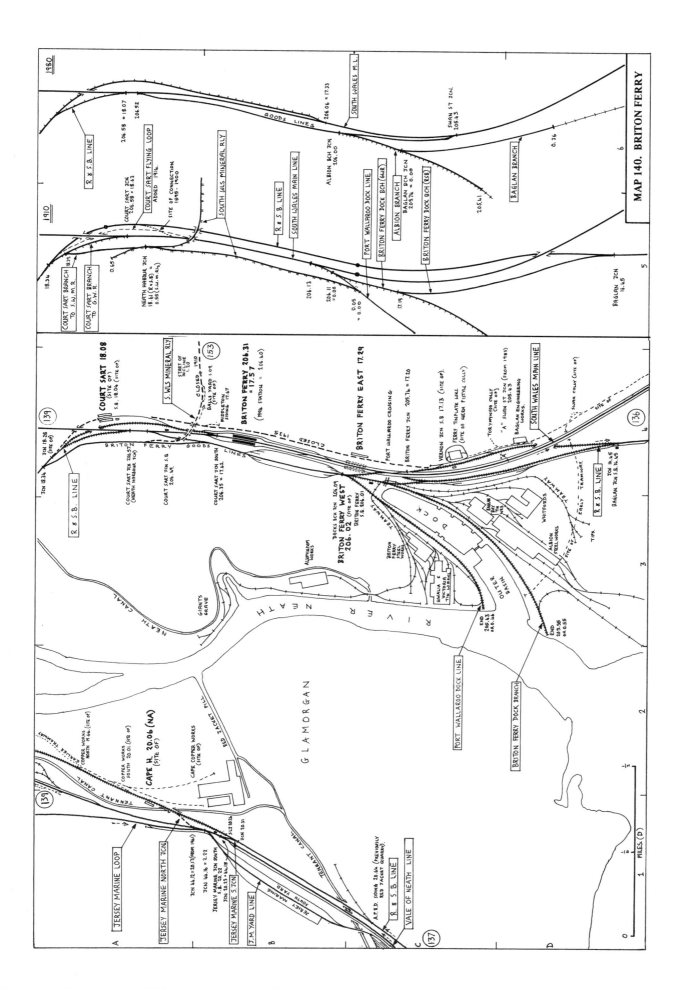

MAP 140. BRITON FERRY

MAP 141. PORT TALBOT ENLARGEMENT

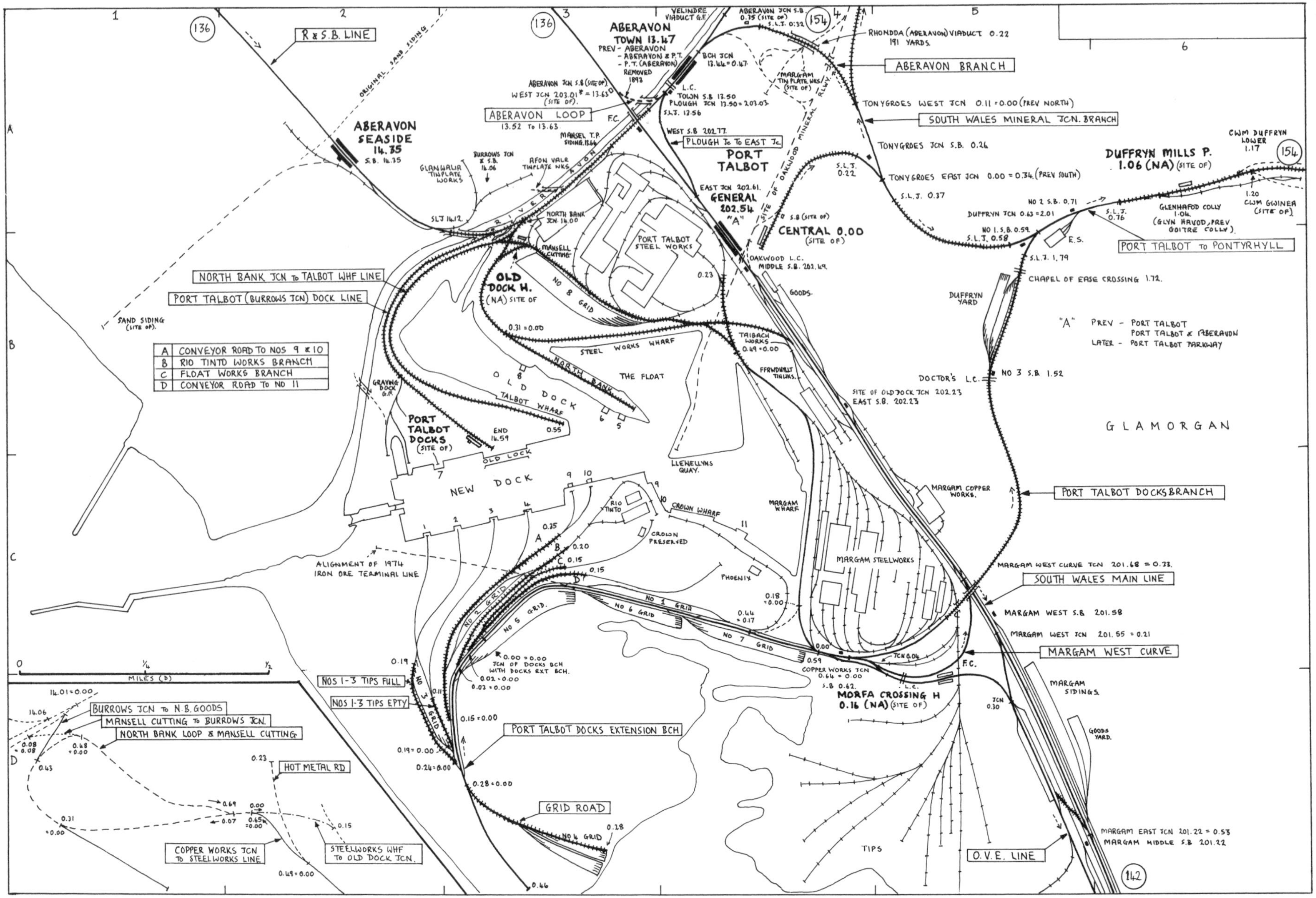

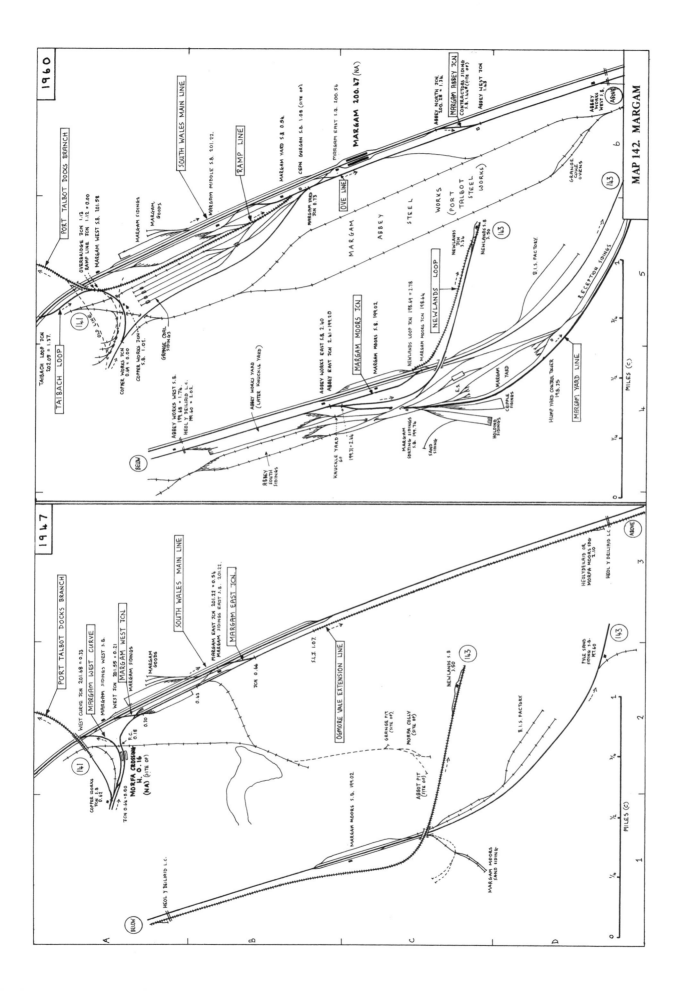

MAP 142. MARGAM

MAP 143. PYLE AND TONDU ENLARGEMENTS

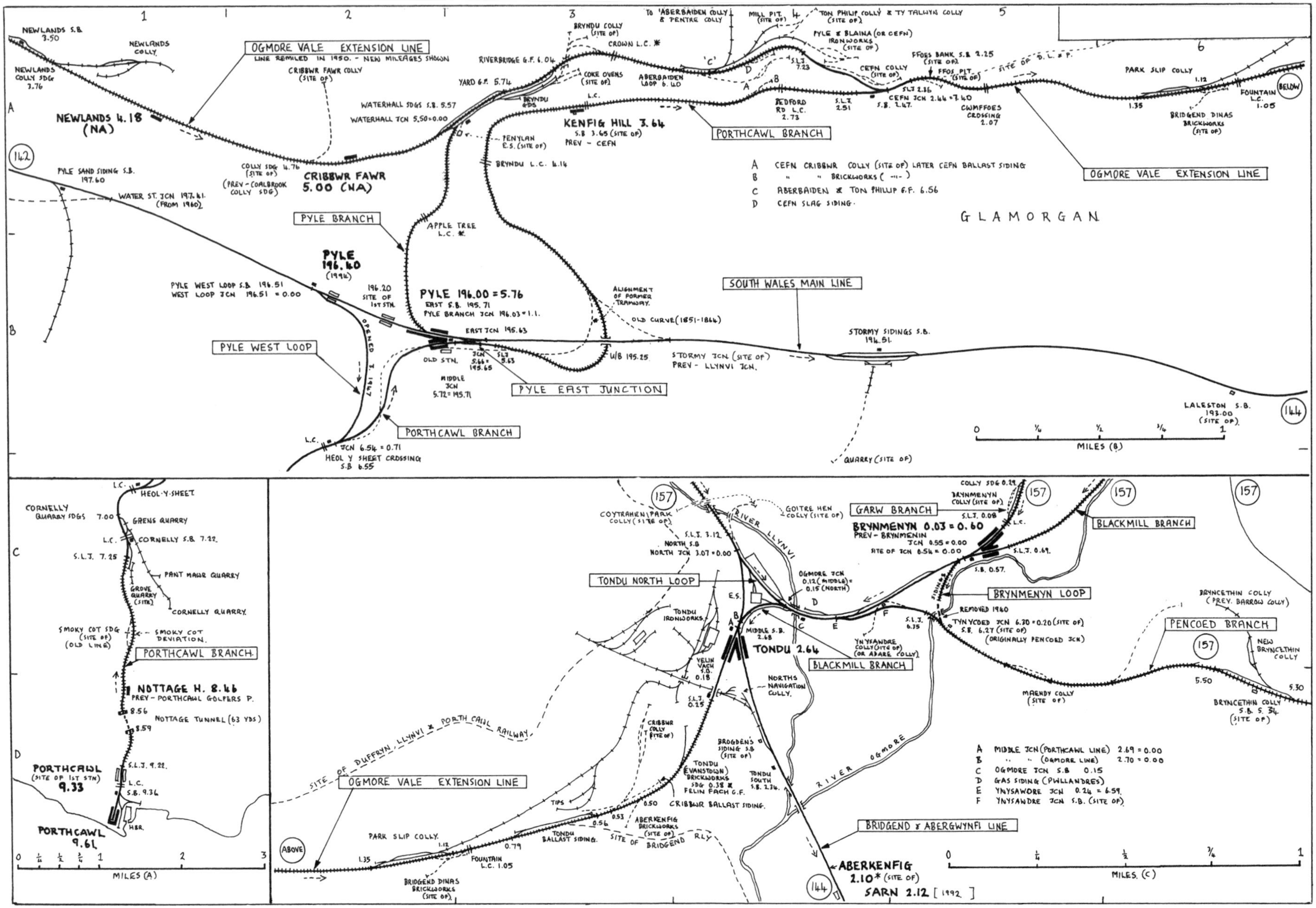

NEWLANDS S.B. 3.50
NEWLANDS COLLY.
NEWLANDS COLLY SDG 3.76
NEWLANDS 4.18 (NA)
OGMORE VALE EXTENSION LINE
LINE REMILED IN 1950. - NEW MILEAGES SHOWN
CRIBBWR FAWR COLLY (SITE OF)
COLLY SDG 4.76 (SITE OF) (PREV - COALBROOK COLLY SDG)
CRIBBWR FAWR 5.00 (NA)
WATERHALL SDGS S.B. 5.57
WATERHALL JCN 5.50=0.00
YARD G.F. 5.74
RIVERBRIDGE G.F. 6.04
BRYNDU COLLY (SITE OF)
CROWN L.C. *
COKE OVENS (SITE OF)
TENYLAN E.S. (SITE OF)
BRYNDU L.C. 6.14
KENFIG HILL 3.64
S.B 3.65 (SITE OF)
PREV - CEFN
ABERBAIDEN LOOP 6.40
TO ABERBAIDEN COLLY & PENTRE COLLY
MILL PIT (SITE OF)
TON PHILIP COLLY & TY TALWYN COLLY (SITE OF)
PYLE & BLAINA (OR CEFN) IRONWORKS (SITE OF)
CEFN COLLY (SITE OF)
FFOES BANK S.B 2.25 (SITE OF)
FFOS PIT (SITE OF)
SITE OF D.L. & P.
CEFN JCN 2.46 = 7.40
S.B. 2.47
CWMFFOES CROSSING 2.07
BEDFORD RD L.C. 2.73
PORTHCAWL BRANCH
PARK SLIP COLLY
BRIDGEND DINAS BRICKWORKS (SITE OF)
FOUNTAIN L.C. 1.05
BELOW
A CEFN CRIBBWR COLLY (SITE OF) LATER CEFN BALLAST SIDING
B " " BRICKWORKS (-"-)
C ABERBAIDEN & TON PHILLIP G.F. 6.56
D CEFN SLAG SIDING
GLAMORGAN
PYLE SAND SIDING S.B. 197.60
WATER ST. JCN 197.41 (FROM 1960)
PYLE BRANCH
APPLE TREE L.C. *
PYLE 196.40 (1994)
PYLE WEST LOOP S.B. 196.51
WEST LOOP JCN 196.51 = 0.00
196.20 SITE OF 1ST STN.
PYLE 196.00 = 5.76
EAST S.B. 195.71
PYLE BRANCH JCN 196.03 = 1.1.
EAST JCN 195.63
OLD STN.
MIDDLE JCN 5.72 = 195.71
PYLE WEST LOOP
OPENED 7. 1947
PYLE EAST JUNCTION
ALIGNMENT OF FORMER TRAMWAY.
OLD CURVE (1851-1866)
W/B 195.25
SOUTH WALES MAIN LINE
STORMY JCN (SITE OF)
PREV - LLYNVI JCN.
STORMY SIDINGS S.B. 194.51
QUARRY (SITE OF)
LALESTON S.B. 193.00 (SITE OF)
JCN 6.54 = 0.71
HEOL Y SHEET CROSSING S.B 6.55
MILES (B)
HEOL-Y-SHEET
CORNELLY QUARRY SDGS 7.00
GRENS QUARRY
CORNELLY S.B 7.22
PANT MAWR QUARRY
GROVE QUARRY (SITE)
CORNELLY QUARRY
SMOKY COT SDG (SITE OF) (OLD LINE)
SMOKY COT DEVIATION
NOTTAGE H. 8.46
PREV - PORTHCAWL GOLFERS P.
NOTTAGE TUNNEL (63 YDS)
PORTHCAWL (SITE OF 1ST STN) 9.33
S.L.J. 9.22
S.B. 9.36
HBR.
PORTHCAWL 9.61
MILES (A)
COYTRAHEN PARK COLLY (SITE OF)
GOITRE HEN COLLY (SITE OF)
RIVER LLYNVI
NORTH S.B
NORTH JCN 3.07 = 0.00
TONDU NORTH LOOP
TONDU IRONWORKS
OGMORE JCN 0.12 (MIDDLE) = 0.15 (NORTH)
MIDDLE S.B. 2.68
TONDU 2.64
BLACKMILL BRANCH
YELIN VACH S.B. 0.18
NORTHS NAVIGATION COLLY.
YNYSAWDRE COLLY (SITE OF) (OR ADARE COLLY)
GARW BRANCH
COLLY SDG 0.29
BRYNMENYN COLLY (SITE OF)
BRYNMENYN 0.03 = 0.60
PREV - BRYNMENIN
JCN 0.55 = 0.00
SITE OF JCN 0.54 = 0.00
S.L.J. 0.69
S.B. 0.57
BRYNMENYN LOOP
REMOVED 1960
TYNYCOED JCN 6.30 = 0.20 (SITE OF)
S.B. 6.27 (SITE OF)
(ORIGINALLY PENCOED JCN)
PENCOED BRANCH
BRYNCETHIN COLLY (PREV. BARROW COLLY)
NEW BRYNCETHIN COLLY
BRYNCETHIN COLLY S.B. 5.34 (SITE OF)
MAENDY COLLY (SITE OF)
SITE OF DUFFRYN, LLYNVI & PORTHCAWL RAILWAY
OGMORE VALE EXTENSION LINE
CRIBBWR COLLY (SITE OF)
BROGDEN'S SIDING S.B (SITE OF)
TONDU (EVANSTOWN) BRICKWORKS SDG 0.38 & FELIN FACH G.F.
TONDU SOUTH S.B. 2.34
CRIBBWR BALLAST SIDING
ABERKENFIG BRICKWORKS (SITE OF)
SITE OF BRIDGEND RLY
TONDU BALLAST SIDING
RIVER OGMORE
BRIDGEND & ABERGWYNFI LINE
ABERKENFIG 2.10* (SITE OF)
SARN 2.12 [1992]
ABOVE
MILES (C)
A MIDDLE JCN (PORTHCAWL LINE) 2.69 = 0.00
B " " (OGMORE LINE) 2.70 = 0.00
C OGMORE JCN S.B 0.15
D GAS SIDING (PWLLANDRES)
E YNYSAWDRE JCN 0.24 = 6.59
F YNYSAWDRE JCN S.B. (SITE OF)

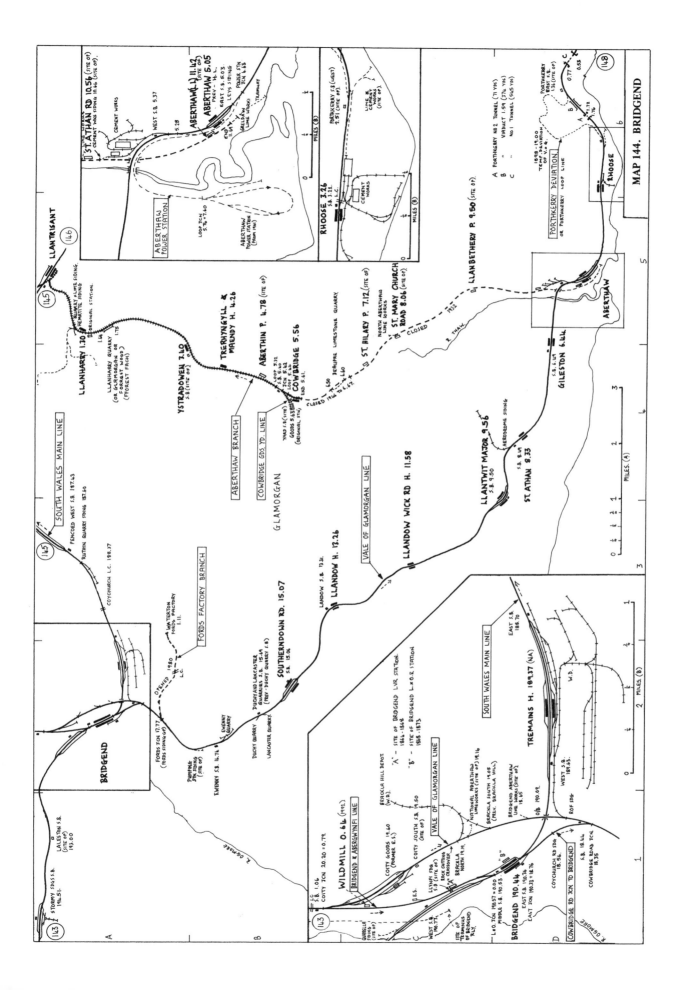

MAP 144. BRIDGEND

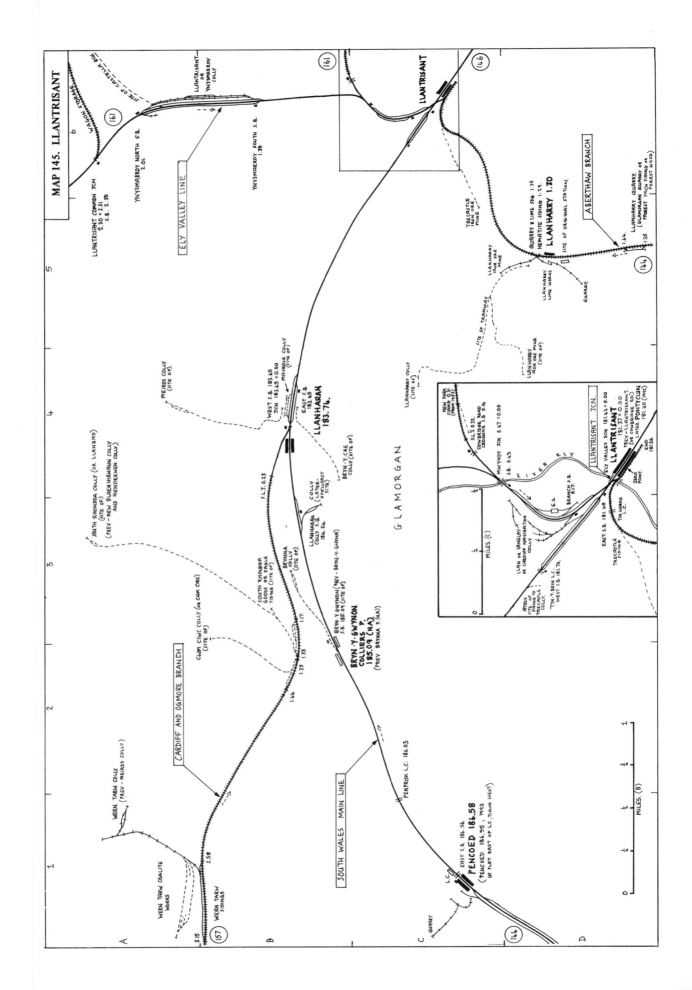

MAP 145. LLANTRISANT

ELY VALLEY LINE

ABERTHAW BRANCH

CARDIFF AND OGMORE BRANCH

SOUTH WALES MAIN LINE

GLAMORGAN

LLANTRISANT

LLANTRISANT COMMON JCN
2.10 = 2.31
S.B. 2.30

YNYSMAERDY NORTH S.B.
2.01.

LLANTRISANT-OR
YNYSMAERDY COLLY

SITE OF CASTELLA BCH

WAGON STORAGE

YNYSMAERDY SOUTH S.B.

YNYSMAERDY S.B.

LLANHARRY 1.70

QUARRY & LIME SDG 1.25
HEMATITE SIDING 1.39.
SITE OF ORIGINAL STATION.

LLANHARRY QUARRY
(GLAMORGAN QUARRY OR
FOREST PACH SIDING OR
FOREST WOOD)

LLANHARRY IRON ORE MINE

LLANHARRY
LIME WORKS

QUARRY.

TRECASTLE
IRON ORE
MINE

LLANHARRY COLLY
(SITE OF)

LLANHARRY IRON ORE MINE
(SITE OF)

LLANHARRY
IRON ORE MINE (SITE OF)

SITE OF TRAMWAY

SOUTH RHONDDA COLLY (OR LLANBAD)
(SITE OF)
(PREV - NEW BLAENHIRWAUN COLLY
AND HENDREWEN COLLY)

MEIROS COLLY
(SITE OF)

WEST S.B. 183.45
LLANHARAN JCN 183.45 = 0.00

PARADISE COLLY
(SITE OF)

EAST S.B.
183.45
LLANHARAN
183.74

BRYN-Y-CAE
COLLY (SITE OF)

COLLY (LATER-OPENCAST
SITE)

LLANHARAN
COLLY S.B.
184.24.

S.L.T. 0.33

BRYNNA
COLLY
(SITE OF)

SOUTH RHONDDA
GOODS OR EAGLE
SIDING (SITE OF)

CWM CINC COLLY (OR CWM CINC)
(SITE OF)

1.17.

1.46

1.35

1.35

BRYN-Y-GWYNON (PREV - BRYN-Y-GWYN)
S.B. 185.09 (SITE OF)

BRYN-Y-GWYNON
COLLIERS P.
185.09 (N.A.)
(PREV BRYNNA P.(N.A))

WERN TARW COLLY
(PREV - MEIROS COLLY)

WERN TARW COALITE
WORKS

2.15

WERN TARW
SIDINGS

2.58

157

PENYRISK L.C. 186.03

PENCOED 186.58
(PENCOED 186.95. 1992
UP FLAT EAST OF L.C. DOWN WEST)

EAST S.B. 186.56.
L.C.

QUARRY

144

GLAMORGAN

[inset box]

NEW PARK
SIDING 0.31
(FROM WEST)

S.L.T. 0.22.
COWBRIDGE ROAD
CROSSING S.B. 0.16

MWYNDY JCN 0.47 = 0.00

S.B. 0.43

LLANTRISANT JCN 181.43 = 0.00
(PREV - LLANTRISANT,
OR COWBRIDGE RD.)
LATER PONTYCLUN 1992

EAST S.B. 181.45

BRANCH S.B.
0.17.

ZERO
POINT.

TIN WORKS

RIVER ELY

LLAN OR URWELYN
OR CARDIFF NAVIGATION
COLLY

E.S.

TYN-Y-BRYN L.C.
WEST S.B. 181.71B.

APPROX
SITE OF
SIDING TO
TRECASTLE
COLLY.

TRECASTLE
SIDING

ELY VALLEY JCN 181.57 = 0.00
PREV - LLANTRISANT.
END
181.10 (1942)
181.26

MILES. (C)

0   ½   1

MILES. (B)

0   ¼   ½   ¾   1

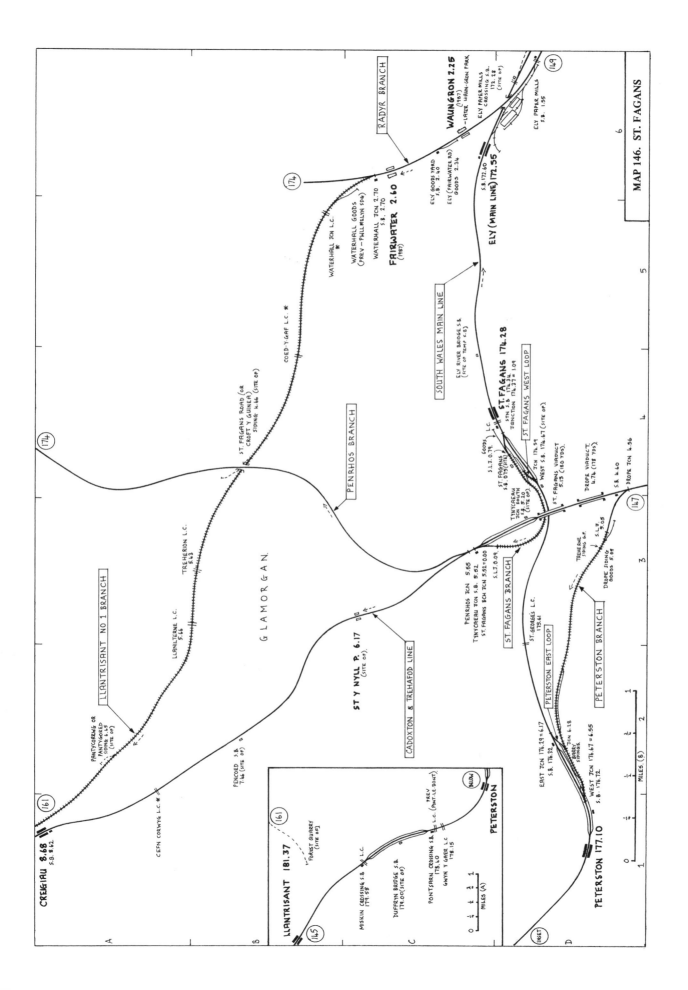

MAP 146. ST. FAGANS

CREIGIAU 8.68
S.B. 8.62

LLANTRISANT NO 1 BRANCH

PANTYGORED OR
PANTYGORED
SIDING 8.45
(SITE OF)

PENCOED S.B.
7.44 (SITE OF)

CEFN CORWYG L.C. ✳

LLANILTERNE L.C.
5.66

TREHERION L.C.
5.43

COED-Y-GRAF L.C. ✳

GLAMORGAN.

PENRHOS BRANCH

ST Y NYLL P. 6.17
(SITE OF)

CADOXTON & TREHAFOD LINE

ST. FAGANS ROAD (OR
CROFT Y GUINEA)
SIDING 4.66 (SITE OF)

WATERHALL JCN L.C. ✳

WATERHALL GOODS
(PREV- PWLLMELYN SDG)

WATERHALL JCN 2.70
S.B. 2.70

FAIRWATER 2.60
(1987)

RADYR BRANCH

WAUNGRON 2.25
(1987)
- LATER WAUN-GRON PARK

ELY GOODS YARD
S.B. 2.40

ELY (FAIRWATER RD)
GOODS 2.34

ELY PAPER MILLS
CROSSING S.B.
1.72.28
(SITE OF)

S.B. 1.72.60

ELY (MAIN LINE) 1.72.55

ELY PAPER MILLS
S.B. 1.55

SOUTH WALES MAIN LINE

ELY RIVER BRIDGE S.B.
(SITE OF TEMP F.B)

ST. FAGANS 174.28
STN. 174.34.
JUNCTION 174.37 = 1.09

ST. FAGANS WEST LOOP

ST. FAGANS
S.B. 0.155 (SITE)

GOODS
L.C.

S.L.I. 0.79

WEST S.B. 174.67 (SITE OF)

JCN 174.59

TYNYCAERAU
JCN SOUTH
S.B. 5.20
(SITE OF)

ST. FAGANS VIADUCT
5.15 (160 YDS.)

DROPE VIADUCT
4.74 (178 YDS.)

S.B. 4.60

DROPE JCN 4.56

PENRHOS JCN 5.65
TYNYCAERAU JCN S.B. 5.62
ST. FAGANS BCH JCN 5.51 = 0.00

S.L.I. 0.09

ST. FAGANS BRANCH

PENRHOS JCN

S.T. GEORGE'S L.C.
175.61

PETERSTON EAST LOOP

PETERSTON BRANCH

TREHANE
SIDING G.F.
S.L.I. 5.05

DROPE SIDING
GOODS 5.08

EAST JCN 174.29 = 6.17
S.B. 174.32

BARRY
SIDINGS

WEST JCN 174.72
S.B. 174.72.

BARRY JCN 6.18

PETERSTON 177.10

PETERSTON

BELOW

MILES (B)

CREIGIAU 161 174
174 161
149
147
145

INSET

LLANTRISANT 181.37

FOREST QUARRY
(SITE OF)

MISKIN CROSSING S.B.
179.58

DUFFRYN BRIDGE S.B.
174.00 (SITE OF)

PONTSARN CROSSING S.B.
178.60

GWYN Y GAER L.C.
178.15

L.C. (PREV
PONTLE BONT)

MILES (A)
0   ¼ ½ ¾ 1

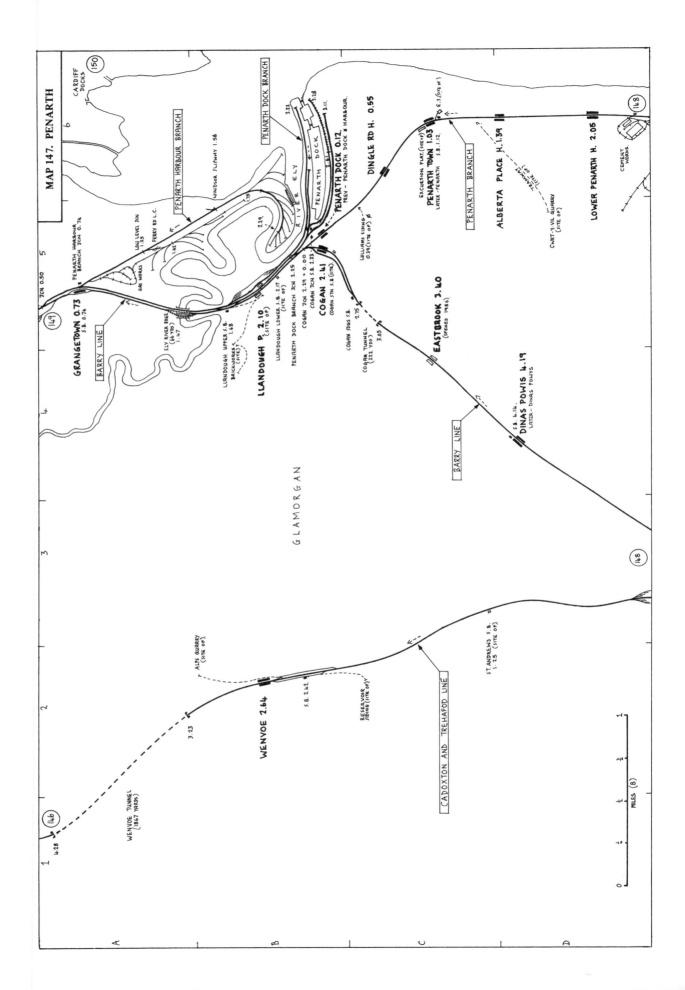

MAP 147. PENARTH

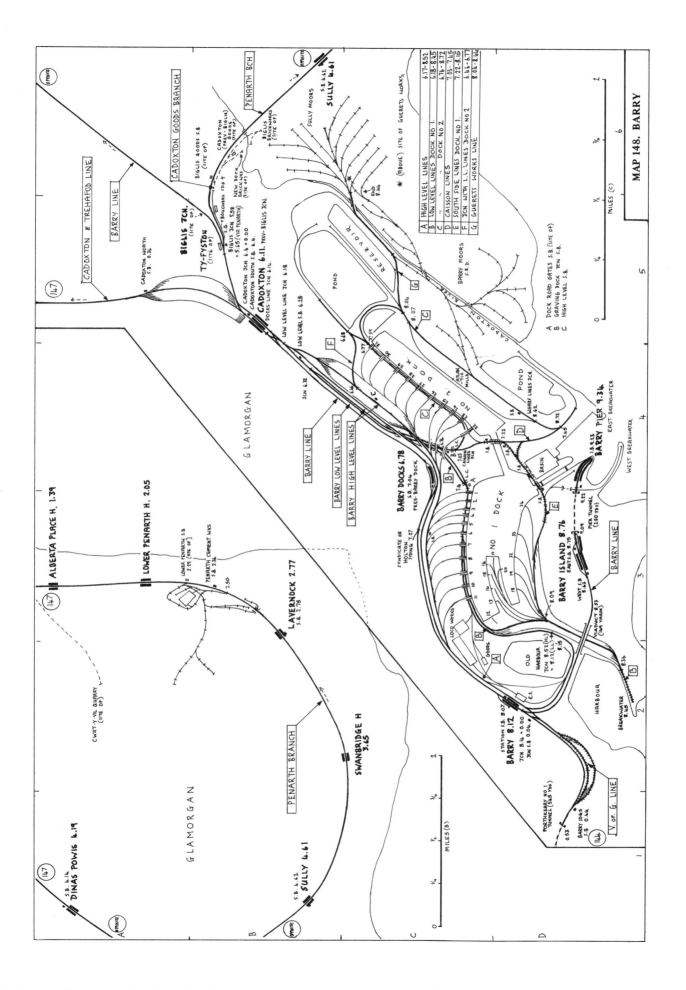

MAP 148. BARRY

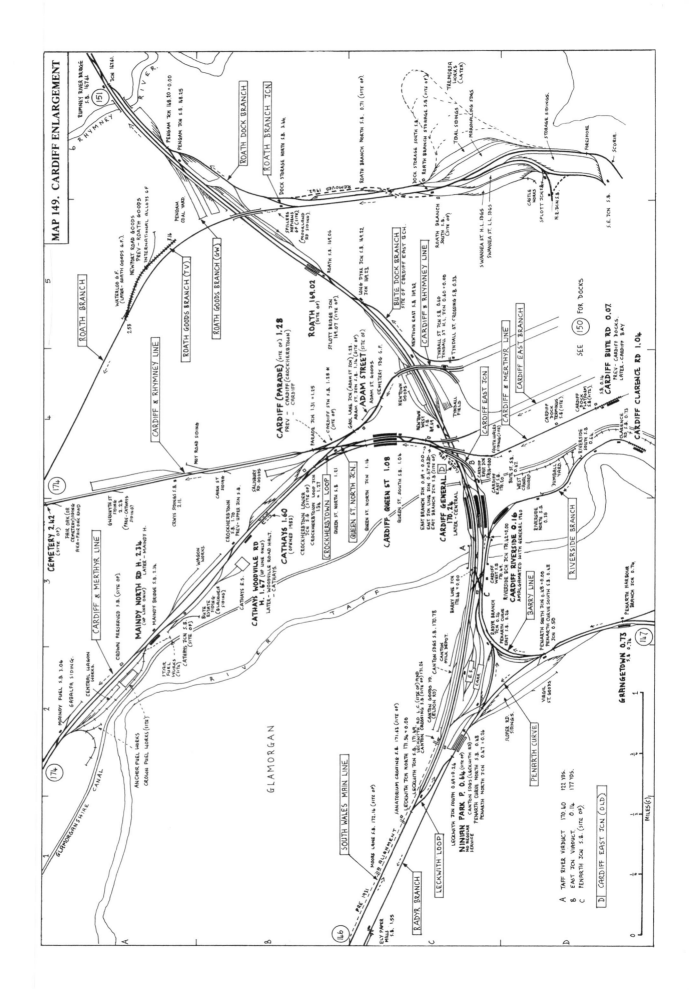

MAP 149. CARDIFF ENLARGEMENT

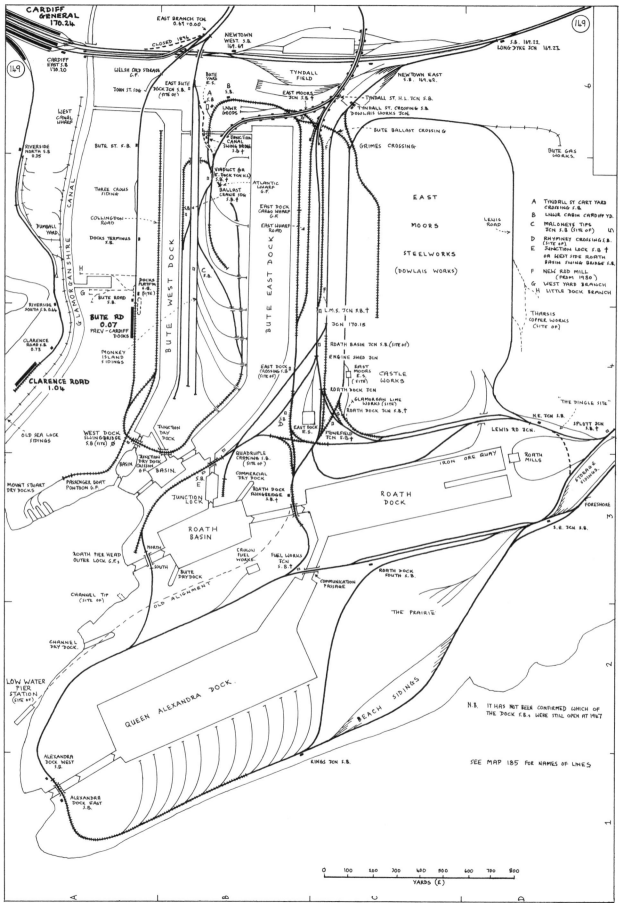

MAP 150. CARDIFF DOCKS ENLARGEMENT

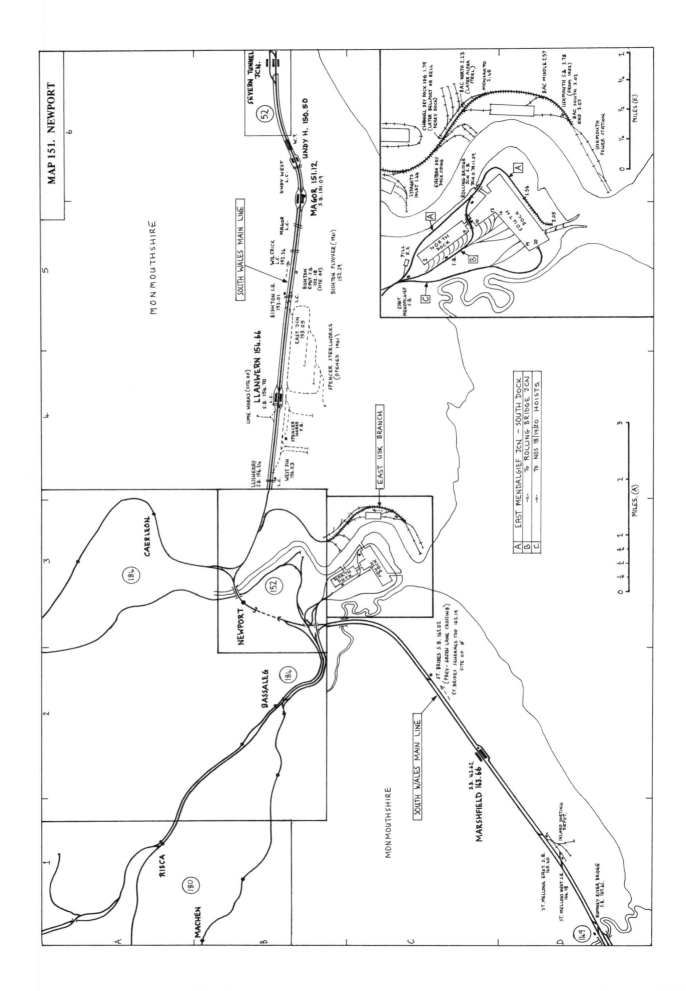

MAP 151. NEWPORT

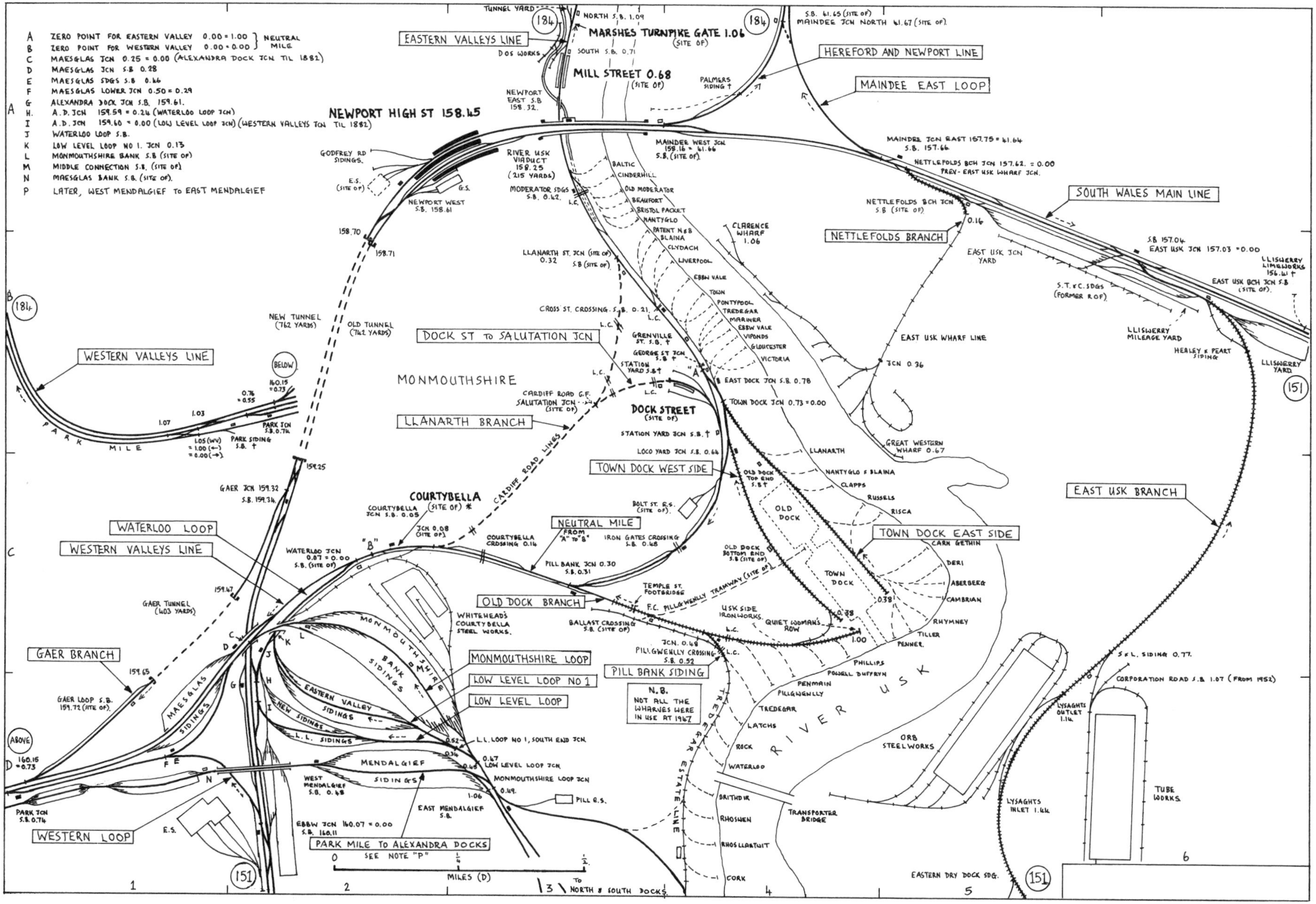

MAP 152. NEWPORT ENLARGEMENT

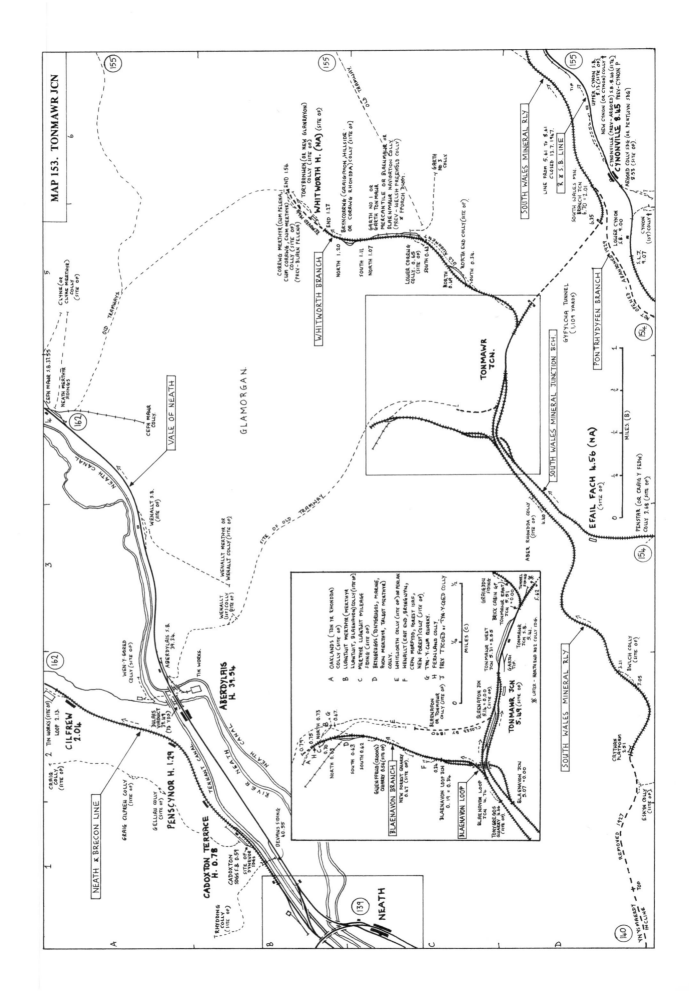

MAP 153. TONMAWR JCN

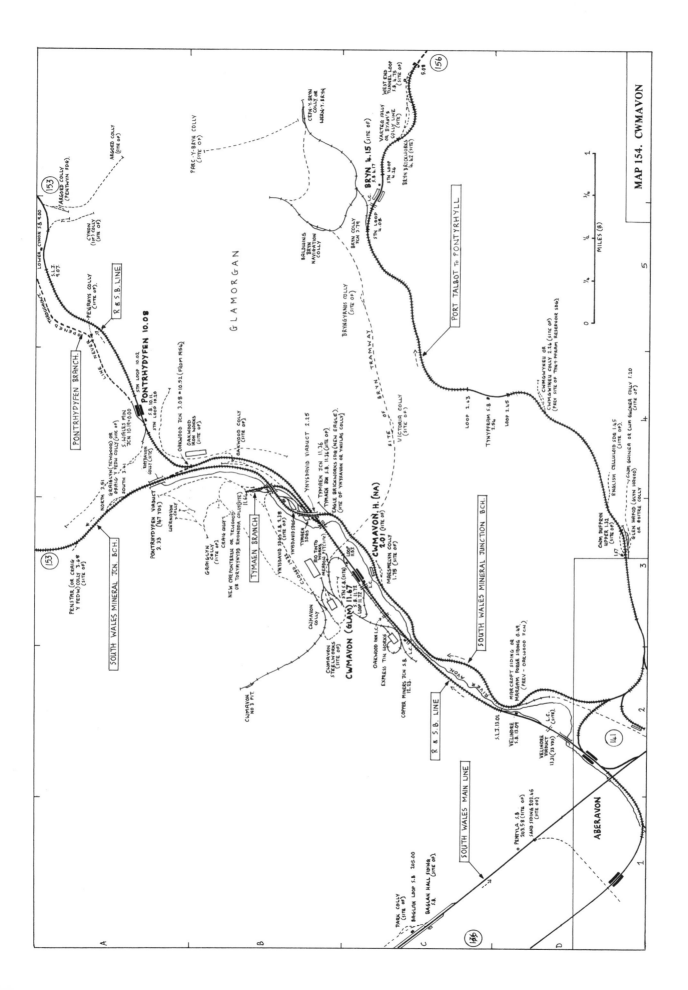

MAP 154. CWMAVON

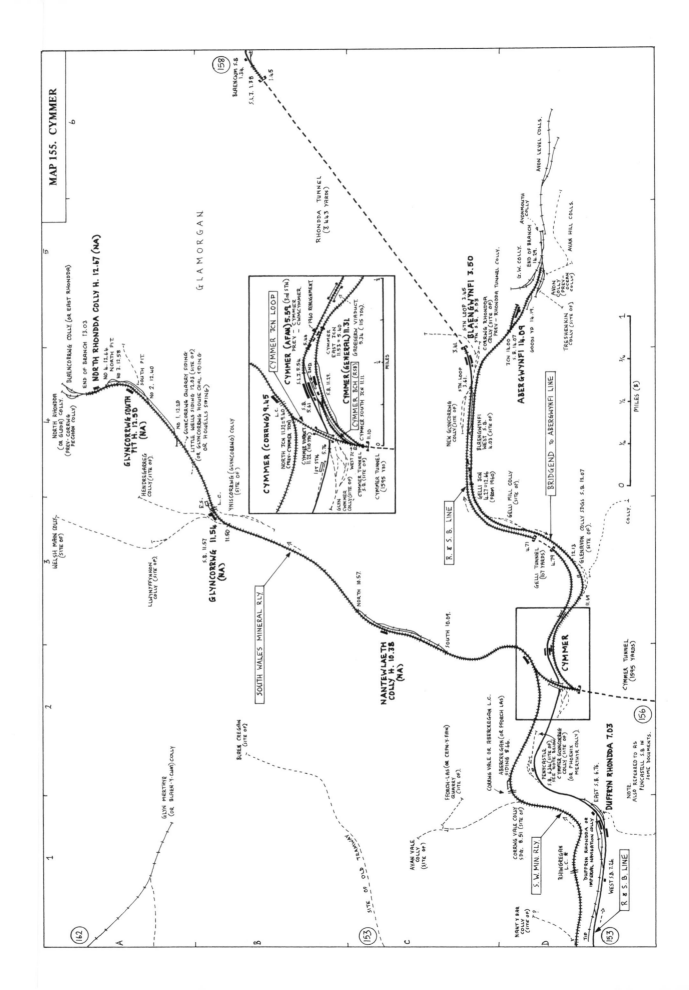

MAP 155. CYMMER

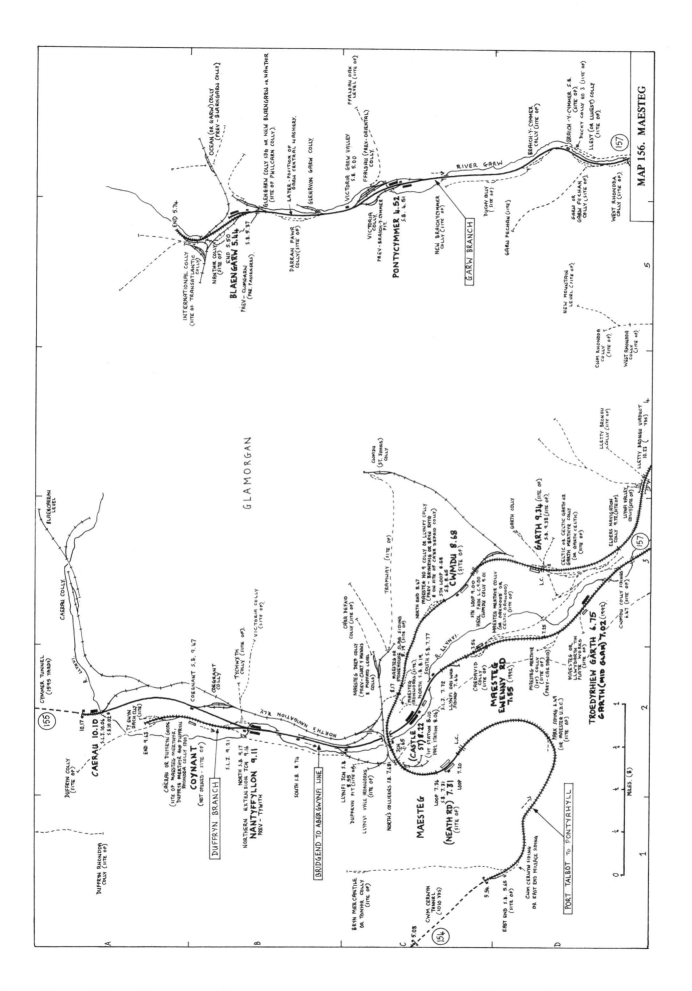

MAP 156. MAESTEG

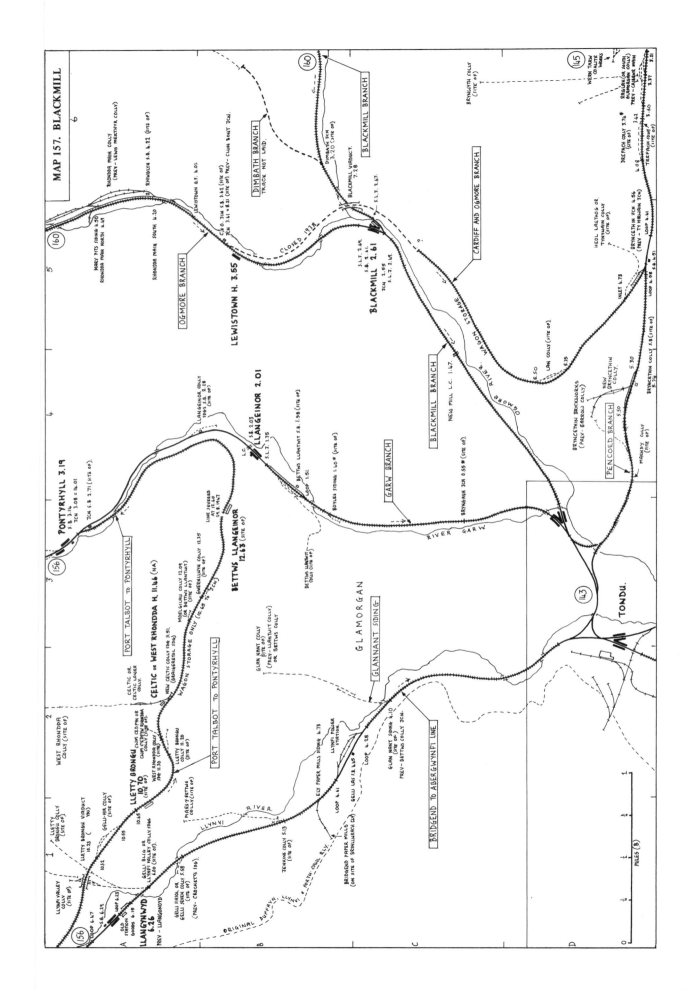

MAP 157. BLACKMILL

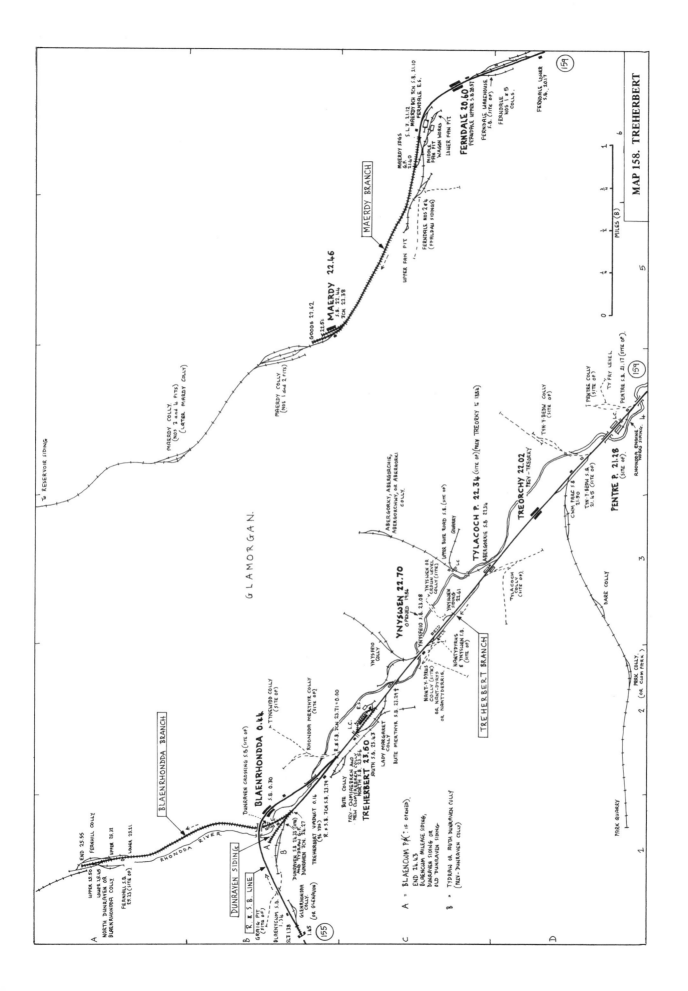

MAP 158. TREHERBERT

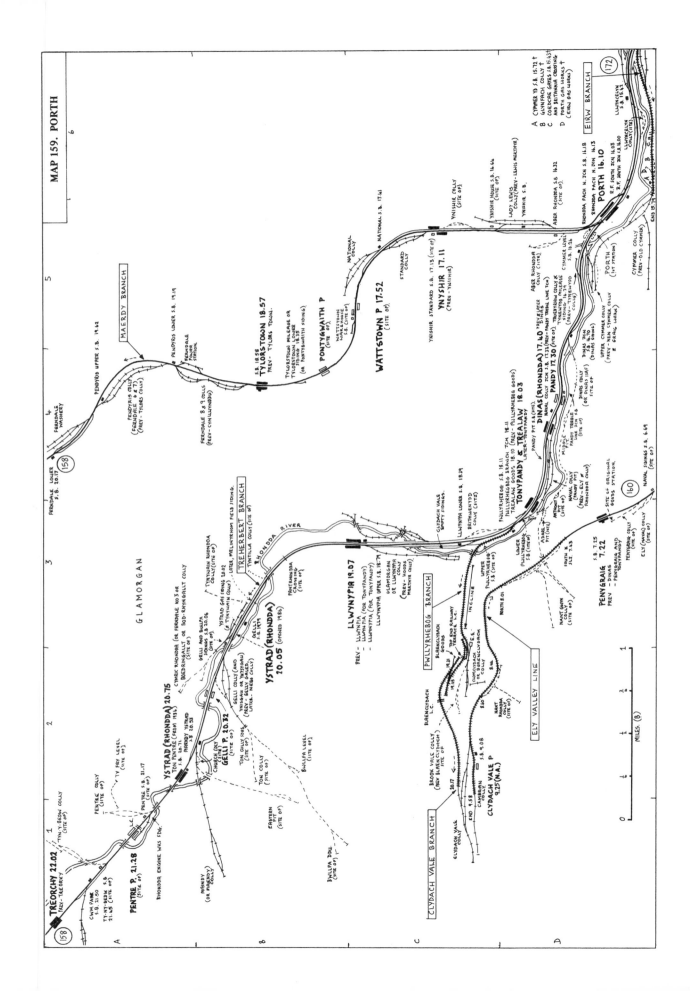

MAP 159. PORTH

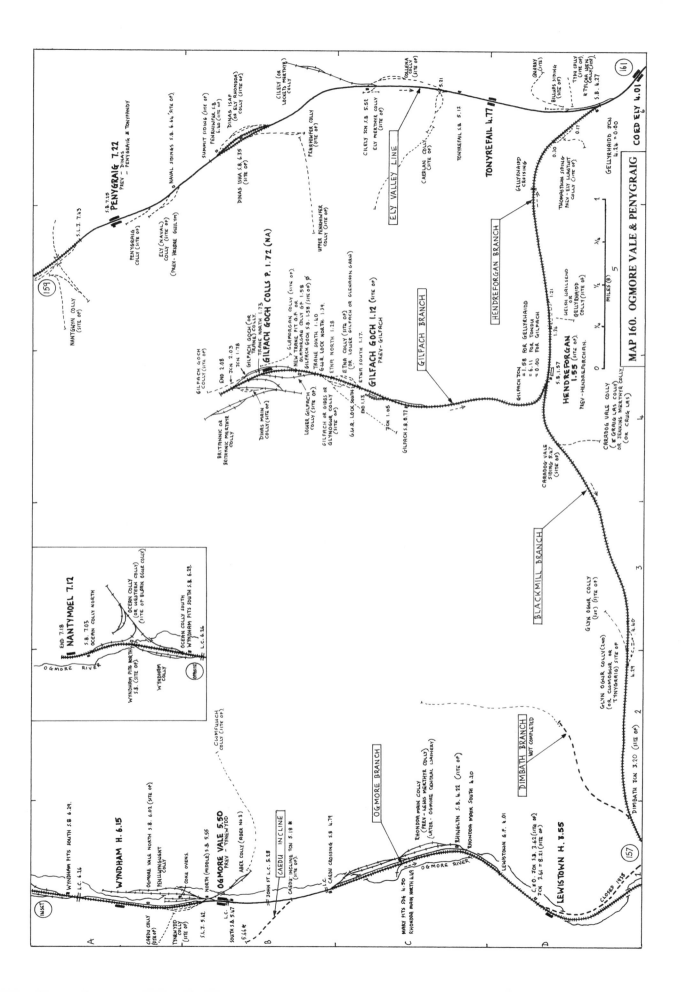

MAP 160. OGMORE VALE & PENYGRAIG

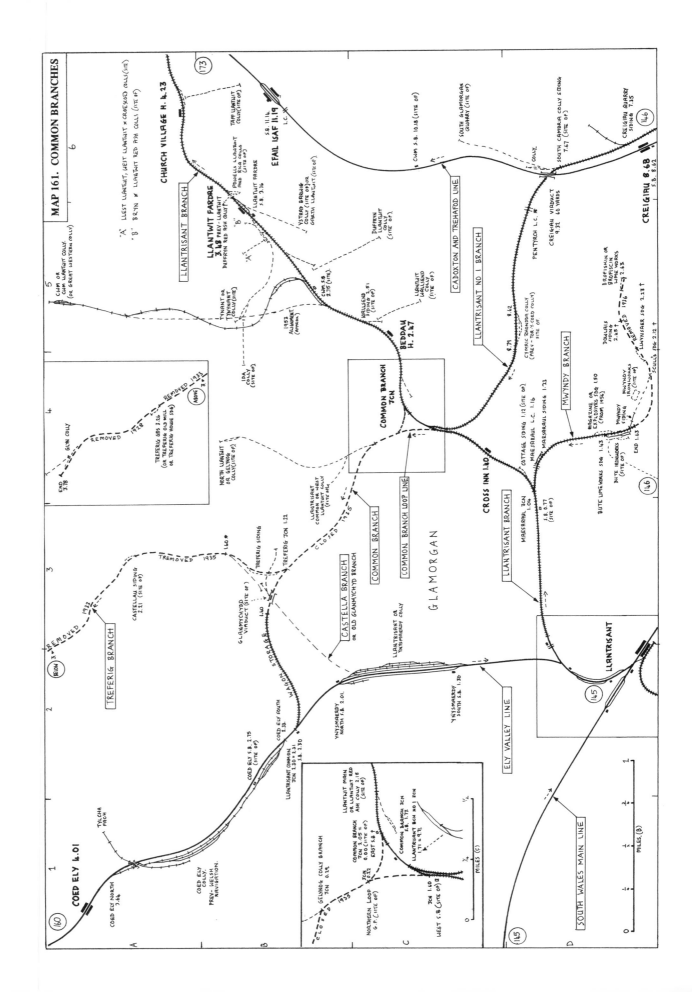

MAP 161. COMMON BRANCHES

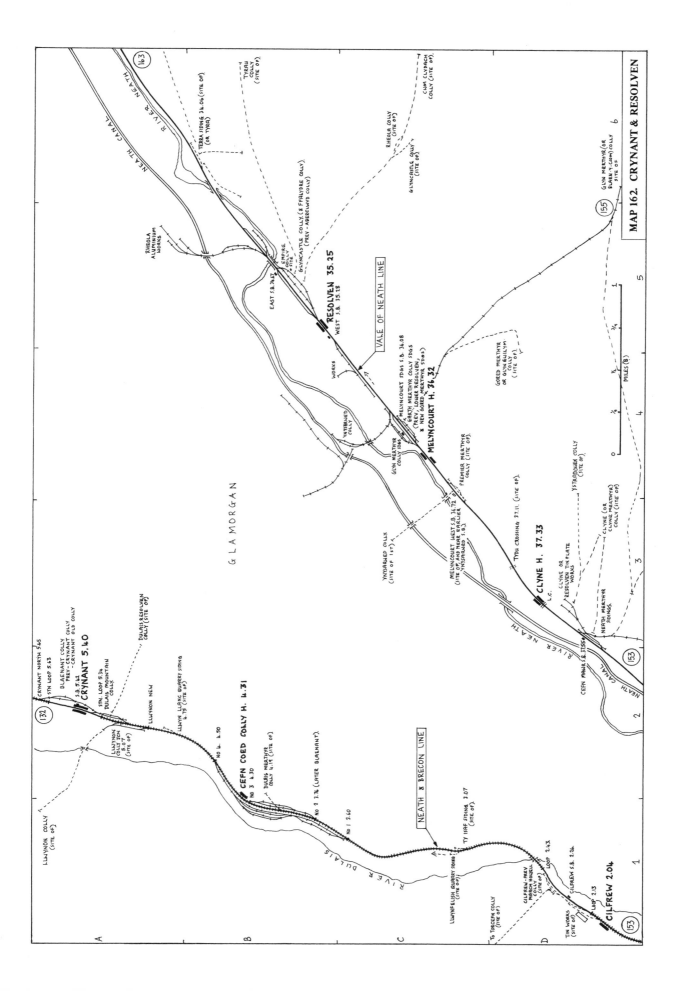

MAP 162. CRYNANT & RESOLVEN

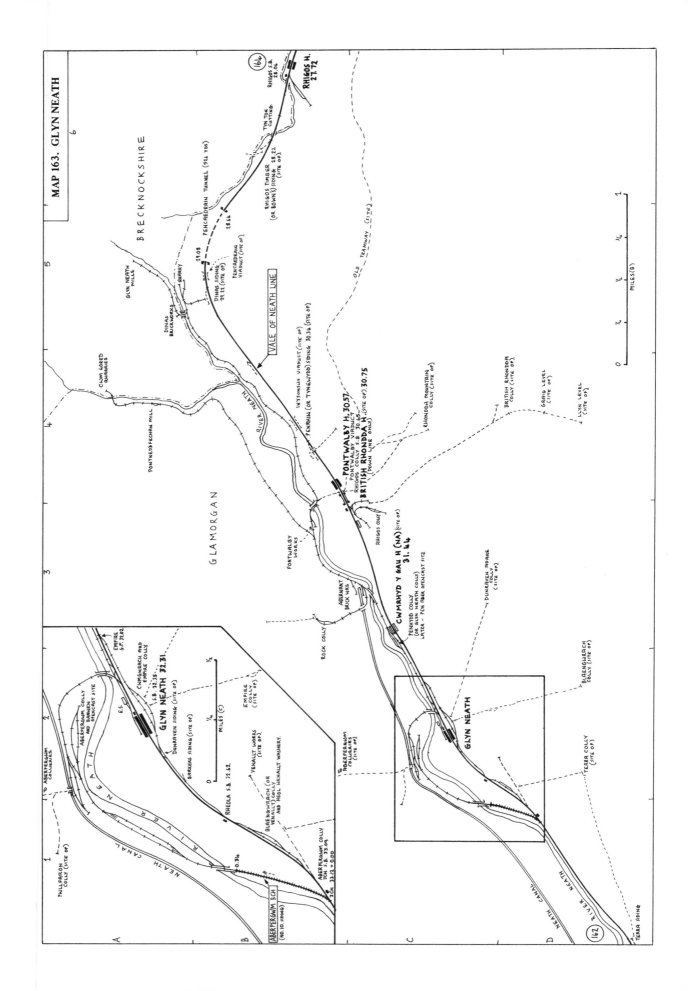

MAP 163. GLYN NEATH

BRECKNOCKSHIRE

GLAMORGAN

VALE OF NEATH LINE

RHIGOS H. 27.72

RHIGOS S.B. 28.04

TYN TON CUTTING

PENCRAEDRAIN TUNNEL (514 YDS)

RHIGOS TIMBER (OR BOWN'S) SIDING 28.22 (SITE OF)

OLD TRAMWAY (SITE)

28.44

29.08

PENCAEDRAIN VIADUCT (SITE OF)

DINAS SIDING 29.21 (SITE OF)

GLYN NEATH MILLS

QUARRY

DINAS BRICKWORKS

CWM GORED QUARRIES

PONTNEDDFECHAN MILL

RIVER NEATH

PENRHIW (OR TYNEWYDD) SIDING 30.34 (SITE OF)

IWYSONSWS VIADUCT (SITE OF)

PONTWALBY H. 30.57

PONTWALBY VIADUCT

RHIGOS COLLY S.B. 30.65

BRITISH RHONDDA (SITE OF) 30.75

(DOWN LINE ONLY)

PONTWALBY WORKS

ABERNANT BRICK WKS

RHIGOS ONLY

RHONDDA MOUNTAIN COLLY (SITE OF)

BRITISH RHONDDR COLLY (SITE OF)

GRAIG LEVEL (SITE OF)

LLYN LEVEL (SITE OF)

ROCK COLLY

CWMRHYD Y GAU R (NA) (SITE OF) 31.44

PENYOD COLLY (OR GLYN NEATH COLLY) LATER – PEN FIBER OPENCAST SITE

DUNRAVEN ARRRE (SITE OF)

TO ABERPERGWM COLLIERIES (SITE OF)

BLAENGWRACH COLLY (SITE OF)

GLYN NEATH

TERRA COLLY (SITE OF)

NEATH CANAL

RIVER NEATH

MILES (B)

0   ¼   ½   ¾   1

PAILLFARON COLLY (SITE OF)

To ABERPERGWM COLLIERIES

ABERPERGWM COLLY AND BARWEN BREAKCAST SITE

ABERPERGWM COLLY

NEATH RIVER

NEATH CANAL

EMPIRE G.F. 32.92

CWMGWRACH AND EMPIRE COLLY

S.B. 32.58

GLYN NEATH 32.31

DUNRAVEN SIDING (SITE OF)

E.S.

EMPIRE COLLY (SITE OF)

VENALLT WORKS

BLAENGWRACH (OR VENALLT) COLLY AND HEOL VENALLT WASHERY.

BARKERS SIDING (SITE OF)

RHEOLA S.B. 32.62

MILES (C)

0   ¼   ½

ABERPERGWM COLLY

ABER S.B. 33.04

0.34

2GH 33.12 = 0.00

2CH

ABERPERGWM BCH

(NO.10. SIDING)

TERRA SIDING

162

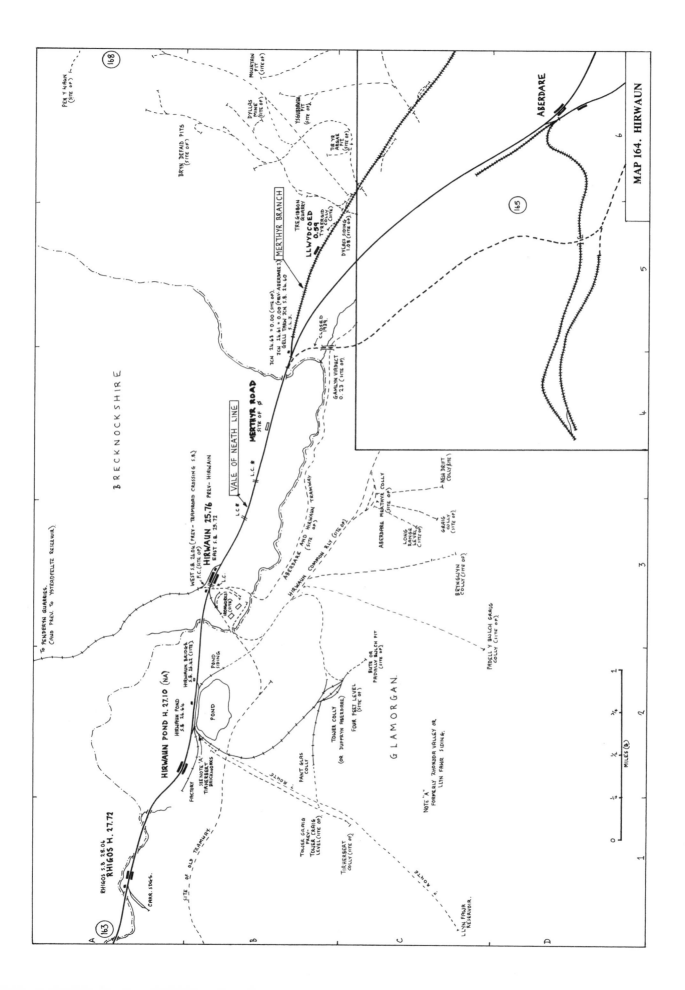

MAP 164. HIRWAUN

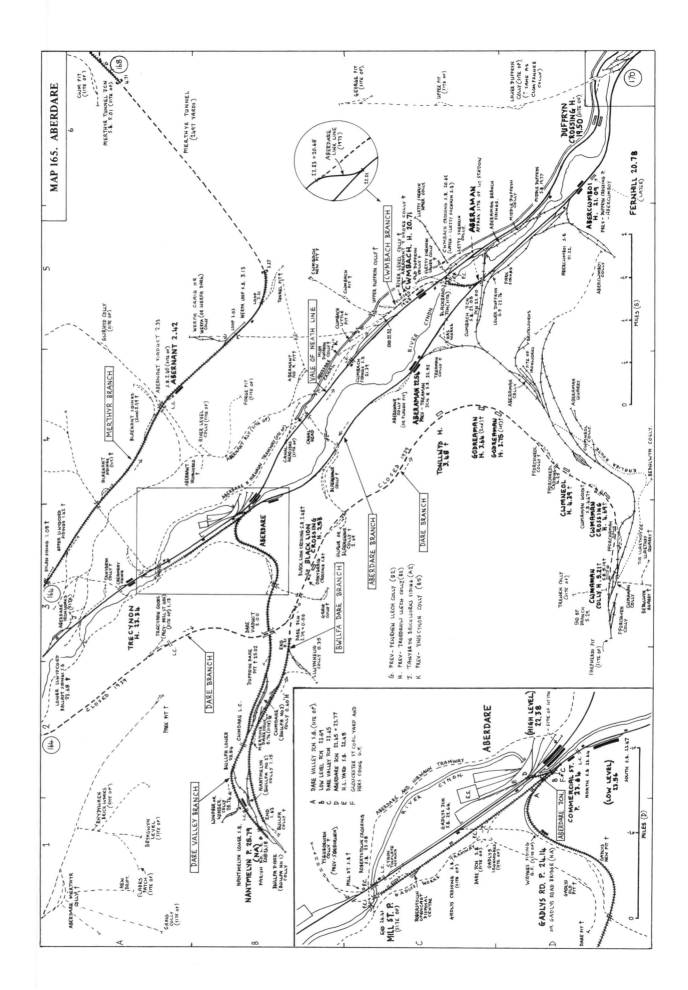

MAP 165. ABERDARE

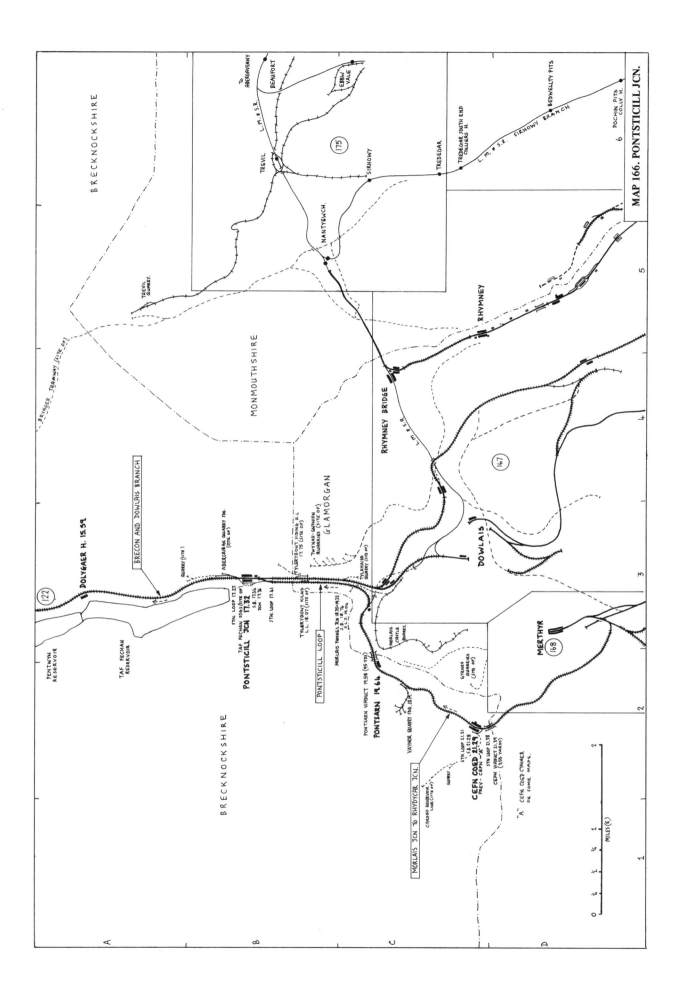

MAP 166. PONTSTICILL JCN.

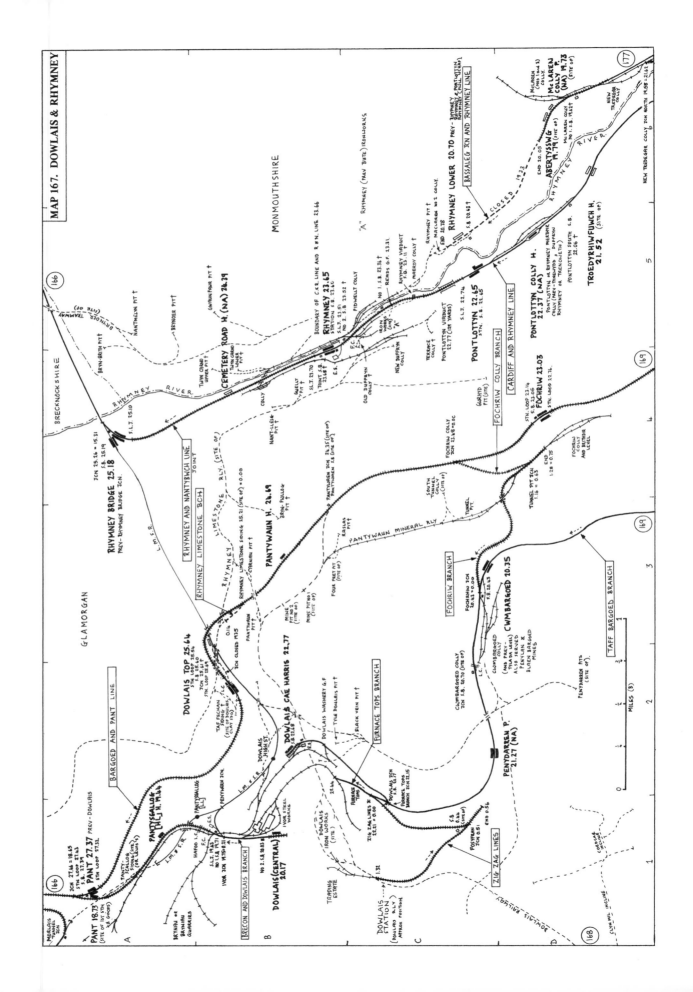

MAP 167. DOWLAIS & RHYMNEY

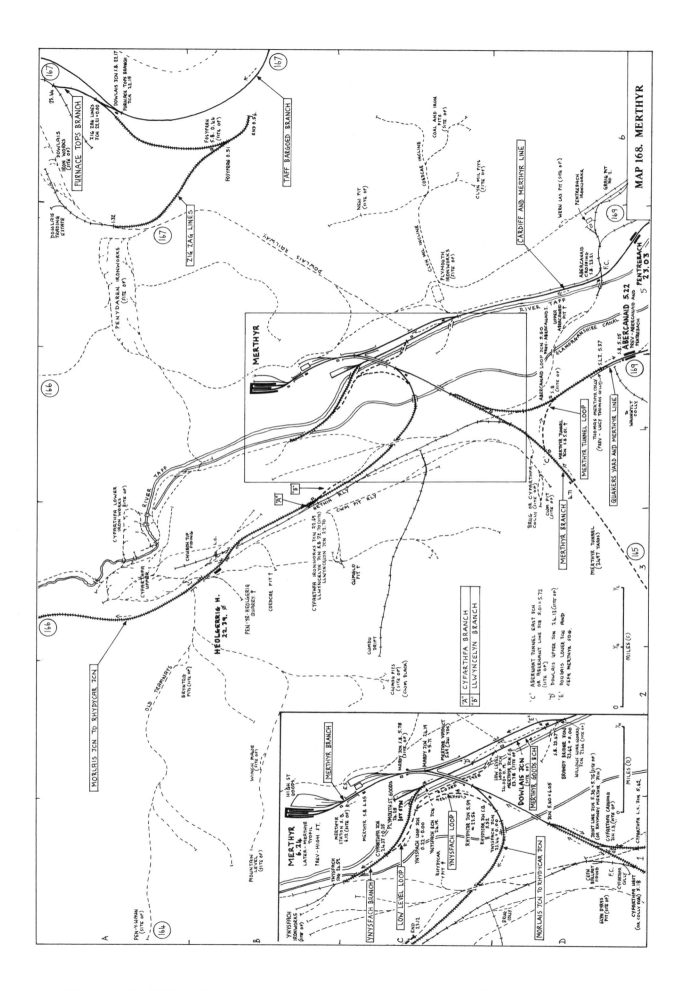

MAP 168. MERTHYR

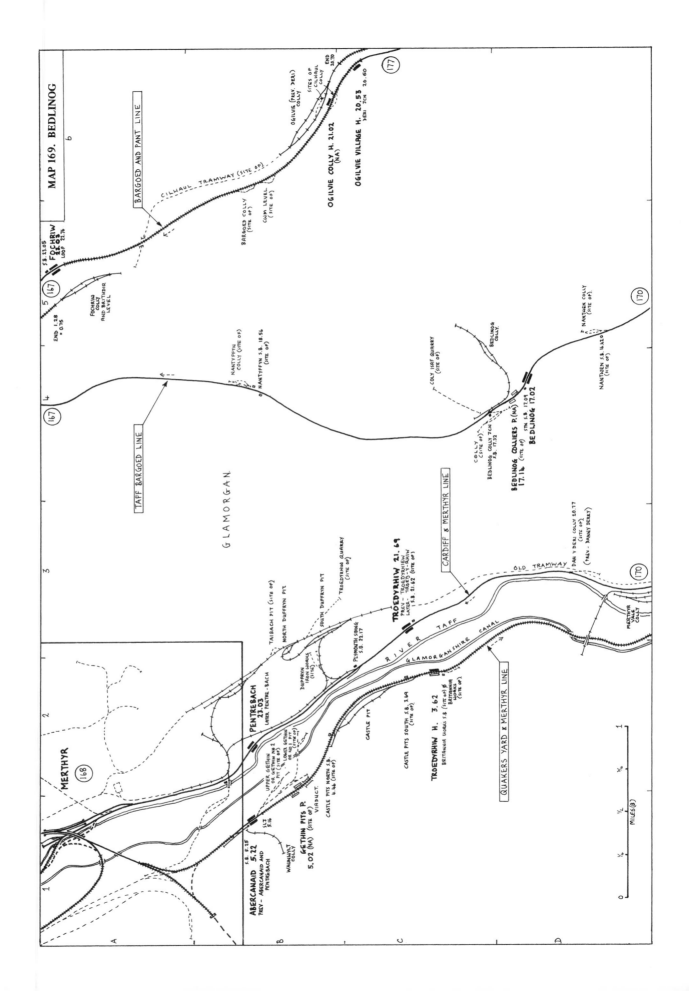

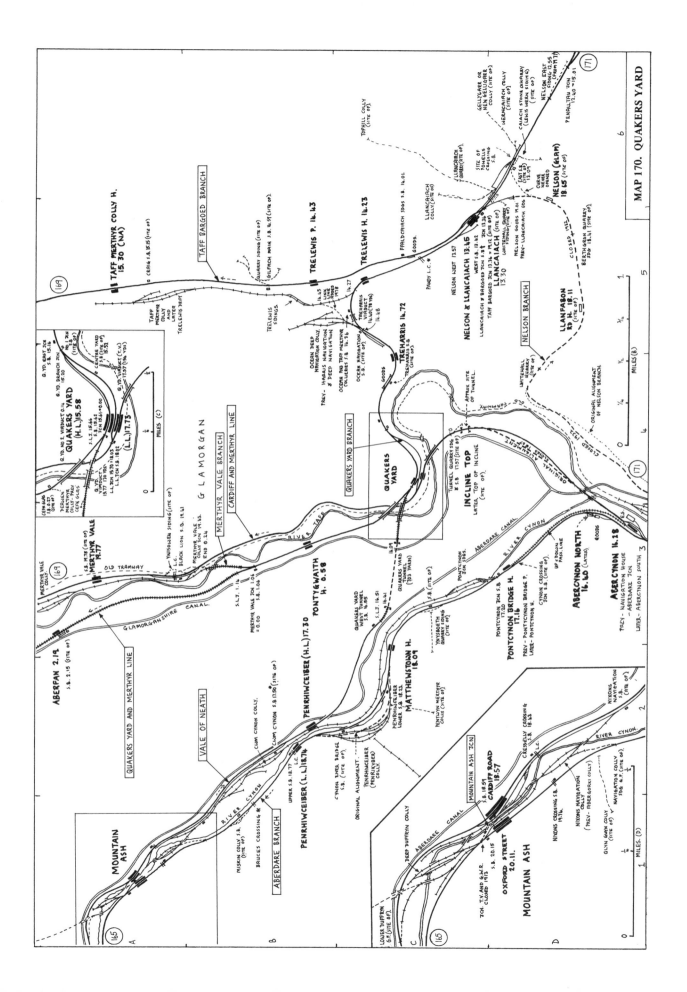

MAP 170. QUAKERS YARD

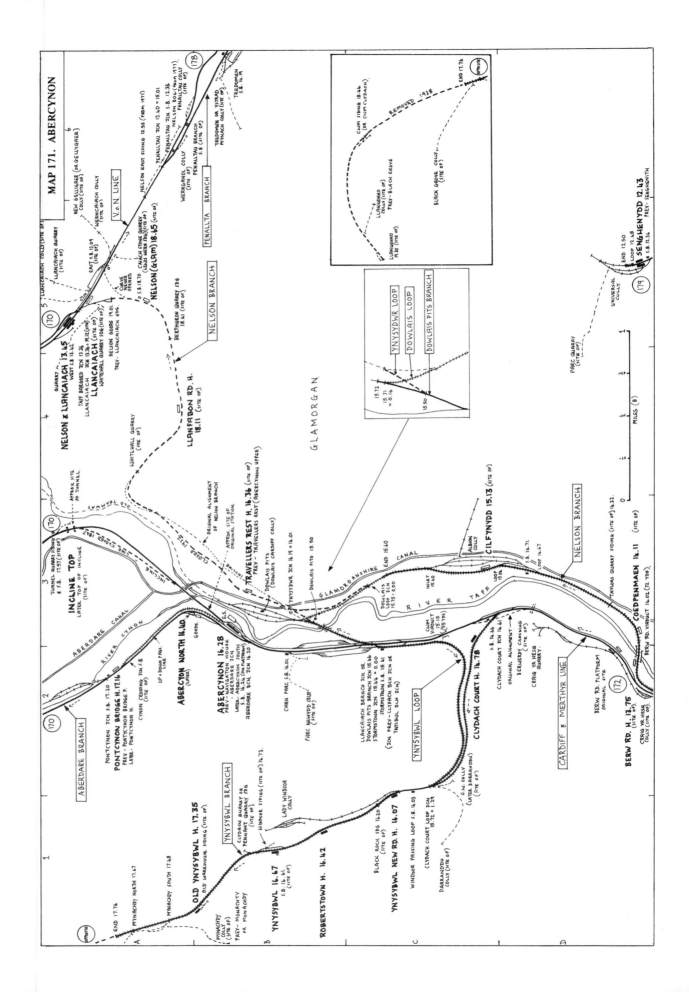

MAP 171. ABERCYNON

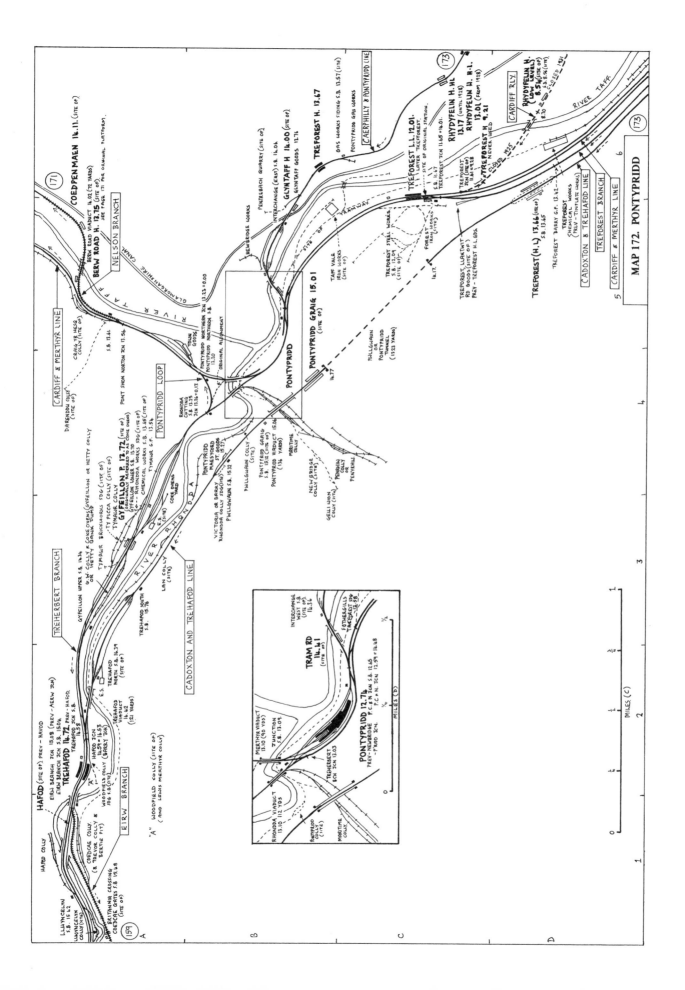

MAP 172. PONTYPRIDD

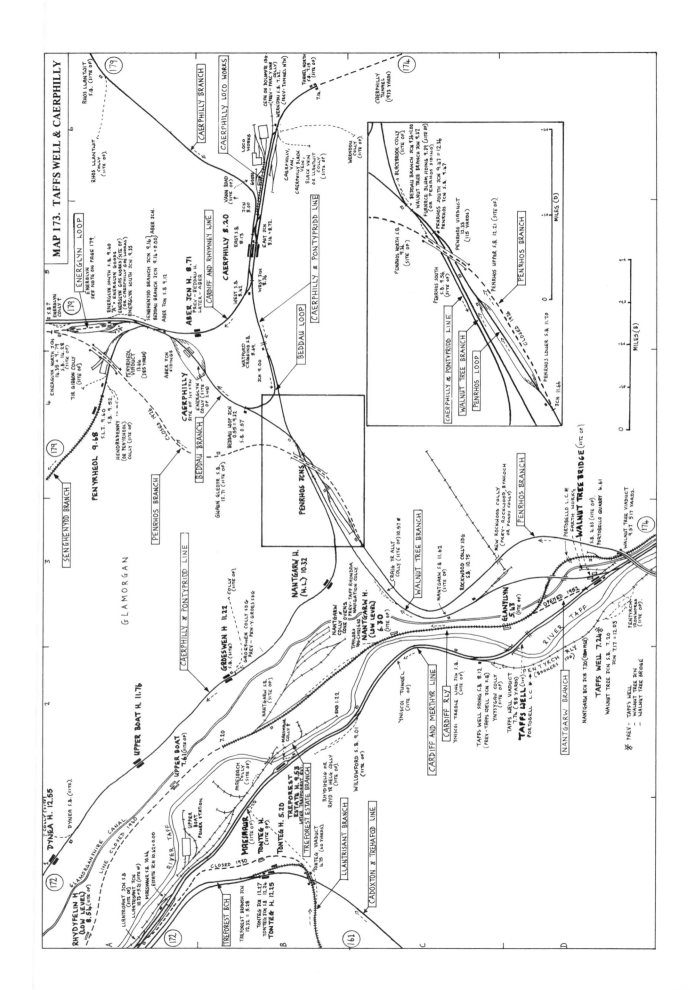

MAP 173. TAFFS WELL & CAERPHILLY

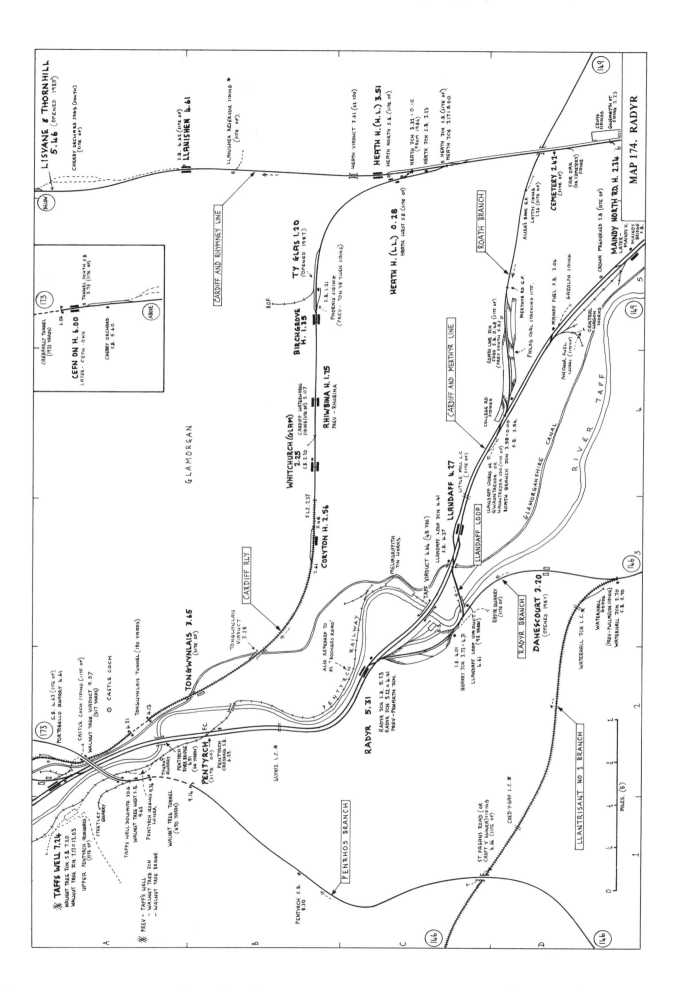

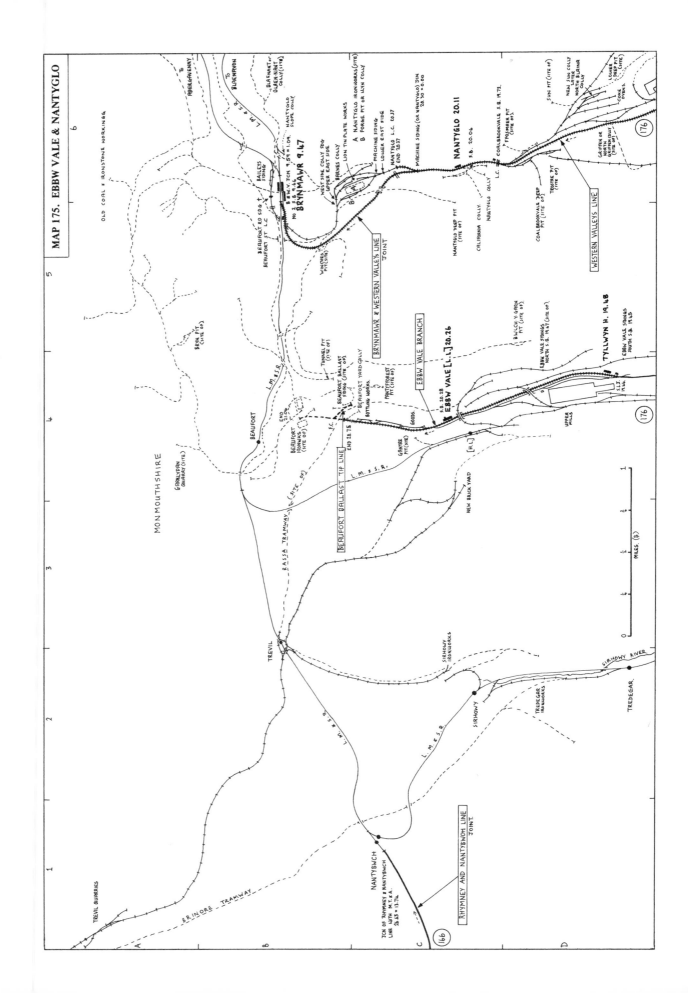

MAP 175. EBBW VALE & NANTYGLO

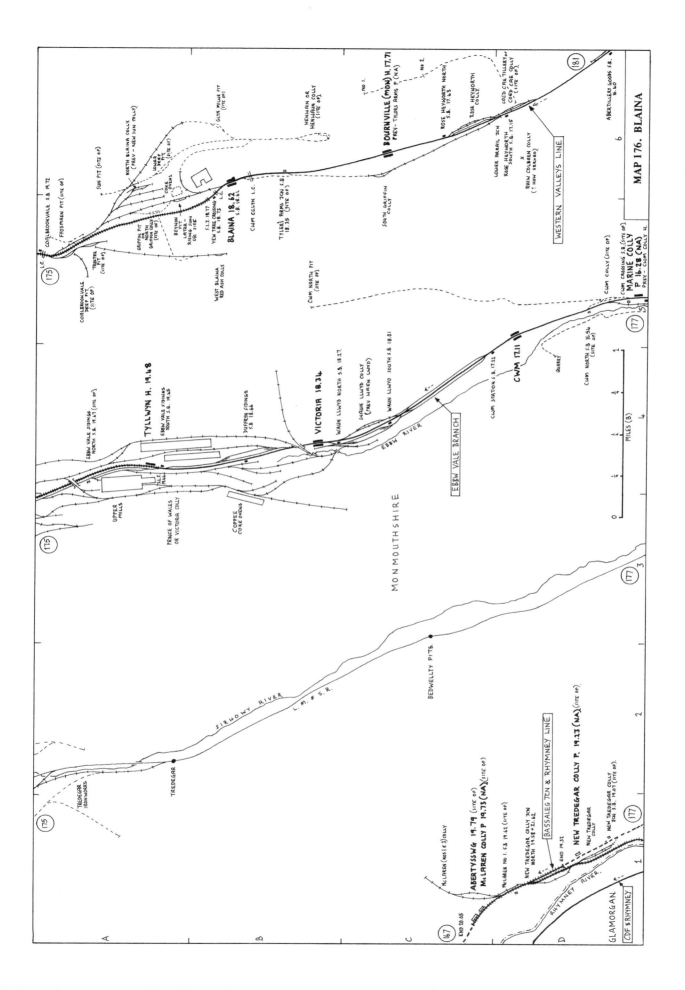

MAP 176. BLAINA

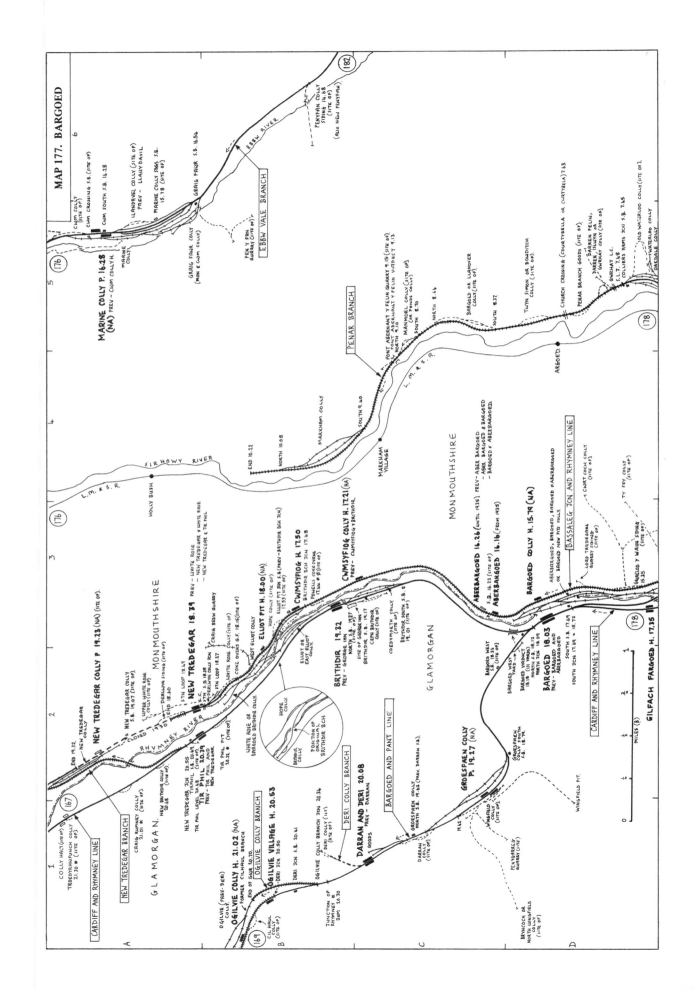

MAP 177. BARGOED

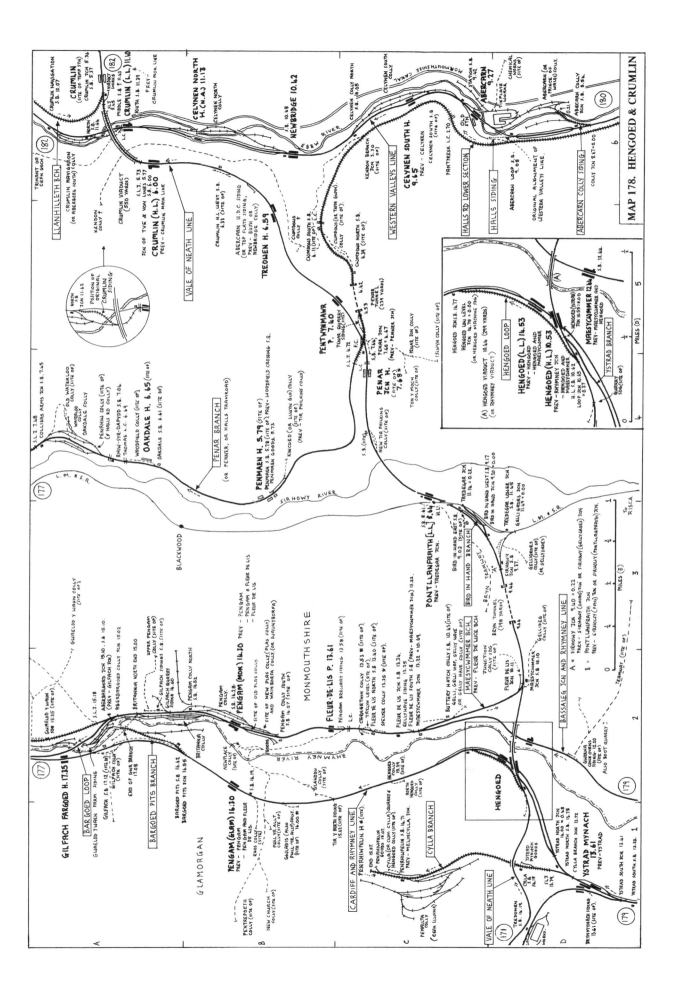

MAP 178. HENGOED & CRUMLIN

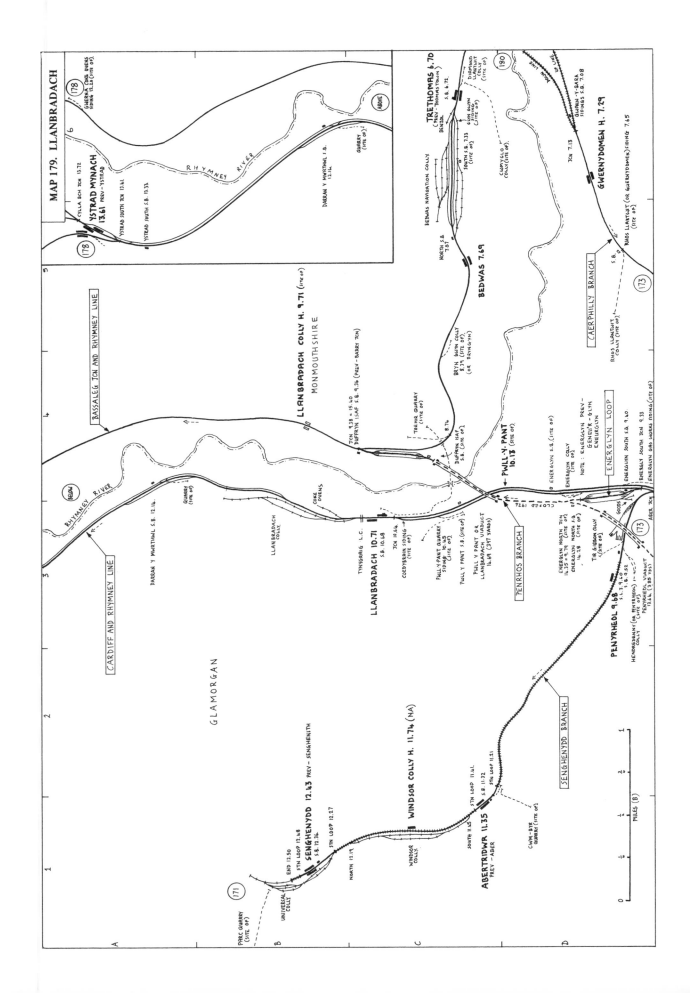

MAP 179. LLANBRADACH

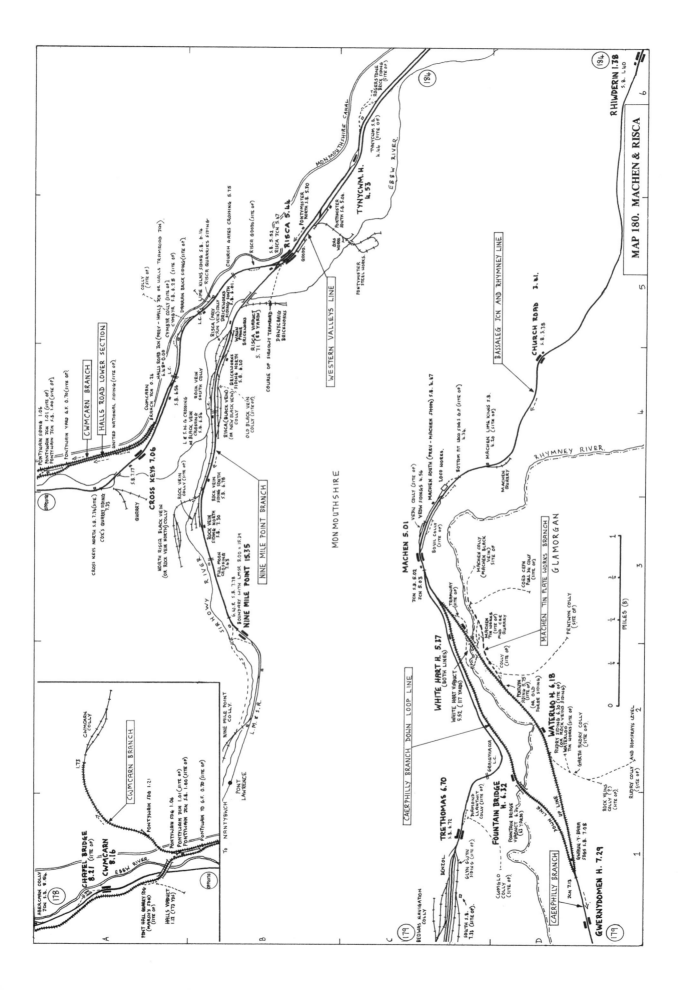

MAP 180. MACHEN & RISCA

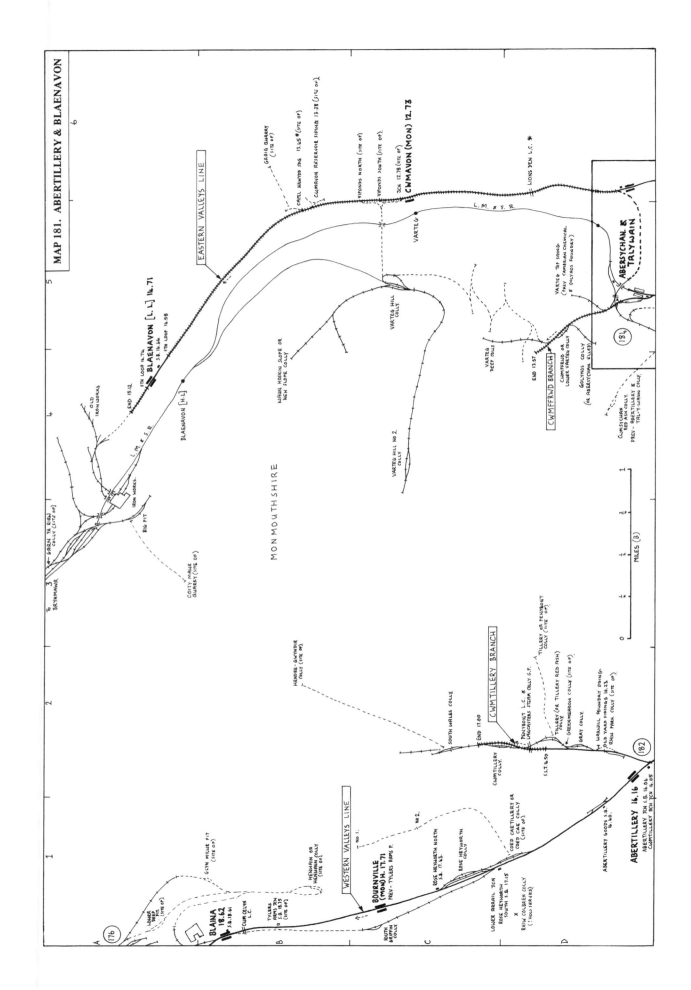

MAP 181. ABERTILLERY & BLAENAVON

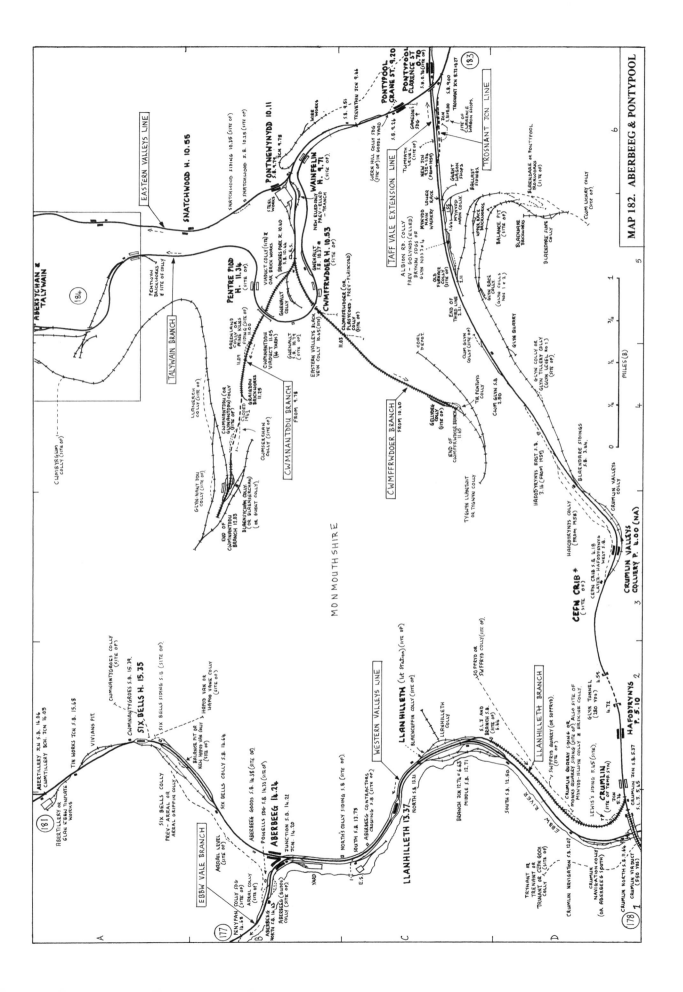

MAP 182. ABERBEEG & PONTYPOOL

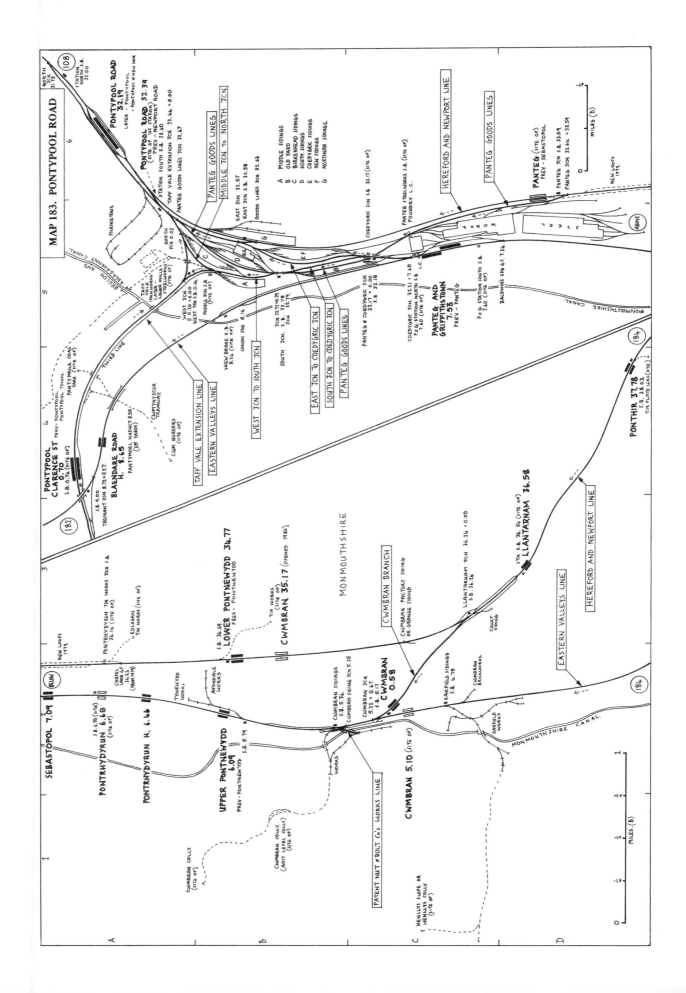

MAP 183. PONTYPOOL ROAD

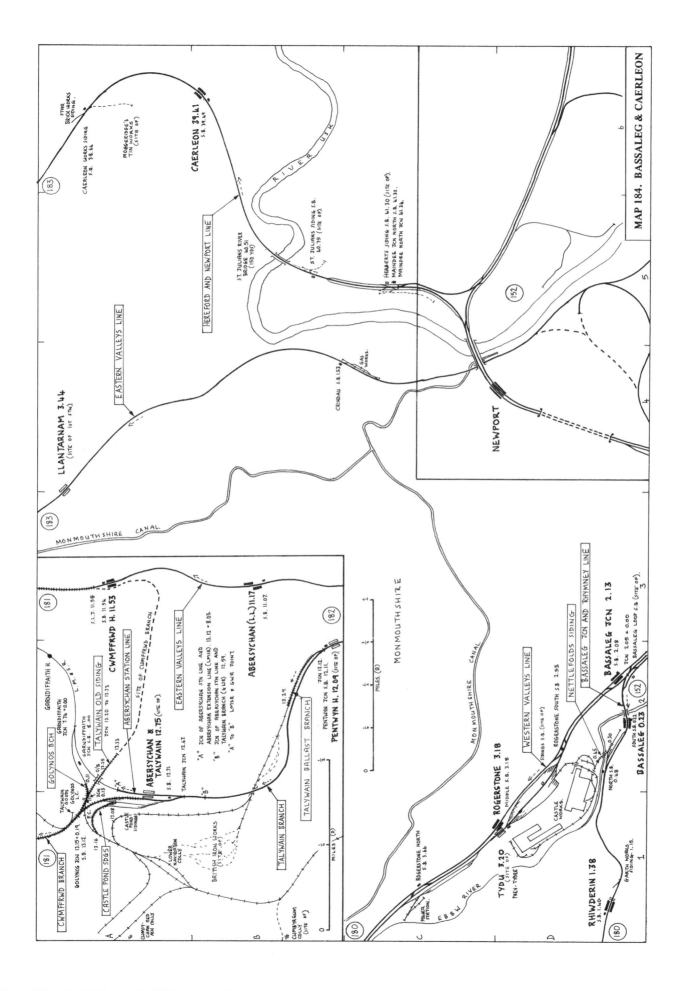

MAP 184. BASSALEG & CAERLEON

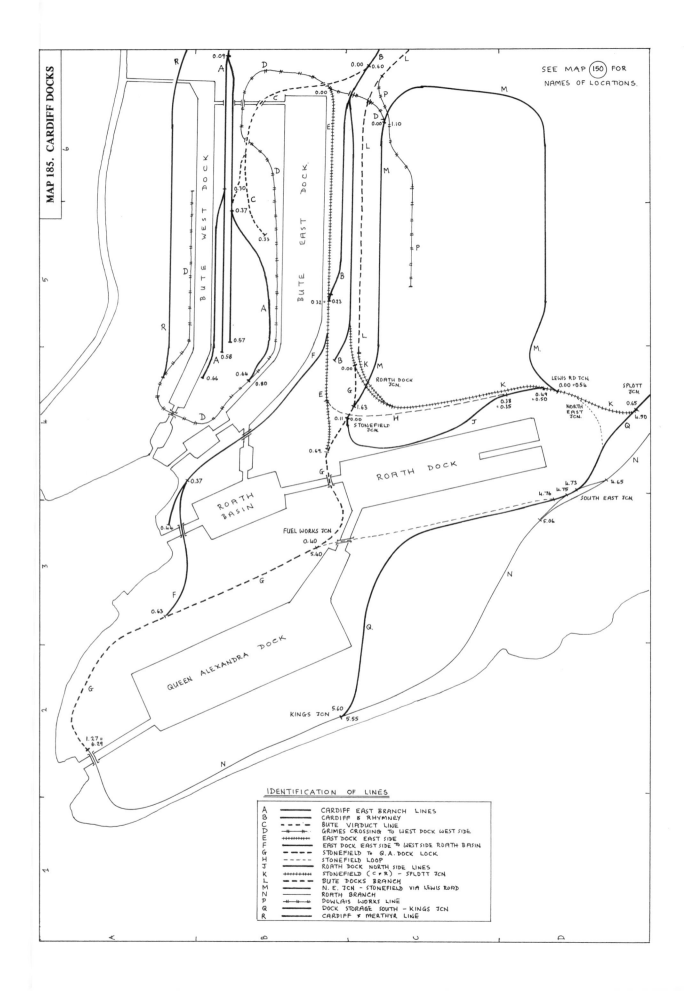

MAP 185. CARDIFF DOCKS

SEE MAP (150) FOR NAMES OF LOCATIONS.

IDENTIFICATION OF LINES

A		CARDIFF EAST BRANCH LINES
B		CARDIFF & RHYMNEY
C		BUTE VIADUCT LINE
D		GRIMES CROSSING TO WEST DOCK WEST SIDE
E		EAST DOCK EAST SIDE
F		EAST DOCK EAST SIDE TO WEST SIDE ROATH BASIN
G		STONEFIELD TO Q.A. DOCK LOCK
H		STONEFIELD LOOP
J		ROATH DOCK NORTH SIDE LINES
K		STONEFIELD (C+R) - SPLOTT JCN
L		BUTE DOCKS BRANCH
M		N. E. JCN - STONEFIELD VIA LEWIS ROAD
N		ROATH BRANCH
P		DOWLAIS WORKS LINE
Q		DOCK STORAGE SOUTH - KINGS JCN
R		CARDIFF & MERTHYR LINE

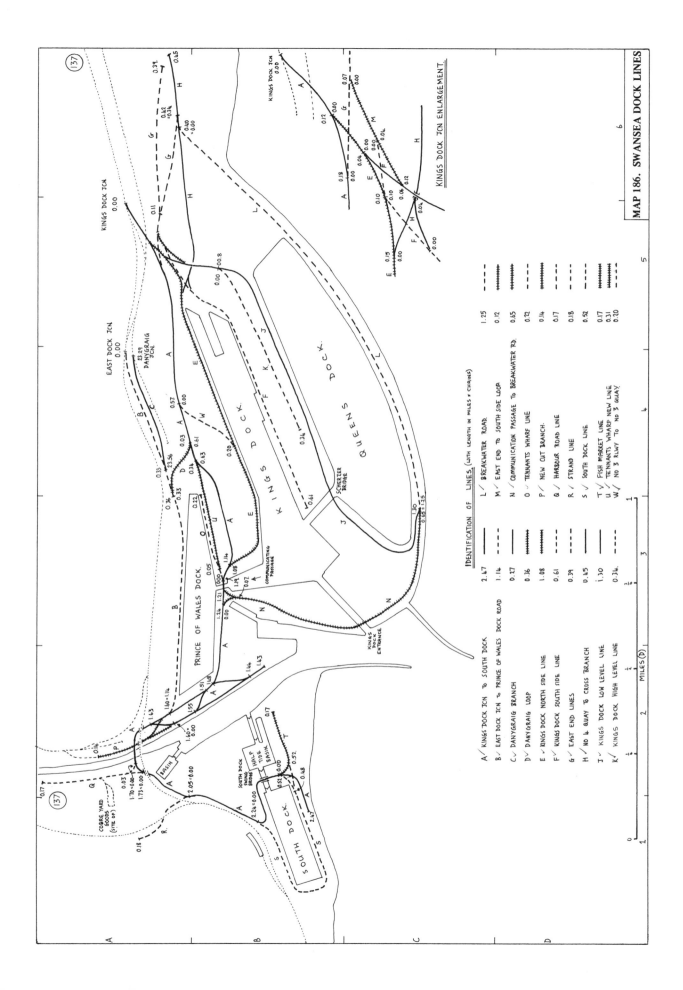

MAP 186. SWANSEA DOCK LINES

KINGS DOCK JCN ENLARGEMENT.

IDENTIFICATION OF LINES. (WITH LENGTH IN MILES & CHAINS)

A	KINGS DOCK JCN TO SOUTH DOCK.	2.47	L	BREAKWATER ROAD.		1.25
B	EAST DOCK JCN TO PRINCE OF WALES DOCK ROAD	1.14	M	EAST END TO SOUTH SIDE LOOP		0.12
C	DANYGRAIG BRANCH	0.27	N	COMMUNICATION PASSAGE TO BREAKWATER RD.		0.65
D	DANYGRAIG LOOP	0.36	O	TENNANTS WHARF LINE		0.72
E	KINGS DOCK NORTH SIDE LINE	1.08	P	NEW CUT BRANCH.		0.14
F	KINGS DOCK SOUTH SIDE LINE	0.61	Q	HARBOUR ROAD LINE		0.17
G	EAST END LINES	0.39	R	STRAND LINE		0.18
H	NO 4 QUAY TO CROSS BRANCH	0.45	S	SOUTH DOCK LINE		0.52
J	KINGS DOCK LOW LEVEL LINE	1.30	T	FISH MARKET LINE		0.17
			U	TENNANTS WHARF NEW LINE		0.31
K	KINGS DOCK HIGH LEVEL LINE	0.34	W	NO 3 RLWY TO NO 3 QUAY		0.10

MILES (D)

APPENDIX A
INDEX TO LINES AND BRANCHES

Many lines will be known by a familiar name; however, the GWR actually allocated most lines, branches and, in some cases, even sidings or depots, a specific name. Unfortunately, over the years conventions for the inclusion or exclusion of lines within this process changed. Furthermore, even the official name sometimes had official alternatives and in some cases a line which had been closed and which was later reopened, received a different name to that used originally.

The pages that follow are an attempt to list all lines and branches including those closed pre-, or opened post-, 1947. Certain entries will no doubt cause eyebrows to be raised, as to how they could be included, witness the Stoneycombe Branch, in reality no more than a siding parallel to the main line, and there are many other such examples. However, any entry appearing in official records has been included, together with a few which, for some equally mysterious reason, were never listed (these have been identified as such in the index). Only those names used colloquially have been excluded.

The list has been culled from various sources, but I am deeply indebted to John Mann, of the WR Area Civil Engineer's office at Bristol, on whose work the majority of this list is based. Without his very considerable advice and assistance, many problems would have remained unresolved. Any errors or omissions, however, remain my sole responsibility.

INDEX TO LINES AND BRANCHES

* = Closed Pre 1947   A = Not listed in GWR/WR records.
≠ = Opened Post 1947   B = Partly or wholly private

193

	Line or Branch	Co.	Map No.	Alternative Name
	Berks & Hants Line		32, 33, 46, 48, 49	
	Bewdley Curve		77	Kidderminster Loop
*	Bicslade Tramway	S&W Jt	54	
	Bilson Loop		54	
	Bilston Branch		75	Hickmans Branch
	Bilston Goods Branch		75	
	Bird-in-Hand Branch		178	
	Birkenhead Goods Extension Line	LNW Jt	90	
	Birmingham & Gloucester Line	Mid	55, 56	
	Birmingham & North Warwickshire Line		80–82	
	Birmingham Loop (at Worcester)		60	Wolverhampton Loop
*	Bishops Wood Tramway	S&W Jt	53, 54	
	Blackmill Branch		143, 157, 160	
	Black Park, Chirk		95	
	Blaenau Festiniog Branch		109, 111	Bala & Festiniog Branch
	Blaenavon Branch	PT	153	
	Blaenavon Loop	PT	153	
	Blaenrhondda Branch	TV	158	
	Bodmin Branch		5, 6	
	Bordesley Junction Branch		80	
*	Bordesley Disused Branch		80	
	Boscarne Extension		5	
	Bradford Branch		27, 46	
	Bradford-on-Avon Loop		46	
	Breakwater Branch Extension	LSW Jt	42	
	Breakwater Road (Swansea)	SHT	186	
	Brecon & Dowlais Line	B&M	122, 166, 167	
	Brecon Curve	LNW Jt	104	
	Brecon Goods Yard Branch	B&M	122	
	Brentford Branch		37	
	Bridgend & Abergwynfi Line		143, 144, 155–157	
A ≠	Bridgwater Chord Line	BR (WR)	19	
	Bridgwater Dock Branch		19	
	Bridport Branch		41	
	Bristol & South Wales Union Line		23, 24, 52	
	Bristol Harbour Branch		24	
	Bristol Loop		24	
	Bristol Relief Line		24	
A	Bristol Temple Meads Old Station		24	
	Brithdir Branch	B&M	177	
	Briton Ferry Dock Branch (GWR)		140	
	Briton Ferry Dock Branch (RSB)		140	
	Brixham Branch		12	
	Brofiscin Branch		161	Mwyndy Branch
	Bromyard Branch		61, 102	
	Brook Lane to Tunnel Junction	LNW Jt	88	Chester Curve
	Brook Street to Shore Road	LNW Jt	90	
A	Brymbo Colly Branch		93	
*	Brynmally Branch		93	
	Brynmawr & Western Valleys Line	LNW Jt	175	
	Brynmenyn Loop		143	
*	Bryn-yr-Owen Branch		94	Legacy Branch
	Bullo Dock Branch		53	
	Burlish Branch		72	
	Burrows Junction to North Bank Goods	PT	141	
	Burry Port & Gwendraeth Valley Bch	BPGV	133, 134	Cwmmawr Branch
	Burry Port Canal Branch	BPGV	134	
	Burry Port Engine Shed Line	BPGV	134	
	Bushbury Branch		74	
	Bute Dock Branch		149, 150	
	Bute Viaduct Lines	Cdf	150	
	Butts Branch		60	
	Bwllfa Dare Branch		165	
	Cadoxton & Trehafod Line	Bry	146–8, 161, 172, 173	
	Cadoxton Goods Branch	TV	148	
*	Caedu Incline		160	
	Caerphilly & Pontypridd Line	ANDR	172, 173	
	Caerphilly Branch	B&M	173, 179, 180	
	Caerphilly Branch Down Loop Line	B&M	180	
	Caerphilly Loco Works	Rhy	173	
	Caerwent Branch		52	
	Caisson Lines (Barry)	Bry	148	
	Caisson Lines to S. Side Lines Dock No. 1	Bry	148	

	Line or Branch	Co.	Map No.	Alternative Name
	Calne Branch		28	
*	Camerton Branch		27	
	Canons Marsh Branch		24	
	Canons Marsh to Corporation Railway		24	
	Carbean Branch		4	
	Carbis Branch		4	
	Cardiff & Merthyr Line	TV	149, 150, 168–174	
	Cardiff & Ogmore Branch		143, 145, 157	
	Cardiff & Rhymney Line	Rhy	149, 150, 167, 173, 174, 176–179	
	Cardiff East Branch	TV	149, 150	
	Cardiff East Junction		149	
*	Cardiff East Junction (Old)		149	
	Cardiff Queen Street North Junction		149	
	Cardiff Railway	Cdf	172–174	
	Cardiff Riverside Branch		149	
	Cardigan Branch		125	Whitland & Cardigan Branch
	Carmarthen & Newcastle Emlyn Line		128, 129	
	Carmarthen West Loop		129	
	Carnarvon Branch		134	
	Carne Point Branch		5	
*	Castella Branch		161	
	Castle Cary & Langport Line		20, 43	
A	Castle Pond Sidings		184	
	Castleton Tramway	LSW Jt	42	
	Cathcart Street Jcn to Goods Shed	LNW Jt	90	
	Cawdor Branch		131	
*	Chacewater West Loop		2	Truro & Newquay West Loop
	Chard Branch		20	
	Cheddar Valley Branch		21, 22	
	Chelsea Basin Branch	WL Jt	38	
	Cheltenham & Honeybourne Line		55, 56, 62, 63	Honeybourne & Cheltenham Line
	Cheltenham Branch		55, 56	
	Cheltenham Loop		56	Gloucester Old Avoiding Line (previously)
	Chester & Birkenhead Line	LNW Jt	88–91	
	Chester Curve	LNW Jt	88	Brook Lane Jcn to Tunnel Jcn
	Chester & Warrington Line	LNW Jt	88, 91	
	Chipping Norton Loop		65	Kingham Loop
≠	Chittening Estate Line	BR (WR)	25	
	Cinderford Branch		53, 54	
	Cinderford North Loop	S&W Jt	54	
	Cinderford South Loop	S&W Jt	54	
	Cirencester Branch		59	
	City Lines (At Paddington)		39	
	Clarbeston Road & Letterston Line		123	
	Clee Hill Branch	LNW Jt	101	
	Cleobury Mortimer & Ditton Priors Bch		71, 72	Ditton Priors Branch
	Clevedon Branch		21	
	Clifton Extension Line	Mid Jt	23, 25	
*	Clifton May Bank Branch		44	
*	Clutton Branch		27	
	Clydach Vale Branch	TV	159	
	Cobre Yard	RSB	137	
	Cockett Goods Branch		135	
	Codsall Loop		74	
	Coegnant Branch		156	Duffryn Branch
A*	Colcerrow Branch		4	
	Coleford Branch (GW)		53	
	Coleford Branch (S&W)	S&W Jt	53, 54	
	Coley Branch		33	
*	Common Branch	TV	161	
*	Common Branch Loop Line	TV	161	
	Communication Psge Bridge to Breakwater Rd	SHT	136	
	Conveyor Road (No. 11) (Port Talbot)	PT	141	
	Conveyor Road (Nos. 9 & 10) (Port Talbot)	PT	141	
	Copper Works Jcn to Steelworks Wharf (Port Talbot)	PT	141	
	Corngreaves Branch		76, 77	
	Cornwall Loop		8	
	Corris Railway	Corris	113	
*	Corris Railway Disused Branch	Corris	113	
	Corwen Junction		112	Denbigh Branch
	Court Sart Branch to GWR	RSB	140	
	Court Sart Bch to S. Wls. Mineral Rly	RSB	140	
	Court Sart Flying Loop		140	

Line or Branch	Co.	Map No.	Alternative Name
Cowbridge Goods Yard Line	TV	144	
Cowbridge Road Junction to Bridgend	Bry	144	
Criggion Branch	S&M	98	
Crimea Yard Line		39	
Crockherbtown Loop	Rhy	149	
Crosshands Branch		131	Mountain Branch
Crumlin Burrows Goods Line		137	
Crumlin Siding		178	
Crystal Palace Loop		39	
Culm Valley Branch		16	
* Cwmaman Branch		165	Dare Branch
Cwmbach Branch	TV	165	
Cwmbran Branch		183	Llantarnam (or Passenger) Branch
* Cwmcapel Branch	BPGV	134	
Cwmcarn Branch		180	
Cwmffrwd Branch		181, 184	
Cwmffrwdoer Branch		182	
Cwmgorse Branch		131	
Cwmmawr Branch	BPGV	133, 134	Burry Port & Gwendraeth Valley Branch
Cwmnantddu Branch		182	
Cwmtillery Branch		181	
A Cyfarthfa Branch		168	
Cylla Branch	Rhy	178	
Cymmer Branch	RSB	155	
Cymmer Junction Loop		155	
Dafen Branch		134	St. David's Branch
Danygraig Branch	RSB	186	
Danygraig Depot		137	
Danygraig Loop	SHT	186	
* Dare Branch		165	Cwmaman Branch
Dare Valley Branch	TV	165	
Denbigh Branch		112	Corwen Junction
Denham & Uxbridge Branch		35	
Denham East Curve		35	
A* Deri Colly Branch		177	
B Devonport Dockyard Branch		8	
Devonport Goods Branch		8	
Didcot & Chester Line		30, 31, 67–70, 74, 75, 79–85, 91–96, 98, 99	
Didcot East Curve		30	
B Didcot Ordnance Depot		30	
B≠ Didcot Power Station	BR (WR)	30	
Didcot West Curve		30	
* Dimbath Branch		157, 160	
Dinas Mawddwy Branch	Cam	115	Mawddwy Branch
Ditton Priors Branch	CMDP	71, 72	Cleobury Mortimer & Ditton Priors Branch
Docks Extension Branch (P. Talbot)	PT	141	
Dock Storage S. Jc to Kings Jc (Cardiff)	Cdf	150	
* Dock Street to Salutation Junction		152	
Dolgelley Branch	Cam	110	
Dorchester Junction		41	
Dovey Junction to Pwllheli	Cam	109, 110, 113	
Dowlais Loop	TV	171	
Dowlais Pits Branch	TV	171	
Dowlais Works Branch (at Cardiff)		150	
Drinnick Mill Goods Branch		4	
Duffryn Branch		156	Coegnant Branch
Dunball Wharf Branch		19	
A Dunraven Siding	TV	158	
Durston Loop		20	
Dynevor Junction to Cardonnel Jcn	RSB	139	
A* Ealing Broadway Junction		38	
* Eardisley Branch		103	
Earls Court Junction	WL Jt	38	
East Dock Branch (Swansea)		137	
East Dock East Side (Cardiff)	Cdf	150	
East Dock E. Side to W. Side Roath Basin	Cdf	150	
East Dock Jc to P. of W. Dock Road	SHT	186	
East End Lines (Swansea)	SHT	186	
East End to South Side Loop	SHT	186	
Eastern Valleys Line		152, 181–184	
East Mendalgief Jc to 18–20 Hoists	ANDR	151	

	Line or Branch	Co.	Map No.	Alternative Name
	East Mendalgief Jc to Rolling Brdge Jc.	ANDR	151	
	East Mendalgief Jc to South Dock	ANDR	151	
	Easton & Church Hope Railway	LSW Jt	42	
	East Somerset Branch		22, 45	
	East Usk Branch		151, 152	
	East Usk Wharf Siding		152	Nettlefolds Branch
*	East Wheal Rose Branch		3	
	Ebbw Vale Branch		175–177, 182	
	Eirw Branch	TV	159, 172	Aerw Branch
*	Ellesmere Loop Line	Cam	96	
	Ely Valley Line		145, 159–161	
*	Energlyn Loop	Bry	173, 179	
≠	Esso Refinery Branch	BR (WR)	124	
	Evesham Junction		62	
	Exeter Basin Branch		13	
	Exeter Low Level Loop		13	
	Exeter Railway		13	
	Exe Valley Branch		16	
	Exleys Tileworks Branch		70	
	Fairford Branch		66–68	
	Falmouth Branch		2	
	Faringdon Branch		29	
≠	Fenny Compton Junction	BR (WR)	83	
*	Ffrwd Branch		93	
	Filton Loop		23	
	Filton West Loop		23	
	Fishguard Harbour Lines		123	
	Fish Market Line (Swansea)	SHT	186	
≠	Fishponds Branch	BR (WR)	93	
	Fleur de Lis Branch (Prev. Fleur de Luce)		178	Maesycwmmer Branch
	Float Works Branch (Port Talbot)	PT	141	
	Fochriw Branch	Rhy Jt	167	
A	Fochriw Colly Branch	B&M	167	
B ≠	Fords Factory Branch	BR (WR)	144	
	Forest of Dean Branch		53, 54	
	Forest of Dean Central Branch		53, 54	
	Fowey Branch		5, 6	
	Frome & North Somerset Line		24, 27, 45	North Somerset Line
	Frome Avoiding Line		45	
	Frome Mineral Loop		45	
	Fron Branch		95	
	Furnace Tops Branch	Rhy Jt	167, 168	
	Futterhill Branch	S&W Jt	54	
	Gaer Branch		152	
	Galton Branch		79	
	Garnant Branch		131	
	Garw Branch		143, 156, 157	
*	Genwen Branch		134	
	Gilfach Branch		160	
*	Glannant Siding		157	
B	Glascoed R.O.F. Branch		108	
	Gloucester Docks Branch		56	
*	Gloucester Old Avoiding Line		56	Later – Cheltenham Loop
*	Gloucester T Line		56	
	Golden Valley Branch		106, 107	
	Golynos Branch		184	
	Goonbarrow Branch		4	
	Grafton Curve		48	
	Grange Court & Hereford Line		53, 104, 105	
*	Gravel Bridge Loop	BPGV	134	
*	Gravel Hill Branch		2	
	Great Bridge Branch		75	
	Greenford East Curve		36	
*	Greyfield Colliery Branch		27	
	Grid Road (No. 4) (Port Talbot)	PT	141	
	Grimes Crossing to West Dock W. Side	Cdf	150	
*	Grove Junction	Met Jt	38	
≠	Grovesend Chord Line		135	
	Gueret's Works Lines (Barry)	Bry	148	
≠	Gulf Oil Refinery Branch	BR (WR)	124	
	Gwaun-Cae-Gurwen Branch		131	
	Gwendraeth Valley Branch	GV	133	

	Line or Branch	Co.	Map No.	Alternative Name
*	Gwersyllt Branch		93	
	Halesowen & Northfield Line	Mid Jt	77, 81	Longbridge & Halesowen Line
	Halesowen Basin Branch		77	
*	Halesowen Basin Loop		77	
	Halesowen Branch		77	
	Halls Road Lower Section		178, 180	
	Halls Siding		178	
	Hammersmith & City Line	Met Jt	39	
	Hammersmith Coal Yard		38	
	Hanwell Loop		37	
	Harbour Road Branch (Swansea)	SHT	186	
	Hatherley Curve		56	Hatherley Loop
	Hatherley Loop		56	Hatherley Curve
	Hatton Curve		82	
	Hay & Brecon Junction Line		104	
	Hayes Creosote Depot		37	
	Hayes Lane Branch		77	
	Hayle Wharf Branch		1	
≠B	Heathrow Link Line	Railtrack	35	
	Helston Branch		1	
	Hendford Goods Branch		44	
	Hendreforgan Branch		160	
	Hendy Loop		133	
	Hengoed Loop	Rhy	178	
*	Henley-in-Arden Branch		82	
	Henley-in-Arden Goods Branch		82	
	Henley-on-Thames Branch		34	
	Hereford & Newport Line		104, 107, 108, 152, 183, 184	
	Hereford Goods Lines		104	
	Hickmans Branch		75	Bilston Branch
	Highbridge Junction		19	
	Highworth Branch		29, 30	
	Hobbs Point Branch		126	
	Holyhead Junction to Joint Boundary	LNW Jt	88	
	Honeybourne & Cheltenham Line		55, 56, 62, 63	Cheltenham & Honeybourne Line
	Honeybourne North Loop		62	
	Honeybourne South Loop		62	
	Hookagate Junction	LNW Jt	98	
	Hooton & Helsby Line	LNW Jt	88, 89, 91	
	Hooton & West Kirby Line	LNW Jt	89, 91	
	Hot Metal Road (Port Talbot)	PT	141	
	Hotwells & Avonmouth Line	Mid Jt	25	
*	Howlerslade Tramway	S&W Jt	54	
	Jersey Marine Loop		138, 139, 140	
	Jersey Marine North Jcn		140	
	Jersey Marine North Loop		139	Neath Loop
	Jersey Marine South Jcn		140	
	Jersey Marine Yard Line		137, 140	
	Joint Line Jc to Rock Ferry New Station	LNW Jt	90	
	Kensington Coal Yard		38	Warwick Rd Coal Depot Branch
	Kerry Branch	Cam	116	
	Ketley Branch		69, 70	
	Kidderminster Loop		77	Bewdley Curve
	Kidwelly Branch	BPGV	133	
	Kidwelly Loop	BPGV	133	
	Kingham Loop		65	Chipping Norton Loop
	Kingsbridge Branch		11	
	Kings Dock High Level Lines (Swansea)	SHT	186	
	Kings Dock Jc to South Dock (Swansea)		186	
	Kings Dock Low Level Lines (Swansea)	SHT	186	
	Kings Dock North Side Lines (Swansea)	SHT	186	
	Kings Dock South Side Lines (Swansea)	SHT	186	
	Kingsland Road Sidings		24	
	Kingswinford Line		73, 74, 76	
	Kington Branch		102, 103	Leominster & New Radnor Branch
	Lambourn Valley Branch		49	
	Lampeter & Aberayron Branch		127	Aberayron Branch
	Landore Western Loop		136	Swansea Loop
*	Latimer Road Jc to Uxbridge Road Jc	Met Jt	38	
	Launceston Branch		7–10	
	Launceston Junction		9	

	Line or Branch	Co.	Map No.	Alternative Name
	Leamington East Junction		83	
≠	Leamington New Junction	BR (WR)	83	
	Leamington West Junction		83	
	Leckwith Loop		149	
	Ledbury Branch		55, 60, 105	
*	Legacy Branch		94	Bryn-yr-Owen Branch
	Leominster & New Radnor Branch		102, 103	Kington Branch
	Limestone Branch		130	
	Limpley Stoke & Camerton Branch		27	
*	Liskeard & Caradon Railway		6	
	Liskeard & Looe Railway		6	Looe & Moorswater Branch
	Liskeard Junction		6	
	Liskeard Loop		6	
*	Llanarth Branch		152	
	Llandaff Loop	TV	174	
	Llandilo Junction to Llanelly Line		134	
	Llandilo Loop Line		134	
	Llanelly & Mynydd Mawr Line		133, 134	Mynydd Mawr Branch
	Llanelly Dock Goods Branch		134	
	Llanelly Dock Loop		134	
	Llanelly Dock North Side		134	
	Llanelly to Llandilo Line		130, 131, 133, 134	
	Llanfyllin Branch	Cam	117, 119	
	Llangollen Goods Branch		112	
*	Llangurig Branch		120	
	Llanhilleth Branch		178, 182	
	Llantarnam Branch		183	Cwmbran (or Passenger) Branch
	Llantrisant Branch	TV	161, 173	
	Llantrisant Junction		145	
	Llantrisant No. 1 Branch	TV	146, 161, 174	
	Llanymynech Curve	Cam	119	
*	Llwyncelyn Branch	B&M/LNW Jt	168	
	Llwynenion Branch		94	
	Longbridge & Halesowen Line		77, 81	Halesowen & Northfield Line
*	Longdon Road Loop		64	
	Looe & Moorswater Branch		6	Liskeard & Looe Branch
	Lostwithiel & Fowey Branch		5, 6	
	Low Level Lines Dock No. 1 (Barry)	Bry	148	Barry Docks Low Level Lines
	Low Level Lines Dock No. 2 (Barry)	Bry	148	Barry Docks Low Level Lines
	Low Level Lines Jc Dock No. 2 (Barry)	Bry	148	
	Lydbrook Branch	S&W Jt	53, 54	
	Lydford Junction		9	
	Lydney East Loop	S&W Jt	54	
	Lydney Lower Dock Branch	S&W Jt	54	
	Lydney Upper Dock Branch	S&W Jt	54	
	Lydney West Loop	S&W Jt	54	
A*	Machen Tin Plate Works Branch	B&M	180	
	Madeley Branch		70	
	Maerdy Branch	TV	158, 159	Rhondda Fach Branch
	Maesycwmmer Branch		178	Fleur de Lis Branch
	Maes-y-Marchog Branch	N&B	132	
	Maindee East Loop		152	
	Main Line		1–8, 11–16, 19–21, 23, 24, 27–35, 37–39	
	Malmesbury Branch		28	
	Mansell Cutting to Burrows Junction	PT	141	
	Margam Abbey Junction		142	
	Margam Moors Junction		142	
	Margam East Junction		142	
	Margam West Junction		142	
	Margam West Curve	PT	141	
≠	Margam Yard Line	BR (WR)	142	
	Market Drayton Branch		69, 97, 99	
	Marlborough Branch		48	
	Marlborough Junction		48	
	Marlow Branch		34	
≠	Marsh Barton Estate Branch	BR (WR)	13	
	Marsh Depot Goods Branch		24	St. Phillips Marsh Goods Branch
	Mawddwy Branch	Cam.	115	Dinas Mawddwy Branch
	Meole Brace Junction	LNW Jt	99	
B≠	Merehead Branch	BR (WR)	45	
A≠B	Merehead East Curve	BR (WR)	45	
	Merthyr Branch		164, 165, 168	

199

	Line or Branch	Co.	Map No.	Alternative Name
	Merthyr Goods Branch	TV	168	
	Merthyr Low Level Loop	B&M/LNW Jt	168	
	Merthyr Tunnel Loop	Rhy Jt	168	Abercanaid Loop
	Merthyr Vale Branch	Rhy Jt	170	
A	Mickle Trafford Jcn	LNW Jt	91	
	Milford Haven Branch		124, 126	Old Milford Branch
	Millbay Docks Line		8	Plymouth Docks Branch
	Minehead Branch		15, 17	
	Mineral Loop	S&W Jt	54	
	Minera Mineral Branch		93	
B	Ministry of Works Loop		26	Westerleigh East Loop
	Minsterley Branch	LNW Jt	98	
	Moat Lane Junction to Talyllyn	Cam	116, 120–122	
B	Monds Works Loop		135	
	Monks Ferry Branch	LNW Jt	90	
	Monmouthshire Loop	ANDR	152	
	Monway Branch		75	Wednesbury Branch
	Moorfields Loop		104	
	Moor Lane Goods Line		76	
A	Moor Street Station		80	
	Moreton & Shipston Tramway		64	Shipston on Stour Branch
	Moretonhampstead Branch		14	
	Morlais Junction to Rhydycar Jcn	B&M/LNW Jt	166, 168	
	Morpeth Dock		90	
	Morriston Branch		136, 138	
	Moss Valley Branch		93	
*	Mountain Ash Junction	TV	170	
	Mountain Branch		131	Crosshands Branch
	Much Wenlock Branch		69, 71, 100	
	Mwyndy Branch		161	Brofiscin Branch
	Mynydd Mawr Branch	LMM	133, 134	Llanelly & Mynydd Mawr Branch
	Mynydd Mawr Loop	LMM	134	
A*	Nant Colly Branch		93	
≠	Nantgarw Branch	BR (WR)	173	
	Nantmawr Branch	Cam	119	
	Neath & Brecon Line	N&B	122, 132, 153, 162	
	Neath Canalside Branch	RSB	139	
	Neath Harbour Junction	SW Min	140	
	Neath Junction		139	
	Neath Loop		139	Jersey Marine North Loop
	Neath Yard Line	N&B	139	
	Nelson Branch	TV	170–172	
	Netherton Branch		76	Withymoor Branch
	Nettlefolds Branch (Newport)		152	East Usk Wharf Siding
	Nettlefolds Siding (Bassaleg)	B&M	184	
	Neutral Mile		152	
	Newbury & Didcot Line		30, 31, 49	
	Newbury & Winchester Line		49–51	
	New Cut Branch (Swansea)	SHT	186	
	Newham Branch		2	
≠	Newlands Loop	BR (WR)	142	
*	New Passage Pier		23	
	Newport Low Level Loop	ANDR	152	
	Newport Low Level Loop No. 1		152	
	Newport Old Dock Branch		152	Pillgwenlly Branch
	Newport Town Dock East Side		152	
	Newport Town Dock West Side		152	
	Newport Western Loop		152	
	Newquay Branch		3, 5	
*	Newquay Harbour Line		3	
	Newtown Goods Depot	Cam	116	
	New Tredegar Branch	Rhy	177	
	Nine Mile Point Branch		180	
	North Acton to Viaduct Junction Line		38, 39	
	North Bank Junction to Talbot Wharf	PT	141	
	North Bank Loop and Mansell Cutting	PT	141	
	North Crofty Branch		1	
	North East Junction to Stonefield	Cdf Rly	150	
	Northolt & Ashendon Line	GC Jt	34–36, 86, 87	
	North Pembroke & Fishguard Line		123	
	North Somerset Line		24, 27, 45	Frome & North Somerset Line
	North Quay Branch (Plymouth)		8	
*	North Wales Junction	S&M	99	Potteries Loop

Line or Branch	Co.	Map No.	Alternative Name
No. 3 Railway to No.3 Quay (Swansea)		186	
No. 4 Quay to Cross Bank (Swansea)	SHT	186	
* No. 8 Railway	RSB	153, 154	Pontrhydyfen Branch
No. 10 Railway		163	Aberpergwm Branch
Nos. 1–3 Tips, empty (Port Talbot)	PT	141	
Nos. 1–3 Tips, full (Port Talbot)	PT	141	
Oakwood Branch	S&W Jt	54	
Ogilvie Colliery Branch	Rhy	177	
Ogmore Branch		157, 160	
Ogmore Vale Extension Line	PT	141–143	
Oldbury Branch		79	
* Old Carway Branch	BPGV	133	
Old Llanfyllin Branch		119	Rock Siding
Old Milford Branch		124, 126	Milford Haven Branch
Oldminster Goods Lines	S&W Jt	58	
Oswestry Branch		96	
Oswestry Loop	Cam	96	
Overbridge Lines (Old Oak Common)		39	
* Oxford Millstream Jc to Old Station		68	
≠ Oxford New Junction	BR (WR)	68	
Oxford North Junction		68	
Oxford, Worcester & Wolverhampton Line		60–62, 64, 65, 67, 68, 74–78	
Paddington Goods Lines		39	
Panteg Goods Lines		183	
Par Docks Branch		5	
Par Harbour Branch		5	
Parkend Goods Branch	S&W Jt	54	
* Parkend Royal Branch	S&W Jt	54	
* Parkgate Colliery Branch	LNW Jt	91	
Park Mile to Alexandra Docks	ANDR	152	
Park Royal Goods Branch		38	
Par Loop		5	
≠ Patchway Curve	BR (WR)	23	
Patent Nut & Bolt Co's Works Line		183	
Peat Moss Company's Siding	Cam	96	
Pembroke & Tenby Branch		124–126	
Penallta Branch	Rhy	171, 178	
Penar Branch		177–178	
Penarth Branch	TV	147, 148	
Penarth Curve	TV	149	
Penarth Dock Branch North Side	TV	147	
Penarth Dock Branch South Side	TV	147	
Penarth Harbour Branch	TV	147	
Pencoed Branch		143, 157	
Penrhos Branch	Bry	146, 173, 174, 179	
Penrhos Loop	Bry	173	
Peterston Branch	Bry	146	
Peterston East Loop	Bry	146	
Pill Bank Siding		152	
Pillgwenlly Branch		152	Newport Old Dock Branch
Pistill Branch		130	
Plasmadoc Branch		94	
Plasmadoc Loop		94	
Plough Junction to East Junction	RSB	141	Port Talbot Jcn to Plough Jcn
Plymouth Docks Branch		8	Millbay Docks Line
Plymouth Loop No. 1		8	
Plymouth Loop No. 2		8	
Ponkey Branch		94	
Pontardawe Branch		138	
Pontrhydyfen Branch	RSB	153, 154	No. 8 Railway
* Pontsmill Ballast Siding		4	
Pontsmill Branch		4	
Pontsticill Loop	B&M	166	
Pontcysyllte Branch		94	
Pontcysyllte Basin Branch		94	
Pontypool Rd E. Jcn to Coedygric Jcn		183	
Pontypool Rd M. Jcn to North Jcn		183	
Pontypool Rd S. Jcn to Coedygric Jcn		183	
Pontypool Rd W. Jcn to South Jcn		183	
Pontypridd Loop	TV	172	
Poplar Goods Depot		40	
Porthcawl Branch		143	

	Line or Branch	Co.	Map No.	Alternative Name
A*	Porthkerry Deviation	Bry	144	
	Porthywaen Branch	Cam	119	
	Portishead Branch		23–25	
	Portishead West Loop		24	
	Portland Goods Branch	LSW Jt	42	
*	Portreath Branch		1	
*	Portskewett Branch		52	
	Port Talbot (Burrows Jc) Dock Line	RSB	141	
	Port Talbot Docks Branch	PT	141	
	Port Talbot Docks Extension Branch	PT	141	
	Port Talbot Junction to Plough Jcn	RSB	141	Plough Jcn to East Junction
	Port Talbot to Pontyrhyll	PT	141, 154, 156, 157	
	Port Wallaroo Dock Line		140	
*	Potteries Loop	S&M	99	North Wales Junction
	Presteign Branch		103	
	Princetown Branch		10	
	Pump House Siding		23	Sea Wall Siding
	Pwllyrhebog Branch	TV	159	
A	Pyle East Junction		143	
	Pyle Branch		143	
	Pyle West Loop		143	
	Pylle Hill Goods Branch		24	
	Quakers Yard & Merthyr Line	Rhy Jt	168–70	
	Quakers Yard Branch		170	
	Quarry Branch (at Pitts Cleave)		10	
	Queens Head Goods Line		79	
	Queen Victoria Road Goods Depot	LMM	134	
	Radyr Branch	TV	146, 149, 174	
	Railway No. 10, Glyn Neath		163	Aberpergwm Branch
≠	Ramp Line	BR (WR)	142	
	Rassa Tramroad		175	
A	Reading Low Level Goods Lines		33	
	Reading New Junction		33	
	Reading West Curve		33	
	Remphrey Siding		4	
	Retew Branch		4	
	Rhondda & Swansea Bay Line	RSB	137, 139–141, 153–155, 158	
	Rhondda Fach Branch		158, 159	Maerdy Branch
	Rhos Branch		94	
	Rhymney & Nantybwch Line	Rhy/LNW J	167, 175	
A*	Rhymney Limestone Branch	B&M	167	
	Rio Tinto Works Branch (Port Talbot)	PT	141	
	Riverside Branch (Llanelly)		134	
	Roath Branch	TV	149, 150, 174	
A	Roath Branch Junction		149	
	Roath Dock Branch		149, 150	
	Roath Dock North Side Lines	Cdf	150	
	Roath Goods Branch (TVR)	TV	149	
	Roath Goods Branch (GWR)		149	
	Rock Siding	Cam	119	Old Llanfyllin Branch
	Roskear Branch		1	
	Ross to Little Mill Junction		53, 105, 108	
	Royal Albert Docks		40	
	Ruabon and Dolgelley Line		94, 95, 110–112	
	Rushey Platt Curve	MSWJ	30	
	St. Austell Goods Branch		3	
	St. Budeaux Junction		8	
	St. Davids Branch		134	Dafen Branch
	St. Dennis Branch		4	
	St. Fagans Branch	Bry	146	
	St. Fagans West Loop	Bry	146	
	St. Ives Branch		1	
	St. Phillips Marsh Goods Branch		24	Marsh Depot Goods Branch
	Salisbury Branch		46, 47	
A	Salisbury Junction		47	
*	Saltash to St. Germans		7	
	Saltney Goods Branch		91	
	Sandy Gate Branch	BPGV	134	
	Sea Wall Siding		23	Pump House Siding
	Senghenydd Branch	Rhy	173, 179	
	Severn & Wye Line	S&W Jt	53, 54, 58	

	Line or Branch	Co.	Map No.	Alternative Name
	Severnside Branch		23	
	Severn Valley Line		69–72, 77, 78, 98, 99	
	Sharpness Dock North Branch	S&W Jt	58	
	Sharpness Dock South Branch	S&W Jt	58	
	Shipston-on-Stour Branch		64	Moreton & Shipston Tramway
≠	Shrewsbury Abbey Branch	BR (WR)	99	
	Shrewsbury & Hereford Line	LNW Jt	98–102, 104	
	Shrewsbury & Wellington Line	LNW Jt	69, 98, 99	
	Shrewsbury & Welshpool Line	LNW Jt	98, 99, 117	
	Shrewsbury Curve	LNW Jt	99	
	Shropshire & Montgomeryshire Light Rly	S&M	98, 99, 117, 119	
	Shropshire Union Canal Line	LNW Jt	90	
	Six Pit Junction	Mid Jt	136	Swansea Valley Jcn with LMSR
	Sling Branch	S&W Jt	53	
	Slough West Curve		34	
	Smithfield Depot		40	
	South Dock N&S Side Lines (Swansea)	SHT	186	
	South Lambeth Depot	SLA	40	
A*	South Sea Ironworks Branch		93	
	South Side Lines Dock No. 1 (Barry)	Bry	148	
	South Wales & Bristol Direct Line		23, 26, 28, 29	
	South Wales Main Line		29, 30, 52–56, 58, 59, 123–126, 129, 133–136, 138–146, 149–152	
	South Wales Mineral Junction Branch	PT	141, 153, 154	
	South Wales Mineral Railway	SW Min	140, 153, 155	
*	Speech House Hill Branch	S&W Jt	54	
	Spinners End Branch		76, 77	
	Staines Branch		35	
	Staines Moor Loop		35	
	Standish Junction		58	
	Stapleton Road Goods Branch		23	
	Steelworks Wharf to Old Dock Jcn	PT	141	
	Stert & Westbury Line		46	
	Stirchley Branch		70	
	Stoke Branch		78	
	Stoke Works Siding		78	
	Stonefield Loop	Cdf	150	
	Stonefield to Queen Alexandra Dk. Lock	Cdf	150	
	Stonefield to Splott Junction	Cdf	150	
	Stoneycombe Branch		12	
	Stourbridge Extension Line		76, 77, 79	
*	Stourbridge Incline		77	
	Stourbridge Junction Goods Branch		77	
	Stourbridge Town Branch		77	
	Strand Lines (Swansea)	SHT	186	
	Stratford Branch		62, 82	
	Stratford Goods Branch		82	
≠	Stratford-on-Avon South Curve	BR (WR)	82	
*	Stratford-on-Avon to Longdon Road		64, 82	
B	Stratton Factory Branch		30	
	Sudbrook Branch		52	
	Sutton Harbour Branch		8	
*	Sutton Harbour Bch to Cattewater Bch		8	
	Swansea Branch		136, 137	
	Swansea District Lines		135, 138, 139	
	Swansea Eastern Loop		137	
	Swansea East Junction Line		137	
	Swansea Harbour Branch	RSB	137	
	Swansea Loop		136	Landore Western Loop
	Swansea North Dock Branch		137	
	Swansea Valley Jcn with LMSR	Mid Jt	136	Six Pit Junction
	Swan Village Branch		75	
	Taff Bargoed Branch	Rhy Jt	167–170	
	Taff Vale Extension Line		182, 183	
≠	Taibach Loop	BR (WR)	142	
A	Talbot Wharf Line (Port Talbot)		141	
	Talyllyn Loop	Cam/B&M	122	
	Talywain Branch		182, 184	
	Talywain Ballast Branch		184	
	Talywain Old Siding		184	
	Tanat Valley Branch	Cam	117, 119	
	Taunton West Loop		20	

Line or Branch	Co.	Map No.	Alternative Name
Teign Valley Railway		13, 14	
Temple Meads Goods Lines		24	
Tenbury Branch		72, 77, 101	
Tenby Goods Branch		124	
Tennants Wharf Lines (Swansea)	SHT	186	
Tetbury Branch		59	
Thame Branch		67, 68, 87	
Three Cocks Junction Line	Cam	121	
Tidworth Branch	MSWJ	51	
Tip Roads Nos. 1–3 (Empty) (Port Talbot)	PT	141	
Tip Roads Nos. 1–3 (Full) (Port Talbot)	PT	141	
Tipton Basin Branch		75	
Tiverton & North Devon Line		15, 16	
Tiverton Branch		16	
Tondu North Loop		143	
Torquay Branch		12, 14	
Totnes Quay Branch		12	
Tranmere Pool Branch	LNW Jt	90	Abbey St. Branch
Treamble Branch		2	
Trecwn Branch		123	
* Treferig Branch	TV	161	
A* Trefonen Branch		119	
A* Treffry Aqueduct Line		4	
Treforest Branch	Bry	172, 173	
Treforest Trading Estate Branch		173	
Treherbert Branch	TV	158, 159, 172	
Treloggan Curve		3	
Trenance Valley Branch		4	
* Tresavean Branch		1	
Trimsaran Branch	BPGV	133	
Trosnant Junction Line		182	
Truro & Newquay Line		2, 3	
Truro & Newquay West Loop		2	Chacewater West Loop
Tycoch Loop	GVR	133	
Tymaen Branch	RSB	154	
A* Tyrcenol Junction		138	
Tyseley Yard Line		80	
Uxbridge Branch		35	
Uxbridge Road Depot		38	
Vale of Glamorgan Line	Bry	144, 148	
Vale of Neath Line		137, 139, 140, 153, 162–165, 170, 171, 178	
Vale of Rheidol Branch	Cam	114	
* Vale of Rheidol Harbour Branch	Cam	114	
Vale of Towy Line	LNW Jt	130	
Van Branch	Cam	116	
Victoria Dock Depot		40	
Victoria Basin Branch		74	Wolverhampton, Herbert St. Branch
Victoria Branch		39	
Victoria Station & Pimlico Railway	SE&C Jt	40	
Vinegar Branch		60	
Vobster Colliery Line		45	
Vron Colliery Branch		93	
Wallingford Branch		31	
Walnut Tree Branch	Rhy	173	
Walsall Street Branch		74	
Walton Old Junc to Ship Canal Sdgs	LNW Jt	88	
Wapping Wharf Branch		24	
Warwick Road Coal Depot Branch		38	Kensington Coal Yard
Waterloo Loop (at Newport)		152	
Watlington Branch		87	
Wednesbury Branch		75	Monway Branch
Welshpool & Llanfair Light Railway	Cam	117, 118	
Westbury Avoiding Line		46	
Westbury East Loop		46	
West Ealing Loop		36, 37	
B Westerleigh East Loop		26	Ministry of Works Loop
Western Valleys Line		152, 175, 176, 178, 180–182, 184	
West London Extension Line	WL Jt	38	
West London Extension No. 1 Branch	WL Jt	38	

Line or Branch	Co.	Map No.	Alternative Name
West London Extension No. 2 Branch	WL Jt	38	
West London Extension No. 3 Branch	WL Jt	38	
West London Line	WL Jt	38, 39	
West London Yard Line		39	
* Weston-super-Mare Branch		21	
Weston-super-Mare Loop		21	
Weymouth & Portland Line	LSW Jt	42	
Weymouth Harbour Line		42	
Weymouth Line		28, 41–46	
Weymouth Tramway	LSW Jt	42	
B≠ Whatley Quarry Branch	BR (WR)	45	
Wheal Virgin Clay Works		4	
Wheatsheaf Branch		93	
Whitchurch & Aberystwyth Line	Cam	95–97, 113–119	
Whitland & Cardigan Branch		125	Cardigan Branch
Whitworth Branch	PT	153	
Wimberry Branch	S&W Jt	54	
* Wimberry Tramway	S&W Jt	54	
Winchester Goods Depot		51	
Windmill End Branch		76	
Windsor Branch		34	
Wind Street Goods Line		137	
Withymoor Branch		76	Netherton Branch
Witney Goods Branch		66	
Wolfhall Loop	MSWJ	48	
Wolverhampton, Herbert St. Branch		74	Victoria Basin Branch
Wolverhampton Loop (at Worcester)		60	Birmingham Loop
Woodside Branch		76	
Woodstock Branch		67	
Woofferton & Tenbury Wells Branch	LNW Jt	101	
Worcester & Hereford Line		60, 61, 104	
Worcester Goods Loop		60	
Worthy Down Loop		51	
Wrexham & Ellesmere Branch	Cam	92, 95, 96	
Wrexham & Minera Extension Line	LNW Jt	92, 93	
Wrexham & Minera Line		93	
Wrexham South Curve		93	
Wrington Vale Branch		21	
Wycombe Branch		34, 87	
Wye Valley Line		52, 53	
Yate Branch		26	
Yealmpton Branch		7	
* Yeo Pumping Station Branch		21	
Yeovil Branch		43, 44	
Yeovil South Junction		44	
Ynysfach Branch	TV	168	
Ynysfach Loop	B&M/LNW Jt	168	
Ynyslas Timber Creosoting Siding	Cam	113	
Ynysybwl Branch	TV	171	
Ynysybwl Loop	TV	171	
Ynysydwr Loop	TV	171	
Yspitty Branch		133	
Ystrad Branch		178	
Ystradgynlais Branch	N&B	132	
Zig Zag Lines	Rhy Jt	167, 168	

APPENDIX B
LIST OF TUNNELS

* = located on Closed Line   † = opened out   ‡ = on Private Line

Aberdovey No. 1	113C3	Dudley	75D1	Newport, New	152B2
Aberdovey No. 2	113C3	East Cliff†	14C5	Newport, Old	152B2
Aberdovey No. 3	113D6	Evershot	44D3	Nightcote	18D5
Aberdovey No. 4	113D6	Fawley	105A2	Nottage	143C1
Ableton Lane	23A3	Flax Bourton	21A6	Oakengates	70B5
Alderton	26C6	Fox's Wood No. 1†	23D5	Old Hill	76D6
Alltycefn	128B2	Fox's Wood No. 2†	23D5	Paddington	39D5
Andoversford	57B4	Frampton	41B5	Parson's	14D6
Ardley	85B3	Frodsham	88C2	Patchway, New	23A4
Balderton	91D4	Gaer	152C1	Patchway, Old	23A4
Ballingham	105A2	Galton	79B4	Patchway, Short	23A4
Barmouth	111C1	Gelli	155D3	Pembroke (Golden Hill)	124D3
Barry Island	148D4	Glyn	182D2	Penar	178B5
Bathealton	15B3	Golden Hill (Pembroke)	124D3	Pencader	128C3
Bedlam‡	45A4	Goonbarrow (Stenalees)	4B4	Pencaedrain	163B5
Berwyn	112B5	Great Elm‡	45A3	Peniel Green (Lonlas)	135B4
Bewdley	77D4	Greenway	12D5	Penllergaer	135B2
Bincombe North	42A6	Greet (Winchcombe)	63C4	Perran	2C2
Bincombe South	42A6	Grenofen	10C4	Perridge	13B3
Blue Rock	54C3	Gulwell	12A1	Phillot	14C6
Box	28D1	Gwersyllt (Summer Hill)*	93A1	Pighill	38D2
Bradford	46B1	Gyfylcha (Tonmawr)	153D5	Pill	25B4
Bradley Hill	54C3	Haden Hill	77A6	Pinnock	6D1
Bridges (Luxulyan)	4B5	Halton	88B3	Plas Madoc	94B2
Bridgnorth	71B5	Harbury	83B2	Polperro	2A4
Brill	86C2	Hatch	20D3	Pontamman	131B4
Bristol Harbour (Redcliffe)	24B3	Hawthorns (Euroclydon)*	105D4	Pontardulais	131D2
Bristol (St. Annes Park) No. 1	24B6	Haymarket	90B4	Pontrilas	107C6
Bristol (St. Annes Park) No. 2	23D5	Higher Town	2A6	Pontypridd (Pwllgwaun)	172C5
Bristol (St. Annes Park) No. 3	23D5	Hockley No. 1	80B5	Porthkerry No. 1	144D6
Brown Queen	6A1	Hockley No. 2	80B5	Porthkerry No. 2	144D6
Brymbo*	93A1	Hook Norton	64C5	Poundbury	41C6
Bryn	178D3	Horsehay	70C1	Pouparts	38D2
Bryn Teify	128B4	Horspath (Wheatley)	67D5	Presthope	71A2
Buckshead	2A3	Hunting Butts	55A6	Pwllgwaun (Pontypridd)	172C5
Bullo	54C3	Kemble	59C3	Quakers Yard	170C3
Caerphilly	173C6	Kennaway	14C6	Rainbow Hill	60B6
Campden	61D6	Knowle Sands	71C5	Reading Low Level	33B5
Cape Horn*	39D3	Lea (Mitcheldean)	105C5	Redbrook, Lower*	53B2
Castle (Maenclochog)	123B5	Ledbury	60B3	Redbrook, Upper*	53B2
Castle Bar (or Drayton Green)	37A5	Leebeer (Shaugh)	10D5	Redcliffe (Bristol Harbour)	24B3
Castle Hill	18C6	Livermead (Torquay)†	12B5	Red Hill	104D1
Charlton	23B4	Llandderfel	111B6	Redruth	1D6
Chedworth	57C3	Llangyfelach	135B3	Rhayader	120B3
Chipping Norton	65B4	Lonlas (Peniel Green)	135B4	Rhondda	155B4
Chipping Sodbury	26C4	Ludlow	101B6	Rodwell	42D3
Chirk	95A1	Luxulyan (Bridges)	4B5	Ruabon Road	94B6
Clerk's	14C6	Lydbrook	105D2	St. Annes Park (or Bristol) No. 1	24B6
Clifton Bridge No. 1	25D6	Maenclochog (Castle)	123B5	St. Annes Park (or Bristol) No. 2	23D5
Clifton Bridge No. 2	25C6	Malmesbury	28B1	St. Annes Park (or Bristol) No. 3	23D5
Clifton Down	25C6	Marlborough	48B4	Saltford	27A2
Cockett	135C2	Marley	11A4	Sandstone	25B5
Cogan	147C5	Marteg	120A3	Sapperton, Long	59B2
Coles Rock	54A1	Merthyr	165A6	Sapperton, Short	59B2
Colwall, New	61D1	Middle Hill	27A6	Saunderton	87D6
Colwall, Old*	61D1	Miery Stock	54A1	Severn	23A3
Combe Hay	27C3	Mitcheldean (Lea)	105C5	Severn Bridge	53D5
Coryton	14C6	Mitre	39B3	Shaugh (Leebeer)	10D5
Culver	13B3	Monks Ferry	90B5	Shillingham (Wivelscombe)	7B2
Cwmcerwyn	156C1	Monmouth	53B1	Shute Shelf	21D4
Cymmer	155D2	Montpelier	23A1	Snow Hill	80B6
Dainton	12A4	Moseley Green	54D2	Somerton	43B2
Danygraig	137D6	Mount Pleasant	72D5	Sorley	11D4
Devizes	46B5	Murdercombe‡	45A3	Sparnick	2B3
Devonport	8C3	Mutley	8C5	Spittal	123C2
Dinedor	104D2	Narberth	124A6	Springs Road Car Park	37B6
Dinmore	102D2	Newland*	53B2	Stenalees (Goonbarrow)	4B4
Drayton Green (or Castle Bar)	37A5	Newnham	53B5	Subway	39D3
Drybrook	53A5	Newquay Harbour*	3A1	Summer Hill (Gwersyllt)*	93A1

APPENDIX C
INDEX TO VIADUCTS

* = located on Closed Line   † = Replaced by embankment

Name	Ref	Name	Ref	Name	Ref
Gloucester Docks No. 2	56B2	Merthyr (Pontypridd)	172B2	River Ithon	121A1
Goonbell	2C5	Midford	27C4	River Loddon	32B6
Gordon Road	87D4	Milltown	6C1	River Rheidol	114A5
Gors y Garnant	131D4	Monmouth Old	53B1	River Rheidol (V of R)	114D1
Gover	3C5	Monmouth River Bridge	53B1	River Severn (Criggion)	98B1
Grand Union Canal	35D4	Moorswater	6C5	River Severn (Caersws)	116D5
Greenhill	124A5	Morfodian	116C2	River Taw	18B5
Greenway (or Maypool)	12D5	Morriston	135B4	River Teme	61B3
Groeserw	155B5	Moulsford	31D6	River Tern	69B1
Grove (Llanfyllin Branch)	119D1	Neath (Neath Jcn line)	139A6	River Tone Bridge	20C3
Grove * (near St. Germans)	7B2	Neath (S. Wales main line)	139A6	River Towy	130B5
Guildford	1B3	Neath Abbey	139A4	River Usk (Newport)	152A3
Gwaun cae Gurwen	131D4	Neath River	139C3	River Usk (Talybont)	122B6
Hackford (Winterbourne)	23B5	Neilson Street	83B6	River Wye (Newbridge)	120D4
Hall's	180A1	New Cut	139C4	Riverford	7A5
Ham Green	7A5	North Row	45C5	Rock Mill	4B5
Ham Meadow	56A2	Noss†	12D2	Royal Albert Bridge	8A1
Hanwell	37B4	Nottar	7B2	Ruddey	69C6
Hayley Dingle	61B2	Nottar*	7B2	St. Austell	3C5
Heath	174C6	Nuneham	31A4	St. Catherine's Meadow	56A2
Hengoed (or Rhymney)	178C4	Old Chapel	111C1	St. Davids Bridge	13C1
Hepworth Foot	111B1	Oldbury (Oldbury)	79B2	St. Erth	1C2
Hinton's	97D2	Oldbury (Bridgnorth)	71B5	St. Fagans	146C3
Holley's	27C4	Over Bridge	56A1	St. Germans	7B1
Hoobrook	77D5	Oxley	74A3	St. Germans*	7B1
Hoodown	12D5	Pantymoel	183A4	St. Ives	1B2
Hook Hill	12C5	Par	5C1	St. James	27D6
Hook Norton No. 1	65B6	Parkhead	76B4	St. Julians	184B5
Hook Norton No. 2	65B6	Pascoe†	2C2	St. Pinnock	6A3
Hughenden Road	87D4	Penadlike	6A2	St. Thomas	13C1
Hunderton River Bridge	104C4	Pencaedrain†	163B5	Sandbourne	77D2
Inysonsws†	163B4	Penpergwm River Bridge	108B2	Sarn Pile	115D6
Ivybridge	11A2	Penponds*	1B4	Sea Mills or River Avon	25B5
K & A Canal (Hungerford)	49D2	Penrhos	173C5	Severn (Salop)	99B2
K & A Canal (Newbury)	49D4	Penryn*	2D2	Severn Arch (Slade)	32B6
Kennet	33B6	Pensarn River Bridge	110A1	Severn Bridge	53D5
Kennington	68D6	Pentyrch River Bridge	174A2	Sharpness No. 1	58A2
Kerne	105D2	Penwithers (main line)	2A3	Sharpness No. 2	58A2
Keyham	8B2	Penwithers† (Falmouth Bch)	2B3	Shawford (LSWR)	51D5
Kidderminster	77D5	Penyrheol	173A4	Sherrington	47B2
Kidwelly	133D1	Penzance†	1D1	Shifnal	69C5
Kilkewydd	118B4	Perran	2C2	Shiplake	34D1
Kingsmill	92D3	Pillowell	54D2	Sir Philip Rose's	34A4
Knowles	14A1	Ponsanooth	2C2	Skewen	139B3
Landore	136B3	Pont Abernant y Felin	177C5	Slade	11A1
Landore Low Level	136B2	Pontlottyn	167C5	Somerford	28A4
Langport	43B1	Pontrhydyfen	154A4	Somerton	43B3
Largin	6A3	Pontsarn	166C2	Souldern No. 1	85A3
Lashbrooke	34D1	Pontsmill	4C6	Souldern No. 2	85A3
Latchmere	38D2	Pontwalby	163C4	Staffords Bridge	13A5
Lavington	46C5	Pontypridd	172B4	Stambermill (Stourbridge)	77B2
Ledbury	60A3	Porthkerry	144D6	Stanway (or Toddington)	63B5
Lee (see Bittaford)	—	Portishead†	23D1	Stapleton Road	23A1
Leonard's Mill	45B5	Poundbury	41C6	Stonehouse Pool	8C4
Leri	113D2	Prideaux	4C6	Stourbridge	77B2
Liskeard	6C6	Probus†	3D3	Strangford	105B2
Llanbradach	179C3	Quakers Yard (Taff Vale)	170A4	Stratford (Stroud)	58C5
Llandaff Loop	174C3	Quakers Yard (Vale of Neath)	170A4	Stratton	41C5
Lletty Brongu	156D4	Quakers Yard No. 2	170A4	Swansea North Dock Branch	137B1
Llwynjack	130A6	Rattery	12B1	Swansea East to South Dock	137B1
Longwood†	12C2	Redbrook	53B2	Swansea St. Thomas	137B2
Loughor (at Loughor)	133D6	Redcliffe (Bristol Hbr)	24B4	Taff	174C3
Loughor (at Morlais)	133C6	Rhondda	172B2	Taffs Well	173D2
Lowertown	1D5	Rhymney	178C4	Tawe	138C4
Lydbrook	54A1	Ringwell†	2B2	Tenby	124A5
Lydbrook River Bridge	53A3	Risca	180B5	Timber Lane	72A6
Magpie	10C4	River Avon or Sea Mills	25B5	Tintern River Bridge	52A5
Maidenhead Bridge	34C4	River Avon (Stratford)	62A6	Tongwynlais	174B3
Main Down (Bristol E D)	24C6	River Caerfanell	122C6	Tonteg	173B1
Main River (Bristol E D)	24C6	River Carno	116D4	Town Hill	92D3
Main Up (Bristol E D)	24C6	River Cherwell	84D4	Traeth Bach	109C3
Marlow	34A1	River Colne	35D4	Traeth Mawr	110A4
Maypool (or Greenway)	12D5	River Dee	95A5	Treffry*	4B5
Merthyr (Merthyr)	168C2	River Frome	45D6	Tregagle	2A4

Tregarne	2A4	Tygwyn	109C3	Westwood	6A3
Trehafod	172A2	Usk	108D4	Wharncliffe	37B4
Treharris	170C5	Velindre	154D2	Wheatley	67D6
Treherbert	158B2	Venn Cross	15B3	White Hart	180C2
Trenance	3A1	Village	116A1	Willow Road	92D3
Trench	95D5	Walkham	10C4	Willow Vale	45D6
Trer'ddol Rover	113D3	Walnut Tree	173D3	Windsor	34D5
Tresulgan	6B6	Watts	58C6	Winterbourne	23B5
Treviddo	6B5	Weaver	88C3	Wivelscombe*	7B2
Trewythen	116B3	Weldon	72A6	Woodbank	57A2
Truro	2A6	West Largin	6A3	Worcester	60C5
Twerton	27D4	Weston	88C3	Ynysdavid	154B4
Twymyn River	115C3	Weston Mill	8B2	Ynysdawley	132C4

APPENDIX D
LINES JOINTLY OWNED

	Joint with	Route Miles	Maintained by
Abersychan and Talywain Joint Station	LMS	0.28	LMS
Avonmouth Dock Branch (5.76 to 6.55)	LMS	0.59	see note A
Banbury Joint Sidings	LMS	—	GWR/LMS
Brecon Curve	LMS	0.18	GWR
Bristol Joint Station	LMS	0.37	GWR
Brynmawr and Western Valleys (0.00 to 1.17)	LMS	1.17	see note B
Chard Joint Station	SR	0.27	GWR
Chester and Birkenhead/Warrington Lines (see Note C)	LMS	56.00	LMS
Chester Joint Station	LMS	1.32	LMS
Chelsea Basin Joint Sidings	LMS	—	GWR
Clee Hill Branch	LMS	6.01	GWR
Clifton Extension Line	LMS	3.24	LMS
Dudley Joint Sidings	LMS	—	GWR/LMS
Halesowen & Northfield Line	LMS	5.70	see note D
Hereford Joint Station	LMS	0.68	GWR
Hotwells to Avonmouth (3.24 to 6.74)	LMS	3.50	see note E
Latimer Rd Jcn to Uxbridge Rd Jcn	Met	0.39	Met
Leamington Joint Sidings	LMS	—	LMS
Minsterley Branch	LMS	4.53	GWR
Morlais Junction–Merthyr Lines (see Note F)	LMS	5.32	?
Oxford Joint Sidings	LMS	—	GWR/LMS
Plymouth North Rd Joint Station Sidings	SR	—	GWR
Pontdardulais Joint Sidings	LMS	—	GWR
Rhymney to Nantybwch	LMS	2.75	?
Severn and Wye & Severn Bridge Lines (see Note G)	LMS	41.08	see Note G
Shrewsbury and Hereford Line	LMS	50.04	GWR
Shrewsbury and Wellington Line (0.32 to 10.56)	LMS	10.24	see note H
Shrewsbury Curve	LMS	0.25	GWR
Shrewsbury and Welshpool Line	LMS	16.22	GWR
Shrewsbury Joint Station	LMS	0.53	GWR
Six Pit Lines	LMS	0.26	LMS
Vale of Towy (18.17 to 29.27)	LMS	11.10	see note I
Westbourne Park to Hammersmith	Met	2.38	Met
West London Line	LMS	2.24	LMS
West London Extension Line	LMS/SR	5.02	GWR
Woofferton and Tenbury Branch	LMS	5.09	GWR
Worcester Shrub Hill Station	LMS	0.78	GWR
Wrexham and Minera Line (0.00 to 0.06)	LMS	2.70	see note J
Yeovil Joint Station Sidings	SR	—	GWR

LINES LEASED OR WORKED OVER

	Joint with	Route Miles	Maintained by
Aylesbury Branch	GW&GC Jt	7.07	LNER
Aylesbury Joint Station	GW&GC&Met	0.19	LNER
Denham West Curve	GW&GC Jt	0.08	GWR
High Wycombe Station	GW&GC Jt	1.10	GWR
High Wycombe to Princes Risborough	GW&GC Jt	7.28	LNER
Northolt Jcn to High Wycombe	GW&GC Jt	16.10	GWR
Princes Risborough to Ashendon Jcn	GW&GC Jt	9.21	LNER
Tidworth Branch	—	2.32	GWR
Weymouth & Portland Line	Southern ⎤	4.40	GWR
Castleton Tramway	,, ⎦		
Weymouth Tramway	,,	1.08	GWR
Easton & Church Hope Line	,,	3.39	GWR
Battersea Pier Jcn–Victoria (until 1932)	,,	0.70	Southern

NOTES

A GWR maintained   6.54 to 6.55, LMS the remainder
B   ,,   ,,   0.00 to 0.01,   ,,   ,,   ,,
C Lines include   Chester (0.36) to Woodside (15.14)
                        Birkenhead Goods Extension Line
                        Brook St. to Shore Road
                        Tranmere Pool Branch
                        Monks Ferry Branch
                        Chester (0.30) to Warrington (Walton New Jcn – 17.10)
                        Acton Grange Jcn to Walton Old Jcn
                        Walton Old Jcn to Ship Canal Sidings
                        Hooton and Helsby Line
                        Hooton and West Kirby Line
D GWR maintained   5.69 to 5.70, LMS the remainder
E   ,,   ,,   6.72 to 6.74,   ,,   ,,   ,,
F Lines include   Morlais Jcn to Rhydycar Jcn
                        Merthyr Ynisfach Loop
                        Merthyr Low Level Loop
G Lines include   Berkeley Road Jcn to Cinderford
                        Mineral Loop
                        Coleford Branch
                        Lydbrook Branch
                        and other minor colly & dock branches
                        LMS maintained all south of Coleford Jcn 12.65 and Tufts Jcn (11.00)
H GWR maintained   0.32 to 0.41,   LMS the remainder
I   ,,   ,,   18.17 to 24.00,   ,,   ,,   ,,
J   ,,   ,,   0.00 to 0.03,   ,,   ,,   ,,

APPENDIX E
LIST OF LOCATIONS WHERE PRECISE POSITION IS UNKNOWN

The following is a complete list of locations which are shown in the index as '?', where the precise position has not been determined. In some cases they may be alternative names for locations shown or possibly in a few instances they may not have been directly rail served, although they have all come from official railway documents.

Of the 121 entries in the first edition, 42 have been removed, but 57 new ones (shown with an asterisk) have been added. I would be especially pleased to hear from anyone who can help pin-point these places, if possible supported by a sketch to show the precise position of the siding.

Location	Approx Position	Location	Approx Position
Aberdare Navigation Colly*	Hirwaun Pond	Jubilee Colly*	Pantyffynon
Aberdare Rhondda Colly*	Hirwaun Pond	Kitchen Hill Colly	Brettell Lane
Abergwybedin Siding*	Aberangell	Lambridge Siding*	Shrewsbury Wolverhampton
Ashton Upper Crossing*	Ashton Gate	Lime Kiln Lane Siding*	Birkenhead
Aston Siding*	Shropshire Union	Lion Black Vein Colly	Nantyglo
Baggeridge Wood Colly	= Baggeridge Colly?	Lion Colly*	Old Hill — Rowley Regis
Bellan*	P. S. & North Wales Rly	Llantwit Basin Colly*	North of Caerphilly
Benallt Colly	Pontardulais	Llantwit Wallsend Colly*	Blaengarw
Blackheath Colly*	Rowley Regis	Llewellyn Merthyr Colly	Merthyr
Black Lane Colly Siding*	Brymbo	Llewellyn Plymouth Colly	Merthyr
Black Pit	Brettell Lane	Llwyn-y-rhidie Colly	Garnant
Black Vein Sirhowy Colly	Ebbw Vale	Lydney & Crump Meadow Colly	Forest of Dean
Blaenavon Siding*	Llynvi & Ogmore Rly	Machynys Crossing	Llanelly
Blaenllecha Colly*	Near Ferndale	Maerdy Colly	Gwaun cae Gurwen
Blaen y Cwm Colly*	Cwmffrwdoer Branch	Mails Cat Pit	Forest of Dean
Blaina Red Ash Colly	Blaina	Marsh Lane Colly	Hallatrow
Botfield Siding*	Stirchley Branch?	Merthyr Rhondda Colly*	Brynmenyn, branch from
Brachty Colly	Newbridge	Millbrook Colly	Newbridge
Bretforton Siding*	Evesham – Honeybourne (? Built)	Mynyddycaeran Siding*	Llynvi & Ogmore Rly
Brithnewynydd Colly*	Near Pandy (? Brithwenydd)	Nantfedw Colly	Abercynon
Browns Pit	Fforchaman	Navigation Colly	Blaenavon
Brynnow*	Llanharan Junction	New Darran Ddu Colly*	near Trehafod
Cabbage Hall Colly	Netherton	New Hulks Pit	Forest of Dean
Canaan Colly	Tumble	New Regulator Pit	Forest of Dean
Catherton Colly Siding*	Clee Hill	Ogmore Colly*	Branch from Hendreforgan
Cefn Merthyr Colly	Cefn Mawr (Vale of Neath)	Old Chester Road Siding*	Birkenhead
Cemetery Level	Ebbw Vale	Old Mill Colly	Ystrad Mynach
Chapel Farm Quarry Siding*	Clee Hill	Old Tunnel Colly	Ebbw Vale
Cinder Colly	Blaina	Old Windmill Siding*	Wolverhampton Herbert St
Clee Hill Colly Siding*	Clee Hill	Panteg Colly	Pontypool
Coed y goe Siding*	Llynclys – Porthywaen	Penrhiwfer Rhondda Colly	Dinas Isha
Corrwg Navigation Colly	Glyncorrwg	Pentwyn Rhondda Colly	Dinas
Craig Colly*	Near Aberdare	Penwaingoch Colly*	near Pontlottyn
Crowthers Crossing	Kidderminster	Penygaer*	near Llanelly
Crumlin Colly	Skewen	Penyrheol Colly	Newbridge
Cuba Colly	Round Oak	Plantation Colly	Ebbw Vale
Cwmnantmoel Colly	Brynamman	Pont Meredith*	Llanymynech – Nantmawr
Dandy Pit	Shut End	Pontypool Colly	Pontypool
Danybryn Colly	Pontycymmer	Quarry Level Colly	Pontypool
Dark Lane Siding (GWR)*	Stirchley Branch?	Rakes Colly	Upper Llwydcoed
Derwen Merthyr Colly*	north of Bargoed	Reddinghorn Pit	Forest of Dean
Dock Colly	Brettell Lane	Rhiew Colly	Newbridge
Duffryn Clydach Colly	Neath	Rhoslas Colly*	
Duffryn Colly	Gowerton	Rock Fawr Colly	Tondu
Duffryn Gower Colly	Gowerton	Rosemount Colly	Abertillery
Duffryn Rhondda Golden Vein Colly*	Bryn	Russell Hall Siding*	Parkhead
Dyllas Isha Colly	Gilfach	Sirhowy Level	Ebbw Vale
Dynevor Main Colly	Neath	Star Colly*	Trimsaran
East Blaina Colly	Blaina	Street End Colly*	Brettell Lane
Faldydre Colly*	Resolven	Talywaun Colly	
Foce Colly*	Cefn Junction	Tir Waen Clwydd Colly*	Victoria – Cwm
Foy Siding*	BP & GV	Tirfounder Level	Mountain Ash – Aberaman
Freehold Colly	Hollinswood	Ton Teilwr Colly	Nelson & Llancaiach
Ganister Level	Ebbw Vale	Ton Tyler Colly	Nelson & Llancaiach
Garth Rhondda Colly*	Taffs Well (on Pentyrch Rly?)	Trebanog Colly	Porth
Gelliargwellt Colly	Ystrad Mynach	Tweedle Colly	Resolven
Gibbons Crossing	Pengam	Tynoming Crossing*	Sarnau – Whitland
Glnhowey Elled Colly	Ebbw Vale	Tyr Nicholas Colly*	Abertillery
Glyn Road Level	Blaendare Jcn	Tyr Pentir Colly Siding*	
Glynteg Colly	Resolven	Verdun Colly	Aberbeeg
Gorllwyn Colly	Nantmelyn	Waresley Siding*	Hartlebury
Graig Colly*	at Marchowell	Warren Lane Siding*	Wheatsheaf Jcn – Gresford
Gwernygasseg Colly*	Minera Branch	Waynes Merthyr Colly	Aberdaqre (Gadlys)
Gwernynoel Crossing	Common Branch Jcn	Wernbwll Colly	Brynamman
Hafod Rhondda Colly	near Hafod Jcn	Wilkins Colly	Upper Llwydcoed
Hall Street Siding	Rhos	Wynots Hill Pit	Forest of Dean
Hendre Colly*	Ebbw Vale – Beaufort	Ynis-y-bwt*	Black Mill – Hendreforgan
Hoole Siding*	Chester – Mickle Trafford	Ynysfarm Crossing	Tonygrugos – Tonmawr

APPENDIX F
LOCATION NAMES NOT ADOPTED

Occasionally a proposed new scheme might refer to a location name which was not finally used, as the proposal was dropped or another name was adopted. The original name may appear in Committee Minutes, on plans or in correspondence with the Board of Trade. The list that follows has only recently been compiled and is expected to be far from complete. Further examples of such locations would be very welcome. (Locations on projected lines have not been included.)

Original Name	Name Adopted	Date	Comments
Aberavon Jubilee Road	Aberavon Seaside	1894	
Alfrick	None	1932	Halt near Knightwick. 128¼ m.p. Not built.
Ashley Road Bridge	None	1958	Halt near Culkerton 3¾ m.p. Not built.
Bailey's Bridge	Ellerdine	1930	
Bath Road	None	1906	Halt between Slough and Windsor. Not built.
Blackminster	Littleton & Badsey	1883	
Blaenllynvi Sidings	Caerau Sidings	1898	
Bryn Bridge	Wynnville	1933	
Bulwark	None	1928	Halt near Chepstow. Not built.
Carey Road Bridge	Ballingham	1908	
Chyandour	–	1878	Name given to old engine shed site.
Cutter Hill	Ponkey Crossing	1904	
Cwmsaebron	Treherbert	1862	
Devonport Tunnel	Dockyard	1905	
Dowlais Cwm Cinnel St	Dowlais Cae Harris	1875	
Dunch Lane	None	1941	Halt near Melksham 99m 50c. Not built.
East Twerton	Oldfield Park	1928	
Evesham Road Bridge	Cheltenham Racecourse	1911	
Froxfield	None	1929	Halt, Hungerford and Bedwyn. Not built.
Glue Pot Bridge	Llandow Wick Road	1943	
Gornal Crossing	Gornal	1924	
Gurrey Fach	Llandilo	1857	
Hailes Bridge	Hailes Abbey Halt	1928	
Halford Lane	Hawthorns	1931	
Hampton Lovett	Cutnall Green	1928	
Heathfield (Pembs)	Mathry Road	1923	
Leckwith Road	Ninian Park	1912	
Lower & Upper Penn	Penn	1924	
Melincylla	Penrhiwfelin	1910	
Moor Lane	Brockmoor	1924	
Newtown	Ledbury Town Halt	1928	
Pandy Bridge	Rhosrobin Halt	1932	
Phoenix Bridge	None	1929	Halt near Caerphilly. Not built.
Rogiet	Severn Tunnel Jcn	1884	
Shut End	Pensnett	1924	
Stocks Lane	Newland Halt	1929	
Thicket Mead	None	1949	Halt near Midsomer Norton 10m. 14c. Not built.
Thomastown	Coed Ely	1924	
Tile House Lane	Whitelocks End Halt	1936	
Tredworth Road Bridge	None	1928	Halt near Gloucester Cen 112m. 51c. Not built.
Truthall Bridge	Truthall	1905	
Tudorville	None	1944	Halt near Ross on Wye 1m. 25c. Not built.
Whitehall Halt	Rushwick Halt	1923	
Wilton Park	Beaconsfield Golf Links	1914	
Windmill End	Stoulton	1897	
Wraggs Wharf	Bromham & Rowde	1908	

INDEX TO LOCATIONS

This index, which contains over 9,200 entries, fulfils two roles. Firstly, of course, it is the index to this atlas, but secondly it is also the master index to the series of booklets 'Track Layout Diagrams of the GWR and BR (WR)'.

INDEX TO ATLAS

Hopefully every station, halt, junction, signal box, level crossing, colliery etc, is listed and where necessary a location such as Cardiff Queen St. will be found twice, both under Cardiff and Queen St. Places with the same name occurring in different localities have an indication of their location shown in a bracket. So, the six Waterloo locations which are to be found at, or near, Oakdale, Kingsland, Caerphilly, Cardiff, Newport and Upper Lydbrook, are shown as such in the index, although the bracket played no part in their true name.

A location will generally only be shown once, unless separate entries are required because of differing map references (or page numbers in respect of Track Layout Diagrams). So whilst Bilston has seven entries for its halt, junction and sidings, other entries such as Wyllie Halt only have one, despite there being a colliery and signal box as well as the halt.

Sidings which had a purely local name, such as 'Burma Road', 'The Klondyke' or 'Happy Valley' (at Goodrington) have not been included.

Any location in capital letters indicates a passenger station, platform or halt.

Each entry gives the map number on which that particular location can be found. For the many locations that appear on two or more pages, as a result of page overlaps, it is the number of the first map upon which they appear that is given. The full reference is the page number followed by the position on the page in accordance with the grid markings e.g. ABBOTSBURY 17/13 42A3 will be found on Map 42 in square A3 using the left hand margin to locate A and the horizontal margin for 3.

Entries which do not have a map number, e.g. Avonside Wharf 19/41 refer to locations which were not part of the Great Western Railway, but which are included in the Track Layout Diagrams series, as they fell at some time under Western Region control.

Entries shown with a question mark '?' indicate a location where the precise position is not known (see Appendix E).

INDEX TO TRACK LAYOUT DIAGRAMS

The first reference against an entry gives firstly the section number and secondly the page number within that section (e.g. ABBOTSBURY will be found on page 13 of Section 17). Locations without a reference number have not yet been covered in the series, which commenced publication in 1973. The page number always refers to the latest editions in the case of those sections which have been reissued in an expanded form. Southern Railway locations, originally contained in Nos. 9, 13 and 15, are not included in this index.

A complete list of Sections will be found at the rear of this atlas.

INDEX

Locations with an asterisk indicate new entries in this second edition.

Aberthaw Cement Works	44/36	144B6
ABERTHAW HIGH LEVEL	44/36	144B6
ABERTHAW LOW LEVEL	44/22	144B6
Aberthaw Power Station	44/37	144B6
ABERTHIN PLATFORM	44/24	144B4
ABERTILLERY	40/57	181D2
Abertillery and Talywain Colly		181D4
Abertillery Goods	40/57	176D6
Abertillery Old Yard	40/58	181D2
Abertillery Tin Plate Works	40/59	182A1
ABERTRIDWR		179C1
ABERTYSSWG	42/9	167D5
ABERYSTWYTH		114A5
Aberystwyth Harbour		114B5
ABINGDON	27/30	31A4
ABINGDON JUNCTION	27/15	31A4
ABINGDON ROAD (Culham)	27/16	31B4
ABINGDON ROAD HALT (Hinksey)	27/14	68C5
* Ableton Lane (Main Line)	19/51	23A3
Ableton Lane Crossing (Severn Beach)	19/95	23A3
Abovecombe Siding	17/8	42C1
Achddu Brickworks	57/47	134A3
ACOCKS GREEN	30/8	81A5
ACOCKS GREEN & SOUTH YARDLEY	30/8	81A5
Acorn Colly	57/63	134B6
Acorn Patch Depot	37/23	54C2
ACREFAIR HIGH LEVEL		94C2
Acrefair Low Level Goods		94C1
* Acrefair Quarry Siding		94B1
ACTON	25/2	38B2
Acton Burnell Crossing	32/18	98D6
Acton Grange Viaduct S.B.		88A4
ACTON MAIN LINE	25/2	38B2
Acton Wells Junction	25/4	39B1
ADAM STREET, CARDIFF	46/105	149C4
Adare Colly (Tondu)		143C4
Adare Pit (Tonypandy)	46/25	159D3
ADDERBURY	28/34	84D3
ADDERLEY	32/43	97D5
Addis Hill Colly	37/28	54A5
ADDISON ROAD	25/27	38C5
ADDLESTROP	28/13	64D2
ADDLESTROP AND STOW ROAD	28/13	64D2
Adit Level Colly		183B1
ADLESTROP	28/13	64D2
ADMASTON	32/2	69B2
Admiralty Junction (Portland)	17/9	42B1
* Adnock Siding — error for Hadnock		
Aerodrome Siding (Bicester)	27/29	—
Aerodrome Siding (Brize Norton)	27/23	66B2
Aerw Branch Junction	46/32	172A2
Afon Colly	53/25	_
Afon Vale Tinplate Works	50/33	141A3
AFON WEN		190A2
A.F.R.D. Siding	56/36	137C5
* Aish Crossovers		11A3
ALBERTA PLACE HALT	44/61	147D6
Albert Quay (Penzance)	10/1	1D1
Albert Road Goods (Llanelly)	57/58	134C2
ALBERT ROAD HALT (Devonport)	12/5	—
Albion Branch Junction		140B6
Albion Colly (Cilfynydd)		171C3
Albion Dockyard (Bristol)	19/37	24B2
Albion Road Colly (Pontypool)	47/109	182C5
Albion Road Crossing (Parkend)		56B2
Albion Steel Works (Briton Ferry)	50/20	140D3
ALBRIGHTON	32/17	69D5
ALCESTER	34/18	82C1
ALDERMASTON	23/26	32D2
* Alderminster		64A4
Aldington Sidings S.B.	28/6	62C3
Alexanders Siding	18/28	—
Alexandra Dock S.B.'s (Cardiff)	43/84	150A1
Alexandra Dock Jcn S.B. (Newport)	38/7	152A1

ALFORD HALT	16/48	43A5
Alfred Road Sidings	25/16	39D3
Allen's Bank G.F.	46/113	174D6
Aller Junction	14/12	14D1
Aller Siding	14/12	14D1
Allerford Siding	15/14	15B6
Allscott Siding	32/2	69B2
Allscott Sugar Works	32/2	69B2
ALL STRETTON HALT	63/2	100B5
ALLTDDU HALT	58/34	126D6
Alltwen Colly	54/53	—
ALMELEY	63/39	103D4
Alpha Steel Siding		151C6
ALPHINGTON HALT	14/45	13B4
Alphington Road Goods	14/21	13D1
Alps Quarry Siding	44/29	147B2
* Alscot Park		64A4
Alston	35/12	—
ALVECHURCH	34/18	—
ALVELEY COLLY HALT	32/24	71D6
ALVESCOT	27/23	66C3
Amblecote Works		77A2
Amey Sidings G.F. (Appleford)	27/16	31B4
Amman Colly (Brynamman GW)	54/45	131C5
* Amman Colly (Brynamman Mid)	53/33	—
Amman Siding S.B. (Brynamman Mid)	53/34	—
* Amman Tin Plate Works	54/42	131C3
AMMANFORD	54/38	131B3
AMMANFORD (Tirydail)	54/3	131B3
AMMANFORD AND TIRYDAIL	54/3	131B3
AMMANFORD COLLY HALT	54/39	131B4
* Amman Valley Colly		131C3
Amoco Junction	58/23	124B1
* Anchor Fuel Works (Cardiff)	46/99	174D5
Anchor Siding	11/28	4C1
* Ancient Druid Siding		—
ANDOVERSFORD	22/1 & 28/28	57B5
ANDOVERSFORD & DOWDESWELL	22/1	57C6
ANDOVERSFORD JUNCTION	22/1 & 28/28	57B5
ANGARRACK	10/8	1B3
ANGARRACK (Hayle Rly)		1B3
Anthony Pit	46/26	159D3
Appleford Crossing	27/16	31B4
APPLEFORD HALT	27/16	31B4
Appleshaw Siding		51D2
Apple Tree Crossing		143A2
Aqueduct G.F.	57/44	133B3
ARDDLEEN		117C5
ARDLEY	26/1	85B4
ARENIG		111A3
ARGOED	41/34	—
Argoed Colly (Cwm Creeich)	41/34	—
Argoed Colly (Cynonville)	51/29	153D6
Argoed Depot (S & M Line)		98A1
* Ariscot Siding — error for Allscott Siding		
ARLEY	32/25	72B4
* Arlscot Siding — error for Allscott Siding		
Armoury Crossing		117C1
Armscroft Road Depot		56D4
Arrail Level	40/61	182B1
Arral Colly	40/61	182A1
Arral Griffin Colly	40/60	182A1
Arrol's Works (Swansea)		137D2
Arscott Colly		98D4
ARTHOG		110D3
Arthur and Edward Colly	37/44	54A1
ASCOTT	28/17	65D4
ASCOTT UNDER WYCHWOOD	28/17	65D4
Ashburnham Colly	57/47	133C3
Ashburnham Tin Plate Works	57/8	134B2
ASHBURTON	14/33	12A1
Ashburton Junction	14/9	12D1
Ashbury Crossing S.B.	23/1	29B5
ASHCHURCH	34/1	—

Ashchurch W.D. Siding	34/15	—
ASHCOTT & MEARE	18/28	—
Ashendon Junction S.B.	26/3	86C1
Ashendon North S.B.	26/3	86C1
Ashford Bowdler Crossing	63/8	101D3
Ashford Crossing S.B.	63/8	101D3
Ashill Crossing	16/44	20A6
Ashley Crossing S.B.	21/8	27A5
ASHLEY HILL	19/59	23C4
Ashley Hill Junction	19/66	23A1
ASHPERTON	33/1	60A2
ASHTON (Devon)	14/44	13D3
ASHTON (Long Ashton)	16/32	23D3
ASHTON GATE PLATFORM	19/34	24C1
Ashton Ironworks	19/34	24C1
Ashton Junction	19/34	24C1
Ashton Meadows	19/34	24C1
* Ashton Sidings East S.B.	19/34	24D1
* Ashton Sidings West S.B.	19/33	24C1
Ashton Swing Bridge North S.B.	19/37	24A2
Ashton Swing Bridge South S.B.	19/34	24B1
ASHTON-UNDER-HILL	34/15	—
* Ashton Upper Crossing S.B.	19/33	?
Ashton Vale	19/32	24C1
Ashwood Basin		73D1
Askew Bridge	31/55	76A1
Assembly Sidings (Jersey Marine)	56/21	137D1
ASTON BOTTERELL SIDING	33/24	71D3
ASTON CANTLOW HALT	30/37	82C3
Aston Le Walls Siding	29/9	—
Aston Magna	28/12	64C1
ASTON ROWANT	26/33	87C3
* Aston Siding		?
Aston Tirrold S.B.	23/14	31C5
Astrop Sidings S.B.	30/27	84C4
ASTWOOD HALT	33/15	61A4
* Asylum Lane Junction		56B3
ATHELNEY	16/46	20B4
* Atherton Colly		98D3
Atlantic Mills (Barry)	44/66	148C4
* Atlantic Wharf (Cardiff)	43/72	150B5
* Atlas Works (Bristol)	19/50	—
AUDLEM	32/43	97D5
Avington Camp	23/32	51C6
* Avon Bridge Signal Hut (Bristol)	19/9	24D4
Avon Bridge S.B. (Defford)	34/3	—
Avon Bridge S.B. (Warwick)	30/17	82A6
AVONCLIFFE HALT	21/15	27C5
Avoncliffe Siding S.B.	21/15	27C5
Avon Colly	51/38	155D5
Avon Crescent S.B.	19/37	24A2
Avondale Works		183A2
Avon Hill Colly	51/38	155D5
Avon Level	51/38	155D6
Avon Merthyr Colly	51/51	153C2
AVONMOUTH	19/78	25B2
* Avonmouth Bulk Handling Terminal	19/81	25B2
Avonmouth Colly (Cymmer)	51/38	155D3
Avonmouth Crown Brickyard S.B.	19/68	25D3
AVONMOUTH DOCK	19/71	25D2
Avonmouth Dock Junction	19/67	25D3
AVONMOUTH DOCKS	19/74	25C2
* Avonmouth Docks Sidings S.B.	19/69	25D2
AVONMOUTH EAST PIER	19/71	25C1
Avonmouth Gloucester Rd Junction	19/72	25D2
Avonmouth Goods Yard S.B.	19/79	25C2
Avonmouth Light Railway	19/68	25D2
* AVONMOUTH PIER	19/71	25C1
AVONMOUTH ROYAL EDWARD	19/84	25C1
Avonmouth Royal Edward Yard	19/87	25B2
* Avonmouth Smelting Works	19/83	25B3
Avonmouth Town Goods	19/79	25C2
Avonmouth West Sidings	19/70	25D3
Avonside Wharf	19/41	—
* Avon Street Crossing (Bristol)	19/41	—
Avon Vale Mineral Railway	51/43	155C1
AVONWICK	14/33	11A4
AWRE JUNCTION	36/16	53C6
AXBRIDGE	16/34	21D4
AYLESBURY	26/34	86C5
Ayleston Hill S.B.	63/18	104B6
AYNHO	27/3	85A3
Aynho Junction	27/2	85A3
AYNHO PARK PLATFORM	26/1	85A3
B.A.C. G.F. (Filton)	19/98	23B4
B.A.C. Works (East Usk)		151D6
* BABINGTON & MELLS		45A3
BACHE		91C5
Bache Goods		88C5
BACKNEY HALT	36/31	105B2
Backwater Parade Crossing		42C3
BACTON	63/44	106D4
Badgeworth S.B.	35/10	55B5
BADMINTON	20/5	26C5
Baggeridge Colly		73B1
Baggeridge Junction S.B.	31/55	76A1
Baggeridge Wood Colly		?
* BAGLAN		136B5
Baglan Bay Chemical Works	50/18	136B5
Baglan Bay Tinplate Works	50/20	140D3
Baglan Engineering Works, GF	50/13	136A5
Baglan Hall Siding S.B.	50/15	136B5
Baglan Junction S.B.	50/15	136B5
Baglan Loop S.B.	50/16	136B5
Baglan Moors Siding	50/17	136B5
BAGLAN SANDS HALT	50/16	136B5
BAILEY GATE	18/20	—
Bailey Hill Colly		54C2
Bailey's Siding (Abergavenny)	41/17	—
Bailey's Siding (Brynmawr)	41/13	175B6
Bakers Siding	37/1	58C1
BALA		111B5
BALA JUNCTION		111B5
BALA LAKE HALT		111B5
Balance Pit (Blaendare Rd)		182D5
Balance Pit (Six Bells)	40/60	182B2
BALDERTON		91D4
Baldhu S.B.	10/17	2A2
Baldwins Colly (Bryn)	51/4	154B5
BALDWINS HALT (Swansea)	56/26	137D2
Baldwins Siding (Gowerton)	55/1	135C1
Baldwins Siding (Panteg & G.)	39/19	183D5
Ballast Crane Siding S.B. (Cardiff)	43/73	150B5
Ballast Crossing S.B. (Newport)	38/49	152C3
BALLINGHAM	36/31	105A2
Ball's Yard	50/11 & 51/39	140B4
Bampton Aerodrome Siding	27/23	66B4
BAMPTON, DEVON	15/17	15B1
BAMPTON, OXON	27/23	66B4
Banbury Bridge S.B.		84B6
BANBURY GENERAL	30/26	84C6
Banbury Junction	30/24	84B6
BANBURY MERTON STREET	30/26	—
Banbury O.I.C. Sidings	30/23	84A6
Banbury Road Junction (Oxford)	27/27	—
Banbury Yards	30/25	84C6
BANGOR ON DEE		95A5
BANK QUAY, WARRINGTON		88A5
Banwen O.C. Disposal (Onllwyn)	52/20	132C5
Banwen O.C. Site (Glyn Neath)		163A2
BAPTIST END HALT	31/52	76B4
BARBERS BRIDGE	33/20	55B2
Bar End Goods	23/33	51D6
BARGOED	42/23	177D3
BARGOED & ABERBARGOED (Aberbar)	42/23	177C4
BARGOED & ABERBARGOED (Bargoed)	42/23	177D3
Bargoed & Aberbargoed Colly	42/23	177D3

	Bargoed Brithdir Colly		177B2
	Bargoed Colly (Bargoed Pits)	42/24	177D3
	Bargoed Colly (Ogilvie)		169B6
	Bargoed Colly (Penar Branch)	40/63	177C5
	BARGOED COLLY HALT	42/24	177D3
	Bargoed New Pits	42/24	177D3
	Bargoed Pits Junction	42/30	178A2
	Bargoed West S.B.		177C2
	Barkers Siding	47/9	163A2
	Barlby Road Sidings	25/11	39B2
	BARMOUTH		111B1
	BARMOUTH FERRY		111D2
	BARMOUTH JUNCTION		111D2
	Barn Colly		76B4
	Barnes Colly	40/49	175B6
	Barnstaple Branch Junction	15/14	20D1
	BARNSTAPLE VICTORIA ROAD	15/19	18A6
	BARNT GREEN	34/7	—
	Barnwood Junction	35/9	56B4
	Barnwood S.B.	35/7	56B4
	Barrow Colly	49/23	143D4
	Barrow Hill Colly		76A2
	Barrow Lane	19/41	—
	Barrow Road Engine Shed	19/41	—
	BARRS COURT	63/18	104B5
	Barrs Court Junction	63/16	104A5
	BARRY	44/42	148D2
	Barry Caisson Lines Junction	44/51	148C4
	Barry Dock Road Gates S.B.	44/48	148D5
	BARRY DOCKS	44/49	148C4
	Barry Goods	44/43	148D2
	Barry Graving Dock Jcn. S.B.	44/51	148D5
	Barry High Level S.B.	44/51	148D5
	BARRY ISLAND	44/62	148D3
*	Barry Junction (Trehafod)	46/35	172A2
	Barry Junction S.B. (Barry)	44/43	148D2
	Barry Junction S.B. (Duffryn Isaf)	42/42	179C4
	Barry Line Junction (Cardiff)		149C3
	Barry Moors	44/68	148C5
	BARRY PIER	44/64	148D4
	Barry Rhondda Colly (Pontypridd)		172B4
	Barry Sidings (Peterston)	44/18	146D2
	Barry Sidings S.B. (Barry)	44/42	148D1
	Barry S.R.D.	44/68	148C5
	Barry Syndicate Siding	44/48	148C3
	Barry Wharf Lines Junction	44/64	148D4
	Barry Works	44/43	148D2
	BARTON	63/31	104B4
	Barton & Brecon Curve Junction	63/16	104A5
	Barton Curve Junction (Hereford)	63/26	104A5
	Barton Hill Wagon Shops	19/41	24C5
*	Barton Junction (Hereford)	63/16	104B5
*	Barton Road Crossing (Bristol)	19/41	—
*	Barton Vale Crossing (Bristol)	19/41	—
	BARTON STACEY HALT	23/34	51A5
	Barton Street Junction (Gloucester)	35/2	56B3
	BASCHURCH		96D4
	Basildon Signals	23/16	32B2
	BASINGSTOKE	23/41	50C5
	BASON BRIDGE	18/28	—
	BASSALEG	42/51	184D2
	BASSALEG JUNCTION	40/43	184D2
	Bassaleg Loop S.B.	40/43	184D2
	Bassett Road Crossing	10/16	1A6
	Bath Co-Op Siding	18/15	—
	Bath Goods (GWR)	21/5	27D5
	BATH GREEN PARK	18/1 & 20/27	—
	Bath Junction	18/1 & 20/27	—
	Bath Road Crossing (Bridgwater)	16/15	19B6
	Bath Road Engine Shed (Bristol)	19/9	24B4
	Bath Road Junction (Slough)	24/19	34C6
	Bath Road Siding (Bridgwater)		19A6
	BATH SPA	21/6	27D6
	BATHAMPTON	21/7	27A5
	BATHFORD HALT	21/8	27A5
	Bathurst Basin	19/38	24B3
	BATTERSEA	25/31	38D2
	Battersea Power Station	25/33	40D2
	BAWDRIP HALT	18/30	—
	Baylys Wharf (Sutton Harbour)	12/18	8D5
	Baylys Wharf (Turnchapel)	12/29	8D5
	Bays Hill S.B.	35/16	56B6
	Baysmoor Colly		76D5
	Bayston Hill S.B.		98C5
	Bayton Colly		72D3
	Beach Junction (Swansea)	56/1	137C2
	Beach Sidings (Cardiff)	43/88	150C2
	Beach Sidings (Swansea)	54/31	137C2
	Beachley Junction	36/10	52B5
	Beachley Shipyard	36/9	52C5
	Beacon Siding	11/32	4D2
	BEACONSFIELD	26/9	34A5
	BEACONSFIELD GOLF LINKS HALT	26/9	34A6
	BEAG FAIR SIDING	58/31	123C5
*	Beag Siding	58/31	123C5
	BEAM BRIDGE	15/12	15C5
	Beanacre Crossing (Caldicot)		52A4
	BEANACRE HALT (Wilts)	21/24	46A3
	Bearah Tor	11/36	6B3
	Beards Lane Crossing S.B.	20/30	58C5
	BEARLEY	30/37	82B3
	Bearley Junctions	30/38	82C3
	Bearmore Colly		76D5
	Beaufort (Ebbw Vale G.W.R.)	40/1	175B4
	BEAUFORT (Ebbw Vale L.N.W.R.)	41/9	—
	Beaufort Brick Siding (E.V.)	41/9	—
	Beaufort Brick Siding (Stoke Gifford)	20/1	23A6
	Beaufort Colly (Penclawdd)	54/52	—
*	Beaufort G.F. (Morriston Mid)	53/41	—
	Beaufort Iron Works (E.V.)		175B4
	Beaufort Road Siding (Brynmawr)	40/47	175B5
	Beaufort Siding (Stoke Gifford)	20/1	23A6
	Beaufort Street Crossing (Brynmawr)	41/12	175B5
	Beaufort Works (Morriston)	53/38	
	Beaufort Yard Colly (Ebbw Vale)		175C6
	Beaupre Quarry	44/23	144B4
	BEAVER'S HILL HALT	58/26	124D5
	BEBINGTON		89C4
	BEBINGTON & NEW FERRY		89C4
	Beck Colly	54/23	—
	Beckett Street Yard	27/10	68B5
	BECKFORD	34/15	—
	Becks Siding	28/18	67A2
	Beddau Branch Jcn (Aber Jcn)		173A5
	Beddau Branch Jcn (Penrhos Jcn)		173C6
	BEDDAU HALT (Caerphilly)		173B5
	BEDDAU HALT (Common Bch Jcn)	49/76	161C5
	Beddau Loop Junction		173B4
	Beddgelert Sidings		110A3
	Bedford Road Crossing	49/45	143A4
	BEDLINOG		169D4
	BEDLINOG COLLIERS PLATFORM		169D4
	Bedlinog Colly Junction		169C4
	BEDMINSTER	19/6	24C3
	BEDWAS	42/43	179C5
	Bedwas Navigation Colly	42/44	179C6
	Bedwellty Pits Colly	41/30	
	BEDWELLTY PITS HALT	41/31	—
	Bedwlwyn Colly	47/43	165D4
	Bedwlwyn Quarry	47/43	165D3
	BEDWYN	23/19	48C6
*	BEECHWOOD		88C3
	Beechgrove S.B.	21/54	47B6
	Beech Tree Colly		77B4
	Beer Hackett Siding	17/6	44B3
	Bees Ditch Crossing		52B2
	Beili Glas Colly	55/1	133D6
	Belfry Quarry		101B5

* Bellan		?
Belle Isle Colly		76C2
Bell End Colly		79C1
Bell Ferry Dock Siding	38/34	151C6
Bellfield Works		87D3
Bellport	38/34	151C6
* Belle Vue Junction		99D1
Belmont Street Sidings	12/17	8C4
Belvidere Bridge S.B.	32/1	98C6
Bemerton Crossing		47D6
Benallt Colly		?
Bendalls Siding	20/44	—
BENGEWORTH	34/15	—
Benner Fawr Crossing		110B1
Bennett's Siding (Charfield)	20/44	—
* Bennett's Siding (Oakengates)		70A4
Bennett's Mill Siding	20/53	—
Benthall Edge Quarry Siding	32/20	70C1
Bentley Heath Crossing S.B.	30/11	81C5
BERKELEY	37/1	58C1
Berkeley Loop Junction	37/1	58C1
Berkeley Loop South Junction	20/44	58C2
BERKELEY ROAD	20/44 & 37/1	58C2
BERRINGTON (Herefordshire)		102A2
BERRINGTON (Shropshire)	32/18	98D6
BERRINGTON AND EYE	63/10	102A2
Berrington Colly	54/52	—
Berry Croft Crossing	23/4	31B3
Berry Hill Sidings	33/14	78C5
Bersham S.B.		94B6
Berthddu Crossing	59/5	—
Berthgron Quarry Siding		170D5
Berthllwyd Colly	54/52	—
Bertie Pit	46/33	172A1
Bertwyn Crossing	57/2	133B1
* Berwerdy Crossing		171D3
Berwick Colly		134D6
BERWIG HALT		93C1
BERW ROAD HALT		171D2
BERWYN		112B6
BETTISFIELD		96A5
BETTWS (Derry Ormond)	58/35	127C4
Bettws Colly (Ammanford)	54/39	131B4
Bettws Colly (Llynvi Valley)	49/10	157B2
Bettws Colly Junction (L.V.)		157C2
BETTWS LLANGEINOR	51/14	157B3
Bettws Llantwit Colly (B. Llantwit)	51/14	157A3
Bettws Llantwit Colly (Llangeinor)	49/33	157B4
Bettws Navigation Colly (L.V.)		157B1
* Bettws New Mine (Ammanford)	54/38	131B4
BEULAH HALT	58/31	123B2
Bevans Siding		153B1
BEWDLEY	32/26 & 33/25	77D2
Beynon Colly	40/51	176A6
Bicester C.O.D.	27/28	—
BICESTER LONDON ROAD	27/16	—
BICESTER NORTH	26/1	85C5
BICKLEIGH	14/27	7A5
Bicknor Siding	37/42	53A3
Bicslade Lower Level Colly	37/14	54B3
Bicslade Siding	37/45	54C1
Bicslade Tramway	37/44	54C1
BIDFORD	29/1	—
BIDFORD ON AVON	29/1	—
BIGLIS	44/59	148B5
Biglis Brickworks	44/59	148B6
Biglis Goods S.B.	44/59	148B6
Biglis Junction	44/59	148B5
Big Pit		181A3
BIGSWEIR	36/29	53D2
Bilboa Quarry	21/49	45B2
BILBROOK	32/8	69D6
BILLACOMBE	12/29	7C5
* Bill Brook Siding		69D6

Billingsley Colly	32/25	72A3
Billups Quarry Siding	49/62	160D6
Bilson Ballast Siding	37/32	54B5
Bilson Colly	37/32	54B5
Bilson Exchange Siding	37/32	54B5
BILSON HALT	37/33	54B5
Bilson Junction	37/32	54B5
Bilson North Junction	37/19 & 37/30	54A6
BILSON ROAD PLATFORM	37/19	54B5
Bilson South Junction	37/19 & 37/30	54A6
Bilson Yard	37/32	54B5
Bilston Basin	31/14	75A2
BILSTON CENTRAL	31/14	74D6
Bilston Gas Works	31/36	74D5
Bilston Steelworks	31/36	75A1
BILSTON WEST	31/36	75A2
Bincombe Tunnel S.B.	17/3	41D6
BINEGAR	18/12	—
BINTON	29/1	—
BIRCHES AND BILBROOKE HALT	32/17	69D6
BIRCHGROVE (LMSR)	53/12	—
BIRCHGROVE HALT (GWR)		174B5
Birchrock Colly		135A1
Birchrock Siding S.B.	54/15	—
* Birchwood Siding		23D5
Bird in Hand Junction	41/37 & 47/93	178C3
Birkenhead Abbey Street Yard		90C3
Birkenhead Blackpool St. S.B.		90C3
Birkenhead Brook St. Junction		90B4
Birkenhead Canning St. S.B.'s		90A4
Birkenhead Canning St. Town		90C3
Birkenhead Cathcart St. Goods		90A4
Birkenhead Cavendish Sidings		90A2
Birkenhead Duke Street		90A3
* BIRKENHEAD GRANGE LANE		90B6
Birkenhead Hinderton Road Goods		90C4
Birkenhead Jackson Street Yard		90C3
* Birkenhead Limekiln Lane Siding		?
Birkenhead Mollington Street		90C4
BIRKENHEAD MONKSFERRY		90B5
Birkenhead Morpeth Dock Goods		90A5
* Birkenhead Old Chester Road Siding		?
* Birkenhead Peel Street Siding		90C5
Birkenhead Shore Road		90C3
Birkenhead Sidings (Pontypool Road)	39/6	183B6
BIRKENHEAD TOWN		90C5
* Birkenhead Tranmere Junction		90C4
Birkenhead Tranmere Pool		90C5
Birkenhead Tunnel Rd Yard		90C3
* Birkenhead Union Street Junction		90C5
BIRKENHEAD WOODSIDE		90B5
Birmingham Corp. Water Works	34/19	81B2
* Birmingham Gas Works Siding		75C5
BIRMINGHAM MOOR STREET	30/1	80B1
BIRMINGHAM SNOW HILL	31/26	80B6
BISHOP'S CASTLE	63/33	100C1
Bishop's Castle Junction	63/4	101C1
BISHOP'S CLEEVE	28/19	63D3
BISHOP'S LYDEARD	15/26	15A6
BISHOP'S NYMPTON & MOLLAND	15/20	18D3
BISHOP'S ROAD (PADDINGTON)	25/17	39D5
Bishopsteignton S.B.	14/16	14C4
Bishopswood Tramway		53A4
Bishton S.B.	38/20	52D1
Bishwell Colly (Gowerton GWR)	55/3	135C1
Bishwell Colly (Gowerton LNWR)	54/25	—
BITTAFORD PLATFORM	14/6	11A3
Bittaford Viaduct S.B.	14/6	11A3
Bitterley	63/34	101B4
BITTON	20/48	—
Bixhead Quarries		54A2
Bixslade	37/14	54C1
* Blackband Junction		165C5
Blackbrook Colly		173C6

BLACK DOG HALT	21/27	28D4
Black Grove Colly		171C6
* Blackheath Colly		?
Black Horse Lane Crossing	19/37	24A3
Black Lane Colly Siding		?
BLACK LION CROSSING HALT	47/36	165B3
Black Lion S.B.		170A3
BLACKMILL	49/22	157C5
* Blackminster	28/6	62C3
Black Mountain Colly	53/51	—
Black Park S.B.		95C3
Black Pit		?
BLACKPOLE HALT	33/15	61A4
Blackpool Street S.B.		90C3
BLACK ROCK HALT (Criccieth)		109C1
Black Rock Quarry (Tenby)	58/27	124A4
* Black Rock Siding (Ynysybwl Branch)		171C1
BLACKTHORN	26/2	85D6
Black Vein Colly (Caerphilly)		173B6
Black Vein Crossing S.B. (Risca)	41/45	180B4
Black Vein Pit (Dowlais)		167C2
Black Vein Sirhowy Colly		?
Blackwater Junctions	10/15	2A1
* Blackwater Viaduct	10/16	2A1
Blackweir Siding	46/103	149B3
BLACKWELL	34/7	—
BLACKWOOD	41/35	—
Blaenafon Colly	51/24	153C2
Blaenant Colly (Abernant)		165A4
Blaenant Colly (Brynmawr)		175B6
Blaenant Colly (Cefn Coed)	52/7	162A1
Blaenant Colly (Crynant)	52/8	132D4
* Blaenau Colly	54/34	131A1
BLAENAU FESTINIOG		109A5
Blaenavon Colly (Tonmawr)	51/51	153B2
BLAENAVON HIGH LEVEL (Mon)	41/23	—
Blaenavon Ironworks (Mon)	41/21	181A3
Blaenavon Junctions (Tonmawr)	51/40	153C2
BLAENAVON LOW LEVEL (Mon)	39/21	181A4
* Blaenavon Siding (L. & O.)		?
Blaen Bargoed Mine		167D2
Blaen Cae Gurwen Colly	53/32	—
Blaencaerau Level	49/1	156A3
Blaen Clydach Colly	46/55 & 49/55	159C4
Blaen Clydach Goods	46/55	159C4
Blaencorrwg Colly	51/48	155A4
Blaen Cregan		155B2
Blaencuffin Colly		182C2
Blaencwm Colly Sidings S.B.	53/25	—
Blaencwm Mileage Siding		158B1
BLAENDARE ROAD HALT	39/18	183A4
Blaendare Ironworks		182D5
Blaendare Sidings S.B.	47/103	182D4
Blaendare Slope Colly	47/110	182D5
BLAENGARW	49/27	156B5
* Blaen Graigola Colly	53/15	—
Blaengwawr Colly (Aberdare)	47/52	165B4
Blaengwawr Colly (Dare Junction)	47/35	165B3
Blaengwrach Colly	47/9	163B1
BLAENGWYNFI	51/37	155C4
Blaenhirwaun Colly	57/50	133A6
* Blaenllecha Colly		?
Blaenmawr Colly	51/53	153C5
* Blaenmawr Navigation Colly		153C5
Blaenant Colly (Abernant)	47/50	165A4
Blaenant Sidings (Abernant)	47/48	165A4
Blaennant Colly (Brynmawr)		175B6
Blaenogwr Colly		160A3
Blaenpelena Colly	51/54	153B5
BLAENPLWYF HALT	58/41	127C3
BLAENRHONDDA	46/2	158B1
Blaenrhondda Colly	46/58	158A1
Blaenserchan Colly	39/24	182B3
Blaensychan Colly	39/24	182B3
Blaen Waen Siding	53/20	—
* Blaenycwm S.B. (Blaenrhondda)	46/3	158B1
Blaenycwm (Llanvihangel)		107B1
Blaen y cwm Colly (Melyn Court)		155A1
* Blaen y Cwm (Blaenrhondda)	46/3	158B1
* Blaeny Cwm Colly (Cwmffrwdoer)		?
* Blaen y Maen Colly	53/19	—
BLAGDON	16/43	21C6
BLAINA	40/53	176B6
Blaina and Raven Colly		131B1
Blaina Colly (Pantyffynon)	54/5	131B1
Blaina Ironworks	40/52	176B6
Blaina Red Ash Colly		?
BLAISDON HALT	36/33	53A6
Blaise S.B.	19/97	23B3
BLAKEDOWN	33/11	78B2
Blakedown Viaduct S.B.		78B2
Blakeney Goods	37/44	54C3
* Blakstads Siding	59/32	116C3
Blaneney Road Bridge	37/22	54C2
BLAKESLEY	29/10	
Blanch's Siding	20/6	28A6
BLANDFORD	18/19	—
BLANDFORD FORUM	18/19	—
Blatchbridge Junction	21/28	45B4
Blackford Viaduct S.B.	14/4	11A1
Blaynea Colly	54/34	131A1
BLEADON AND UPHILL	16/21	21D2
Bledington Sidings	28/15	65C6
BLEDLOW	27/22	87B4
BLEDLOW BRIDGE HALT	26/33	87B4
BLENHEIM AND WOODSTOCK	27/30	67A2
BLETCHINGTON	27/4	85D2
Bletchington Cement Sidings S.B.	27/5	67A3
Blinkhorn Siding	16/2	20D2
* Blists Hill Ironworks	32/54	—
BLISWORTH	29/15	—
Blisworth Ironstone Siding	29/13	—
BLOCKLEY	28/12	64B1
Blockleys Siding (Hadley Jcn)	32/50	—
BLODWELL JUNCTION		119B2
Bloomfield Crossing S.B.	31/37	75C2
* Bloomfield Junction		75B2
BLOWERS GREEN	31/41	76B4
Blowers Green Junction	31/41	76B4
BLOXHAM	28/33	84D2
Bloxham Ironstone Sidings	28/33	84D2
BLUE ANCHOR	15/24	17A2
Blue Lias Lime Works		82C3
* Blundells Siding	63/10	102B6
BLUNSDON	22/5	29A2
Board's Siding	18/30	—
Bockhampton Crossing	23/40	49B2
Bodinnick S.B.	11/2	3C4
BODMIN GENERAL	11/35	5D5
BODMIN NORTH	11/35	—
BODMIN PARKWAY	11/10	5D6
BODMIN ROAD	11/10	5D6
Bod-rhyngallt Colly	46/18	159B3
Bodriggy Crossing	10/8	1A3
* Bodtalog Mill Siding		113C1
Boedringallt Colly	46/18	159A2
Bojea Siding	11/13	4D4
BOLHAM HALT	15/17	15D1
Bolney Crossing		34C1
Bolt Street Siding	38/58	152C4
Bomford's Siding	28/2	62B1
BONCATH	58/32	125C3
* Bone Mill Siding (Ruckley)		69C5
BONTNEWYDD		110C6
Bonville's Court Colly	58/28	124C6
BONWM HALT		112B3
* Bookers Siding	46/77	173D2
* Boot Quarry		178D2

BORDESLEY	30/2	80C1
Bordesley Junction (Midland)	30/4	80B2
Bordesley Junction Yards	30/3	80C2
Bordesley Sidings S.B.	30/3	80C2
Borough Bounds Wharf	11/35	—
BORTH		114A1
Borth Harbour Sand Siding		114A1
BOSCARNE EXCHANGE PLATFORM	11/35	5A6
Boscarne Junction	11/35	5A6
Boskell Siding	11/18	4C4
Botany Bay Colly		70A2
* Botfield Siding		?
Botley Road Crossing		68B5
Bottomcombe Siding	17/8	42D2
Bottom Pit Loco Sidings	42/48	180C4
* Bouchers Siding		148B5
BOUGH ROOD	59/24	121B5
BOUGH ROOD AND LLYSWEN	59/24	121B5
BOUGHTON HALT	33/9	61B4
Boundary Siding	53/14	—
BOURNE END	24/38	34A1
Bourne Lane Crossing	16/43	21C5
BOURNEMOUTH WEST	18/24	—
BOURNVILLE (Birmingham)	34/11	—
BOURNVILLE (MON) HALT	40/55	176C6
BOURTON (Flax Bourton)	16/32	21A6
Bourton Crossovers (Shrivenham)	21/1	29B5
BOURTON-ON-THE-WATER	28/29	57A6
BOVEY	14/40	14B2
Bovey Granite Siding	14/40	14B2
Bovey Lane Crossing	14/43	14B3
Bovey Pottery Siding	14/40	14B2
Bovil Colly	42/46	180C3
BOWBRIDGE CROSSING HALT	20/32	58D6
Bowditch Colly	40/53	177D5
Bowleys Crossing	35/2	—
Bown's Siding	47/14	163B6
Bowson Colly	37/28	54A5
BOW STREET		114C2
BOX	21/9	27A5
BOXFORD	23/40	49C4
Box Hill		28D1
BOX (MILL LANE) HALT	21/9	27A6
Box Tunnel East S.B.	21/9	28D2
Boyd Avon S.B.	20/48	—
Boyes Siding	24/41	35C1
Boyles Siding		157B3
BOYNE HILL, MAIDENHEAD		34C3
Brabazon Crossing	19/101	23B4
Brachty Colly		?
Brackla Hill Siding	44/32	144C2
Brackla Siding	44/32	144C1
* BRADDIN BRIDGE	29/18	—
Bradford Crossing (Somerset)	15/14	15B6
Bradford Crossing (Wilts)	22/15	27C6
Bradford Junctions (Wilts)	21/18	46B2
BRADFORD-ON-AVON	21/15	27C6
BRADFORD PEVERELL & STRATTON H.	17/4	41C5
BRADLEY AND MOXLEY	31/14	75A3
Bradley Siding (Much Wenlock)	32/32	69D2
Bradley's Works (Stourbridge)		77B1
Bradpole Crossing Siding	17/14	41C1
Braichbach Quarry		113A6
Braich-y-Cymmer (1st Colly)	49/31	156C5
Braich-y-Cymmer S.B.	49/31	156D6
Brains Trafalgar Tramway	37/18	54A5
BRAMLEY	23/42	50B6
BRAMPFORD SPEKE	15/16	16D1
Branches Fork Junction	39/23	182B5
Brandey Crossing		94D4
Brandie Pit		94D4
Brandy Bottom Colly	20/40	—
Brandy Bridge Junction		168D2
BRANKSOME	18/23	—

BRANSFORD ROAD	33/8	61B3
Bransford Road Junction	33/8	61B3
Braysdown Colly Sidings	18/6	—
BREAN ROAD HALT	16/21	21D1
BRECON	52/16	122C3
Brecon Boat Siding (Brynmawr)	41/13	—
Brecon Curve Junction (Hereford)	63/18	104A5
Brecon Forest Tramway		132C4
BREDON	34/3	
BREIDDEN		98C1
Bremell Sidings S.B.	20/35	29B2
Brendon Hill		17C2
BRENT	14/8	11A3
BRENTFORD	24/42	37D6
Brentford Dock	24/44	37D6
Brentford Town Goods	24/42	37D5
BRENTHAM	26/23	36A6
BRENT KNOLL	16/21	19A2
Brentor Siding	14/24	9D5
Bres Pit		134C3
BRETFORTON & WESTON-SUB-EDGE	28/20	62C4
* Bretforton Siding		?
BRETTELL LANE	31/47	76D2
Brewens Crossing	28/17	65D3
Brewery Siding (Bath)	20/48	—
Brewery Siding (Fleur de Lis)	42/36	178C2
Brewham Siding S.B.	16/51	45C3
Brick Cabin G.F. (Whitworth)	51/53	153C3
Brick Pit Siding	37/21	54C2
Brickworks Siding S.B.'s (Risca)	41/45	180B4
* Bridge Bolt G.F. (Bristol)	19/37	24A2
Bridge Inn Siding		136C4
BRIDGEND	44/1	144D1
Bridgend & Aberthaw Lime Works	44/24	144D1
Bridgend Brackla Siding	44/24	144C1
Bridgend Coity Goods	44/22	144C1
Bridgend Coity Junction	44/22	144B1
Bridgend Colly (Bromley)		76C2
Bridgend Cowbridge Road Jcn	44/25	144D1
Bridgend Dinas Brickworks (Tondu)	49/50	143A6
Bridgend Paper Mills (Tondu)	49/9	157B1
BRIDGES	11/24	3B6
BRIDGE STREET, NEATH	56/49	139A6
BRIDGNORTH	32/23	71B5
BRIDGWATER (G.W.R.)	16/14	19B6
BRIDGWATER (S. & D.)	18/30	—
Bridgwater Docks	16/15	19B5
Bridgwater Works	16/13	19B6
BRIDPORT	17/14	41C1
* BRIDPORT HARBOUR		41C1
BRIERLEY HILL	31/45	76C2
BRIERLEY HILL AND ROUND OAK	31/45	76C2
Brierley Siding	37/43	54A1
BRILL & LUDGERSHALL	26/3	86B1
BRIMLEY HALT	14/40	14B2
* BRIMSCOMB	20/32	58D5
BRIMSCOMBE	20/32	58D5
BRIMSCOMBE BRIDGE HALT	20/32	58D4
Brimspill		53C6
Brindley Street Siding	32/27	72A5
BRINKWORTH	20/8	28A5
Brinsea Road Crossing	16/43	21C4
BRISLINGTON	21/43	24D6
* Bristol Bulk Handling Terminal	19/81	25B2
* Bristol Canons Marsh	19/39	24B2
Bristol East Depot	19/19	24B6
* Bristol Goods Junction S.B.	19/41	—
* BRISTOL HARBOUR	19/40	24B2
Bristol Harbour Goods	19/40	24B2
Bristol Harbour Junction		24B4
Bristol Loop Junction	19/15	24B5
* Bristol No. 1 Tunnel S.B.	19/18	23B6
BRISTOL PARKWAY	20/2	23A6
Bristol Road Crossing (Bridgwater)	16/15	19B6

Bristol Road Crossing (Dunball)	16/18	19C2		Brook Street S.B. (Birkenhead)		90B3
BRISTOL ST PHILIPS	19/41	—		Brookthorpe Crossing	35/1	55D3
Bristol St Philips Marsh	19/21	24B4	*	Brook Vale Colly	46/57	159C2
BRISTOL TEMPLE MEADS	19/9	24B4		BROOME	59/14	—
Bristol Water Works (Cheddar)	16/35	22A1		Broome Crossing (Swindon)		29C3
Bristol West Depot	19/2	24D1		BROOM JUNCTION	29/1 & 34/17	—
Britannia Colly (Pengam)	42/34	178B2		Brothers Pit	53/12	—
Britannia Crossing (Eirw Branch)	46/33	159D6		Broughton Colly		93C4
BRITANNIA HALT (Kingswear)	14/34	12D5		Broughton Crossing S.B.		93B4
Britannic Colly	49/69	160B4		Broughton Forge S.B.		93C4
Britannic Merthyr Colly	49/70	160B4		BROUGHTON GIFFORD HALT	21/21	46A2
BRITHDIR	42/20	177B3		Broughton Hall Ironworks		93C4
Brithdir and Cwmdu Colly	55/18	139A1		Broughton Solvay Coke Sidings		93C4
Brithdir Branch Junction	42/18	177B3		Brownlands	56/13	137D6
Brithdir Colly (nr. Bargoed)	42/18	177B3		Browns Pit		?
Brithdir Colly (Skewen)	56/40	139A1		Bruces Crossing		170B1
Brithdir Level (Fochriw)		167D4		Bruern Crossing	28/17	65D3
Brithwenydd Colly	46/22	159C3		Brug Colly		168D4
British Aluminium Sdg (Uskmouth)	38/34	151C3		Brug Colly (2nd)		168D1
British Ironworks (Abersychan)		184B1		Brunsdon Bridge S.B.	23/20	49D2
* British Mannesmann Tube Co G.F.	53/37	—		BRUTON	16/51	45D2
BRITISH RHONDDA HALT	47/12	163C4	*	Bruton Jcn (Glastonbury)		—
BRITON FERRY	50/12	140B4		BRYMBO		93B4
Briton Ferry Docks	50/19	140D3		Brymbo Colly		93B3
BRITON FERRY EAST	50/11	140C4		Brymbo Junction		93B4
Briton Ferry Junction	50/11	140C4		Brymbo Sidings (Hook Norton)	28/33	65A6
BRITON FERRY ROAD	56/32	137C5		Brymbo Silica Sdg (Llanfynydd)		92B2
Briton Ferry Steelworks	50/19	140D3		Brymbo Steel Works		93B4
BRITON FERRY WEST	50/11	140C4		BRYMBO WEST CROSSING HALT		93A4
Britannia Works (Troedyrhiw)		169C2		BRYN	51/4	154C6
BRIXHAM	14/36	12C6		Brynamman Colly	54/44	131C4
Brixham Branch Junction	14/35	12C5		BRYNAMMAN EAST	53/33	131C5
BRIXHAM ROAD	14/35	12C5		BRYNAMMAN WEST	54/45	131C5
BRIXTON ROAD	12/30	7C6		Brynau Quarries		167A1
BRIZE NORTON & BAMPTON	27/23	66B4		Bryn Brickworks Siding	51/5	154C6
BROAD MARSTON HALT	28/23	62B5		Bryn Brith Pits		167A4
Broadmoor Siding	37/30	54A5		BRYNCELYNOG HALT		111B1
Broadoak Colly (Loughor)	55/1	133D6		Bryncethin Colly	49/23	143D6
Broadoak Crossing (Rossett)		92B4		Bryncethin Junction	49/24	157D5
BROADSANDS HALT	14/36	12C5		Bryncoch Colly (Groesfaen)		177D1
* BROAD SOMERFORD		28A4		Bryncoch Colly (Rockwood)		173D3
BROADSTONE	18/13	—		Bryncoch Colly (Wernddu)		135A6
Broadstone Junction	18/13	—		Bryncock Colly	53/15	—
BROADWAY (Dorset)		42A5		Bryn Colly (Dafen)		133C5
BROADWAY (Worcs)	28/20	62D4	*	Bryn Colly (Llantwit Fardre)	49/79	161B5
BROADWEY		42A5		Bryncorrwg Colly	51/54	153B5
Brockhampton Siding	33/22	102D6		Bryn Defaid Pits		164A6
BROCKMOOR HALT	31/46	76C2		Brynderi Colly	53/25	—
BROCKWEIR HALT	36/29	52A5		BRYNDERWEN	59/18	122B4
Brofiscin Limeworks	49/83	161D5		Bryn Dewi Colly		135B5
* Brofiskin	49/83	161D5		Bryndu Colly	49/43	143A3
Brogdens Siding S.B.	49/16	143D4		Bryndu Crossing	49/44	143A3
Broken Cross Crossing	36/21	55C1		Bryndu Goods	49/44	143A3
BROMBOROUGH		89C4		Bryndu Sidings (Blaendare)		182C5
Bromborough Port		89A5		Bryngavn Junction	49/33	157C3
BROMBOROUGH RAKE		89C4		Bryngrugos Colly	51/52	153C2
BROMFIELD	63/6	101B2		BRYNGWYN (Llanfyllin)		117B3
BROMHAM & ROWDE HALT	21/26	46B4		Bryngwyn Colly (Bedwas)	42/41	179C4
Bromley Basin S.B.	31/57	76C2		Bryngwyn Colly (Blaenavon)	51/52	153C2
Bromley Colly (Bromley)	31/57	76C2		Bryngwyn Colly (Dafen)	57/60	134C5
Bromley Colly (Pensford)	21/43	27B1		Bryngwyn Colly (Hirwaun)		164C3
BROMLEY HALT	31/57	76C2		Bryngwyn Siding (Gorseinon)	54/22	
Brompton and Fulham Goods	25/30	38D6		Bryngyn Colly		179C5
BROMSGROVE	34/6	—		Bryngyrnos Colly		154C5
BROMYARD	33/21	102D6		Brynhenllish Colly	53/51	—
Bromyard Junction (Bransford Rd)	33/8	61B3		Brynhenllish Junction	53/29	—
Bromyard Junction (Leominster)	63/10	102B6		Brynhenllys Colly	53/51	—
* BRONGWYN		117B3	*	Brynhellyshigg		
BRONWYDD ARMS	58/37	129B4		Bryniau Quarries		167A1
Bronybuckley Crossing		117C2		Brynkinalt Colly		95C3
Brook Bridge Crossing		103A6		Brynllais Colly	54/50	—
Brook Lane Junction		88C5		Bryn Lliw Colly	54/16 & 55/40	135A1
Brooksby Crossing		34A1		Brynlloi Colly	54/40	131A5
BROOK STREET HALT		94D4		Brynllwrack Colly	49/9	157B1

Brynllynfell Colly	53/51	—
Brynmally Colly		93A4
Brynmally Crossing		93A1
Brynmarlais Crossing	54/3	130D6
BRYNMAWR	40/46 & 41/11	175B6
Brynmawr and Bishwell S.B.	54/25	—
Brynmawr and Western Valleys Jcn	41/11	175B6
Brynmawr Colly (Gowerton)	54/25	—
Brynmelyn Quarry		132B1
BRYNMENIN	49/20	143C5
BRYNMENYN	49/20	143C5
Brynmenyn Colly	49/21	143C4
Bryn Mercantile Colly		156C1
Brynmorgan Colly	53/28	—
Brynmynach Siding		178D1
Brynna Colly	44/8	145B3
BRYNNA PLATFORM		145C3
Bryn Navigation Colly	51/4	154B5
* Brynnow		?
Brynoer Pit		167A5
Brynoer Tramway	59/16	166A4
Brynog Drive Crossing	58/41	127B2
Brynpwllog Pit		167B3
Brynrhig Colly	51/10	156C3
Brynrhug Colly (Brymbo)		93A3
Brynrhug Colly (Maesteg)		156C3
Brynteg Colly (Seven Sisters)	52/9	132C4
Brynteg Pits (Cyfarthfa)		168B2
BRYN TEIFY	58/36	128B4
* Bryn Tramway Siding		—
Bryn Whilach Colly		138C3
* Bryn Works (Yniry Geinon)	53/19	—
Brynwyth Colly	49/25	157C6
Bryn Yard (Llanelly)	57/17	134D3
Bryn-y-Cae Colly		145B4
Brynygroes Colly	53/49	—
* Bryn-y-Gwyna		145B3
BRYNYGWYNON PLATFORM	44/8	145B2
Bryn yr Owen Colly		94C4
BUCKFASTLEIGH	14/33	12A1
Buckland Colly	54/49	131B6
BUCKNELL	59/13	—
Buckshead Tunnel S.B.	11/1	2A3
Budbrook S.B.	30/17	82A5
Budds Colly		182B1
* Budds Road Siding	53/23	—
Budock Crossing		2D2
Buffery Colly	31/52	76B5
BUGLE	11/23	3B6
BUILDWAS	32/19	69C1
* Buildwas Crossing	32/18	69B1
* Buildwas Sand Siding	32/18	69B1
BUILTH ROAD HIGH LEVEL	59/7	—
BUILTH ROAD LOW LEVEL	59/26	121A3
BUILTH WELLS	59/25	121B2
Bulkamore Siding		12A1
Buller Quay	11/37	6D5
Bullocks Mill Crossing		103B3
Bullocks Siding		115A4
BULLO CROSS HALT	37/37	53B5
Bullo Pill	36/17	53B6
Bullo Pill Docks	36/17	53B6
Bullpoint	12/2	8B2
* Bulls Bridge		35C2
Bulls Lock S.B.	23/24	49A5
Bulwark Camp	36/5	52C5
Bumble Hole Sidings	31/52	76C5
Bunford Flax Mill Siding	17/16	44A2
Burbage S.B.	21/42	48A1
Burcott Road Crossing	63/18	104A5
Burgedin Crossing		117C5
BURGHCLERE	23/36	50B1
Burghfield S.B.	23/43	32D4
Burgotha Siding	11/28	4C1
BURLESCOMBE	15/11	15D4
Burlish Branch	32/27 & 33/25	72A5
BURLISH HALT	32/27 & 33/25	72A5
* Burlish Lodge Crossing	32/27	7A5
BURN HALT	15/16	16C1
BURNGULLOW	11/3	3C5
Burngullow West Siding	11/32	4D3
BURNHAM (BUCKS)	24/18	34C5
BURNHAM BEECHES	24/18	34C5
BURNHAM ON SEA	18/25	—
Burnt Mill Junction S.B.		99D2
BURRATOR HALT	14/32	10C5
BURRINGTON	16/43	21C5
Burrows Junction (Aberavon)	50/34	141B3
Burrows Junction (Swansea)	56/17	137D6
Burrows Lodge Goods	56/1	137B2
Burrows Siding S.B.	56/17	137D6
Burrows Sidings (1–2 Sets)	56/21	137D1
Burrows Sidings (3–4 Sets)	56/26	137D3
Burrows Sidings (5 Set)	56/30	137C4
* Burrows Yard G.F.		137D4
BURRY PORT	57/8	134A2
Burry Port Dock Junction	57/8	134A2
BURTON DASSETT	29/7	—
Burton Hill Siding	29/7	—
BURWARTON HALT	33/24	71D3
Bush Colliery	47/99	178B5
Bushbury Junction	31/3	—
Bushbury Sidings S.B.	31/3	74B4
* Bute Ballast Crossing	43/62	150C6
Bute Colly (Treherbert)	46/4	158B2
* Bute Dry Dock	43/79	150A2
* Bute Estate Siding (Cathays)		149A3
Bute Gas Works (Cardiff)	43/53	150D6
* Bute Ironworks (Mwyndy)		161D4
* Bute Ironwords (Rhymney)		167C6
Bute Limeworks Siding (Mwyndy)	49/82	161D4
Bute Merthyr S.B.	46/4	158C2
Bute Pit (Hirwaun)		164C2
BUTE ROAD, CARDIFF	43/77	149D4
Bute Street S.B.	43/72	149D4
Bute West Yard	43/76	150A5
* Bute Yard Engine Shed	43/72	150B6
Buttery Hatch Colly	42/37	178C2
Buttery Hatch S.B.	42/38	178C2
BUTTINGTON		117D5
Buttington Gates S.B.		118A4
Butts Branch	33/10	60C4
Bwlch Colly (Tonmawr)	51/39	153D2
Bwlch S.B. (N. & B. Rly.)	52/14	122C1
Bwlchgwyn Siding		93A3
Bwllfa Colly	47/32	165B1
Bwllfa Dare Colly	47/32	165B1
Bwllfa Ddu Colly (Llangyfelach)	55/42	138B2
Bwllfa Ddu Colly (Ystrad)	46/18	159B1
Bwllfa Level (Ystrad)	46/18	159B2
Bwllfa Lower		165B2
Bwllfa No. 1 Colly (Bwllfa Dare)	47/32	165B1
Bwllfa No. 2 Colly (Nantmelyn)	47/32	165B2
Bwllfa No. 3 Colly (Cwmdare)	47/34	165B2
Byass's Colly Siding	51/5	154C6
Bye Colly		76B3
BYFIELD	29/9	—
Byfield Ironstone Siding	29/9	—
BYNEA	55/31	133D5
Bynea Steelworks	55/33	133D5
C. & O. Junction S.B.	49/40	157B5
CABAN COCH		120D1
Cabbage Hall Colly		?
Cadbury's Siding (Bournville)	34/11	—
Cadbury's Siding (Ellesmere Line)		92D4
CADELEIGH	15/16	16B1
CADELEIGH & BICKLEIGH	15/16	16B1

CADOXTON (Barry)	44/53	148B5
Cadoxton High Level S.B. (Barry)	44/51	148D5
Cadoxton Junction (Neath)	52/1	139A5
Cadoxton Low Level S.B. (Barry)	44/53	148B5
Cadoxton North S.B. (Barry)	44/56	148A5
Cadoxton Sidings S.B. (Neath)	52/5	153B1
CADOXTON TERRACE HALT (Neath)	52/5	153B1
Cadoxton T.V. Goods (Barry)	44/59	148B6
Cae Colly (Dafen)	57/60	134C4
Caebad Colly	57/56	133C4
Cae David Colly	49/6	156C2
* Caedy Colly	49/36	160A1
Caedu Crossing S.B.	49/38	160B1
Caedu Incline Junction	49/38	160B1
Cae Duke S.B.	55/1	133D6
CAEDYAH HALT		95B5
Cae Glas Colly (L & MMR)	57/52	133A4
Cae Glas Crossing (Minera)		93C2
CAE HARRIS DOWLAIS		167B2
Caelliau Branch Junction	53/29	—
Caello Siding		93A3
Cae Newydd Pit		135B1
Caepenty Colly		93A4
Caepontbren Colly	57/39	133A4
Cae Quarry (Machen)	42/57	180C3
CAERAU	49/1	156A2
Caerau Colly		156A3
Caerbryn Colly	54/33	131A1
Caer Cynydd Colly		—
Cae'r Defaid Colly	51/5	156C3
Caergwyndd Colly	54/25	—
Caergwynydd Down S.B.	54/25	—
Caerlan Colly	49/61	160C6
CAERLEON	39/12	184B6
Caerleon Works Siding		184A6
CAERPHILLY		173B5
CAERPHILLY (1st Station)		173A4
Caerphilly Black Vein Colly		173B6
* Caerphilly Gas Works Siding		173A5
Caerphilly Loco Works		173B6
Caerphilly Tunnel North S.B.		173B6
Caerphilly Tunnel South S.B.		174A5
CAERSWS		116C5
Caerwent	36/1	52C3
Caerwent Branch Junction	36/1	52B1
Cae Twpa Crossing		115C5
Caiach Stone Siding		170D6
Caia Road Goods		92D3
Cairn Street Siding		149B4
Caisson Lines Junction S.B.	44/51	148C4
Cakemore Sidings	31/33	79D2
Calciner & New Buell Siding	11/30	4B2
Calcot S.B.	23/32	32C4
CALDICOT HALT	38/24	52A4
Caldicot Junction	36/1	52B1
CALDY		89C1
Calenick Siding	10/18	2B3
California Colly (Mountain Branch)	54/32	131A1
California Colly (Nantyglo)	40/51	175C6
California Crossing (Gloucester)	35/2	—
California Crossing (Mountain Branch)		131A2
Callow Hill Quarry		98D1
CALNE	21/27	28D5
Calthorpe Crossing	23/26	49D4
CAM	20/53	—
* CAM & DURSLEY		—
CAMBORNE	10/10	1C5
* Cambria Works	54/12	—
* Cambrian Chemical Siding		181D5
Cambrian Colly (Clydach)	49/55	159C2
Cambrian Junction (Whitchurch)		97D2
Cambrian Mercantile Colly	52/17	131D2
CAME BRIDGE HALT	17/3	41D6
CAMELS HEAD HALT	12/3	—

CAMERTON	21/52	27C2
Camerton Branch Junction		27C1
Cam Mills Siding	20/53	—
CAMPDEN	28/12	62D6
Canaan Colly		?
* Canada Brick Works	29/1	—
Canal Branch Junction (Lifford)	34/11	—
Canal Bridge S.B. (Gloucester)	35/17	—
Canal Head (Aberdare)	47/54	165B4
Canal Head (Swansea)	55/23	136C2
CANALSIDE, NEATH		139B5
Canal Swing Bridge S.B. (Cardiff)	43/72	150B6
Canning Street S.B.'s		90A4
* Cannock Chase Siding		69D2
Cannock Road Junction S.B.	31/3	74B4
Cannop Bridge Colly		54B1
Cannop Colly	37/17	54B1
Cannop Sidings	37/15	54B1
Cann Quarry	14/28	7B5
Canons Marsh	19/39	24B2
Canons Road Crossing		24B2
Canton		149C2
Canton Siding (Eldon Road)		149C2
Canton Siding (Leckwith Road)		149C2
Cantrell Siding	14/6	11A3
Cap Crossing		107C2
Cape Colly (Ffrwd)	57/45	133C2
Cape Colly (Gowerton)		135B1
Cape Copper Works	56/38	140B2
CAPEL BANGOR		114D2
CAPEL CELYN HALT		111A3
CAPEL COLBREN JUNCTION	52/12	132B5
Capel Ifan Colly	57/38	133A4
* Capel Newydd Siding		181B6
Capel Soar Crossing		114A1
CAPENHURST		91A4
CAPE PLATFORM	56/38	140A1
Capern's Siding	16/28	21B4
Cape Yard (Warwick)	30/18	82A6
Capponfield Siding		75A2
CARADOG FALLS HALT	58/34	126C6
Caradog Vale Colly	49/67	160D4
Caradon	11/36	6C3
Carbean	11/33	4C4
CARBIS BAY	10/21	1B2
Carbis Wharf	11/23	4A4
Cardiff and Ogmore Junction	49/40	157B5
CARDIFF, ADAM STREET	46/105	149C4
Cardiff, Alexandra Dock S.B.'s	43/84	150A1
* Cardiff, Atlantic Wharf G.F.	43/72	150B5
Cardiff, Allens Bank	46/113	174D6
* Cardiff, Anchor Fuel Works		149A2
Cardiff, Ballast Crane Siding S.B.	43/73	150B5
Cardiff, Barry Line Junction		149C3
* CARDIFF BAY		149D4
Cardiff, Beach Sidings	43/88	150C2
* Cardiff, Bute Ballast Crossing	43/62	150C6
* Cardiff, Bute Dry Dock	43/79	150A2
* Cardiff, Bute Estate Siding (Cathays)		149A3
Cardiff, Bute Gas Works	43/53	150D6
CARDIFF, BUTE ROAD	43/77	149D4
Cardiff, Bute Street S.B.	43/72	149D4
Cardiff, Bute West Yard S.B.	43/76	150A5
* Cardiff, Bute Yard Engine Shed	43/72	150B6
Cardiff, Cairn Street Siding		149B4
Cardiff, Canal Swing Bridge S.B.	43/72	150B6
Cardiff, Canton		149C2
Cardiff, Castle Works	43/66	149D6
CARDIFF, CATHAYS	46/104	149B3
CARDIFF, CEMETERY		149A3
* Cardiff, Cemetery Siding G.F.		149C4
CARDIFF, CENTRAL		149C3
* Cardiff, Channel Dry Dock	43/80	150A2
* Cardiff, Channel Tip	43/79	150A2

223

	CARDIFF, CLARENCE ROAD		149D4
	Cardiff, College Road Sidings	46/97	174D4
	Cardiff, Communication Passage	43/81	150C3
	CARDIFF, CROCKHERBTOWN	46/105	149B4
*	Cardiff, Crown Fuel Works	43/80	150B3
	Cardiff, Crown Preserved S.B.	46/102	149A2
	Cardiff, Crwys Sidings, S.B.		149A4
*	Cardiff, Dingle Site	43/95	150D4
	CARDIFF, DOCKS	43/76	149D4
	Cardiff, Docks Platform S.B.	43/77	150A5
	Cardiff, Dock Storage North S.B.	43/104	149B6
*	Cardiff, Dock Storage South S.B.	43/99	149B6
	Cardiff, Dock Terminus	43/72	149D4
	Cardiff, Dowlais Works	43/54	150C5
*	Cardiff, Dowlais Works Junction	43/63	150C6
	Cardiff, Dumball Yard		150A5
	Cardiff, East Branch Junction	46/105	149C4
	Cardiff, East Bute Dock Junction	43/72	150B6
*	Cardiff, East Dock Cargo Wharf G.F.	43/69	150B5
	Cardiff, East Dock Crossing S.B.	43/67	150B4
	Cardiff, East Dock Engine Shed	43/67	150B4
	Cardiff, East Dock Junction H.L.	43/72	150B5
	Cardiff, East Junction		149C4
*	Cardiff, East Moors Engine Shed	43/68	150C4
	Cardiff, East Moors Junction S.B.	43/62	150B6
	Cardiff, East Moors Steelworks	43/58	150C5
	Cardiff, Eldon Road Siding		149C2
	Cardiff, Engine Shed Junction	43/68	150C4
	Cardiff, Fair Oak Siding		149A3
	Cardiff, Foreshore	43/94	149D6
	Cardiff, Fuel Works Junction S.B.	43/81	150B3
	Cardiff, Gabalfa Siding	46/100	149A2
	Cardiff, Gaol Lane Junction	46/105	149B4
	CARDIFF, GENERAL		149C3
*	Cardiff, Glamorgan Lime Works	43/67	150C4
	Cardiff, Goods (Newtown)		149C4
	Cardiff, Grimes Crossing	43/63	150C6
	Cardiff, Gwennyth Street Siding		149A4
*	Cardiff, International Alloys G.F.		149A5
*	Cardiff, John Street Siding	43/73	150A6
	Cardiff, Junction Canal Swing Bridge	43/72	150B6
*	Cardiff, Junction Dry Dock Caisson S.B.	43/77	150B4
	Cardiff, Junction Lock S.B.	43/77	150D5
	Cardiff, Kings Junction S.B.	43/87	150B1
	Cardiff, Latty's Siding		174D6
	Cardiff, Leckwith Junctions		149C2
	Cardiff, Leckwith Road Siding		149C2
	Cardiff, Lewis Road Junction	43/58	150D4
*	Cardiff, Little Dock	43/54	150D5
	Cardiff, L.M.S. Junction S.B.	43/62	150C4
*	Cardiff, L.N.W.R. Cardiff Yard S.B.	43/72	150D5
	Cardiff, L.N.W.R. Goods	43/72	150B6
	Cardiff, Long Dyke Junction		149C5
*	CARDIFF, LOW WATER PIER	43/79	150A2
	Cardiff, Maloneys Tip Junction S.B.	43/73	150D5
	Cardiff, Maindy Bridge S.B.	46/102	149A3
	Cardiff, Maindy Fuel S.B.	46/99	149A2
	CARDIFF, MAINDY NORTH ROAD HALT	46/102	149A3
	Cardiff, Merthyr Road G.F.		174D6
*	Cardiff, Monkey Island Sidings	43/72	150B5
	Cardiff, Moors Lane S.B.		149C1
*	Cardiff, Mount Stuart Dry Docks	43/76	150A3
	Cardiff Moy Road Siding		149A4
	Cardiff Navigation Colly	44/13	145D3
	Cardiff, Newport Road Goods	46/113	149A5
	Cardiff, New Rod Mill	43/66	150D5
	Cardiff, Newtown Goods		149C4
	CARDIFF, NINIAN PARK PLATFORM		149C2
	Cardiff, N.E. Junction S.B.	43/93	149D6
*	Cardiff, Old Sea Lock Sidings		150A4
	CARDIFF, PARADE	46/105	149B4
*	Cardiff, Passenger Boat Pontoon G.F.	43/78	150A3
	Cardiff, Penarth Curve Junctions		149C2
	Cardiff, Pengam		149A6
*	Cardiff, Prairie Sidings	43/91	150C3
	Cardiff, Quadruple Crossing S.B.	43/67	150B3
*	Cardiff, Queen Alexandra Dock S.B.'s	43/84	150A1
	CARDIFF, QUEEN STREET	46/105	149C4
	Cardiff Reservoir Line (Cefn Coed)		166C2
	Cardiff, Rhymney Crossing S.B.	43/68	150D5
	CARDIFF, RIVERSIDE		149D3
	Cardiff Road Lines (Newport)	38/46	152C3
	CARDIFF, ROATH		149B5
	Cardiff, Roath Basin Junction	43/67	150C4
*	Cardiff, Roath Basin G.F.	43/69	150B3
	Cardiff, Roath Branch Junction	46/95	174D4
	Cardiff, Roath Branch S.B.'s	43/98	149C6
	Cardiff, Roath Branch Storage	43/98	149B6
	Cardiff, Roath Dock Junction	43/68	150C4
	Cardiff, Roath Dock South S.B.	43/90	150C3
	Cardiff, Roath Dock Swing Bridge	43/68	150B3
	Cardiff, Roath Goods (GWR)		149B5
	Cardiff, Roath Goods (TVR)	46/113	149A5
	Cardiff, Roath Line Junction Sidings	46/95	174D5
*	Cardiff, Roath Mills	43/59	150D4
*	Cardiff, Roath Pier Head Outer Lock G.F.s	43/78	150A3
	Cardiff, Rumney River Bridge		149A6
	Cardiff, Salisbury Road Goods		149B4
	Cardiff, Sanatorium Crossing S.B.		149C2
	Cardiff, Scoria Sidings	43/59	149D6
	Cardiff, S.E. Junction S.B.	43/93	149D6
	Cardiff, Sloper Road Sidings		149D2
	Cardiff, South Wales Siding		149C4
	Cardiff, Spillers Nephews G.F.	43/104	149B5
	Cardiff, Splott Bridge Junction		149B5
	Cardiff, Splott Junction	43/93	149D6
*	Cardiff, Star Fuel Works		149A3
	Cardiff, Stonefield Junction	43/68	150C4
	Cardiff, Swansea Street Sidings	43/99	149C6
	Cardiff, Tharsis Copper Works	43/57	150D4
*	Cardiff, Three Crows Siding	43/73	150A5
	Cardiff, Tidal Sidings	43/99	149C6
	Cardiff, Tremorfa Works	43/100	149D6
	Cardiff, Tyndall Field		149C4
	Cardiff, Tyndall St. Cart Crossing	43/73	150D5
	Cardiff, Tyndall St. Crossing	43/62	149C4
	Cardiff, Tyndall St. H.L. Junction	43/62	150C6
	Cardiff, Viaduct S.B.	43/72	150B5
	Cardiff, Virgil Street Goods		149D2
	Cardiff, Waterloo G.F.	46/114	149A5
*	Cardiff Welsh Cold Storage G.F.	43/73	150A6
*	Cardiff, West Canal Wharf		149D4
*	Cardiff, West Dock Swing Bridge S.B.	43/77	150A4
	Cardiff, West Side Roath Basin	43/77	150D5
	CARDIFF, WOODVILLE ROAD HALT	46/104	149B3
	CARDIGAN	58/32	125A2
	Cardigan Junction	58/7	125D4
*	Cardner's Siding		93C1
	Cardonnel East S.B.	56/42	139D2
	CARDONNEL HALT	56/42	139C3
	Cardonnel Junction S.B.	56/42	139D2
	Cardonnel Sidings S.B.	56/38	139D2
	Cardonnel Tin Works	56/38	139D5
	Cardonnel West S.B.	56/39	139D5
	Carloggas Siding	11/32	4C2
	Carlyon Farm Siding	11/18	4D4
	Carmarthen Bay Power Station	57/9	134B3
	Carmarthen Goods Yard	58/38	129A2
	CARMARTHEN JUNCTION	58/9	129B1
	Carmarthen River Bridge S.B.	58/9	129B1
	Carmarthenshire Dock Siding		134D1
	CARMARTHEN TOWN	58/39	129B1
	Carmarthen Valley Junction	59/1	130D3
	Carmears Incline	11/25	4B6
	Carnarfon Colly	55/30	134D6
	Carnau Drift		167B3
	CARN BREA	10/11	1B5
*	Carn Brea Quarry	10/12	1B5

Name		
Carne Point S.B.	11/27	5C2
Carngethin Colly	42/36	178C2
CARNO		115D6
* Carnon Viaduct	10/39	2B2
Carn Parc S.B.		171B2
Carnsmerry Siding	11/33	4B4
Carpella Siding	11/32	4C2
CARREGHOFA HALT		119D3
Carreg Llwyd Quarry	57/45	133C2
* Carriers Dock Depot		90A1
CARROG		112B4
Carters Siding	18/21	—
CARTERTON	27/23	66B4
Carthew Crossing		4C4
Carway Colly	57/40	133B3
CASHES GREEN HALT	20/30	58C4
CASSINGTON HALT	27/25	67B2
Castellau Branch	49/84	161B2
Castellau Siding	49/84	161A3
* Castell Coch Siding	46/82	174A2
CASTLE BAR PARK HALT	26/20	36D6
CASTLEBYTHE HALT	58/31	123A3
CASTLE CAEREINION		118B2
* CASTLE CAREY	16/49	45D1
CASTLE CARY	16/49	45D1
Castle Cary Road Crossing		43A6
Castle Coch Siding	46/82	174A2
Castle Colly (Llanelly)	57/56	133C4
Castle Foregate Goods		99B2
CASTLE HILL (Filleigh)	15/19	18C5
CASTLE HILL (West Ealing)	24/33	37B5
Castle Meads Power Station		56B2
* Castle Mill Siding		75D2
Castle Piggin Crossing	58/42	—
Castle Pits S.B.s		169C2
Castle Pond Sidings	39/14	184A1
CASTLE STREET, MAESTEG	49/5	156C2
Castle Works (Bassaleg)	42/52	184D1
Castle Works (Cardiff)	43/66	149D6
Castle Works (Rogerstone)	40/38	184D1
Castleton Junction	17/9	42B1
Castleton Siding	17/9	42B1
Cathan Crossing		131B3
CATHAYS	46/104	149B3
Cathays Junction S.B.	46/102	149A3
* Cathays Siding (Rhymney)		149A3
CATHAYS (WOODVILLE RD) PLATFORM	46/104	149B3
Cathcart St. Goods		90A4
* Catherton Colly Siding		?
Cattedown	12/24	—
Cattewater	12/24	—
Cattewater Junction	12/20	8C6
CATTISTOCK HALT	17/5	41A4
Cattle Pens Crossing	19/37	24A2
Cattybrook Siding S.B. (Pilning)	19/55	23A4
Cattybrook Siding (Dr. Days Bridge)	19/15	24B5
Caudledown Siding	11/33	4B4
CAUSELAND	11/37	6B5
Causeway Crossing	23/4	31B3
Cavendish Sidings		90A3
* Cawdon Quarry Siding	14/23	9D2
Cawdor Branch (Garnant)	54/46	131D4
Cawdor Colly (Garnant)	54/40	131D3
Cawdor Colly (Glanamman)	54/40	131B5
Cawdor Crossing (Glanamman)	54/40	131A5
Cawdor Siding (Glanamman)	54/40	131A5
Cawdron Quarry Siding	14/23	9D2
CEFN (Cefn Coed)		166C2
CEFN (Denbighshire)		94D2
CEFN (Kenfig Hill)	49/43	143A3
Cefn Ballast Siding (Merthyr)		168D1
Cefn Ballast Siding (nr. Tondu)		143A4
Cefn Brithdir Colly	42/40	177C3
Cefn Celfi Colly	53/Ind	—
CEFN COED		166C2
CEFN COED COLLY HALT	52/7	162B1
* CEFN COED CYMMER		166D2
Cefn Colly (nr. Tondu)	49/49	143A4
Cefn Corwyg Crossing	44/54	146A1
CEFN CRIB	47/103	182D3
Cefn Cribbwr Colly	49/45	143A4
Cefn Crossing (Acrefair)		94C1
Cefn Glas S.B. (Merthyr line)		170A4
Cefn Glas Siding (Vale of Neath)	47/77	170A4
Cefn Goch		178A6
Cefn Goleu Colly	54/52	—
Cefn Gurgan S.B.	50/55	142B6
Cefngyfelach Colly	55/8	138C2
Cefn Ironworks (nr. Tondu)	49/46	143A4
Cefn Junction (nr. Tondu)	49/48	143A5
Cefn Llwyna Colly		178C1
* CEFN MAWR (Acrefair)		94C2
Cefn Mawr S.B. (Vale of Neath)	47/2	153A4
Cefn Merthyr Colly (Cefn Mawr)		?
* Cefn Merthyr Siding (Merthyr)		168D2
Cefn Morfydd Colly	51/52	153C2
Cefn on Dolomite Siding		173B6
Cefn On Halt		174A5
CEFN ONN		174A5
Cefn Quarry Siding (Acrefair)		94C2
Cefn Stylle Colly	54/52	—
CEFN TILLA HALT	36/23	108D4
Cefn Wharf Siding (Denbighshire)		94C2
* CEFN-Y-BEDD	59/7	
Cefn y Bryn Colly	51/4	154B6
Cefn y Coed Colly		92B2
Cefn y Fan Quarry	51/43	155C2
Celtic Colly	51/14	156D3
Celtic Garth Colly	49/7	156D3
CELTIC HALT	51/14	157A2
Celtic Lowr Colly	51/14	157A2
Celtic Oakwood Colly	49/6	156D3
CELYNEN HALT	40/25	178C6
Celynen North Colly	40/21	178B6
CELYNEN NORTH HALT	40/21	178A6
Celynen North S.B.	40/22	178C6
Celynen South Colly	40/25	178C6
CELYNEN SOUTH HALT	40/25	178C6
Celynen South S.B.	40/24	178C6
Cement Sidings S.B.	27/5	67A3
CEMETERY (nr. Cardiff)		149A3
Cemetery Level (Ebbw Vale)		?
CEMETERY ROAD HALT (Rhymney)	42/1	167B4
* Cemetery Sidings G.F. (Cardiff)	46/108	149B4
Cemetery Road S.B. (Acton)	26/31	38A2
CEMMAES		115B3
CEMMES		115B3
CEMMES ROAD		115C3
Cendros Colly	57/45	133C2
Central Treviscoe Siding	11/31	4D1
Central Wagon Works (Cathays)	46/101	149A2
Central Wales Junction	63/4	101D1
Centre Beat S.B.	56/6	137B3
CERIST		116C1
CERNEY & ASHTON KEYNES	22/5	59C5
Cerrig Gwynion Siding	59/28	120C3
CHACEWATER	10/16	2A1
CHALFORD	20/32	58D6
Chalk Hill Quarry		119A3
Chalk Sidings (High Wycombe North)	26/7	87D3
Chalk Sidings (High Wycombe South)	26/8	87D3
CHALLOW	23/2	29D6
* Chaloner Street Depot		90B1
CHALVEY HALT	24/40	34D5
CHAMBERS CROSSING HALT	28/26	62A6
Chance and Hunts Siding	31/35	79B3
* Channel Dry Dock (Cardiff)	43/80	150A2
Channel Dry Dock Siding (Newport)	38/33	151C6

*	Channel Tip (Cardiff)	43/79	150A2
	CHAPEL BRIDGE	40/28	180A1
	Chapel Crossing (Llanbrynmair)		115C5
	Chapel Crossing (Quintrel Downs)	11/21	3A2
*	Chapel Farm Quarry Siding		?
	CHAPEL LANE (Criggion Branch)		98A1
	Chapel Lane G.F. (Panteg)	39/11	183A2
	Chapel of Ease Crossing	51/1	141B5
	Charbridge Lane Crossing	27/29	—
	CHARD	16/44	20C6
	CHARD CENTRAL	16/44	20C6
	CHARD JOINT	16/44	20C6
	Chard Junction (Creech Jcn)	16/9	20C2
	CHARD TOWN	16/44	20C6
	CHARFIELD	20/43	—
	CHARLBURY	28/17	65D5
	Charles Pit	53/9	—
	Charlton Crossing (Hartlebury)	32/28	72D6
	CHARLTON HALT (Bristol)	19/98	23B4
	CHARLTON HALT (Oxon)	27/28	—
	CHARLTON KINGS	28/27	55B6
	CHARLTON MACKRELL	16/47	43B4
	CHARLTON MARSHALL	18/20	—
	Charlton Siding S.B.	28/2	62B2
	Chawson Crossing		78C5
	CHEDDAR	16/33	22A1
	Cheddar Branch G.F.	16/28	21B4
	Cheddar Valley Junction	16/27	21B4
	CHEDWORTH	22/2	57C3
	Chedworth Woods Siding	22/2	57C3
	CHEESEHILL, WINCHESTER	23/33	51D6
	Cheesewring Quarry	11/36	6C3
	CHELSEA & FULHAM	25/31	38C1
	Chelsea Basin	25/31	38C1
	Cheltenham Alston Junction	35/12	56B6
	CHELTENHAM HIGH STREET	35/13	56A6
	CHELTENHAM HIGH STREET HALT	35/15	56A6
	CHELTENHAM LANSDOWN	35/12	56B5
	Cheltenham Lansdown Junction	35/11	56B5
	CHELTENHAM LECKHAMPTON	28/27	55B6
	CHELTENHAM MALVERN ROAD	35/15	56B6
	CHELTENHAM RACECOURSE	35/15	55A6
	CHELTENHAM ST. JAMES	35/16	56B6
	CHELTENHAM (S.) & LECKHAMPTON	28/27	55B6
	Cheltenham Tewkesbury Road	35/13	56A6
*	Chemical Works S.B. (Gyfeillon)	46/39	172A4
	Chemical Works Siding (Oldbury)	31/35	79B3
	Chemical Works Siding (Ynysddu)	41/40	—
	CHEPSTOW	36/6	52B5
	CHEPSTOW EAST		52B5
	Chequers Road Junction	35/7	56C4
	Cherry Orchard S.B.		174A5
	Cherry Tree Brickworks		70B1
	Cherwell S.B.	27/4	85C2
	CHESIL, WINCHESTER	23/33	51D6
	Chester, Bache Goods		88C5
	Chester, Brook Lane Junction		88C5
	CHESTER, GENERAL		88D5
	Chester, Holyhead Junction		88D5
	Chester, Tunnel Junction		88D4
	CHESTERTON LANE HALT	20/38	59B4
	CHETNOLE HALT	17/5	44C3
	CHILCOMPTON	18/11	—
*	Chillington Works		74C5
	CHILTON SIDING	33/24	72C2
	CHINNOR	26/33	87B3
	CHIPPENHAM	21/12	28C3
	CHIPPING CAMPDEN	28/12	62D6
	CHIPPING NORTON	28/31	65B4
	CHIPPING NORTON JUNCTION	28/14	65C6
	CHIPPING SODBURY	20/5	26C3
	CHIRK		95A1
	CHISELDON	22/8	29D4
	CHISELDON CAMP HALT	22/8	29D4

*	CHITTENING FACTORY	19/92	23B3
	Chittening Junction S.B.	19/92	23A3
	CHITTENING PLATFORM	19/92	23B3
	Chittening Estate	19/93	23A3
	CHOLSEY & MOULSFORD	23/15	31D6
	CHRISTIAN MALFORD HALT	21/13	28B4
	CHRISTOW	14/44	13C3
	CHUDLEIGH	14/43	14B3
	CHUDLEIGH KNIGHTON HALT	14/43	14B3
	CHUDLEIGH ROAD	14/41	14C3
	Chunes Crossing	32/20	70C1
	Church Bridge Colly		79C2
	Church Colly (Ystrad Rhondda)		159B2
	Church Crossing (Oakdale)	40/64	177D5
	Church Crossing (Tidenham)		52B5
	CHURCHDOWN	35/10	55B4
	Church Gates Crossing	40/33	180B5
	CHURCHILL	33/11	78B2
	CHURCHILL AND BLAKEDOWN	33/11	78B2
	Churchill Crossing (Sarsden)	28/30	65C3
	Church Hill Pit	20/49	—
	Church Lane Crossing (Grange Court)	36/33	53A6
	Church Quarry (Grovesend)	20/51	—
	CHURCH ROAD (Birmingham)	34/12	—
	CHURCH ROAD (Machen)	42/50	180D4
	Church Road Junction	34/12	—
	Church Street Crossing (Bridgwater)	16/15	19B6
	Church Street Crossing (W. & L.)		117D2
	CHURCH'S HILL HALT	20/38	59C2
	CHURCH STRETTON	63/2	100B4
	CHURCH VILLAGE HALT	49/80	161A6
	Church Tip Siding (Cyfarthfa)		168A3
	Churchway	37/27	54A4
	CHURN	23/38	31D4
	CHURSTON	14/35	12C5
*	CHWARELAN — error for CHWRELA		
*	CHWRELA		94C1
	Cilely Colly	49/59	160B6
	Cilely Junction S.B.	49/59	160C6
	Cilcennin Crossing	58/41	127A2
	Cil Cewydd Mills		118B4
*	Cilfack — error for Gilfach.		
	CILFREW	52/6	153A2
	CILFYNYDD		171C3
	Cilgwrgan Wharf		116B6
	Cilhaul Colly		169B6
	CILIAU AERON HALT	58/41	127A2
	Cille Colly	57/57	133C4
	CILMERY	59/7	—
	Cilrhedyn Colly	57/44	133B2
	Cilwern Colly	54/35	131A1
	Cilybebyll Colly	53/20	—
	Cilyrychen Crossing	54/1	130C6
	Cincoed Siding	54/2	130C6
	Cinder Colly (Blaina)		?
	CINDERFORD	37/20	54B6
	CINDERFORD (OLD STATION)	37/19	54A5
*	CINDERFORD (RUSPIDGE)		54C6
	Cinderford Crossing	37/31	54A6
	Cinderford Goods (Town)	37/20	54B6
	Cinderford Goods (Whimsey)	37/30	54A5
	Cinderford Ironworks	37/34	54B6
	Cinderford Junction	37/19	54B5
	Cinderford South Loop Junction	37/19	54A6
	Circourt S.B.	23/42	31C1
	CIRENCESTER TOWN (GWR)	20/38	59B4
	CIRENCESTER WATERMOOR (MSWJ)	22/4	59B4
	City Basin (Exeter)	14/21	13C2
	City Basin Junction (Exeter)	14/21	13D1
	Clandown Pit	18/10	—
	CLAPHAM JUNCTION	25/32	38D2
	Clapps Wharf	40/60	181A2
	Clarbeston Junction	58/6	123C3
	CLARBESTON ROAD	58/6	123C3

Name	Ref	Grid
Clarbeston Road West S.B.	58/18	123C3
Clarbeston S.B.	58/7	123D4
CLARENCE ROAD		147D4
Clarence Wagon Shops		182C6
Clarence Wharf (Newport)	38/28	152B4
Clatter Crossing S.B.		116A2
CLAVERDON	30/37	82B4
Claverham S.B.	16/29	21B4
Claverton S.B.	21/14	27B5
Clay & Newmans Siding	33/14	78C5
Claydon Crossing S.B.	30/21	84A3
Clayfield Crossing	28/6	62C4
Clayphon Wharf	53/50	—
Clayton Works	54/12	131D2
CLEARBROOK HALT		10D5
Cleaves Siding	11/33	4B4
Clee Hill	63/35	101C5
* Clee Hill Colly Siding		?
* Clee Hill Granite Siding (Dettonford)		72B2
Clee Hill Junction S.B.	63/7	101A6
CLEEVE	34/1	—
CLEOBURY MORTIMER	33/23	72C3
CLEOBURY NORTH CROSSING	33/24	71D3
CLEOBURY TOWN HALT	33/24	72C2
CLEVEDON	16/33	21A3
Clevedon Junction	16/27	21B4
CLEVEDON ROAD	16/27	21B4
CLIFFORD (Golden Valley)	63/44	106A1
Clifford Sidings (Stratford)	29/5	—
CLIFTON (Hotwells)	19/64	25D6
CLIFTON BRIDGE	19/32	24B1
CLIFTON DOWN	19/65	23C4
Clifton Junction	19/47	24A5
Clifton Maybank Goods	17/6	44D6
Clifton Tunnel West S.B.	19/63	25C6
Clink Road Junction	21/33	45A5
Clink Yard (Bridgwater)	16/16	19B6
Closucha Colly	57/37	133A3
Closyryn Colly	57/35	133A3
Cloud Hill Quarry	21/44	27C1
CLOY HALT		95B5
* Clun Bont Junction		157B6
CLUNDERWEN	58/7	123D5
CLUTTON	21/44	27C1
CLYDACH (nr. Brynmawr)	41/16	—
Clydach Branch Junction		171C2
* Clydach Colly (Waenavon)	41/19	—
CLYDACH COURT HALT		171C3
Clydach Court Junction		171C1
Clydach Court Loop Junction		171C3
Clydach Goods (on Tawe North)	55/49	138A5
Clydach Graigola Colly	53/43	—
Clydach Merthyr Colly	53/43	138A4
Clydach-on-Tawe North Goods	55/49	138A5
CLYDACH-ON-TAWE SOUTH	53/43	—
* Clydach Quarry Siding (Ynysybwl)		171B1
Clydach Siding (Brynmawr)	41/19	—
CLYDACH VALE	49/55	159C2
Clydach Vale Colly	46/54	159C1
Clydach Vale Empty Sidings	46/54	159C3
CLYNDERWEN	58/7	123D5
Clyne Colly (Cefn Mawr)	47/2	153A5
Clyne Colly (Killay LNWR)	54/26	—
CLYNE HALT (nr. Cefn Mawr)	47/3	162D3
Clyne Merthyr Colly		153A5
* Clyne Valley Colly	54/27	—
Clyne Wood Colly	54/27	—
Clyn Mill Incline		168C5
Clyn Mil Pit		168C5
Cnewr Siding		122C1
* Coalbrook Colly Siding		143A2
COALBROOKDALE	32/33	70B1
Coalbrookvale Deep Pit		175D6
Coalbrookvale S.B.	40/51	175C6
COALEY	20/46	—
COALEY JUNCTION	20/46	—
Coaley Road Crossing	20/53	—
COALPIT HEATH	20/3	26C1
Coalpit Heath Colly	20/49	26D1
Coalpit Heath (Mid)	20/49	—
COALPORT	32/22	70D3
COALPORT EAST	32/55	—
COATES	20/33	59B3
Coates Crossing (Longville)	32/29	71B1
Cobden Mill Siding		93D6
Cobre Yard Goods	56/4	137A2
COCKETT	55/7	135C2
Cockett East S.B.	55/7	135C2
Cockett Goods	55/5	135C2
Cocklebury Sidings	20/20	30C2
Cockley Brake Junction	29/18	—
CODFORD	21/55	47B2
Codford Camp		47A2
CODSALL	32/17	69D6
Codsall Colly (Cradley)		77A5
Coed Amman Colly	54/60	131A4
Coed Bach Colly	57/43	133B2
Coedcae Colly (Rose Heyworth)		176D6
Coedcae Colly (Eirw Branch)	46/32	172A1
Coedcae Gates S.B. (Eirw Branch)	46/32	159D6
Coedcae Incline (Merthyr)		168C6
Coedcae Pit (Cyfarthfa)		168B3
Coedcaetillery Colly	40/56	176D6
Coed Cefn Pwll Du Colly	42/56	180D3
COED ELY	49/64	161A1
Coedffalddau Colly	53/Ind	—
COEDPENMAEN		171D3
COED POETH		93C2
Coed Talon Joint Line Junction		92B2
Coed y Brain Siding (Ffrwd)		93A4
Coedybrain Siding (Llanbradach)		179C3
Coed y gaf Crossing		146B4
* Coed-y-goe Siding		?
Coedygric Junction	39/4	183C5
Coedygric Sidings	39/6	182C6
Coedymoeth Colly	42/20	177C3
Coegnant S.B.	49/1	156B2
Cofton Siding	34/8	—
COGAN		147B5
Cogload Junction	16/10	20B3
Coity Goods	44/30	144C1
Coity Junction	44/30	144B1
Coity Mawr Quarry		181A3
Coke Ovens Jcn (New Tredegar)	42/16	177B2
Coke Ovens Yard (Pontypridd)	46/39	172A3
COLBREN JUNCTION	52/12	132B5
Colcerrow	11/25	4B6
* Cold Halton Siding	32/45	99C6
COLDHARBOUR HALT	15/18	16A4
Coldrennick Viaduct S.B.	11/13	5B6
COLE	18/16	—
COLEFORD	37/39	53B3
Coleford Junction	37/12	54C1
COLEFORD JUNCTION PLATFORM	37/13	54C1
Coleham S.B.		99C2
Coley Goods	24/35	33C4
College Bridge Sidings (Hereford)	63/19	104A5
College Road Sidings (Cardiff)	46/97	174D4
College Sidings (Bearley)	30/38	82C3
* Collegewood Viaduct	10/38	2D2
Collena Colly	49/59	160C6
Colliers Arms Junction	40/67	177D5
Colliers Crossing (Trimsaran)	57/44	133B2
COLLINGBOURNE	22/16	51B1
COLLINGBOURNE KINGSTON HALT	22/16	51A1
* Collingdon Road (Cardiff)	43/72	150A5
Collins Lane Crossing	20/35	29B2
COLLOMPTON	15/8	16B3

COLNEBROOK	24/41	35C1
COLNEBROOK ESTATE HALT	24/41	35C1
Colthorp Siding S.B.	23/26	32D1
Colthurst & Symons Siding	18/25	—
Colton Mine		17C3
COLWALL	33/4	60A4
Colwall Park Quarry Siding		60A4
Coly Isaf Quarry		169C4
COMBE HALT	28/18	67A1
COMBE HAY HALT	21/53	27C4
Comberow		17C2
Commercial Road Crossing	12/18	—
COMMERCIAL ST. PLATFORM	47/28	165D2
COMMINS COCH HALT		115C3
Commissioners Dock Junction	57/13	134C2
Common Branch Junction S.B.	49/34	161C1
Communication Passage (Cardiff)	43/81	150C3
COMPTON (Berkshire)	23/38	49A6
COMPTON HALT (Wombourn)	31/54	74C1
CONDOVER	63/1	98D5
Congreaves	31/30	77A4
CONGRESBURY	16/34	21B4
* Contractor's Siding S.B. (Bristol)	19/18	24B5
Contractors Siding S.B. (Margam)	50/58	142C6
CONWIL	58/37	129A3
COOKHAM	24/38	34B3
Cooks Bridge Siding	57/38	133A4
Cooks Kitchen Siding	10/27	1B6
Cook's Wood Quarry Siding	21/27	45A2
COOLE PILATE HALT	32/43	97C5
COOMBE JUNCTION	11/37	6C5
Coombe Mill Siding (nr. Handborough)	28/18	67A1
* Coombes Mill Siding (Thorverton)	15/16	16C1
COOMBES HOLLOWAY HALT	31/53	77B6
Coombs Wood Colly	31/53	77B6
Coopers Crossing	27/22	67D5
Coopers Siding (Soudley)	37/37	54C3
Coppee Coke Ovens		176B3
COPPERHOUSE		1B3
COPPERHOUSE HALT	10/8	1B3
Copper Miners Junction	51/21	154C3
Copper Pit Colly	55/26	138D3
COPPER PIT PLATFORM	55/26	138D3
Copper Works Junction (Llanelly)	57/17	134D3
Copper Works Junction (Margam)	50/48	141C4
Copper Works Siding (Cape)	56/38	140A2
Coppice Colly (Pensnett)		76B2
Coppice Lane Crossing (W. & L.)		118B2
Copthorne Lane Crossing	16/43	21C5
Copy Works Siding		94C4
Corbyns Hall Siding	31/56	76B2
Cores End Crossing	24/38	34A1
CORFE MULLEN HALT	18/21	—
Corfe Mullen Junction	18/21	—
Cornelly S.B.	50/79	143C1
Corngreaves Branch	31/30	77A4
Corngreaves Siding S.B.	31/30	77B4
Cornish Kaolin Siding	11/3	4D3
Cornwall Junction	12/17	8C4
Cornwall Loop Junction	12/7	8C4
Coronation Road Crossing		38A2
Coronation Sidings		39A2
CORNWOOD	14/4	11A1
CORNWOOD ROAD	14/4	11A1
Corporation Railway Jcn (Bristol)	19/22	24B2
Corporation Road S.B. (Newport)	38/32	152D5
CORRIS		113A5
Corrwg Fechan Colly	51/47	155A4
Corrwg Merthyr Colly	51/54	153B5
Corrwg Navigation Colly		?
Corrwg Rhondda Colly (Blaengwynfi)	51/37	155C5
Corrwg Vale Colly	51/43	155D1
CORSHAM	21/9	28D2
Corton Siding	17/13	42A5
CORWEN		112B3
CORYATES HALT	17/13	42A4
* Cory Navigation Colly	54/19	—
CORYTON (Devon)	14/23	9D4
CORYTON HALT (Glam.)		174B3
Coseley Goods	31/37	75C2
COSFORD	32/16	69C6
COSFORD AERODROME HALT	32/16	69C6
Cosford Siding S.B.	32/16	69C6
COSSINGTON	18/30	—
Coswarth Crossing	11/21	3A2
Cotfield S.B.	14/21	13B5
Cotland Siding	23/13	30C6
Coton Hill		99A1
Cotswold Lime Siding	22/3	57D3
Cottage Siding	49/73	161D4
Cottomfield Siding	17/8	42C1
COUGHTON	34/18	—
Council Hill Siding	28/33	64C5
COUND HALT	32/18	69C1
Courtaulds Siding	31/54	74A2
Court Herbert Colly	56/48	139B4
COURT SART	50/8	140A4
Court Sart Junction	50/8	140A4
Court Siding (Llantarnam)	39/11	183C3
Court Works (Madeley Court)		70B3
COURTYBELLA (Newport)		152B2
Courtybella (Oakdale)	40/64	177D5
Courtybella Crossing (Newport)	38/47	152B3
Courtybella Junction (Newport)	38/46	152B2
COVE HALT	15/17	15C1
* Covercroft Salt Works		78C5
COWBRIDGE	44/23	144B4
* COWBRIDGE ROAD		145D4
Cowbridge Road Crossing	49/73	145C4
Cowbridge Road Junction	44/33	144D1
Cowbridge Road S.B.	44/33	144D1
* Cowden Quarry — error for Cawdon		
Cow Lane S.B.	24/2	33B3
COWLEY	24/39	35B1
Cowley Bridge Junction	15/4	13A1
Cowley Freight Terminal	27/21	67D5
COXBANK HALT	32/43	97D5
Coxside		8D5
Cox's Lane Crossing S.B.	31/52	76C5
Cox's Quarry Siding	40/29	180A3
Coychurch Crossing	44/7	144A3
Coychurch Road Siding	44/33	144D1
COYNANT	49/1	156B2
Coypool Siding	14/30	8A5
Coythrahen Park Colly	49/13	143C4
Crabtree Siding	12/15	8A5
Crabtreehill Colly	37/25	54C4
CRADLEY	31/29	76D4
Cradley Colly	31/27	77B4
CRADLEY HEATH AND CRADLEY	31/29	76D4
Cradley Park Colly	31/27	77B4
CRADOC	52/15	122A4
Craig (Taff Bargoed Branch)		170A5
Craigavon Colly	51/54	153B5
Craig Bedw Quarry		177B3
* Craig Colly (Aberdare)		?
Craig Colly (Cadoxton)		153A2
Craig Colly (Tymaen Junction)		154B3
Craig Ddu Quarry		109A6
* Craigfryn Siding	59/32	116C3
CRAIG GOCH		120D1
Craigllyn Colly	51/40	154A3
CRAIGLON BRIDGE HALT	57/45	133C2
Craig Merthry Colly		138A4
Craig Rhiwarth Colly		117A1
Craig Rumney Colly	42/11	177A1
Craig y fedw Colly	51/40	153D3
CRAIGYNOS	52/13	122D1

Craig yr allt (Elan Valley)		120B1
Craig yr allt Colly (Penrhos Jcn)		173C3
Craig yr Hesq Colly		171D2
Craig yr Hesq Quarry		171D3
Crane Street Junction	31/8	—
CRANMORE	16/40	22C6
Crantock St. Crossing		3A2
CRAVEN ARMS	63/4	101D1
CRAVEN ARMS AND STOKESAY	63/4	101D1
CRAY	52/14	122B1
Cray Water Works Siding	52/14	122C1
CREDENHILL	63/43	—
Creech Junction	16/9	20C2
Creech Mills Siding	16/9	20C3
CREECH ST. MICHAEL HALT	16/9	20C3
CREEKMOOR HALT	18/22	—
CREIGIAU	44/26	146A1
Creigian Quarry Siding	49/85	161D6
Crelake Siding	14/26	10B4
Cremorne Wharf		38C1
CRESSAGE	32/18	69D1
Cresselly Crossing S.B.	47/67	170D2
Crewe Gresty Lane		97A6
Crewe Junction (Shrewsbury)		99B2
CREW GREEN		98B1
Cibbwr Ballast Siding	49/52	143D4
Cribbwr Colly	49/51	143D3
CRIBBWR FAWR	49/42	143A2
Cribbwr Main Colly	49/25	157D6
CRICCIETH		109A4
Crickheath Wharf		119A6
CRICKLADE	22/5	59D6
Cricklade Road Crossing (Highworth)	20/29	29A3
CRIGGION		98B1
Crimea Sidings	25/12	39D3
Crindau S.B.	38/64	184B4
Croborn Mine		18B1
* Crocketts Siding		157A1
Crockham Siding	14/43	14A3
CROCKHERBTOWN, CARDIFF	46/105	149B4
Crockherbtown Lower S.B.	46/105	149B4
Crockherbtown Upper S.B.	46/102	149B3
* Croescoed Colly	49/79	161B5
Croes Newydd East Junction		93D6
Croes Newydd North Fork		93D6
Croes Newydd South Fork		93D6
Croes Newydd West S.B.		93D5
Croes Newydd Yard		93D6
Crofton Crossing	23/19	48D6
Croftyguinea Siding	49/85	146B4
Crooks Stone Quarry	51/52	153C2
Crookwood S.B.	21/41	46C6
CROPREDY	30/23	84A3
CROSS GATES	59/10	98C3
Cross Hands (L. & M.M.)	57/50	133A6
Cross Hands (Mountain Branch)	54/32	131A1
CROSS HANDS HALT (Avonmouth)	19/52	23A3
CROSS INN (Ammanford)	54/38	131B3
CROSS INN (Common Branch)	49/74	161C4
CROSS INN (LLANFIHANGEL)		128B4
CROSS KEYS (Glanamman)	54/40	131A5
CROSS KEYS (Risca)	40/31	180A4
Cross Keys North S.B. (Risca)	40/30	180A3
Cross Road Crossing (Corris)		113A5
Cross Street Crossing S.B. (Newport)	38/58	152B3
CROSSWAYS HALT	58/41	127A2
CROWCOMBE	15/26	17C5
CROWCOMBE HEATHFIELD	15/26	17C5
Crowell Crossing		87C3
Crown Brickyard S.B. (Avonmouth)	19/48	25D3
Crown Colly (Moseley Green)	37/21	54C2
Crown Colly (Sandygate)	57/48	134A5
Crown Crossing (Cefn Junction)		143A3
Crown Dale Siding		92B2
* Crown Fuel Works (Cardiff Docks)	43/80	150B3
* Crown Fuel Works (nr. Cathays)	46/99	149A2
Crown Level Colly		158C3
Crown Preserved S.B.	46/102	149A2
Crown Siding (Serridge Jcn)	37/18	54B1
Crown Siding (Soudley)	37/37	54C3
Crown Works (Cardonnel)	56/40	139C3
Crown Works (Swansea)	56/17	137B6
Crows Nest Mine		98D1
Crowthers Crossing		?
Cruckmeole Colly		98D3
Cruckmeole Junction		98D4
CRUCKTON		98C4
CRUDGINGTON	32/45	99D6
Crug Las Colly		160D4
Crugwallins Siding	11/32	4D3
CRUMLIN (Temporary Station)		178A6
Crumlin Burrows Colly	56/32	137C5
Crumlin Colly (Skewen)		?
CRUMLIN HIGH LEVEL	47/101	178A6
Crumlin High Level West S.B.	47/100	178B6
CRUMLIN LOW LEVEL	40/19	178A6
Crumlin Navigation S.B.	40/19	178A6
* Crumlin Quarry Siding		182D1
CRUMLIN VALLEY COLLS PLATFORM	47/104	182D3
Crump Meadow Colly (Bilson Jcn)	37/32	54B5
Crump Meadow Colly (Mineral Loop)	37/26	54B4
Crundale Crossing	58/18	123D2
Crwys Siding S.B.		149A4
Crymlyn Quarry		138D5
CRYMMYCH ARMS	58/32	125D2
CRYNANT	52/8	132D3
CRYNANT NEW COLLY HALT	52/8	132D4
Crystal Palace Loop	25/12	39D3
Crythan Platform	51/39	153D2
Cuba Colly		?
Cuckoo Nest Siding	41/16	—
CULHAM	27/16	31B4
CULKERTON	20/38	59C1
CULLOMPTON	15/8	16B3
Culm Davy Siding		16A6
CULMSTOCK	15/18	16A5
Culm Valley Branch Junction	15/9	16B6
Cumberland Siding	19/37	24A2
Cummings Crossing	33/4	60A4
Curry Rivel Crossing	16/46	20B5
Curry Rivel Junction	16/46	20B6
CUTNALL GREEN	33/13	78B5
CWM (Ebbw Vale)	40/8	176D5
CWM COLLIERS HALT (Ebbw Vale)	40/8	176D5
Cwm Colliery (Ebbw Vale)	40/8	176D5
Cwm Colliery (Llantwit Fardre)	49/76	161A5
Cwm Level (Ogilvie)		169B6
Cwm North Pit (Ebbw Vale)		176B5
Cwm Pit (Merthyr)		168D3
Cwm Quarries (Pontypool)		183A4
Cwm S.B. (Barry Rly)	44/26	161C6
Cwm S.B. (Llantwit Fardre)	49/36	161B5
Cwm Siding (Ynysbwl)		171C6
* Cwmamman Brickworks (Glanamman)	54/41	131A5
CWMAMAN COLLIERY HALT	47/46	165D3
CWMAMAN CROSSING HALT	47/44	165D3
CWMAVON (MON)	39/21	181C6
CWMAVON (GLAM)	51/22	154C3
CWMAVON HALT (GLAM)	51/22	154C3
Cwmavon Reservoir Siding (Mon)		181B5
Cwmbach Colly (Cockett)	55/5	135C2
Cwmbach Crossing S.B.	47/58	165C5
CWMBACH HALT	47/60	165C5
Cwmbach Junction S.B.	47/58	165C5
Cwmbach Little Pit	47/56	165B5
Cwmbach New Pit	47/57	165B5
Cwmbach Sidings S.B.	47/56	165C4
CWMBARGOED		167C3

Cwmbargoed Branch (LNWR)	41/4	—
Cwmbargoed Colly Jcn S.B.		167C2
Cwmbargoed Junction (LNWR)	41/3	—
Cwm Black Colly		168C2
Cwmblawd Goods	57/52	133A5
Cwmbowydd Crossing		109A5
CWMBRAN	39/20	183C2
CWMBRAN (1986 Station)		183B2
Cwmbran Colly		183B1
Cwmbran Factory Siding	39/11	183C3
Cwmbran Junction S.B.	39/20	183C2
Cwmbran Sidings S.B.	39/20	183B2
Cwmbwrla Sidings S.B.	55/7	136C1
Cwmbyrgwm Colly		182A4
Cwm-byr Quarry		179D1
Cwm Capel	57/47	133C3
CWMCARN	40/28	180A1
Cwmcarn Branch Junction	40/29	180A4
Cwmcarn Colly	40/30	180A2
Cwm Cedfw Rhondda Colly	51/14	157A2
Cwmcedfyn Colly		157A2
Cwm Ceiros Colly	53/16	—
Cwm Celyn Crossing		176B6
Cwm Cerwyn Siding	51/5	156D1
Cwm Circ Colly		145A3
Cwm Ciwc Colly	49/26	145A3
Cwm Click Colly	53/19	—
CWM CLYDACH	53/43	
* Cwm Clydach (Ynysybwl)		171C6
Cwm Clydach Colly (Blaenclydach)	46/55	159C2
Cwm Clydach Colly (Resolven)		162C5
Cwm Corrwg Colly	51/54	153B5
Cwm Creeich Colly	41/34	—
Cwm Cylla Quarry		178C1
CWM CYMMER	51/34	155B4
Cwm Cynon S.B.	47/69	170B2
Cwmdare Colly	47/34	165B2
Cwmdows Colly	40/73	178C5
Cwmdrisein Colly	54/46	131D4
CWMDU (Port Talbot Rly)	51/10	156C3
Cwmdu Colly (Neath Abbey)	56/40	139A1
Cwmdu Colly (Skewen)	55/18	139B1
Cwmdu Drift (nr Merthyr)		168C2
* Cwmdu Quarry	53/19	—
Cwmdu St. Johns Colly	51/5	156C4
Cwmdu Sidings (Llynfi Valley)	49/7	156D3
Cwm Duffryn Siding	51/3	141A6
Cwmdyffryn Colly	51/3	147A6
Cwm Farm Siding	57/52	133A5
Cwmfelin Tinplate Works	55/8	136A1
Cwmfelin and Cwmbwrla S.B.	55/9	136A1
Cwmfelinfach Goods	41/40	—
Cwmffoes Crossing	49/49	143A5
Cwmffrwd Colly	39/22	181D5
CWMFFRWD HALT	39/22	184A3
Cwmffrwdoer Colly	39/24	182C5
CWMFFRWDOER HALT	39/16	182B5
Cwmfuwch Colly		160B1
* Cwm Garw		156B5
* Cwmgeidd Colly	53/Ind.	—
Cwm Gelly Colly	41/36	—
Cwmglas Quarry	52/17	132D3
Cwmglo Pit (Merthyr)		168C3
Cwm Glyn S.B.	47/107	182D4
Cwm Gored Quarries		163A4
CWMGORSE	54/49	131B6
Cwmgorse Branch Junction	54/47	131D4
Cwmgorse Colly (new line)	54/49	131C6
Cwmgorse Colly (old line)	54/47	131B6
Cwm Gwenea Colly	51/2	141A6
Cwm Gwinea Colly	51/2	154C4
Cwmgwineu Colly	51/3	141A6
Cwmgwrach Colly	47/9	163A2
Cwmgwyneu Colly	51/3	154D2
Cwm Lickey Colly		182D5
Cwm Llantwit Colly	49/76	161A5
CWMLLYNFELL	53/31	
CWMMAWR	57/35	133A3
Cwm Merthyr Colly	51/54	153B5
Cwmnant Colly		—
* Cwmnant Du Colly (Swansea Vale)	53/19	—
Cwmnantddu Colly (Branches Fork)	39/24	182B4
Cwmnantgan Crossing	41/15	—
Cwmnantllwyd Colly	53/18	—
Cwmnantmoel Colly		?
Cwmnantygroes S.B.	40/60	182A2
Cwmneol Colly	47/41	165D4
CWMNEOL HALT	47/42	165D4
Cwmogwr Colly	49/67	160D2
Cwm Park Colly	46/11	158D2
Cwm Park S.B.	46/11	158D4
Cwm Pelena Colly	51/54	153B5
Cwmpennar Colly		165D6
* Cwmphil Sidings S.B.	53/24	—
CWM PRYSOR		111A2
Cwm Rhondda Colly		156D5
CWMRHYD-Y-GAU HALT	47/11	163C3
* Cwmsaebran Colly	46/4	158C2
Cwmscwm Colly	57/46	134A2
Cwmserchan Colly		182B4
Cwmsychan Red Ash Colly		181D4
CWMSYFIOG	42/21	177B3
CWMSYFIOG AND BRITHDIR	42/20	177B3
CWMSYFIOG COLLY HALT	42/21	177B3
CWMSYFIOG HALT	42/19	177B3
Cwmtawe Colly (Abercrave)	52/21	132A3
Cwmtawe Siding (Pontardawe)	53/33	—
Cwmteg Colly (Brynamman)	53/33	—
Cwmteg Colly (Garnant)	54/44	131C4
Cwmtillery Branch Junction	40/57	181D2
Cwmtillery Colly	40/58	181C5
Cwmtrupit Colly	54/46	131D4
CWMTWRCH WELL HALT	53/27	—
* Cwm Vale Colly	54/50	—
Cwmynyscos Tramway	47/112	183A4
Cwrt Coch Colly		177D4
Cwrtybela Crossing		177D5
Cwrt y bettws Colly	56/38	139D2
Cwrt y Clafdy Crossing		139B2
* Cwmyglo Colly	42/43	179C6
Cwrt y mwnws Colly	51/8	156C2
Cwrt y vil Quarry		147D5
Cyfarthfa Colly		168D1
Cyfarthfa Crossing S.B.		168D1
Cyfarthfa Ironworks		168A3
Cyfarthfa Ironworks Junction		168B3
Cyfarthfa Junction		168C1
Cyfarthfa Siding		168D1
CYFRONYDD		118A2
Cylla Quarry		178C1
Cylla S.B.		178D1
Cymbyr S.B.	40/32	180A5
Cymerau Quarry Siding		113A4
CYMMER	51/33	155B4
CYMMER AFAN	51/33	155B4
Cymmer Colly (Eirw Branch)	46/29	159D5
CYMMER CORRWG	51/34	155B4
CYMMER GENERAL	51/33	155B4
Cymmer Glyncorrwg Colly	51/32	155D2
Cymmer Level S.B. (Porth)	46/28	159D5
Cymmer Tunnel S.B.	51/33	155C4
Cymmer Upper Colly		159D5
Cymmer Yard S.B. (Eirw Branch)	46/30	159D6
Cymric Rhondda Colly (Common Bch)	49/85	161D5
Cymric Rhondda Colly (Ystrad)	46/19	159A2
CYNGHORDY	59/5	—
Cynheidre	57/53	133B4
Cynllwynddu Colly		159B4

Cynon Colly	51/29	153D5	Days Road Wagon Shops		24C5
Cynon (New Cynon) Colly	51/30	153D6	Daywell Crossing		95D3
Cynon Crossing Jcn		170D3	Deadman's Bay Quarry	12/24	—
CYNON PLATFORM	51/30	153D6	* Deakins Siding	28/2	62C2
* Cynon River Bridge S.B.		170B2	Decoy Crossing		96C2
Cynon Tin Plate works (Aberdare)	47/25	165C1	Dee Junction		91D2
CYNONVILLE HALT	51/30	153D6	Dee Oil Works Siding		91D1
CYNWYD		112B2	Deep Duffryn Colly	47/65	170C1
			Deepfield Colly		70D1
Dafen Goods	57/61	134B5	Deep Navigation Colly	47/81	170B5
Dafen Loop	57/61	134C4	Deer Park Siding	10/34	2B6
Dafen Tinplate Siding	57/61	134C5	Deeside S.B.		112B5
Dainton	14/11	12A4	* Deeside Slate Quarry		112C4
* DAISEY BANK	31/37	75A2	DEFFORD	34/3	—
DAISY BANK	31/37	75A2	DEFIANCE PLATFORM	11/15	7B3
DAISY BANK AND BRADLEY	31/37	75A2	Delph Brickworks Siding		94B2
Dam Head Crossing		54A5	Denbigh C.C. Siding		93D6
Dandy Pit		?	DENHAM	26/10	35D3
DANES COURT	46/93	174D3	DENHAM GOLF CLUB PLATFORM	26/10	35D2
Danes Hill Siding	23/42	50C6	Denham Junctions	26/11	35D4
Daniels Mill Siding	20/53	—	* Deniford Siding		15A6
* Danny Derry Colly		169D3	Dennis's Quarry Siding		94C2
Danybryn Colly		?	Denty's Timber Yard Crossing	19/37	24A2
Dan y deri Colly		169D3	Deri Colly		169B6
Danycraig Brickworks (Risca)	41/46	180B5	Deri Colly (1st Location)		177B1
DANYGRAIG (RSB)	56/12	137B5	Deri Junction		177B1
DANYCRAIG HALT (VoN)	56/13	137B4	Derlwyn Siding	42/17	177A2
Danygraig Crossing (Black Lion)	47/35	165B2	Derlyn Colly	42/16	177B3
Danygraig Corssing (Swansea)	56/13	137D6	Derrington G.F.	32/21	—
Danygraig Engine Shed (Swansea)	56/21	137D2	DERRY ORMOND	58/35	127C4
Danygraig Freightliner Terminal	56/24	137D3	* Derwenlas Siding		113C4
Danygraig Junction S.B. (RSB)	56/13	137B4	* Derwen Merthyr Colly (Quakers Yard)		170A4
Danygraig Junction S.B. (SHT)	56/12	137B4	Derwen Merthyr Colly (Rhym)		?
Danygraig Sidings G.F.	56/15	137B5	DERWYDD ROAD	54/1	130C5
Danylan Colly	54/51	—	DETTONFORD	33/24	72B2
DANZEY	30/31	81D4	DEVIL'S BRIDGE		114D4
DARBY END HALT	31/52	76C5	DEVIZES	21/26	46B5
Dare Colly (Treorchy)	46/14	158D3	Devon Basalt Quarry	14/44	13C3
Dare Junction (Aberdare GWR)	47/35	165B3	DEVONPORT ALBERT ROAD	12/5	8C3
Dare Junction (Aberdare TV)	47/27	165C1	DEVONPORT ALBERT ROAD HALT	12/5	—
Dare Valley Junction	47/27	165B2	DEVONPORT BARRACKS	12/32	8B2
Daren Colly	55/49	138A5	Devonport Dockyard	12/32	8C2
Darenddu Colly		172A4	Devonport Junction	12/6	8C4
DARESBURY		88B3	DEVONPORT KINGS ROAD	12/5	—
Darkhill Sidings	37/41	54A5	Devonshire Street Crossing	16/14	19B6
Darkhill & Winnall Pit		54C1	Devon Valley Mill	15/7	16C3
Dark Lane Colly	32/11	70C5	Devoran		2C3
Dark Lane Crossing	32/41	70C5	DEVYNOCK	52/14	122A2
* Dark Lane Siding (GWR)		?	DEVYNOCK & SENNYBRIDGE	52/14	122A2
Dark Lane Siding (LNWR)	32/52	—	Dew Siding	63/44	106B2
Darlingscott Green Crossing	28/36	64A2	Dhu Quarry		101C5
Darlingscott Junction	28/36	64A2	Diamond Colly	53/50	—
DARRAN		177C1	Diamond Jubilee Pit		79A5
DARRAN AND DERI		177C1	Diamond Llantwit Colly	42/43	179C6
Darran Brick Works Siding (Cymbyr)	40/32	180A5	Dibdale Colly		76A3
Darran Fawr Colly	49/27	156B5	DIDCOT	23/8	30B5
Darran y Mwrthwl		179A3	Didcot East Junction	23/13	30C6
Darranddu Colly		171C1	Didcot Ordnance Depot	23/45	30B4
Darren Colly (Penar Branch)	40/64	177D5	Didcot Ordnance Depot G.F.	23/6	30B4
Darren Felin Siding	40/64	177D5	DIDCOT PARKWAY	23/8	30B5
Dart Valley G.F. (Totnes)	14/9	12D1	DILLWYN & BRYNTEG HALT	52/9	132C4
DAUNTSEY	21/13	28B5	Dillwyn Colly	52/9	132C4
Dauntsey Rd. Crossing	20/7	28A4	DILTON MARSH HALT	21/54	46D2
Davies Siding	36/23	108A5	Dimbath Branch	49/67	157B6
Dawley (Middlesex)	24/26	35B2	Dimmer S.B.	17/7	43A6
Dawley Brook		73C1	DINAS (Penycraig)	49/56	159D3
Dawley Ironwork	32/i	70D1	DINAS (Rhondda)	46/25	159D5
Dawley Magna Colly	32/i	70D1	Dinas Brickworks Siding (Kidwelly)	57/34	133D2
Dawley Parva Colly	32/i	70A2	Dinas Colly (Dinas Rhondda)		159D4
Dawley Parva Crossing	32/40	70A2	Dinas Isaf Colly (Penygraig)	49/58	160B6
DAWLEY & STIRCHLEY	32/43	—	Dinas Isaf Colly (Porth)		159D4
DAWLISH	14/19	14C6	Dinas Isha S.B.	49/58	160B6
DAWLISH WARREN	14/19	14B6	Dinas Junction S.B. (Dinas Rhondda)		159D5
Day House Crossing		72B2	Dinas Main Colly (Gilfach)	49/69	160B4

DINAS MAWDDY		115A4
DINAS POWIS	44/59	147D4
DINAS POWYS	44/59	147D4
DINAS (RHONDDA)		159D4
Dinas Siding (Rhigos)	47/14	163B5
* Dinas Siding S.B. (Pandy)	46/27	159D5
* Dinas Works (Kidwelly)		133D1
DINASTOW	36/24	108B5
DINGESTOW	36/24	108B5
Dingle Colly		77B3
DINGLE ROAD PLATFORM	44/61	147C6
* Dingle site (Cardiff)	43/95	150D4
Dinham G.F.	36/2	52C3
DINMORE	63/13	102D2
* Diphwys Junction		109D5
DITTON PRIORS	33/24	71C3
Dock Colly		?
Dock Gates Lane Crossing (Bristol)	19/37	24A3
Dock Road Gates S.B. (Barry)	44/48	148D5
DOCK STREET (NEWPORT)	38/58	152B3
Dock Storage North S.B. (Cardiff)	43/104	149B6
* Dock Storage South S.B. (Cardiff)	43/99	149B6
Docks Platform S.B. (Cardiff)	43/77	150A5
Docks Terminus S.B. (Cardiff)	43/72	149D4
DOCKYARD HALT	12/4	8C2
Doctor's Crossing		141B5
Doctor Days Bridge Junction	19/10	24B5
Dodmore Green Crossing	20/41	—
Dodsdown Siding	22/16	48C6
DOLARDDYN		118B2
DOLAU	59/10	—
Dolau Junction	57/17	134D3
DOLCOATH HALT	10/11	1C6
Dolcoath Mine Siding	10/27	1B6
Dolcoath Siding S.B.	10/11	1C6
DOLDDERWEN CROSSING		113B5
DOLDOWLOD	59/27	120C3
Dolemeadow Crossing	63/13	104A2
DOLGELLAU		110C5
DOLGELLEY		110C5
Dolgelley Branch Junction		111D2
DOLGELLY		110C5
Dolgoch Quarry		119A4
Dolgwili Siding	58/37	129B4
Dolomite Siding		174A2
Dolphin Junction S.B.	24/22	34C6
Dolrhyd Crossing		118A1
DOLSERAU HALT		110C5
Dolyfonddu Siding		115B3
DOLYGAER HALT	59/15	166A3
DOLYHIR	63/37	103B2
DOLWEN	59/32	116C2
DONNINGTON	32/47	—
* DONNINGTON WOOD	32/47	—
Donnington Wood Colly		—
DONYATT HALT	16/44	20B6
DORCHESTER WEST	17/4	41D6
DORRIDGE	30/12	81C5
DORRINGTON	63/1	100A1
Dorrington Ballast Pit S.B.	63/1	100A1
DORSTONE	63/44	106B3
DORTON HALT	26/3	86C2
Dos Works	38/64	152A3
DOSELEY HALT	32/40	70A1
Doseley Quarries	32/39	70D1
DOUBLEBOIS	11/12	6A4
Doulting Siding	16/39	22D6
DOUSLAND	14/32	10C5
Dousland Barn Crossing	14/32	10C5
DOVEY JUNCTION		113C4
DOWDESWELL	22/1	57C6
DOWLAIS (later Pant)		167A1
* DOWLAIS (Dowlais Rly)		167C1
DOWLAIS CAE HARRIS		167B2

Dowlais Cardiff Colly (Abercynon)		171B3
DOWLAIS CENTRAL	41/1	167B1
Dowlais Clay Level Siding		167B2
DOWLAIS HIGH STREET	41/3	—
Dowlais Iron Works		167B1
* DOWLAIS JUNCTION		168D2
Dowlais Junction S.B.		167A1
Dowlais Loop Junction		171C3
Dowlais Loop Line (Abercynon)		171B3
Dowlais Lower Junction (Merthyr)		168D2
Dowlais Pits (Abercynon)		171B3
Dowlais Pits Branch Junction		171C2
Dowlais Siding (Brofiscin)	49/83	161D5
DOWLAIS TOP (HIGH LEVEL)		167B2
DOWLAIS TOP (LOW LEVEL)	41/5	—
Dowlais Upper Junction (Merthyr)		168D2
Dowlais Washery G.F.		167B2
Dowlais Works (Cardiff)	43/54	150C5
* Dowlais Works Junction (Cardiff)	43/63	150C6
Downend Siding	16/18	19C2
DOWNFIELD CROSSING HALT	20/30	58C5
Downend Quarry Siding		45B2
Downside Quarry	18/13	—
* Dragons Site Siding		—
DRAYCOTT (Wells)	16/35	22B2
Draycott Camp (MSWJ)	22/8	29D4
Draycott Mill Siding	20/53	—
DRAYTON GREEN HALT	26/20	37B5
* Drayton Green Siding (Main Line)		37B5
Dr. Days Bridge Junction	19/14	24B5
Drefach Colly	49/25	157D6
Drinnick Mill S.B.	11/32	4C2
DROITWICH ROAD	34/4	—
DROITWICH SPA	33/14	78C5
Drope Goods	44/29	146D3
Drope Junction	44/29	146D4
Drump Lane	10/14	1C6
Drwllas Colly		—
DRWS-Y-NANT		110B6
DRYBROOK HALT	37/29	53A5
Drybrook Quarry	37/29	53A5
DRYBROOK ROAD	37/18	54B4
Dry Kiln Siding	11/29	4B1
Drym Colly	52/11	132B5
Drymma Colly	53/Ind	—
DRYSLLWYN	58/42	—
Dubbers Sidings	11/32	4C2
Duchy and Lancaster Quarries S.B.	44/34	144B2
Duchy Colly	49/32	156D6
Duchy Quarry Siding	44/34	144B2
Duck Colly	37/30	54A5
DUDBRIDGE	20/55	—
Dudgeley	63/2	100A5
DUDLEY	31/39	75D1
Dudley East Castle Works	31/39	75D2
DUDLEY SOUTH SIDE & NETHERTON	31/41	76B4
Duff Sidings (Felin Fran)	55/45	135B4
DUFFRYN (TIRYDAIL)	54/3	131B3
Duffryn Aberdare Colly		164B2
Duffryn Amman Colly	54/40	131A4
DUFFRYN ARDUDWY		110B1
Duffryn Bridge S.B.	44/17	146C1
Duffryn Chemical Works (Ynysddu)	41/40	—
Duffryn Clydach Colly	56/44	?
Duffryn Colly (Brynmawr)	41/12	—
Duffryn Colly (Gowerton)		?
Duffryn Colly (Nantyffyllon)	49/1	156A2
DUFFRYN CROSSING HALT (GWR)	47/65	165D6
DUFFRYN CROSSING PLATFORM (TV)	47/63	165D6
Duffryn Crossing S.B. (Llandilo Jcn)	57/33	134D6
Duffryn Dare Colly (Aberdare)	47/34	165B2
Duffryn Goods (Nantyffyllon)	49/1	156A2
Duffryn Gower Colly		?
Duffryn Iron Works (Pentrebach)		169B2

Duffryn Isaf S.B.'s	42/42	179C4	
Duffryn Junction S.B. (P. Talbot)	51/1	141B5	
Duffryn Lantwit Colly	49/78	161C5	
Duffryn Main Colly		135A6	
Duffryn Main S.B. (Neath)	56/47	139B4	
Duffryn Merthyr Colly (Nantyffyllon)	49/1	156A2	
DUFFRYN MILLS PLATFORM	51/3	141A6	
Duffryn Pit (Maesteg)	49/3	156C2	
Duffryn Red Ash Colly	49/79	161B5	
Duffryn Rhondda Colly		156A1	
* Duffryn Rhondda Golden Vein Colly		?	
DUFFRYN RHONDDA PLATFORM	51/31	155D1	
Duffryn Rhymney Colly	42/7	167D5	
Duffryn Sidings S.B. (E. Vale)	40/5	176B4	
Duffryn Tawe Colly	53/19	—	
Duffryn Yard (Port Talbot)	51/1	141B5	
* Duffws Junction		109D5	
Duke Colly (Abernant)	54/49	131C6	
* Duke Lock Junction		68B2	
Duke Siding (Swansea)	56/4	137B2	
Duke Street Goods		90A3	
* Dukes Dock Depot		90B2	
Dulais Colly (Onllwyn)	52/11	132B5	
Dulais Merthyr Colly	52/7	162B1	
Dulais Mountain Colly	52/8	132D3	
Dulais Resolven Colly		162A2	
* Dulais Works	54/12	—	
* Dulas Colly	54/51	—	
Dulcote Quarry Siding	16/39	22C4	
DULVERTON	15/21	18D6	
Dunball Yard		150A5	
DUNBALL	16/18	19C2	
Dunball Pottery Siding S.B.	16/18	19C2	
Dunch Lane Crossing	21/22	46A3	
DUNHAM		88D1	
DUNHAM HILL		88D1	
DUNHAMPSTEAD	34/4	—	
DUNKERTON	21/53	27C3	
DUNKERTON COLLY HALT	21/53	27C3	
Dunkirk S.B.		91B4	
Dunkirk Siding	20/56	—	
DUNMERE HALT	11/35	—	
Dunmere Junction	11/35	—	
Dunmere Wharf	11/35	—	
Dunraven Adare Colly (Glynn Neath)	47/10	163C3	
* Dunraven Colly (Treherbert)	46/3	158C1	
Dunraven S.B. (Treherbert)	46/2	158B1	
Dunraven Siding (Glyn Neath)		163A2	
DUNSFORD HALT	14/45	13C3	
DUNSTALL PARK	31/3	74A3	
DUNSTER	15/23	17A1	
DUNVANT	54/25	—	
Dunvant Penlan Colly		—	
Durn Siding		115C4	
DURSLEY	20/53	—	
DURSLEY JUNCTION	20/46	—	
DURSTON	16/11	20C3	
Dwrllas Colly	54/50	—	
Dyehouse Siding	20/56	—	
DYFFRYN		110B1	
DYFFRYN ARDUDWY		110B1	
DYFFRYN ON SEA		110B1	
* Dyffryn Works	53/39	—	
Dylass Colly Siding	47/48	164B5	
Dylass Isha Colly		?	
DYMOCK	33/20	60C3	
Dynant Colly	57/36	133A3	
Dynant Siding	57/36	133A5	
Dynea Colly		173A1	
DYNEA HALT		173A1	
DYNEVOR (Skewen)	55/18	139B2	
Dynevor Colly Siding (Glanamman)		131A5	
Dynevor G.F. (Neath River Bridge)	56/43	139D6	
Dynevor Junction (Neath River Bridge)	56/41	139D5	
Dynevor Main Colly	56/44	?	
Dynevor Sidings (Neath)	52/5	153B1	
Dynevor Sidings (Skewen)	55/18	138D6	
Dynevor Tin Plate Wks (Pantyffynon)	54/7	131C1	
Dysynni Gas Siding		113C1	
Dyvatty Crossing	57/48	134A3	
Eagle Brickworks Siding (Cwmavon)	51/26	154B3	
Eaglebush Colly	50/5	139C5	
Eaglebush G.F. (Canal Branch)	50/6	139B5	
Eagle Sidings (nr. Hollinswood)	32/8	70C5	
Eagle Siding (nr. Llanharan)		145B3	
Eagle Tin works (Neath)		139C5	
EALING	25/1	37B6	
EALING BROADWAY	25/1	37B6	
EARDINGTON	32/24	71C5	
EARDISLEY	63/41	—	
Eardisley Branch Junction		103B4	
Eardisley Junction		103D3	
Earl Dudley's Lines		76C4	
Earley Power Station	24/13	32B6	
Earls Court Junction	25/29	38D5	
EARLSWOOD	30/30	81C4	
EARLSWOOD LAKES	30/30	81C4	
East & West Junction S.B.	30/36	82C6	
EAST ACCESS HALT	36/22	108A4	
EAST ACTON	25/22	38B3	
East Adderbury Pits	27/1	84D3	
EAST ANSTEY	15/20	18D4	
East Beat G.F. (Neath)	50/5	139B6	
East Blaina Colly		?	
East Branch Junction (Cardiff)	46/105	149C4	
EASTBROOK		147C4	
Eastbrook Crossing		147C4	
EASTBURY	23/40	49B2	
East Bute Dock Junction S.B.	43/72	150B6	
East Caradon	11/36	6C4	
East Castle works (Dudley)	31/39	75D2	
East Central S.B. (Swansea)	56/8	137C3	
East Cliff Siding		14C5	
East Colly (Gwaun cae Gurwen)		131B6	
East Depot (Bristol)	19/19	24B6	
East Dock (Cardiff)		150B5	
EAST DOCK, SWANSEA	56/7	137B3	
* East Dock Cargo Wharf G.F.	43/69	150B5	
East Dock Crossing (Cardiff)	43/67	150B4	
East Dock Engine Shed (Cardiff)	43/67	150B4	
East Dock Junction (Cardiff)	43/72	150B6	
East Dock Junction (Newport)	38/58	152B4	
East Dock Junction (Swansea)	56/11	137D6	
East Elliot Colly	42/18	177B3	
East End Colly (Blaenavon)	51/52	153C2	
East End S.B. (Cwm Cerwyn)	51/6	156D1	
East End Sidings (Swansea)	56/22	137D1	
Eastern Depot (Swansea)	56/6	137B3	
Eastern Dry Dock (Uskmouth)	38/33	151C6	
Eastern Pit	46/17	159B1	
Eastern United Colly	37/36	54B2	
Eastern Valley Colly		182B5	
Eastern Valleys Sidings (Newport)	38/44	152D2	
EAST GARSTON	23/40	49B2	
* EASTHAM RAKE		89D4	
EASTHOPE HALT	32/29	71B2	
East Llansamlet Sidings	55/18	138D4	
East Loop Junction (Lydney Jcn)	37/5	54C5	
East Mendalgief S.B.	38/43	152D3	
* East Moors Engine Shed	43/68	150C4	
East Moors Junction S.B.	43/62	150B6	
East Moors Steelworks	43/58	150C5	
EASTON	17/8	42C1	
EASTON COURT	33/23	101D4	
Easton Neston Siding	29/16	—	
Easton Road Junction	19/47	24A5	
EAST PIER AVONMOUTH		25C1	

East Pool Siding	10/8	1A5	
East Rhondda Colly		155A5	
East Slade Colly	37/27	54A2	
EAST SOMERSET, WELLS	16/37	22A4	
* East Somerset Junction (Witham)	16/51	45C3	
EAST STREET	17/13	41C1	
East Street Crossing (Newquay)		3A2	
East Tramway Crossing (Portmadoc)		110A3	
* East Tyndall Street	43/53	150C6	
East Usk Junction	38/17	152B6	
East Usk Wharf	38/28	152B4	
* East Wharf Road (Cardiff)	43/62	150B5	
East Wheal Rose	10/31	3C1	
EATON	63/33	100B2	
* Eaton Crossing (Leominster)	63/10	102B6	
Eaton Hall Tramway		91D4	
Ebbw Junction	38/3	152D2	
Ebbw Vale Goods	40/1	175C4	
EBBW VALE HIGH LEVEL	41/10	—	
Ebbw Vale Junction	41/9	—	
EBBW VALE LOW LEVEL	40/2	175C4	
Ebbw Vale Sidings S.B.	40/3	175D4	
EBLEY CROSSING HALT	20/30	58C4	
ECKINGTON	34/3	—	
Eclipse Brickworks Siding	57/54	133C4	
* Edgar St. Sidings	63/19	104B6	
EDGEBOLD		98C4	
Edge Hill Light Rly	29/4	—	
EDGERLEY		98A2	
EDINGTON & BRATTON	21/41	46D3	
EDINGTON JUNCTION	18/28	—	
* Edlogan Works Siding		183A3	
Edstone Crossing		82B4	
Edward's Private Line		94C1	
EFAIL FACH	51/40	153D3	
EFAIL ISAF	44/26	161B6	
Egerton Dock Goods		90C3	
Eggworthy Siding	14/32	10C5	
Eirw Branch Junction	46/32	172A2	
* Eirw Gas Works	46/30	159D6	
Elan Valley Junction	59/28	120B3	
Elba Colly (Gowerton)	54/54	—	
Elba Steel Works S.B. (Gowerton)	54/53	—	
Elba Works (Gowerton)	55/2	135C1	
Elba Works (Swansea Docks)	56/27	137D3	
ELBURTON CROSS	12/29	7C5	
Elders Navigation Colly	51/12	156D3	
Eldon Road Siding		149C2	
Electric House G.F.	11/27	5D3	
Elled Colly	39/17	182B5	
ELLERDINE HALT	32/45	99C6	
ELLESMERE		96C5	
Ellesmere Dump Siding		96C4	
ELLESMERE PORT		90D1	
Elliot Colly Sidings (Brithdir)	42/20	177B3	
Elliot Colly Sidings (New Tredegar)	42/16	177B3	
ELLIOT PIT HALT	42/19	177B3	
Elliot Pit Junction	42/18	177B3	
Elliotts Crossing (Bramley)	23/42	50B6	
Ellwoods Siding	41/13	—	
Elm Bridge (Pontrilas)	63/44	107B6	
Elm Bridge S.B. (Gloucester)	35/10	55B4	
Elm Farm Siding		107B6	
Elmley Lovett S.B.	33/21	78D1	
* Elm Park	63/44	107B6	
ELMS BRIDGE	36/23	108C4	
Elms Colly	54/25	—	
ELSON HALT		95D5	
* Ely & Rhondda Colly		159D4	
Ely Colly (Penygraig)	49/57	159D3	
Ely Fairwater Road Goods	46/93	146C6	
Ely Goods Yard S.B.	46/93	146C6	
Ely Llantwit Colly	49/62	160D6	
ELY MAIN LINE		146C6	
Ely Merthyr Colly	49/59	160C6	
Ely Paper Mills Crossing S.B.		146C6	
Ely Paper Mills (nr. Tondu)	49/9	157B2	
Ely Place (Brecon)	52/16	122B2	
Ely Rhondda Colly	46/25	160B6	
Ely River Bridge S.B. (St. Fagans)		146C4	
Ely Valley Junction (Llantrisant)	44/11	145D4	
Emily Pit	53/12	—	
Emlyn Colly	54/33	131A1	
Emlyn Sidings G.F. (Gloucester)	35/8	56B4	
Empire Colly (Glyn Neath)	47/11	163A2	
Empire Colly (Resolven)		162B5	
Enborne Junction	23/20	49A2	
Energlyn Colly (1st)		173A5	
Energlyn Colly (2nd)		173B4	
Energlyn Junctions		173A5	
Eneurglyn		179D4	
* Engine House Beat S.B.		136D2	
Engine Shed Junction (Cardiff)	43/68	150C4	
Engine Shed Junction (Gloucester)	35/7	56B4	
Engine Shed Junction (Lydney)	37/5	54C4	
* Engine Shed S.B. (Bath Road)	19/10	24B4	
Engine Shed S.B. (Leamington)	30/19	83C6	
Engine Shed Siding (Gloucester)	35/7	56B4	
Engine Shed Sidings S.B. (Barrow Road)	19/41	—	
English Bridge Junction S.B.		99C2	
English Celluloid Siding	51/2	154D3	
Erskine Colly	40/19	182D2	
ERWOOD	59/24	121D3	
ESGAIRGEILIOG		113A5	
Eskyn Colly	51/39	153D2	
Estateways G.F.	56/43	139D5	
Etna Colly	49/72	160D4	
Eton S.B.	24/40	34D5	
ETTINGTON	29/6	—	
Ettington Lime Works	29/6	—	
Evans Bridge Crossing		113A5	
Evanstown Brick Works	49/53	143D3	
EVERCREECH JUNCTION	18/14	—	
EVERCREECH NEW	18/14	—	
EVERSHOT	17/5	44D3	
EVESHAM	28/3 & 34/16	62C1	
* Evesham North S.B.	28/2	62C1	
EVESHAM ROAD CROSSING HALT	29/3 & 30/36	82C6	
* Evesham Road Siding		82C6	
* Ewyas Harrold G.F.	63/44	107B6	
Ewenny S.B.	44/34	144B2	
* EWENNY ROAD, MAESTEG		156C2	
* Exe Bight (Pier) Siding		14A6	
Exeter Basin Junction	14/21	13D1	
Exeter City Basin	14/21	13C2	
Exeter Marsh Barton	14/45	13D1	
Exeter Railway Junction	14/21	13D1	
Exeter Riverside	15/3	13B1	
EXETER ST. DAVIDS	15/1	13B1	
EXETER ST. THOMAS	14/21	13C1	
Exhibition Sidings (Plymouth)	12/6	8C3	
Exley Tileworks Branch	32/22	70D4	
EXMINSTER	14/20	13C5	
* Express Tin Works	51/21	154C3	
Exwick Crossing	15/1	13B1	
EYNSHAM	27/24	67C2	
Eynsham Beet Factory	27/24	67C2	
Eyton Crossing		98A4	
FAIRBOURNE		111D1	
Fairfield Crossing (Hungerford)	23/19	49D1	
Fairfield Crossing (Portreath)	10/28	1A5	
Fairfield Siding (Portreath)	10/28	1A5	
FAIRFORD	27/23	66C1	
Fair Oak Siding		149A3	
* Fair Oak Road Siding		149A3	
FAIRWATER	46/93	146C6	
Fairwater Siding (Ely)		146C6	

Fairwater Yard (Taunton)	16/2	20D2
Fairwood Crossing S.B. (Westbury)	21/33	46D1
Fairwood Junction S.B. (Westbury)	21/33	46C2
Fairwood Tinplate Works (Gowerton)	55/4	135C1
Falcon Lane Goods	25/32	38D2
* Fald y dre Colly		?
FALMOUTH1	10/35	2D3
* FALMOUTH DOCKS	10/38	2D3
* FALMOUTH TOWN	10/38	2D3
Fal Valley Siding	11/29	4B1
FARINGDON	23/39	29C5
FARINGDON ROAD	23/2	29D6
Farleigh Down S.B.	21/8	27A5
FARLEY HALT	32/32	69D2
Farnham Road S.B.	24/18	34B5
Farrington Colly	21/45	27D1
FARRINGTON GURNEY	21/45	27D1
Fawler Siding S.B.	28/18	67A1
FAWLEY	36/31	105B2
FEARNALL HEATH	33/15	61A4
Feeder Bridge Junction	19/17	24B5
FELINDYFFRYN HALT	58/34	126B5
FELIN FACH	58/41	127B3
* Felin Fach		143D4
Felin Fach Crossing (Llangynog)		117A1
FELIN FOEL COLLIERS HALT	57/56	133C5
Felin Foel Goods		133C4
Felin Fran Colly (Midland)	53/11	—
Felin Fran Colly (G.W.R.)	55/49	138B5
Felin Fran Duff Sidings	55/45	138B5
FELIN FRAN HALT	55/45	138C5
Felin Fran Junction	55/44	138C4
FENCOTE	33/21	102C4
FENNANT ROAD HALT		94C4
FENNS BANK		96A6
FENNY COMPTON	29/8 & 30/22	83C1
FERNDALE	46/44	158C6
Ferndale Lower S.B.	46/46	158D6
Ferndale No. 1 Colly	46/46	158D6
Ferndale No. 2 Colly	46/43	158C6
Ferndale No. 3 Colly	46/18	159A2
Ferndale No. 4 Colly	46/43	158C6
Ferndale No. 5 Colly	46/46	158D6
Ferndale No. 6 Colly	46/47	159A4
Ferndale No. 7 Colly	46/47	159A4
Ferndale No. 8 Colly	46/48	159B4
Ferndale No. 9 Colly	46/48	159B4
* Ferndale Power Station	46/48	159A4
Ferndale Washery	46/46	159A4
* FERNHILL (Abercwmboi)		165D6
FERNHILL HEATH	33/15	61A4
Fernhill S.B. (Blaenrhondda)	46/58	158A1
Fernland Colly	51/52	153C3
Ferry Road (Grangetown)		147A5
Ferry Road Junction (St. Budeaux)	12/1	8A2
FERRYSIDE	57/1	133A1
Ferry Tinplate Works	50/14	140C4
FESTINIOG		109B6
Fetterhill Siding	37/40	54C1
FFAIRFACH	54/1	130D3
Ffaldcaiach Sidings S.B.	47/84	170C5
Ffaldau Colly (Pontycymmer)	49/30	156C6
Ffaldau Oak Level	46/43	156C6
Ffaldau Sidings (Ferndale)	46/43	158C6
Ffalydre Colly		162B6
Ffochriw Colly		167D4
Ffoes Bank S.B.	49/49	143A5
Fforchaman Colly	47/43	165D3
Fforch Dwm Colly	51/53	153C5
Fforchlas Siding	51/43	155D2
Fforchneol Colly	47/41	165D4
Fforchwen Colly	47/46	165D3
Ffordd Crossing		117A1
Fforest Fach Siding	44/24	144A4

Fforest Goch Colly		135A6
Ffosddu Colly	52/12	132B5
Ffosfach Colly	55/32	133D6
Ffosmaen Pit	40/51	175D6
Ffos Pit	49/46	143A5
Ffos y Go Colly		93A4
FFRIDD GATE		113B5
FFRITH		93A3
Ffrith Colly		93A3
Ffrith Quarries		92B1
FFRONFRAITH HALT		116A6
Ffrwd Branch Junction		93A1
Ffrwd Colly (Brymbo)		93A4
Ffrwd Colly (B.P. & G.V.)	57/45	133C2
Ffrwd Ironworks		93A4
Ffrwdwyllt Tin Works	50/30	141B4
Ffynnongain Crossing	58/9	125D6
* Fiddington Crossing		—
Field Sidings (Pontyberem)	57/37	133A2
* Fields Sand Siding (Foley Park)	32/26	77D4
FILLEIGH	15/19	18C5
FILTON	19/58	23B5
* FILTON ABBEY WOOD	19/58	23B5
FILTON HALT	19/99	23B4
Filton Incline	19/59	23B4
Filton West Junction	19/99	23A5
Findall Mine		54C2
FINSTOCK HALT	28/18	65D5
Fire Engine Pit		135B6
Firestone S.B.	24/42	37D5
Fishers Lane Crossing	23/37	49C5
Fisherton Sidings	21/58	47D6
FISHGUARD & GOODWICK	58/1	123A6
FISHGUARD HARBOUR	58/1	123A6
Fish Market (Swansea)	56/1	137C3
* Fishmore Siding	63/7	101A6
FISHPONDS (Bristol)	19/49	—
Fishponds Siding (Brymbo)		93B4
Five Fords Crossing (Culmstock)	15/18	16A5
Five Fords Siding (Marchwiel)		92D4
FIVE WAYS	34/12	—
FLADBURY	28/2	62B2
FLAG STATION HALT		111C4
FLAX BOURTON	16/32	21A6
Flax Bourton Cutting S.B.	16/32	23D3
FLEUR DE LIS	42/34	178B2
Fleur de Lis Junction (B & M)	34/37	178C2
Fleur de Lis Junction (V. of N.)	47/92	178D2
FLEUR DE LIS PLATFORM	34/37	178B2
* Fleur-de-Luce Branch		178C2
Flood Gates Crossing		103B2
Florence Siding	15/20	18C1
Florries Crossing	57/59	134C2
Flour Mill Colly		54D1
* Foce Colly		?
FOCHRIW		167D4
Fochriw Colly Junction		167C4
Fochriw Junction		167C3
Fochriw Pits		167D4
Foggintor Quarry		10B6
FOLEY PARK HALT	32/26 & 33/25	77D4
Folly Point Siding	32/25	72C4
FORD (LSWR)	12/4	—
FORD (S & M Line)		98C3
FORD AND CROSSGATES		98C3
FORD BRIDGE	63/12	102D2
FORD PLATFORM (Plymouth)	12/4	8B2
FORDEN		118C4
Fordgate S.B.	16/12	20A4
Fords Siding (Bridgend)	44/33	144A2
FOREGATE STREET, WORCESTER	33/10	60C5
Foreshore Sidings (Cardiff)	43/94	149D6
* Forest Iron Works (Treforest)	46/67	172C5
Forest Isaf Colly	51/51	153C2

Garth Works (Rhiwderin)	42/54	184D1
* Garth Works (Taffs Well)	—	173D3
Garw Central Washery	49/27	156B6
Garw Colly (Blaengarw)	49/27	156B6
Garw Colly (Pontyrhyll)	49/31	156D6
Garw Fechan Colly	49/31	156D6
* Gas Ferry Road Crossing	19/39	24B2
Gas House Siding S.B. (Torquay)	14/38	12B5
Gas Lane Sidings (Bristol)	19/16	24B4
Gas Lane Sidings (Portishead)	19/29	23C1
* Gas Siding G.F. (Portishead)	19/27	23C1
Gas Siding S.B. (Reading)	24/10	—
Gas Works Junction S.B. (Bournemouth)	18/23	—
Gas Works Lane Crossing (Bristol)		24B2
Gas Works Siding S.B. (Newland)	33/8	61C3
GATCOMBE		53D5
Gatehampton Siding	23/16	32A2
Gate Lane Siding	16/38	22A5
Gatewen Colly		93C5
GATEWEN HALT		93C5
Gaverigan Siding	11/22	4B1
Gayton Wood Mines	29/13	—
Gegin Crossing		93B2
Gelert Sidings		110A3
Gellavalln Junction S.B.	41/15	—
Gelli and Bwllfa Sidings S.B.	46/18	159B2
* Gelli Blig Colly	49/8	157A1
Gelli Colly (Buttery Hatch)	42/36	178C2
Gelli Junction (Blaengwynfi)	51/37	155C4
GELLI PLATFORM (Ystrad Rhondda)	46/19	159B2
Gelli S.B. (Ystrad Rhondda)	46/18	159B3
Gelliargwellt Colly		?
Gelliau Colly		153A1
Gellideg Colly (Cwmffrwdoer)		182C4
Gellideg Colly (Maesycwmmer Jcn)		178D3
Gelli Dwyll Colly	41/35	—
Gellierllwyn Colly	54/50	—
GELLI FELEN HALT	41/15	—
Gelligroes Colly	41/37 & 47/93	178D3
Gelligroes Junction	41/37 & 47/93	—
Gelli Haf Colly	42/36	178C2
Gellihir Colly	51/13	157A1
Gelli Las S.B.	49/10	157B2
* Gelly Leven — error for Gelly Seven		
Gelli Mill Colly	51/36	155D3
Gelli Seven Colly	49/9	157A1
Gelli Siriol Colly	49/9	157A1
Gelli Tarw Junction	47/20	164B4
Gelli Wion Colly	46/59	172B4
* GELLYCEIDRIM		131A5
Gellyceidrim Colly	54/41	131A5
Gellydeg Colly	39/24	182C4
Gellydwyllt Colly		—
Gellygaer Colly		171A6
* Gelly Galed Colly		159B2
* Gellygroes Colly		178D3
Gellyhave Siding		178C2
* Gelly Havr Colly		178C2
Gellynog Colly Branch Junction	49/84	161B1
Gellynudd Colly	53/18	—
Gellyonen Colly	53/14	—
Gellyrhaidd Colly	49/68	160D5
Gellyrhaidd Junction	49/62	160D6
Gelynog Colly	49/84	161B4
Geneu'r-glyn Colly		179D4
Genwen Colly	55/32	134C6
Genwen Junction S.B.	55/29	134D6
Genwen Quarry	55/32	134C6
GEORGE INN	42/20	177B3
George Pit		165C6
George Street Junction S.B.	38/58	152B3
GERRARDS CROSS	26/10	34A6
GETHIN PITS HALT		169B2
Giants Grave		140B3
Gibbons Crossing		?
Gibbs Colly	49/72	160B4
GILESTON	44/35	144D5
GILFACH (Gilfach Goch)	49/72	160C4
Gilfach Colly (B & M)	42/26	178A2
Gilfach Colly (Gilfach Goch)	49/72	160B4
Gilfach Colly (Gwys)	53/29	—
Gilfach Colly (Mountain Branch)	54/32	131A1
Gilfach Colly (Rhymney)	42/26	178A2
GILFACH FARGOED HALT	42/28	177D3
Gilfach Goch Colly	49/69	160B4
GILFACH GOCH COLLY PLATFORM	49/69	160B4
Gilfach Junction (Aberbargoed)	42/26	178A2
Gilfach Junction (Hendreforgan)	49/68	160D4
* Gilfach Loop	49/71	160D4
Gilfach Main S.B. (Trelewis)		170B5
Gilfach Quarry (Aberbargoed	42/32	178A2
Gilfach S.B. (Rhymney)	42/26	178A2
Gilfach Sidings S.B. (B & M)	42/33	178A2
Gillwyn Sidings	53/18	—
Gilwen Colly	53/27	—
GILWERN	41/16	—
Gilwern Quarry Siding	41/16	—
* Gilwyn Sidings	53/27	—
Gisellfield Siding	32/22	70D4
Gladstone Sidings	44/54	148B5
GLAIS	53/13	—
Glamorgan Colly (Gilfach)	49/31	160B4
Glamorgan Colly (Llwynpia)	46/20	159C3
* Glamorgan Lime Works (Cardiff)	43/67	150C4
Glamorgan Quarry (Llanharry)	44/24	144A4
Glamorgan works (Pontardulais)	54/12	131D2
* Glamorgan Works (Six Pit Jcn)	53/7	—
GLANAMMAN	54/40	131A5
* Glanamman Works	54/41	131A5
Glancynon Siding		159C3
Glanddu Colly	42/31	178B2
GLANDOVEY		113D4
GLANDOVEY JUNCTION		113D4
GLANDYFI		113D4
Glan Ebbw Tinworks		181A1
Glan Garnant Colly	54/46	131D4
Glanhowy Elled Colly		?
Glanlash Colly	54/33	131A1
GLAN LLYN HALT		111C4
* Glanmorlais Colly	54/50	—
Glan Mwrwg Colly	55/35	133C5
Glan Nant Colly	49/10	157C2
GLANRAFON HALT		114D1
GLANRHYD HALT	59/2	130C4
* Glanrhyd Works (Swansea Vale)	53/17	—
Glantawe Siding	53/17	—
Glantowy Crossing	58/42	—
Glantwelly Crossing	58/41	128B4
Glantwrch Colly	53/25	—
Glanwalia Tinplate Works	50/34	141A3
Glanygors Siding		109A6
GLANYLLYN		173D3
* Glanyrafon Works	53/43	—
GLANYRAFON (Tanat Valley)		117A5
GLAN-YR-AFON HALT (Mid Wales Line)	59/29	120A6
Glanyrwyth Isaf Crossing		130C3
Glasbrooks Colly Line (Gowerton)	55/3	135B1
Glasbrooks Colly S.B.	54/23	—
Glasbury Junction		121B6
GLASBURY-ON-WYE	63/40	—
GLASCOED CROSSING HALT	36/22	108A3
GLASCOED FACTORY	36/22	108A3
GLASCOED HALT	36/22	108A3
GLASCOED R.O.F.	36/22	108A3
Glascoed Siding (Brymbo)		93A3
GLASTONBURY	18/29	—
Glebe Siding		37C2
Glenavon Colly (Blaengarw)	49/27	156B5

*	Glenavon Colly (Blaenrhondda)	46/1	158B1	Glyn Ogwr Siding (Gilfach)	49/72	160B4
	Glenavon Colly Sidings S.B. (Cymmer)	51/36	155D3	Glyn Quarry (Pontypool)	47/107	182D5
	Glenavon Garw Colly (Gilfach)		160C5	Glyn Race Colly		182C5
	Glengarw Colly	49/27	156B5	Glyn Road Level		?
	Glenhafod Colly	51/3	141A6	GLYNTAFF HALT		172B5
	Glenrhondda Colly	46/1	158B1	Glynteg Colly		?
*	Globe Colly	53/28	—	Glyn Tillery Colly	47/107	182D4
	Gloda Colly		155A4	Glyn Valley Siding (Onslow)	11/10	6A2
	GLOGUE	58/32	125D3	Glyn Valley Tramway (Chirk)		95C1
	Gloucester, Abbey Road Crossing		56B2	Gnoll Colly Siding	50/2	139B5
*	Gloucester, Asylum Lane Junction		56B3	GNOSALL	32/21	—
	Gloucester Barnwood Junction	35/7	56B4	* Goat Crossing		56B2
	Gloucester Barnwood S.B.	35/9	56B4	GOBOWEN		95D3
	Gloucester Barton St. Junction	35/2	56B3	Godfrey Road Sidings	38/12	152A2
	Gloucester Castle Meads		56B2	GODREAMAN HALT	47/42	165C4
	GLOUCESTER CENTRAL	35/4	56B3	Godscroft S.B.		88C2
	Gloucester Chequers Road Junction	35/7	56C4	GOGARTH HALT		113C3
	Gloucester Docks	35/16A	56B2	Goitre Colly (Duffryn Yard)	51/3	141A6
	Gloucester Docks Junction	35/19	56A1	GOITRE HALT (Kerry Branch)		116B6
	GLOUCESTER EASTGATE	35/4	56B3	Goitre Hen Colly		143C4
	Gloucester Engine Shed Junction	35/7	56B4	GOLANT	11/27	6C2
	Gloucester Engine Shed Siding	35/7	56B4	GOLDEN GROVE	58/42	—
	Gloucester Goods Junction S.B.	35/4	56C4	GOLDEN HILL PLATFORM	58/26	124D3
	Gloucester Horton Road Crossing	35/7	56B4	Golden Valley Junction		107C6
	Gloucester Junction (Swindon)	20/13	30C1	Golden Vein Colly		—
	Gloucester Loop Junction (Cheltenham)	35/11	56C5	GOLDHAWK ROAD	25/24	38C4
	Gloucester Millstream Junction	35/7	56C4	GOLFA		118A3
	Gloucester Road Junction (Avonmouth)	19/72	25D2	Golynos Colly		181D4
	Gloucester South Junction	35/7	56C4	Golynos (Elled) Colly		182C5
	Gloucester Street Yard (Aberdare)		165C2	* Golynos Foundry Siding		181D5
	Gloucester Stroud Road Junction	35/2	56B3	Golynos Junction	39/14	184A1
	GLOUCESTER 'T' STATION	35/7	56B4	Gommes Siding	26/8	87D5
	Gloucester Tramway Junction	35/7	56B4	Gonamena	11/36	6C3
	Gloucester Yard Junction	35/9	56C3	Gonnamarris Works	11/31	4D1
	GLYN ABBEY HALT	57/40	133B3	GOODRINGTON HALT	14/36	12B5
	Glynbeudy Siding	54/44	131D4	GOODRINGTON SANDS HALT	14/36	12B5
	Glyncastle Colly	47/6	162B5	Goodrington S.B.	14/36	12B5
	Glyncoch Colly	55/43	135B3	GOODWICK	58/1	123A6
*	Glyncock Colly	53/44	—	Goodwick Brickworks	58/1	123A6
	Glyncoed Colly	57/63	134B6	Goodwick Junction S.B.	58/4	123A1
	Glyn Colls Nos. 1 and 2		182D5	Goonbarrow Junction	11/24	3B6
	Glyn Colls Nos. 3 and 4		182C5	Goonbarrow Siding	11/33	4B4
	Glyn Colly (Brynmawr)		—	GOONBELL HALT	10/30	2D4
	Glyn Colly (Pontypool)	47/107	182D4	GOODHAVERN HALT	10/30	2C6
	Glyn Colly (Treferig)	49/84	161A4	Goonvean Siding	11/31	4D1
	GLYNCORRWG	51/45	155B3	* Gordon's Siding	54/52	—
*	Glyncorrwg Colly	51/47	155A4	Gored Merthyr Colly		162C4
*	Glyncorrwg Quarry Siding	51/47	155A4	GORING	23/15	32A2
	GLYNCORRWG SOUTH PIT HALT	51/48	155A4	GORING AND STREATLEY	23/15	32A2
	Glyncymmer Colly	51/34	155B3	Gorllwyn Colly		?
*	GLYNDYFRDWY		112B5	GORNAL HALT	31/55	76A2
	Glyndyle Graigola Colly	53/Ind	—	Gors Colly	57/61	134B5
	Glyn Dyrys Pit		168D1	Gorse Hill Siding (Swindon)	20/23	30C3
	Glynea Colly	55/31	133D5	Gorse Works (Dafen)	57/62	134C5
	Glynfach Colly	46/29	159D6	GORSEINON	54/18	—
	Glyngoch Colly		138C2	Gorseinon Colly	55/4	135B1
	Glyngwilym Colly		162D4	Gorseinon Line Jcn (Swansea)	54/29	137C1
	Glyn Gwyn Colly (Mount. Ash)		170D1	Gors Goch Colly	54/52	131A1
	Glyn Gwyn Siding (Trethomas)	42/43	179C6	Gorsllan Colly	55/42	138C2
	Glyn Havod Colly		141A6	Gors y Garnant Colly	54/46	131D4
	Glynhebog Colly	57/36	133A2	GORS Y GARNANT HALT	54/46	131D4
	Glynhir Siding S.B.	54/11	131D2	Gorwydd Colly	54/23	—
	Glynis Crossing		174B2	Gospel Oak S.B.	31/14	75B3
	Glyn Level Colly		182D4	Gossington S.B.	20/44	—
	Glynllech Colly	52/21	132B5	Goss Moor Siding (Gothers)	11/30	4A2
	Glyn Merthyr Colly		155A1	GOTHERINGTON	28/19	63C3
	Glyn Merthyr Colly Sidings	47/4	162C4	Gothers Siding	11/30	4A2
	Glyn Milwr Pit		176B6	Gover Colly (Cwmllynfell)	53/Ind	—
	Glynmoch Colly	54/40	131B4	Gover Viaduct S.B. (Burngullow)	11/4	3C5
	Glynnantddu Colly	39/24	182B4	GOVILON	41/17	—
	GLYN NEATH	47/9	163A2	Govilon Canal Wharf	41/17	—
	Glyn Neath Colly		163C3	Gower Gorwydd Colly	55/3	135C1
	Glyn Neath Mills		163A5	GOWER ROAD (GWR)	55/3	135C1
	Glyn Ogwr Siding (Blackmill)	49/67	160D2	GOWER ROAD (LNWR)	54/23	—

238

*	Gower Tinplate Works	54/51	—
	Gowerton Junction	55/2	135C1
	GOWERTON NORTH (GWR)	55/3	135C1
	GOWERTON SOUTH (LNWR)	54/23	—
	Graesser's Siding		94C1
	GRAFTON	22/16	48D5
	GRAFTON AND BURBAGE	22/16	48D5
	Grafton Curve S.B.	22/14 & 23/18	48B3
	Grafton East Junction	22/14 & 23/18	48B3
	Grafton Goods	22/16	48D5
	Grafton South Junction	22/14	48B3
	GRAIG (PONTYPRIDD)		172B4
	Graig Cilfrew Colly		153A2
*	Graig Colly (Pontardawe)	53/16	—
	Graig Colly (Dare Junction)	47/35	165B3
	Graig Colly (Hirwaun)		164C3
*	Graig Colly (Marchowell)		?
	Graig Colly (Trebanos)	55/49	138A5
	Graigavon Colly	51/54	153B5
*	Graig Cwm Colly	53/Ind	—
	Graigddu Brickworks (Cwmnantddu)	39/24	182B4
	Graigddu Colly (Whitworth)	51/53	153C3
	Graigeretol Sidings	51/14	157A2
	Graigfach Colly	53/Ind	—
	Graig Fawr Quarry (Minera)		93C2
	Graig Fawr S.B. (Ebbw Vale)	40/8	177A5
	Graig Las Colly	49/67	160D4
	Graig Level (Pontwalby)		163D4
	Graiglon Colly	57/45	133C2
	Graiglyn Colly		154B3
	Graig Merthyr Colly (LNWR)	54/15	—
	Graig Merthyr Colly Sdgs (GWR)	55/41	135A1
	Graigola Fuel Works	53/14	—
*	Graigola Merthyr Colly (Birchrock)	54/15	—
*	Graigola Merthyr Colly (Skewen)	55/41	139A1
*	Graigola Merthyr Colly (Swansea Vale)	53/43	—
	Graig Pit (Abercanaid)		168D6
	Graig Pit (Blaenrhondda)		158B1
*	Graig Wern Colly		159D5
*	Graig-y-fedw Colly	51/40	154A4
	Graighacca Crossing	42/43	180C2
*	Graig-y-llyn Colly	51/40	154A4
	GRAMPOUND ROAD	11/2	3D3
	Granby Sidings	57/24	134D3
*	Grange Coke Ovens (Margam)		142D6
	Grange Colly (Stirchley)		69D5
	Grange Colly (Hollinswood)		70A6
	GRANGE COURT	36/20	53A6
*	GRANGE LANE		90B6
	Grange Lane Sidings (Birkenhead)		90C3
	Grange Pit (Margam Moors)		142C2
	Grange Sidings (Banbury)	30/24A	84B6
	Grange Siding (Llantarnam)	39/11	183C3
	Grange Sidings (Port Talbot)	50/60	142A5
	GRANGETOWN		147A5
	Grangetown Ferry Road		147A5
	Granville Colly	32/48	70A6
	Granville & Gorsty Hill Colly		77B4
	Gravel Bridge	57/8	134B2
	Gravel Hill	10/33	2B6
	Graving Dock G.F. (Port Talbot)	50/39	141B2
	Graving Dock Junction (Barry)	44/51	148D5
	Gray Colly	40/58	181D2
	Grayfield Colly	21/24	27C1
	Grays Lane Siding	28/13	64C1
	Grazebrook Colly	31/41	76B4
	GREAT ALNE	30/37	82C2
	Great Beam Siding	11/23	4A4
	Great Bedwyn S.B.	23/19	48C6
	GREAT BRIDGE SOUTH	31/18	75D4
	Great Halvyggan Siding	11/3	4D4
	Great Halwyn Siding	11/29	4B1
	GREAT MALVERN	33/7	61D2
	GREAT MARLOW	24/39	34B3
	Great Mountain Nos. 1 & 2 Collys	57/51	133A5
	Great Mountain No. 3 Colly	57/52	133A5
	Great Rollright Siding	28/32	64D4
	GREAT SHEFFORD	23/40	49B3
	GREAT SOMERFORD	20/7	28A4
	Great Treviscoe Siding	11/31	4D1
*	Great Western Colly (Abergwynfi)	51/38	155D5
	Great Western Colly (Bristol)	19/19	24B5
	Great Western Colly (Coleford Branch)	37/41	54D1
	Great Western Colly (Gyfeillon)	46/38	172A3
	Great Western Colly (Llantwit)	49/76	161A5
*	Great Western Colly (Ynysybwl)		171C1
	Great Western Wharf (Newport)		152B4
	Great Wheal Prosper Siding	11/23	4A4
	Greaves Siding S.B.	30/21	83C3
	GREEN BANK HALT	32/35	70B1
	Greenfields Siding		99A2
	GREENFORD	26/17	36C5
	Greenford Junctions	26/20	36C5
	Green Grove Siding	58/41	127B2
	Greenham Junction S.B.	23/20	49A4
	Greenland Colly (Branches Fork)		182B5
	Greenland Mill Crossing	21/15	27C6
*	Greenland Quarry (Netham)	19/31	25C6
*	Green Lane Crossing (St Brides)		151C2
	Green Lane Crossing (Saltney)		91D2
	Green Lane Crossing (Severn Beach)	19/96	23A3
	Green Lane Crossing (Swindon)	20/27	30B3
	Green Lane Junction (Birkenhead)		90C5
	Green Lane Junction (London)	25/12	39D3
	Green Meadow Colly		181D2
	Greens Norton Junction	29/11	—
	GREEN'S SIDING	63/44	106B2
	GREENWAY HALT (Gloucs)	33/20	60C3
	Greenway Siding (Talyllyn)		122A6
*	Greldaw Limeworks	44/22	144B6
	Grenfells Siding	53/5	—
	Grenville Street S.B.	38/58	152B3
	GRESFORD		92B3
	Gresford Colly		92C3
	Gresty Lane		97A6
	GRETTON HALT	28/19	63C4
	Greyfield Pits	21/44	27C1
	Grey Tree Crossing	36/32	105B2
	Griffin & Morris S.B.	31/7	—
	Griffin Pit	40/52	176A5
	Grimes Crossing (Cardiff)	43/63	150C6
	GRIMES HILL PLATFORM	30/30	81C4
	GRIMES HILL & WYTHALL	30/30	81C4
	GRIMSTONE	17/4	41C5
	GRIMSTONE & FRAMPTON	17/4	41C5
	Grists Mill	20/56	—
	GROESFAEN COLLY PLATFORM		177C2
	GROESFFORDD HALT		122A5
	GROESWEN HALT		173B2
	GROGLEY HALT	11/34	—
	Grooms Siding	63/17	104A5
	Grosvenor Colly		93C2
	Groveley Wood Crossing	21/56	47C5
	Groveley Wood Siding	21/56	47B3
	Grove Quarry (Cornelly)	50/80	143C1
	Grove Road Junction	25/24	38C4
	GROVESEND (LNWR)	54/19	—
	Grovesend Colly (LNWR)	54/17	—
	Grovesend Colly Loop S.B.	55/40	135A1
	Grovesend Colly Sidings S.B. (LNWR)	54/17	—
	Grovesend Goods Junction	55/40	135A1
	Grovesend Quarry (Thornbury)	20/52	—
*	Grovesend Works (Gorseinon)	54/19	—
	Grove Mill	20/56	—
	Grove Siding	11/28	4C1
	Grwyne Fawr Reservoir		107B1
*	Guent Colly		182B3
	Guerets Graigola Colly	53/46	—

239

Guerets Works (Barry)	44/67	148C6	
Guilden Sutton		91C5	
* Guildford Viaduct	10/8	1B3	
Guinness's Brewery	26/11	38A2	
Gulf Branch Junction	58/22	124B2	
Gulley's Siding		4B2	
Gulston Junction (Mountain Branch)	54/34	131A3	
Gulston Siding (Derwydd Road)	54/1	130C6	
Gulston Siding (Mountain Branch)	54/34	131A3	
Gunheath	11/33	4C4	
Gupworthy		17C1	
Gurnos Colly	53/50	—	
* Gurnos Goods (first location)	53/27	—	
Gurnos Junction	53/24	—	
G.W. Colly (Abergwynfi)	51/38	155D5	
G.W. Colly (Bristol)	19/19	24B5	
* G.W. Colly (Coleford Branch)	37/41	54C1	
G.W. Colly (Gyfeillon)	46/38	172A3	
* G.W. Colly (Llantwit)	49/76	161A5	
* G.W. Colly (Ynysybwl)		171C1	
* G.W. Ironworks (Soudley)	37/36	54C3	
* G.W. Wharf (Newport)		152B4	
Gwaelod y Waen Colly	42/26	178A3	
Gwaelod y Waen Farm Siding	42/28	178A2	
Gwalia Tin Plate Works	50/21	140C3	
GWAUN CAE GURWEN	54/47	131D4	
Gwaun cae Gurwen Collieries	54/48	131D5	
GWAUN CAE GURWEN HALT	54/49	131D4	
* GWAUN CAE GURWEN COLLY HALT	53/31	—	
Gwaun cae Gurwen Incline	54/47	131D4	
Gwaun cae Gurwen S.B. (Mid)	53/31	—	
Gwaunfawr Pit		167B5	
Gwaun Gledyr S.B.		173B4	
Gwaunton Opencast	52/21	132A3	
* Gwaun Tre Oda Siding	46/95	174C4	
Gwaun y Bara Sidings	42/53	179D6	
Gwaun y Clawdd Colly	52/20	132B4	
Gwawr Colly		165C3	
Gwellt Pit		167B4	
Gwenallt Colly	39/23	182B5	
Gwenallt S.B.	39/16	182B5	
Gwendraeth Colly (Pontyates)	57/39	133B4	
Gwendraeth Siding (Pembrey)	57/47	134A3	
Gwenffrwd Quarry	51/52	153B2	
Gwennyth St. Siding		149A4	
Gwent Wagon Shops		182C6	
Gwerna Coke Ovens	42/39	178D2	
Gwernllwyn Colly	51/14	157A3	
Gwern Pit	53/11	—	
GWERNYDOMEN HALT	42/53	179D6	
Gwernydomen Siding		179D5	
* Gwernygasseg Colly		?	
Gwernynoel Crossing		?	
Gwersyllt Brickworks		93B5	
Gwersyllt Colly		93A5	
GWERSYLLT HILL HALT		93B5	
Gwerwydd Colly	55/34	133D6	
GWINEAR	10/9	1B4	
GWINEAR ROAD	10/9	1B4	
Gwladis Colly	42/31	178B1	
Gwrhay Colly	40/64	177D5	
Gwrhyd Colly (Abernant)		165A5	
Gwrhyd Colly (Rhymney)		167C5	
G.W.R. Lock G.F.s (Gilfach)	49/72	160D4	
Gwscwm Colly	57/46	134A2	
Gwyns Drift Colly	53/15	—	
GWYS	53/29	—	
GYFEILLON PLATFORM	46/40	172A3	
Gyfeillon Lower S.B.	46/39	172A3	
* Gyfeillon Upper S.B.	46/37	172A3	
Gyrnos Quarries		166C2	
Hack Green S.B.	32/43	97B5	
Hackney S.B.	14/15	14B1	
HADDENHAM	26/4	86D3	
HADDENHAM & THAME PARKWAY	26/4	86D3	
HADLEY	32/46	—	
Hadley Junction	32/46	—	
Hadley Lodge Siding	32/50	—	
Hadley Moor Crossing (Bucknell)	59/13	—	
HADLOW ROAD		89D3	
HADNOCK HALT	36/25	53A2	
Hadnock Quarry Siding	36/25	53A2	
Hadnock Siding	36/25	53A2	
HAFOD (Trehafod)	46/32	172A1	
Hafod Colly (Johnston & Hafod)		94D5	
Hafod Colly (Trehafod)	46/32	172A1	
Hafod Crossing (Dowlais)		167A1	
Hafod Junction (Swansea)	55/23	136C2	
Hafod Junction (Trehafod)	46/110	172A2	
Hafod Loop Junction (Swansea)	55/23	136C3	
Hafod Rhondda Colly		?	
Hafod Sidings (Johnston & Hafod)		94D5	
Hafod Vane Colly (Abertillery)	40/60	182B2	
* Hafod y Broch Colly		94C5	
Hafod-y-bwch Colly		94B5	
Hafodyrnys East S.B.	47/107	182D4	
HAFODYRNYS PLATFORM	47/104	182B2	
Hafodyrnys West S.B.	47/105	182D3	
HAGLEY	33/11	78B3	
Hakin Road Crossing	58/17	124A2	
HALBERTON HALT	15/17	16A3	
Halesfield Colly		70B4	
HALESOWEN	31/53	77B6	
Halesowen Basin	31/53	77B6	
Halesowen Junction	34/8	81C1	
Half Way Crossing	57/60	134B4	
HALLATROW	21/44	27C1	
Hall Colly		70C5	
HALLEN HALT	19/97	23B3	
Hallen Marsh Junction S.B.	19/90	25A3	
* Hallen Moor Siding	19/101	23B3	
HALL GREEN	30/30	81A4	
Hallivet Siding	11/24	4B5	
HALLOON	11/21	3A3	
Halloon Crossing	11/21	3A3	
Halls Junction	40/31	180A4	
* Halls Road Colly		178A4	
Halls Road Junction	40/31	180A4	
* Halls Tramroad Junction	40/31	180A4	
Hall Street Siding (Rhos)		?	
HALTON		88C2	
* Halton Jcn (Frodsham Jcn)		88C2	
Hamblin Yorkley Colly		54A2	
HAM GREEN HALT	19/30	25B4	
Ham Hill Siding	16/19	45B1	
Ham Sidings	37/40	53C3	
HAMMERSMITH	25/24	38D4	
* Hammersmith Junction		39B6	
HAM MILL CROSSING HALT	20/32	58B5	
HAMPSTEAD NORRIS	23/37	49B6	
HAMPTON	32/24	71D6	
Hampton Lane Crossing	20/32	58D6	
HAMPTON LOADE	32/24	71D6	
Hampton Lovett S.B.	33/13	78B5	
HAMPTON ROW HALT	21/7	27A4	
Hamstead Crossing S.B.	23/20	49D4	
Hamwood Quarry Siding	18/13	—	
HANDBOROUGH	28/18	67A2	
HANDSWORTH	31/21	79B5	
HANDSWORTH AND SMETHWICK	31/21	79B5	
Handsworth Junction	31/20	79B5	
Hanger Lane S.B.	26/23	36A6	
HANNINGTON	20/29	29A4	
HANWELL	24/33	37B4	
HANWELL AND ELTHORNE	24/33	37B4	
Hanwell Bridge Sidings	24/30	37B3	
Hanwell West S.B.	24/30	37B4	

HANWOOD		98C4
Hanwood Colly		98D4
HANWOOD ROAD		98C4
Hapsford Loop	21/51	45A3
Harbour Branch Sdgs S.B. (Swansea)	53/1	—
Hardwick Siding		96C4
Harefield Embankment Siding	26/11	35D4
HAREFIELD HALT	26/11	35D5
HARESFIELD	35/1	55D3
HARLECH		109D3
* Harris Navigation Colly		170C5
Harrow Hill Sidings	37/29	53A5
HARTLEBURY	33/13	78D1
HARTON	32/29	100C5
HARTON ROAD	32/29	100C5
HART'S HILL AND WOODSIDE	31/42	76B3
Harvey's Siding (Camborne)	10/7	1C5
Harvey's Siding (Roskear)	10/15	1C6
HARVINGTON	34/17	—
Harwell Street S.B.,	12/17	8C4
Hatherley Junction S.B.	35/11	56C5
HATCH	16/44	20D3
HATTON	30/14	82A5
HAUGHTON (Staffordshire)	32/21	—
HAUGHTON HALT (nr. Rednal)		96D3
Haughton Sidings S.B.	96D3	
Haven Road Crossing	14/21	13C2
HAVERFORDWEST	58/17	124A2
Haverfordwest Bridge West S.B.	58/17	124A2
HAVOD		172A1
Hawkeridge Junction	21/39	46B4
Hawkeridge W.D. Sidings	21/16	46B3
Hawkes Point Crossing		1B2
HAWKMOOR HALT	14/40	14A1
Hawkwell Siding	37/27	54A5
Hay & Brecon Junction S.B.	63/25	104A5
Haybridge Colly (Stirchley)		70D5
Haybridge Siding (Wellington)	32/5	69A5
HAYES (Middlesex)	24/26	35C2
HAYES AND HARLINGTON	24/26	35C2
Hayes Colly (Hayes Lane)	31/27	77B3
Hayes Creosote Works	24/27	37C1
Hayes Lane Branch	31/27	77B4
Hayes Lane Junction S.B.	31/27	77B3
* Hayes Siding (Brentford Bch)		37D5
Hay Junction		106B1
Hay Lane S.B.	20/9	29C2
HAYLE	10/7	1A2
Hayle Explosive Branch	10/25	1B3
HAYLES ABBEY HALT	28/19	63C5
Hayle Wharves	10/22	1A2
Hay Mill S.B.	24/18	34B4
HAY ON WYE	63/40	—
Haystack Siding		119A5
Hay Tor Granite Siding	14/40	14B2
Hay Tor Quarries		14B1
Haywood S.B.	63/21	104D4
Healey & Peart Siding	38/17	152B6
HEATH HALT HIGH LEVEL		174C6
HEATH HALT LOW LEVEL		174C6
HEATHFIELD	14/41	14C3
Heath Hill Colly		70D1
Heath Junction		174C6
* HEATHROW		35C2
* HEATHROW INTERCHANGE		35C2
Heath Town Junction	31/9	—
* Hedge End		51C1
Hedge G.F.	27/27	68A2
* Heks Siding G.F.		165C2
HELE	15/7	16C3
HELE AND BRADNINCH	15/7	16C3
Helland Siding	11/35	—
HELMDON	29/18	—
HELSBY		88D1

HELSTON	10/26	1D5
Hematite Siding (Llanharry)	44/25	145D5
Hemerdon Junction S.B.	14/3	11A1
Hemerdon Sidings S.B.	14/3	7B6
Hempstead Wharf	35/17	56D1
Hempstone Quarry Siding	14/11	12B3
HEMYOCK	15/18	16A6
HENBURY	19/98	23B3
HENDFORD HALT	17/16	44C4
Hendra Down	11/30	4B2
* Hendre Colly		?
Hendredenny Colly		173A4
* Hendre Forchan	49/68	160D4
HENDREFORGAN	49/68	160D4
Hendreforgan Colly (Cwmllynfell)	53/30	—
Hendregarreg Colly	51/45	155A3
* Hendre Gwilym Colly	49/57	160A5
Hendre-Gwyndir Colly	40/58	181B2
Hendreladis Colly	53/50	—
Hendrewen Colly	49/14	145A3
Hendryd Siding		132B6
Hendy Junction	55/39	133C6
Hendy Merthyr Colly (Pontardawe Branch)	55/49	138B5
* Hendy Merthyr Colly (Clydach-on-Tawe)	53/44	—
Hendy Siding	55/39	133C6
HENGOED AND MAESYCWMMER (GWR)		178D5
HENGOED AND MAESYCWMMER (Rly)		178D5
Hengoed Colly (Cylla Branch)		178C1
Hengoed Colly (Hengoed)		178C2
Hengoed Colly (Rhym Line)		178C2
HENGOED HIGH LEVEL	47/90	178D5
HENGOED LOW LEVEL		178D5
Hengoed Low Level Junction		178C5
Hengoed Machine Siding		178C5
Hengoed Ystrad Junction	47/91	178D5
HENIARTH		118A1
HENIARTH GATE		118A1
HENLEY (Henley on Thames)	24/37	34C1
HENLEY IN ARDEN	30/31	82A3
HENLEY ON THAMES	24/37	34C1
HENLLAN	58/41	128B2
Henllys Colly (Cwmbran)		183C1
Henllys Slope Colly (Cwmbran)		183C1
Henllys Vale Colly (Gwys)	53/51	—
Hensbarrow Siding	11/25	4A6
HENSTRIDGE	18/18	—
Henwain Colly	40/53	176B6
Henwaun Colly	40/53	176B6
HENWICK	33/9	60D4
Heol Fain Crossing		156C3
Heol Fawr Crossing	57/15	134C2
HEOLGERRIG HALT		168B3
Heol Lladron Junction		122C3
Heol Llaethog Colly	49/24	157D5
Heol Wenallt Washery		163B1
Heol y Deiliaid Crossing	50/61	142A1
Heolydelaid Siding	50/61	142A1
Heol y Sheet Crossing S.B.	50/81	143B2
Herberts Siding S.B.	38/13	184C5
Herbert Street Goods	31/7	74A5
Herbrandston Junction	58/22	124B1
Herbrandston Refinery	58/23	124B1
Hereford, Ayleston Hill S.B.	63/18	104B6
HEREFORD, BARRS COURT	63/18	104B5
Hereford, Barrs Court Junction	63/16	104A5
HEREFORD, BARTON	63/31	104B4
Hereford, Barton & Brecon Curve Jcn	63/16	104A5
* Hereford, Barton Junction	63/16	104B5
Hereford, Barton Curve Junction	63/26	104A5
Hereford, Brecon Curve Jcn	63/18	104A5
Hereford, College Bridge Sidings	63/19	104A5
* Hereford Edgar Street Sidings	63/19	104B6
* Hereford, Groom's Sidings	63/17	104A5
Hereford, Hay & Brecon Junction	63/25	104A5

	HEREFORD, MOORFIELDS	63/25	104B4		Holmbush Crossing		3B6
	Hereford, Moorfields Junction	63/25	104B4	*	HOLME LACEY	36/31	104D3
	Hereford, Red Hill Junction	63/21	104D1		HOLME LACY	36/31	104D3
*	HEREFORD ROTHERWAS FACTORY	63/20	104D6		Holmes Colly	54/25	—
	Hereford, Rotherwas Junction	63/20	104D6		HOLT JUNCTION	21/21	46B2
	Hereford, Shelwick Junction	63/16	104B2		Holton Siding		148C3
*	Hereford, Show Yard Siding	63/16	104B6		Holyhead Junction		91C2
*	Hereford, Widemarsh Junction	63/16	104B5	*	Holyoake's Quarry Siding		69C6
	Hereford, Worcester Sidings	63/26	104B5		HOLYWELL		3A5
	HERMITAGE	23/27	49C5		Homer Hill Colly	31/28	77A4
	Herveth Crossing		116C1		Homfrays Level	42/54	180D2
	HESWALL		89D2		HONEYBOURNE	28/8	62A1
	Hetty Bank Dump	46/38	172A4		Honeybourne East Loop Junction	28/21	62A2
	Hetty Colly		172A4		Honeybourne North Loop Junction	28/11	62A2
	HEYFORD	27/4	85C2		Honeybourne South Loop Junction	28/11	62A2
	Heyford Bridge S.B.	27/4	85B3	*	Honeybourne W.D.	28/7	62A2
	Heyope Crossing	59/11	—		Honeybourne West Loop Junction	28/21	62A2
	HEYTESBURY	21/55	47C6		Hoobrook Siding S.B.	33/12	77D5
	Heywood Road Junction S.B.	21/39	46B4		Hoods Merthyr Colly	46/20	159C3
	Hickmans Branch Junction	31/36	75A2	*	Hood Street Depot		90B1
	HIGHBRIDGE (GWR)	16/20	19B2		Hookagate		98C5
	HIGHBRIDGE (S & D)	18/27	—		HOOKAGATE AND REDHILL		98C5
	HIGHBRIDGE AND BURNHAM ON SEA	18/27	19B2		Hook Colly	58/16	124B3
	Highbridge Wharf	18/25	—		HOOK NORTON	28/32	64C5
	HIGHCLERE	23/36	50A1	*	Hoole Siding		?
	High Duffryn Colly	47/56	165C5		HOOTON		89D4
	High Ercal Colly		76D2		Hope Colly (New Tredegar)	42/18	177B2
	Higher Gothers		4B2		Hope Level Crossing S.B. (Dinmore)	63/13	102D2
*	High Home Quarry		69D5		HOPESBROOK		105D5
*	High Lanes Crossing	10/8	1A3		Hopewell Pits	37/47	54A2
	HIGHLEY	32/24	72B4		Hopmead G.F.	18/3	—
	High Meadow Siding	36/26	53A2	*	HOPTON HEATH	59/14	—
	High Orchard	35/18	56B2		HORDERLEY	63/33	100C3
	HIGH STREET (Newport)	38/10	152A2		Horeb Brickworks	57/54	133C4
	High St G.F. (Llanelly)	57/59	134C2		Horeb Goods	57/54	133B4
	High Street Siding (Burngullow)	11/32	4D2		HORFIELD	19/59	23C4
	HIGHTOWN HALT		92D3		Horns Lane Crossing	16/34	21D4
	HIGHWORTH	20/29	29A4		HORRABRIDGE	14/26	10C4
	Highworth Junction	20/22	30C3		HORSEHAY AND DAWLEY	32/39	70D1
	HIGH WYCOMBE	26/7	87D4		Horsepool Crossing		106C4
	Hillside Colly	51/54	153B5		Horse Shoe Point S.B.	19/62	25A5
	Hills Lane Colly		70B3		Horsington Crossing	18/17	—
*	Hills Merthyr Colly	53/43	—		Horseley Fields Jnction	31/18	75C4
	HIMLEY	31/54	73C4		HORSPATH HALT	27/22	67D5
	Himley Colly		76B2	*	Horton Lane		98C4
	Hinderton Road Goods		90C4		Horton Road Crossing	35/7	564
	Hingleys Siding	31/52	76C5		HOSPITAL HALT (Portland)	17/9	42B1
	HINKSEY HALT	27/13	68C5		HOTWELLS	19/64	24A1
	Hinksey North S.B.	27/12	68C5		Howbeach Colly	36/24 & 37/44	54C2
	Hinksey South S.B.	27/14	68C5	*	Howells Siding	51/47	155A4
	Hinksey Yards	27/13	68C5		Howey S.B.	59/8	—
	Hinkshay Siding	32/52	70D5		Howlerslade Tramway	37/46	54B1
	HINTON (nr Ashchurch)	34/15	—		Hughes and Lancaster Siding		94B2
	Hinton Crossing (Bledlow)	27/22	87A3		Huish Colly (Radstock)	21/47	27B3
	Hinton Road Crossing		106C3		Huish Crossing (Yatton)	16/27	21B3
	HIRWAIN	47/15	164B3		HULLAVINGTON	20/6	28A3
	HIRWAUN	47/15	164B3		Hungary Hill Colly		77B2
	Hirwaun Bridge	47/16	164B2		HUNGERFORD	23/19	49D2
	Hirwaun Common Railway	47/15	164B3		HUNNINGTON	34/19	81A1
	Hirwaun Crossing (Cwmmawr)	57/35	133A3		Hunthouse Level Colly	33/23	72D3
	HIRWAUN POND	47/15	164A2		Huntingford Mill	20/44	—
	Hobbs Point	58/24	126D1		Huntspill S.B.	16/20	19B2
	Hobbs Quarry Siding	52/13	122D1	*	Hutching's Siding		64A6
	HOCKLEY	31/26	80A5		Hutton S.B.	16/26	21C2
	HODNET	32/44	99D4				
	Holes Bay Junction	18/22	—		Ida Colly	49/78	161B4
	Holesmouth Junction S.B.	19/87	25A2		Idanfawr Lane Crossing		118A2
	Hollies Siding		96D5		IDE	14/45	13B4
	Hollinswood (GWR)	32/11	70C5		IFFLEY HALT	21/17	68D6
	Hollinswood Siding (LNWR)	32/51	—		Ifton Colly (Weston Rhyn)		95D3
	HOLLY BUSH	41/32	—		Ifton Quarry (Severn Tnl. Jcn)	38/24	52A3
	Holly Hill Crossing		81B1		Illogan Gate Crossing	10/28	1A5
	Hollymoor Hospital	34/19	81B1		Illogan Highway Siding	10/28	1A5
	Holman's Siding	10/27	1B5		ILMER HALT	26/4	87A4

242

* Ilmington		64A4
ILMINSTER	16/44	20B6
Ilsley Signals	23/38	31D4
ILTONHALT	16/44	20A6
Imperial Navigation Colly		155D1
* Imperial Salt Works		78B6
Imperial Siding	11/33	4B4
INCE		91A6
INCE AND ELTON		91A6
Ince Marshes		88C1
* INCLINE TOP		171A3
INGRA TOR HALT	14/32	10B6
Interchange Sidings		172B5
* International Alloys G.F. (Cardiff)	46/114	149A5
International Colly (Abercrave)	52/20	132B4
International Colly (Blaengarw)	49/27	156A5
Ipplepen Siding	14/11	12A4
IRON ACTON	20/51	—
IRONBRIDGE	32/20	70C1
IRONBRIDGE AND BROSELEY	32/20	70C1
Ironbridge Power Station	32/19	69B2
Iron Gates Crossing S.B.	38/58	152C4
Ironstone Branch S.B.	30/23	84A6
Ironworks Junction (Yniscedwyn)	53/48	—
ISLIP	27/28	—
Isllwyn Colly (Penar Bch)	40/64	177D5
Isllwyn Colly (Penar Junction)		178C5
IVER	34/23	35B1
Ivor Junction	41/1	167B1
Ivor Steelworks	41/1	167B1
IVYBRIDGE	14/5	11A2
Ivybridge Siding Goods	14/5	11A2
Iwood Lane Crossing	16/43	21C5
JACKAMENTS BRIDGE HALT	20/38	59C2
JACKFIELD HALT	32/22	70C2
* Jackfield Siding	32/21	70C2
Jackson Street Yard		90C3
* James Street Depot		90B1
* Jaynes Colly Branch	41/19	—
Jefferies Siding S.B.	20/30	58B4
* Jenkins Brickworks Siding	52/23	—
Jenkins Colly	49/9	157B1
Jenkins Merthyr Colly	49/68	160D4
JERSEY MARINE	56/32	137C5
Jersey Marine Down Hump Yard	56/30	137D3
Jersey Marine Hump Line G.F.	56/30	137C4
Jersey Marine Jcn North S.B.	55/48	139C2
Jersey Marine Jcn South S.B.	56/35	140B1
Jersey Marine South Yard	56/35	140B1
Jersey Marine Up Hump Yard	56/33	137C5
Jersey Sidings (Danygraig)	56/11	137B5
Jersey Sidings (Weymouth)	17/1	42C3
* JEWELLRY QUARTER		80A5
JOHNSTON (PEMBROKE)	58/15	124B2
JOHNSTOWN AND HAFOD		94D5
John Street Crossing (Ogmore Vale)		160B1
* John Street Siding (Cardiff)	43/73	150A6
Joint Line Junction (Merthyr)		168D1
JORDANSTON HALT	58/4	123C6
* Jubilee Colly (Pantyffynon)	54/5	?
Jubilee Sidings (Weymouth)	17/1	42C3
Junction Canal Swing Bridge (Cardiff)	43/72	150B6
Junction Colly		178D2
* Junction Dry Dock Caisson S.B. (Cardiff)	43/77	150B4
Junction Lock S.B. (Bristol)	19/37	24A2
Junction Lock S.B. (Cardiff)	43/77	150D5
KEINTON MANDEVILLE	16/47	43A4
KELMSCOTT AND LANGFORD HALT	27/23	66C3
KELSTON	20/48	—
Kelston Bridge S.B.	20/48	—
Kemberton Colly	32/37	70A4
KEMBLE	20/34	59B3

Kempsters Siding		117B5
Kendon Branch Junction	40/22	178C6
Kendon Colly	40/73	178A6
KENFIG HILL	49/43	143A3
Kennaway S.B.	14/18	14C6
Kennels Crossing		71C3
Kennet Bridge S.B.	24/13	33B6
Kennington Junction	27/14	68D6
Kensal Green	25/10	39B5
Kensham Siding	15/8	16C3
KENSINGTON (ADDISON ROAD)	25/27	38C5
KENSINGTON (OLYMPIA)	25/27	38C5
Kentsford S.B.	15/24	17A3
* Kenyon Siding		94A4
KERNE BRIDGE	36/27	105D2
Kernick S.B.	11/31	4C2
KERRY		116B6
Kerry Branch Junction		116A6
KETLEY	32/38	69A6
* Ketley Brickworks Siding (Bromley)		76B1
Ketley Junction	32/5	69A6
KETLEY TOWN HALT	32/38	69B3
KEYHAM	12/3	8B2
KEYNSHAM	21/2	27A2
KEYNSHAM AND SOMERDALE	21/2	27A2
KIDDERMINSTER	33/12	77C5
Kidderminster Viaduct S.B.		77D5
KIDLINGTON	27/5	67A3
Kidnalls Siding	37/9	53C3
KIDWELLY	57/2	133D1
Kidwelly Branch Junction	57/41	133B2
Kidwelly Bridge S.B.	57/2	133D1
KIDWELLY FLATS HALT	57/5	133C2
Kidwelly Junction S.B.	57/41	133B3
Kidwelly Loop Junctions	57/41	133B2
Kidwelly Quay	57/2	133D1
Kidwelly Tinplate Works	57/34	133B2
KILGERRAN	58/32	125B3
KILGETTY	58/29	124B6
KILGETTY AND BEGELLY	58/29	124B6
Kilkewydd Siding		118B4
Killan Colly	54/25	—
Killan and Voilarts Colly	54/25	—
KILLAY	54/26	—
Kilmar Tor	11/36	6B3
Kilmersdon Colly	21/47	27C2
Kilver Street Crossing	16/39	22C5
Kimberley Sidings	25/5	39B2
Kimmins Siding (Dudbridge)	20/56	—
Kimmins Siding (Charfield)	20/44	—
Kincoed Colly	40/70	178B4
KINETON	29/6	—
King Barrow Quarries		42C1
KINGHAM	28/14	65C6
* Kingham East Junction	28/30	65C6
* Kingham West Junction	28/30	65C6
KINGSBRIDGE	14/33	11D4
Kingsbridge Branch Junction	14/8	11A3
KINGSBRIDGE ROAD	14/8	11A3
Kings Dock Junction S.B. (Swansea)	56/17	137B6
Kings Dock Works	56/26	137D3
Kingsdown Road S.B.	20/29	29A3
Kings Junction S.B. (Cardiff)	43/87	150B1
KINGSKERSWELL	14/39	12A5
KINGSLAND	63/39	102B1
Kingsland Road Goods (Bristol)	19/14	24B5
Kingsmead Crossing	20/7	28C1
Kings Meadow Sidings (Reading)	24/11	33B5
Kingsmill Siding		92D3
KINGS NORTON	34/9	—
KING'S SUTTON	27/1	84D4
King Street G.F. (Plymouth)	12/17	8C4
KINGSTON CROSSING HALT	26/33	87C3
KINGSWEAR	14/34	12D5

KINGSWEAR CROSSING	14/34	12D5
* Kings Wharf (Bristol)	19/38	—
Kingswinford Junction	31/45	76D2
KINGSWOOD		81S6
* Kingswood Collieries	19/50	—
Kingswood Junction	19/49	—
KING'S WORTHY	23/33	51C6
KINGTON	63/37	103B3
Kington Junction	63/10	102A6
KING TOR HALT	14/32	10B6
Kinlet and Billingsley Sdgs S.B.	32/25	72B4
Kinlet Colly	32/25	72B3
KINNERLEY	63/42	98A2
KINNERLEY JUNCTION	63/42	98A2
KINTBURY	23/20	49D3
KIRBY PARK		89B1
KIRTLINGTON	27/4	85D2
Kitchen Hill Colly		?
Knightcote S.B.	30/21	83C3
KNIGHTON	59/12	—
Knighton Crossing (Chudleigh Knighton)	14/43	14B3
Knighton Crossing (Uffington)	23/1	29A6
KNIGHTWICK	33/22	61A1
Knook Camp	21/55	47B2
KNOWLE	30/12	81C5
KNOWLE AND DORRIDGE	30/12	81C5
Knowle Limeworks (Presthope)	32/30	71A2
Knowle Sand Siding (Bridgnorth)	32/33	71C5
KNUCKLAS	59/11	—
Knuckle Yard	50/62	142B4
L. & O. Junction	44/1	144D1
L. & S.W. Co. Crossing S.B.	41/45	180B4
LACOCK HALT	21/24	28D3
Ladbroke Bridge S.B.	25/10	39B5
LADBROKE GROVE (H & C)	25/24	38B5
Ladbroke Grove S.B. (GWR)	25/10	39B5
Lady Lewis Colly	46/52	159C5
Lady Margaret Colly	46/6	158C2
Lady Windsor Colly		171B1
LAIRA GREEN		8B3
LAIRA HALT	12/11	8B3
Laira Junction	12/10	8B4
Lake View Crossing	57/56	133C4
Laleston S.B.	50/75	143B6
* Lambridge Siding		?
Lamb Colly (Gors y Garnant)	54/46	131D4
Lamb Siding (Mountain Branch)	54/32	131A1
LAMBOURN	23/40	49A1
Lambourn Valley Junction	23/21	49A3
LAMPETER	58/35	127D4
* LAMPETER ROAD		130B5
LAMPHEY	58/26	124D4
* Lancasters Steam Colly G.F.		181D2
Lan Colly (C. & O. Line)	49/22	157D5
Lan Colly (Pontypridd)		172A3
Lancaster Quarry Siding		144B2
Lando Ordnance Factory	57/5	133C2
LANDO PLATFORM	57/5	133C2
LANDORE	55/10	136B2
LANDORE LOW LEVEL	55/25	136B2
Landore Mile End G.F.	55/10	136B2
Landore Steelworks (Mid)	53/37	—
Landore Steel Works S.B. (GWR)	55/13	136A3
Lane Junction	11/20	3A1
Lanelay Colly	44/13	145D3
Lanes Siding	20/54	—
LANGFORD (Wiltshire)	21/56	47B3
LANGFORD (Wrington Vale)	16/43	21C5
LANGFORD LANE	27/5	67A3
Langford Lane Crossing	27/28	—
LANGLEY	24/22	34C6
LANGLEY (BUCKS)	24/22	34C6
Langley Crossing S.B. (Chippenham)	21/13	28C3
LANGLEY GREEN	31/34	79C3
LANGLEY GREEN AND ROOD END	31/34	79C3
Langley Green Crossing S.B.	31/34	79C3
LANGLEY MARSH	24/22	34C6
LANGPORT EAST	16/47	43B1
LANGPORT WEST	17/15	43B1
* Langston & North Dock Depot		90A1
Lanjeth Crossing	11/32	4D3
Lansalson Siding	11/18	4C4
LANSDOWN	35/12	36B5
Lansdown International (Didcot)	23/44	30B4
Lansdown Junction (Cheltenham)	35/11	36B5
LAPWORTH	30/13	81D6
Largin S.B.	11/11	6A3
Latchmere Junctions	25/32	38D2
LATIMER ROAD	25/24	38D5
Latteridge Crossing	20/51	—
Latty's Siding		174D6
LAUNCESTON	14/23	9D1
LAVERNOCK	44/60	148B3
LAVERTON HALT	28/20	63B5
LAVINGTON	21/41	46C5
LAWLEY BANK	32/39	70C1
Lawley Colly		70C5
Lawn Colly		70C1
LAWRENCE HILL	19/47	24A5
Lawrence Hill Junction	19/41	24A5
Lawton Siding	32/15	69C5
Laymoor Junctions	37/19	54A6
Leamington G.W. Junction S.B.	30/19	83C6
LEAMINGTON SPA AVENUE	30/19	—
LEAMINGTON SPA GENERAL	30/19	83B5
Leapgate Siding	32/28 & 33/25	72A6
Leat Mill Siding	14/23	9D2
LEATON		98A5
LECHLADE	27/23	66C2
LECKHAMPTON	28/27	55B6
Leckhampton Quarries Siding	28/27	55B6
Leckhampton Sand Pit Siding	28/27	55B6
Leckwith Junctions		149C2
Leckwith Road Crossing		149C2
LEDBURY	33/3	60A3
Ledbury North End S.B.	33/3	60A3
LEDBURY TOWN HALT	33/20	60B3
LEDSHAM		91A3
Ledsham Junction S.B.		91A4
LEEBOTWOOD	63/2	100B1
Lee Moor Crossing S.B.	14/29	7B5
LEGACY		94B4
Legacy Colly		94B4
Legges Siding	32/54	
Leigh Bridge S.B.	15/26	17C4
LEIGH COURT	33/22	61B2
* Leigh Valley Quarry	19/31	25C6
Leigh Wood Crossing	15/26	17C5
LELANT	10/21	1B2
Lelant Quay	10/21	1B2
LELANT SALTINGS	10/21	1C2
Lemington Lane Crossing	28/36	64C2
Lent Rise Siding	24/17	34C4
LEOMINSTER	63/10	102B6
Leominster Junction (Bransford Rd.)	33/8	61B3
Lester's Lime Works		93C1
LETTERSTON	58/30	123A2
Letterston Junction S.B.	58/4	123A1
* Lever Bros Sidings		89A5
* Lewis & Sons G.F.	54/22	—
Lewis Graigola Colly	53/Ind	—
Lewis Merthyr Colly (Ogmore Vale)	49/39	157A6
Lewis Merthyr Colly (Trehafod)	46/33	172A1
Lewis Merthyr Colly (Ynyshir)	46/52	159D5
Lewis Road Junction (Cardiff)	43/58	150D4
Lewis's Siding (Crumlin Junction)	40/19	182D1
* Lewis's Siding (Pantysgallog)		167A1

Lewis's Siding (Ystradgynlais)	52/18	132C3	Llan Colly (Llantrisant)	44/13	145D3
LEWISTOWN HALT	49/40	157B5	Llanarth St. Jcn. S.B.	38/58	152B3
Lewis Wern Siding		170D6	LLANARTHNEY	58/42	
LEWKNOR BRIDGE HALT	26/33	87C2	Llanayron L.C.	58/41	127A1
Ley Crossing (Grange Court)	36/21	55C1	Llanbad Colly	49/26	145A4
Leys Siding (Aberthaw)	44/36	144B6	Llanbadarn Crossing S.B.		114B6
Libanus Siding	41/37	—	LLANBADARN HALT (V o R)		114B6
LIDDATON HALT		9D4	LLANBEDR		110A1
LIDFORD	14/24	9C4	LLANBEDR & PENSARN		110A1
LIFFORD	34/10	—	LLANBER HALT		110C2
LIFTON	14/23	9D2	LLANBETHERY PLATFORM	44/23	144C5
Lightmoor Colly (Bilson Jcn)	37/32	54B5	LLANBISTER ROAD	59/10	—
Lightmoor Colly (Mineral Loop)	37/23	54B2	Llanboidy Crossing	58/7	125C5
Lightmoor Junction (Shrops.)	32/34	70B2	LLANBRADACH		179C3
LIGHTMOOR PLATFORM (Shrops)	32/34	70B2	LLANBRADACH COLLY HALT	42/42	179B4
Lightmoor Railway (F. of Dean)	37/23 & 37/32	54B5	LLANBRYN MAIR		115C4
Lilleshall Siding (Blodwell Jcn)		119A2	LLANCAIACH	47/85	170D5
Lilleshall Siding (Hollinswood)	32/11	70B5	Llancaiach & Bargoed Jcn S.B.	47/84	170D5
Lilleshall Siding (Presthope)	32/29	71A2	Llancaiach Branch Junction		171C2
Lillie Bridge Sidings S.B.	25/29	38D6	Llancaiach Colly		110C6
* Lime Kiln Lane Siding		?	LLANDAFF	46/93	174C3
Lime Kilns S.B. (Machen)	42/48	180C4	* Llandaff Girder Works Siding	46/95	174C4
Lime Kilns Siding S.B. (Risca)	40/32	180B5	Llandaff Loop Junction	46/93	174C3
Limestone Branch Junction	54/1	130C6	LLANDANWG HALT		110A1
Limmer Junction	16/41	45B2	LLANDARCY PLATFORM	55/48	139D1
LIMPLEY STOKE	21/14	27B5	Llandarcy S.B.	55/47	138D6
LINLEY	32/23	71A5	Llandavel Colly	40/8	177A5
Linton Mill Crossing		102D6	LLANDDERFEL		112D1
Lion Black Vein Colly		?	Llanddu Junction		119B2
* Lion Colly		?	Llanddu Quarry		119B2
Lion Siding (Waenavon)	41/15	—	LLANDEBIE	54/3	130D6
Lion's Den Crossing		181D6	Llandebie Colly	54/35	131A3
Lion Tinplate Works (Nantyglo)	40/49	175B6	Llandebie Lime Works	54/35	131A3
Lipson Junction	12/10	8B3	LLANDECWYN HALT		109C3
LIPSON VALE HALT	12/7	8B5	LLANDEILO	59/1	130D3
LISKEARD	11/12	6C6	Llandeilo Junction	57/30	134D5
Liskeard Viaduct S.B.	11/13	6C6	LLANDENNY	36/23	108D4
Listers Siding	20/53	—	LLANDERFEL		112D1
LISVANE AND THORNHILL		174A6	LLANDILO	59/1	130C3
LITCHFIELD (HANTS)	23/35	50C1	LLANDILO BRIDGE	58/42	—
Little Bedwyn S.B.	23/19	48C6	Llandilo Jcn (Llanelly)	57/30	134D5
Little Bourton Crossing		84B3	LLANDINAM	59/32	116C3
Little Dark Lane Colly		70C5	* Llandinam Timber Siding	59/32	116C3
* Little Dock (Cardiff)	43/54	150D5	LLANDOGO HALT	36/29	53D2
LITTLE DRAYTON HALT	32/44	99B5	LLANDOUGH PLATFORM		147B5
Little Faringdon Crossing	27/23	66C2	Llandough S.B.'s		147B5
Littlefield Crossing	17/11	42C3	LLANDOVERY	59/4	130A6
Little Hereford Crossing		101D4	LLANDOW HALT	44/34	144B3
LITTLE KIMBLE	26/34	87A5	LLANDOW WICK RD HALT	44/35	144C3
LITTLE MILL	39/3	108D2	LLANDRE		114B2
Littlemill Crossing (Cropredy)	30/23	84B3	LLANDRILLO		112C2
Little Mill Crossing (Llandaff)		174C4	LLANDRINDOD WELLS	59/9	—
LITTLE MILL JUNCTION	39/3	108D2	LLANDRINIO ROAD		98B1
LITTLEMORE	27/17	67D4	LLANDYBIE	54/3	130D6
Little Rock Quarry		119A4	Llandyry Colly	57/44	133B3
LITTLE SOMERFORD	20/6	28A4	LLANDYSSIL	58/41	128B3
LITTLE STRETTON HALT	63/3	100B4	LLANDYSSUL	58/41	128B3
LITTLE SUTTON		91A4	LLANDYSUL	58/41	128B3
LITTLETON AND BADSEY	28/6	62C3	Llanelay Colly	44/12	145D3
Little Treviscoe Siding	11/31	4D2	LLANELLY	57/15	134C3
Little Wells Siding	51/47	155A4	Llanelly Albert Road Goods	57/58	134C2
* Liverpool, Carriers Dock		90A1	Llanelly Commissioners Dock Jcn	57/13	134C2
* Liverpool, Chaloner Street		90B1	Llanelly Copper Works	57/16	134D2
* Liverpool, Dukes Dock		90B1	LLANELLY DOCK	57/17	134D3
* Liverpool, Hood Street		90B1	Llanelly Dock Goods	57/24	134D3
* Liverpool, James Street		90B1	Llanelly Dock Junction	57/17	134D3
* Liverpool, Langton & North Docks		90A1	Llanelly Dock Loop Junction	57/17	134D3
* Liverpool, Manchester Basin		90B1	Llanelly Foundry G.F.	57/49	134C1
* Liverpool, Ranelagh Street		90B1	Llanelly Gas Works	57/15	134C3
* Liverpool, South End Depot		90B1	Llanelly High Street G.F.	57/59	134C2
* Liverpool, Stanley Dock		90B1	Llanelly Low Level Junction	57/58	134C2
LLAFAR HALT		109C6	Llanelly Morfa Junction	57/22	134D4
Llamarch Colly		—	Llanelly Mynydd Mawr Stages	57/13	134D2
Llan Colly (C. & O. Branch)	49/22	157D4	Llanelly Nevilles Dock Rlwy	57/16	134C2

Llanelly New Dock	57/22	134D3	
Llanelly North Dock S.B.	57/13	134C2	
Llanelly Old Castle Crossing	57/12	134C2	
Llanelly Queen Victoria Road Gds	57/58	134B2	
Llanelly St. David's Dock Crossing S.B.	57/17	134D4	
Llanelly Siding S.B. (Clydach)	41/15	—	
Llanelly Steelworks	57/58	134C1	
Llanelly Trevose Head Siding	57/15	134C2	
Llanelly West Junction	57/13	134C2	
Llanelwydd Quarry Siding	59/25	121B2	
LLANERCH AYRON HALT	58/41	127A1	
Llanerch Colly (Cwmnantddu)	39/24	182B3	
Llanerch Siding (Upper Bank)	53/5	—	
LLANFABON ROAD HALT		170D5	
LLANFAIR CAEREINION (W & L)		118A1	
Llanfair & Guilsfield Road L.C. (W & L)		117D1	
LLANFALTEG	58/33	125C4	
LLANFAREDD HALT	59/24	121C3	
LLANFECHAIN		117B4	
LLANFIHANGEL (Mon)	63/24	107D1	
Llanfoist Siding	41/17	—	
LLANFYLLIN		117B3	
Llanfyllin Branch Junction		119B3	
LLANFYNYDD		92B2	
LLANFYRNACH	58/33	125A5	
LLANGADOCK	59/2	130B4	
LLANGADOG	59/2	130B4	
* LLANGAMMARCH	59/6	—	
LLANGAMMARCH WELLS	59/6	—	
Llangar L.C.		122B2	
Llangasty Crossing	59/17	112D5	
LLANGEDWYN		117A4	
LLANGEINOR	49/33	157B4	
Llangeinor Colly Siding S.B.	49/33	157B4	
LLANGELYNIN HALT		113A1	
LLANGENNECH	55/34	133C6	
Llangennech Colly (Dafen)	57/63	134C6	
* Llangennech Park Depot	55/36	133C6	
Llangennech Tin Works	55/34	133C6	
LLANGLYDWEN	58/33	125B4	
LLANGOLLEN		95B1	
Llangollen Line Junction		94C2	
LLANGOLLEN ROAD		95C3	
Llangollen Road Crossing		94C2	
LLANGOLLEN ROAD HALT		95C3	
LLANGONOYD	49/8	157A1	
LLANGORSE LAKE HALT	59/21	121D5	
LLANGOWER HALT		111C5	
LLANGUNLLO	59/11	—	
Llangurig		120A4	
LLANGYBI	58/35	127C5	
LLANGYFELACH	55/42	138B2	
LLANGYNOG		117A1	
LLANGYNWYD	49/8	157A1	
LLANHARAN	44/9	145B4	
Llanharan Colly	44/8	145B3	
Llanharan Opencast Site	44/8	145B3	
LLANHARRY	44/24	145D5	
LLANHILLETH	40/16	182C1	
Llanhilleth Branch Junction	40/17	182C2	
LLANIDLOES	59/31	116D1	
Llanidloes Road Crossing		116D5	
LLANILAR	58/34	126A4	
Llanilterne Crossing		146A2	
LLANION HALT	58/24	126D2	
LLANISHEN		174A6	
Llanlay Colly	44/13	145D3	
Llanmore Iron Works		134C3	
LLANMORLAIS	54/50	—	
Llanmorlais Wern Colly	54/50	—	
Llannon Valley Colly	57/53	133B4	
Llanover Colly	40/63	177C5	
LLANPUMPSAINT	58/36	128D3	
Llanrhaiadr Crossing		117A3	

LLANRHAIADR MOCHNANT			117A2
LLANRHYSTYD ROAD	58/34		114D1
LLANSAMLET (First Station)	55/17		138C5
LLANSAMLET NORTH (GWR)	55/16		138C4
LLANSAMLET SOUTH (LMSR)	53/11		—
* Llansamlet Works (Six Pit Jcn)	53/7		
LLANSANTFFRAID			117B5
LLANSILIN ROAD			117A4
Llansilio S.B.	63/24		107C3
Llanstephan Crossing S.B.	58/9		129B1
LLANSTEPHAN HALT	59/24		121A4
LLANTARNAM	39/11		183D3
Llantarnam Junction S.B.	39/11		183C3
Llanthony Docks (Gloucester)	35/20		56B2
LLANTRISANT	44/11		145D4
Llantrisant Branch No. 1 Junction	49/75		161C1
Llantrisant Colly	49/65		145B6
Llantrisant Common Colly	49/84		161B4
Llantrisant Common Jcn S.B.	49/64		145A6
Llantrisant Jcn S.B. (Treforest)	46/72		173A1
* LLANTRISSANT	44/11		145D4
LLANTWIT (Llantwit Fardre)	49/78		161B5
* Llantwit Basin Colly			?
* Llantwit Colly (Caerphilly)			173B6
Llantwit Colly (Glannant)	49/10		157B2
Llantwit (Tyn-y-Nant) Colly	49/78		161B5
LLANTWIT FARDRE	49/79		161B5
Llantwit Main Colly	49/74		161C1
LLANTWIT MAJOR	44/35		144D3
Llantwit Merthyr Colly	51/51		153B2
Llantwit Red Ash Colly (Common Bch.)	49/74		161C1
Llantwit Red Ash Colly (Llantwit)	49/79		161B5
Llantwit Road Goods (Treforest)	46/69		172C5
* Llantwit Wallsend Colly (Blaengarw)			?
Llantwit Wallsend Colly (Common Bch Jcn)	49/76		161C5
LLANUWCHLLYN			111C4
LLANVIHANGEL (Cambrian)			114B2
LLANVIHANGEL (Mon)			107D1
Llanvihangel Crossing (Talyllyn Jcn)	59/21		121D4
Llanwddyn Siding			96C5
LLANWERN	38/19		52D1
Llanwern Steelworks	38/22		52D1
Llanwonno Colly			171C5
LLANWRDA	59/3		130A5
LLANWRTYD WELLS	59/6		—
Llanwrthwl Crossing	59/27		120C3
LLANYBLODWELL (Blodwell Jcn)			119B2
LLANYBLODWELL (Llanyblodwell)			119B1
LLANYBYTHER	58/35		128A6
LLANYCEFN	58/31		123C5
* Llanydavil Colly			177A5
LLANYMYNECH			119D4
LLECHRYD	59/26		121A3
Llest Colly	49/31		156D6
Llest Llantwit Colly	49/78		161B5
LLETTY BRONGU	51/13		157A1
Lletty Brongu Colly (G.W.)	49/8		156D4
Lletty Brongu Colly (P.T.R.)	51/6		157A2
Lletty Shenkin S.B.	47/58		165C5
Llewellyn Merthyr Colly			?
Llewellyn Plymouth Colly			?
Llewellyn Quay	50/26		141C4
Lliew Common Crossing	54/17		—
* Lliswerry Limeworks			152B6
Liswerry S.B.	38/18		151B4
Liswerry Yard (Newport)	38/17		152B6
LLIWDY (Corris)			113B5
Lloyds Siding (Blisworth)	29/12		—
Lluest Colly	49/31		156D6
Llwydarth Tin Works	49/7		156D3
LLWYDCOED	47/48		164B5
Llwyn Colly	57/60		134C4
Llwynada Colly	54/34		131A1
Llwyncelyn Junction S.B. (Merthyr)			168B3

246

Llwyncelyn S.B. (Trehafod)	46/32	159D6
Llwyndu Colly	53/14	—
Llwyneinon Siding		94C4
Llwynfelish Quarry	52/7	162C1
Llwyn Glo Colly	40/70	178B4
LLWYNGWERN		113B5
LLWYNGWRIL		113A1
Llwynhelig Colly	47/34	165B2
Llwynhendy Colly	55/29	134D6
Llwynjack Siding	59/3	130A6
Llwynllafrod Colly	52/20	132B4
Llwynllanc Quarry	52/8	162A2
Llwynon Colly	52/8	132D4
LLWYNPIA	46/20	159C3
LLWYNPIA AND TONYPANDY	46/20	159C3
Llwynsaer Siding	49/83	161D5
Llwynyffynon Colly	51/22	155A3
Llwyn-y-rhidie Colly		?
* LLYNCOCH	59/11	—
LLYNCLYS		119A5
Llynclys Junction		119A5
Llyn Colly (Nantyglo)	40/49	175C6
Llyn Fawr Siding		164C2
Llynfi Gas Works	49/6	156C2
* Llynfi Colly		156C3
Llynfi Junction S.B.	49/3	156C2
Llynfi Power Station	49/10	157B2
Llynfi Siding S.B. (Bridgend)	44/1	144C1
* Llynfi Vale Iron Works	49/3	156C2
Llynfi Valley Colly	49/8	157A1
* Llynfi Valley Gas Works	49/6	156C2
Llyn Level (Pontwalby)		163D4
* Llynvi Junction		143B4
Llynvi Vale Ironworks	49/3	156C2
LLYS HALT		111D4
L.M.S. Junction S.B. (Cardiff)	43/62	150C4
L.M.S. Junction S.B. (Stratford)	30/36	82C6
* L.N.W.R. Cardiff Yard S.B.	43/72	150D5
* L.N.W.R. Goods (Cardiff)	43/72	150D5
* Loam Bank Siding (Ruckley)		69C5
Lockets Merthyr Colly		160B6
Lockinge S.B.	23/3	31B2
LOCKING ROAD, WESTON-SUPER-MARE	16/23	21C1
Lockyers Quay	12/18	8D5
Loco Yard Junction S.B. (Newport)	38/58	152B4
LODDISWELL	14/33	11C4
Lode Sidings	34/14	—
Loders Siding	17/14	41C1
Lodge Bridge S.B.	23/35	51A5
Lodge Colly		70C5
Lodge Farm Crossing		6B5
LODGE HILL	16/35	22B2
Lodge Sidings (Stratford)	30/34	82C6
LOGIN	58/33	125C4
LONDON (PADDINGTON)	25/17	39D5
London Yard (Worcester)	33/17	60C6
LONG ASHTON	16/32	23D3
LONGBRIDGE	34/19	81C1
LONGDON HALT	32/45	69A2
LONGDON ROAD	28/36	64A2
LONGDOWN	14/45	13B3
* Long Drive Siding	26/19	36C4
Long Dyke Junction S.B.		149C5
Longfield Avenue S.B.	25/1	37B6
Longhedge Junction	25/32	38D3
LONGHOPE	36/33	105D5
Long Lane Crossing S.B.	63/4	101C1
Longleat Park Siding	21/54	47B6
LONG MARSTON	28/23	62B5
* Long Marston W.D.	28/25	62B5
* Longnor Forge Siding		100B1
Long Range Level		164C3
Long Rock S.B.	10/3	1D1
LONG SUTTON AND PITNEY	16/47	43B2
LONGVILLE	32/29	71B1
Lonlas Junction S.B.	55/47	138D5
Lonlas South S.B.	55/47	138D6
LONSDALE		98A3
LOOE	11/37	6D5
Lord Dynevor's Siding (Ammanford)	54/38	131B3
Lord Hills S.B.'s	25/17	39D4
Lord Tredegars Quarry Siding	42/22	177D3
Lord Tredegars Siding	41/40	—
LOSTWITHIEL	11/9	6B2
Lotts Road	25/31	38C1
LOUDWATER	24/38	34A4
LOUGHOR	55/1	133D6
* Loughor & Spitty Copper Wks		133D6
Loughor Bridge S.B.	55/1	133D5
* LOUGHOR COMMON		—
* Lovells Quarry	19/31	25C6
Lovely Cottage Crossing		1A5
LOVERINGS SIDING	11/18	4D4
Lovers Lane Crossing	20/7	28B1
LOVESGROVE		114D2
Lower Arrail Junction	40/56	176C6
Lower Brynhellish Colly	53/51	
* Lower Brynhen Ilys Colly	53/51	—
Lower Burgotha Siding	11/28	4D1
Lower Conygre Colly	21/52	27C2
Lower Corrwg Colly	51/53	153C5
Lower Cwm Gelli Colly	41/36	
Lower Cwmgoy Colly		107C1
Lower Cwmtwrch Crossing	53/27	—
Lower Cwmtawe Colly	52/18	132C3
Lower Cynon S.B.	51/30	153D6
Lower Deep Pit (Blaina)	40/53	175D6
Lower Delph Colly	31/27	77B4
Lower Duffryn Colly	47/65	165D6
Lower Duffryn G.F. (Cwmbach)	47/60	165C5
Lower Duffryn G.F. (Mountain Ash)		170C1
Lower East Side (Nantyglo)		175C6
Lower Fan Pit	46/44	158C6
Lower Farm Siding	41/31	—
* Lower Forest Works	53/39	—
Lower Forge (Lydney)	37/5	54C4
Lower Gethin Pit		169B2
Lower Gilfach Colly	49/72	160D4
Lower Gothers		4B2
Lower Graigola Colly	55/18	139A1
* Lower Llanmorlais Colly	54/41	—
Lower Llwydcoed Ballast Sidings	47/22	165A2
Lower Lodfin Crossing	15/17	15B1
LOWER LYDBROOK	37/42	54A1
Lower Mills Steelworks	39/5	183A5
Lower Navigation Colly		184A1
LOWER PENARTH HALT	44/60	147D6
Lower Penarth S.B.		148A4
LOWER PONTNEWYDD	39/11	183B3
Lower Race	47/108	182C5
Lower Resolven Colly	47/5	162C4
* Lower Rhoswen Colly		—
Lower Rosemarket Crossing	58/15	124B2
Lower Ruddle Siding	11/18	4D4
Lower Varteg Colly	39/14	181D5
Lower Writhlington Colly	18/6	27D3
Lower Yard (Avonside)	19/41	—
Lower Yard S.B. (Stafford Road)	31/4	74B4
Low Level Loop Junction (Exeter)	14/21	13D2
Low Level Loop Junction (Merthyr)		168D2
Low Level Loop Junction (Newport)	38/44	152A1
Lowry Road Crossing	14/32	10C5
* LOW WATER PIER, CARDIFF	43/79	150A2
Loxdale Siding	31/14	75A3
Lucas Siding S.B. (Leamington)	30/19	—
LUCAS TERRACE HALT	12/21	—
Lucy Thomas Colly		168D4
Ludgate Junction	25/32	38D2

LUDGERSHALL	22/17	51C1	
LUDLOW	63/7	101B6	
Ludlows Colly	18/8 & 21/47	27B3	
Lukes New Siding	11/31	4D1	
Lukes Old Siding	11/31	4D1	
LUSTLEIGH	14/40	14A1	
Luxborough Road		17C1	
LUXULYAN	11/24	3B6	
LYDBROOK	36/27	53A3	
LYDBROOK JUNCTION	36/27	53A3	
Lydbrook Tin Works	37/41	54A1	
LYDFORD	14/24	9C4	
LYDHAM HEATH	63/33	100C2	
Lydney and Crump Meadow Colly		?	
Lydney Docks Branch Junction	37/6	54C4	
Lydney Engine Shed S.B.	37/5	54C4	
LYDNEY JUNCTION	36/11 & 37/5	54D4	
Lydney Lower Docks	37/38	54D6	
Lydney Lower Forge	37/5	53D6	
Lydney Middle Forge	37/9	53D3	
Lydney Road Crossing (Parkend)	37/14	54B3	
Lydney Tin Works Junction	37/6	54C4	
LYDNEY TOWN	37/9	53D4	
Lydney Upper Docks	37/38	54D5	
Lydney Upper Forge	37/9	53C3	
LYDSTEP HALT	58/26	124D6	
LYE	31/27	77B3	
Lympsham S.B.	16/21	21D1	
* Lynch Colly	54/50	—	
* Lyng Bridge Siding		20B4	
LYNG HALT	16/12	20B4	
LYONSHALL	63/39	103C4	
Lysaghts G.F.	38/31	152D5	
M. & S. Tramway Junction	28/6	64C1	
M.T. & A. Junction	39/1	108A2	
McLaren Colly No. 1	42/9	167D6	
McLaren Colly No. 2	42/7	167C5	
McLAREN COLLY PLATFORM	42/10	167D6	
MACHEN	42/46	180C3	
Machen Black Vein Colly	42/57	180C3	
Machen Lime Kilns	42/46	180C4	
Machen Pit	42/57	180C3	
Machen Quarry	42/49	180D4	
Machen Shops	42/46	180C3	
Machen Tin Plate Works	45/56	180C3	
Machine Road G.F. (Kidwelly Jcn)	57/41	133B2	
Machine Siding (Nantyglo)	40/50	175C6	
Machine Siding (Porthywaen)		119A5	
Machine Siding Junction (Nantyglo)	40/50	175C6	
MACHYNLLETH		113B5	
Machynys Crossing		?	
Mackintosh Colly	21/51	45B1	
Maclarens Siding	11/29	4B1	
Maconochie's Siding	58/22	124B1	
MADELEY COURT	32/36	70A3	
Madeley Junction	32/14	70C6	
MADELEY MARKET	32/54	—	
MADELEY, SALOP	32/36	70A3	
Madeley Wood Colly (Kemberton)	32/37	70B4	
Madeley Wood Siding	32/54	—	
Maelor Siding		92D4	
MAENCLOCHOG	58/31	123B5	
Maendy Colly (nr. Tondu)	49/23	143D5	
Maendy Colly (Ystrad Rhondda)	46/17	159B1	
Maendy Ystrad S.B.	46/16	159A2	
MAENTWROG ROAD		109B5	
MAERDY	46/42	158B5	
* Maerdy Branch Junction	46/44	158C6	
Maerdy Colly (Gwaun cae Gurwen)		?	
Maerdy Colly (Rhymney)	42/3	167C5	
Maerdy Colly Nos. 1 and 2 Pits	46/42	158B4	
Maerdy Colly Nos. 3 and 4 Pits	46/42	158A4	
Maerdy Sidings G.F.		158D6	
Maesaraul Junction	49/73	161D3	
Maesaraul Siding	49/73	161D4	
Maesarddafen Colly	57/60	134C4	
Maesbach Colly		173B3	
MAESBROOK		98A1	
Maes Crossing		107C1	
Maesglas Bank S.B.	38/37	152A1	
Maesglas Junction S.B.	38/38	152A1	
Maesglas Lower Junction	38/36	152A1	
Maesglas Sidings S.B.	38/36	152A1	
* MAESMAWR	46/74	173B2	
Maesmawr Colly (Crynant)		132D4	
Maesmawr Colly (Treforest)		173B1	
Maesmawr Crossing (Pontyberem)	57/37	133A2	
Maesmawr S.B. (Treforest)	46/72	173A1	
Maesmelyn Colly	51/23	154C3	
Maespoeth Junction (Corris)		113A5	
MAESTEG (CASTLE ST)	49/5	156C2	
Maesteg Council (Park) Siding	51/6	156D2	
Maesteg Deep Colly	51/8	156C2	
* MAESTEG EWENNY ROAD		156C3	
Maesteg Ironworks	49/5	156C2	
Maesteg Merthyr Colly (Troedyrhiew)	49/6	156D3	
Maesteg Merthyr Pit (Maesteg)	49/6	156C2	
Maesteg Merthyr (Duffryn) Colly	49/1	156A2	
MAESTEG (NEATH ROAD)	51/7	156C2	
Maesteg No. 9 Colly	51/10	156C3	
Maesteg Slag Tip Siding	51/8	156C2	
* Maesteg Tin Plate Works	49/7	156D3	
Maes y Bettws Colly	49/9	157A1	
Maescycoed Street Goods		172B4	
MAES-Y-CRUGIAU	58/35	128B5	
MAESYCWMMER	42/39	178D5	
MAESY CWMMER AND HENGOED	42/39	178D5	
Maesycwmmer Junction (B. & M.)	42/36	178C2	
Maesycwmmer Junction (V. of N.)	47/92	178D2	
Maesyddhirion Crossing		130C6	
Maes y Marchog Colly	52/11	132C6	
Magazine Siding (Ellesmere)		96C4	
Magazine Siding (Mwyndy)	49/82	161D4	
MAGOR	38/21	52D2	
Magpie Grove S.B.	57/55	133C4	
MAIDENHEAD	24/16	34C3	
MAIDENHEAD AND TAPLOW		34C4	
MAIDENHEAD, BOYNE HILL		34C3	
Maidenhead Bridge S.B.	24/16	34C4	
MAIDENHEAD, WYCOMBE BRANCH		34C3	
MAIDEN NEWTON	17/4	41B4	
Mails Cat Pit		?	
Main Collieries Nos. 3 and 4 Pits	56/44	139A2	
Main Collieries No. 7 Pit		139B3	
Main Colly		135A6	
Maindee Junctions	38/13	152A4	
Maindy Bridge S.B.	46/102	149A3	
Maindy Colly (Ystrad Rhondda)		159B1	
Maindy Fuel S.B.	46/99	149A2	
MAINDY HALT	46/102	149A3	
MAINDY NORTH ROAD PLATFORM	46/102	149A3	
Malago Vale	19/5	24D2	
Malehurst Siding		98D1	
MALINS LEE	32/52	—	
Maliphant S.B.	55/23	136C2	
MALLWYD		115A4	
MALMESBURY	20/7	28B1	
Maloneys Tips Junction S.B.	43/73	150D5	
MALSWICK HALT	33/20	55A1	
Malvern & Tewkesbury Junction	33/6	61C1	
MALVERN LINK	33/37	61C3	
* Malvern Quarries Siding		60A4	
MALVERN ROAD (Cheltenham)	35/15	56B6	
Malvern Sidings S.B. (Mid)	33/6	—	
MALVERN WELLS (GWR)	33/5	61D1	
MALVERN WELLS (Mid)	34/14	—	
* Manchester Basin, Liverpool		90B1	

MANGOTSFIELD	20/39	—	
Mangotsfield South Junction	20/39	—	
Mangotsfield Stone Siding	20/39	—	
Manmoel Colly	40/63	177C5	
Mannamead S.B.	12/7	8B5	
MANNINGFORD HALT	21/42	48D3	
MANOD		109A6	
MANORBIER	58/26	124D5	
Manorbier Newton Crossing	58/26	124D4	
Manor Farm Siding	23/43	32C4	
Manor Way Siding	24/39	35B1	
Manorwen S.B.	58/4	123B6	
Mansel Colly (Cwmfelin)	55/8	136A1	
Mansel Tin Plate Works (Port Talbot)	50/26	141A3	
* Mansell Cutting		141B3	
* Mansell Lacy Siding	63/42	—	
Mapleford Colly	37/45	54B3	
MARAZION	10/5	1D1	
MARAZION ROAD	10/5	1D1	
March Howell Colly (Cilfrew)		162D1	
* Marchowell Colly (Pontardawe)	53/15	—	
MARCHWIEL		92D4	
Marcroft Siding G.F.	51/19	154D2	
* Mardon's G.F.	19/38	24B3	
* Mardy Colly (Maerdy)	46/42	158A4	
Mardy Junction		168C2	
* Mardy Works	54/22	—	
Marford S.B.		92B4	
MARGAM HALT	50/58	141C6	
Margam Abbey Works	50/61	141C5	
Margam Copper works	50/30	141C5	
Margam Forge Siding	51/19	154D2	
Margam Goods	50/48	141D5	
Margam Knuckle Yard	50/62	142B4	
Margam Moors S.B.	50/63	142C1	
Margam Sidings	50/46	141D5	
Margam Steel Works	50/31	141C4	
Margam Tin Plate Works		141A4	
Margam West Curve Junction	50/47	141C5	
Margam Wharf	50/30	141C4	
Margam Yard	50/69	142D4	
Margam Yard S.B.	50/55	142B5	
Marina Crossing		34A1	
Marine Colly (Blaenavon)	51/51	153C2	
MARINE COLLY PLATFORM	40/10	176D5	
Marine Colly Sdgs S.B. (Graig Fawr)		177A5	
Maritime Colly	46/59	172B4	
* Markers Siding	54/52	—	
MARKET DRAYTON	32/44	99B5	
Market Drayton Junction (Nantwich)	32/43	97B5	
Market Drayton Junction (Wellington)	32/3	69A4	
Market Siding (Frome)	21/27	45C5	
Marke Valley Mine	11/36	6C4	
Markham Colly	40/62	177B4	
MARKHAM VILLAGE	41/32	—	
MARLBOROUGH HIGH LEVEL	22/10	48B4	
MARLBOROUGH LOW LEVEL	22/10	48B4	
Marlborough South Junction	22/10	48B4	
MARLOW	24/39	34B3	
MARLOW ROAD		34A1	
Mardon and Proctors Siding	19/38	24B3	
Marsh S.B. (Midgham)	23/26	32D1	
Marsh Barton Estate	14/45	13D1	
MARSHBROOK	63/3	100C4	
Marsh Crossing (Leominster)		102A5	
MARSHES TURNPIKE GATE		152A3	
Marsh Farm Junction	63/3	100C4	
MARSHFIELD	38/2	151C2	
Marshfield Tin Works (Llanelly)	57/15	134C2	
* Marsh Depot (Bristol)	19/25	24D4	
Marsh Goods (Bristol)	19/19	24B4	
Marsh Junction (Bristol)	19/19	24B5	
Marsh Lane Colly		?	
Marsh Lane Crossing	26/34	86C5	

	MARSH MILLS	14/30	8A5
*	Marsh Pit	53/9	—
	Marsh Pond Sidings	19/21	24D5
	Marsh Sidings (Parkend)	37/12	54D1
	Marsh's Quarry Siding	40/29	180A1
	MARSTON (Marston Magna)	17/7	43C5
	Marston Crossing S.B. (Swindon)	23/1	29B4
	MARSTON HALT (Titley)	63/39	103B4
	MARSTON LANE (Titley)	63/39	103B4
	MARSTON MAGNA	17/7	43C5
	MARTEG HALT	59/30	120A2
	MARTELL BRIDGE HALT	58/31	123A3
	Martins New Siding	11/23	4A4
	MARTOCK	17/15	43D2
	Martock Drove Crossing		43D2
	Martyn Colly	52/9	132C4
	Mary Pit Siding	49/39	157A5
	MARYTAVY	14/24	10A4
	MARYTAVY AND BLACKDOWN	14/24	10A4
	MASBURY	18/13	—
	MATHRY ROAD	58/5	123A1
	Matthews Mill Siding (Corris)		113A4
	MATTHEWSTOWN HALT	47/74	170C3
	Maws Siding	32/22	70D2
*	Maxwell Road Crossing (Cattedown)		—
	May Hill Siding	36/24	53B1
	Mayrose Colly	44/9	145B4
	Mayshill Colly	20/51	26D1
	Mays Siding (Bath G.P.)	18/5	—
	Meadowcliffe Colly	37/27	54A4
	Meadow Colly (Donnington)		69B4
	Meadow Pit (Cwmavon)		154B3
	Meads Crossing S.B.	16/12	19D2
	Meerbrook Siding	37/35	54B2
	Meiros Colly	44/9	145A2
	Melangoose Mill	11/28	4C1
	Melbur Siding	11/28	4C1
	MELCOMBE REGIS	17/1	42C3
	Meledor Loop Siding	11/28	4C1
	Meledor Mill Siding	11/28	4C1
	Melincrythan Crossing	50/5	139C5
	Melincrythan Siding	50/3	139B5
*	Melincylla Junction S.B.		178C1
	Melingriffiths Tin Works	46/86	174C3
*	Melinyrhom Field	46/19	159B3
	MELKSHAM	21/22	46A3
	MELLS	21/49	45A2
	MELLS AND BABINGTON	21/49	45A3
	Mells Quarry	21/51	45B2
	MELLS ROAD	21/49	45A2
	MELVERLEY		98B1
	Melyn Colly	55/19	139B1
	MELYNCOURT HALT	47/4	162C4
	Melyncourt West S.B.	47/3	162C3
	Mendalgief Sidings	38/44	152D2
	Mendip Mountain Quarry		22C6
	Mendip Paper Mills	16/36	22C3
	MENHENIOT	11/13	6B6
	MEOLE BRACE		98C5
	Meole Brace Junction		99D1
	Mercantile Colly	51/53	153C5
	Merchants Dock Siding	19/37	24A2
*	Merchants Road Siding	19/37	24A2
*	Merchants Venturer Siding	19/37	24A2
	Merehead Quarry	16/41	45B2
	Merehead Quarry Junction	16/41	45B2
	Merllyn Crossing		109C1
	Mersey Ironworks		90D2
	Mersey Junction S.B.		90D5
	Methrose Siding	11/31	4D3
	MERTHYR		168B1
	Merthyr Dare Colly		165B2
	Merthyr High Street Goods		168B1
	Merthyr Junction S.B.		168D2

Merthyr Llantwit Colly (Blaenavon)	51/51	153B2
Merthyr Low Level Loop Junction		168D2
Merthyr Plymouth St. Goods		168C1
* Merthyr Rhondda Colly		?
* MERTHYR ROAD (V. of N.)		164B4
Merthyr Road G.F. (Cardiff)		174D6
Merthyr Tunnel Junction S.B.		168D4
MERTHYR TYDFIL		168B1
MERTHYR VALE		170A3
Merthyr Vale Colly		169D3
Merthyr Vale Junction S.B.		170B3
Metropolitan Junction S.B.		39C6
MICKLETON HALT	28/12	62C5
MICKLE TRAFFORD		91B6
Micklewood S.B.	63/2	100B1
Middle Amman Colly	54/32	131A5
Middle Connection S.B. (Newport)	38/44	152A1
Middle Duffryn S.B.	47/61	165D6
Middle Fan Pit	46/43	158C6
Middle Forge (Lydney)	37/9	53C3
Middle Mill Crossing		116A6
Middle Pit (Dinas Rhondda)		159D4
Middle Pit (Radstock)	18/10	—
Middleton Siding (Bristol Ferry)		140B4
Middleton Siding (Ludlow)	63/34	101B3
MIDDLETOWN		98C1
MIDDLETOWN HILLS		98C1
Middleway Bridge Crossing	11/26	5C1
MIDFORD (S & D)	18/15	—
MIDFORD HALT (GWR)	21/53	27C4
MIDGHAM	23/26	32D1
Midland Bridge Road Goods (Bath)	18/1	—
Midland Junction (Bristol)	19/16	24B4
MIDSOMER NORTON & WELTON (GWR)	21/46	27D2
MIDSOMER NORTON & WELTON (S & D)	18/11	—
Mierystock Siding	37/43	54A1
MILCOTE	28/26	62A6
* MILCOTE & WESTON	28/26	62A6
Mile End Siding (Landore)	55/10	136C3
MILFORD HAVEN	58/19	126A1
MILFORD HAVEN (Neyland)	58/12	126C2
* MILFORD, NEW (Neyland)	58/12	126C1
* MILFORD, OLD (Milford Haven)	58/19	126A1
MILFORD ROAD	58/15	124B2
Milfraen Colly	41/19	—
* Milfraen Hill Colly	41/19	—
MILKWALL	37/40	53C3
MILLBAY (PLYMOUTH)	12/17	8C4
Millbay Crossing	12/16	8D4
Millbay Docks	12/16	8D4
Millbrook Colly		?
Millbrook Works (Landore)	55/10	136A2
Milldown Siding	18/19	—
Millfield Siding		74D6
Mill Lane Crossing S.B.	24/37	34C1
Mill Pit	49/46	143A4
Millstream Junction (Gloucester)	35/7	56C4
Millstream Junction (Oxford)	27/13	68C5
MILL STREET, NEWPORT	38/64	152A3
Mill Street Crossing (Aberdare)	47/27	165C1
Mill Street Goods (Trecynon)	47/20	165A3
MILL STREET PLATFORM (Aberdare)	47/25	165C1
Milltown Viaduct S.B.	11/8	6C1
Milton Aircraft Factory	23/44	30B4
Milton S.B.	23/5	30A2
MILTON HALT (Adderbury)	28/33	84D3
Milton Trading Estate	23/44	30B4
MILVERTON	15/22	15A5
MINEHEAD	15/23	17A1
Minehead Branch Junction	15/14	20D1
Mine Kiln Siding	39/24	182B5
Mine Pits		167B3
Minera Limeworks		93C1
Minera Mineral Branch Junction		93C1
Minera Mines Siding		93C2
Mineral Loop Junction (Frome)	21/28	45D6
Mines Royal Works	56/44	139B3
MINETY	20/35	59D4
MINETY AND ASHTON KEYNES	20/35	59D4
MINFFORDD		110A5
Minions	11/36	6C3
MINSTERLEY		98D1
Miskin Colly (Mountain Ash)	47/70	170B1
Miskin Crossing S.B. (Llantrisant)	44/17	146C1
MITCHELDEAN ROAD	36/33	105C4
MITCHELL AND NEWLYN HALT	10/31	3B1
MITHIAN HALT	10/30	2D5
Mitre Bridge Junction	25/25	—
Moat Hall Colly		98D4
MOAT LANE	59/32	116D5
MOAT LANE JUNCTION		116D6
Moderator Sidings S.B.		152A3
* Moelferna Quarry		112C4
Moelgilau Colly	51/14	157A3
Moelygest Quarry Siding		109B2
Moffats Level	51/8	156C2
* Moggeridge's Siding		184A6
Mold Road Crossing		91D2
Molinnis Crossing	11/23	3B6
MOLLAND	15/20	18D3
MOLLINGTON		91B4
Mollington Street (Birkenhead)		90C4
Mon and Cwm Colly		177B5
* Monachdy Colly		171B1
* Monachty Colly		171B1
Mond Loop (GWR)	55/50	138B5
Mond Nickel Works (GWR)	55/50	138D5
Mond Siding (Mid)	53/67	—
Monk & Newell Siding		94A4
* Monkey Island Sidings	43/72	150B5
MONKS FERRY		90B5
Monks Meadow	35/17	56C1
Monksmoor Bridge S.B.		11A3
Monksmoor Siding	14/7	11A3
Monks Quarry Siding	40/19	182D1
MONKS RISBOROUGH	26/34	87A5
MONKS RISBOROUGH & WHITELEAF H.	26/34	87A5
MONKTON AND CAME HALT	17/3	41D6
MONKTON COMBE	21/53	27B4
MONMORE GREEN (LNWR)	31/11	—
MONMOUTH MAY HILL	36/24	53B1
MONMOUTH TROY	36/24	53B1
Monmouthshire Bank S.B.	38/44	152A1
Monsanto Siding (Newport)	38/34	151C6
Monsanto Siding (Trevor)		94C1
MONTACUTE	17/15	43D3
MONTGOMERY		118D3
MONTPELIER	19/66	23C4
Monway Siding	31/16	75A5
Moodys Graigola Colly		—
Moons Hill Quarry Siding		45B1
MOORE		88B3
Moore's Siding	12/28	—
Moortown Colly	55/18	139B1
Moorewood S.B.	18/12	—
MOORFIELDS	63/25	104B4
Moorfields Junction S.B.	63/25	104B4
MOORHAMPTON	63/42	—
* Moorland Road Siding		149B5
Moor Lane (Brierley Hill)	31/45	76C2
Moor Lane Crossing (Portishead)		23C1
Moors Lane S.B. (Cardiff)		149C1
MOOR STREET, BIRMINGHAM	30/1	80B1
MOORSWATER	11/37	6B5
MORDEN		113C4
MOREBATH	15/21	15B1
MOREBATH JUNCTION HALT	15/21	15B1

	MOREDON HALT	22/5	29B2
	Moredon Power Station	22/5	29B2
	MORETON (Moreton in Marsh)	28/13	64C2
	MORETON (Moreton on Lugg)		104B2
*	Moreton (Shropshire)		95D3
	Moreton Colly (Gardden Lodge)		94D5
	Moreton Colly (Saundersfoot)	58/28	124C6
	Moreton Colly (Weston Rhyn)		95B2
	Moreton Cutting S.B.	23/14	31C5
	Moreton Hall Colly		95B1
	MORETONHAMPSTEAD	14/40	14A2
	MORETON IN MARSH	28/13	64C2
*	MORETON IN THE MARSH	28/13	64C2
	MORETON ON LUGG	63/14	104B2
	Morfa Colly (Margam)	50/54	142C2
	Morfa Copper Works (Landore)	55/25	136B3
	MORFA CROSSING HALT (Margam)	50/48	141D5
	Morfa Junction S.B. (Llanelly)	57/22	134D4
	MORFA MAWDDACH		111D2
	Morfa Moors Siding (Margam)	50/61	142D3
	Morfa Siding (Harlech)		109D3
*	Morfa Siding (Swansea)		136B2
	Morlais Colly	55/37	133C6
	Morlais Junction East	55/38	133C6
	Morlais Junction South	55/37	133C6
	Morlais Tin Works	55/35	133C5
	Morlais Tunnel Junction (nr. Pant)		166B3
*	Morlais Vale Colly	54/50	—
	Morpeth Dock Goods		90A5
	MORRIS COWLEY	27/19	67D5
	MORRISTON EAST (Mid)	53/39	—
	MORRISTON WEST (GWR)	55/27	138C3
	Morriston Junction	55/28	138C3
*	Morriston Junction (Mid)	53/42	—
	MORTIMER	23/43	50A6
	MORTON PINKEY	29/10	—
	Moseley Green Sidings	37/22	54C2
	Moseley Green Tunnel Van Siding	37/21	54D2
	MOSS AND PENTRE HALT		—
*	Moss Junction		93A1
	MOSS PLATFORM		93A1
	Moss Quarry		93B1
	Moss Siding S.B.		93A1
	Moss Valley Junction		93D5
	MOULSFORD	23/15	31D6
	Moulsford River Bridge S.B.	23/15	31D6
*	Mount Colly	54/38	131B3
	MOUNTAIN ASH CARDIFF ROAD (GWR)	47/67	170D1
	MOUNTAIN ASH OXFORD ST (TV)	47/67	170D1
	Mountain Branch Junction (Cross Hands)	54/3	131A3
	Mountain Colly (Gorseinon)	54/18	—
*	Mountain Engine Shed	54/32	131A1
*	Mountain Incline	54/33	131A2
	Mountain Level (Cwmgorse)		131B6
	Mountain Level (Cyfarthfa)		168B1
	Mountain Pit (Llwydcoed)		164A6
	Mount Colly (Ammanford)		131B4
	Mount Gould Junction	12/10	8C6
	MOUNT GOULD AND TOTHILL HALT	12/21	8C6
	MOUNT HAWKE HALT	10/30	2A1
	MOUNT STREET, BRECON	52/16	122B2
*	Mount Stuart Dry Docks (Cardiff)	43/76	150A3
	Mousehole Sidings G.F.	25/15	39D3
	Moy Road Siding		149A4
	MUCH WENLOCK	32/31	69D2
	MUMBLES ROAD	54/28	—
	MUTLEY	12/7	8C4
	Mwrwg Vale Colly	55/35	133C5
	Mwyndy Iron Works	49/81	161D4
	Mwyndy Junction S.B.	44/11	145C4
	Mwyndy Siding	49/82	161D4
	Mynachdy Colly		171A1
*	Mynyadyganey		133B3
	Mynydd Bach Colly (Cwmfelin)	55/8	135B3
	Mynydd Bach Colly (Gwys)	53/28	—
	Mynydd Bach-y-Glo S.B.	55/5	135C1
	Mynydd Isllwyn Colly	40/19	182D1
	Mynydd Maen Colly	47/109	182C5
	Mynydd Mawr Loop Junction	57/13	134C2
	Mynydd Mawr Stages	57/13	134D2
	Mynydd Newydd Colly (Landore)	55/10	135C2
	Mynydd Newydd Colly (Llangyfelach)	55/42	138B2
	Mynydd Selen Colly	57/54	133C4
*	Mynyddycaeran Siding		?
	Mynydd y Gareg	57/34	133B2
*	Mynyddellyganey		133B3
	Myrtle Hill Junction S.B.	58/9	129B1
	N. & B. Junction S.B.	47 v. 52/1 & 56/49	139A6
	Naas Crossing (Gloucester)	35/1	55D3
	Naas Crossing (Lydney)	36/16	53D5
	Nagersfield Works		76D1
	NAILBRIDGE HALT	37/29	54A2
	NAILSEA	16/31	21A5
	NAILSEA AND BACKWELL	16/31	21A5
	Nailsea Brickworks S.B.	16/30	21A5
	Nailsea Colly	16/30	21A5
*	Nailsea Pond	16/30	21A5
	NAILSWORTH	20/56	—
	NANCEGOLLAN	10/26	1D4
	Nanpean Siding	11/32	4C2
	NANSTALLON	11/34	
	Nant Colly		93B4
	Nantcyff Siding		115B3
	Nantdyrus Colly	46/7	158C2
	NANTEWLAETH COLLY HALT	51/44	155C3
	Nantfedw Colly		?
	NANTGAREDIG	58/42	
	Nantgarw Branch Junction		173D2
	Nantgarw Colly		173B2
	NANTGARW HALT HIGH LEVEL		173B3
	NANTGARW HALT LOW LEVEL		173C3
	Nantgarw S.B. (Rhymney Rly)		173C3
	Nantgwyn Colly (Cwmllynfell)	53/30	—
	Nantgwyn Colly (Penygraig)	49/56	159D3
	Nanthir Colly	49/27	156B5
	Nant-Llesg Pit		167B4
	Nantmawr		119A2
	Nantmawr Branch Junction		119B2
	Nantmawr Junction		119D3
	Nantmelyn Colly (Bwllfa)	47/32	165B2
	Nantmelyn Pit (Rhymney)		167A5
	NANTMELYN PLATFORM	47/32	165B1
	Nant Rhondda Colly	49/55	159C2
	Nantricket Siding	54/49	131B6
	Nantwen S.B.		169D5
	NANTWICH	32/43	97A5
	Nant y bar Colly		155D1
	NANTYBWCH	41/6	166B5
	NANTYCAFN COLLY HALT		132C4
	Nantyderris Colly		158C2
	NANTYDERRY	39/3	108C2
*	NANTYDERRY & GOITRE	39/3	108C3
	Nanty dyrus Colly		158C2
*	Nantydyrus & Ynyswen	46/9	158C2
	NANTYFFYLLON	49/2	156B2
	Nantyffyn S.B.		169B4
	Nantygasseg Siding	54/49	131C6
	NANTYGLO	40/51	175C6
	Nantyglo Crossing	40/50	175C6
	Nantyglo Deep Pit	40/48	175C5
	Nantyglo Ironworks	40/48	175C6
	Nantyglo Junction	40/50	175C6
	Nantyglo Slope Colly (Brynmawr)	41/13	175C6
	NANTYMOEL	49/34	160A2
*	Nantymyn Lead Mines Siding	59/4	130A6
	NANTYROWEN		114D3
	Nantywrach Siding	54/34	131A3

NARBERTH	58/29	124A6
NARBERTH ROAD	58/7	123D5
Narroways Hill Junction	19/60	23A1
National Aberthaw Lime Works		144C2
National Colly	46/49	159C5
Naval Colly (Penygraig)	49/57	159D3
Naval Colly Junction (Dinas Rhondda)	46/27	159D4
Naval Ely Colly (Penygraig)	49/57	159D3
Naval Sidings S.B. (Penygraig)	49/57	159D3
Navigation Colly (Bedwas)	42/44	179C6
Navigation Colly (Blaenavon)		?
Navigation Colly (Crumlin)	40/20	178A6
Navigation Colly (Mountain Ash)		170D2
NAVIGATION HOUSE		171B2
N.E. Junction S.B. (Cardiff)	43/93	149D6
* Neachley Siding		69C6
NEATH ABBEY	56/44	139B3
Neath Abbey Colly	56/47	139B4
Neath Abbey Ironworks	55/20	139A4
Neath Abbey Wharves	56/40	139D3
Neath and Brecon Junction S.B.	47/v	139A1
Neath Branch Junction		139D4
NEATH BRIDGE STREET	47/v, 52/1 & 56/49	139A6
NEATH CANAL BRIDGE	50/3	139B5
NEATH CANALSIDE	50/3	139B5
Neath Canalside G.F. (Neath Jcn)	50/10	139D5
Neath East Beat G.F.	50/4	139B6
Neath Engine Shed S.B.	50/5	139D5
NEATH GENERAL	50/1	139B6
Neath Harbour Junction	50/7	140A4
Neath Junction S.B. (R.S.B.)	50/8	139D4
Neath Junction S.B. (V o N)	47/v	139A6
Neath Loop Junction (Dynevor)	55/48 & 56/41	139D6
Neath Loop Junction (Neath Gen.)	50/1	139A6
NEATH LOW LEVEL	47/v, 52/1 & 56/49	139A6
Neath Merthyr Colly	47/2	153A4
Neath River Bridge Sidings	56/42	139D5
NEATH RIVERSIDE	47/v, 52/1 & 56/49	139A6
NEATH ROAD, MAESTEG	51/4	156C2
Neath Yard S.B.	47/v & 52/1	139A6
* Nebo Colly	46/19	159B2
Neen Lane Crossing		72C2
NEEN SOLLARS	33/23	72D2
Nell Bridge Quarry Siding	27/2	84D4
NELSON (Glam.)		170D6
NELSON AND LLANCAIACH	47/84	170C5
* Nelson Bog	47/88	171A6
Nelson Brick Yard Siding (Churchway)	37/27	54A4
Nelson East Siding (Nelson & L.)	47/88	170D6
NESSCLIFF		98B2
NESSCLIFF AND PENTRE		98B2
NESCLIFF CAMP		98A2
Neston Colly		89D2
NESTON SOUTH		89D3
Netham Quarries S.B. (Clifton Bridge)	19/31	25C6
Netham Siding (Bristol)	19/20	24B6
Netherend Colly	31/27	77B3
NETHERHOPE HALT	36/29	52B5
NETHERTON	31/41	76B4
Netherton Basin	31/52	76C5
Netherton Ironworks		76B4
Netherton Junction S.B.	31/41	76B4
Netherton Sidings S.B.	31/41	76B4
Netley Crossing		4B4
Nettlefolds Branch	38/28	152B4
Nettlefolds Branch Junction	38/17	152A5
Nettlefolds Siding (Bassaleg)	42/52	184D2
Neutral Mile	38/46	152C3
Nevilles Dock Railway	57/16	134C2
New Berthlwyd Colly		—
New Black Vein Colly	41/45	180B4
New Blaengarw Colly		156B6
New Blaenhirwaun Colly (Cross. Hands)	57/50	133A5
New Blaenhirwaun Colly (Llanharan)		145A3

* Newbold		64A4
New Bowson Colly	37/27	54A4
New Braichy Cymmer Colly		156C6
NEWBRIDGE (Crumlin)	40/22	178B6
NEWBRIDGE (Pontypridd)	46/59	172C2
* New Bridge Colly (Bromley)		76B2
Newbridge Colly (Pontypridd	46/59	172B4
Newbridge Colly Sdgs (Crumlin)	47/99	178B6
NEWBRIDGE-ON-WYE	59/27	120D4
Newbridge Works (Interchange Sdgs)		172B5
New Brithdir Colly	42/14	177A2
* New British Coal Siding		94C3
New British Ironworks (Acrefair)		94C2
New British Pit (Llynclys)		117A6
New British Rhondda Colly	47/12	163C4
New Bromley Colly		76B2
New Brook Colly	53/31	—
New Broughton Colly		93C4
New Bryncethin Colly	49/23	143C6
New Brynmally Colly		93A4
New Buell Siding	11/30	4B2
Newburn P.A.D. Sidings	20/12	30D1
NEWBURY	23/21	49A3
Newbury Colly (Mells Road)	21/51	45A2
NEWBURY RACECOURSE	23/22	49A4
NEWBURY WEST FIELDS HALT	23/40	49A3
New Caepontbren Colly	57/39	133B4
* New Caepontben Colly (Tymaen)	51/26	154B3
New Carpella Sidings	11/32	4D2
New Carway Colly	57/39	133B3
NEWCASTLE EMLYN	58/41	128B1
New Caudledown Siding	11/33	4B4
New Cawdor Colly	54/46	131D4
New Celtic Colly	51/14	157A2
New Church Colly	42/31	178B1
New Clydach Colly	41/19	—
New Consolidated Siding	11/25	4A6
New Cross Hands Colly	57/50	133A6
New Cut Drawbridge S.B.	56/4	137B2
New Cwmgorse Colly	54/49	131B6
New Cwmmawr Colly	57/35	133A3
* New Cwmsaebren Colly		158C2
New Cymmer Colly	46/28	159D5
New Cynon Colly	51/30	153D6
NEW DALE HALT	32/39	69B3
* New Darran Ddu Colly		?
New Diamond Colly	53/30	—
New Dock Brickworks	44/59	148B6
New Dolcoath Siding		1B6
New Drift (Hirwaun)		164C4
New Drive Crossing		118A3
New Duffryn Colly	42/3	167C5
New Dunvant Colly	54/25	—
New Dynant Colly	57/35	133A3
New Eagle Brickworks	51/26	154B4
New Elba Colly	54/55	—
New Elled Colly	39/17	182B5
Newell's Siding		113C1
New Engine Colly (Forest of Dean)	37/21	54C2
New Engine Yard (Coalpit Heath)	20/49	26D1
NEWENT	33/20	60D4
New Fancy Colly (F. o D.)	37/22	54C2
New Fancy Colly (S. & W.)	37/22	54C2
New Fancy Junction	37/22	54C2
New Fancy (Moseley Green) Sidings	37/22	54C2
New Florence Mine	15/20	18B2
New Forest Colly (Blaenavon)	51/40	153B2
New Forest Colly (Ynysygeinon)	53/20	—
New Frome Quarry	21/27	45B3
New Gelligaer Colly		170C6
New Glanravon Colly	51/54	153B5
New Glyncorrwg Colly	51/37	155C4
New Glynea Colly	55/31	133D5
New Gored Merthyr Colly	47/4	162C3

New Gorseinon Colly	55/4	135B1
New Gorsllan Colly	55/42	138B2
New Gorwydd Colly	55/4	135C1
New Gunheath Siding	11/33	4C4
NEW HADLEY HALT	32/6	69D6
* New Hafod Van Colly		182A2
* New Hafod Yard		136C2
New Halwyn Siding	11/28	4B1
Newham Branch Junction	10/11	2A5
Newham Goods	10/18	2A3
New Hawne Colly		77B5
New Henllys Colly	53/52	—
* New Hoskyn Waen		—
New Hulks Pit		?
NEW INN BRIDGE HALT	58/31	123A4
NEWLAND (Mon)	37/39	53B2
NEWLAND HALT (Worcs)	33/8	61C3
Newlands Colly		143A1
NEWLANDS HALT	49/41	143A1
Newlands Junction		142C5
Newlands Loop Junction		142C4
New Lodge Brickworks	57/48	134A4
New Lych Colly	54/50	—
New Marchowell Colly	53/15	—
New Meledor Siding	11/28	4C1
New Melyn Colly	55/19	139B1
NEW MILFORD	58/12	126C2
New Mill Crossing (Brynmenyn)	49/22	157C4
New Mills Works (Lydney)	37/9	53C3
New Mountain Level		156D5
NEWNHAM (Grange Court)	36/20	53B5
NEWNHAM (Tenbury Wells)	33/23	101D6
NEWNHAM BRIDGE	33/23	101D6
New Park Siding (Llantrisant)	49/73	145C4
New Park Siding (Weymouth)	17/2	42C3
NEW PASSAGE	19/52	23A3
NEW PASSAGE HALT	19/52	23A3
NEW PASSAGE PIER	19/52	23A3
* New Penlan Colly	54/52	—
* New Penyfan Colly		177B6
Newplace Colly	42/31	178B2
New Plas Colly	42/32	178B2
New Pool Colly	57/48	134A4
NEWPORT (Salop)	32/49	—
Newport Alexandra Dock Junction	38/7	152A1
Newport Alpha Steel Siding		151C6
Newport B.A.C. Siding	38/34	151D6
Newport Ballast Crossing S.B.	38/49	152C3
Newport Bell Ferry Dock Siding	38/34	151C6
Newport Bellport	38/34	151C6
Newport Bolt Street	38/58	152C3
Newport Cardiff Road Lines	38/46	152C3
Newport Channel Dry Dock	38/33	151C6
Newport Clarence Wharf	38/28	152B4
Newport Corporation Road S.B.	38/32	152D5
NEWPORT COURTYBELLA		152C2
Newport Courtybella Crossing	38/47	152C3
Newport Courtybella Junction	38/46	152C2
Newport Crindau	38/64	184B4
Newport Cross Street Crossing	38/58	152B3
NEWPORT DOCK STREET	38/58	152B4
Newport East Dock Junction	38/58	152B4
Newport Eastern Dry Dock	38/33	151C6
Newport Eastern Valleys Sdgs	38/44	152D2
Newport East Mendalgief	38/43	152D3
Newport East Usk Junction	38/17	152B6
Newport East Usk Wharf	38/28	152B4
Newport Ebbw Junction	38/3	152D2
Newport Gaer Junction	38/7	152C2
Newport Gaer Loop S.B.	38/38	152D1
Newport George Street Junction	38/58	152B4
Newport Godfrey Road Sidings	38/12	152A2
Newport Great Western Wharf	38/28	152B5
Newport Grenville Street Junction	38/58	152B4
Newport Healey & Peart	38/17	152B6
Newport Herberts Siding	38/13	184C5
NEWPORT HIGH STREET	38/10	152A2
Newport Iron Gates Crossing	38/58	152C3
Newport Llanarth Street Junction	38/58	152B3
Newport Loco Yard Junction	38/58	152C4
Newport Low Level Loop	38/44	152A1
Newport Lysaghts G.F.	38/31	152D5
Newport Maesglas Bank	38/37	152A1
Newport Maesglas Junction	38/38	152A1
Newport Maesglas Sidings	38/36	152A1
Newport Maindee Junctions	38/13	152A4
NEWPORT MARSHES TURNPIKE GATE		152A3
Newport Mendalgief Sidings	38/44	152D2
Newport Middle Connection S.B.	38/44	152A1
NEWPORT MILL STREET	38/64	152A3
Newport Moderator Sidings	38/63	152A3
Newport Monmouthshire Bank	38/44	152A1
Newport Monsanto Siding	38/34	151C6
Newport Nettlefolds Branch	38/28	152B5
Newport Nettlefolds Branch Jcn	38/17	152A5
Newport Neutral Mile	38/46	152C3
Newport Old Dock	38/53	152C4
Newport Orb Steelworks	38/31	152D5
Newport Palmers Siding	38/14	152A4
Newport Park Junction	38/36	152D1
Newport Park Mile	38/37	152B1
Newport Park Siding	38/37	152B2
Newport Pill Bank Junction	38/46	152C3
Newport Pill Engine Shed	38/52	152D3
Newport Pillgwenlly Crossing	38/49	152C4
Newport Quiet Woman's Row	38/49	152C4
NEWPORT ROAD (Pontypool Road)	39/4	183A6
Newport Road Goods (Cardiff)	46/113	149A5
Newport Rolling Bridge Junction		151C6
Newport Salutation Junction	38/46	152B3
Newport Station Yard Jcn S.B.	38/58	152B4
Newport Temple Street Footbridge	38/51	152C3
Newport Town Dock	38/53	152C4
Newport Tredegar Estates	38/49	152D4
Newport Tunnel Yard	38/64	152A3
Newport Uskmouth	38/35	151D6
Newport Waterloo Junction	38/46	152C2
Newport Waterloo Loop	38/7	152A1
* Newport Western Valleys Junction		152A2
Newport West Mendalgief	38/44	152D2
Newport Whiteheads Steelworks	38/48	152C3
New Potlid Level	37/47	54A2
New Quarry Mawr Siding	57/55	133C4
NEWQUAY	11/19	3A1
Newquay Harbour	11/19	3A1
Newquay Junction	11/19	3A1
NEW QUAY ROAD	58/36	128B4
Newquay Siding (Burgotha)	11/28	4D1
NEW RADNOR	63/37	103A1
New Regulator Pit		?
* New Rhoswen Colly		—
New Rock Colly (Blackwood)	41/36	—
New Rock Colly (S. & D. Rly)	18/11	—
New Rockwood Colly		173C3
New Rod Mill (Cardiff)	43/66	150D5
New Slope Colly		181B5
New Sun Colly		176A6
New Tir Philkins Colly		178C4
NEWTON	14/13	14C1
* Newton S.B. (Kelston)	20/50	—
NEWTON ABBOT	14/13	14C1
Newton Abbot Clay Sidings	14/42	14B1
Newton Abbot Goods	14/42	14B1
Newton Noyes	58/19	126B3
NEWTOWN		116B5
Newtown (Cardiff)		149C4
New Trane Pit	49/71	160D4
NEW TREDEGAR	42/17	177A2

NEW TREDEGAR AND TIRPHILL	42/16	176D1
NEW TREDEGAR AND WHITE ROSE	42/16	176D1
New Tredegar Colly	42/13	167D6
NEW TREDEGAR COLLY HALT	42/11	176D1
New Tredegar Junction	42/14	177A2
New Trerice Siding	11/29	4B1
New Tylerybont Siding		166B3
New Waenycoed Colly	53/19	—
New Wernddu Colly	53/15	135A6
New Yard Works (Oakengates)		70A5
NEYLAND	58/12	126C2
Nibley Colly	20/50	26D1
NIGHTINGALE VALLEY HALT	19/31	25D6
NINE MILE POINT	41/42	180B3
Nine Mile Point Colly	41/41	180B2
NINIAN PARK PLATFORM		149C2
Nixons Crossing S.B. (T.V.)	47/67	170D2
Nixons Navigation S.B. (GWR)	47/67	170D2
Nobels Siding (Trimsaran Junction)	57/44	133B2
Norchard Colly	37/9	53C3
Norcot Siding	24/1	33A1
North Aberthaw Limeworks	44/23	144C5
NORTH ACTON	26/31	39B1
* North Acton Filling Factory	26/36	38A2
NORTH ACTON HALT	25/22 & 26/31	38A2
North Acton Junction	26/31	38A2
North Amman Colly	54/46	131D4
North Bank (Port Talbot)		141B3
North Blaina Colly	40/52	175D6
North Crofty	10/27	1B6
North Crofty Junction	10/11	1C6
North Dock Branch Jcn (Swansea)	55/21	137A2
North Dock Drawbridge S.B.	56/4	137B2
North Dock Goods (Swansea)	53/1	137A2
North Dock S.B. (Llanelly)	57/13	134C2
North Dock S.B. (Swansea)	56/3	137B2
North Duffryn Colly		169B2
North Dunraven Colly	46/58	158A1
NORTH END (SMJ)	29/7	—
North End Colly	51/53	153C5
* North End No. 2 Colly Siding		153D3
Northern Extension Junction	49/2	156B1
* Northern Loop G.F. (Llantrisant Common)	49/75	161C1
Northern Sidings (Pontypool Road)	39/6	183B6
Northern United Colly	37/28	54A4
Northey's Siding	12/21	8D5
NORTHFIELD	34/8	—
Northfield Road Crossing	31/52	76C5
Northfield Siding (Brixham)	14/36	12C5
NORTH FILTON PLATFORM	19/99	23B4
North Fork (Croes Newydd)		93D6
North Gate Road Crossing	16/15	19B5
North Griffin Colly	40/52	175D6
North Hengoed Colly		178C2
North Kilmar		6B3
* North Llangynog Lead Mine		117A1
North Llantwit Colly		161B4
NORTHOLT	26/16	36B4
NORTHOLT JUNCTION	26/15	36B4
North Parade Crossing	10/27	1B6
* North Pole Depot		39A5
North Pole Junction	25/25	39B4
North Pool Siding	10/28	1A5
North Quay (Plymouth)	12/18	8D5
NORTH RHONDDA COLLY HALT	51/48	155A4
North Risca Black Vein Colly	41/45	180A3
NORTH ROAD, PLYMOUTH	12/7	8C4
North Poskear	10/27	1B6
North Savernake Siding	22/12	48C4
North Somerset Junction	19/14	24B5
North's Collieries S.B. (Maesteg)	51/8	156C2
North's Colly S.B. (Aberbeeg)	40/13	182C1
North's Navigation Railway	51/8	156B2
* Norths Navigation Colly (Tondu)		143D4

North Town Level Crossing S.B.	24/38	34C3
North Wales Junction		99C3
North Wales Power Siding		94B4
Northway G.F.	34/2	—
North Wingfield Colly		177D1
NORTHWOOD HALT	32/25	72C4
Northwood Street Carriage Sdgs	31/26	80B5
NORTON		88B3
Norton Cawdor Colly		131A5
NORTON FITZWARREN	15/14	15B6
Norton Hill Colly	18/11	—
NORTON JUNCTION (Worcs)	33/15	61B5
Norton Siding (Norton Fitizwarren)	15/26	15B6
Norton Siding (Norton Jcn)	33/15	61B5
Noss Siding	14/35	12D3
NOTGROVE	28/29	57A4
NOTGROVE AND WESTFIELD	28/29	57A4
NOTTAGE HALT	50/79	143D1
NOTTING HILL	25/24	38B5
Nova Scotia Place Crossing	19/37	24A2
Noyadd Colly (Garnant)	54/44	131C4
Noyadd Crossing (Garnant)	54/43	131C3
Noyadd Sidings (Elan Valley)	59/28	120B2
Nuneham S.B.	27/15	31A4
Nut Tree Wharf		119A4
Oak Brickworks Siding	39/23	182B5
Oakdale Colly	40/67	177D5
OAKDALE HALT	40/69	178A4
Oakdale S.B.	40/69	178A4
OAKENGATES (GWR)	32/6	70B4
OAKENGATES MARKET ST. (LNWR)	32/51	—
OAKENGATES WEST (GWR)	32/6	70B4
Oak Farm Siding	31/55	76A1
Oakfield Sidings S.B.	39/20	183C2
Oaklands Colly	51/52	153B2
OAKLE STREET	36/21	55C1
OAKSEY HALT	20/35	59D3
Oakwood Branch (Tufts Jcn)	37/10	54D1
Oakwood Colly (Cwmavon)	51/25	154B4
Oakwood Colly (Maesteg)	49/6	156D3
Oakwood Crossing (Port Talbot)	50/25	141B4
Oakwood Inn Crossing (Cwmavon)		154C3
Oakwood Iron Works (Cwmavon)		154B4
Oakwood Junction (Aberavon)	51/20	154D2
Oakwood Junction (Cwmavon)	51/28	154B4
Oakwood S.B. (Clifton Bridge)	19/30	25B5
Ocean & Taff Merthyr Colls S.B.	47/82	170C5
Ocean Colly (Abergwynfi)		155D5
Ocean Colly (Blaengarw)	49/28	156B6
Ocean Colly (Nantymoel)	49/34	160A3
Ocean Deep Navigation Colly	47/81	170B5
Ocean Navigation S.B.	47/81	170C5
Ocean Siding (Plymouth)	12/15	8B4
Oddingley	34/4	—
ODDINGTON HALT	27/28	
Oerffrwd Crossing		116A2
* Offenham Siding	28/6	62C3
OGBOURNE	22/8	48A4
Ogbourne St. Andrew	22/8	48A4
Ogilvie Colly Branch Junction		177B1
OGILVIE COLLY HALT		169B6
OGILVIE VILLAGE HALT		169C6
* Ogmore Centre Washery	49/39	160C1
* Ogmore Colliery		?
Ogmore Junction S.B.	49/12	143C4
OGMORE VALE	49/36	160B1
Oil Siding	11/33	4C4
Old Beam Siding	11/33	4B4
Old Black Vein Colly	41/45	180B4
OLDBURY	31/35	79B2
OLDBURY AND LANGLEY GREEN	31/34	79C3
Oldbury Junction S.B.	31/34	79B3
Old Carpella Siding	11/32	4C2

Old Carway Colly	57/40	133B3	
Old Castle Crossing S.B.	57/12	134C1	
Old Castle Works	57/57	134C1	
Old Cawdor Colly		131B5	
Old Chapel Crossing		115C5	
* Old Chester Road Siding		?	
Old Craigola Colly		—	
Old Cymmer Colly		159D5	
Old Dark Lane Colly	32/11	70C5	
Old Dee Works		91D1	
* OLD DOCK HALT (Port Talbot)		141B3	
Old Dock Junction (Port Talbot)		141B4	
Old Dock S.B.'s (Newport)	38/53	152C4	
Old Down Siding	18/12	—	
Old Duffryn Colly (Cwmbach)	47/58	165C5	
Old Duffryn Colly (Rhymney)	42/1	167C4	
* Old Dunraven Siding	46/3	158C1	
Old Ends Crossing	20/46	—	
OLDFIELD PARK	21/5	27D4	
Old Forge Siding	42/56	180D2	
Old Furnace Colly	47/109	182C5	
* Old Glanmychyd Branch	49/84	161B2	
* Old Graigola	53/14	—	
OLD HILL	31/32	76D6	
Old Hill Goods	31/31	76D5	
* Old Hill Ironworks		76C5	
OLD HILL HIGH ST. HALT	31/52	76D5	
* Old Hill Siding		76C6	
Old Hill Wharf		76C5	
OLDLAND COMMON	20/48	—	
Old Lane Crossing		72B2	
Old Level Colly		76C3	
* Old Llanmorlais Colly	54/50	—	
* Old Llwyndu	53/14	—	
Old Lodge Ironworks (Llanelly)	57/15	134C2	
Old Lodge Ironworks (Oakengates)		70A6	
Old Main Colly		135A6	
OLD MILFORD	58/21	126A1	
Old Milford Branch Junction	58/15	124B2	
Old Mill Colly (Ystrad Mynach)		?	
Old Mill Siding (Wimberry)	37/16	54B1	
Old Mills Colly	21/45	27D2	
Oldminster Junction	37/1	58B2	
Old Moat Lane Crossing		116D5	
Oldnall Colly		77B3	
Old Oak Common	25/5	39B3	
Old Oak Common Loco Shed	25/8	39B2	
OLD OAK LANE HALT	26/31	39B1	
Old Park Colly (Pensnett)		76A2	
Old Park Ironworks (Stirchley)	32/41	70D5	
Old Park Siding (Stirchley)	32/52	—	
Old Pit (Radstock)	18/10	—	
Old Plas Colly	42/36	178B2	
Old Quay (Teignmouth)	14/16	14C5	
* Old Sea Lock Sidings (Cardiff)		150A4	
* Old Station Crossing (Moat Lane)	59/32	116D6	
OLD TOWN, STRATFORD	29/3	—	
Old Tunnel Colly		?	
Old Vobster Colly	21/27	45B2	
Old Waencoed Colly	53/18	—	
Old Warehouse Siding (Ynysybwl)		171B2	
Old Waterloo Colly	40/65	177D5	
Old Welton Colly	21/46	27D2	
* Old Windmill Siding		?	
Old Wood Colly	20/43	—	
OLDWOODS HALT		98A4	
Old Yard Sidings (Abertillery)	40/58	181D2	
OLD YNYSBWL HALT		171B1	
OLMARCH HALT	58/35	127B5	
OLTON	30/8	81A5	
OLYMPIA, KENSINGTON	25/27	38C5	
ONIBURY	63/6	101B2	
ONLLWYN	52/11	132B5	
Onllwyn No. 3 Colly		132C6	

Onslow Sidings	11/10	6A2	
Orb Steelworks	38/31	152D5	
ORESTON	12/28	—	
Oriental Colly		156C6	
OSWESTRY		96D5	
Oswestry Branch Junction		95D3	
Otters Pool Junction	37/6	54C5	
Overbridge Junction (Margam)	50/50	142A5	
Over Junction S.B. (Gloucester)	35/19	56A1	
* OVERPOOL		91A4	
Over Siding (Cattybrook)	19/53	23A4	
Over Sidings S.B. (Gloucester)	35/19	56A1	
OVERTON-ON-DEE		95C5	
OXFORD	27/10	68A5	
OXFORD (First Terminus)	27/12	68B5	
Oxford Banbury Road Junction	27/27	68A3	
Oxford Beckett St. Yard	27/10	68B5	
Oxford Engine Shed	27/8	68A5	
Oxford Gas Works	27/12	68B5	
Oxford Goods	27/10	68B5	
Oxford Hinksey Yards	27/13	68C5	
Oxford Millstream Junction	27/13	68C5	
Oxford North Junction	27/9	68D3	
OXFORD REWLEY ROAD	27/10	68A5	
OXFORD ROAD HALT	27/27	68A3	
Oxford Road Junction (Oxford)	27/27	68A3	
Oxford Road Junction (Reading)	24/36	33B3	
Oxford Road Junction (Yarnton)	27/25	68A1	
Oxford South End Yard	27/10	68B5	
Oxley Branch Junction	31/54	69D6	
Oxley North Junction	31/1	69D6	
Oxley Yards	31/1	74A3	
P. & T. Junction (Whitland)	58/8	125C6	
P. & T. Loop Junction	58/9	129B1	
P. C. & N. Junction	46/59	172C2	
Packers Siding	54/10	131B3	
Packington Crossing		78C5	
Padally Bwlch Pit		164C2	
PADDINGTON	25/17	39D5	
Paddington Goods	25/17	39D5	
Paddington New Yard	25/13	39D3	
Paddock Colly		70D1	
Padell y Bwlch Graig Colly		164D3	
* Padmores Siding	32/6	70A4	
Padmore Street Crossing	33/19	60C5	
PADSTOW	11/34	—	
Padworth Sidings	23/27	32D2	
PAIGNTON	14/37	12B5	
Painswick Road Crossing	35/2	—	
Palleg Colly	53/28	—	
* Palleg Sidings	53/48	—	
Palmers Siding	38/14	152A4	
PANDY (Dinas Rhondda)	46/27	159D4	
PANDY (Pontrilas)	63/24	107C2	
Pandy Crossing (Nelson & L.)		170C5	
Pandy Pit S.B. (Tonypandy)	46/25	159D4	
Pandy Treble Line Junction S.B.		159D4	
PANGBOURNE	23/16	32B3	
PANS LANE HALT	21/26	46B5	
PANT (Glamorgan)		167A1	
PANT (Shropshire)		119C5	
Pant Brick Works Sidings (Rhos)		94D4	
PANT HALT (Rhos)		94D4	
PANTEG	39/4	183D6	
PANTEG (Panteg & Griffithstown)	39/19	183C5	
Panteg & Coedygric Junction	39/5	183C5	
PANTEG AND GRIFFITHSTOWN	39/19	183C5	
Panteg Colly		?	
Panteg Goods Lines Junction	39/4	183A5	
Panteg Junction	39/4	183D6	
Panteg Steelworks S.B.	39/4	183C5	
Pant Glas Colly		164B2	
Panthowell Colly	57/48	134A3	

*	Penylan Engine Shed (Waterhall Jcn)			143A3
	Penylan Mine (Cwmbargoed)			167D2
	PENYRHEOL			173A4
	Penyrheol Colly (Newbridge)			?
	Pen-yr-heolgerig Quarry			168B3
	Penyrhiw Colly		46/59	172C4
	Pen y Val Hospital Siding		39/1	108A1
	Pen y waun			164A6
	Penywern Junction		41/1	—
	PENZANCE		10/1	1D1
	PEPLOW		32/45	99D4
	Perham S.B.		22/17	51C1
	PERIVALE HALT		26/23	36C6
	PERRAN		10/39	2B2
	PERRANPORTH		10/30	2C5
	PERRANPORTH BEACH HALT		10/30	2C5
	PERRANWELL		10/39	2B2
	Perryfield Quarry			42D2
	Perry Wood Siding			60D6
	Perseverance Iron Works Siding		37/36	54B2
	PERSHORE		28/1	61C6
	PETERCHURCH		63/44	106C3
	PETERSTON		44/18	146D1
	Petfu Siding		18/29	—
	Pethicks Siding		13/4	10B6
	Pew Hill Siding		21/12	28C3
	PEWSEY		21/42	48D3
*	Pheasant Quarry		19/31	25C6
	Pheasant St. Crossing			60C5
*	Phillips Siding		59/24	121A4
*	Philog Siding		46/97	174C4
	Phipps Siding		37/21	54D2
	Phoenix Merthyr Colly			155D2
	Phoenix Mine (Cornwall)		11/36	6C3
	Phoenix Siding (Glam)			174B5
*	Phoenix Siding (Gurnos)		53/27	—
	PICKHILL HALT			92D4
	Pictors Siding		21/9	27A6
	Pidwellt Colly		42/5	167C5
	PILL		19/50	25B3
	Pill Bank Junction (Newport)		38/46	152C3
	Pill Crossing (Lostwithiel)			6B1
	Pill Engine Shed (Newport)		38/52	152D3
	Pillgwenlly Crossing S.B.		38/49	152C4
	Pillowell Colly		37/21	54D2
	PILNING HIGH LEVEL		19/52	23A3
	PILNING LOW LEVEL		19/52	23A3
*	Pilning West G.F.		19/51	23A3
	Pine End		37/38	54D5
	PINEWOOD HALT		23/37	49C6
	PINGED HALT		57/44	133C2
	Pinkwood S.B.		16/51	45D3
	Pinnock S.B.		11/27	6D2
	Pirton Sidings		34/4	—
	Pistill Branch		54/1	130C6
	Pitts Cleave Quarry		14/25	10B4
	Plaiscoed Colly			182C5
	Planet Colly			76B2
	Plantation Colly			?
	Plas Bach Colly (Pontyates)		57/39	133B3
	Plas Bach Crossing (Mountain Bch)		54/35	131A3
	Plas Bennion Colly			94A2
	Plas Bennion Crossing			94B2
	Plas Colly		42/32	178B2
	Plas Isaf Colly		55/34	133C5
	Plasissa Colly		55/35	133C5
	Plas Kynaston Colly			94C2
	Plas Madoc Junction			94B3
	Plas Madoc Loop Junction			94B2
	PLAS MARL		55/25	136A3
	PLAS POWER (GC)			—
	PLAS POWER (GWR)			93C4
	Plasycoed Colly		39/24	182C5
	PLAS Y COURT HALT			98C1
	Plas ynwern Siding			94C1
	Plas y Wern Junction			94B2
	PLEALEY ROAD			98D3
	Plessey Sidings		20/19	20B3
	Plough Junction (Aberavon)		51/15	141A4
	Plough Pit (Aberaman)			165C4
	PLOWDEN		63/33	100C3
	PLYM BRIDGE PLATFORM		14/29	7B5
	PLYMOUTH FRIARY		12/18	—
	Plymouth Ironworks (Merthyr)			168C5
	PLYMOUTH MILL BAY		12/17	8C4
	PLYMOUTH NORTH ROAD		12/17	8C4
	Plymouth Siding S.B. (Merthyr)			169C2
	Plymouth Street Goods (Merthyr)			168C1
	PLYMPTON		14/3	7B6
	PLYMSTOCK		12/28	8D6
	POCHIN PITS COLLY HALT		41/31	—
	Pochins Siding (St. Dennis Junction)		11/30	4A2
	Pint Quarry Sidings		37/41	54C1
	Poldice Tramway			2B1
	Polperro Tunnel S.B.		11/1	2A4
	Polwrath		11/36	6C3
	Pond Rock Siding		41/36	—
	Ponds Colly (Penar Branch)		40/63	177C5
	Ponds Colly (Rockwood)			173C3
	Pond Siding (Hirwaun)			164B2
	Ponkey Branch Junction			94B3
*	Ponkey Colly			94D4
	PONKEY CROSSING HALT			94D4
	Ponsandane S.B.		10/2	1D1
*	Ponsanooth Viaduct		10/39	2C2
	Pont Abernant y Felin Quarry		40/63	177C5
	Pontamman Siding		54/39	131B4
	PONTARDAWE		53/15	—
	Pontardawe Branch			138B5
	PONTARDDULAIS		54/11	131D2
	PONTARDULAIS		54/11	131D2
	PONTCYNON BRIDGE HALT			170D3
	PONTYCYNON HALT		47/76	170D3
	Pontcynon Junction		47/76	170D3
	Pontcysyllte Basin			94C1
	PONTDOLGOCH			116A3
	PONTESBURY			98D3
	Pont Hall Quarry Siding		40/29	180A1
	PONTHENRY		57/38	133A4
	PONTHIR		39/12	183D4
*	Ponthir Road Crossing (Cae Glas)			93C2
	Pontithel Siding (Three Cocks Jcn)		59/22	121B6
*	Pontithel Chemical Works (Moorhampton)		63/41	—
	Pont Lash Colly			131A2
	PONT LAWRENCE HALT		41/41	—
*	Pont-le-Bont Crossing			146C1
	PONTLLANFRAITH HIGH LEVEL		41/37	—
	PONTLLANFRAITH LOW LEVEL		47/93	178C3
	PONT LLANIO		58/35	127B6
	PONT LLIW		55/51	135A1
	PONTLOTTYN		42/6	167C5
	PONTLOTTYN COLLIERY HALT		42/7	167D5
	Pontlottyn South S.B.		42/8	167D5
*	Pont Meredith			?
	Pontneddfechan Mills			163A4
	PONTNEWYDD (Lower Pontnewydd)		39/11	183B3
	PONTNEWYDD (Upper Pontnewydd)		39/19	183B2
	PONTNEWYDD HALT (Glyn Abbey)		57/40	133B3
	PONTNEWYNYDD		39/17	182B6
	Pont Nichol Crossing		59/21	121C5
	PONTRHYDYFEN		51/29	154A4
	PONTRHYDYRUN		39/19	183A2
	PONTRHYDYRUN HALT		39/19	182A2
	Pontrhydyrun Tin Works Siding		39/11	183A2
	PONTRILAS		63/22	107C6
	PONTSARN (Merthyr)			166C2
	Portsarn Crossing S.B. (Peterston)		44/17	146C1
	Pont Shon Norton Junction			172A5

	Pritchard's Down Loop G.F.	56/30	137D6	Quiet Woman's Row	38/49	152C4
	Pritchard's Siding S.B.	56/21	137D2	Quinta Colly		95B1
	PROBUS AND LADOCK PLATFORM	11/2	3D3	QUINTREL DOWNS PLATFORM	11/21	3A2
	Probus S.B.	11/2	3D3	Quintrel Siding	11/21	3A2
	Provendor Stores (Didcot)	23/9	30B5			
	Providence Works		76D4	R & S.B. Junction S.B.	46/4	158B2
	Prowse's Crossing	14/32	10C5	Race Marsh Crossing	14/9	12D1
	Pudley Hill Colly		70B5	RADFORD AND TIMSBURY HALT	21/52	27C2
*	Pudley Hill Siding	32/51	—	RADIPOLE HALT	17/2	42B3
	Pugham Crossing	15/11	15D3	RADLEY	27/15	31A4
	Puleston Mill Siding		94A6	Radstock Branch Junction (Frome)	21/28	45D6
	Pulford Siding		92A4	Radstock Junction	18/9	27B2
	PULLABROOK HALT	14/40	14A1	RADSTOCK NORTH (S & D)	18/7	—
	Pullman Factory Siding	54/37	131B2	RADSTOCK WEST (GWR)	21/47	27B2
	Pumewart Colly	57/40	133B3	RADYR	46/86	174C2
	Pump House Siding	19/96	23A3	Radyr Branch Junction (Cardiff)		149C3
	PUNCHESTON	58/31	123A3	Radyr Quarry Junction	46/86	174C2
	Puriton R.O.F.	16/20	19B2	RAGLAN	36/23	108C4
	Purley Signals	23/16	32B3	Raglan Colly (Wern Tarw)	49/25	157D6
	PURTON	20/35	29B1	RAGLAN FOOTPATH	36/23	108C4
	Purton Common Crossing	20/35	29B1	RAGLAN ROAD CROSSING HALT	36/23	108C4
	PUXTON	16/27	21C3	Railway Terrace Siding	57/52	133A5
	PUXTON AND WORLE	16/27	21C3	Rainbow Hill Junction	33/16	60C6
	Puxton Siding	16/27	21B3	Rakes Colly		?
	Pwllandres Gas Siding	49/13	143D5	Ram Hill Pit	20/49	—
	Pwll Colly	57/39	134A5	Ramp Line Junction	50/50	142A5
	Pwllbach Colly	53/21	—	Ramrod Colly		79C1
	Pwllcarn Colly	49/27	156B5	Randlay Siding (Stirchley Branch)	32/41	70D5
	Pwllfaron Colly		163A1	* Randley Siding (Malins Lee)	32/52	—
	PWLL GLAS		116B2	Ranelagh Bridge Sidings (Paddington)	25/18	39D4
	Pwllgwaun S.B.	46/111	172B4	* Ranelagh Street Depot (Liverpool)		90B1
	PWLLHELI		109A1	Rangeworthy S.B.	20/43	—
	Pwllheli Granite Siding		110A4	Raslas Pit		167C3
	Pwll Hir Quarries		123A6	Rassa Tramway	40/1	175B3
	Pwllmawr Colly	53/7	—	Rassau Crossing	41/8	
	Pwllmelyn Siding	46/93	146C6	Ratgoed Quarry		113A4
	PWLL UCHAF, RHYMNEY	42/7	167C6	Rattery Mill Siding	14/9	12B1
	PWLL Y PANT		179D4	Rattery S.B.	14/9	12B1
	Pwll y Pant Quarry		179C3	Raven Central Coal Plant	54/43	131C3
	Pwll yr allt Colly	42/31	178B1	Raven Colliery	54/42	131C3
*	Pwllyrhebog Goods	46/55	159D3	Raven Crossing	54/42	131D3
	Pwllyrhebog Junction	46/55	159D3	RAVEN SQUARE		117D1
	PYLE (S & D)	18/29	—	Ravenstone Wood Junction	29/17	—
	PYLE (Glamorgan)	50/72	143B2	Raven Tin Plate Works	54/41	131A5
	Pyle and Blaina Ironworks		143A4	Rea Bridge S.B.	33/2	60A2
	Pyle Sand Siding	50/70	142D2	Reading Central Goods	24/35	33C4
	Pyle West Loop S.B.	50/71	143B2	Reading Engine Shed	24/2	33B3
	Pyle Hill Goods	19/7	24C3	READING GENERAL	24/5	33B4
	Pylle Limeworks Siding	18/29	—	Reading Junction (SEC)	24/9	33B5
				* Reading Loop Line Junction		33B3
	Quadruple Crossing S.B. (Cardiff)	43/67	150B3	Reading Oxford Road Junction	24/36	33B3
	Quakers Yard East Junction S.B.	47/79	170A4	READING SOUTH	24/5	—
	QUAKERS YARD HIGH LEVEL	47/77	170A4	Reading Spur S.B.	24/11	33B6
	QUAKERS YARD LOW LEVEL		170A4	Reading Triangle G.F.	24/36	33B3
	Quakers Yard West Tunnel S.B.	47/74	170C3	Reading Vastern Road	24/6	33B4
	Quarella Siding	44/2	144C1	READING WEST	24/36	33B3
	Quarry & Lime Siding (Llanharry)	44/25	145D5	Reading West Junction	24/2	33B2
	Quarry Bank		76D4	Read's G.F. (Rhymney)	42/5	167C5
	Quarry Close Siding		4D1	Red Ash Colly (Common Bch)	49/74	161C1
	Quarry Cottage Crossing		117D1	Red Ash (West Blaina) Colly		176B5
	Quarry Junction S.B. (Radyr)		174C3	REDBROOK	36/28	53B2
	Quarry Level Colly		?	REDBROOK-ON-WYE	36/28	53B2
	Quarry Mawr Siding	57/55	133C4	Redcliffe Goods	19/38	24B3
	Quarry S.B. (Ford & Crossgates)		98B3	Red Cow Crossing	15/1	13B1
	Quarry Sidings (Bronwydd)	58/37	129B3	Reddinghorn Pit		?
	Quarry Tip Siding (Easton)	17/8	42D2	REDDITCH	34/18	—
	Quedgeley Sidings	35/1	55D3	REDHILL		98D5
*	Queen Alexandra Dock S.B.s	43/84	150A1	Red Hill Junction S.B.	63/21	104D1
	Queens Head S.B.	31/22	79B6	RED HOUSE (Van Branch)		116B2
	QUEEN STREET, CARDIFF	46/105	149C4	Red House Crossing (Abermule)		116A6
	Queen Street Goods (Wellington)	32/3	69A4	Red Jacket Sidings	56/35	137C5
	Queen Victoria Road Goods	57/58	134B2	Redlake Siding	14/6	11B3
	Quidchurch Siding	37/36	54B2	REDLAND	19/65	23C4
	Quidhampton Siding	21/57	47D5	RED LION CROSSING HALT	54/46	131D4

REDNAL		96C2
REDNAL AND WEST FELTON		96C2
Red Post Junction	22/20	51D3
REDRUTH	10/13	1D6
Redruth Junction	10/13	1D5
Redruth West Yard (Old Station)	10/13	1D5
Relief Sidings (Cwm Prysor)		111A2
Remphrey Siding	11/29	4B1
Reservoir Siding (Cwmavon)	39/21	181B5
Reservoir Siding (Trawsfynydd)		109C6
Reservoir Storage Sdg (Felin Foel)	57/55	133C4
RESOLVEN	47/6	162B5
Resolven Tin Plate Works	47/3	162C3
RESPRYN		6A1
Restowrack Siding	11/31	4D1
Retew Siding	11/29	4B1
Retew Loop Siding	11/28	4B1
Rewe S.B.	15/5	16D2
REWLEY ROAD, OXFORD	27/10	68A5
Reynalton Colly	58/28	124B5
RHAYADER		120B3
Rhayader Quarry Siding		120C3
RHEIDOL FALLS HALT		114D4
Rheola Colly		162C6
Rheola S.B.	47/9	163B1
Rheola Works	47/7	162A5
Rhiew Colly		?
Rhigos S.B.	47/14	163B6
Rhigos Colly S.B.	47/12	163C4
RHIGOS HALT	47/14	163B6
Rhigos Timber Siding		163B6
RHIWBINA HALT		174B4
Rhiw Colbren Colly		175D6
RHIWDERIN	42/50	180D6
RHIWFRON		114D4
Rhiwglyn S.B.	49/39	157A6
Rhiwgregan Crossing		155D1
Rhiwlas Colly	57/47	133C3
Rhiw Park Colly		181D2
Rhiw Syr Dafydd S.B.	40/64	178A4
Rhondda Cutting S.B.	46/59	172B4
Rhondda Engine Works	46/15	158D4
Rhondda Fach Junction	46/30	159D5
Rhondda Main Colly	49/38	157A6
Rhondda Merthyr Colly	46/4	158B2
Rhondda Mountain Colly		163C4
Rhondda Tunnel Colly	51/37	155C5
Rhondda Valley Siding		164C2
* Rhondda Works Siding	46/39	172A3
RHOOSE	44/38	144B5
RHOS		94D4
RHOS (First Station)		94C6
Rhos Amman Colly	53/32	—
Rhos Colly (Pantyffynon)	54/4	131B2
Rhos Colly (Pengam Glam)	42/30	178B1
Rhosddu Engine Shed		93C6
RHOS-DDU HALT		—
* Rhosferig Sidings	59/7	—
Rhos Hall Siding		94C4
Rhos Junction		94B6
* Rhoslas Colly		?
Rhosllanerchrugog		94C4
Rhos Llantwit Colly	42/53	173A6
RHOSROBIN HALT		93B6
RHOSTYLLEN		94B5
Rhoswen Sidings S.B.	41/33	—
* RHOSYMEDRE		94D2
RHOSYMEDRE HALT		94C2
RHUBINA		174B4
Rhyd Colly		132A3
* Rhydavon Colly	51/29	154A4
Rhydding Colly	52/1	153B1
* Rhydhelig Siding		173B2
Rhydmeredydd Siding		119C2

RHYDOWEN	58/33	125A4
Rhyd-whimen Crossing		118C3
Rhydycar Junction		168C1
Rhydycar Pit		168C1
Rhydydefed Siding	54/26	—
Rhydydrain Crossing		111D3
RHYDYFELIN HALT HIGH LEVEL		172C6
RHYDYFELIN HALT LOW LEVEL		172D6
Rhyd yr helg Colly	46/75	173B2
Rhydywaen Brickworks		165A1
RHYMNEY	42/1	167B5
RHYMNEY AND PONTLOTTYN	42/7	167C6
RHYMNEY BRIDGE	41/6	167A4
Rhymney Crossing S.B. (Cardiff)	43/68	150D5
Rhymney Ironworks	42/3	167B5
Rhymney Joint S.B.	42/2	167B4
RHYMNEY JUNCTION (Hengoed)	47/90	178D5
Rhymney Limestone Siding		167B3
RHYMNEY LOWER	42/7	167C5
Rhymney Merthyr Colly (Rhymney)	42/7	167D5
Rhymney Merthyr Junction (Merthyr)		168D1
Rhymney Pit	42/7	167C5
RHYMNEY PWLL UCHAF	42/7	167C6
Rhymney Viaduct S.B.	42/4	167C5
Rica Colly	49/78	161B6
Rice Meadow Mill	20/54	—
Richmond Junction	25/27	38C5
Rich's Siding	23/13	30C6
Riddling Sidings	56/27	137D3
RIFLE RANGE HALT	32/26 & 33/25	77D3
* Rigwell Siding	12A4	
Rillaton		6C3
* Ringwell Viaduct	10/39	2B2
RIPPLE	34/14	—
RISCA	40/33	180B5
Risca Black Vein Colly	41/45	180B4
Risca Colly	41/46	180B5
Risca Quarries Siding	41/46	180B5
* Rising Sun Opencast Site		176A5
* Riverbridge G.F. (Waterhall Jcn)	49/44	143A3
River Dart Siding	14/9	12D1
River Level Colly		165B4
RIVERSIDE, CARDIFF		149D3
RIVERSIDE, NEATH	56/49	139A6
RIVERSIDE, SWANSEA	56/8	137B3
Riverside Branch (Bath)	18/1	—
Riverside Branch (Worcester)	33/10	60D5
Riverside Yard (Exeter)	15/3	12B1
ROADE	29/17	—
Roade Junction	29/17	—
Roadwater		17C2
ROATH		149B5
* Roath Basin G.F.	43/69	150B3
Roath Basin Junction S.B.	43/67	150C4
Roath Branch S.B.'s	43/98	149C6
Roath Branch Junction S.B.	46/95	174D4
Roath Branch Storage S.B.	43/98	149B6
Roath Dock Junction	43/68	150C4
Roath Dock South S.B.	43/90	150C3
Roath Dock Swingbridge S.B.	43/68	150B3
Roath Goods (G.W.R.)		149A6
Roath Goods (Newport Road)	46/113	149A5
Roath Line Junction Sidings S.B.	46/95	174D5
* Roath Mills	43/59	150D4
* Roath Pier Head Outer Lock G.F.'s	43/78	150A3
Robert and Lewis Siding	36/25	53A2
Robertstown Crossing S.B. (Aberdare)	47/24	165B1
Robertstown Disposal Centre	47/26	165C1
ROBERTSTOWN HALT (Ynysybwl)		171B1
Robeston Refinery	58/23	124B1
ROCHE	11/22	3A5
Rock Castle Siding (Cross Hands)	54/32	131A2
Rock Colly (Glyn Neath)	47/11	163B3
* Rock Cottage Siding	59/17	122B6

	Rock Cutting Crossover (Bridgend)	44/32	144C1		* Ruabon Colly		94A3
	Rock Fawr Colly		?		RUBERY	34/19	81B1
	ROCK FERRY		90D5		Ruckley Siding	32/16	69C6
	Rock Hill Siding	11/33	4B4		RUDDLE ROAD HALT	36/18	53B5
*	ROCKINGHAM	19/92	23B3		* Rudmore Park S.B.	20/50	—
	ROCK LANE (Rock Ferry)		89B3		Rudry Colly	42/54	180D2
	Rock Lane Crossing (Ludlow)	63/8	101C3		RUISLIP AND ICKENHAM	26/13	36A1
	Rock Level	41/36	—		RUISLIP GARDENS	26/15	36A2
	Rock Siding (Blackwood)	41/36	—		Rumney River Bridge S.B.		149A6
	Rock Siding (Llanymynech)		119D4		RUNCORN (HALTON)		88C2
	Rock Siding (Talybont)	59/17	122B6		RUNCORN EAST		88B3
	Rocks Siding (Cornwall)	11/24	4B5		RUNCORN ROAD (HALTON)		88C2
	Rock Vein Colly (Machen)	42/54	180D2		RUNEMEDE HALT	24/41	35D1
	Roch Vein North Colly	41/43	180A3		RUNEMEDE RANGE HALT	24/41	35D1
	Rock Vein Siding S.B.	41/43	180B3		Rushcombe S.B.	24/15	34D2
	Rock Vein South Colly		180B4		RUSHBURY	32/29	71C1
	Rockwood Colly Siding S.B.		173C3		RUSHEY PLATT	22/6	30D1
	Rodbourne Lane S.B.	20/13	30D1		Rushey Platt Junction (GWR)	20/10	30D1
	RODMARTON PLATFORM	20/38	59C2		Rushey Platt Junction (MSWJ)	22/6	30D1
	RODWELL	17/11	42D3		Rush Lane Crossing	32/44	99B5
	Roebuck Crossing	15/26	17C5		RUSHWICK HALT	33/9	61B3
	ROGERSTONE	40/39	184D1		RUSPIDGE HALT	37/34	54C6
	Rogerstone Brick Siding	40/36	180C6		Ruspidge Mill Siding	37/35	54B2
	Rogerstone North S.B.	40/37	184C1		* Russell Hall Siding		?
	Rogerstone South S.B.	40/39	184D2		Ruthern Bridge	11/34	
	Rolling Bridge Junction		151C6		Ruthin Quarry Siding (Pencoed)	44/7	144A3
	ROLLRIGHT HALT	28/32	64D4		Ruthin Road Goods (Coed Poeth)		93C2
	Roman Road Siding		132C5		Ryecroft Quarry Siding	14/44	13D3
	ROOD END		79B3		RYEFORD	20/54	—
	Rood End Yard	31/34	79B3				
	Rooksmoor Mill	20/56	—		S & M Junction S.B.	29/3 & 30/36	82C6
	ROSEBUSH	58/31	123A4		S & R Colly	57/50	133A6
	Rose Heyworth Colly	40/56	176C6		ST AGNES	10/30	2D4
	Rosemarket Crossings	58/15	124B2		St Andrews Junction (Avonmouth)	19/74	25C2
	Rosemellyn Siding	11/23	4A4		ST ANDREWS ROAD	19/79	25B2
	Rosemont Colly		?		St Andrews S.B. (nr. Cadoxton)	44/29	147C3
	Rosevallon Siding	11/28	4D1		ST ANNE'S PARK	19/19 & 21/1	24B6
	Rosevear Siding	11/24	4B5		St Anne's Pumping Station	21/1	23D5
	Rosevear Siding S.B.	11/24	3B6		ST ATHAN	44/35	144D4
*	Rosevear Moor Siding		3A6		St Athan Aerodrome Siding	44/35	144D4
	Rosevidney Crossing	10/6	1C2		ST ATHAN ROAD	44/22	144A6
	Roskear	10/27	1B6		ST AUSTELL	11/5	3C6
	Roskear Junction	10/10	1C5		St Austell Road Crossing S.B.	11/5	3C6
	Roskear Road Crossing	10/27	1C6		ST BLAZEY	11/26	5C1
	ROSS	36/32	105C3		St Blazey Bridge Crossing S.B.	11/26	4C6
	Rossers Siding	54/52	—		St Botolph's Crossing	58/23	124B1
	ROSSETT		92B4		ST BRIAVELS	36/29	53D2
	Rossett Sand Siding		92B4		ST BRIAVELS AND LLANDOGO	36/29	53D2
	ROSS ON WYE	36/32	105C3		St Brides S.B.	38/2	151C2
	Rostowrack	11/31	4C2		ST BUDEAUX (FERRY ROAD)	12/2	8A2
	ROTHERWAS FACTORY	63/20	104D6		ST BUDEAUX (VICTORIA ROAD)	12/2	
	Rotherwas Junction	63/20	104D6		ST CLEARS	58/9	125D6
	Roundham Crossing	27/6	67A3		St Cleer	11/36	6D3
	ROUND OAK	31/43	76C3		St Clements Siding	33/9	60D4
	ROUND OAK AND BRIERLEY HILL	31/45	76C2		ST COLUMB ROAD	11/21	3A3
	Round Pit Colly	53/11	—		* St Cuthbert Paper Mills	16/36	22C3
	ROWDEN MILL	33/21	102C5		ST DAVID'S, EXETER	15/1	13B1
	Rowington Junction S.B.	30/13	81D6		St David's Colly (Llanelly)	57/63	134C6
	ROWLEY	31/33	79D2		St David's Dock Crossing S.B.	57/16	134D3
	ROWLEY AND BLACKHEATH	31/33	79D2		St David's Incline	57/61	134C6
	Rowley Hall Colly		79C1		St David's Tin Works	55/32	133D6
	ROWLEY REGIS	31/33	79D2		* St David's Works (Morriston)	53/40	—
	ROWLEY REGIS AND BLACKHEATH	31/33	79D2		St Dennis Junction	11/22	3A4
*	Rowley Station Colly		79D2		ST DEVEREUX	63/22	107A5
	ROWTON HALT	32/45	99C6		ST ERTH	10/6	1C2
	Royal Albert Bridge S.B.	12/1	8A1		St Ervans Road Goods	25/16	39D2
	Royal Albert Dock Goods	25/37	40D6		ST FAGANS	44/20	146D4
	ROYAL EDWARD, AVONMOUTH		25C1		St Fagans Branch Junction	44/27	146C3
	Royal Edward Yard	19/87	25B2		St Fagans Road Siding	49/85	146B4
	ROYAL OAK	25/17	39D4		St Georges Colly (Llanelly)	57/60	134C4
	Royal Oak Crossing (Moss)		93A1		St Georges Crossing (Peterston)	44/19	146D3
	Royal Oak Siding (Princetown)	14/32	10B6		ST GERMANS	11/15	7B1
	RUABON		94B3		St Germans Crossing S.B.	11/14	7B1
	Ruabon Brick Works Siding		94A3		St Germans Viaduct S.B.	11/16	7B2

	Name				Name		
	ST HARMONS	59/30	120A3		SCORRIER GATE	10/14	1A6
	St Helens Siding	54/28	—		Scours Lane	24/1	33A1
	ST HILARY PLATFORM	44/23	144C4		Sculls Siding	49/82	161D4
	ST IVES	10/21	1B2		S.E. Junction S.B. (Cardiff)	43/93	149D6
	ST IVES ROAD	10/6	1C2		Sea Lane Crossing	15/23	17A1
	ST JAMES, CHELTENHAM	35/16	56B6		SEA MILLS	19/63	25B5
	St John's Colly (Cwmdu)	51/10	156C4	*	Sea Mills Junction		25B6
	St John's Siding (Henwick)	33/9	60D4		Sea Wall Pumping Station	19/96	23A3
	St Julians Siding S.B.	38/13 & 39/12	184B5		SEBASTOPOL	39/19	183A2
	ST KEYNE	11/37	6B5		SEBASTOPOL (Panteg)	39/19	183D6
	ST LAWRENCE PLATFORM`		5D4		Sedbury Camp		52C5
	ST MARY CHURCH ROAD	44/23	144C5		SEEND	21/25	46B3
	ST MARY'S CROSSING HALT	20/32	58D5		SEER GREEN	26/9	34A5
	St Mellons S.B.'s	38/1	151D1		SEER GREEN AND JORDANS	26/9	34A5
	ST QUINTIN PK & WORMWOOD SCRUBS	25/25	39B4		SELLY OAK	34/12	—
	ST PHILIPS, BRISTOL	19/41	—	*	Semington Canal Junction		46B3
	St Philips Marsh	19/21	24B4		SEMINGTON HALT	21/25	46B3
	ST THOMAS, EXETER	14/21	13C1		SENGHENITH		171D5
*	ST THOMAS, SWANSEA	53/1	—		SENGHENYDD		171D5
	ST Y NYLL PLATFORM	44/27	146C3		Senghenydd Branch Junction		173A5
	SALCEY FOREST	29/17	—		Serridge Junction	37/18	54B1
*	Salcombe Siding		14C5		Serridge Pit (Coalpit Heath)	20/49	—
	SALFORD PRIORS	34/17	—		SERRIDGE PLATFORM	37/18	54B1
	SALISBURY	21/58	47D6		SESSWICK HALT		92D4
	Salisbury Branch Junction	21/34	46C3		Sets 1–2 (Burrows Sidings)	56/21	137D1
	Salisbury Road Goods (Cardiff)		149B4		Sets 3–4 (Burrows Sidings)	56/26	137D3
	SALTASH	11/17	8A1		Set 5 (Burrows Siding)	56/30	137C4
	SALTFORD	21/4	27A2		SEVEN SISTERS	52/10	132C4
	SALTFORD (Kelston)	20/48	—		SEVEN STARS		117D2
	Saltmore Crossing	63/8	101D3		SEVERN BEACH	19/95	23A3
	SALTNEY		91D2		SEVERN BRIDGE	37/4	53D5
	Saltney Dee Junction		91D2		Severn Bridge Junction (Shrewsbury)		99C2
	Saltney Junction		91D2		Severn Foundry (Coalbrookdale)		70C1
	Saltney Lower Yard		91D2		Severn Mills Siding (Sharpness)		58B2
	Saltwells Colly		76C4		Severn Road Siding (Welshpool)		117D3
	Salutation Junction	38/46	152B3		Severnside Works	19/94	23A3
	Samlet Colly	53/11	—		Severn Tunnel East S.B.	19/51	23A3
	SAMPFORD PEVERELL HALT	15/10	15D3		SEVERN TUNNEL JUNCTION	38/23	52A3
	Sampford Siding	15/10	15D3		Severn Tunnel West S.B.	38/24	52A4
	Samson Colly		79C2		Severn Valley Junction		99C2
	Sanatorium Crossing S.B.		149C2		Shacklesford Siding	56/17	137B6
*	Sandfield Colly		76A2		Shadwell Rock Quarry	32/32	69D2
	SANDFORD (Sandford & Banwell)	16/34	21C4		Shakemantle Quarry Siding	37/36	54B2
	SANDFORD AND BANWELL	16/34	21C4	*	Shapters Way Crossing (Cattedown)		—
	Sandford Quarry (S. & Banwell)	16/34	21C4		SHAPWICK	18/28	
	Sandford Siding (Oxford)	27/15	67D4	*	SHARPNESS (First Station)	37/2	58B2
	Sandilands Crossing		113C1		SHARPNESS	37/1	58A2
	SANDPLACE	11/37	6C5		Sharpness Docks	37/1	58A2
	SANDSFOOT CASTLE HALT	17/11	42C6		Sharpness Swing Bridge S.B.	37/4	58A2
*	Sanduck Wood Siding		14A2		Sharp Tor	11/36	6B3
	Sandwell Park Colly S.B.	31/20	79A4		SHAUGH BRIDGE PLATFORM	14/27	7A5
	Sandygate Junction	57/48	134B2	*	Shaugh Siding		7A4
	Sandy Junction S.B.	57/59	134B2		Shawford Junction	23/18	51D6
	Sandy Lane Crossing (Kidlington)	27/6	67B3		Sheenhill S.B.	28/7	62C4
*	Sandy Lane Crossing (Gwinear Road)	10/10	1B4		Sheepcroft Sidings	17/8	42C1
	Sandy Siding	57/49	134B1		Sheephouse Crossing (Bruton)		45D2
	Sapperton Sidings S.B.	20/33	59B2	*	Sheephouse Siding (Three Cocks Jcn)		—
	Sapperton Tunnel S.B.	20/33	59B2		Shelwick Junction S.B.	63/16	104B2
	Sardis Crossing	57/44	133B2		SHEPHERDS	10/31	2C6
*	SARN		143D4		SHEPHERDS BUSH	25/24	38C5
	SARNAU	58/9	129C2		Shepherds Bush Goods	25/26	38C5
	Saron Colly	54/5	131B1		Shepherds Pit		165D3
	SARSDEN HALT	28/30	65C3		SHEPTON MALLET CHARLTON ROAD	18/13	
	SAUNDERSFOOT	58/28	124C6		SHEPTON MALLET HIGH STREET	16/39	22C5
	SAUNDERTON	26/6	87C5		Sherfield S.B.	23/42	50C6
	SAVERNAKE HIGH LEVEL	22/13	48A2		Sherrington Crossing S.B.	21/55	47B2
	SAVERNAKE LOW LEVEL	23/17 & 22/13	48A2		SHIFFNAL	32/15	69C5
*	Scars Line Works Siding		101B1		SHIFNAL	32/15	69C5
	Scatter Rock Quarry Siding	14/44	13C3		Shillingham S.B.'s	11/16	7B2
	SCAFELL		116B4		SHILLINGSTONE	18/18	
	Schrills Bridge S.B.	24/39	35B1		SHIPLAKE	24/37	34C1
	Scilly Point Siding	37/37	54C3		SHIPSTONE	28/36	64A3
	Scoria Sidings	43/59	149D6		SHIPSTON ON STOUR	28/36	64A3
	SCORRIER	10/14	1A6		Shipston Road Crossing (Shipston)	28/36	64A3

*	Shipston Road Siding (Clifford Siding)	29/5	—
	SHIPTON	28/17	65D3
	SHIPTON-ON-CHERWELL HALT	27/30	67A2
	SHIREHAMPTON	19/62	25A4
	SHIRLEY	30/30	81B4
	Shoddesdon Crossing		51C3
	SHOOT HILL		98C4
	Shopland Crossing		5C2
	Shore Road Junction		90C3
	Short Hill Colly		98D3
	Short Hill Crossing		98D3
	Shortwood S.B.	20/40	—
	SHOSCOMBE AND SINGLE HILL	18/5	—
	Shottery Footpath S.B.	20/36	82C6
	Shottesbrook S.B.	24/15	34D2
*	Show Hill Junction		74A4
	Show Siding (Hereford)		104A5
	Showsley Pits	29/16	—
*	Show Yard G.F. (Hereford)	63/16	104A5
	Show Yard Sidings S.B. (Shrewsbury)		99B3
	SHRAWARDINE		98B3
	SHREWSBURY ABBEY		99C2
	Shrewsbury Abbey Foregate Junction		99B2
	Shrewsbury Abbey Junction		99D3
	Shrewsbury Bayston Hill		98C5
	Shrewsbury Burnt Mill Junction		99D2
	Shrewsbury Castle Foregate Goods		99B2
	Shrewsbury Coleham		99C2
	Shrewsbury Coton Hill		99B2
	Shrewsbury Crewe Junction		99B2
	Shrewsbury English Bridge Junction		99C2
	SHREWSBURY GENERAL		99B2
	Shrewsbury North Wales Junction		99C3
	Shrewsbury Potteries Junction		99B3
	Shrewsbury Severn Bridge Junction		99C2
	Shrewsbury Severn Valley Junction		99C2
	Shrewsbury Show Yard Sidings		99B3
	Shrewsbury Shropshire Union Yard		99B2
	Shrewsbury Sutton Bridge Junction		99C2
	Shrewsbury Wellington Junction		99C2
	Shrewsbury Welshpool Junction		99C2
	SHREWSBURY WEST		99D2
	SHRIVENHAM	23/1	29B5
	Shropshire Union Branch (E. Port)		91A5
	Shropshire Union Yard (Shrewsbury)		99B2
	Shrubbery Basin	31/10	—
	SHRUB HILL, WORCESTER	33/16	60C6
	Shut Castle Pit	37/41	54C1
	Shut End Collieries	31/55	76B1
	Shut End Ironworks		76A2
	Shut End New Colly		76B2
	Shutfield Brickworks		70A1
	Sierford S.B.	28/29	57A3
*	Siemens Sidings	53/37	—
	SILIAN HALT	58/41	127C4
	Silchester Crossing	23/43	50A6
	Silk Mill Crossing S.B.	16/1	20D2
	Silverdale Junction	32/44	99B5
	SILVERTON	15/6	16D2
	SIRHOWY	41/25	—
	Sirhowy Junction (Pontllanfraith)	47/93	178D3
	Sirhowy Level		?
	Sirhowy Navigation Colly		—
	Sirhowy Valley Colly	41/41	—
	Sisters Pit	53/13	—
	Six Bells Colly (Aberbeeg)	40/60	182B1
	SIX BELLS HALT (Aberbeeg)	40/60	182A2
	SIX BELLS HALT (LMSR)	39/14	—
*	Six Pit Colly	53/9	—
	Six Pit Junction	53/7	138D4
	Skew Bridge S.B.	39/19	183B5
	SKEWEN	55/18	139B2
	Skewen Cutting S.B.	55/20	139A4
	Skewen East Junction	55/18	139B2

	Skewen West S.B.	55/17	138D5
*	Skinner's Lock S.B.		49D2
	Slades Patch		165A1
	Slag Tip Sidings (Maesteg)	51/8	156C2
*	Slaney's Siding (Ruckley)		69C5
	Slant Colly (Glanamman)		131B4
	Slants Colly (Pontyberem)	57/36	133A2
	Slaughter Siding	36/26	53A2
	Slimbridge Munitions Depot	20/45	—
	Sling Branch	37/40	54C3
	Slip Siding	11/31	4D1
	Sloper Road Sidings		149D2
	SLOUGH	24/19	34C6
	SLOUGH ESTATE	24/18	34B5
	SMALL HEATH	30/5	80C3
	SMALLHEATH AND SPARKBROOK	30/5	80C3
	Small Hill Colly		70C1
	Smelt Siding		93A3
*	SMETHWICK GALTON BRIDGE H.L.		79B4
	SMETHWICK JUNCTION	31/35	79B4
	SMETHWICK WEST	31/35	79B4
	Smithfield Goods	25/35	40D4
	Smithfield Road Crossing		117D2
	Smithfield Siding (Welshpool)		117D2
*	Smoky Cot Siding		143C1
	Snailbeach Siding		98D3
	SNATCHWOOD HALT	39/22	182A5
	Snatchwood Siding S.B.	39/22	182B5
*	Snedshill Brick Works	32/8	70B5
	Snedshill Ironworks	32/6	70B5
	Sneyd Park Junction	19/63	25B5
	Snipehill Junction		52B5
	SNOW HILL, BIRMINGHAM	31/26	80B6
	Soffrydd Quarry Siding	40/19	182D2
	SOHO	31/23	79B6
	SOHO AND WINSON GREEN	31/23	79B6
	Soho Junction S.B.	31/23	79B6
	SOLIHULL	30/9	81B5
	Solvay Coke Ovens		93C4
	Somerdale Siding	21/2	27A2
	SOMERFORD	20/18	28A4
	Somerset Quarry Siding	21/50	45A4
	SOMERSET ROAD	34/12	—
	SOMERTON (Oxon)	27/3	85B3
	SOMERTON (Somerset)	16/47	43B2
*	Somervilles Siding	16/9	20C2
	Sonning S.B.'s	24/13	32B6
	Soudley Furnaces	37/37	54C3
	Soudley Siding	37/37	54C3
	Souldern S.B.	26/1	85A3
	SOUTHALL	24/28	37C3
	SOUTHAM ROAD AND HARBURY	30/21	83B3
	Southam Road North S.B.		83B2
	SOUTH AYLESBURY HALT	26/34	86C5
	South Cambria Colly	49/85	161D6
	South Caradon	11/36	6C3
	SOUTH CERNEY	22/5	59C5
	Southcote Junction	23/32	33D2
	South Crofty Siding		1B6
	South Dock S.B. (Swansea)	56/1	137B2
	South Duffryn Colly		169B3
	South Dunraven Colly	46/3	158B1
*	South End Chaloner Street Depot		90B1
	South End Yard (Oxford)	27/10	68B5
	SOUTHERNDOWN ROAD	44/34	144B2
	Southfield Crossing	20/56	—
	South Fraddon Siding	11/29	4B1
	Southgate St Crossing	35/18	—
	South Glamorgan Colly (Wern Tarw)	49/25	157D6
	South Glamorgan Quarry (Creigiau)	49/85	161C6
	SOUTH GREENFORD HALT	26/20	36C5
	South Griffin Colly	40/55	176C6
	South Hams Siding	12/30	7D6
	SOUTH HAREFIELD HALT	26/11	35D5

South Hill Siding	28/32	64C5
South Lambeth Goods	25/33	40D2
SOUTH LEIGH	27/24	66B6
South Liberty Junction	19/1	24D1
* South Liberty Lane Siding	19/3	24D1
South Marston Factory	20/29	29A4
SOUTH MOLTON	15/20	18D1
SOUTH PIT HALT	51/48	155A4
South Reserve Sidings		90A5
South Rhondda Colly	49/26	145A3
South Rhondda Siding	49/26	145B3
South Roskear	10/27	1B6
SOUTH RUISLIP	26/15	36B2
SOUTH RUISLIP & NORTHOLT JCN	26/15	36B2
South Sea Ironworks		93C4
South Stoke S.B.	23/15	31D6
South Tunnel Colly		167C4
South Wales Colly (Cwmtillery)	40/58	181C2
South Wales Junction (Bristol)	19/14	24B4
South Wales Mineral Branch Junction	51/43	153D6
South Wales Mineral Junction	51/29	154A4
South Wales Siding (Cardiff)		149C4
South Wales Union S.B.	19/14	24C5
South Wales Works (Llanelly)	57/22	134D1
SPARKFORD	17/7	43B5
* Sparrows Siding	29/13	—
Speculation Colly	37/44	54B1
Speech House Hill Colly	37/16	54B1
SPEECH HOUSE ROAD	37/15	54B1
Speedway Junction		8B3
* Speedwell Pit (Bristol)	19/50	—
Speedwell Siding	37/29	53A5
SPEEN	23/40	49D4
Spekes Wood Crossing	16/44	20A6
Spelter Colly (Fleur de Lis)	42/36	178C2
Spelter Works S.B. (Morriston)	55/26	135B3
Spencers Crossing		82C2
Spencer Works S.B.	38/22	151B4
Spero Siding	37/30	54A6
SPETCHLEY	34/4	—
SPETISBURY	18/20	—
Spicers Crossing		34A4
Spillers Nephew G.F.	43/104	149B5
Spinners End	31/31	76D4
Spion Kop Quarry		54A2
SPITAL		89B5
Spittal S.B.	58/5	123C2
* Spitty Tin Works		133D6
Splott Bridge Junction S.B.		149B5
* Splott Junction	43/93	150D4
Springfield Crossing		139B3
Springfields Colly	21/45	27D2
SPRING ROAD	30/30	81A4
* Spring Vale Siding		75A1
Squborwen Colly		165B2
Stafford Colly (Hollinswood)		70C6
Stafford Junction S.B. (Wellington)	32/5	69A5
Stafford Road Junction (Wolverhampton)	31/3	74A3
Stafford Road Works	31/3	74A3
Staines Moor Junction	24/41	35D1
STAINES WEST	24/41	35D1
STALBRIDGE	18/18	—
Standard Colly	46/51	159C5
Standard Quarry Siding		117D1
Standhill Rock Quarry	32/32	69D2
Standhills Colly		76B1
Standish Junction	35/1	58A4
STANLEY BRIDGE HALT	21/27	28C4
* Stanley Dock Depot		90B1
Stanley Mill Siding	20/54	—
Stanleys Pit		134A1
STANLOW AND THORNTON		90D3
Stanlow Refinery		90D3
STANNER	63/37	103B2
STANTON	20/29	29A3
Stanton Cutting S.B.	28/20	63B6
Stanton Wood Siding	20/29	29A3
STANDWARDINE HALT		96D4
STANDWELL MOOR AND POYLE	24/41	35D1
STAPLE EDGE HALT	37/36	54B2
STAPLE HILL	19/49	—
STAPLETON ROAD	19/60	23A1
Stapleton Road Gas Siding (Mid)	19/66	—
Starch Products G.F.	24/22	34C6
* Star Brickworks (Caerleon)		184A6
* Star Colly (Trimsaran)		?
* Star Fuel Works (Cardiff		149A3
STARCROSS	14/20	13D6
Station Rd Crossing (Newquay)		3A2
Station Yard S.B. (Newport)	38/58	152B4
STAVERTON (Devon)	14/33	12A2
STAVERTON HALT (Wiltshire)	21/18	46B2
STEAM FERRY CROSSING	14/34	12D5
STEAM MILLS CROSSING HALT	37/29	54A2
Steam Packet Corner Crossing		1A2
Steel Works Wharf (Port Talbot)		141B3
STEENS BRIDGE	33/21	102C3
Steer Colly	54/48	131D5
STEER POINT	12/30	7D6
Steetley Quarry		174A1
Stenalees Engine Shed	11/33	4B4
* Stepaside Iron Works		124C6
* Sterry's Mountain Colly	54/19	—
Stert Junction S.B.		46B6
STEVENTON	23/4	31B3
Stewarts Lane Junction	25/32	40D2
* STIRCHLEY	32/53	—
Stirchley Branch	32/41	70D5
STOCKCROSS AND BAGNOR	23/40	49D4
* Stockley Bridge Jcn		35B2
Stock Shed, Swindon	20/17	30C1
Stocks Lane S.B. (Newland)	33/8	61C3
Stocks Lane S.B. (Steventon)	23/4	31B3
Stockton Crossing		47B2
Stock Yard G.F.	57/53	133B4
STOGUMBER	15/26	17C4
STOKE BRUERN	29/16	—
STOKE CANON	15/5	13A5
STOKE EDITH	33/1	60A1
Stoke Gifford	20/1	23A6
* Stoke Gifford Tip Siding	19/100	23A6
STOKE PRIOR HALT	33/21	102C2
Stoke Prior Junction (Stoke Works)	34/5	78B5
Stokesay Crossing	63/6	101A1
Stokeswood Crossing	63/6	101A1
STOKE WORKS	34/5	78B5
Stonefield Junction S.B.	43/68	150C4
STONEHOUSE BRISTOL RD	20/46	—
STONEHOUSE BURDETT RD	20/30	58B4
Stonehouse Pool (Plymouth)	12/31	—
Stonehouse Slag Siding (Maesteg)		156C2
Stonehouse Wharf	20/54	—
Stonehouse Wool Siding	20/46	—
Stoneycombe Siding S.B.	14/11	12A4
Storeton Quarry		89C3
Stormstown Junction		171C2
* Stormy Junction		143B4
Stormy Sidings S.B.	50/75	143B4
STOTTESDON HALT	33/24	72B2
STOULTON	28/1	61C6
STOURBRIDGE (First station)	31/49	77B2
Stourbridge E.S. Sdgs S.B.	31/48	77B2
Stourbridge Extension Colly		76A1
Stourbridge Incline	31/51	77B1
STOURBRIDGE JUNCTION	31/49	77C2
STOURBRIDGE TOWN	31/51	77B1
Stour Colly		77A4
STOURPAINE AND DURWESTON	18/19	—

Stourpaine Loop S.B.	18/19	—	
STOURPORT	32/27 & 33/25	72A5	
STOURPORT-ON-SEVERN	32/27 & 33/25	72A5	
Stourport Sand Siding	32/28 & 33/25	72A6	
Stourton Siding		89B4	
* Stour Valley Junction		75C2	
Stover Siding	14/41	14C3	
Stow Heath S.B.	31/10	74C5	
STOW-ON-THE-WOLD	28/29	65C1	
* Stradey Line		134B2	
Straits Green Colly		76A2	
Strand Line (Swansea)	56/3	137A2	
STRAP LANE HALT	16/51	45C3	
STRATA FLORIDA	58/34	126C6	
Stratfield Saye S.B.	23/43	50A6	
* STRATFORD (S. & M. Tramway)		82D4	
STRATFORD, EVESHAM RD CROSSING H	30/36	82C6	
STRATFORD ON AVON (GWR)	30/33	82C6	
STRATFORD ON AVON (Mid)	29/3	—	
STRATFORD RACECOURSE	30/36	82D6	
* Stratford Sewerage Works Siding	28/26	62A6	
STRATTON	20/29	29B3	
Stratton Factory	20/26	30C3	
Stratton Green Sidings	20/25	30C3	
STRATTON PARK HALT	20/25	29B4	
Stray Park Crossing	10/27	1C6	
Stream Hall Siding		102D6	
* Street End Colly		?	
Street Las Crossing		94D4	
STRETFORD BRIDGE	63/33	100D4	
Stretford Bridge Junction	63/4	101C1	
Stretton Heath Crossing		98C2	
STRETTON-ON-FOSSE	28/36	64B2	
Stretton Road Crossing	28/36	64B2	
Strip and At It Pit		54A3	
STROUD (GWR)	20/31	58C6	
STROUD (Mid)	20/55	—	
Stroud Road Jcn (Gloucester)	35/2	56B3	
STUDLEY (Redditch)	34/18	—	
Studley S.B. (Wootton Bassett)	20/9	29C1	
Stump Oak Siding	11/35	—	
STURMINSTER NEWTON	18/18	—	
Styches Colly		70C2	
Subway Junction S.B.	25/12	39D3	
Succours Lane Crossing		106A1	
SUCKLEY	33/22	61B1	
* SUCKLEY ROAD		61B1	
Sudbrook Branch	36/1	52B2	
Sugar Loaf	59/5	—	
SULLY	44/60	148B1	
Sully Moors	44/70	148B6	
Summerhill Engine Shed		93B5	
SUMMERTOWN HALT		68D3	
* Summit Siding	49/58	160B6	
SUN BANK HALT		95B2	
Sun Pit		176A6	
Sunset Siding		1C6	
Sun Vein Colly	41/45	180B5	
SUTTON (Little Sutton)		91A4	
* SUTTON (Ledsham)		91A3	
Sutton Bridge Junction		99C2	
Sutton Dock (Halton)		88C2	
Sutton Harbour	12/18	8D5	
Sutton Harbour Branch G.F.	12/22	8C6	
Sutton Road L.C. S.B.	12/18	8D5	
SUTTON SCOTNEY	23/34	51A5	
Sutton Veny Camp	21/55	47C6	
Sutton Wharf	12/11	8D5	
SWANBRIDGE HALT	44/60	148C2	
Swan Colly	50/13	136B5	
SWANSEA BAY	54/28	—	
Swansea Beach Sidings	54/31	137C2	
Swansea Branch Junction (Landore)	55/10	136B2	
Swansea Brownlands	56/13	137D6	
Swansea Burrows Lodge Goods	56/1	137B2	
Swansea Canal Head Sidings		136C2	
Swansea Centre Beat S.B.	56/6	137B3	
* Swansea Chemical Works Siding	53/9	—	
Swansea Cobre Goods	56/4	137A2	
Swansea Complex Ore Sidings	55/15	138D5	
Swansea Corporation Power Station	56/5	137B2	
SWANSEA DOCKS	56/8	137B3	
Swansea Duke Siding	56/4	137B2	
Swansea East Central S.B.	56/8	137B3	
SWANSEA EAST DOCK	56/7	137B3	
Swansea East Dock Junction	56/11	137B4	
Swansea Eastern Depot	56/6	137B3	
* Swansea Engine Home Beat S.B.		136D2	
Swansea Fish Market	56/1	137C3	
Swansea Gorseinon Line Junction	54/30	137B1	
Swansea Harbour Branch Sdgs S.B.	53/1	—	
SWANSEA HIGH STREET	55/21	136D2	
Swansea Kings Dock Junction	56/17	137B6	
Swansea Loop East Junction	55/23	136C2	
Swansea Loop West Junction	55/11	136C2	
Swansea Maliphant Sidings	55/23	136C2	
Swansea Navigation Colly	54/19	—	
Swansea New Cut Drawbridge S.B.	56/4	137B2	
Swansea North Dock Branch Jcn	55/21	136D2	
Swansea North Dock Drawbridge S.B.	56/4	137B2	
Swansea North Dock Goods	53/1	—	
Swansea North Dock S.B.	56/3	137B2	
Swansea Ore Siding S.B.	55/15	135B4	
Swansea Paxton St Engine Shed	54/30	—	
Swansea Prince of Wales Dock Jcn	56/19	137D6	
SWANSEA RIVERSIDE	56/8	137B3	
SWANSEA ST THOMAS	53/1	137B3	
Swansea South Dock S.B.	54/29 & 56/1	137B2	
Swansea Station S.B. (RSB)	56/8	137B3	
Swansea Street Sidings (Cardiff)	43/99	149C6	
Swansea Tir John Power Station	56/19	137A6	
Swansea Vale Junction	53/1	137A3	
* Swansea Vale Works	53/9	—	
Swansea Valley Junction S.B.	55/15 & 53/9	136A5	
SWANSEA VICTORIA	54/29	137B2	
* Swansea Waterworks Siding (CRAY)		122B1	
Swansea West Central S.B.	56/8	137B3	
* SWANSEA WIND ST		137B2	
Swansea Wind St Jcn S.B.	56/3	137B2	
Swan Street Junction	50/24	140C4	
SWAN VILLAGE	31/18	75C5	
Swan Village Basin	31/18	75C5	
Sweeney Siding		96D1	
Swell Tor Siding	14/32	10B6	
Swffryd Quarry		182C2	
Swifts Siding	28/2	62C3	
SWIMBRIDGE	15/19	18B4	
SWINDON	20/18	30C2	
Swindon Cocklebury Sidings	20/20	30C2	
Swindon Engine Shed	20/13	30C1	
Swindon Gloucester Junction	20/13	30C2	
Swindon Goods Yard S.B.	20/22	30C3	
Swindon Gorse Hill Siding	20/23	30C3	
Swindon Highworth Junction	20/22	30C3	
Swindon Loco Yard S.B.	20/13	30C1	
Swindon Newburn P.A.D.	20/12	30D1	
Swindon Rodbourne Lane	20/13	30D1	
Swindon Rushey Platt Jcn	20/10	30D1	
SWINDON TOWN	22/7	29C3	
Swindon Transfer Yard	20/23	30C3	
Swing Bridge G.F. (Hayle)	10/23	1A2	
Swing Bridge S.B. (Sharpness)	37/4	58A2	
Sydenham Sidings S.B.	28/35	84D4	
Sylan Colly	57/54	133C4	
Sylen Mountain Colly	57/54	133C4	
SYLFAEN FARM		118B3	
SYLFAEN HALT		118B3	
SYMONDS YAT	36/26	53A3	

Syndicate Siding	44/48	148C3	
Syon Lane G.F.	24/42	37D5	
T Sidings (Gloucester)	35/7	56D4	
T STATION (Gloucester)	35/7	56B4	
TACKLEY HALT	27/4	85D2	
Taff Bargoed Junction	47/84	170C5	
Taf Fechan Siding (Dowlais Top)		167B2	
Taf Fechan Siding (Pontsticill Jcn)		166B3	
Taff Llantwit Colly	49/80	161B6	
Taff Merthyr Colly	47/81	170A5	
TAFF MERTHYR COLLY HALT		170A5	
Taff Rhondda Navigation Colly		173B3	
Taff Vale Extension Junction	39/5	183A5	
Taff Vale Ironworks (Pontypool Rd)	39/4	183A5	
Taff Vale Ironworks (Pontypridd)	46/64	172B5	
TAFF'S WELL	46/80	173D3	
* TAFFS WELL (First station)	46/79	173D3	
Taffs Well Dolomite Siding		174A1	
Taffs Well Junction S.B.	46/80	173C2	
Taffs Well Siding S.B.	46/77	173C2	
Taf Vale Junction	58/7	125D4	
Taibach Loop Junction	50/32	142A5	
Taibach Pit		169B3	
Taibach Tinplate Works	50/25	141B4	
Talbot Merthyr Colly	51/51	153C2	
Talbot Wharf	50/38	141B3	
TALERDDIG		115D5	
Talfon Colly		131D2	
TALGARTH	59/21	121C5	
TALLEY ROAD	59/2	130C3	
TALSARNAU		109C3	
TALSARN HALT	58/41	127B3	
Talvan Colly	54/13	131D2	
TALWRN BACH HALT		110A1	
Talwrn Colly (Vron)		93C3	
Talwrn Crossing (Legacy)		94C4	
TALYBONT	59/17	122C6	
TALYBONT HALT (Barmouth)		110B1	
TALYBONT ON USK	59/17	122C6	
Talyclyn Colly	55/37	133C6	
Talyfan Colly		131D2	
TALYLLYN	59/18	122C5	
TALYLLYN (BRYNDERWEN)	59/18	122B4	
TALYLLYN JUNCTION	59/18	122C4	
Talywain Goods	39/14	184A1	
Talywain Junction	39/14	184A2	
Talywain Old Ballast Siding	39/14	184B2	
Talywaun Colly		?	
Tamar Bridge S.B.	12/1	—	
Tan Lane Crossing	14/21	13C2	
Tanllan Siding		118A1	
Tanners Lane Crossing	14/36	12B5	
Tansey Green Colly		76A2	
Tany Bryn Colly	47/22	165A3	
Tanymanod S.B.		109A6	
Tanyrallt Colly	53/Ind	—	
Tanyrheol Colly		—	
TAPLOW	24/17	34C4	
Tareni Coly	53/20	—	
Tatham Siding		94B3	
TAUNTON	16/3	20D3	
Tavistock Junction	14/1	8A5	
Tavistock Junction G.F.	12/15	8A5	
TAVISTOCK SOUTH	14/36	10B4	
Tawe Clay Works Siding	52/17	132C3	
* Tawe Foundry Siding	53/11	—	
Tawe Vale Colly	53/15	—	
* Tawe Valley Gas Works	53/22	—	
Taylors Quarry Siding (Nelson Branch)		171D3	
* Taylors Siding (Nantgarw)		173C3	
Techon Fach Colly	55/29	134D6	
Techon Siding S.B.	55/29	134D6	
TEIGL HALT		109A6	
Teignbridge Siding	14/41	14C3	
TEIGNGRACE	14/41	14C3	
Teign House Siding	14/44	13C3	
TEIGNMOUTH	14/16	14C5	
Teign Valley Junction	14/41	14B3	
Teilo Works	54/12	131D2	
TELFORD CENTRAL	32/13	70B5	
Temple Cloud Quarry	21/44	27C1	
TEMPLECOMBE	18/17	—	
TEMPLE MEADS, BRISTOL	19/9	24B4	
Temple Street Footbridge	38/51	152C3	
TEMPLETON	58/29	124B6	
TENBURY	33/23	101D5	
TENBURY WELLS	33/23	101D5	
TENBY	58/27	124A5	
TERN HILL	32/44	99C4	
Terra Colly		163D2	
Terra Siding	47/8	162B6	
Terrace Colly (Rhymney)	42/3	167C5	
Terrace Sidings (Tumble)	57/52	133A5	
Terras Crossing	11/37	6C5	
TETBURY	20/38	59D1	
TETBURY ROAD	20/33	59B3	
TETTENHALL	31/54	74B2	
Tewgood Colly	51/40	154B4	
TEWKESBURY	34/13	—	
Tewkesbury Quay	34/13	—	
THAME	27/22	87A2	
Tharsis Copper Works	43/57	150D4	
THATCHAM	23/25	49D6	
THEALE	23/28	32C3	
THE DELL	10/38	2D3	
THE HAWTHORNS HALT	31/20	79A5	
The Kennels Crossing		71C3	
THE LAKES HALT	30/31	81C4	
THE LODGE HALT		93B4	
Thingley Junction	21/10	28D3	
Thingley West Junction	21/10	28D3	
Third Line (Blaendare Road end)	47/109	182C5	
Third Line (Pontypool Road end)	39/4	182B5	
Thomas Crossing (Penar Branch)	40/66	178A4	
Thomas Merthyr Colly		168D4	
Thomas's Siding (Bourne End)	24/38	34B4	
Thomas's Siding (Builth Rd)	59/27	121B1	
* Thomastown (Trethomas)		179C6	
Thomastown Siding (Gellyrhaidd Jcn)	49/63	160D6	
THORNBURY	20/52	—	
THORNE	16/44	20C3	
THORNE FALCON	16/44	20C3	
THORNEY AND KINGSBURY HALT	17/15	43C1	
Thorney Mill Sidings	24/41	35C1	
Thorney Siding	17/15	43C1	
THORNFALCON	16/44	20C3	
THORNFORD BRIDGE HALT	17/6	44B3	
Thornton Refinery		90D3	
Thornwood S.B.	36/5	52C5	
THORVERTON	15/16	16C1	
THREE COCKS JUNCTION	59/22	121B6	
* Three Crows Siding	43/73	150A5	
THURSTASTON		89C1	
Tidal Sidings	43/99	149C6	
TIDDINGTON	27/22	87A1	
TIDENHAM	36/29	52B5	
TIDWORTH	22/21	51C1	
Tigley S.B.	14/3	12B2	
TILEHURST	23/16	32B4	
Tile Mills Siding	23/28	32D3	
Tillery Colly	40/58	181D2	
Tillery Red Ash Colly		181D2	
Timber Jetty Junction (Portishead)	19/27	23C1	
Timber Mill G.F.	20/48	—	
Timbertree Colly		77A5	
Timmis's Siding S.B.	31/27	77B2	
Timsbury Colly	21/52	27C2	

Tinkerpit Siding	21/57	47D5	
TINKERS GREEN HALT		96C1	
Tinny Bonny Works		131D2	
TINTERN	36/30	52A5	
Tintern Quarry	36/29	52A5	
Tintern Wire Works	36/30	52A5	
Tin Works Crossing (Llantrisant)	44/13	145D3	
Tin Works Junction (Abertillery)	40/59	182A2	
Tin Works Junction (Lower Lydbrook)	37/42	54A1	
Tin Works Junction (Lydney)	37/6	54C4	
Tipton Basin	31/37	75C2	
TIPTON FIVE WAYS	31/37	75C2	
Tipton Junction S.B.	31/37	75C2	
Tirbach Colly	53/23	—	
Tircanol Pit	53/42	—	
TIRCELYN	59/24	121D3	
Tircelyn Quarry Siding (Minera)		93C2	
Tirclay Crossing	57/35	133A3	
Tirdonkin Colly	55/42	138C2	
Tirffordd Colly	55/42	138B2	
Tirfounder Level		?	
Tir Gibbon Colly		173A4	
Tir Herbert Brickworks	47/15	164B2	
Tir Herbert Colly		164C1	
Tir Isaf Pit	53/5	—	
Tir John Power Station	56/19	137A6	
Tir Llaethdy Quarry		165D3	
Tirllewellyn Fuel Works	55/42	138D2	
Tir Pentwys Colly	39/24	182C4	
TIR PHIL	42/17	177A2	
TIR PHIL AND NEW TREDEGAR	42/16	177A2	
Tir Philkins Colly	40/70	178B4	
Tir Phil Level	42/16	177A2	
Tir Phil Pit	42/16	177B2	
* Tir-Waen-Clwydd Colly		?	
Tir-y-Berth Siding	42/30	178B1	
TIRYDAIL	54/3	131B3	
Tirydail Colly	54/36	131A3	
Tir yr Argae Pit		164B6	
TITLEY	63/38	103B4	
Titterstone Quarry	63/34	101B5	
TIVERTON	15/17	16A2	
Tiverton and North Devon Junction	15/17	16A2	
TIVERTON JUNCTION	15/9	16B6	
TIVERTON PARKWAY	15/10	16A4	
TIVERTON ROAD	15/9	16B6	
Tobacco Warehouse Crossing	19/37	24A2	
TODDINGTON	28/20	63C5	
Todenham Lane Crossing	28/36	64B2	
Todenham Road Crossing	28/36	64C2	
Tokenbury	11/36	6C4	
Tolbenny Siding	11/28	4C1	
Tolcarn Junction	11/20	3A1	
Toldish Siding	11/21	3A3	
Tollbridge Crossing		110C4	
TOLLER	17/15	41B3	
Tomperrow Crossing	10/17	2A2	
Ton Colly	46/18	159B2	
TONDU	49/11	143C4	
Tondu Ballast Siding	49/50	143D3	
* Tondu Brickworks	49/54	143D4	
* Tondu Ironworks	49/16	143C4	
TONFANAU		113B1	
* Tonfanau Quarry Siding		113A1	
Tongue Head Crossing	19/37	24A2	
TONGWYNLAIS		174B2	
Tonhir Colly	51/6	156C1	
TONLLWYD HALT	47/42	165C4	
Tonmawr Colly	51/51	153C2	
TONMAWR JUNCTION	51/40	153D2	
TON PENTRE	46/18	159A2	
Ton Philip Colly	49/46	143A4	
TONTEG HALT (Cadoxton Line)	46/112	173B1	
TONTEG HALT (Llantrisant Line)	46/112	173B1	

TONTEG HALT (T.V. Rly)	46/112	173B1	
Tonteg Junction	46/112	173B1	
Ton Teilwr Colly		?	
Ton Tyler Colly		?	
Tonygregos Quarry	51/41	153C1	
Tonygroes Junction	51/15	141A5	
Tonygrugos Colly	51/52	153C2	
Ton y March Colly		178C5	
TONYPANDY		159D3	
TONYPANDY AND TREALAW	46/23	159D3	
TONYREFAIL	49/61	160C6	
Ton yr Rhondda Colly	51/52	153B2	
Ton yr ywen Siding		174B5	
Top End Railway Terrace Crossing		159C3	
Top Flats Siding	47/100	178B6	
* TOP OF INCLINE		171A3	
Tophill Colly		170C6	
Topsham Bridge Crossing	14/33	11C3	
Topyard Colly		70A2	
Torcefn Colly		162D1	
TORPANTAU	59/15	122D5	
TORQUAY	14/38	12B5	
Torquay Gas Works	14/14	12B5	
Torquay Junction	14/12	14D1	
TORRE	14/39	12A5	
Torr Works		45B2	
Torybanwen Colly	51/54	153B5	
Torycoed Colly	49/85	161D5	
Torymynydd Colly (Briton Ferry)	50/13	140C4	
Torymynydd Colly (Cwmavon)	51/25	154B4	
Tothill Crossing	12/20	8C6	
TOTNES	14/9	12D1	
Totnes Loop (DVR)	14/9	12C1	
Totnes Quay	14/9	12D1	
TOTNESS	14/9	12D1	
Towans Sidings	10/22	1A2	
TOWCESTER	29/11	—	
* Towcester Brickworks Siding	29/12	—	
Towcester Ironstone Siding	29/16	—	
Tower Colly	47/15	164B2	
Tower Craig Level		164B1	
* Tower Graig Colly		164B1	
TOWERSEY HALT	27/22	87A3	
Town Dock (Newport)	38/53	152C4	
Towney Crossing	23/27	32D2	
* Towy Bridge Junction		129B1	
Towy Castle S.B.	57/1	129D3	
TOWYN		113C1	
Towyn Rivers S.B.	57/1	129D3	
Traeth Mawr Crossing		110A3	
Trafalgar Colly (Bilson Junction)	37/19 & 37/32	54B5	
Trafalgar Coly (Drybrook Rd)	37/18	54B3	
Trafalgar Tramway	37/18	54A4	
TRAM INN	63/22	104D1	
Tramroad Crossing (Hirwain)	47/17	164B3	
TRAM ROAD HALT		172B2	
Tramway Junction (Gloucester)	35/7	56B4	
Tramway Junction (Weymouth)	17/1	42C3	
Tranch Colly	39/17	182B5	
Trane Colly	49/70	160B4	
* Tranmere Junction		90C4	
* Tranmere Branch Jcn		90C4	
Tranmere Pool		90C5	
Transatlantic Colly		156A5	
Transfer Sidings (Swindon)	20/9	30C3	
Transformer Sidings G.F.	24/27	35B2	
TRAVELLERS REST (Abercynon)		171B3	
Travellers Rest S.B. (Parkend)	37/12	54C1	
TRAVELLERS REST ABERCYNON UPPER		171B3	
TRAWSCOED	58/34	126B5	
TRAWSFYNYDD		109C6	
TRAWSFYNYDD CAMP		109C6	
Trawsfynydd C.E.G.B.		109B5	
TRAWSFYNYDD LAKE HALT		109B5	

Trealaw Goods		46/22	159D3
TREAMAN		47/56	165C4
Treaman Sidings		47/39	165C4
Treamble		10/33	2B6
Trebanog Colly			?
Trebanos Siding		55/49	138A5
Trecastle Siding		44/11	145C5
Trecwn		58/30	123A2
Trecynon Creamery Siding		47/23	165A3
Trecynon Goods (Mill St)		47/20	165A3
TRECYNON HALT		47/23	165A3
TREDEGAR		41/28	—
Tredegar Estate Line (Newport)		38/49	152D4
Tredegar Iron Works		41/27	—
TREDEGAR JUNCTION		41/37 & 47/93	178C3
Tredegar Junction Lower S.B.		41/37 & 47/93	
TREDEGAR SOUTH END COLLY HALT		41/28	—
Tredomen S.B.		47/88	171B6
Treduston Crossing		59/21	121C5
Trefach Colly		49/25	157D6
TREFEGLWYS			116B2
TREFEINON		59/21	121D5
Treferig Goods		49/84	161A4
Treferig House Siding		49/84	161A4
Treferig Junction		49/84	161B3
Treferig Old Mill Siding		49/84	161A4
Treffgarne S.B.		58/5	123B2
Treffry Siding		11/24	3B6
Trefonen			117A6
* Treforest Barry G.F.		46/71	172D6
Treforest Branch Junction		46/112	173B1
* Treforest Chemical Works		46/71	172D6
TREFOREST ESTATE HALT		46/75	173B2
Treforest Estate Junction			173A1
TREFOREST HALT			172B6
TREFOREST HIGH LEVEL		46/111	172D6
* Treforest High Level Goods		46/68	172C5
Treforest Junction		46/68	172C6
Treforest Llantwit Road Goods		46/68	172C5
TREFOREST LOW LEVEL		46/67	172C6
Treforest Steel Works S.B.		46/68	172C5
Treforest Tin Plate Works		46/70	172D6
* Treforest Trading Estate		46/74	173B2
Trefynant Brickworks			94C1
Tregagle S.B.		11/1	2A4
TREGARON		58/34	127A6
Tregibbon Quarry			164B5
Tregonissey Crossing		11/5	3D6
Tregoss Moor S.B.		11/22	3A4
TREHAFOD		46/35	172A2
Trehafod S.B.'s (Barry Rly)		46/110	172A3
TREHARRIS		47/80	170C4
TREHERBERT		46/5	158C2
Treherbert Branch Jcn (Pontypridd)		46/62	172B2
* Treherne Siding		44/29	146D3
Treherion Crossing			146B3
Trehir Quarry		42/41	179C4
TREHOWELL HALT			95A1
Trelavour Siding		11/30	4B2
Trelewis Drift			170A5
TRELEWIS HALT (Vale of Neath)		47/82	170C5
TRELEWIS PLATFORM (Taff Bargoed)			170B5
Trelewis Sidings			170B5
Treloggan Junction		11/20	3A1
Trelyn Level		42/36	178C2
Tremabe S.B.		11/12	6A4
TREMAINS HALT		44/6	144D2
Trembear S.B.		11/4	3C5
* Tre-mellens Siding			—
Tremorfa Works		43/100	149C6
Trenance Junction S.B.		11/4	3C6
Trenance Siding S.B.		11/4	3C5
Trenance Viaduct G.F. (Newquay)		11/19	3A1
Trenant		40/19	182D1
* TRENCH CROSSING		32/46	—
TRENCH HALT (Ellesmere)			95C5
* Trench Ironworks		32/50	—
Trench Sidings S.B. (Hadley Jcn)		32/46	—
Trencreek G.F.'s		11/20	3A1
Trenoweth Colly			167D5
TREORCHY		46/11	158D3
* TREORKY		46/9	158D3
TREOWEN HALT		47/99	178B5
TRERHYNGYLL AND MAENDY HALT		44/24	144B4
Trerice Siding		11/29	4B1
Trerule S.B.		11/14	7B1
Tresarrett Siding		11/35	—
Tresavean		10/29	1B6
Treshenkin Colly		51/38	155D5
Treskilling Siding		11/24	3B6
Tresulgan Viaduct S.B.'s		11/14	6B6
TRETHOMAS		42/44	179C6
Trethosa Siding		11/31	4D1
Trevanny Siding		11/25	4C6
Trevemper Siding		10/32	3A1
Treveor Siding		10/11	1C6
Treverne Terrace Crossing			3A2
Treverrin S.B.		11/8	6C1
Trevethin Junction		39/17	182C6
Treviddo Viaduct S.B.'s		11/13	6B5
TREVIL		41/7	—
Trevil Quarries		41/7	175A1
Treviscoe Crossing			4C1
Treviscoe Siding		11/31	4C2
TREVOR			94C1
Trevor Colly (Trehafod)		46/33	172A1
* Trevor Mills Siding			94B1
Trevose Head Siding		57/15	134C2
Trewen Colly			165D3
TREWERRY AND TRERICE HALT		10/31	3B1
Trewerry Siding		10/31	3B1
Trewheela Siding		11/29	4B1
TREWYTHAN			116B2
Triangle G.F. (Reading)		24/36	33B3
Triley S.B.			107D1
Trimley Hall Siding			92B2
Trimsaran Branch Junction		57/44	133B2
TRIMSARAN ROAD		57/41	133B3
Trimsaran Upper Colly		57/44	133B3
Trimsaran Waun-Hir Colly		57/44	133B2
Trinant			178A6
* Troedrhiw Llech Colly			165C3
TROEDYRHIEW			169C3
TROEDYRHIEW GARTH		49/7	156D3
* TROEDYRHIW (B & M Jt)			169C2
TROEDYRHIW (T.V.)			169C3
* Troedyrhiw Colly		46/28	159D5
Troedyrhiw Quarry			169B3
Troed y Rhiw Fedwin Crossing		59/11	—
Troedyrhiwfwch Colly		42/12	177A1
TROEDYRHIWFUWCH HALT (Pontlottyn)		42/9	167D5
TROEDYDHIW HALT (G.W.R.)			169C2
Trosnant Junctions		39/18 & 47/111	182C6
Trostre Crossing (Dafen)		57/60	134C4
Trostre Pit (Nantyglo)		40/51	175D6
Trostre Tin Plate Works		57/32	134D5
TROUBLE HOUSE HALT		20/38	59C1
TROWBRIDGE		21/16	46C1
* TROY HOUSE, MONMOUTH			53B1
TRUMPERS CROSSING HALT		24/42	37C4
TRURO		10/19	2A6
Truro and Newquay Junction		10/16	2A1
Truro Cattle Pens, S.B.		11/1	2A6
Truro, Newham		10/18	2A4
TRURO ROAD		10/17	2A5
Truro Viaduct S.B.		11/1	2A6
TRUSHAM		14/43	14A3
TRUTHALL PLATFORM		10/26	1D5

* Trynant Colly		182D1
Tubbs Mill Crossing	27/29	—
TUCKER STREET, WELLS	16/37	22A4
Tucking Mill Siding	10/27	1B6
Tuffley Branch	35/17	—
Tuffley Junction	35/2	56D2
Tuffley Siding S.B.	35/2	—
Tufts Junction S.B.	37/10	54D2
Tumble Goods	57/52	133A5
Tunnel Junction (Chester)		88D4
Tunnel Junction (Worcester)	33/16	60C6
Tunnel Pit (Abernant)	47/51	165B5
Tunnel Pit (Beaufort)		175B4
Tunnel Pit (Fochriw)		167C3
Tunnel Pit Junction (Fochriw)		167D4
Tunnel Quarry Siding (Quakers Yard)		170C4
Tunnel Road Yard (Birkenhead)		90C3
Tunnel S.B.'s (Cherry Orchard)		173B6
Tunnel Siding (Tonmawr)	51/42	153D3
Tunnel Yard (Newport)	38/64	152A3
TURNCHAPEL	12/29	—
Turners Crossing		5C2
TUTSHILL HALT	36/9	52B5
Tweedle Colly		?
TWERTON	21/4	27D4
TWERTON ON AVON	21/4	27D4
Twerton Tunnel S.B.	27/4	27A3
Twmpath Level		182C6
TWYFORD	24/14	34D1
TWYFORD ABBEY HALT	26/23	36A6
* Twyford Abbey Sidings	26/26	38A2
Twynau Gwynion Quarry		166B3
* Twyn Blainant		—
Twyn Carno Pot	42/1	167B5
Twyn Disgwyth Quarry		122D1
Twyn Gwyn Colly		178B5
Twyn Simon Colly	40/63	177D5
Ty Cerrig Sidings		93B4
Tychwyth Colly	49/2	156B2
TYCOCH	57/43	133D2
Tycoch Loop Junction	57/2	133D1
Tycoed Colly	51/41	153C1
TYDDYN BRIDGE HALT		114A4
* TYDDYN GWYN		109D5
* TYDEE		184D1
Tydraw Colly	46/3	158B1
TYDU (Rogerstone)	40/38	184D1
Tydu Colly (Coed Ely)	49/62	160D6
Tydu Crossing (Ynisarwed)	47/3	162D3
Tyfedw S.B.	63/24	107D2
Ty Fry Colly (Aberbargoed)		177D4
Ty Fry Level (Pentre)		158D4
TY-FYSTON HALT	44/59	148B5
TYGLAS		174B5
Ty Gwyn Colly (Cwmffrwdoer)	40/73	182C4
* Tygwyn Colly (Gurnos)	53/Ind	—
Ty Gwynn Bach Colly (Nantyffyllon)	49/1	156A2
TYGWYN HALT		109C3
Tygwyn-Llantwit Colly		182C4
Ty Hirwain Junction		157D5
Ty Isaf Quarry	52/7	162C1
Tyisha Siding	55/35	133C6
Tylacoch Colly	46/9	158D3
TYLACOCH PLATFORM	46/9	158C3
Tyla Du Level		167D2
Tylahaidd Quarry	59/15	122D5
Tylcha Fach Colly	49/64	161A1
* Tylcha Wen Colly	49/62	—
Tyle Dowlais Pit		167B2
Tye Penlan Colly	53/Ind	—
Tylers Arms Junction	40/53	176B6
TYLERS ARMS PLATFORM	40/55	176C6
Tylers Green S.B.	26/9	34A4
Tylerybont Siding (High Level)		166B3
Tylerybont Siding (Low Level)		166B3
Tyllwyd Colly	54/41	131A5
TYLLWYN HALT	40/4	175D4
Tylors Colly		159A4
TYLORSTOWN	46/48	159B4
Tylorstown Lower Siding	46/49	159B4
TYLWCH	59/29	120A6
Tymaen Branch	51/24	154B4
Tymaen Junction S.B.	51/24	154B3
Tymawr Colly (Gyfeillon)	46/37	172A3
Tymawr S.B. (B.P. & G.V.)	57/45	133C2
Tynant Colly (Llantwit Fardre)		161B5
* Tynant Quarry (Pentyrch)	46/84	174A2
Tyndall Field Sidings		149C4
Tyndall St Cart Yard Crossing	43/73	150D5
Tyndall St Crossing S.B.	43/62	149C4
Tyndall St High Level Junction	43/62	150C6
* Tynebedw Colly	46/11	158D4
* Tyne Bone Works		—
TYNEWYDD	49/36	160B1
Tynewydd Colly (Ogmore Vale)	49/36	160A1
Tynewydd Colly (Pontlottyn)	42/7	167D5
Tynewydd Colly (Porth)	46/28	159D5
Tynewydd Colly (Treherbert)	46/4	158B2
Tynewydd Crossing (Llangynog)		117A1
Tynewydd Mileage Siding (Porth)	46/28	159D5
Tynewydd Siding (Glyn Neath)	47/13	163B4
Tynewydd Works (Upper Pontnewydd)		183A2
Tyning Pit	18/7	—
* Tynoming Crossing		?
Tynpant Colly	52/21	132B5
Tyntesfield Siding	16/32	21A6
* Tyntilla Colly		159B3
Tyn Ton Cutting	47/14	163B6
Tynybedw S.B.		158D4
Tynybryn Crossing	44/11	145D3
Tynycaeau Junction	44/27	146C3
Tyncerig S.B.	54/10	131C3
Tyncoed Junction	49/20	143C5
* Tyn y Coed Colly	51/41	153D1
TYNYCWM HALT (Risca)	40/36	180C6
Tyn-y-cwm Quarry (Tonmawr)	51/51	153C3
Tyn-y-ffram S.B.	51/3	154C4
Tyn-y-ffram Reservoir Siding	51/3	154D4
Tyngraig Colly (Blackmill)	49/67	160D2
Tynygraig Crossing (Llanbradach)		179C3
Tynynant Colly	49/78	161B5
Tynywain Colly (Bryncethin Jcn)	49/24	157D5
* Tynywain Colly (Ystrad Rhondda)	46/19	159B3
Tynywain Rhondda Colly		159B3
Tyn-y-waun Colly	57/38	133A4
* Ty Picca Colly	46/39	172A3
Tyra Siding	47/8	162B6
Tyrau Colly		162B6
Tyrcenol Junction	53/42 & 55/28	138C4
Tyrcenol Siding	53/42	—
Tyre Mill S.B.	41/21	—
Tyrergyd Colly		164B5
Tyrissa Colly	53/5	—
* Tyr Nicholas Colly		?
* Tyr Pentir Colly Siding		?
TYSELEY	30/6	80D4
Ty Talwyn Colly		143A4
TYTHERINGTON	20/51	—
Ty Trist Colly	41/28	—
Ty Trist Siding S.B.	41/29	—
* Ty Uchaf Crossing	54/42	131A5
Ty Ucha Colly	54/35	131A1
TYWITH	49/2	156B2
TYWYN		113C1
UFFCULME	15/18	16A4
UFFINGTON	23/2	29D5
Ufton Crossing S.B.	23/27	32D2

270

Undy Crossing S.B.	38/24	52A1
UNDY HALT	38/21	52D2
* Union Road Crossing (Bristol)	19/41	—
Union Siding	39/19	183B5
* Union Street Junction		90D5
United Colly Siding S.B.		93B6
United National Colly G.F.	41/45	—
United National Siding	40/31	180A4
* United Westminster & Wrexham Colly		92C4
Universal Colly		171D5
UP EXE AND SILVERTON	15/16	16C1
UP EXE HALT	15/16	16C1
UPHILL	16/21	21D2
Uphill Junction	16/21	21D2
Upper Abercanaid Colly		168D5
UPPER BANK	53/4	
Upper Bank Copper Works	53/4	136B3
Upper Bedwellty Sidings	41/29	—
UPPER BOAT		173A1
UPPER BOAT HALT		173A1
* Upper Boat Power Station	46/73	173A1
* Upper Bute Road S.B.	46/9	158D3
Upper Corris		113A6
Upper Cwm Gelly Colly	41/36	—
Upper Cwmtwrch Colly	53/28	—
Upper Cymmer Colly	46/28	159D5
Upper Cynon S.B.	51/30	153D6
Upper Duffryn Colly	47/56	165C5
Upper East Side (Nantyglo)		175B6
Upper Fan Pit	46/43	158C5
Upper Forge (Lydney)	37/9	53C3
* Upper Forest Works	53/39	—
Upper Gethin Pit		169B2
Upper Llwydcoed Sidings	47/48	165A3
UPPER LYDBROOK	37/43	54A1
Upper Pengam Colly	42/32	178A3
Upper Penrhiwfer Colly		160B5
Upper Pit (Mountain Ash)		165C6
UPPER PONTNEWYDD	39/19	183B2
* Upper Pwllyrhebog S.B.	46/22	159C3
Upper Race	47/108	182C5
Upper Rosemarket Crossing	58/15	124B2
UPPER SOUDLEY HALT	37/37	54C3
Upper White Rose Colly	42/16	177A2
Upper Writhlington Colly		27D3
UPTON (Midland)	34/14	—
UPTON (Upton & Blewbury)	23/38	31C4
UPTON AND BLEWBURY	23/38	31C4
UPTON BY CHESTER HALT		91B5
Upton Lovell Siding	21/55	47A1
UPTON MAGNA	32/1	69B1
Upton Scudamore S.B.	21/54	46A5
Upton S.B. (Chester)		91C5
Upton Siding (Shifnal)	32/16	69C6
UPWEY	17/13	42A5
UPWEY AND BROADWEY	17/3	42A6
UPWEY JUNCTION	17/3	42A6
UPWEY WISHING WELL HALT	17/3	42A6
USK	36/23	108A5
Uskmouth S.B.	38/35	151C6
* Uskside Ironworks		152C4
UXBRIDGE HIGH STREET	26/11	35A1
UXBRIDGE ROAD (West London)	25/26	38C5
UXBRIDGE VINE STREET	24/39	35B1
Vallis Quarries	21/51	45B3
VAN		116C1
Van Branch Junction		116D5
* Van Colly (Caerphilly)		173B6
Van Mines		116C1
* Vann Road (Caerphilly)		173B6
Van Siding (Moseley Green)	37/21	54D2
Varcoe Siding		4D1
VARTEG (Blaenavon)	39/13	—

Varteg Brickworks (Ystradgynlais)	52/18	132C3
Varteg Colly (Ynisygeinon)	52/17	132C3
* Varteg Colly (Bryn)	51/5	154C6
Varteg Deep Colly (Cwmffrwd)		181C5
Varteg Hill Colly	39/13 & 41/24	181C5
Varteg Hill No 2 Colly		181C4
* Varteg Top Siding		181D5
Vastern Road Goods	24/6	33B4
Vauxhall Colly Sdgs S.B. (Ruabon)		94D5
Vauxhall Quay (Plymouth)	12/18	8D5
Vauxhall Wharf (Plymouth)	12/11	8D4
Vaynor Quarry Siding		166C2
Vedw Sidings	42/48	180C3
Velindre S.B. (Aberavon)	51/16	154D2
Velindre Viaduct G.F. (Aberavon)	51/16	141A4
Velindre Works (Llangefelach)	55/43	135B2
Velin Vach S.B.	49/16	143C4
Venallt Colly	47/9	163B1
Venallt Fuel Works	47/8	163B2
* Veness's Siding		49C6
VENN CROSS	15/22	15B3
Venus Colly	37/41	54D1
Verdun Colly		?
Vernon Junction S.B.	50/13	140C4
Viaduct 199 S.B. (Dorchester)	17/4	41C5
Viaduct 202 S.B. (Dorchester)	17/4	41C5
Viaduct Colly (Branches Fork)	39/23	182B5
Viaduct Junction S.B. (London)	25/26	38B4
Viaduct S.B. (Cardiff Docks)	43/72	150B5
Viaduct Works Siding (Crumlin)	47/101	178A6
Vicarage Crossing (Llandre)		114B2
VICARAGE CROSSING HALT (Coed Poeth)		93C2
VICTORIA (Ebbw Vale)	40/7	175B4
VICTORIA, LONDON		40C2
VICTORIA (Roche)	11/22	3A5
Victoria Basin S.B. (Wolverhampton)	31/7	74B4
Victoria Colly (Cwmavon)		154C4
Victoria Colly (Ebbw Vale)	40/5	176A3
Victoria Colly (Nantyffyllon)	49/2	156B2
Victoria Colly (Pontycymmer)	49/30	156C5
Victoria Colly (Pwllgwaun)		172B4
Victoria Dock Goods (London)	25/37	40D5
Victoria Garw Valley S.B.	49/27	156C5
Victoria Pier (Plymouth)	12/24	—
Victoria Road Sidings (Bristol)	19/16	24C5
Victory Siding S.B.	15/14	15B6
* Villiers Estate Siding (Tymaen)	51/24	—
* Villiers Works (Six Pit Junction)	53/7	—
Vinegar Branch	33/19	60C5
Viponds Sidings	39/21	181C6
Virgil Street Goods		149D2
Virginia Siding	11/28	4C1
* Vittoria Dock		90A4
Vivian's Pit (Abertillery)	40/59	182A2
Vivians Sand Siding (Port Talbot)	50/16	136D6
Vivians Works (Port Talbot)	50/30	141C5
Vobster Breach Colly	21/49	45B1
Vobster Colly	21/49	45B2
Vobster Quarry	21/49	45A2
Voilart Colly	54/26	—
VOWCHURCH	63/44	106D4
Vron Colly		93C3
Vron Junction		93A4
Vron Lodge Crossing		93B4
* Vulcan Foundry Siding		60C6
WADBOROUGH	34/4	—
WADEBRIDGE	11/34	—
WAENAVON	41/19	—
Waenavon Nantyglo Colly	41/13	—
Waenavon Slope Colly	41/19	—
* Waencaegurwen Siding	53/32	—
Waen Llwyd Colly		176C4
Waen Nantyglo Colly		—

271

Waenycoed Old Colly	53/18	—	
* Waenycoed New Colly	53/19	—	
Wagon Works Siding (Bristol)	19/47	—	
Wainborfa Colly	42/32	178B2	
WAINFELIN HALT	39/17	182B6	
WAINHILL HALT	26/33	87B4	
WALCOT	32/1	69B1	
WALFORD HALT	36/27	105D2	
Walkhampton Common Siding	14/32	10C5	
WALLBRIDGE, STROUD	20/55	—	
Walleroo Crossing	50/12	140D3	
WALLINGFORD	23/39	31C6	
WALLINGFORD ROAD	23/15	31D6	
Wallsend Colly (Forest of Dean)	37/44	54C2	
Wallsend Siding (Common Bch)		161C5	
Walnut Tree Branch Junction		173C5	
WALNUT TREE BRIDGE	46/80	173D2	
WALNUT TREE JUNCTION	46/80	173D2	
Walnut Tree Junction S.B.	46/80	173D3	
Walnut Tree West S.B.		174A2	
Walsall Street Goods	31/11	74C4	
Waltham Siding S.B.	24/15	34C3	
Walton New Junction		88B5	
Walton Old Junction		88B5	
Wansborough Siding	15/24	17A3	
WANSTROW	16/41	45C3	
WANTAGE ROAD	23/3	31B2	
Wapley Common S.B.	20/4	26C2	
WAPPENHAM	29/18	—	
Wapping Wharf	19/38	24B2	
* Waresley Siding		?	
WARGRAVE	24/37	34D1	
WARMINSTER	21/54	47B5	
WARMLEY	20/48	—	
WARREN HALT	14/19	14B6	
* Warren Lane Siding		?	
WARRINGTON		88A5	
WARWICK	30/18	82A6	
WARWICK ROAD (SMJ)	29/7	—	
Warwick Road Goods (Kensington)	25/29	38C5	
* Warwill Foundry Siding		181D2	
WASHFORD	15/24	17B3	
WATCHET	15/25	17A3	
Watchet Paper Mills Siding	15/24	17A3	
Water Eaton Crossing	27/28	—	
Waterhall Goods (Ely)	49/85	146C6	
Waterhall Junction (OVE Line)	49/44	143A3	
Waterhall Junction S.B. (Ely)	46/93	146C6	
Water Lane Crossing	14/21	13C2	
Waterlip Quarry Siding	16/40	22C6	
Waterloo Colly (Oakdale)	40/65	177D5	
Waterloo Crossing (Kingsland)		102B1	
Waterloo G.F. (Cardiff)	46/114	149A5	
WATERLOO HALT (Caerphilly)	42/55	180D2	
Waterloo Junction S.B. (Newport)	38/46	152C2	
Waterloo Loop S.B. (Newport)	38/7	152A1	
Waterloo Pit (Upper Lydbrook)	37/43	54A1	
Waterloo Road S.B. (Winsor Hill)	18/13	—	
Waterloo Tin Works (Caerphilly)	42/54	180D2	
WATERMOOR, CIRENCESTER	22/4	59B4	
Waterston Refinery	58/23	124C2	
Water Street Junction		143A1	
Waterton		144A3	
Water Works Siding (Blagdon)	16/43	21C6	
Water Works Siding (Cheddar)	16/35	22A1	
Water Works Siding (Whitchurch)		174B4	
Watery Lane Goods		93D6	
Watford Crossing S.B.		173B5	
Watling Street Crossing		101C1	
WATLINGTON	26/33	87D2	
Watson's Siding	28/1	61C6	
WATTON, BRECON	52/16	122C3	
Watts Siding	59/27	120D4	
WATTSTOWN PLATFORM	46/49	159B5	

Wattsville Goods	41/42	—	
* Waun Siding	53/30	—	
Waunarlwyd Works		135C2	
Waun Fawr Siding	41/46	180B5	
WAUNGRON	46/93	146C6	
* WAUN GRON PARK	46/93	146C6	
Waun-Hir Colly	57/44	133B2	
Waun Hoskins Slope		181B5	
Waunllech Colly		134B6	
Waun Llwyd Colly	40/7	176C4	
* Waun Siding			
Wauntreoda Siding	46/95	174C4	
Waunwyllt Colly		168D4	
Waunyborfa Colly	42/32	178B2	
Waunycoed Colly	53/18	—	
Way and Works Siding	53/13	?	
Waynes Merthyr Colly			
Waynes Siding		165D1	
Wearde S.B.	11/15	7B3	
Weavings Siding	28/9	62A1	
Webber and Pangbournes G.F.	17/8	42C1	
Websters Crossing		6B5	
WEDNESBURY CENTRAL	31/16	75A6	
Weighbridge Siding S.B.		93C5	
Weighing Machine Siding		94B2	
Weig Lane Crossing		116B3	
WELFORD PARK	23/40	49C3	
Wellfield Siding		121B2	
WELLINGTON (Salop)	32/5	69A4	
WELLINGTON (Somerset)	15/13	15C5	
* Wellington Goods (Shrops)	32/3	69A4	
Wellington Crossing (Moreton on Lugg)	63/13	104A2	
Wellington Junction (Shrewsbury)		99C2	
Wellington Wharf (Dudley)		76A4	
WELLOW	18/15	—	
Wells Branch Junction (Glastonbury)	18/29	—	
WELLS EAST SOMERSET	16/37	22A4	
WELL PRIORY ROAD	16/37 & 18/31	22A4	
WELLS TUCKER STREET	16/37	22A4	
Wellsway Colly	21/46	27B2	
WELSHAMPTON		95D6	
* Welsh Cold Storage G.F.	43/74	150A6	
Welsh Freehold Colly	51/53	153C5	
WELSH HOOK HALT	58/5	123B1	
Welsh Main Colly	51/45	155A3	
Welsh Navigation Colly		161B1	
WELSHPOOL		117D3	
Welshpool Junction (Shrewsbury)		99D2	
Welsh Wallsend Colly	49/68	160D5	
WELTON	21/46	27D2	
WELTON AND MIDSOMER NORTON	21/46	27D2	
Welton Hill Colly	21/46	27D2	
Wenallt Colly (Aberdylais)	47/1	153B3	
Wenallt Colly (Blaenavon)	51/52	153C2	
Wenallt Merthyr Colly		153B3	
Wenallt S.B. (Aberdylais)	47/2	153A3	
WENDLEBURY HALT	27/28	—	
Wenford Bridge	11/35	—	
Wentlodge Colly	41/40	—	
WENVOE	44/29	147B2	
Wen-y-gored Colly		153A2	
Werfa Colly	47/51	165B5	
Werfa Craig Colly		164B5	
Werfa Dare Colly		165B5	
Werfa Loop S.B.	47/51	165B5	
Wernavon Colly		154B3	
Wernbwll Colly		?	
Werncaiach Colly	47/85	170D6	
* Wern Colly	54/40	—	
Wernddu Colly (Neath area)	53/15	135A6	
Wernddu Colly (Caerphilly)		173C6	
Wernddu S.B. (Caerphilly)		173B6	
Wern Fawr Colly		—	
Wernganol Colly		171A6	

272

Name		
Wern Hill Colly		182C6
WERN HIR HALT	36/22	108A3
Wern Ironworks (Llanelly)	57/15	134C2
Wern Lane Siding		93B6
WERN LAS (S & M Line)		98A1
Wern Las Pit (Merthyr)		168D6
Wernos Colly	54/5	131C1
Wern Pistyll Colly	50/13	140C4
Wernplumis Branch	53/50	—
Wern Siding (Portmadoc)		109B2
Wern Tarw Colly	49/26	145A1
* Wern y Bryn Colly		154B6
Wesley Hill Crossing		3A2
WEST ACCESS HALT	36/15	108A3
WEST ACTON	25/22	38B1
West Adderbury Pits	27/1	84D3
WEST BAY	17/13	41C1
West Blaina Red Ash Colly		176B5
Westbourne Bridge S.B.	25/17	39D4
WESTBOURNE PARK	25/12	39D3
* WESTBOURNE PARK & KENSAL GREEN		39C4
WEST BROMPTON	25/30	38D6
* WEST BROMPTON & LILLIE BRIDGE		38D6
WEST BROMWICH	31/20	75D6
WESTBROOK	63/44	106B2
WESTBURY (Salop)		98C2
WESTBURY (Wilts)	21/34	46C3
WESTBURY-ON-SEVERN HALT	36/20	53A6
* West Canal Wharf (Cardiff)		149D4
West Caradon		6C3
West Central S.B. (Swansea)	56/8	137B3
West Cheshire Junction		88D1
Westcott S.B.	15/8	16C3
West Depot (Bristol)	19/2	24D1
* West Dock Swing Bridge S.B.	43/77	150A4
Westdown Quarry Siding		45B2
WEST DRAYTON	24/23	35B1
WEST DRAYTON AND YIEWSLEY	24/23	35B1
West Drayton Coal Yard	24/41	35C1
WEST EALING	24/33	37B5
West Elliot Colly	42/18	177B2
West End (Burton Dassett)	29/7	—
West End Colly (Nailsea)	16/30	21A5
West End Tunnel Loop S.B.	51/5	154C6
Westerleigh Junctions (GWR)	20/3	26C2
Westerleigh Yards (Mid)	20/40	—
Western Colly		160A3
* Western Gas Colly	54/51	—
* Western Valleys Junction		152A2
WEST EXE HALT	15/16	16A2
Westfield Mill Crossing	58/15	124B3
* Westfields Siding	63/28	—
West Gloucestershire Power Station	37/9	53C3
West Goonbarrow Siding	11/23	4A4
WESTHAM HALT	17/11	42D3
WEST KIRBY		89B1
Westland Siding		44A2
Westleigh Quarries	15/11	15C4
West Llantwit Colly	49/79	161B4
West London Carriage Sidings	25/10	39B4
WEST LONDON JUNCTION		39B6
West London Junction (Clapham)	25/32	38D2
West London Junction (O.O.C.)	25/5	39B3
West Loop North Junction (Bristol)	19/2	24D1
West Mendalgief S.B.	38/44	152D2
Westminster Colly		93A1
* WEST MOOR	63/42	—
Westmoreland Road Sidings	21/5	27D5
West of England New Siding	11/32	4D1
WESTON (Bath)	20/48	—
Weston Crossing (Knighton)	59/13	—
WESTON JUNCTION (W-super-M.)	16/26	21C2
WESTON MILL HALT	12/2	—
WESTON MILTON HALT	16/25	21C2
WESTON RHYN		95B2
WESTON-SUB-EDGE	28/20	62C4
WESTON-SUPER-MARE	16/22	21C1
WESTON-UNDER-PENYARD HALT	36/33	105C4
Weston Wharf (Oswestry)		96C1
Westover Crossing		43B1
WEST PENNARD	18/29	—
West Quay Road Crossing		19B5
West Rhondda Colly (Lletty Brongu)	51/6	157A2
West Rhondda Colly (Pontyrhyll)	49/31	156D5
WEST RHONDDA HALT	51/14	157A2
WEST RUISLIP	26/13	36A1
WEST SHEFFORD	23/40	49B3
West Side Colly Siding (Nantyglo)		175B6
West Side Roath Basin S.B.	43/77	150D5
West Swansea Colly		135C1
West Town Crossing		25D3
West Treviscoe	11/28	4C1
WESTWOOD HALT (Salop)	32/31	71A3
Westwood Quarry (Wiltshire)	21/15	27C5
Westwood S.B. (Cornwall)	11/11	6A3
WEST WYCOMBE	26/6	87D5
WEYHILL	22/19	51D2
WEYMOUTH	17/1	42C3
Weymouth Quay	17/12	42D4
Wharf Colly		70C5
Wharf Lines Junction (Barry)	44/56	143D4
Whatley Quarry	21/51	45A3
Wheal Agar Siding	10/28	1A5
Wheal Anna Siding	11/24	4B5
Wheal Beauchamp Siding	10/29	1B6
Wheal Benallick Siding	11/28	4C1
Wheal Buller Siding	10/29	1B6
Wheal Busy Siding	10/14	2A1
Wheal Crelake Siding	14/26	10B4
Wheal Henry Siding	11/24	4B5
Wheal Louisa Siding	11/3	4D3
Wheal Rashleigh Siding	11/25	4A6
Wheal Remfrey Siding	11/29	4B1
Wheal Rose Siding	11/23	4A4
Wheal Virgin Siding	11/30	4A4
WHEATLEY	27/22	67C6
Wheatsheaf Goods		93B5
Wheatsheaf Junction		93B6
Wheatsheaf Sidings		93B5
Wheldons Siding	29/13	—
Whetcombe Quarry Siding	14/44	13D3
Whimsey Goods	37/30	54A5
WHIMSEY HALT	37/31	54A5
Whimsey Junction	37/32	54B5
WHITBY LOCKS		90D1
WHITCHURCH (GLAM)		174B4
WHITCHURCH (HANTS)	23/35	50D1
WHITCHURCH (Salop)		97D2
WHITCHURCH DOWN PLATFORM	14/26	10B4
WHITCHURCH HALT (Somerset)	21/43	27A1
WHITCHURCH TOWN (Hants)	23/35	50D1
Whiteball Tunnel S.B.	15/12	15C4
WHITEBROOK HALT	36/28	53C2
WHITE CITY	25/24	38B4
Whitecliffe Quarry Siding	37/39	53D3
WHITECROFT	37/10	54D1
Whitecroft Level Colly	37/10	54D1
Whitefield Crossing		29D4
Whitegate Siding (Parkandillack)	11/30	4B2
Whitegates Crossing (Nantmawr)		119A3
Whitegates Junction (Proposed)	37/18	54B1
WHITEHALL HALT	15/18	16A6
* Whitehall Quarry (Nelson Branch)		171A4
Whitehall Quarry Siding (Nelson & L)		170D5
WHITE HART HALT	42/57	180C2
Whitehaven Quarry		119A3
Whiteheads Siding (Weymouth)	17/10	42C5
Whiteheads Steel Works (Newport)	38/48	152C3

WHITEHURST HALT		95C3
Whitehurst Goods		95C3
* WHITE LADIES ROAD		23D4
WHITEMILL	58/42	—
White Oak Colly	16/30	21A5
Whiterleys Ballast Siding		—
White Rocks Siding	53/4	—
WHITE ROSE	42/16	177A2
White Rose Colly	42/16	177B2
Whites Crossing		45B2
* Whitestone Quarry	19/31	25C6
Whitford Steel Works	50/21	140D3
WHITLAND	58/8	125C6
WHITLOCK'S END HALT	30/30	81B4
WHITNEY-ON-WYE	63/40	—
* Whitterley's Ballast Pit	59/11	—
* Whittington Ballast Siding		96B1
WHITTINGTON HIGH LEVEL		96B2
WHITTINGTON LOW LEVEL		96C2
Whitworth Colly (Blaenavon)	51/52	153C2
Whitworth Colly (Tredegar)	41/28	—
WHITWORTH HALT (Whitworth Bch)		153B5
* Whitworth Siding (Llandovery)	59/4	—
Wick Crossing (Curry Rivel Junction)	16/46	20B5
* Wick S.B. (Berkeley Road)	20/44	—
WICKWAR	20/43	—
* Widemarsh Junction	63/16	104A5
WIDNEY MANOR	30/10	81B5
Wigfach Colly	55/5	135C2
Wigpool Iron Mine		105D4
Wilcrick Crossing		52D2
Wilderness Siding		93B6
* WILDMILL		144C1
Wildon Iron Works (Govilon)	41/17	—
Wilds Siding (Bridgwater)	18/30	—
WILEY		47B3
Wilkins Colly		?
WILLERSEY HALT	28/20	62D4
* Wilham's Siding		147C6
Willingsworth Siding	31/17	75A4
WILLITON	15/26	17B4
Willowford S.B.	46/76	173C2
Willows Wire Works Junction		168D2
WILMCOTE	30/32	82C3
WILTON NORTH	21/57	47D5
Wilton Park S.B.	26/9	34A5
Wimberry Branch Junction	37/15	54B1
Wimberry Sidings	37/16	54B1
Wimberry Tramway	37/47	54B1
* Wimblow Junction	37/15	54B1
Wimborne Junction	18/21	—
WINCANTON	18/16	—
WINCHCOMBE	28/19	63C4
WINCHESTER	23/33	51D6
Winchester Camp Railway	23/33	51C6
Winchester Junction	23/34	51C6
Winch Mawr		168B2
Windber Colly	47/32	165A1
WINDMILL END	31/52	76C5
Windmill End Junction	31/52	76B5
WINDSOR	24/40	34D5
WINDSOR AND ETON	24/40	34D5
WINDSOR COLLY HALT		179C1
Windsor Passing Loop S.B.		171C1
* Windsor Siding (Ynysybwl)		171B1
* Windsor Slipway Siding (Cardiff)		147B5
WIND STREET (Swansea)	56/1	137B2
Wind Street Junction	56/3	137B2
Wingfield Colly		177C1
WINGFIELD VILLAS HALT	12/2	8C3
Winnall Down Siding	23/33	51D6
* Winnall Pit		54C1
Winnall Siding	23/33	51C6
WINSCOMBE, SOMERSET	16/34	21D4
Winsel Crossing	58/17	124A2
WINSON GREEN	31/23	79B6
Winsor Hill S.B.	18/13	—
WINTERBOURNE	20/2	23B6
Wireworks Branch (Tintern)	36/30	52A5
Wirral Colly		89D2
Wirral Junction		89B1
WISHFORD	21/56	47C4
WISTANSTOW HALT	63/3	100D4
* WITHAM FRIARY	16/51	45C4
WITHAM, SOMERSET	16/51	45C3
WITHINGTON, GLOS	22/1	57B3
WITHINGTON (Hereford)	33/1	104B3
Withymoor Basin	31/52	76C5
Withymoor Ironworks	31/52	76C5
Witley Colly		77B5
WITNEY	27/24	66B5
Witney Junction (Yarnton)	27/25	68A1
WIVELISCOMBE	15/22	15A4
Wivelscombe S.B. (St. Germans)	11/16	7B2
WIXFORD	34/18	—
WNION HALT		110B5
WOBURN GREEN	24/38	34A4
Wolfhall Junction	22/14 & 23/18	48B2
WOLF'S CASTLE HALT	58/5	123B2
WOLHAMPTON	23/26	32D1
WOLLERTON HALT	32/44	99C4
Wolvercot Junction	27/6	68B2
* Wolvercot Mill Siding		68B2
WOLVERCOT PLATFORM	27/7	68B2
Wolvercot Siding S.B.	27/7	68B2
WOLVERCOTE HALT	27/26	68B3
Wolverhampton Herbert Street	31/7	74A5
WOLVERHAMPTON LOW LEVEL	31/8	74A6
Wolverhampton New Depot	31/12	74C4
Wolverhampton North Junction	31/7	74B4
Wolverhampton Steam Shed S.B.	31/3	74A3
Wolverhampton Walsall Street	31/10	74C4
Wolverhampton Wednesfield Road	31/9	—
Wolverton Crossing	32/29	100C5
WOMBOURN	31/54	73B1
* Wombridge Branch	32/50	—
Wombridge Crossing	32/6	69A6
* Wombridge Ironworks	32/51	—
* Wombridge Old Quarry Siding	32/51	—
WOOBURN GREEN	24/38	34A4
WOODBOROUGH	21/42	48D2
WOODBOROUGH (Winscombe)	16/36	21D4
WOODCHESTER	20/56	—
WOOD END	30/31	81D4
Woodfield Colly (Penar Branch)	40/69	178A4
Woodfield Colly S.B. (Trehafod)	46/32	172A2
Woodfield Crossing S.B. (Penar Branch)	40/69	178B4
WOODFORD & HINTON	29/10	—
WOODFORD HALSE	29/10	—
Woodford West Junction	29/9	—
Wood Green Crossing	36/33	105D5
WOODHAY	23/36	50A1
Woodhouse Colly		70B6
Woodlands Crossing (Little Stretton)	63/3	100B4
Woodlands S.B. (Somerset)	21/28	45B4
WOOD LANE (White City)	25/24	38C4
Wood Lane Junction S.B.	25/23	38B4
Wood Lane Milk Depot	25/22	38B4
Woodley Bridge S.B.	24/13	32B6
WOODSIDE, BIRKENHEAD		90B5
Woodside Branch (Round Oak)	31/43	76C3
WOODSTOCK (Bletchington)	27/4	85D2
Woodstock Junction (LNWR)	27/26	—
WOODSTOCK ROAD (Bletchington)	27/4	85D2
WOODSTOCK ROAD (Kidlington)	27/5	67A3
Woodstock Road G.F. (LNWR)	27/26	—
* Woodtown Siding		10C5
WOODVILLE ROAD HALT	46/104	149B3

WOOFERTON	63/8	101D3	YARDLEY WOOD	30/30	81B4
WOOFFERTON	63/8	101D3	Yarnbrook S.B.	21/16	46C2
WOOKEY	16/36	22C3	YARNTON	27/25 & 28/11	68A1
Woolascot Crossing		98B5	Yarnton Lane Crossing	27/6	67B3
WOOLASTON	36/10	52A6	YATE	20/41	—
WOOLHAMPTON	23/26	32D1	Yate Collieries	20/43	—
Woorgreens Pit Siding	37/24	54B2	Yate South Junction	20/41	26C2
WOOTTON BASSETT	20/8	29C1	YATTON	16/27	21B4
Wootton Bassett Incline S.B.	21/13	28A6	Yatton East S.B.	16/29	21B4
WOOTTON BASSETT ROAD		29C2	YEALMPTON	12/30	7D6
Wootton Bassett West Crossovers	20/5	28A6	YEARSETT		61B1
WOOTTON RIVERS HALT	21/42	48C4	YELVERTON	14/27	10D5
WOOTTON WAWEN PLATFORM	30/32	82B3	YEO MILL HALT	15/20	18D4
Worcester Butts Branch	33/10	60C4	Yeo Pump House Siding	16/43	21C6
Worcester Colly (Cockett)	55/5	135C2	YEOVENEY HALT	24/41	35D1
Worcester Corporation Siding	33/9	60D4	Yeovil Clifton Maybank Goods		44D6
WORCESTER FOREGATE STREET	33/10	60C5	YEOVIL HENDFORD	17/16	44C4
Worcester Rainbow Hill Junction	33/16	60C6	YEOVIL PEN MILL	17/6	44B6
Worcester Riverside Branch	33/10	60D5	Yeovil South Junction	17/6	44C6
WORCESTER SHRUB HILL	33/16	60C6	YEOVIL TOWN	17/16	44B5
Worcester Sidings S.B. (Hereford)	63/26	104B5	YETMINSTER	17/5	44B3
Worcester Tunnel Junction	33/16	60C6	Yetminster Mill Crossing		44B3
Worcester Vinegar Branch	33/19	60C5	Yew Tree Crossing S.B.	40/53	176B5
* Worcester Works (Morriston)	53/39	—	Ynisallen	55/49	135A4
Workmans Mill	20/53	—	YNISCEDWYN (N. & B.)	52/19	132C3
Workshop Sidings (Swindon)	20/17	30C1	Yniscedwyn Branch G.F. (Gurnos)	53/46	—
WORLE	16/26	21C2	Yniscedwyn Colly	53/50	—
* WORLE (1990 Station)	16/26	21C2	Yniscedwyn Ironworks Branch	53/48	—
WORLE (Puxton and Worle)	16/27	21C3	Ynisci Colly	52/17	132C3
Worle Junction	16/26	21C2	* Yniscoi Treble Line Junction	46/77	173C3
Wormleighton Crossing	30/21	83D4	Yniscorrwg Colly	51/45	155B3
WORMWOOD SCRUBS	25/25	39B4	* Yniscynon Colly		165C3
Wormwood Scrubs Siding		39C6	Ynisdawla Siding	54/44	131C4
WORTHY DOWN PLATFORM	23/34	51B5	Ynisfawr Siding	57/39	133B3
WRANGATON	14/7	11A3	Ynisfechan Colly	53/Ind.	—
Wraysbury Sand Siding	23/28	32C3	Ynisgau Colly	46/77	159B2
Wrekin Chemical Works Siding	32/42	70D5	* YNISGEINON JCN		132D3
Wrekin Foundry Siding	32/38	69A6	* YNISHIR	46/51	159C5
Wrexham and Acton Colly		93C6	Ynismardy Colly		145A6
Wrexham Caia Road Goods		92D3	* Ynisowen Siding		170A3
WREXHAM CENTRAL		93D6	* Ynis y bwt		?
Wrexham Colly S.B.		93C6	Ynisygeinon Colly	52/17	132C3
WREXHAM EXCHANGE		93D6	Ynisygeinon Junction S.B.	52/17 & 53/20	132D2
WREXHAM GENERAL		93D6	Ynisygeinon Sidings S.B.	53/20	—
Wright's Siding (Trevor)		95B2	Ynysallen Siding	55/49	138B4
WRINGTON	16/43	21C5	Ynysamman Colly	54/44	131C4
Writhlington S.B. (S & D)	18/6	—	Ynysarwed Colly	47/4	162C4
Writhlington Sidings (GWR)	21/47	27B3	Ynysarwed Colly S.B.	47/3	162C3
Wroxton		84B2	Ynysawdre Colly	49/20	143C3
Wychall Earth Siding	34/9	—	Ynysawdre Junction	49/20	143D4
* WYCOMBE BRANCH, MAIDENHEAD		34C3	Ynysavon Colly	51/25	154B3
* Wycombe Junction		34C3	Ynysboeth Quarry Siding S.B.	47/74	170C3
* Wye Colly		54B1	Ynys Crossing (Dovey Jcn)		113C4
WYESHAM HALT	36/28	53B1	Ynysdavid Sidings S.B.	51/24	154B3
Wyesham Junction	36/28	53B2	Ynysdawley S.B.	52/10	132C4
Wye Valley Junction S.B.	36/9	52B5	YNYSDDU	41/40	—
WYKE REGIS HALT	17/10	42C5	Ynysddu Lower Goods	41/40	—
Wyke S.B.	16/50	45D1	Ynysdwr Junction		171B3
Wykey Crossing		96D3	Ynysfach Branch Junction		168B1
Wyld's Lane S.B.	33/16	60D6	Ynysfach Ironworks		168C1
WYLLIE HALT	41/39	—	Ynysfach Junction		168C1
WYLYE	21/56	47B3	Ynysfach Loop Junction		168C1
WYNDHAM HALT	49/35	160A1	Ynysfach Siding		168B1
Wyndham Pits	49/34	160A1	* Ynys-faig Siding		111D1
WYNN HALL HALT		94A2	Ynysfarm Crossing		?
Wynnstay Colly (Plas y Wern)		94B2	Ynysfeio S.B.	46/7	158C2
Wynnstay Colly (Ruabon)		94C3	Ynysforgan Colly	53/43	—
WYNNVILLE HALT		94B3	Ynysgau Colly	46/19	159B2
Wynots Hill Pit		?	Ynys Hafren Birkcworks	57/39	133A4
Wyre Common Crossing		72C2	YNYSHIR	46/51	159C5
WYRE FOREST	33/23	72C3	Ynyshir House S.B.		159C5
WYRE HALT	28/2	62B1	Ynyshir Standard S.B.		159C5
WYTHALL	30/30	81C4	YNYSLAS		1213D2
			Ynyslas Colly (Cwmavon)	51/25	154B4

TRACK LAYOUT DIAGRAMS OF THE GWR AND BR(WR)

by R.A. COOKE

(Published by the author and available from the address given below)

For full details of track layouts, showing all sidings and branches including historical details and dates of alterations, the above series provides comprehensive information. It commenced publication in 1973 and will probably take another ten years to complete. The full list of sections is as follows:

Currently (Winter 1997) those sections shown * have not yet been published and several older ones are now out of print. For full details, including prices and availability, send a s.a.e. to the author at Evergreen, School Lane, Harwell, nr Didcot, Oxon OX11 0ES.